W9-ATQ-919

www.wadsworth.com

wadsworth.com is the World Wide Web site for Wadsworth Publishing Company and is your direct source to dozens of online resources.

At *wadsworth.com* you can find out about supplements, demonstration software, and student resources. You can also send e-mail to many of our authors and preview new publications and exciting new technologies.

wadsworth.com
Changing the way the world learns®

Texas Politics

SEVENTH EDITION

Richard H. Kraemer
Emeritus Professor of Government
University of Texas at Austin

Charldean Newell
Regents Professor of Public Administration
University of North Texas

David F. Prindle
Professor of Government
University of Texas at Austin

WEST/WADSWORTH

I(T)P® **An International Thomson Publishing Company**

Belmont, CA • Albany, NY • Boston • Cincinnati • Johannesburg • London • Madrid • Melbourne
Mexico City • New York • Pacific Grove, CA • Scottsdale, AZ • Singapore • Tokyo • Toronto

Political Science Editor: Clark Baxter

Senior Development Editor: Sharon Adams Poore

Editorial Assistant: Melissa Gleason

Marketing Manager: Jay Hu

Print Buyer: Barbara Britton

Permissions Editor: Robert Kauser

Production: Matrix Productions

Interior and Cover Design: Christy Butterfield

Copy Editor: Alice Manning

Cover Image: Sunrise over the state capitol build-ing, viewed from the hills west of Austin. Courtesy of the State Department of Transportation.

Back Cover Image: Sunrise finds early risers angling from the Horace Caldwell Pier on the Gulf of Mexico in Port Aransas. Courtesy of the State Department of Transportation.

Compositor: Parkwood Composition Service, Inc.

Printer: Courier, Kendalville

Page 1: Courtesy of the Texas Department of Transportation. *Page 32:* The Center for American History, The University of Texas at Austin. *Page 60:* David Kennedy/Austin American-Statesman. *Page 99:* (top) Texas Senate Media Services; (bottom) David Kennedy/Austin American-Statesman. *Page 125:* (top) Bob Daemmrich Photography; (bottom) David Kennedy/Austin American-Statesman. *Page 155:* David Kennedy/Austin American-Statesman. *Page 188:* Ralph Barrera/Austin American-Statesman. *Page 219:* (both photos) Ralph Barrera/Austin American-Statesman. *Page 247:* David Kennedy/Austin American-Statesman. *Page 272:* David Kennedy/Austin American-Statesman. *Page 302:* David Kennedy/Austin American-Statesman. *Page 331:* Courtesy of Travis County Sheriff's Department. *Page 361:* David Kennedy/Austin American-Statesman. *Page 391:* Bob Daemmrich Photography. *Page 428:* (top) Courtesy of the Texas Department of Transportation; (bottom) David Kennedy/Austin American-Statesman.

This book is printed on acid-free recycled paper.

COPYRIGHT © 1999 by Wadsworth Publishing Company
A Division of International Thomson Publishing Inc.
I(T)P The ITP logo is a registered trademark under license.

Printed in the United States of America
1 2 3 4 5 6 7 8 9 0

For more information, contact Wadsworth Publishing Company, 10 Davis Drive, Belmont, CA 94002, or electronically at http://www.wadsworth.com

International Thomson Publishing Europe
Berkshire House
168-173 High Holborn
London, WC1V 7AA, United Kingdrom

Nelson ITP, Australia
102 Dodds Street
South Melbourne
Victoria 3205 Australia

Nelson Canada
1120 Birchmount Road
Scarborough, Ontario
Canada M1K 5G4

International Thomson Publishing Southern Africa
Building 18, Constantia Square
138 Sixteenth Road, P.O. Box 2459
Halfway House, 1685 South Africa

International Thomson Editores
Seneca, 53
Colonia Polanco
11560 México D.F. México

International Thomson Publishing Asia
60 Albert Street
#15-01 Albert Complex
Singapore 189969

International Thomson Publishing Japan
Hirakawa-cho Kyowa Building, 3F
2-2-1 Hirakawa-cho, Chiyoda-ku
Tokyo 102 Japan

Library of Congress Cataloging-in-Publication Data
Kraemer, Richard H.
    Texas politics / Richard H. Kraemer, Charldean Newell, David F. Prindle. — 7th ed.
        p. cm
    Includes index.
    ISBN 0-534-54936-5
    1. Texas—Politics and government—1951– I. Newell, Charldean.
II. Prindle, David F. (David Forrest), 1948– . III. Title
JK4816.K7 1999
320.4764—dc21   98-27072

Table of Contents

Preface xi

Preface

Because this edition of the book marks the move to a new publishing house and thus the beginning of a new "tradition," we thought it appropriate to look backwards a bit. In the nineteen years since this book was first published, the government and politics of Texas have changed a great deal. The state has added 8.5 million more residents. The Republicans have moved from being a decidedly minority political party to an increasingly dominant party. A candidate who places a full-page advertisement in a daily newspaper will pay five times as much as in 1979, although a 30-second spot on television costs only about 20 percent more. Citizens find it easier to register to vote and to cast their ballots. One elective office—that of state treasurer—has disappeared.

Other aspects of government and politics have not changed much at all. The Texas Constitution is still a patchwork of detailed provisions and numerous amendments—in fact, more each year—rather than a streamlined document. The judicial system still consists of a hodgepodge of courts with overlapping jurisdictions. Business and economic interests continue to be the dominant influence on the legislature. The executive branch remains confusing because of the myriad boards and commissions that dominate state administration. Special districts continue to increase in number at the local level while council-manager government remains the favorite of home-rule municipalities. Change and the lack of it are part of what makes studying Texas politics interesting.

The reader will encounter three themes in *Texas Politics*. In each case, the authors are describing reality and challenging the readers to make their own assessment. In doing so, we often rub against long-held political notions and biases.

First, the overriding theme is a *comparison of the reality of Texas government and politics to the democratic ideals* of participation, majority rule, and protection of minority rights. Throughout, the authors raise the question of whether a particular political decision meets the test of being good for society as a whole or whether only special interests are served. As political scientists, the authors are trained to be analysts, not merely observers, of politics. Our mission is not to offer a defense or an apology for the present system but to identify the differences between governmental practices and the sense of fair play and equity expected in a democratic system. Thus, we point out where the system works well, but we also examine the faults of the system and suggest needed changes. The study questions that end each chapter often ask the reader to make the same analysis and agree or disagree with the suggested changes.

Second, the theme of *conservatism* is echoed throughout the book. The Democrats have long been divided into liberal and conservative wings, with "conservative" mainly meaning protection of business interests and a paternal attitude toward ethnic minorities and the poor. The Republicans seem destined to a division between economic conservatives and social conservatives.

Third, because political ideologies are so different among the various political factions and because the ethnic and racial composition of the state is changing rapidly, we introduce a theme of *conflict*. We particularly call attention to conflicts among the rich, the poor, and the middle class; among and between Anglos, Mexican Americans, and African Americans; between ideologies; and between religious traditions.

Faculty members who use this book have available to them an instructor's manual, including a test bank; a computerized test bank that is available in both Mac and Windows format; and transparency acetates. Students as well as faculty members also should find the research guide in the appendix to be helpful. Because the Dallas County Community College District has adopted *Texas Politics* for their telecourses, individuals with access to DCCD programming on public television may find the content familiar.

Many people have helped in the preparation of the seventh edition of this book. Professors Henry Flores, St. Mary's University; Richard Gutierrez, University of Texas at El Paso; Gary Lipscomb, Texas A&M University, Kingsville; Naomi Robertson, Southwest Texas State University; John Ben Sutter, Wharton County Junior College; and Carter Whatley, Texas A&M University, Corpus Christi, served as formal reviewers of the sixth edition and made many helpful suggestions for revision. Our colleagues at the University of Texas at Austin and the University of North Texas also made many useful suggestions. Sometimes we agreed with the reviewers but were unable to comply with their suggestions because of page limitations. Nevertheless, many changes in this edition are due to their comments and the comments of colleagues across the state who called our attention to points deserving coverage or correction. We are similarly indebted to our students who raised provocative questions and pointed out places where greater clarity would be appreciated.

We gratefully acknowledge the work of David Dillman of Abilene Christian University who used his knowledge of and interest in Texas politics to prepare the instructor's manual. We appreciate the research assistance of Mindi Hurley. We thank the many elected officials, legislative staff members, and state agency staff members who provided us with information, clarification, and graphics material. We especially thank Ben Sargent, winner of the 1982 Pulitzer Prize for editorial cartooning, for again graciously permitting the use of his outstanding cartoons.

Of course, any errors of fact or interpretation are ours alone.

Richard H. Kraemer
Emeritus Professor of Government
The University of Texas at Austin

Charldean Newell
Regents Professor of Public Administration
University of North Texas

David F. Prindle
Professor of Government
The University of Texas at Austin

Texas Politics

SEVENTH EDITION

5. Detailed provisions in the constitution: For example, each time more funding is needed for welfare payments or the veterans' land program, a constitutional amendment must be passed. Thus, another area for reform is removing from the constitution details that are better left for statutory law, which can be changed more readily as situations demand.

RECENT REFORM EFFORTS

Attempts have been made to modernize the Texas Constitution from time to time since its adoption in 1876. Serious interest in constitutional reform/ revision was evident in 1957–1961 and 1967–1969, but the only reform effort that resulted in an opportunity for the electorate to decide on a new document came in 1975.

1971–1974

The 1971–1974 effort was important for two reasons. First, it clarified a long-standing concern about whether the legislature had the constitutional right to convene itself as a constitutional convention. A 1972 constitutional amendment authorized the Sixty-third Legislature to convene itself as a constitutional convention. This constitutional convention was quickly labeled the "Con-Con." Second, the Texas Constitutional Revision Commission, created by the same amendment, provided a detailed study of the state constitution that served as the basis for new constitutions proposed in 1974 and 1975. The proposal drafted by the constitutional convention was defeated when two issues, pari-mutuel (that is, racetrack) betting and right-to-work, which is an antiunion provision, were introduced that became the red herrings for foes of reform. (Red herrings are diversions intended to draw attention away from the main issues.) They brought opposition from Bible Belt conservatives and organized labor. The proposal died before ever reaching the voters.

1975

Interest in constitutional reform remained high. When the Sixty-fourth Legislature convened in January 1975, constitutional revision was a principal issue. Senate Joint Resolution 11 (with amendments) emerged as the vehicle for accomplishing constitutional change. Although the legislature did not adopt all the changes suggested by the 1973 revision commission, legislators did draw heavily on that work.[22] Highlights of SJR 11 included annual

---

22. A detailed analysis of the 1975 document is available in George Braden *Citizen's Guide to the Proposed Constitution* (Houston: Institute of Urban Studies, University of Houston, 1975). The University of Houston served as a research and information center during the revision efforts and published numerous reports beginning in 1973. Scholars from across the state were involved in the Houston research. One, Janice C. May, published a book-length study, *Texas Constitutional Revision Experience in the '70s* (Austin: Sterling Swift, 1975). A summary of the general literature on the revision efforts and of voting behavior can be found in John E. Bebout, "The Meaning of the Vote on the Proposed Texas Constitution, 1975," *Public Affairs Comment* 24 (February 1978): 1–9, published by the Lyndon B. Johnson School of Public Affairs at the University of Texas at Austin.

legislative sessions, a streamlined judicial system, and modernization of county government. SJR11 eliminated such details as the welfare ceiling. It gave more power to the governor coupled with a limit of two terms. It also provided for property tax relief and a tax on petroleum refining.

Powerful interests lined up on both sides of this proposed constitutional reform, with vested economic interests and emotionalism acting as important components of the struggle for ratification of the document. In spite of the efforts of most state officials to convince the voters of the worth of the proposed state charter, voters defeated the entire proposal by a two-to-one margin on November 4, 1975. Governor Dolph Briscoe, fearful of higher taxes and government expansion, and county officials, concerned for their jobs, helped to bring about defeat. A combination of interests worried that the "equal educational opportunity" provisions would upset the scheme of funding public schools helped to convince citizens to vote against the proposal. Texans clearly preferred the old, lengthy, familiar document to one they saw as possibly promoting more spending and allowing greater governmental power.

1976–1991

Little interest in constitutional revision was evident in the fifteen years following the defeat of the proposed new state constitution. The League of Women Voters was the only organized group to show a consistent concern for constitutional revision. Too many problems demanding immediate solutions filled the recent legislative sessions. Legislators did not have time to give consideration to constitutional change beyond proposing more amendments. Besides, virtually every group with interests protected by the current constitution, from veterans to the University of Texas and Texas A&M systems to county commissioners, was anything but encouraging of constitutional change.

1992 AND BEYOND

Following the 1991 legislative session, Senator John Montford drafted a joint resolution that proposed a new constitution for consideration in 1993. The Montford proposal includes such features as:

★ Six-year terms for senators and four-year terms for House members

★ A limit of two consecutive terms for a senator and three for a House member

★ A sixty-day budget session of the legislature in even-numbered years

★ Empowerment of the legislature to meet to reconsider bills vetoed by the governor

★ The only elected executives to be the governor, lieutenant governor, and comptroller, each with a limit of two terms

★ Simplification of the court system and provision for nonpartisan elections

★ Creation of five regional university systems, each of which would share in the Permanent University Fund (PUF)

★ Ordinance power for counties, subject to local voter approval[23]

As is so often the case, immediate problems such as the budget shortfall, school finance, and a prison system unable to cope with the volume of state prisoners crowded out constitutional revision in 1993. When Senator Montford prepared the draft constitution, he was one of the most powerful state senators in Texas, but even he had other issues to address in 1995. Subsequently, he left the legislature to become head of Texas Tech University. Without a champion, constitutional revision was not considered by the 1997 legislature.

Rob Junell, chair of the powerful Appropriations Committee in the House of Representatives, has expressed interest in constitutional revision. Junell reportedly liked some but not all of Montford's proposal, and apparently had some legislative colleagues who might join him in a reform effort.[24] Whether he will try to act on his interest in 1999 or beyond remains to be seen.

Meanwhile, patches in the form of constitutional amendments will continue to be applied to the creaky Texas Constitution. By the end of 1997, citizens had been asked to consider 162 amendments since 1980, and they approved 139 of them. These amendments have been as varied as changes in the property tax exemptions allowable by local government, elimination of the need for a statewide vote for a county to abolish the office of county surveyor, authorization of bonded indebtedness to fund such functions as prisons and water development, and even cleaning out part of the constitutional deadwood.

In addition to amendments, the Texas legislature has used statutory law to alleviate some of the shortcomings of the constitution. Modifying the election code to ensure that the qualifications for voting in Texas conform to national requirements is one example.

Constitutional Politics

Making a constitution, like other lawmaking processes, is highly political. Whether the issue is general constitutional reform or an individual amendment, changing a constitution will benefit some groups and disadvantage others. Because the requirement of a two-thirds legislative vote plus public approval makes constitutional change more difficult than ordinary lawmaking, the political stakes are greater when alteration of a state's fundamental charter is at issue.

SOMETHING FOR EVERYONE

Various special-interest groups attempt to embody their political, social, economic, and/or moral viewpoints in the constitution by either advocating a

23. Draft resolution and "Comparison of Current and Proposed Constitutions" provided by the office of Senator John Montford, January 1992.
24. William McKenzie, "Constitutional Retooling," *Dallas Morning News,* November 4, 1997, p. 15A.

particular change or working against it. If a group can embed its particular policy concern in the constitution, the issue is likely to remain there, perhaps forever. In other words, it is easier to "amend in" a provision than to "amend it out." The relative ease of amending the state charter contributes to this attitude of using the constitution as a security blanket. The constitution has become a political "goody" store with something for everyone in it.

One strategy used by these groups is to seek an authorizing provision in the constitution that will result in economic gains for the group. For example, a set of 1985 amendments about funding for water supply benefits small cities, farmers, and ranchers, all of whom vigorously advocated passage of the proposals.

Similarly, tax relief has been a frequent subject for constitutional amendment since 1978. Almost everyone got something from the amendments and the accompanying legislation. Farmers and ranchers thought that they had been shortchanged by 1978–1980 amendments when other economic groups gained substantial advantages. Consequently, a 1981 amendment exempted livestock and poultry from all taxation, much as lumber interests had earlier managed to get trees excluded. By 1987, after four years of economic difficulty, oil producers sought their share of tax relief and managed to secure an amendment exempting from taxation certain kinds of offshore drilling equipment that was not in use. A 1997 amendment authorizes the legislature to cap increases in residential property tax appraisals and school districts to permit an elderly person to transfer a property tax freeze (already a benefit) to a different residence.

Sometimes a group tries to prohibit a state from taking, or being able to take, a particular action. When the foes of pari-mutuel betting helped to destroy the efforts of the 1974 constitutional convention, their goal was to prevent the constitutional authorization of gambling in Texas. As noted in the previous section, this issue was a political red herring dragged in by general opponents of constitutional reform and illustrates tactics that were used to defeat change. The proposed constitution did not specifically provide for pari-mutuel betting, but it did not prohibit it. Opposition to pari-mutuel betting has since lessened, and in November 1987 voters approved it in a referendum held at the time of a constitutional amendment election. A 1991 amendment authorized more gambling through a state lottery.

The strategy of getting something for everyone by opposition to particular policies has more recently focused on various proposed amendments that would prohibit a state income tax. In 1993 voters overwhelmingly approved an amendment that mandates a voter referendum if the legislature should ever pass an income tax. The amendment also requires that at least two-thirds of the revenue from an income tax be pledged to reduce property taxes that support public schools, with the remainder to go to support education.

At other times a group seeks to advance some special interest that is already the subject of a constitutional guarantee. The periodic amendment of the legislative article on the Veterans Land Board is an example. This constitutional provision authorizes the state to sell bonds both to purchase land for veterans and to underwrite low-cost loans for home purchasers. It must be amended each time an authorization for more bond sales is needed.

A similar case is the periodic introduction of amendments to the welfare section of the legislative article to provide funds to pay for aid to the state's needy citizens. Mainly a device for limiting the amount of money that can be spent for welfare, the constitutional provision about welfare has not been a political "plum" or guarantee for the state's poor people. Still, a 1982 amendment authorizes the legislature to provide funds for this purpose up to a maximum of 1 percent of the state budget, beginning in 1983–84. There is still a ceiling on welfare expenditures, but the 1982 provision is somewhat more generous than the old provision and is elastic—that is, the amount available for welfare goes up as the budget goes up.

Another example of the politics of constitution making concerns branch banking, which the Texas Constitution prohibited before a 1986 constitutional amendment. Larger banks wanted branch banking because they wanted to establish branches in other parts of a city or even in other cities. Smaller, independent banks, fearing the competition that a change would permit, opposed the practice. From 1987 through 1990, Texas banks and savings and loans suffered many failures. Because branch banking had been legalized, finding purchasers for the failed Texas financial institutions was easier. Larger, more stable banks both in Texas and in other states could acquire the troubled banks and make them into branches. In 1997, financial institutions were major advocates of a proposal that would allow Texas homeowners, like the citizens of all other states, to take out a second mortgage on their residence. Voters, viewing home equity loans as a type of easy credit, went along with the banks and savings and loans.

Private interests are not always the only ones seeking constitutional change. Sometimes elected officials want changes in the constitution to enhance their power. In 1980 and 1981, for example, the governor tried to gain greater control over the state's budgeting and spending processes through constitutional amendment, but the public defeated both of the proposed amendments. Public officials may also try to prevent constitutional change through fear of losing powers. Members of the Texas Association of County Officials (TACO) were a potent lobbying force against the proposed 1975 constitution. They were afraid of losing political control if county governments were modernized.

THE POLITICAL PROCESS

The political process involved in constitutional change is essentially the same as other activities designed to influence public policy. Elected officials, political parties, special interests and their lobbyists, and campaigning are all involved. A brief illustration of the process is provided by a situation that began in 1979 and was resolved by an amendment approved by the voters in 1984—namely, the issue of building funds for the state's universities. The University of Texas at Austin and Texas A&M University at College Station, through provisions in Article VII of the state constitution, were the sole beneficiaries of the Permanent University Fund (PUF). The PUF is now worth about $6 billion. These funds can be used for buildings, other permanent improvements, and enrichment activities. The PUF gets its money from the proceeds of the oil and gas leases on a million acres of public land granted to the two universities. Seventeen other state universities originally received money for buildings directly from the legislature and then, beginning in 1947, from a dedicated fund fed by the state property tax. Institutions created after 1947 were dependent on legislative appropriations.

In 1979, as part of a general tax-relief movement, the legislature reduced the rate for the state property tax to almost zero. In the 1979 and 1981 sessions of the legislature, a variety of proposals to establish an alternative to financing college building programs were introduced. Neither the legislators nor the universities could agree on a proposal. The legislature subsequently proposed a constitutional amendment to abolish the state property tax altogether, and the voters approved the amendment in late 1982. Also in 1982, the universities received some building funds in a special legislative session to tide them over until the larger issue could be decided.

The 1983 legislature then had to deal with the issue of funding university construction. The legislators agreed on a basic plan that provided PUF coverage for other institutions in the UT and A&M systems and established a separate fund to cover the other state institutions. This separate fund would cover repairs and renovations, new construction, library and equipment purchases, and land acquisitions. They also agreed on a special infusion of funds to the two predominately Black institutions in the state, Texas Southern University and Prairie View A&M. The UT and A&M representatives wanted to ensure that the PUF was not opened to other universities. They feared a significant reduction in the funds available to the two flagship institutions. Their willingness to include their branch campuses in the PUF avoided the need to include these branch campuses in the new construction fund. At the same time, UT and A&M also gained the agreement of the other universities not to seek inclusion in the PUF.

In spite of agreement on the basics of the plan, three controversies arose. First, the Texas Higher Education Coordinating Board, which oversees the entire state university system, strongly opposed the dollar amount proposed for the new fund. The board argued that the universities were already overbuilt and would squander the money. The Texas House of Representatives yielded to coordinating board pressure and established a $75 million annual fund in its version of the amendment. The Senate and the governor, on the other hand, preferred the $125 million annual funding level favored by the institutions. A second controversy was the prospective source of revenue for the construction fund, especially when the Senate suggested an increase in the oil and gas production (severance) tax. The third controversy was over the best date to vote on an amendment to extend the PUF to the branch campuses and establish the second fund. However, the two legislative houses agreed to a vote in conjunction with the 1984 general election and compromised on a $100 million fund. Oil and gas interests prevented a severance tax increase, so that, initially at least, general revenue sources had to be tapped for the construction fund.

The saga of university construction involved many people. Legislators themselves had diverse interests. Some came from districts with one or more state universities. Others were budget conscious; still others were strong alumni supporters of the institutions they had attended. The governor supported the higher amount favored by the Senate, calling it a goal. The state's universities agreed that some solution must be found, and the Council of (state university) Presidents saw to it that the disagreements that had surfaced in 1979 and 1981 were contained. Taxpayers wanted assurance that tax increases would not be necessary to fund college construction. The coordinating board strongly urged a low level of funding. It also argued that the authority should keep a tight rein on university construction.

Business and industrial interests were a part of the picture in three ways. First, spokespersons for high-technology fields were concerned about the adequacy of training in their areas if university facilities became outmoded. Second, the Texas Research League, an influential private organization financed by business interests, joined the coordinating board in saying that the twenty-six institutions covered by the new fund were asking for too much money. It also used its report on college construction as a vehicle for advocating tuition increases. Third, when the Senate looked toward an increase in the severance tax as a source of revenue for the college construction fund, the oil and gas industry quickly rallied against the proposal.

Minority interests and the U.S. Office of Civil Rights pressed for the special funding for Texas Southern and Prairie View. Finally, individual college presidents said that they intended to ask their students to vote for the amendment and to ask their parents and spouses to vote for it. The voters overwhelmingly approved the proposal, and higher education was elated with having "Prop Two" funds beginning in 1985. (The proposal was the second one on the 1984 ballot, hence the nickname Prop Two for Higher Education Assistance Funds [HEAF]).

This issue of university construction was resolved more broadly as an issue about financing "capital" improvements (those of long-term duration). It gives us a portrait of how many varied interests can become involved in constitutional change. Different constitutional change issues have different casts of characters, of course, but they all are fraught with similar complex political relationships.

Subsequent implementation of HEAF funds also proved to be politically interesting. The antipathy of the coordinating board, subsequently buttressed by legislators, to new construction resulted in HEAF dollars being spent primarily for renovation until the mid-1990s. The dollars were spent only secondarily for research and instructional equipment and for libraries. Still, colleges and universities rely on the HEAF dollars. Administrators and faculty members alike were relieved when a new ten-year round of funding set at $175 million a year was approved by the Seventy-third Legislature, beginning in fiscal year (FY) 1996. By then, even the coordinating board approved the funding and was authorizing new construction on most campuses.

Summary

Texans were so unhappy with Reconstruction government that, given the opportunity to draft and ratify a new constitution in 1876, they concentrated their attention on two of the four purposes of constitutions: legitimacy and limiting government. The intent of the framers was to curb governmental power. Thus they largely ignored the importance of assigning sufficient power to government officials. Also, they subverted the purpose of organizing government by creating a fragmented set of institutions and offices designed to diffuse authority. Although this approach limits government, it also makes citizen participation more difficult because state government is confusing to most people. Partisans of democracy are frustrated because the state constitution makes the people's ability to govern themselves more difficult.

Lacking the farsightedness of the framers of the U.S. Constitution, the authors of the Texas charter produced a restrictive document that today impedes the development and implementation of needed policies and programs. By the end of 1997, lawmakers had had to resort to amending the Texas Constitution 377 times to make possible programs that otherwise would have been consigned to legislative dreamland. In one sense, the element of democratic theory that holds that public input into policy is important is satisfied by such a practice, but policies are very hard to modify once they are written into the constitution. Dynamic public issues such as funding for water quality, prison expansion, and public education could be handled more smoothly without the necessity of proposing and ratifying a constitutional amendment. Now, if a policy proves to be ineffective, only another amendment can solve the problem.

The most cumbersome and/or unnecessarily restrictive provisions in the 1876 constitution and their consequences are the following:

1. The governor, although held responsible by the public for overall state leadership and the action of state agencies, in reality has limited direct control over most major policy-making offices, boards, and commissions.

2. The legislature is caught between the proverbial "rock and a hard place." While constantly being criticized by the citizenry for poor legislative performance, it nevertheless must operate within the constraints of poverty-level salaries, short and infrequent sessions, and innumerable restrictions on legislative action.

3. Texas judges are well aware of the lack of cohesiveness in the judicial system, but they are virtually powerless to provide simpler, more uniform justice because of the overlapping and parallel jurisdictions of the state's courts and the lack of effective supervision of the whole judicial system.

4. County governments, even when county commissioners are progressive in attitude, are restricted by their constitutional structure and scope.

5. In spite of frequent amendments, the constitution still does not conform to current federal law.

6. The 377 amendments exacerbate the poor organization of the charter, making it even more difficult for the layperson to read.

Some modern legislatures have shown an interest in constitutional revision; two have devoted considerable time and energy to reform efforts. Whether such efforts will succeed is uncertain. The electorate still lacks sufficient understanding of the shortcomings of the present constitution to be receptive to increases in governmental power. Citizens are far too concerned about state taxes, public education, social services, crime and punishment, and many other pressing issues to give constitutional revision much attention. Although the current constitution "creaks and groans," the state still takes care of its business.

In addition, special interests have found it easy to amend the current document by influencing key legislators, then mounting serious campaigns to elicit voter support. They prefer the protection of a constitution to more easily changed statutes. Thus, a successful revision effort may have to wait not only until the citizens of Texas are more aware of the pitfalls of the present document, but also until powerful special interests can be persuaded to work for, not against, constitutional reform. Article I of the Texas Constitution as quoted at the beginning of this chapter is ironic: The emphasis has come to be more on the phrase "political power" than on the intended phrase "inherent in the people."

Key Terms

Bill of Rights
Checks and balances
Constitution

Constitutional amendment
Constitutional revision
Home rule

Separation of powers

Study Questions

1. What are the four purposes of constitutions? Which ones are most reflected in the Texas Constitution? Which ones are least reflected?

2. How many constitutions has Texas had? Why have there been so many? Do you think there needs to be another one? Why or why not?

3. Why is the Texas Constitution so frequently amended? What types of interests are involved when constitutional change is advocated?

4. Why do you think that the constitution, the legal framework of a state, is so important?

5. The U.S. Constitution is considered to be a durable, flexible document, whereas the Texas Constitution is considered to be an inflexible, archaic document. Do you agree with these judgments? Why or why not?

6. What similarities and differences do you see in the U.S. and Texas constitutions?

7. "Texas seems to govern itself despite the criticisms of the state constitution. Consequently, constitutional reform is unnecessary." Do you agree or disagree with this statement? Why?

8. Consider the short list of features of the Montford proposal for a new constitution provided in this chapter and whatever other knowledge you have. What chance do you think the proposal has of being adopted? Why? Who do you think will be for and against it?

9. Do you think that you, personally, could get interested in constitutional revision? Why or why not?

Internet Assignment

Internet site: www.capitol.state.tx.us/txconst/toc.html

Click on search; then click on "concept search." Type in "land grants." Choose three of the listed references, selecting different articles of the constitution. Why do you think the Texas Constitution has so many references to land grants? What is there about the history of the state that makes them so important?

Chapter Three

Local Government

Fire services are among the most basic functions of local government. Along with police services, they often command the lion's share of the municipal budget.

The new city manager is (1) invisible, (2) anonymous, (3) nonpolitical, and (4) none of the above. Increasingly, modern city managers are brokers, and they do that brokering out in the open.

Alan Ehrenhalt, 1990, *Deputy Editor,* Governing: The States and Localities

When Congress began swinging its ax in earnest . . . at the Federal deficit, somebody forgot to tell Amarillo to duck.

Michael Wines, 1996, New York Times

Introduction

When the Texas Constitution was being written in 1875, only 8 percent of the state's population lived in urban areas. By the 1970 federal census, Texas was already 80 percent urban. The U.S. Bureau of the Census forecasts that Texas will grow faster than any other state through 2000 and will gain 45 percent more population by 2025 than it had in 1990. Much of this population growth will be in special populations that have unique problems—Hispanics and the elderly in particular[1]—and most of it will be in urban areas. Much of the state's history and many of its problems are linked to urbanization and population growth.

Once one of the most rural states, Texas is now one of the most urban. Most of the change has taken place since 1950, when the development of such industries as petrochemicals and defense began luring rural residents into cities. Like most American cities, Texas cities are virtually unplanned. Growth patterns are largely determined by developers, who give little thought to the long-range effects of their projects on the total community. Only in the past two decades has community planning come to be taken seriously. In Texas and elsewhere, the nation's domestic problems—racial strife, unemployment, inflation, delinquency, crime, substance abuse, inadequate health care, pollution, inadequate transportation, taxation, and the shortage of energy—seem to be focused in the cities. But before examining city government and its problems, this chapter will step back in time and look at the first unit of local government: the county.

Local government is an especially rich field for exploring whether the tests of democratic government outlined in Chapter 1 have been passed. Americans have long viewed local government as the government that is closest and most responsive to them. In looking at the organization, finance, and politics of Texas's local governments, Chapter 3 also will look closely at whether citizens really are most involved at the local level and whether differences exist between general-purpose local governments (cities and counties) and special-purpose local governments (special districts).

---

1. David LaGesse, "Texas Predicted to Grow Faster than Other States," *Dallas Morning News,* October 23, 1996, 1A, 8A.

Counties: Horse-Drawn Buggies?

HISTORICAL AND LEGAL BACKGROUND

The county is the oldest form of local government in America, and in rural Texas it is still the most important. Today there are approximately 3,100 counties in the forty-seven states that have this form of government. Texas has the largest number of counties—254—of any state in the nation.[2]

Across the nation, counties vary enormously in size and importance. The largest in area is San Bernardino County in California, with 20,131 square miles. Arlington County, Virginia, is the smallest, with only 24 square miles. The largest county in Texas is Brewster, with 6,028 square miles; the smallest is Rockwall, with 147 square miles. Even more striking contrasts exist in population size. The 1990 census registered Loving County in west Texas as having a grand total of 110 people. Harris County, which includes Houston, has more than 3 million.

In Texas, as in other states, the county is a creation of state government. Since citizens could not be expected to travel to the capital to conduct whatever business they had with the state, counties were designed to serve as units of state government that would be geographically accessible to citizens. Until city police departments assumed much of the role, the sheriff and the sheriff's deputies were the primary agents for enforcement of state law. County courts still handle much of the judicial business of the state (see Chapter 11), and they remain integral to the state judicial system. Many state records, such as titles, deeds, and court records, are kept by the county; many state taxes are collected by the county; and counties handle state elections. Counties also distribute large portions of the federal funds that pass through the state government en route to individuals, such as welfare recipients. Thus most dealings that citizens have with the state are handled through the county. Yet, strangely, state government exercises virtually no supervisory authority over county governments. They are left to enforce the state's laws and administer the state's programs pretty much as they choose.

County officials are elected by the people of the county and have substantial discretion in a number of areas. For example, they can appoint some other county officials and set the tax rate. The result is a peculiar situation in which the county is a creation of state government, administering state laws and programs—with some discretion on the part of its officers—but county officials are elected by the people of the county and are in no real way accountable to the state government for the performance of their duties. Not surprisingly, county officials view themselves not as agents of the state but rather as local officials. One result is that enforcement of state law varies considerably from county to county.

Home rule allows local governments to adopt their own charters, design their organizations, and enact laws within limits set by the state. Following

---

2. Our discussion of county government in Texas relies in part on Robert E. Norwood, *Texas County Government: Let the People Choose* (Austin: Texas Research League, 1970). Norwood's monograph is the most extensive work available on the subject. A second edition, coauthored with Sabrina Strawn, was published in 1984.

the successful example of advocates of home rule for Texas cities, adherents of county home rule succeeded in 1933 in amending the state constitution with a home-rule provision. However, the amendment was badly written. The required procedures were difficult to follow, and some were so obscure that fear of lawsuits precluded any adoption of home rule. For example, the home-rule charter could not "abridge the sovereignty of the state, affect its established policies, impair the homestead exemption, or 'inconstantly' affect the operation of the laws of the state relating to the judicial, tax, fiscal, education, police, highway, and health systems."[3]

ORGANIZATION AND OPERATION OF COUNTY GOVERNMENT

The Constitution of 1876, which established the state government, also set out the organization and operation of county government. The same concerns and styles are manifested for both governments, and there are close parallels in their organization and operation. For example, the decentralized executive found at the state level is reproduced at the county level in the county **commissioners court,** the governing body in all Texas counties, and in semi-independent county agencies.

STRUCTURE

Since the county is the creation of the state and home-rule provisions, which would allow the individual counties to choose their own form of government, do not apply, the organization and structure of county government are uniform throughout Texas. Tiny Loving County and enormous Harris County have substantially the same governmental structure, a structure that, unfortunately, is a burden to both. Unlike counties in many other states, Texas counties do not have the option of having a form of government with an appointed professional administrator, such as the council-manager type described later in this chapter. Neither can they choose a form of government with an elected chief executive similar to the strong mayor-council form of city government.

Counties have often found themselves saddled with unnecessary offices, such as treasurer, school superintendent, or surveyor. In November 1993, Texas voters were asked once again to vote on eliminating the position of county surveyor in two specific counties (McLennan and Jackson). But they also got to vote on whether, in the future, only residents of the county involved would need to vote to abolish an office. The vote was more than six to one in favor of eliminating the need for the whole state to vote on the business of one county.

3. Caleb Perry Patterson, Sam B. McAlister, and George C. Hester, *State and Local Government in Texas,* 3rd ed. (New York: Macmillan, 1961), 404.

FIGURE 3–1
Organization
of County
Government
in Texas

Source: George D. Braden, Citizens' Guide to the Texas Constitution, *prepared for the Texas Advisory Commission on Intergovernmental Relations by the Institute of Urban Studies, University of Houston (Austin, 1972), 51. Used by permission.*

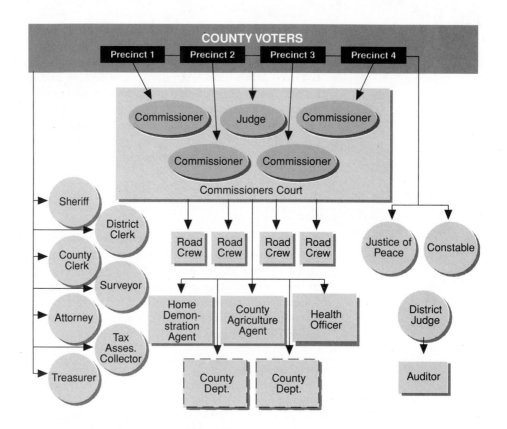

Figure 3–1 illustrates the organization of Texas county government. The county is divided into four precincts, each of which elects a commissioner to the commissioners court. The presiding officer of the commissioners court is the county judge. The county commissioners and the administrative agencies constitute the executive branch of county government, but the commissioners court performs as a legislature as well. Figure 3–1 also illustrates that counties have a large number of elected officials, ranging from a sheriff to constables to an attorney.

Each of the four commissioners is elected from a precinct, but the county judge is chosen in an **at-large election**—that is, one in which all registered voters in the county are eligible to participate. They and all other county officials are chosen in partisan elections; that is, candidates run as Democrats, Republicans, or minor party candidates.

APPORTIONMENT

In the past, when county commissioners drew county precinct lines, they drew those lines on some basis other than population. Unlike gerrymandering, where the object is to perpetuate the position of the dominant party or faction, county precinct apportionment was for the purpose of reelecting incumbent commissioners and dividing the county road mileage on an equal basis. Roads, a major county function, were often more important than people. Not only were roads the lifeline for the state's rural population, which was once in the majority, but also contracts for road work represented the best opportunity for individual commissioners to wheel and deal. As a result, county commissioners often created precincts with great disparities in population.

During the 1960s, one precinct in Travis County contained almost 60 percent of the county's population, including most of the African Americans, Mexican Americans, and poor Whites. Another precinct contained only 6 percent of the county's population, mainly upper-middle-class Whites. Midland County carried bias against city dwellers to the ultimate extreme: One precinct, composed of the City of Midland, contained 97 percent of the people. The remaining 3 percent lived in the other three districts.

In 1968, the U.S. Supreme Court, acting in a case against Midland County, ruled that all counties had to abide by the one-person, one-vote rule that had been applied earlier to the U.S. House of Representatives and to state legislatures (*Avery* v. *Midland County,* 88 S.Ct. 1114, 1968). This rule requires that electoral districts must be roughly equal in population. After this ruling, some commissioners courts voluntarily redistricted on the basis of population; in other counties, federal judges ordered population-based redistricting. County apportionment has resurfaced as an issue in recent years in disputes over adequate opportunities for ethnic minorities to contend for county offices, in counties with substantial political party competition, and in urban counties with fast-growing suburbs.

COMMISSIONERS[4] COURT

The term *commissioners court* is a misnomer. It is not a judicial body but an executive (policy-administering) and legislative (policy-making) body for the county.

Although technically the county is nothing more than an administrative arm of the state, the commissioners court does have functional latitude in several areas. In addition to setting the tax rate for the county (a legislative function), it exercises discretion in the administration of state programs (an executive function). Some of these state programs are mandatory, but the county may choose among others and may determine the amount of money to be allocated to each. For example, the state and counties are responsible for health care for the indigent, including care for individuals who are not qualified for the federally funded Medicaid program, and counties must ensure that hospital service is provided. An individual county, however, may elect to operate a public hospital, pay a public hospital in an adjacent county for services, or pay a private hospital for care of the indigent. Counties also are responsible for building and maintaining county jails, generally for providing health and safety services in rural areas, and for subdivision regulation in unincorporated areas. Perhaps the most important power of the commissioners court is that of controlling the county budget in most areas of county government. If it chooses, it can institute a variety of different programs, many of which are major undertakings such as county hospitals, libraries, and various welfare programs. Counties also are active in economic development activity.

---

4. Although one often sees commissioners court written as "commissioners'" with an apostrophe, Chapter 81 of the *Texas Local Government Code* is explicit in the lack of an apostrophe.

Chapter 6 describes how the county commissioners court has the responsibility for conducting general and special elections. The court also has the power to determine the precinct lines for the justice of the peace precincts, as well as for the precincts of the four commissioners themselves. This power is a potent political weapon that can be used to advance the cause of some individuals and groups and to discriminate against others. When these lines are not drawn fairly and equitably, malapportionment results, as was the case in the Midland situation noted earlier.

COUNTY OFFICIALS

The *county commissioners* also perform important functions as individuals. Each is responsible for his or her own precinct, including the establishment of road- and bridge-building programs, which represent a major expenditure of county funds. Since 1947, counties have had the authority to consolidate the functions of building and maintaining roads and bridges. In twenty-four counties, a countywide unit system has been established, enabling commissioners in those counties to take advantage of volume purchasing, share heavy road equipment, and so on. When she was a Travis County commissioner, former Governor Ann Richards led an unsuccessful campaign for statewide adoption of the unit system. In more than 90 percent of Texas's counties, individual commissioners still tend to roads and bridges in their individual precincts. One reason is the importance of these transportation facilities to residents in outlying areas, and thus the potential effect on reelecting the commissioner. Another reason is that individual commissioners simply like the power implicit in hiring personnel and letting contracts for road and bridge work. They also like the political advantage to be gained from determining just where new roads will go and which existing roads and bridges will be improved.

The *county judge* performs many functions. As a member of the commissioners court, the judge presides over and participates fully in that body's decision making. As a member of the county election board, the county judge receives the election returns from the election judges throughout the county, presents the returns to the commissioners court for canvassing, and then forwards the final results to the secretary of state. In counties with a population of fewer than 225,000, county judges serve also in an administrative capacity as county budget officer. They also have the authority to fill vacancies that occur on commissioners courts. They are notaries public, can perform marriages, and issue beer, wine, and liquor licenses in "wet" counties. Many citizens see the county judge as a representative of the people and ask him or her to intervene with other elected officials and county bureaucrats. Many county judges have strong countywide power bases and are influential politicians.

The county judge also presides over the county court, although the position does not require legal credentials other than "being well-informed in the law." County judges devote time to such matters as probate of wills, settlement of estates, appointment of guardians, and, in many counties, hearing lawsuits and minor criminal cases. However, in larger counties the county commission usually relieves the judge of his courtroom responsibilities by creating one or more county courts at law (see Chapter 11 for a discussion of the Texas judiciary).

One of the most visible officers of the county is the *sheriff,* who is elected at large. The sheriff has jurisdiction throughout the county but often also makes informal agreements involving a division of labor with the police of the municipalities in the county. Particularly where large cities are involved, the sheriff's office usually confines itself to the area of the county outside the city limits. The county sheriff has comprehensive control of departmental operations and appoints all deputies, jailers, and administrative personnel. In fact, the principal function of the sheriff is to serve as administrator of the county jail system. County jails house defendants awaiting criminal trial, individuals convicted of a misdemeanor and sentenced for a term up to a year, and felony (serious crime) convicts waiting to be transported to a state prison. Some counties have found it profitable to build larger jails than they require and rent space to the state and to other states. Depending on the size of the county, the sheriff's department may be quite complex and may have a substantial annual budget. A 1993 amendment to the state constitution authorizes the legislature to impose qualifications on sheriffs, such as mandatory training as a peace officer.

A recent phenomenon among county sheriffs has been the election of four women in Armstrong, Bowie, Kerr, and Travis counties. As the executive director of the Sheriffs' Association of Texas pointed out, women have served at other times in the state's history, but largely because they were named to the job when their sheriff-husbands died in office. These four were all elected in their own right.

Source: Victoria Loe, "Badges of Distinction," *Dallas Morning News,* December 22, 1996, 1A, 30A; Ellen Sweets, "Woman behind the Badge," *Dallas Morning News,* October 29, 1997, 1C, 9C.

Another prominent county official is the *county attorney,* also elected at large. As the head of the county's legal department, the county attorney provides legal counsel and representation of the county. The attorney also prosecutes misdemeanors in the justice of the peace and county courts.

Another of the important elective offices in the county is that of *county clerk,* who is also elected at large. The county clerk is the recorder of all legal documents, such as deeds, contracts, and mortgages; issues all marriage licenses; and is the clerk of both the county court and the commissioners court. Many of the responsibilities for the conduct of elections, which formally rest with the commissioners court, actually are performed by the county clerk. For example, absentee voting is handled by the county clerk (see Chapter 6).

The *assessor-collector of taxes* collects the ad valorem (general property) tax for the county, collects fees for license plates and certificates of title for motor vehicles, and serves as the registrar of voters. This last duty is a holdover from the days of the poll tax, which was a fee paid to register to vote. The assessor-collector's job has been changed in recent years by the creation of the uniform appraisal system, to be discussed later in this chapter. In counties of 10,000 or more population, a separate assessor-collector is elected at large; in smaller counties, the sheriff serves as assessor-collector.

Other legal officers of the county are the *justices of the peace* (JPs) and the *constables*. In most but not all counties there is at least one justice of the peace and one constable for each of the four precincts. Larger counties may have as many as eight JP districts. In the largest counties, numerous deputy constables assist the elected constables. The justice of the peace is at the bottom of the judicial ladder, having jurisdiction over only minor criminal cases and civil suits. The constable has the duty of executing judgments, serving subpoenas, and performing other duties for the justice of the peace court. Like the commissioners, the constables and JPs are elected for four years on a partisan basis by district.

Another elected official is the *county treasurer*, who is the custodian of public funds. Some counties have a *county school superintendent* to oversee rural schools.

The county has a number of other officers, some of whom perform important functions. In larger counties, a *county elections coordinator* is appointed to supervise elections. In counties with a population of more than 35,000, the state law requires that an *auditor* be appointed by the district judge having jurisdiction in the county for the purpose of overseeing the financial activities of the county and assuring that they are performed in accordance with the law. A *county health officer* to direct the public-health program is also required by state law, and in most counties a *county agricultural agent* and a *home demonstration agent* are appointed by the commissioners court for the purpose of assisting (primarily) rural people with agriculture and homemaking. The last two officers are appointed in conjunction with Texas A&M University, which administers the agriculture and home demonstration extension programs.

COUNTY FINANCE

The largest single source of income for the county is the property tax. The state constitution permits counties to tax real property, such as land and buildings, within their boundaries. Prior to the tax relief measures of 1978 to 1982, some county commissioners courts used the discretion described earlier in this chapter to tax tangible personal property, such as automobiles, and intangible personal property, such as bank deposits. The commissioners court is required to meet annually to set the tax rate, which may not exceed $0.80 per $100 valuation. Rates in excess of that, if authorized by the legislature and approved by the voters of the county, can be imposed for special projects such as farm-to-market roads. The worth of all property is determined by a countywide tax appraisal district that is required by law to use the market value.

Certain counties have been authorized to collect a sales tax. Counties also receive funding from federal grants and from various state programs. State maintenance of rural farm-to-market roads and state highways is an important financial aid to Texas counties.

Figures 3–2 and 3–3 illustrate how the central counties of the state's two largest population centers get and spend money. The major difference on the revenue side is that Dallas County gets considerably more money from national, state, and other local governments than does Harris County. Intergovernmental transfers include federal and state grants for public health, highways, and hospitals. The difference between the two counties is in wel-

FIGURE 3–2

Revenues in Dallas County and Harris County, 1993–94 ($791 million in Dallas, $1.5 billion in Harris)

Source: Finances of Individual County Governments Having 1,000,000 Population or More, 1993–94, cntydoc.txt at www.census.gov

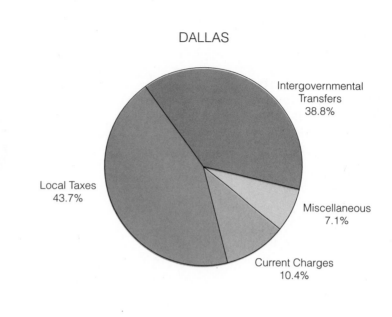

DALLAS

Intergovernmental Transfers
38.8%

Local Taxes
43.7%

Miscellaneous
7.1%

Current Charges
10.4%

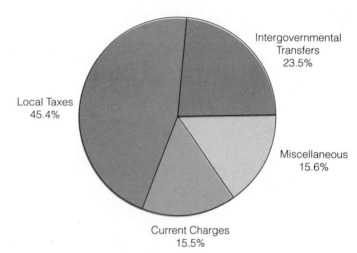

HARRIS

Intergovernmental Transfers
23.5%

Local Taxes
45.4%

Miscellaneous
15.6%

Current Charges
15.5%

fare grants. Both rely to about the same degree on local taxes, which are mainly property taxes. As one would expect given its lower proportion of intergovernmental transfers, Harris County gets a larger proportion of its funds from current charges and miscellaneous sources of revenue. Current charges include revenues collected from hospitals, toll roads, and recreation facilities; fines, special assessments, and interest earned constitute miscellaneous income.

Figure 3–3 illustrates expenditures for the two counties. The first difference one notes is that Harris County spent more money than it brought in, while Dallas County had a surplus. Harris County was either spending a previous surplus (known as reserve funds) or using borrowed money. The expenditure

FIGURE 3–3

Expenditures in Dallas County and Harris County, 1993–94 ($765 million in Dallas, $1.6 billion in Harris)

Source: Finances of Individual County Governments Having 1,000,000 Population or More, 1993–94, cntydoc.txt at www.census.gov

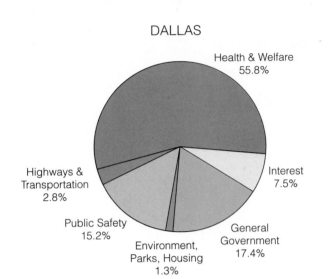

DALLAS

Health & Welfare
55.8%

Interest
7.5%

Highways &
Transportation
2.8%

Public Safety
15.2%

Environment,
Parks, Housing
1.3%

General
Government
17.4%

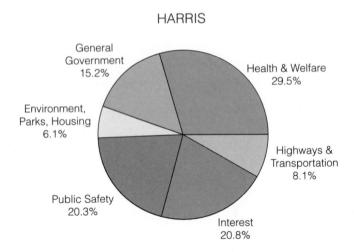

HARRIS

General
Government
15.2%

Environment,
Parks, Housing
6.1%

Health & Welfare
29.5%

Highways &
Transportation
8.1%

Public Safety
20.3%

Interest
20.8%

side reflects the same difference that the revenue side shows—namely, that Dallas County spends a much higher proportion of its funds on health and welfare programs. However, Harris County spends the single largest share of its budget on welfare, hospitals, and health. Again, fitting with the fact that Harris County spent more money than it generated, the share of Harris County's budget expended for interest payments is more than twice that of Dallas County. Both governments spend a goodly share of their budgets on public safety—chiefly the sheriff's operations and jails—and on general government, which includes the courts and county administration. Both spend a lesser share on highways and transportation and on environment, parks, and public housing.

Under a 1985 state law, counties are responsible for health care for the indigent, and so health costs have increased in virtually all Texas counties.

Another cost that has risen over the past decade is that of jails, as counties struggle to meet court-imposed minimum jail standards.

Of course, individual Texas counties vary greatly in both revenue and expenditures, depending on whether they are rural or urban, rich or poor, large or small. They also vary according to the services demanded by the residents.

COUNTY POLITICS

County politics is characterized by three interrelated qualities: partisanship, precincts, and a long ballot. With the exception of the professional appointments noted earlier, such as a home demonstration agent and health officer, all the county officials discussed earlier in this chapter are elected. The key electoral units are the four commissioners' precincts, which also serve as the electoral base for constables and JPs. All contenders run under a political party banner and are elected during general elections when major officials such as president, governor, and members of Congress are elected. Because the form of government is the same in all counties, so also are the electoral arrangements. Thus, to a great extent, a description of state parties and elections (Chapters 5 and 6) also describes county politics.

County government, especially in urban areas, is growing more sophisticated, particularly as counties become key players in economic development. However, even on the outskirts of major metropolitan cities, the stereotype of county politics as rural, good ol' boy, and socially conservative comes to life. In Denton County, immediately north of Dallas–Fort Worth, Scott Armey, son of the majority leader of the U.S. House of Representatives, was elected as a commissioner at the age of twenty-three. He has spent considerable energy trying to enlist commissioners in other counties to pass a resolution calling for the restoration of voluntary prayer in public schools, although the issue of school prayer is not in the county's jurisdiction. County commissioners in Williamson County—just north of Austin—almost lost a major Apple Computer installation when they at first turned down a package of economic development incentives for the company because Apple grants health benefits to homosexual couples.

Sources: Melinda Hoffman-Rice, "Scott Armey: Leading the March for School Prayer," *Denton Record-Chronicle,* February 6, 1994, 1A, 2A; Sam Howe Verhovek, "Texas County Retreats over Apple's Gay Policy," *New York Times,* December 8, 1993, A10.

AN EVALUATION OF COUNTY GOVERNMENT

When industrial firms experience problems, they call in teams of management consultants, who make a searching examination and a critical evaluation of the firm's operation. If one could arrange for a management consulting firm to make a thorough examination of county government in Texas, its report would very likely include the following topics.

STRUCTURE AND PARTISANSHIP

The county in Texas is a nineteenth-century political organization struggling to cope with twentieth-century society—hence the "horse-drawn buggy" title of this section. In many states, counties have the same flexibility as cities to choose a *form of government* that is appropriate for the size and complexity of that particular jurisdiction. In Texas, all county governments have the same structure, and the emphasis is on *party politics* because all officials are elected on a partisan basis. The positive aspect of partisanship is that the average voter can understand more clearly what a candidate's approximate political position is when the candidate bears the label "Republican" or "Democrat" than when the voter has no identifying tag. One negative aspect is a heavy reliance on a spoils system, that is, on the appointment of deputy sheriffs, assistant clerks, and road workers on a political basis.

Nationally, although most counties operate with a commission, urban counties serving the majority of the nation's citizens operate with a county manager or appointed administrator.[5] Texas, of course, offers no such flexibility for the larger counties. Although the current structure is uniform and simple, it also makes it difficult to produce decisions for the benefit of all or most county residents because of the emphasis on precincts. Commissioners tend to see themselves as representing their precinct rather than the county as a whole. In turn, the precinct focus makes it difficult to enjoy economies of scale, such as purchasing all road paving materials at one time.

The partisanship and restrictive structure can lead to governance problems. Commissioners often squabble over petty matters. Citizens have difficulty deciding whom to blame if they are dissatisfied with county government, since the commissioners serve as a collective board of directors for the county. For example, a troublesome sheriff—a not uncommon situation—may be reelected while the voters blame the county commissioners for the sheriff's behavior. Similarly, the voters may focus on the county judge, who has one vote on the commissioners court just like the other members, when other members of the court should be the object of attention. Such confusion can happen in any government, but the large number of elected officials—mirroring the state pattern—compounds the problem.

A plus for counties is that they are less bureaucratic than other governments, and so the average citizen can more easily deal with a county office. One reason may be that, unlike the state government, county government does not have a clear-cut separation between legislative and executive branches and functions. The merger of executive and legislative functions, which is called a unitary system, also is found in some city and special district governments. It can sometimes produce a rapid response to a citizen problem or request.

One county judge assessed county government by noting that many county officials are highly responsive to public demands when they must face competitive elections. In fact, he argued that counties are the last true bastions of "grassroots politics," whereby government is close to all the people in the county. Although the court sets much of the policy and the tone for the conduct of county operations, it lacks the authority to give explicit orders to subordinate officials. Nevertheless, this county judge pointed out, by controlling the budget, the commissioners court can often dictate the behavior of

---

5. Robert E. Norwood and Sabrina Strawn, *Texas County Government: Let the People Choose,* 2d ed. (Austin: Texas Research League, 1984), 157.

other elected officials. Additionally, counties have the lowest tax rates of all the governments in Texas.[6] Another county judge put it this way: "We do meat-and-potatoes government . . . not flashy, press-release government, but good government."[7]

Thus, the evaluation of county organization and politics is mixed. The public often shows little interest in county government. Voter turnout is low, and even the media tend to ignore county government and focus instead on big city, state, and national political events. The county is a horse-drawn buggy in structure. It is often highly democratic, especially when it advocates the interests of groups ignored by other governments, since the commissioners must secure support for reelection. However, the willingness of commissioners and other elected officials to attend to the needs of individuals and to deal with details can easily lead to corruption.

MANAGEMENT PRACTICES

With the exception of a few of the larger counties, county government in Texas is one of the last bastions of the *spoils system* in which people are appointed to government jobs on the basis of whom they supported in the last election and how much money they contributed. While a spoils system helps to ensure the involvement of ordinary citizens in government, it also leads to the appointment of unqualified people, especially in jobs requiring specialized training. A spoils system can lead to a high turnover rate if the county tends to usher new elected officials into office on a regular basis. For example, a common practice is for a newly elected sheriff to fire several deputies and bring in his or her own people. Democratic government demands that citizens not only be willing to obey the law but also be able to count on public officials being scrupulous in their own behavior, not merely partisan.

From a management standpoint, a merit system—a *civil service* or a *merit system* of recruitment, evaluation, promotion, and termination is one based on qualifications—and a pay scale that would attract and hold competent personnel would help to improve governmental performance. These also would be fair: to employees for their labors, and to taxpayers as a return on their dollars. The larger counties have made significant strides toward developing professional personnel practices such as competitive hiring, merit raises, and grievance processes, but 90 percent of the counties have a long way to go. In a larger county, commissioners also appoint a wide array of professionals, such as a budget officer, personnel director, and economic development coordinator.

Two other features of county government illustrate its tendency toward inefficient management: *decentralized purchasing* and the road and bridge system. Decentralized purchasing means that each department and each commissioner makes separate purchases. Quantity discounts, which might

---

6. Bell County Judge John Garth, in a conversation with one of the authors on February 21, 1991.
7. Travis County Judge Bill Aleshire in "Elected County Officials—Unlike City—Actually Run Government," *Austin American-Statesman*, September 26, 1996, A15.

be obtained with a centralized purchasing agent, are unavailable on small-lot purchases. Also, the opportunity for graft and corruption is great. To be sure that they will get county business, sellers may find themselves obligated—or at least feel that they are—to do a variety of favors for individual officials in county government. This situation is not unknown in the other governmental units but becomes more widespread in highly decentralized organizations.

Unless a Texas county belongs to the elite 10 percent that have a unit system for countywide administration of the *roads and bridges*, individual commissioners may plan and execute their own programs for highway and bridge construction and maintenance at the precinct level. The obvious result is poor planning and coordination, and also duplication of expensive heavy equipment. These inefficiencies are important because counties, like other local governments, must cope with taxpayer resistance to providing more funding for government. Thus, efficient performance is a must.

In rural areas, the lack of county ordinance power has created a new kind of "range war." The eight hundred indoor and outdoor gun ranges in the state are primarily in rural areas, and counties lack the authority to control the noise or even the straying bullets.

Source: Tara Trower, "Range War," *Austin American-Statesman,* March 4, 1997, B1, B6.

LACK OF ORDINANCE POWER

Texas counties have no general power to pass ordinances—that is, laws pertaining to the county. They do have authority to protect the health and welfare of citizens, and through that power they can regulate the operation of a sanitary landfill and mandate inoculations in the midst of an epidemic. They can regulate subdivision development in unincorporated areas, sometimes sharing power with municipalities and the federal government (for flood control). However, the lack of general ordinance power means that, for example, they cannot zone land to ensure appropriate and similar usage in a given area.

RECOMMENDATIONS

Having reviewed Texas county government, our mythical management consultants probably would recommend greater flexibility in this form of government, particularly in heavily populated areas, to encourage more professional management of personnel, services, purchasing, and all other aspects of county government. They would urge counties to take advantage of economies of scale by centralizing purchasing and adopting a unit system of road and bridge construction and maintenance. They probably would not yet explore any of the forms of city-county cooperation that exist in such areas as San Francisco, Honolulu, or Nashville, since counties in Texas are not yet ready to function as cities. The one exception is El Paso County, where the county and the city have

Texas counties have no authority to pass general ordinances that could, for example, regulate land use in rural areas. The colonias on the outskirts of Texas cities along the Mexican border are an example of unregulated growth.

Courtesy of Ben Sargent.

explored consolidation.[8] The Austin newspaper has also urged some consideration of "government modernization" on the Travis County commissioners.[9]

PROSPECTS FOR REFORM

Given the obvious disadvantages of the current structure, what are the prospects for changing county government in Texas? County commissioners, judges, sheriffs, and other county officers, acting individually as well as through such interest groups as TACO (Texas Association of County Officials), are potent political figures who can and do exercise substantial influence over their state legislators. Unfortunately for the taxpayers, most county

8. Maggie Rivas, "El Paso Still Fights for Government Consolidation," *Dallas Morning News*, July 2, 1989, 47A, 50A.
9. Richard Oppel (editor of the paper), "Time to Ask Right Questions about County Government," *Austin American-Statesman*, September 22, 1996, E3.

officials have shown little willingness to accept change in the structure and function of county government. The exceptions are usually county commissioners in more heavily populated counties, who have taken a number of steps to professionalize government, including the appointment of personnel and budget experts. They are outnumbered ten to one by commissioners in less populous areas. Thus, substantially more citizen participation will be necessary if change is to occur. If city residents, who tend to ignore county politics, were to play a much more active role, reform might be possible because of the sheer numbers they represent when approaching legislators.

Cities: Managed Environments

Unlike the county, the city has a long history of independence and self-government. The power of Greece was concentrated in city-states such as Athens and Sparta, which as early as 700 B.C. were centers of culture and military might. In the Middle Ages, European cities received crown charters that established them as separate and independent entities. One of their major functions was to protect their citizens from external danger; for this reason, the cities of the period were surrounded by high walls, and the citizens paid taxes for this protection. In America this tradition continued, and early American cities sought charters initially from the British crown and later from the state legislatures. In Texas, San Fernando de Béxar (now called San Antonio) was the first city. Its settlement was ordered by the king of Spain and began with fifteen families in 1731.

State legislatures traditionally have been less than sympathetic to the problems of the cities, partly because of rural bias and partly because they wished to avoid being caught in the quagmires of city politics. Therefore, in the nineteenth century the states (including Texas) established **general laws**—statutes that pertained to all municipalities—for the organization of the city governments, to which municipalities were required to conform. But these general laws were too inflexible to meet the growing problems of the cities, and around the turn of the century there was a movement toward municipal home rule. The home-rule laws permitted the cities, within limits, to organize as they saw fit.[10]

In Texas the *municipal home-rule* amendment to the constitution was adopted in 1912. It provides that a city whose population is more than 5,000 is allowed—within certain procedural and financial limitations—to write its own constitution in the form of a city charter, which becomes effective when approved by a majority vote of the citizens. A city charter is the local equivalent of a constitution. Home-rule cities may choose any organizational form or policies as long as they do not conflict with the state constitution or the state laws. General-law cities may organize according to any of the traditional forms of municipal government discussed later in this chapter, but with a number of restrictions. A rather complex categorization of general-law cities based on combinations of population and land area exists.

---

10. Provisions for how both home-rule and general-law municipalities can organize are found in Chapters 9 and 21 to 26 of the *Texas Local Government Code.*

Two legal aspects of city government in Texas that are growing in importance are extraterritorial jurisdiction (ETJ) and annexation. ETJ gives cities limited control over unincorporated territory contiguous to their boundaries; that is, cities get some control over what kind of development occurs just outside the city limits. The zone ranges from a half-mile in distance for cities under 1,500 in population to five miles for those over 100,000. Within these zones, municipalities can require developers and others to conform to city regulations regarding construction, sanitation, utilities, and similar matters. In this way, cities can exercise some positive influence on the quality of life in the immediate area around them. Socially irresponsible individuals and businesses sometimes locate outside both city limits and a city's extraterritorial jurisdiction for the dual purposes of avoiding city taxes—usually higher than the county's—and city regulation—such as building codes. The lack of county ordinance power encourages such behavior, while ETJ helps to correct it.

Annexation power allows cities to bring adjacent unincorporated areas inside the municipal boundaries. Doing so helps prevent suburban developments from incorporating and blocking a large city's otherwise natural development. It also allows a city to expand its tax base. However, municipalities are limited by the need to provide fair notice to residents of the area to be annexed, by the requirement that they provide city services within a reasonable time, and by a restriction that limits the amount of annexed territory in any given year to 10 percent of the city's land area prior to the annexation.

Unincorporated areas and municipal utility districts formed the Annexation Reform Committee during the 1997 legislative session to attempt to curtail municipal annexation powers. Typical of the protests was the situation in North Texas when the small city of Red Oak tried to annex a rural area, causing a major legal battle between the city and the property owners.[11] However, legislators represent people, and the vast majority of people live in cities, and so the curtailment effort did not succeed.[12]

Annexation laws in Texas help to prevent a phenomenon that is very common in other cities, such as New Orleans and Denver. There, more affluent residents have fled to upscale suburbs in what is often called "white flight." They leave the inner cities with inadequate tax revenues and decaying facilities. They no longer pay city taxes but continue to use and enjoy such services as airports, libraries, utilities, and museums, which city residents pay taxes to support. In exercising their annexation powers, municipalities are interested not only in protecting their tax base but also in preserving a pathway for future growth.[13] Although the larger cities are surrounded by suburbs, many of which are upscale, they have been somewhat successful in counteracting white flight and the erosion of their tax bases. Houston is the best (or worst) example of a city using annexation to protect itself. In 1995,

---

11. Judy Jennings, "No Need to Go to War on Annexation Policy," *Austin American-Statesman,* February 15, 1997, A13; and Mike Jackson, "Rage in Red Oak," *Dallas Morning News,* March 7, 1997, 35A, 40A.
12. An excellent summary of legislation pertaining to municipalities can be found in the July (No. 7) issue of *Texas Town & City,* published by the Texas Municipal League, in legislative years.
13. See Terrell Blodgett's letter to the editor of the *Austin American-Statesman* on the topic of annexation law in Texas, November 23, 1994, A8. Blodgett is a former city manager and long-time professor at the LBJ School at the University of Texas at Austin.

Houston, along with Austin, Nederland, and Longview, was the target of special legislation advocated by suburbanites to limit annexation power. Again, the cities prevailed.

Houston has long been known as the only major American city without zoning ordinances that dictate what can be built where—homes, offices, factories. In the past, city leaders have used such terms as *Communist plot* and *socialized real estate* to describe zoning. Voters have explicitly and repeatedly rejected it, most recently in 1993. As a result a church, an office tower, and a home can be found adjacent to one another.

Sources: See, for example, " `Anything Goes' Houstonians May Go the Limit: to Zoning," *New York Times,* October 27, 1993, 1.

ORGANIZATION OF CITY GOVERNMENT

As of 1996, Texas had 284 home-rule municipalities. These municipalities overwhelmingly describe their form of government by standard terms such as "mayor-council," "commission," and "council-manager." Occasionally, one finds a city council that calls itself a commission or a board of aldermen. In a few cases, two of the standard forms of local government have been combined. However, one of the standard forms of municipal government dominates: 250 of the 284 home-rule municipalities prefer council-manager government. Only 33 operate with the mayor-council form, and only 1 uses the mayor-manager form. None uses a straight commission form.[14] The basic forms of local government are described below, with emphasis on the two most popular forms, council-manager and mayor-council.

THE COUNCIL-MANAGER FORM

San Antonio and Dallas are two of the largest cities in the country—along with San Diego and Cincinnati—using this organizational model (Figure 3–4), but smaller cities such as Bay City, Gainesville, and Yoakum also operate with this form of government. Under this system, a city council of five to fifteen members is elected at large or by districts and, in turn, appoints a city manager who is responsible for the hiring and firing of department heads and for the preparation of the budget. A mayor, elected at large or by the council, is a member of the council and presides over it, but otherwise has only the same powers as any other council member.

Proponents of council-manager government, including many political scientists, traditionally have argued that this form of government allows at least some separation of politics and administration. They believe that the council makes public policy and that, once a decision is made, the manager is charged with administering it. In reality, however, politics and administration cannot be separated: The city manager must make recommendations to the council on

---

14. *Texas Almanac and State Industrial Guide, 1998–1999* (Dallas: A. H. Belo, 1997), 436–443.

FIGURE 3–4
Council-Manager
Form

Source: Adapted from Forms of
City Government *(Austin: Institute of Public Affairs, University
of Texas, 1959), 23. Used by
permission.*

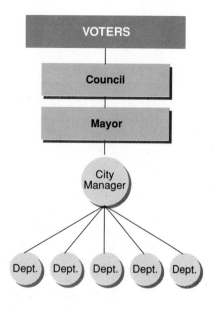

such highly political matters as tax and utility rates and zoning,[15] as the brokering role cited by Alan Ehrenhalt in the chapter-opening quotation indicates. Nevertheless, some citizens claim to perceive a distinction in this type
of government between politics and policy making on one hand and administration on the other, and many are convinced that it is the most efficient form
of city government. States with a large number of council-manager cities
include Texas, California, Maine, and Michigan, among others.

On Becoming a City Manager

How does one become a city manager? A city manager usually has a master's degree in public
administration, public policy, or public affairs. The most common route is an internship in a city
while still in school followed by a series of increasingly responsible general management positions:
administrative assistant, assistant to the city manager, assistant city manager, then city manager.
Alternatively, an individual may begin in a key staff area—for example, as a budget analyst, then
budget director, then director of finance—or in a major operating department—for example, as an
administrative assistant in the public works department, then as an assistant director, then director.
Usually these positions are in more than one city.

For all its efficiency and professionalism, council-manager government
does have some problems. First, council members are part-time and often
serve short tenures, and so rely heavily on the manager for policy guidance.

---

15. A thorough look at modern council-manager government can be found in George Frederick-
son, ed., *Ideal and Practice in Council-Manager Government,* 2d ed. (Washington, D.C.: International City/County Management Association, 1995).

Because the manager is not directly responsible to the voters, this practice makes it more difficult for the average citizen to influence city hall, and many citizens react negatively to reading in the local newspaper about the city manager's policy recommendations, even though the council must approve them. Second, the comparison is frequently drawn between council-manager government and the business corporation because both involve policy-making "boards" and professional managers. When coupled with the emphasis on efficiency, this image of a professionally trained "business manager" also tends to promote the values of the business community. The result is that festering political problems, especially those involving ethnic minorities and the poor, may not be addressed in a timely manner. However, district elections and direct election of the mayor in council-manager cities has reduced this problem somewhat, as representation on city councils has become more diversified. In Dallas, the issues of how many districts there should be and whether any council members should be elected at large seriously divided the city along ethnic lines in 1990–1991. The upshot, after several unsuccessful compromise efforts, was the implementation in 1993 of a 14-1 plan—fourteen council members are elected by districts, and the mayor is elected at large.

THE MAYOR-COUNCIL FORM

In the mayor-council form of municipal government, council members are elected at large or by geographic districts, and the mayor is elected at large. At large means citywide. The mayor-council form has two variants: the *weak mayor–council* form and the *strong mayor–council* form. In the weak mayor–council form, other executives such as the city attorney and treasurer also are elected, whereas in the strong mayor–council form, the mayor has the power to appoint and remove other city executives. In the strong mayor–council form, the mayor also prepares the budget, subject to council approval. In both mayor–council forms, the mayor can veto acts of the city council, but typically fewer council votes are needed to override the mayor's veto in a weak mayor–council city than in a strong mayor–council city. An individual city charter may combine elements of both strong–mayor and weak mayor–council government—for example, giving the mayor budget control while also allowing for some other elected positions. Figure 3–5 illustrates the strong mayor–council form.

The words *strong* and *weak* are used in reference to a mayor's powers in the same way that the word *weak* is applied to the Texas governorship. The terms have to do with the amount of formal power given to the chief executive by the city charter. An individual mayor, by dint of personality, political savvy, and leadership skills, can heavily influence local politics regardless of restrictions in the city charter.

The strong mayor form is most common among the nation's largest cities, whereas the weak mayor form prevails in smaller communities. In Texas, among the state's largest cities, only El Paso and Houston operate with mayor-council government. The other large cities have council-manager government. Small-city examples include Hitchcock and Olney.

FIGURE 3–5
Strong
Mayor-Council
Form

In a number of strong mayor-council cities, the chief of police and some other department heads are elected, although that is not the case in Texas. #Common departments are fire, police, streets and sanitation, utilities, parks and recreation.

Source: Forms of City Government *(Austin: Institute of Public Affairs, University of Texas, 1959), 10. Used by permission.*

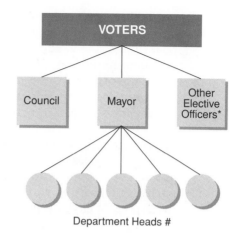

Because mayor-council government is what is called an "unreformed" or a "political" model,[16] it may experience more efficiency problems than a professionally managed city and have less ability to arrive at consensus on policy. To overcome some of its problems, mayor-council cities—particularly larger ones—often have a deputy mayor or chief administrative officer appointed by the mayor who tends to the internal business of the city while the mayor tends to political matters.[17] The leading character in a popular television show in the mid-1990s, *Spin City,* was a deputy mayor.

Many political scientists favor the strong mayor-council form of government because they think that it seems most likely to provide the kind of leadership needed to cope with the growing problems of major urban areas and that it focuses on an elected, not an appointed, official. One reason for this opinion is that the mayor and council members, especially in larger cities, are full-time paid officials who can devote their time to the development of public policy and oversight of government services. Thus, policy proposals come directly from elected officials. If these officials represent a broad public interest, as opposed to narrow interest groups, democracy is well served.

MAYOR-MANAGER FORM

The mayor-manager form of government, also called the chief administrative officer (CAO) form of government, is growing in popularity nationwide. This plan has generated interest because it combines the overt political leadership of a mayor-council plan with the professional management skills identified with council-manager government. Typically, it arises when the mayor recognizes a need for managerial assistance. In this form of government, the city

16. See Robert B. Boynton, "City Councils: Their Roles in the Legislative System," *Municipal Year Book 1976* (Washington, D.C.: International City Management Association, 1976), 67–77, for a detailed discussion on the characteristics of the two models.
17. See Jane Mobley, "Politician or Professional? The Debate over Who Should Run Our Cities Continues," *Governing,* February 1988, 41–48, for an excellent discussion of the advantages and disadvantages of mayors versus city managers as executive officers of cities.

manager reports only to the mayor, not to the council as a whole, and focuses on fiscal/administrative policy implementation. The mayor provides broad policy leadership in addressing major problems such as crime and economic development. In Texas, only Bedford lists itself as having this form of government although the Houston mayor and the budget director have a mayor-manager relationship. Elsewhere, mayor-manager government is practiced in major cities such as San Francisco and New Orleans.

A variant of mayor-manager government is arising in larger municipalities. In Texas and across the country, large cities using the council-manager plan have seen disputes develop among the mayor, council members, and managers as assertive mayors try to carve out a larger role for themselves. The growing interest of big-city mayors in controlling both the political and the administrative aspects of city government is illustrated by events in Dallas. First, in 1992–1993 Mayor Steve Bartlett, a former U.S. congressman, and City Manager Jan Hart struggled for control, with Hart ultimately leaving in 1993 to enter the private sector. In 1997 Mayor Ron Kirk struggled more with the Dallas City Council, which resisted his bid for greater power, than he did with City Manager John Ware, but his intent was the same as Bartlett's: to gain control of the city's executive establishment. A more cooperative mayor-manager relationship existed in San Antonio during the mayoralty of Henry Cisneros (1981–1989), who enjoyed widespread popularity as an elected official but who also worked well with City Manager Lou Fox.[18]

 Disagreements between the mayor and the manager are not limited to home-rule cities. In Gun Barrel City southeast of Dallas, the words *civil war* were used to describe the feud between the mayor and the city manager over most local policy issues.

Source: Kevin O'Hanlon, "Turmoil Sires Chaos in Gun Barrel City," *Austin American-Statesman*, December 3, 1995, B7.

THE COMMISSION FORM—A HISTORICAL FOOTNOTE

The commission form of city government is said to have originated in Galveston. In 1900 the city lost 7,200 persons in a disastrous tidal wave that swept the Texas coast in the wake of a fierce hurricane. The city then applied for and received permission from the state legislature to adopt a commission form of government to meet its emergency needs.

Under this type of organization, the elected commissioners collectively compose the policy-making board and, as individuals, are administrators of various departments such as public safety, streets and transportation, finance, and so on. They are usually elected at large. Although initially widely copied, the commission system has more recently lost favor because many think that the commissioners tend to become advocates for their own departments rather

---

18. See Melvin G. Holli, "America's Mayors: The Best and the Worst since 1960," *Social Science Quarterly* 78, no. 1 (March 1997): 149–157. Holli's survey ranks Cisneros as the second best mayor of the modern era and the best minority mayor in the United States since 1960. Richard J. Daley of Chicago was ranked number one.

than public-interest advocates who act on behalf of the entire city. Also, the city commission is subject to many of the same problems as the county commission, including corruption and unclear lines of responsibility. Although some cities still call their city councils "commissions," Texas home-rule cities have abandoned this form of government. Some general-law cities still have commission government.

FORMS USED IN GENERAL-LAW CITIES

There are almost 900 general-law cities in Texas—cities whose population is fewer than 5,000 or somewhat larger cities that, for one reason or another, have not opted for home rule. These cities can organize under any of three basic forms of government: aldermanic (a variant of the mayor-council type), council-manager, or commission. However, state law limits the size of the council, specifies other municipal officials, spells out the power of the mayor, and places other restrictions on matters that home-rule cities can decide for themselves.[19] Because of their small size, most of the general-law cities have chosen the aldermanic model—basically mayor-council government. The council-manager form, calling for the hiring of a professional city manager, is thought to be too expensive and unnecessary in a small city. There is also the problem of finding a trained city manager who is knowledgeable about small-town issues. However, many smaller cities, such as Anthony and Nolanville, have designated the city clerk as the chief administrative officer without bothering to adopt council-manager government formally. A few, such as Oak Point, have hired a part-time manager—usually a graduate student in a nearby public administration program—or have banded with other small communities to hire a "circuit-riding" city manager. Whatever their official title—city manager, city clerk, city secretary, or assistant to the mayor—administrators in smaller cities more than earn their salaries. They usually serve as general managers, personnel directors, tax assessor-collectors, and so forth because often they are the only full-time professional in the city's government.

WHAT FORM IS PREFERABLE?

The only clear answer is that council-manager government seems to work best in middle-sized cities (from 25,000 to 250,000 or so in population). These cities are largely suburban and prefer the council-manager form's emphasis on businesslike efficiency and the distance it maintains from party politics and from state and national political issues. Smaller cities that can afford a city manager also often do well with that form, but most use a mayor-council form. The really large cities often fare best with either a mayor-council form or a mayor-manager form since they need the political focus provided by the elected mayor.[20]

---

19. See *Texas Local Government Code,* Chapters 22–25.
20. See, for example, Boynton, "City Councils: Their Role in the Legislative System"; Tari Renner and Victor S. DeSantis, "Contemporary Patterns in Municipal Government Structures," *The Municipal Year Book, 1993* (Washington, D.C.: International City/County Management Association, 1993), 57–68; and Daniel R. Morgan and Robert E. England, *Managing Urban America,* 4th ed. (Chatham, N.J.: Chatham House, 1996), 58–80.

FIGURE 3–6
**Revenues in San
Antonio and
Houston, 1993–94
($1.7 billion in San
Antonio, $2 billion
in Houston)**

*Source: Finances of Individual
City Governments Having
500,000 Population or More,
1993–94, citydoc.txt at
www.census.gov*

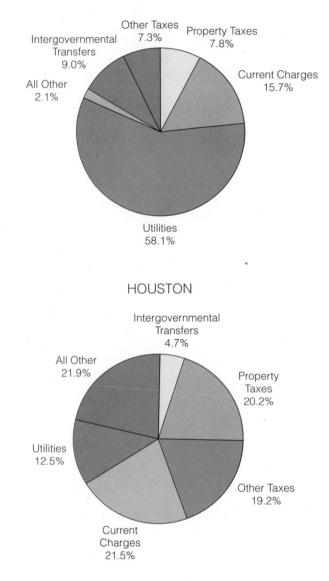

SAN ANTONIO

Other Taxes 7.3%
Property Taxes 7.8%
Intergovernmental Transfers 9.0%
Current Charges 15.7%
All Other 2.1%
Utilities 58.1%

HOUSTON

Intergovernmental Transfers 4.7%
All Other 21.9%
Property Taxes 20.2%
Utilities 12.5%
Other Taxes 19.2%
Current Charges 21.5%

CITY FINANCE

REVENUES AND EXPENDITURES

Besides utilities, the most important sources of municipal funding are the
property tax, general and selective sales taxes, borrowing through bonds, and
current charges—everything from fees for using municipal golf courses to airport landing fees. Other sources include intergovernmental transfers and miscellaneous fees and fines, such as liquor licenses and traffic fines collected by
the municipal court. Figure 3–6 shows how the state's two largest cities,

FIGURE 3–7
Expenditures in San Antonio and Houston, 1993–94 ($1.7 billion in San Antonio, $2.1 billion in Houston)

Source: Finances of Individual City Governments Having 500,000 Population or More, 1993–94, citydoc.txt at www.census.gov

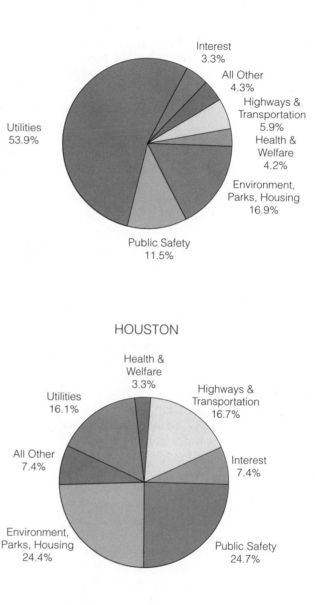

SAN ANTONIO

Interest
3.3%

All Other
4.3%

Highways &
Transportation
5.9%

Health &
Welfare
4.2%

Environment,
Parks, Housing
16.9%

Public Safety
11.5%

Utilities
53.9%

HOUSTON

Health &
Welfare
3.3%

Highways &
Transportation
16.7%

Interest
7.4%

Public Safety
24.7%

Environment,
Parks, Housing
24.4%

All Other
7.4%

Utilities
16.1%

Houston and San Antonio, raise money. The most striking difference is in utilities revenues and expenditures. Because San Antonio's utilities include electricity, both the revenues and the expenditures are much higher than those of Houston. Another obvious difference is that the percentage of San Antonio's revenues that comes from federal government transfers is almost double that of Houston's. The U.S. government makes payments in lieu of taxes when federal installations occupy land that might otherwise generate property taxes. San Antonio is a major military center.

Cities spend their money on diverse services. For most cities, the largest areas of expenditure are police and fire protection, streets, solid-waste disposal, parks and recreation, and interest on municipal debt. Figure 3–7 shows how Houston and San Antonio raise and spend their money. Again, one of the most obvious differences is in utilities. The other marked difference is in the area of environment, parks, and housing, which includes everything from sewage to parks and recreation to community development. A third notable difference is Houston's spending on public safety, the percentage of which is almost double that of San Antonio.

FISCAL PROBLEMS AND SOLUTIONS

Municipalities, like the state (see Chapters 13 and 14), have had to adapt to changing economic conditions and shrinking sources of income coupled with burgeoning population growth.[21] In the almost-thirty-year period since 1970, the state has gone through a boom-bust-boom cycle. Today, Texas cities find themselves with heightened demands for services as a result of growth but with more restrictions on how to pay for them.

The financial problems of Texas cities have *six principal causes*.[22] First, beginning in 1978, taxpayers across the country began to *revolt against rapidly rising property (real estate) taxes,* then and now the most important source of local revenues. In all, forty-five of the fifty states have passed some type of taxpayer protective measure, such as Proposition 13 in California, Proposition 2½ in Massachusetts, the Hancock Amendment in Missouri, and the Texas 8 percent rollback law. The Texas rollback law stipulates that any combination of an increase in *tax rate* or *tax base* of 8 percent or more is subject to an election to roll back the increase if the revenue is to be used to support regular government operations. Tax rate is the amount per $100 of property valuation due in taxes; tax base is the real estate that is assessed and assigned a value. This provision applies to all local governments.

Second, *national priorities and responsibilities have changed* as a result of increased political conservatism and growing budget deficits. However, although less federal funding was available, the needs of the cities did not diminish.[23] The statement at the beginning of the chapter that "somebody forgot to tell Amarillo to duck" applies to all Texas municipalities.

Third, *both the national and state governments have shifted service burdens to the cities*. These shifts involve many basic but costly services. For example, the state legislature mandated in 1987 that the Texas Highway Department would no longer maintain rights-of-way along farm-to-market roads inside the city limits of cities whose population is 50,000 or greater; thus, the cities had to increase their maintenance staffs and budgets. Stringent standards for water quality, including sewage treatment, are still imposed, but

---

21. Texas, the second most populous state in the country, was seventh in rate of growth from 1990 to 1995 and was projected to lead the nation in growth rate until the year 2000. See Andrea Stone, "California on the Upswing," *USA Today,* December 31, 1996, 6A, and Bruce Nichols, "Texas Leads All States in Population Growth," *Dallas Morning News,* November 11, 1997, 43A, 60A.
22. This discussion of municipal finance relies heavily on the remarks of Lloyd V. Harrell, then city manager of Denton, in an April 23, 1988, address to political science honors students at the University of North Texas. His observations are still valid, and most of the material presented here on the causes of fiscal stress and strategies for addressing them is from him.
23. Michael Wines, "Cities Digging Deep and Wide as Congress Tightens Purse," *New York Times,* April 8, 1996, A1.

the national government no longer provides most of the funding for improvements in municipal water and sewage treatment plants as it once did. Since 1994, both cities and counties have had to bear the additional expense of "motor voter" registration (see Chapter 6), and as of 1997, all governmental units conducting elections must provide an additional ballot box in each location for use by voters who must sign an affidavit that they are registered voters because they did not carry their registration card with them to the polling place or were otherwise challenged as to being a legal voter. In 1997, the legislature also created the Unfunded Mandates Interagency Workgroup to review and provide notice of all *unfunded mandates* imposed on local governments by the state.[24] An unfunded mandate is a requirement set by a higher level of government that costs money to meet but for which no financial support is forthcoming from the higher government.

Fourth, *changes in federal policy*, especially in the 1986 federal income tax reform, have fundamentally affected municipal debt flexibility and costs. When the maximum tax rate was lowered, both individuals and banks had less incentive to invest in tax-free municipal bonds, which typically pay lower interest rates than do taxable investments. Moreover, cities can no longer invest the proceeds from bond sales and add the interest earned to the funds available for the project for which the bonds were sold. Beginning in 1988, the purchasers of state and municipal bonds had to be registered, a requirement that increases the cost to cities. Furthermore, municipalities were beginning to be concerned that the national government would eliminate the tax-free status of local bonds in an effort to find another source of federal revenue. The upshot is that cities have less revenue.

Fifth, *Texas municipalities have become increasingly reliant on the local sales tax*. Cities can assess a 1 percent retail sales tax, or 1.5 percent if the city is outside a metropolitan transit district, which also assesses a sales tax. In addition, cities can add another half percent to offset revenues lost if property taxes are lowered and yet another half percent to support economic development. Any sales tax authorization requires citizen approval. During periods of economic decline, municipalities tend to become very interested in the additional sales tax possibilities in order to meet revenue demands.

Sixth, *competition among the nation, states, and local governments over revenue sources has intensified*. For example, most citizens are particularly resentful of sharp increases in property taxes; indeed, property tax resentment is the root cause of taxpayer revolt. (See Chapter 10 for a discussion of taxation at the state level.) Cities often find themselves particularly constrained with regard to the property tax not because of their own sharp increase in the tax rate but because of school district increases that affect basically the same people. Both state and local governments have looked askance at federal proposals to institute a type of national sales tax, given the reliance of other governments on this type of tax.

The combination of these factors has resulted in cities facing steady or even increasing demands for services but stable or declining revenues. Moreover, the problem of mandates—services or programs required by the state or the national government—reduces the discretion of the municipality in determining how to spend what money it does have.

---

24. "Seventy-fifth Texas Legislature Adjourns," *Texas Town & City*, Number 7, 1997, 14.

Sometimes fiscal issues cause divisiveness among Texas cities. In 1997 a major legislative issue in Texas was deregulation of electric utilities. Municipalities that bought their electric power from private companies, cooperatives, or other cities were in favor of deregulation in the hope of securing lower rates for themselves, local businesses, and citizens. But municipalities that generated and sold electric power and depended significantly on the revenue from the sales were opposed to deregulation. The position of power companies varied according to whether they held a monopoly or wanted to break an existing monopoly. A major issue was the debt both municipalities and private companies had incurred to build new facilities and how they would pay off that debt if they lost customers or had to reduce their rates. That issue waylaid the bill in the legislature. Eight states had passed deregulation legislation by mid-1997, and pressures were being applied to Congress to pass national legislation mandating deregulation of electric utilities.

Source: Glenn Hodges, "Brace Yourself for a Shock: Deregulated Electricity Will Go the Same Way as Planes and Phones—More Money for Less Service," *Washington Post Weekly Edition,* April 14, 1997, 21; Matthew H. Brown, "Standing the Electric Industry on Its Head," *State Legislatures,* March 1997, 12–18; Tom Arrandale, "Electrical Storm," *Governing,* July 1996, 20–24; "Governor on Electric Dereg: It's Good for Texas," *Texas Government News,* November 4, 1996, 1; Homer Jones, "Deregulation of the Utilities Industry Puts Texas Companies on Top of the World," *Texas Business,* November 1996, 23–29; "Deregulation Sparks," *Fiscal Notes,* published by John Sharp, Texas Comptroller of Public Accounts, December 1996, 1, 6–10, which points out that the state has rates below the national average but higher total bills because of the hot summers; "Snap, Crackle, Fizz: Electric Dereg Bills to Generate Interest," *Texas Government News,* March 3, 1997, 1.

Cities have engaged in *six tactics* in response to the tightening revenue picture. First, they have placed greater emphasis on *public-private cooperation* in everything from joint funding of arts centers to private sponsorship of Fourth of July celebrations. Second, cities have turned to *privatization*—that is, turning some services over to the private sector. The most frequent example is solid-waste disposal. Instead of the city hauling away garbage, the homeowner or business pays a private company to dispose of solid wastes. Third, cities are *asking citizens to volunteer* to perform some services that were formerly provided by paid employees. Examples include picking up litter and supervising and even constructing playgrounds. Fourth, cities have turned to *productivity enhancement,* a package of management techniques ranging from flexible scheduling of employees' time to workload standards and pay-for-performance, to make scarce financial resources stretch further. Fifth, cities have sought *new revenue sources.* One is user fees, charges paid directly by the consumer of services. Although municipalities have long had user fees for services such as water, they are charging new or higher fees for other services, such as recreational facilities. The other is special fees, including so-called impact fees charged to developers for the effect that land development has on streets, utilities, and other basic services. Sixth, municipalities have simply *terminated certain services;* the most obvious example is refusal to accept grass clippings at the local landfill in an effort to extend the life of the landfill.

All these strategies have worked in part. The problem for municipalities is how to respond to a disaster such as the tornado that struck downtown Lancaster in 1994, to a major economic upheaval such as the closing of a military base, or to yet more federal and state mandates for, say, clean air, when they are just holding their own. Making the problem worse, some traditional sources of local revenue are being considered by state and national governments as likely revenue sources for them. For example, the national government periodically debates a value-added tax, which is an elaborate form of a sales tax.

CITY POLITICS

Our discussion of forms of city government and city finance gives us a substantial amount of factual information about the operation of the city but tells us little about how city government really works. Who gets the rewards, and who is deprived? Which individuals and groups benefit most from city government, and which groups bear the burdens?

The electoral system used by Texas cities is an indication of how the rewards and deprivations are distributed. Although the partisanship of candidates is well known in cities like Beaumont and El Paso, all Texas cities hold **nonpartisan elections.** The irony is that the municipalities are surrounded by counties with highly partisan elections. In most Texas cities, municipal elections are held during the spring in a further attempt to separate city government from party politics. In this electoral setting, a private interest group such as a local Realtors' association or homeowners may sponsor a slate of candidates for municipal office, just as a political party would, under the guise of a civic organization that purportedly has no goals of its own except efficient and responsive government. Such is not the case, however. These groups do have goals and are highly effective in achieving them. In some cities, a charter association or good government league exists; these organizations inevitably reflect the interests of conservative business elements in the community. In other cities, environmentalists or neighborhood advocates or antitax groups may launch well-organized single-issue campaigns. In addition, a number of more or less ad hoc groups usually appear at election time to sponsor one or more candidates; and in all Texas cities, independent candidates also come forth with their own campaigns to seek public office.

Changes in Texas politics are most evident in the major cities where leaders and interest groups reflect newer interests and where the sacrosanct principle of nonpartisanship is sometimes violated. Austin, San Antonio, Houston, Dallas, El Paso, Fort Worth, and Galveston have had women mayors, as have more than 200 smaller communities. El Paso and San Antonio have elected Mexican American men as mayors, and Dallas and Houston have elected African American men.

Austin, Houston, and Dallas have become the homes of large groups of politically active homosexuals. In all three cities, politicians of many ideological persuasions seek the support of the Gay and Lesbian Political Caucus.

In Dallas and Houston, although party labels were not officially used, recent mayors' races have clearly pitted prominent Republicans against prominent Democrats.

In the big cities, the importance of neighborhood representation and ethnic representation has intensified to such an extent that it is difficult to gain a workable consensus for establishing public policy. Instead, individual council members sometimes advocate the needs of their districts to the exclusion of concerns about the city as a whole.

Closely associated with nonpartisan elections is the system of electing candidates for the city council at-large. All voters select all the members of the council and vote for as many candidates as there are positions on the council. In another practice widely followed in Texas cities, the **place system,** the seats on the council are designated as Place One, Place Two, and so on. In this type of election, candidates who file for a particular place run only against other candidates who also file for that place. Voting is still citywide. The at-large, by-place system predominates in smaller cities.

Increasingly, however, Texas cities whose population is 50,000 or more are amending their charters to provide for a **district system,** wherein candidates are required to live in a particular geographic area within the city and run against only those candidates who also live in the district. Voters choose only among candidates within their district, although the mayor is usually elected at large. In other cities, some council members are elected by district and some at large. Often the change to district elections occurs as the result of a successful court suit alleging discrimination against minorities, who find it difficult to win election in a citywide race (see Chapter 12). Running in districts costs less money and has the advantage of allowing minority candidates to concentrate their campaigning in neighborhoods with large numbers of individuals who share the candidate's ethnic background. Often, additional council seats are created when a city switches to district elections.

Advocates of at-large and by-place elections argue that the council focuses on citywide concerns, but district elections result in a fragmented council whose members concentrate on only the problems of their electoral district. They also think that district elections are incompatible with council-manager government, which predominates in the state's home-rule cities, because they make local elections "too political." Advocates of district elections think that the council is more representative when members are elected by wards or districts because minorities, spokespersons for citizens' groups, and individuals without personal wealth have a better opportunity to be elected and will be more inclined to address "local district" problems. They believe government by its very nature is political, and so all political viewpoints should be represented.

Questions about the organization of elections and the nature of representation are at the heart of the democratic process. One measure of a city's democratic morality is the extent to which the council is diversified ethnically, economically, and geographically. Thus, democratic theorists usually recommend district over at-large elections except in small municipalities where all candidates are likely to be known by most voters.

Controversy also exists over whether elections should be nonpartisan. As discussed in Chapter 6, nonpartisan elections rob the voters of the most important symbol that they have for making electoral choices: the party label. Without knowing whether a candidate is a Democrat, a Republican, or a member of some other party, how does the voter decide how to vote?

In answering this question, critics of nonpartisan elections say that voters depend on personalities and extraneous matter. For example, television personalities and athletes frequently win elections simply because they are better known than their opponents are. These critics also think that nonpartisan elections rob the community of organized and effective criticism of the government in power. Since most candidates win as individuals rather than as members of an organized political party with common goals and policies, such criticism is sporadic and ineffectual, and meaningful policy alternatives seldom are stated. Chapter 5 points out that Texas political parties are not well organized. The blame for weak party organizations is often placed on nonpartisan local elections because the parties have no strong grassroots input. A fourth criticism is that nonpartisan elections encourage the development of civic organizations that are, in essence, local political parties whose purposes and policy proposals are not always clear to the voters.

Advocates of nonpartisan elections obviously disagree. They think that the absence of a party label allows local elections to focus on local issues and not on national issues about which the municipal government can do little or nothing. They note that television personalities, athletes, and actors are also elected under party banners. Moreover, they point to the fact that local civic groups clarify, not confuse, local issues. Homeowners, taxpayers, and consumers have become political forces that stand in contrast to the traditional, business-oriented civic associations. As a result, participation is enhanced, although resolving political disagreements has become more difficult.

At-large elections, nonpartisan voting, and holding elections in the spring apparently do contribute to low voter turnout. A municipal election in which as many as 25 percent of the eligible voters participate is unusual. Many local elections are decided on the basis of the preference of only 5 or 10 percent of the eligible voters. Moreover, statistics on voting behavior for all elections show that older, affluent whites vote more frequently than do the young, the poor, and ethnic minorities. The structure of municipal elections in Texas, particularly when those elections are at-large, tends to perpetuate the dominant position of the white middle-class business community. Thus, when one examines municipal government against the criteria for a democratic government, one finds some problems of participation, especially among the less affluent and among ethnic minorities.

Special Districts: Our Hidden Governments

Perhaps the best way to introduce the topic of special districts is to look at the changes in Texas local government shown in Table 3–1. The table shows that the number of counties in Texas has remained the same during the period cited, the number of municipalities has increased by 35 percent, the number of school districts has decreased by approximately 25 percent (due to consolidation), and the number of special districts (our hidden governments) has increased by 226 percent.

WHAT IS A SPECIAL DISTRICT?

A special district is a unit of local government created by an act of the legislature to perform limited functions. Its authority is narrow rather than broad, as in the case of the city or the county. Any further definition is almost impossible; special districts vary enormously in size, organization, function, and importance.

There are about two dozen different types of special districts in Texas. About one-fourth of these are housing and community-development districts, while another fourth are concerned with problems of water—control and

TABLE 3–1

Units of Local Government in Texas, 1962–1992

Type of Government	1962	1972	1982	1992
Counties	254	254	254	254
Municipalities	866	1,000	1,121	1,171
School Districts	1,474	1,157	1,125	1,101
Special Districts (nonschool)	733	1,215	1,692	2,393
Total	3,327	3,626	4,192	4,919

SOURCES: David W. Tees, *A Fresh Look at Special Districts in Texas* (Austin: Texas Urban Development Commission, 1971); *Texas Almanac and State Industrial Guide, 1978–79* (Dallas: A. H. Belo, 1978), 582; Bureau of the Census, *Statistical Abstract of the United States, 1984* (Washington, D.C., 1984) and *Statistical Abstract of the United States, 1994.*

improvement, drainage, navigation, supply, and sanitation. Other frequently encountered types of special districts are airport, soil conservation, municipal utilities, hospital, fire prevention, weed control, and community college districts.

Every county has a tax appraisal district that is responsible for assessing property and providing up-to-date tax rolls to each taxing jurisdiction—county, municipalities, school districts, and other special districts. In addition to assessment, the uniform appraisal district may have a formal agreement with one or more of the taxing jurisdictions to collect taxes.

No single state or county agency is responsible for supervising the activities or auditing the financial records of all these special districts. Such supervision depends on the type of district involved. For example, community college districts are supervised by the Texas Higher Education Coordinating Board and the Texas Education Agency. Average citizens, however, have a hard time keeping track of the many special districts surrounding them.

WHY SPECIAL DISTRICTS?

Why does Texas have so many special districts? And why is this form of government growing so rapidly?

INADEQUACY OF ESTABLISHED GOVERNMENTS

First, our established governments—the cities and counties—are inadequate to solve many of the increasingly diverse problems of government. The problem of flood control can seldom be solved within a single city or county, for example; in fact, it frequently goes beyond state boundaries, thus requiring an interstate authority. Cities and counties may find it difficult to finance needed projects. Hospital and community college districts are sometimes created because the debt limitations on established governmental units make taking on a major new activity all but impossible. Then, too, local units may be incapable of coping with governmental problems for other reasons, such as poor organizational structure and a lack of personnel. Special districts are part of the price paid for governmental institutions such as counties that were fashioned a century ago and that are not always capable of addressing complex modern problems.

These inadequacies make the creation of a new unit of government an attractive solution. Perhaps nowhere does one see the need for, and advantages of, special districts more than in the various water-supply districts. The Lower Colorado River Authority, for example, owns and operates six lakes.

EASE OF ORGANIZATION AND OPERATION

Part of the attraction of special districts is that they are easy to organize and operate. Political leaders of cities and counties frequently promote a special district as a solution to what might otherwise become "their problem," and the legislature is willing to go along. Creating a hospital district, for example, means that the city and the county don't have to raise their taxes. Indeed, the cost may be spread over several cities or counties included in the special district.

PRIVATE GAIN

In a few instances, special districts have been created primarily for private gain. Land speculators and real estate developers create special districts called municipal utility districts (MUDs) on the outskirts of urban areas to increase the value of their holdings. Once enabling legislation has been obtained from the state, it requires only a handful of votes in the sparsely settled, newly created district to authorize a bond issue for the development of water, sewer, and other utilities. This development increases the value of the property in the district, to the benefit of the developers. Ultimately, of course, the taxpayers pay for the bonds, sometimes through very high utility rates. MUDs are a good example of the consequences of a lack of effective state regulation of special districts.

FLEXIBILITY

Special districts offer great flexibility to government organizations and have the added attraction of rarely conflicting with existing units. A two-city airport such as Dallas–Fort Worth International is the result of a flexible airport authority. In 1997–1998, however, DFW proponents did find themselves in conflict with airlines that wanted to expand operations at Dallas's Love Field.

APOLITICAL

With highly technical problems such as flood control, the special district offers the opportunity to "get it out of politics." In other words, it is possible to take a businesslike approach and bring in technical specialists to attack the problem. Of course, other types of special districts—most notably, those whose purpose is economic development—tend to be highly political.

ASSESSMENT OF SPECIAL DISTRICTS

Special districts other than school districts are *profoundly undemocratic.* They are indeed "hidden governments," with far less visibility than city or county governments. It is not an exaggeration to say that every reader of this book is under the jurisdiction of at least one special district, yet it will be a very rare reader who knows which districts affect her or him, how much they cost in taxes, who the commissioner or other officials of each such district are, whether they are elected or (as is more frequently the case) appointed, and what policies they follow. Special district government is hidden government, unseen by and frequently unresponsive to the people. Thus, when one applies the test of democratic morality, one finds that special districts fail to meet the standards of participation and public input.

Most special districts are small in size and scope. Because of this, they are *uneconomical*. Their financial status is often shaky, and so the interest rates that taxpayers must pay on the bond issues used to finance many types of special district projects are exceptionally high. Economies such as large-scale purchasing are impossible.

Finally, one of the most serious consequences of the proliferation of special districts is that *they greatly complicate the problems of government, particularly in urban areas*. With many separate governments, the likelihood is greater that haphazard development, confusion, and inefficiency will occur. No single government has comprehensive authority, and coordination among so many smaller governments becomes extremely difficult. Texans have been reluctant to experiment with a comprehensive urban government. Their individualism demands retention of the many local units, although metropolitan areas such as Miami and Nashville have succeeded with comprehensive government.

Instead, Texans rely on one of the twenty-four *regional planning councils*, also known as *councils of governments* (COGs), to provide coordination in metropolitan areas. These voluntary organizations of local government provide such functions as regional land-use and economic planning, police training, and fact-finding studies on problems such as transportation.

Given the inadequacies of comprehensive planning and revenue shortfalls at the local level, special districts will surely continue to proliferate. Under current conditions, they are too easy to create and operate as short-range solutions to governmental problems. Such continued proliferation, without adequate planning and supervision, will result not in the solution but rather in the worsening of the problems of local and particularly urban government.

SCHOOL DISTRICTS

School districts are an exception to much of the foregoing discussion of special districts for several reasons. First, school board members are publicly elected, most commonly in an at-large, by-place system. Second, their decisions are usually well publicized, with the local newspapers and broadcast media paying careful attention to education decisions. Third, the public has considerable interest in and knowledge about school-district politics. Indeed, although county or city public hearings sometimes fail to attract a crowd, as soon as a school board agenda includes a topic such as determining attendance districts—basically, who gets bused and who doesn't—or sex education, the public turns out for the debate. Fourth, the number of school districts has been steadily declining for fifty years. Finally, although the local boards have a substantial amount of control over such matters as individual school management, location of schools, and personnel, the state is the ultimate authority for basic school policies and shares in the funding of public schools.

Public school finance has been a dominant issue in Texas politics at several points in the state's history, but particularly since 1987. The fact that more than 1,000 school districts exist is one of the factors contributing to considerable unevenness in the quality of education provided from one district to the next. This unevenness and the quest for solutions to public school finance are examined in detail in Chapter 12.

Local Government: Prospects for the Future

The trends toward urbanization and suburbanization no doubt will continue, with the result that metropolitan problems will become more acute than they are today. Nowhere is the problem of rapid growth and dealing with a sprawl that even cuts across county lines more obvious than in the Austin Metropolitan Area,[25] which topped 1 million in population in 1996. What are the prospects for local governments in Texas under these circumstances?

Texas has twenty-eight metropolitan areas: Houston, Dallas, Fort Worth–Arlington, San Antonio, Austin–San Marcos, El Paso, McAllen–Edinburg–Mission, Beaumont–Port Arthur, Corpus Christi, Brownsville–Harlingen–San Benito, Killeen–Temple, Galveston–Texas City, Lubbock, Brazoria, Waco, Amarillo, Longview–Marshall, Tyler, Laredo, Bryan–College Station, Wichita Falls, Abilene, Odessa, Texarkana, Midland, San Angelo, Sherman–Denison, and Victoria. It has two consolidated metropolitan statistical areas (CMSAs) (a U.S. Bureau of the Census term for two or more primary metropolitan statistical areas that are consolidated and that have more than a million people): Dallas–Fort Worth and Houston–Galveston–Brazoria. An official metroplitan area has at least 100,000 people, although when the Census Bureau reorganized its categories in 1983, it "grandfathered in" metropolitan areas with between 50,000 and 100,000 people. Sherman–Denison and Victoria fall into the grandfathered category.

There are several developments worth noting. As urban problems and local finance problems become more acute, national and state governments are being forced to pay more attention to them. One major consideration in the 1997 legislative struggle over utility deregulation was the recognition that the legislature would have to find a way for both cities and private companies to retire their debt on power plants. This recognition came about in part because *the legislature is becoming more "citified."*

Another significant development occurred in August 1978, when the voters of Houston and six of its suburbs approved the creation of a Metropolitan Transit Authority with taxing power and authority to establish transit systems as alternatives to Houston's increasingly congested freeways. Other Texas metropolitan areas such as Dallas are following suit. It has long been obvious that the practice of virtually every person using his or her own motor vehicle for personal and business travel is incompatible with increasing urbanization. Smog, congestion, and even rush-hour gridlock do not make for a high quality of life. *Mass-transit systems* must be established if the trend toward further

---

25. See, for example, Chuck Lindell, "Recharging the City's Heart," *Austin American-Statesman,* January 5, 1997, A1, A10; Joe Grey, "Austin City Unlimited," *Texas Business,* November 1966, 30–41; and Sylvia Moreno, "Some Worry Boom Is Spreading Austin's Aura Too Thin," *Dallas Morning News,* December 29, 1996, 1A, 7A. In the last article, the Austin city manager is quoted as saying that Austin is "not the town you went to college in."

urbanization is to continue, especially given the inability of the state to build roadways fast enough to move traffic at peak times.

Another development is that of *strategic planning*, a type of planning that focuses on identifying a mission and pursuing it in an opportunistic manner by taking advantage of any favorable situation that comes along. A community that strives to be high technology might aggressively seek to persuade electronics plants to locate there, perhaps even ignoring some of their environmental problems.

A fourth area of concern for the future is *interlocal cooperation*. COGs are one example of an arrangement that allows the many kinds of local governments—counties, cities, special districts—to work together to solve their common problems. Cooperative ventures such as city-county ambulance service, city-school playgrounds and libraries, and multiple-city purchasing are other examples. Indeed, interlocal agreements are the most dynamic element of modern intergovernmental relations and can help to overcome some of the negative effects of the growing number of governments.

A fifth area of concern is *ordinance-making power for counties*. The lack of ordinance-making power is developing into a serious problem for safety, environmental, and aesthetic standards, as well as other matters. For example, an issue of growing concern is the lack of control over adult bookstores and massage parlors that set up shop just outside a municipality, where control of them becomes a problem for the county. Indeed, counties asked for legislative relief in 1989 on this specific issue. Counties want and need ordinance-making power but have thus far been denied it, primarily because of the opposition of real estate businesses and developers, who can, for example, create developments in unincorporated areas outside the extraterritorial jurisdiction of the cities that do not have to meet rigorous city building codes.

A sixth major problem that will continue to plague local governments is *funding*. With an improved economy, some of the financial strains have been alleviated, but, unlike those of many enterprises, the costs of local government are not subject to economies of scale. In manufacturing, for example, producing more cars or soap bars results in lowered unit costs—the cost of one car or bar of soap. This principle doesn't hold true for picking up more bags of garbage or cleaning more streets. Burgeoning populations that move farther and farther away from the central city make delivery of services more costly.

Leadership in Local Government

Historically, genuine differences have existed between county leadership and the leadership of other local governments. Elected officials in county government hold full-time positions that pay decent salaries and represent starting points in party politics. In most other local governments, a strong tradition of amateurism prevails: Elected officials are paid parking-and-lunch money and give their time as merely an extension of the same service orientation that leads them to accept office in Kiwanis or Rotary or the Business and Professional Women's Club. The decentralized nature of county governments has often led to rural fiefdoms of commissioners or sheriffs, but in urban counties, candidates as diverse as ethnic minority candidates with major social agendas and young conservatives contemplating a lifetime in politics are beginning to seek county office. Former Governor Ann Richards, for example, began her political career as a county commissioner. In large cities, serving on the city council also can be a step into big-time politics, and mayors have gone on to both the state and national capitols. City councils and school boards are becoming increasingly diversified in terms of gender, ethnicity, and viewpoint.[26]

How to Get Involved in Local Government

Local government is the logical starting point for exercising your democratic rights and getting involved as a participant in government. Here are a few suggestions for how to go about getting involved:

★ Go to the party precinct conventions, held immediately after the primary elections (see Chapter 6).
★ Attend a public hearing and speak out.
★ Organize a petition drive on a matter of importance to you—saving the trees along a planned freeway route, for example.
★ Attend a neighborhood meeting.
★ Attend a meeting of the city council, county commission, or school board.
★ Talk to the city clerk or the county clerk to find out how to volunteer for an advisory committee or citizen task force.
★ Volunteer to work for a local candidate during an election.

Summary

Local governments are the governments most likely to have a daily impact on the citizen, and much of this effect is critical to the quality of life. Will our children get a good public education, or should we save to send them to private school? Is our neighborhood safe, or will we have to live behind triple-locked doors with a guard dog for a companion? Will we enjoy a reasonably efficient and economical transportation system, or will we have to fight dangerous and congested freeway traffic two or three hours a day to get to and from our jobs?

The answers to these and a hundred other critical questions are given by the units of local government. And Texas counties, cities, special districts, and COGs seem ill prepared to provide optimum solutions. County governments must cope with modern problems despite having an inflexible, outmoded organizational structure. City governments are better organized and have more comprehensive powers, yet they too are handicapped by a variety of factors, including the rapid increase in urban population, the proliferation of independent special districts, and the limited and frequently reluctant cooperation of state and national government. COGs, as voluntary organizations, provide only very limited solutions to problems of organized, coordinated planning. All local governments will face serious revenue problems for the foreseeable future.

Texas, like most states, will undoubtedly continue to become more and more urbanized. Consequently, problems such as congestion, poor housing,

---

26. See, for example, Edward C. Olson and Laurence Jones, "Change in Hispanic Representation on Texas City Councils Between 1980–1993," *Texas Journal of Political Studies* 18 (Fall/Winter 1996): 53–74; and Laurence F. Jones, Edward C. Olson, and Delbert A. Taebel, "Change in African-American Representation on Texas City Councils: 1980–1993," *Texas Journal of Political Studies* 18 (Spring/Summer 1996): 57–78.

inadequate schools, and crime will grow. It is imperative that local governments both represent the diversity of the state and govern effectively. Democracy is about both participating and getting things done.

Key Terms

At-large elections

Commissioners courts

District system

General laws

Home rule (defined originally in Chapter 2)

Mandates

Nonpartisan elections

Place system

Study Questions

1. Why do you think the authors of this book called county government a "horse-drawn buggy"? Do you agree or disagree with that label?

2. What is a home-rule city? What are the forms of government used in home-rule cities? Why do you think most home-rule cities have council-manager government?

3. Pretend you are consultant to a city of 250,000 people. Your advice is sought on how to structure municipal elections. How would you advise this city with regard to the time when city elections should be held and whether to have nonpartisan candidates and at-large elections? Why?

4. Why does Texas have so many special districts, and what are some of the problems associated with them?

5. Based on what you have read, what do you think life will be like in a Texas city in the year 2010? Why?

6. Which type of local government do you think is truly at the "grass roots"—that is, which type more nearly represents all the citizens and works hardest to solve human problems?

7. Attend a meeting of your local city council, school board, or county commission. Then, describe for your fellow students what you learned by attending the meeting.

8. Would you consider a career in local government management? Why or why not?

Internet Assignment

Internet site: www.ci.name.tx.us/ or www.co.name.tx.us ("Name" is the name of a city or county; if you prefer a state other than Texas, then substitute the two-letter abbreviation for the state.)

Choose a city or county other than the one that is your home town or home county. Then—and these Web sites will vary a lot—learn everything you can about the history and the form of government of that city or county. You may then want to explore the Web site for your home local government.

Chapter Four

Interest Groups and Lobbying

Texas politicians are constantly besieged by a variety of interest groups. Senator Gonzalo Barrientos, Democrat of Austin, addresses a rally of the Combined Law Enforcement Association of Texas (CLEAT) at the capitol during Law Enforcement Week, May 1989 (top). Even children may demonstrate for special interests, as shown by their banner for a tobacco-free workplace bill (bottom).

As soon as several of the inhabitants of the United States have taken up an opinion or a feeling they wish to promote in the world, they look around for mutual assistance; and as soon as they have found each other out, they combine. From that moment they are no longer isolated men, but a power seen from afar, whose actions serve for an example, and whose language is listened to.

Alexis de Tocqueville
Democracy in America, *1835*

Money doesn't talk, it swears.

Bob Dylan
"It's Alright Ma (I'm Only Bleeding)," *1965*

Introduction

Politics is concerned with the making of *public* policy, but a great many of its actions have *private* consequences. When government imposes a tax, or begins to regulate an industry, or writes rules about the behavior of individuals, it makes an impact, not just on the public in general, but on citizens in particular. Human nature being what it is, people often tend to judge the action not so much on the basis of its value to everyone in general as on the basis of its utility to themselves.

Seeking to obtain more favorable policies, people organize to try to influence government. When they do, they create a problem for democracy. We want our government to take account of the impact of its laws on individuals, but we do not want the special wants of some people to be more important than the common needs of us all. To the extent that public policy is made or modified at the behest of private interests, democracy is crippled.

In Texas, as elsewhere in the United States, special, organized interests are always busy trying to influence what government institutions do. Citizens have to decide whether these groups are merely presenting their point of view to public authorities, or whether instead they are attempting to corrupt the process of self-government.

In this chapter the discussion will first focus on the definition and classification of interest groups, then describe and analyze their activities, and move on to consider some major groups in Texas. Some of the efforts that have been made to regulate lobbying will then be examined. The interest-group system in Texas will be evaluated in the light of democratic theory.

Interest Groups

DEFINITION

An *interest* is something an individual or individuals have that has value, and is therefore worth defending. It can be economic, religious, ethnic, or, indeed, based on almost anything. People who produce oil have an interest, as do Catholics, as do *Star Trek* fans.

Interests affect politics in two general ways. One topic of Chapter 5 will be the manner in which they form the basis for much of the battle between political parties. In this chapter, the subject is the direct effect of interests and interest groups on Texas government.

In the broad sense, an interest group is a private organization of individuals who have banded together because of a common cause or interest. We are concerned here, however, only with **political interest groups**—those that try to influence politicians to make public policy to the advantage of their membership. When people join such groups, they exercise their right—guaranteed by the First Amendment to the U.S. Constitution—to "assemble" and "petition" the government.

Interest groups can be usefully contrasted with political parties. The focus of a party is broad, encompassing many different interests, whereas the focus of a group is narrow, comprising just one interest. Parties attempt to gain power by running candidates in elections, whereas groups try to affect power by influencing officeholders. Therefore, while parties are forced to appeal to the citizenry to marshal support, groups may work entirely behind the scenes. By joining groups, people gain the ability to affect government decisions beyond what they achieve with just their vote.

CLASSIFICATION

Interest groups may be classified according to five main concerns:

1. Economic groups, such as manufacturers' associations or labor unions

2. Spiritual or ideological groups, such as churches or the right-to-life and pro-choice organizations

3. Artistic-recreational organizations, such as the Symphony League or the Texas Association of Bass Clubs

4. Public interest groups, such as Common Cause or the League of Women Voters

5. Ethnic groups, such as the League of United Latin American Citizens (LULAC) or the National Association for the Advancement of Colored People (NAACP)

Interest-Group Activities

WHO IS ORGANIZED?

The two most important things to understand about interest groups are that *not all interests are organized*, and that *organized interests are much more powerful than unorganized interests*. Although the famous quotation from de Tocqueville at the beginning of this chapter might lead us to believe that every potential interest spawns an interest group, in fact some interests are far more likely to be organized than others. Those that are organized are relevant to policy making; those that are not organized are usually irrelevant.

For example, oil and gas producers are well organized and politically powerful in Texas. Oil and gas consumers, however, are not organized, except insofar as general consumers' groups (which theoretically represent everybody but never have a very large membership) include petroleum among the many products of interest to them. As a result, petroleum consumers are not usually of much concern to policy makers. Unless a question concerning oil and gas policy gets into the media and becomes a topic of public discussion, therefore, government policy makers are likely to pay much more attention to petroleum producers than to petroleum consumers.

There are three general rules of interest-group formation. First, economic producing groups are more likely to be organized than are consuming groups (as in the oil and gas example above). Second, regardless of the type of group, people with more education and income are more likely to join than are people with less education and income. Third, citizens who join groups out of personal involvement—as opposed to economic stake—tend to feel very strongly about the particular issue that is the group's reason for existence. They are therefore much more likely to contribute money, write letters, attend rallies, and in other ways engage in actions that get the attention of government officials. Consequently, because they are more likely to be organized, producers tend to exert more political influence than consumers, the middle and upper classes more influence than the working classes, and passionate believers more influence than citizens who are less emotionally involved.

FUNCTIONS

Interest groups attempt to *persuade* both the public and individual government officials to take a particular point of view on specific public policies. In trying to be persuasive, they perform five important functions in the political process:

1. They furnish information to officeholders in all branches of government. This activity includes both communicating their collective opinion on public policy and supplying policy makers with their version of the facts.

2. They politicize and inform members of their groups, as well as others.

3. They mediate conflict within their groups.

4. They engage in electioneering, especially the contribution of money to candidates, and possibly in other interventions in the governing process, such as filing lawsuits.

5. By disseminating information supporting their own policy stands to citizens, they help to form public opinion.

ACTIVITIES

Interest groups therefore enhance democratic government by supplying information to citizens, contributing to debates about issues, getting people involved in politics, and shaking up the established order by influencing institutions. But because they attempt to skew the process of government to benefit themselves, these groups also can be a corrupting influence. A closer look at their activities will show the extent to which they deflect public policy making into private channels.

ELECTIONEERING

One of the most common ways in which interest groups try to ensure that their future efforts at persuasion will be more effective is by supporting candidates for public office. Interest groups that have helped to elect a politician can be confident that they will not be forgotten when the politician enters government.

Usually, the most effective way to help candidates is to give them money. In this regard, perhaps the most important development in electoral politics in recent years is the increase in **political action committees** (PACs) and their influence on elections. A PAC is a committee formed by an organization, industry, or individual for the purpose of collecting money and then contributing that money to selected political candidates and causes. The cost of campaigning for office goes up every election, and PACs—particularly those that represent corporations and other economic interest groups—are paying an increasingly large percentage of that cost. Almost all observers agree that, in return, they are having an increasingly large influence on public policy. Some states, such as Minnesota, Maine, and California, limit the amount of money that PACs can contribute in state elections, but in Texas these groups may give as much as they wish. There will be more about the connection between money and power in the discussion of elections.

LOBBYING

To **lobby** means to attempt to influence policy makers face-to-face. Everyone has the right to try to make an impact on what government does, and it is obvious that a personal talk with a government official has more impact than one anonymous vote. Because of the rules of interest-group formation, however, some groups are much more likely than others to be able to afford to lobby. It is corporations and trade organizations that employ the most **lobbyists.** Wealthy special interests may have good or bad arguments for their positions, but in either case they employ the most people to make sure that their arguments are heard.

Who Are the Lobbyists? In late 1997 there were 1,596 legislative lobbyists registered with the Texas Ethics Commission.[1] Lobbyists vary as much in their experience and competence as do the legislators they are trying to

---

1. Source: Texas Ethics Commission, October 1997; thanks to Adam Gonzales.

influence. Top-flight freelance lobbyists can make over $2 million per session. State legislators make $7,200.

In the nation's earliest days, members of the national Congress did not have offices. They stayed in hotels or boardinghouses near their legislative chambers and worked "out of their hats." Petitioners hoping to enlist their aid in legislation waited for them in their hotel lobbies, hence the term *lobbyist*. In Texas, it was not until 1965 that all legislators had offices in the capitol.

It is common for a government official, after leaving his or her job representing the people, to go to work as a lobbyist, making very good money trying to persuade old colleagues on behalf of an interest group. In 1996, for example, sixty-seven former lawmakers were earning their living lobbying the legislature on behalf of clients. When Gib Lewis retired as House speaker in 1993, he went to work as a lobbyist for the Dallas/Fort Worth International Airport for a yearly salary of $110,000, a raise over his legislator's paycheck of more than 1,500 percent. By 1996, he was lobbying for thirty clients and was earning at least $340,000 a year.

Sources: Mike Ward, "Ex-Legislators Find Lobbying a Natural Turn, Lucrative Offers," *Austin American-Statesman,* November 15, 1992, A1; "Political Intelligence," *Texas Observer,* February 12, 1993, 4; Suzanne Gamboa and Michele Kay, "Reformers Struggle to Disturb Legislators' Lobbying Dreams," *Austin American-Statesman,* November 3, 1996, H1; Michele Kay, "Lawmakers Urged to Tighten Lobbying Rules," *Austin American-Statesman,* November 12, 1996, B1.

Not all lobbyists come from the ranks of the people they are hired to persuade, not all serve special economic interests, and not all earn fortunes from their work. Some "public interest" lobbyists serve their conception of the common good and take home a modest salary for their efforts. But the biases in the interest-group system mean that most of the people doing most of the lobbying will be serving narrow, wealthy interests.

What Lobbyists Do and How They Do It. The best lobbying technique is direct personal contact. Lobbyists try to see as many legislators as possible every day, buying a lunch, chatting for a few minutes, or just shaking a hand. Most lobbyists are able to get on a first-name basis with each legislator they think might be sympathetic to their goals. The speaker of the House and the lieutenant governor are key figures in the legislature, and lobbyists try, above all else, to ingratiate themselves with these two powerful officials.

Contributions or Bribery? The best way to assure personal access to politicians is to give them money, or the equivalent. This money is contributed in a variety of ways. Groups spend some of it entertaining legislators and executives at parties, taking them to lunch, giving them awards, and attracting them to similar events that give lobbyists the chance to cultivate personal relationships and apply the arts of individual persuasion. As Table 4–1 illustrates, interest groups reported spending slightly over a million dollars to lobby the legislature during the 1997 session.

With only a little exaggeration, Ben Sargent illustrates one of the major aspects of politics in Texas.

Courtesy of Ben Sargent.

Another, more direct way in which groups funnel money to politicians is by giving them campaign contributions. Few lobbyists are as brazen as East Texas chicken magnate Lonnie "Bo" Pilgrim, who, during a fight over a new workers' compensation law in 1989, simply handed out $10,000 checks on the floor of the Senate.[2] But the Capitol is always thronged by representatives of interest groups who are happy to give money in a less public manner.

For example, from the end of the 1995 legislative session to the beginning of the 1997 session, House Speaker Pete Laney received contributions totaling $932,711. Among his most generous donors were PACs representing the Texas State Teachers Association, which contributed $25,000, the Texas Association of Realtors, which gave $20,000, and the Texas Optometric Association, which chipped in $12,500.[3]

---

2. Paul Burka, "Is the Legislature for Sale?" *Texas Monthly,* February 1991, 118; Dave McNeely, "Backslaps Take On New Meaning with Ethics Concerns," *Austin American-Statesman,* February 21, 1991, A13.

3. Stuart Eskinazi, "Laney Walks Softly, Hides a Big Stick," *Austin American-Statesman,* January 5, 1997, A1.

TABLE 4–1

Interest-Group Spending in 1997 Legislature

Type of Spending	Amount Spent
Events to which all legislators were invited	$510,144
Legislative employees (staff)	198,764
Individual House members	193,955
Individual senators	58,260
Others	71,888
Total	$1,032,411

SOURCE: Stuart Eskinazi and Mike Ward, "Lobbyists Focus Gift-Giving on Legislative Staff," *Austin American-Statesman*, August 3, 1997, A1.

Moreover, many would-be influencers find only slightly more subtle ways to give things to legislators. One way to be generous that special interests devise is to invite politicians to address one of their trade meetings in some resort location. For example, in June 1996, seven lawmakers and the executive director of the Texas Natural Resource Conservation Commission spent three days in the Stein Erikson Lodge in Park City, Utah (in the Wasatch Mountains), as the guests of the Consulting Engineers Council of Texas. To make this trip legal, the politicians each gave a talk to the assembled engineers about their areas of expertise.[4]

Another way lobbying groups manage to be nice to government officials is by presenting them with gifts. For example, in 1995 and 1996, ENSERCH Corporation gave eagle statues, valued at $305 each, to Governor George W. Bush, Lieutenant Governor Bob Bullock, and Speaker of the House Pete Laney; GTE Southwest gave sports bags, hats, and umbrellas, costing from $100 to $150, to eight legislators; and Jack Strong, a lobbyist for telecommunications and financial firms, gave mantle clocks valued at up to $200 each to eighty-three legislators.

The Center for Public Policy Priorities is an example of a lobbying group that does not speak for a rich special interest and does not attempt to achieve its objectives through veiled bribery, yet still manages to influence the process of making public policy. Founded in the 1980s by a group of Benedictine nuns, the center attempts to speak on behalf of poor Texans, especially to the legislature. It provides high-quality analysis of the possible effects of proposed government policies on persons of middle and low income.

"They do very good research and very good work," says Republican Representative Harvey Hilderbran of Kerrville, who worked with the group on Texas's 1995 welfare reform law. "I view them as an important and credible resource."

During the legislative discussion of how the state should implement the new federal welfare reform law in 1997, the center managed to convince lawmakers to spend more money for adult education and job search programs that could help welfare recipients find jobs.

Source: Suzanne Gamboa, "Voice for Low-Income Texans Gains Influence in Legislature," *Austin American-Statesman*, March 28, 1997, B1.

---

4. This and the following paragraph are based on Mike Ward and Stuart Eskinazi, "Lobby-Paid Trips Still Fly," *Austin American-Statesman*, April 20, 1997, A1.

Not all lobbyists use money so unashamedly. Some, who represent relatively poor groups, rely upon persistence, information, and the passion they feel for their cause. They sometimes score important victories. Nevertheless, the power of money, day in and day out, to capture the attention of lawmakers makes wealth one of the great resources of politics and ensures that rich interest groups, over the long run, will tend to prevail over poor ones.

The power of money in the interest-group system brings up uncomfortable questions about democracy in Texas. Simply giving money to a politician for personal use is bribery and is illegal. Bribery is a danger to democracy because it means that private wealth has been substituted for public discussion in the making of public policy. When policy is made at the behest of a few rich interests working behind the scenes, then government is plutocratic (that is, government by the wealthy), not democratic. The disturbing fact is that the line between outright bribery (illegal) and renting the attention of public officials with campaign contributions, entertainment, gifts, and speaking fees (legal) is a very thin one. Money talks, and those with more of it speak in louder voices, especially in a state characterized by low legislative salaries and no public campaign finance.

Information. Thousands of bills are introduced in the Texas legislature every session, and legislators can have no more than a passing knowledge of most of the policy areas involved. Even those legislators who may have specialized knowledge need up-to-date, accurate information. Therefore, in Texas as in other states, information is one of the most important lobbying resources. The information furnished is biased, since it represents the group's viewpoint, but it also must be accurate. Getting and keeping a reputation for providing solid information is one of the most important assets a lobbyist can develop.

Information is a tool of influence not only in dealing with the legislature, but also in dealing with the bureaucracy. State executive agencies have a constant need for information, and sometimes no independent means of finding it. They may come to rely on lobbying groups to furnish them with facts. For example, in 1996 Elton Bomer, the state insurance commissioner, chose the Texas Insurance Checking Office to gather the data the commission uses to determine auto insurance rates. The checking office is a subsidiary of an insurance industry lobbying group. An industry group is therefore supplying the information used to regulate the industry it represents. Consumers might suspect that such data will not show that insurance companies are charging too much. (See Chapter 10 for a description of the ways in which agencies themselves lobby lawmakers.)

PERSUADING THE PUBLIC

Although most interest-group energy is expended in lobbying government directly, some groups also attempt to influence government policy indirectly by "educating" the public. They buy television commercial time in order to argue their public policy case to citizens, who, they hope, will then put pressure on their representatives to support the groups' agendas.

The years 1996 and 1997 saw several examples of public-education campaigns waged by interest groups that were concerned about the upcoming legislative session. For example, during the 1997 legislative session, a bill was considered to allow new companies to compete with electric utility monopolies. The Coalition for Affordable Power, sponsored by companies with investor-owned utility monopolies, had spent $2.6 million by the end of 1996 to convince consumers, via television, that allowing such competition would increase utility rates (see Chapter 3 for a discussion of utilities and local finance). Another legislative proposal, to open local telephone service to competition, spawned an additional ad campaign. Consumers watching television could not miss the spots by the Partnership for a Competitive Texas, a lobbying consortium of AT&T, MCI, and the Texas Association of Long Distance Companies. These ads urged consumers to contact their representative and demand a vote for the bill permitting more competition in local phone service.

From the standpoint of democratic theory, the efforts of wealthy special interests to create public support through such television campaigns have both reassuring and troubling aspects. By expending their resources on propaganda aimed at ordinary citizens, interest groups greatly expand the amount of information available to citizens. Millions of people who would otherwise have been unaware that such fights were brewing in the legislature were exposed to arguments and information about utility policy through the 1996–1997 TV spots. Since an informed citizenry is a democratically competent citizenry, such campaigns are worthy additions to public debate. On the other hand, the arguments presented in the ads reflect a private, one-sided viewpoint. The pro- and antimonopoly sides may choose to speak their positions on television, but no one can afford to buy television time to speak for the general public interest. On balance, such campaigns probably do more good than harm, but it is a close call.

INFLUENCING ADMINISTRATORS AND CO-OPTING AGENCIES

The executive branch of government also is an interest-group target. All laws are subject to interpretation, and most laws allow the administrator substantial leeway in determining not only the intent of the lawmakers but also the very meaning of their words. Interest groups attempt to influence the interpretation of laws that apply to them.

As society has become more complex, each individual has become less and less able to provide for her or his own needs. Where once people grew their own food, most must now buy it from large corporations. How can they be sure that it is pure, honestly labeled, and sold at a fair price? Where once people traveled by horses or mules raised on the family homestead, they now drive expensive vehicles that also are supplied by large corporations. How can they be sure that these are safe and honestly advertised?

To protect people's interests in those areas in which they cannot protect themselves, *administrative agencies,* or *bureaus,* have been created in the executive branch of government. Although many agencies provide public services, many others are regulatory. Their function is to protect the public interest by regulating various narrow, private interests.

The concern here is with the regulatory agencies created to ensure that a particular industry provides good services at fair prices. Unfortunately, the history of these agencies is that, over time, they lose their independent role and become dominated by the interest they were created to control. This transition from guardian of the public interest to defender of private interests—called **co-optation**—has several causes.

First, people who serve on regulatory agencies tend to come from the industry being regulated and return to it after their stint in government is over. This is called the **revolving door.** Members of the Federal Communications Commission, for example, usually have spent their work lives in the broadcasting industry. As a result, regulators tend to have the perspective of the industry, to sympathize with its problems and share its values.

Second, it is almost impossible for even the best-intentioned regulators to remain independent from the interest to be regulated because they come to have cordial personal relationships with the people in the industry. Even if they had no connection with the petroleum industry before their election, for example, railroad commissioners soon come to have many friends in the industry. It becomes more and more difficult for commissioners to interpret public policy problems differently from their buddies in oil and gas.

Third, although a serious problem may cause an initial public outcry demanding regulation of a private interest—railroads, meat packers, or insurance companies, for instance—once regulatory legislation is passed, the public tends to lose interest, and the spotlight of publicity moves elsewhere. From that point on, only the regulated industry is intensely interested in the activities of the government agency. Regulators find that representatives of the industry are constantly in front of them in person, bringing information, self-serving arguments, and the force of personality, while there is no one to speak up for the public. When the Texas Department of Health is creating hospital regulations, for example, it is frequently visited by spokespeople for the health industry. In such situations, it is only human to be more influenced by personal persuasion than by an abstract conception of the common good.

This co-optation of government regulators is well illustrated by the recent history of the State Board of Insurance. With more than 2,200 companies and 130,000 agents collecting approximately $34 billion of premiums each year, the insurance business is a significant part of the Texas economy. The state began to regulate the industry in the late 1800s to try to protect consumers from unscrupulous practices. By the late 1980s, however, the board was notorious among consumer representatives for always taking the side of the insurance industry in any dispute with customers.

In 1991, the Travis County grand jury issued a report on its investigation of the insurance industry and the board. The grand jury reported that it was "shocked by the size of the problem, frightened by what it portends for our future economic health, and outraged by the ineffective regulation of the State Board of Insurance. . . . The potential exists for a savings-and-loan type of disaster in the insurance industry. As was true in the savings-and-loan arena, we see embezzlement and self-dealing by insurance company insiders and regulators who are asleep at the switch." The report went on to say that "fraud in the insurance industry is widespread and deep and it is covered by falsified documents filed with the State Board of Insurance."[5]

When Ann Richards became governor in 1991, she moved quickly to try to clean up the mess caused by the co-optation of the State Board of Insurance. Through public attacks and private cajolery, she managed to induce one

5. Report quoted in Elyse Gilmore Yates, "Insure Integrity in the Insurance Industry," *Texas Observer,* February 8, 1991, 11.

of the three board members to resign, and she replaced him and another member whose term had expired with more consumer-oriented people. The board had offended so many citizens, however, that such a change in personnel was not enough. In 1993 the legislature abolished the board, giving some of its former powers to a single commissioner and transferring some of its powers to other state agencies, and renamed the agency the Texas Department of Insurance.

Politicians and citizens hoped that because the new commissioner would have clear responsibility for promulgating and enforcing rules, he or she would more easily be held accountable to the public. Although the verdict is not yet in on whether this hope has been realized, the decision of the insurance commissioner to rely upon an industry lobbying group for information, mentioned earlier, is not an encouraging sign.

INTEREST GROUPS AND THE COURTS

Like the legislative and executive branches, the judicial branch of government also makes policy by interpreting and applying laws. For this reason, interest groups are active in the judicial arena of politics. Groups representing important economic interests make substantial campaign contributions during judicial campaigns, hire lawyers to influence judges with legal arguments, and file suits. Money talks in courtrooms as well as in legislatures and the executive branch.

Courts also can be an avenue of success for interest groups that have been unsuccessful in pressing their cases either through electoral politics or by lobbying the other two branches of government. An outstanding example is the National Association for the Advancement of Colored People (NAACP). Not only has this organization won such profoundly important national cases as *Brown* v. *Board of Education* (347 U.S. 483, 1954), in which segregated schools were declared unconstitutional, but it also has won vital victories at the state level. In *Nixon* v. *Herndon* (273 U.S. 536, 1927), the U.S. Supreme Court held that a Texas law excluding African Americans from the Democratic primary was unconstitutional. The Texas legislature attempted to nullify this decision by writing a new law authorizing party leaders to make rulings to the same effect, but this was struck down in *Nixon* v. *Condon* (286 U.S. 73, 1932). Later, in *Smith* v. *Allwright* (321 U.S. 649, 1944), the Texas NAACP won still another victory when the Court held that racial segregation in party primaries on any basis whatsoever is unconstitutional. Thus, although dominant interest groups may win most of the time, the history of the NAACP in Texas proves that any interest group can sometimes prevail if it organizes and knows how to use the court system.

Major Interest Groups in Texas

Interest groups want publicity for their programs and goals, but they tend to hide their operations. Political scientists have not done extensive research on interest groups in Texas, and the activities of such groups and the precise nature of their influence are difficult to discover. Nevertheless, we will try to describe some of the major interest groups in the state.

THE TEXAS GOOD ROADS AND TRANSPORTATION ASSOCIATION

Since the 1930s, one of the most influential interest groups in the state has been the Texas Good Roads and Transportation Association. It exemplifies the classic pattern of successful interest group activity: an industry effectively organized into a strong interest group that is allied with a strong governmental bureaucracy and that has a number of friends in the legislature.

The Texas Good Roads Association was formed under that name in 1932 by representatives of industries interested in expanding highway construction—automobile makers, the oil industry, and road-building contractors, among others. In the late 1970s, the Good Roads Association added the words "and Transportation" to its name, so that its initials are now TGRTA. The association, which works closely with the Texas Department of Transportation, has arranged its geographical organization within the state to coincide with the twenty-five districts of the highway department. From the beginning, the TGRTA has successfully masked its economic interest behind a facade of civic virtue by choosing as its officers sympathetic community leaders who are not directly connected with highway construction. In 1993 the association had more than one thousand individual and corporate members.

Griffin Smith, Jr., captured the essence of the organization as follows:

> 54 local Chambers of Commerce, 46 cities and counties (some of which pay their annual dues with public funds), and numerous individuals who are prominent in the social and political affairs of their communities. These are the opinion-makers. They are crucial.
>
> Most of the laymen are exactly what they seem: well-respected, public-spirited citizens who honestly believe that the welfare of the state depends on a good network of highways built by a Highway Department unblemished by political chicanery. They are not money-seekers, not crackpots; they are the bed-rock Establishment of Texas. To an impressive extent, TGRA commands their loyalties.
>
> These laymen are indispensable to TGRA's purposes. Without them the Association is naked, a straightforward phalanx of powerful economic interests. With them it is something grander than a lobby; it is a movement, a personification of the Texas automobile-highway-mobility ethos. No other lobby in the state has so successfully camouflaged its basic economic motives.[6]

The proudest achievement of the Texas Good Roads and Transportation Association is the so-called dedicated highway fund. A 1946 amendment to the Texas Constitution allocates most of the state revenue from gasoline taxes and motor vehicle registration fees to this special fund. These monies can be spent only for highway construction and related activities such as maintenance and acquisition of rights-of-way. In fiscal year 1997, this "motor fuels tax" generated almost $1.75 billion, most of which went to the Texas Department of Transportation. Even in a prosperous year, competition for state funds is intense, and this large automatic commitment is a monument to the success of the TGRTA.

---

6. Griffin Smith, Jr., "The Highway Establishment and How It Grew and Grew and Grew," *Texas Monthly,* April 1974, pp. 79–80. Copyright 1974 by Mediatrix Communications Corporation. Used by permission.

THE TEXAS TRIAL LAWYERS ASSOCIATION

Like other occupational groups, attorneys have interests.[7] Lawyers have a great advantage not shared by the members of other occupations, however: Many legislators and all judges share their profession. Lawyers therefore have an automatic advantage in arguing their positions on public policy to legislatures or courts, as they will frequently be addressing people who share their values and point of view.

For this reason, combined with the customarily generous political giving of its members, the Texas Trial Lawyers Association has traditionally been a powerful force during any legislative session. Until the late 1980s, the association was able to block all legislation that threatened the income of attorneys. In 1969, for example, the TTLA dominated efforts to reform the workers' compensation system in Texas, thereby preserving it as a fountain of employment for its members.

By the 1990s, however, the TTLA's influence was on the wane. Attorneys were a traditional part of the Texas Democratic Party's coalition (see Chapter 5), and their power declined with their party's. On the other hand, business, the traditional ally of the Republican Party, grew in power as the GOP's star ascended in Texas.

In the 1995 legislature, business made a determined push to overhaul the state's tort system. Torts are wrongful acts, and the loser of a civil lawsuit concerning such an act can be forced to pay an amount of money to compensate a victim, and may be required to pay an extra amount as punishment. People in business hate such lawsuits because of their costs in time, legal fees, and sometimes punitive damages, while lawyers love them because they constitute the stuff of their livelihood. The TTLA, along with many Democratic representatives and many consumer groups, fought tort reform.

But Republican Governor George Bush, riding a tremendous national and state victory by his party in the 1994 elections (see Chapter 6) and aided by a powerful and wealthy pro-business interest group, Texans for Lawsuit Reform, pushed through major changes in Texas's tort laws. These made it more difficult to win punitive damages against a business, lowered the maximum amount of damages that could be awarded, decreased the percentage of an award that one company among many defendants could be forced to pay, limited the ability of attorneys to "shop around" for a sympathetic judge, and made other similar changes.

In 1997 the legislature limited lawsuits even more, although the pace slowed from 1995. Future sessions are likely to see additional changes in the tort laws.

The Texas Trial Lawyers Association therefore looks to be a giant in decline. As its traditional party continues to lose ground, it faces a hard future.

THE CHRISTIAN RIGHT

In the late 1970s a number of national organizations arose, calling for a return to "Christian values," as they defined them, in American government

---

7. This section is based on the information in Charles P. Elliott, Jr., "The Texas Trial Lawyers Association: Interest Group under Siege," in Anthony Champaigne and Edward J. Harpham (eds.), *Texas Politics: A Reader* (New York: W. W. Norton, 1997), pp. 162–176.

and in society. The groups' purposes were to inform religious, politically conservative voters of a candidate's positions on certain issues and to persuade them to participate more actively in local politics. By the 1990s, these groups were a formidable presence at virtually every level of American politics. They have been especially important in the South, and thus were well represented in Texas. Together, the conservative religious interest groups are known as the "Christian Right."

The best-known and probably the largest of these organizations is the Christian Coalition, the successor to the Moral Majority, led by televangelist Pat Robertson from his office in Chesapeake, Virginia. Others are Focus on the Family, headquartered in Colorado; Family Research Council of Washington, D.C.; Citizens for Excellence in Education, working out of California; and the American Family Association, based in Mississippi. Members of these groups tend to overlap, and they often work together on specific political issues. All, especially the Christian Coalition, are active in Texas.

Although Christian Right groups do not all place the same emphasis on each individual issue, they share a cluster of strongly conservative positions on the substance of government. Kirk Ingels, Austin coordinator of the Christian Coalition, summarizes the movement's concerns by saying that "The primary focus" of his group "is to affect public policy so it reflects biblical truth."[8] Members interpret the Bible so as to be antiabortion, anti-gay rights, anti-gun control, anti-tax policies they view as subversive of families, and in favor of constitutional amendments that would mandate a balanced federal budget and permit organized prayers in public schools. They also organized in opposition to the national health-care reform package sponsored by President Bill Clinton in 1993 and 1994.

Despite its relatively small size, in the 1990s the Christian Right has had a strong impact on Texas politics and society. The American Family Association pressured thirteen of seventeen ABC television affiliates in the state to take the often-raunchy police drama *NYPD Blue* off the air. In Austin, a local group called Concerned Texans mustered enough petition signatures to place on the city ballot a referendum question about keeping the city's "domestic partner" ordinance, which gave health insurance to the live-in lovers of hetero- and homosexual city workers, then mobilized enough voters to pass the referendum. In Denton, the Christian Coalition distributed a "Pro-Family Voter's Guide" in local churches the Sunday before the 1994 election, outlining the positions of various state and congressional candidates on a variety of issues: vouchers for public schools, a balanced budget amendment to the U.S. Constitution, and outlawing abortion except to save the life of the mother, among others.

One of the areas in which the Christian Right is most active is local schools. Elections to fill positions on the governing boards of Texas's 1,048 school districts generally draw fewer than 10 percent of the eligible voters to the polls. An organized, disciplined group can easily elect those it favors. Robert Simonds, president of Citizens for Excellence in Education, claims that his group has helped elect more than 7,000 school board members nationally. Other observers place the number at closer to 300.[9] Since there is no official

8. Quoted in Chuck Lindell, "Pulpit to Polls Movement Gathers Steam," *Austin American-Statesman,* March 6, 1994, A1.
9. *Ibid.*

compilation of such election statistics, it is impossible to say which estimate is closer to the truth, or how many of the victorious elections were in Texas. Nevertheless, the Christian Right is undoubtedly a powerful force on the state's local school boards.

The most dramatic flexing of the Christian Right's muscles occurred at the state Republican Party conventions in 1994 and 1996. These events are discussed in detail in the next chapter.

The Christian Right has become so important in Texas and national politics that it may sometimes give the impression that all believing Christians are politically conservative. In fact, political ideology is not the same thing as religious belief. There are many famous examples of devout Christians who are liberal in politics. Father Robert Drinan, a Jesuit priest and president of Boston College, served for some years as a very liberal member of the U.S. House of Representatives from Massachusetts. M. William Howard, the former president of the National Council of Churches of Christ, was one of the original members of the executive board of the liberal organization People for the American Way. Former President Jimmy Carter, no conservative, is a born-again Baptist.

The success of the Christian Right has inspired liberal Christians to organize. Jim Wallis, a Washington, D.C., evangelical pastor, has founded Call to Renewal, a national group of liberal evangelicals. Within Texas, Cecile Richards, elder daughter of former Governor Ann Richards, created the Texas Freedom Network in 1995 to try to mobilize moderate and liberal Christian Democrats to oppose Christian Right candidates. Liberal pastors have formed the Texas Faith Network to counter the efforts of the Christian Coalition. At the group's first gathering in September 1996, forty ministers from around the state met to call on fellow religious leaders not to allow the distribution of Christian Coalition voters' guides in their churches.

In other words, organization among the Christian Right has sparked counterorganization among the Christian Left. Interest-group politics in Texas thus promises to be more fervently oriented toward moral questions than it has been in the past.

THE OIL AND GAS INDUSTRY

As befits its historical status as the most important sector in the Texas economy, the oil and gas industry has a close working relationship with state government and is well represented by several interest groups. Principal among these are the Midcontinent Oil and Gas Association (MOGA), which represents the industry as a whole but is dominated by the large producers, and the Texas Independent Producers and Royalty Owners (TIPRO), which is dominated by the smaller producers and royalty owners.

MOGA, TIPRO, and other groups keep track of the voting records of members of the legislature, contribute generously to the campaigns of representatives who are friendly to their interests, and are tireless in providing information to the legislative staff on conditions within the industry. Since oil and gas production is widely distributed within the state, and oil and gas business offices are even more widely distributed, petroleum's interest groups have a great deal of influence over a large majority of legislators, whether they are liberal or conservative on other issues. Just as there are very few

Iowa state politicians who will oppose the wishes of corn farmers and virtually no politicians in North Carolina who will criticize the tobacco industry, Texas politicians are nearly unanimous in supporting the positions of the petroleum producers.

ORGANIZED LABOR

Many Texans think of organized labor as a powerful interest group that has great influence on state policy, but there is little evidence to support this assumption. The primary explanation for this lack of power is cultural.

As we discussed in Chapter 1, the conservative political culture that dominates most of the southern states is hostile to labor unions. Texas is no exception. In 1997 the AFL-CIO had a national membership of 13.1 million, but only 218,000 in the Lone Star State. Texas is second in size of population of the United States, but only eighth in union membership.

Politically, unions have traditionally allied themselves with the Democratic Party nationally, and with the liberal wing of that party within the state (see Chapter 5). But the relative weakness of liberals in Texas has meant that labor unions are even less powerful than their membership figures would suggest. Their weakness is reflected in the relatively antilabor nature of Texas's laws. Workers' compensation insurance, unemployment insurance payments, and other benefits are lower than those of most other industrial states, and the laws regarding unions are restrictive rather than supportive. Unions are forced to make public disclosure of virtually all their major activities. This is not, of course, true of corporations. There are prohibitions against secondary boycotts, checkoff systems for union dues, and mass picketing and other such activities, and the "right-to-work" law prohibits the closed shop and the union shop.[10] In addition to these crippling regulations on organized labor in the private sector, Texas joins Georgia as the state with the most restrictive legislation dealing with public-sector unions. Organized labor would like nothing better than to get rid of this array of restrictions, but it lacks the political power to do so.

Developments in the 1990s do not suggest that the future will be brighter than the past for Texas organized labor. For one thing, the state's labor leaders cannot even control the political behavior of unionized workers. The Texas AFL-CIO's own polls show that 45 percent of its members voted for Republican George Bush for governor in 1994, despite the fact that the organization endorsed incumbent Democrat Ann Richards.[11] In 1996, when Governor Bush appointed David Perdue, a labor official whom most union leaders considered a probusiness turncoat, to head the new Texas Workforce Commission, organized labor's utter lack of influence was emphasized.

---

10. A *secondary boycott* occurs when one union boycotts the products of a company being struck by another union. The *checkoff system* is a method of collecting union dues in which an employer withholds the amount of the dues from workers' paychecks. *Mass picketing* occurs when so many people picket a firm that traffic is disrupted and the firm cannot conduct business. A *closed shop* is in effect when workers must already be members of a certain union in order to even apply for work in a given firm. A *union shop* is in effect when workers do not have to be members of the union to apply for work, but must join the union if they get a job.
11. Stuart Eskinazi, "Labor Unions Finding Friends in Former Foes," *Austin American-Statesman,* January 16, 1996, A1.

The most venerable of the Hispanic organizations, the League of United Latin American Citizens (LULAC) was formed in Corpus Christi in 1929.[12] Its members were much concerned about discrimination against Mexican Americans, especially in public education. In its first three decades, LULAC pursued the goal of equal education as both a private charitable organization and a public crusader. Privately, LULAC formed local self-help organizations to advance Latino education. Its "Little School of the 400" program of the 1950s, for example, which taught Spanish-speaking preschoolers the 400 English words they needed to know in order to survive in first grade in public schools, was so successful that it inspired the national program Head Start. Publicly, the organization persuaded the U.S. Supreme Court to forbid Texas to segregate Mexican Americans in public schools in 1948.

Branching out to other issues, in 1953 LULAC won another suit against Texas's practice of excluding Mexican Americans from juries. Then in 1959 it persuaded the state legislature to sponsor its program to teach Latino preschoolers English. Soon the Texas Education Agency was paying up to 80 percent of the program's funding. LULAC may have represented a struggling minority, but it had become part of the state's political establishment; it was a success.

Into the 1970s, LULAC continued to be the standard-bearer for Mexican American aspirations for full citizenship in the United States in general and Texas in particular. But in that decade, the organization began to falter. For one thing, with many of its original goals achieved, it began to experience internal dissension about what course to set for the future. For another, as an organization dispensing millions of dollars in foundation grants, it began to attract members who were more interested in advancing themselves than in advancing their ethnic group. Most seriously, the financially reckless administration of President Joseph Benetes in the mid-1970s nearly bankrupted the organization, plunging it more than $200,000 in debt. Benetes was indicted by LULAC's Supreme Council for financial mismanagement and was impeached by the general organization. The group's troubles, however, continued.

The year 1994 was a typically turbulent one for LULAC in the modern era. Many local and former activists were complaining that LULAC's national administration was dominated by a group that was more interested in enjoying power than in bettering the lives of citizens of Latin American ancestry. "LULAC's gone from a result-oriented organization of activists to a banquet-oriented bunch of blow-hards and do-nothings," protested Ruben Sandoval, its former special counsel. He was not alone. "What issues have you seen the national LULAC address in the last six months, the last year, the last two years? Give me one issue," said Rafael Acosta, a restaurateur and Houston politician who was one of many to agree with Sandoval.[13]

Although LULAC's leadership could be criticized for not pursuing an activist agenda, it could not be accused of doing nothing. In 1994 the presi-

---

12. This account of the history of LULAC through the 1980s relies upon Benjamin Marquez, *LULAC: The Evolution of a Mexican-American Political Organization* (Austin: University of Texas Press, 1993), passim.

13. Quoted in Lori Rodriguez, "Fretting over 'Fratricide,'" *Houston Chronicle*, June 26, 1994, A1.

dent, Jose Velez, together with three Taiwanese gangsters, was indicted by a federal grand jury on charges of collecting millions of dollars in a scheme to smuggle Asians and Hispanics into the United States illegally.

Given that Velez was under an ethical cloud, it might have been expected that his power in LULAC would be extinguished. But the national convention held in July 1994 provided several surprises. Rosa Rosales, a labor organizer from San Antonio, was the reform candidate and a favorite to be elected president. But Velez made a deal with a contingent of Puerto Rican delegates who bloc-voted for his hand-picked candidate, Belen Robles. The Puerto Rican delegation numbered 120 of the 604 delegates, larger than the entire Texas delegation. Their support, added to that of Velez loyalists, enabled Robles to beat Rosales by 5 votes. What the Puerto Ricans received in return for their loyalty to Velez has not been made public.

Not only were many in LULAC outraged by the defeat of a reform presidential candidate, but they were also stunned by the loss of power of Mexican Americans. Although words such as *Hispanic* and *Latino* may give the impression that everyone with a Spanish-language background is culturally the same, the terminology hides considerable differences in economic class and national origin. After the defeat of Rosales, journalist Lori Rodriguez wrote a column in the *Houston Chronicle* in which she expressed Mexican American resentment at the rise of a rival Hispanic group. "Puerto Ricans are, after all, a very different breed of Hispanics," she asserted. "Beyond style, their focus on pet issues like international politics, statehood for their commonwealth and minority procurement contracts for their businessmen raise fears among more traditional LULAC members that the group will stray too far from its original civil rights mission." Rodriguez also quoted an unnamed "longtime leader" of LULAC who believed that "the Puerto Ricans are good for LULAC in a way, they bring in so much energy and enthusiasm and we need that. But we have to watch them. We wouldn't want them to take over our group."[14]

As of 1997, therefore, Texas's historically most important Hispanic organization was in trouble. Although still influential, especially at the local level, it was riven with disagreements over strategy, racked by ethnic conflict, and possibly enfeebled by corruption. It may be that the modern realities of Texas politics demand a different kind of Mexican American organization. LULAC may be an ethnic interest group that has outlived its usefulness.

TEACHERS

Schoolteachers in Texas have been disgruntled for years. Their complaints are many, but the major ones fall into three areas: inadequate compensation, inadequate participation in decision making, and stress—the last brought on by too-large classes, too much paper work, too little time to eat lunch, and a host of other conditions.

Politically, Texas's teachers are marked more by disorganization and competition than by coordination and cooperation. Like Texas's other white-collar workers, most teachers resist unionization, and fully a third belong

---

14. Lori Rodriguez, "LULAC Turning Puerto Rican," *Houston Chronicle*, July 9, 1994, A25.

to no teachers' organization at all. The others are divided among seven statewide and dozens of local groups, all fiercely competitive.

The largest of these organizations is the Texas State Teachers Association (TSTA), with a 1997 membership of 95,000 teachers and administrators. The members of teachers' organizations are well educated and politically active. TSTA and other groups file thousands of grievances yearly with the Board of Education and with local school boards, and the statewide groups aggressively lobby the legislature. Yet teachers have little to show for their political activity. Their salaries, class size, state spending per student, dropout rates, and other measures of state support and educational effectiveness are well below the national average (see Tables 1–1 and 1–3 in Chapter 1).

Although it might be supposed that teachers would have such similar interests that they would unite into one organization, teachers are so divided in their beliefs and values that it takes many organizations to cover their differences. Here is a summary of the most important statewide organizations as of 1997:

TSTA Texas State Teachers Association
TFT   Texas Federation of Teachers
TCTA Texas Classroom Teachers Association
ATPE Association of Texas Professional Educators

	TSTA	TFT	TCTA	ATPE
Membership (some teachers belong to more than one)	95,000	25,000	40,000	74,000
Endorses candidates?	Yes	Yes	No	No
Supports pay raises?	Yes	Yes	Yes	Yes
Supports collective bargaining?	Yes	Yes	No	No
Supports publicly-funded vouchers for private schools?	No	No	No	No

Source: Compiled by David Prindle in October 1997.

Part of the problem is cultural. The quality of public education has rarely been a major concern of the conservative culture that dominates the state. Texas law limits teachers in achieving their political and economic goals by forbidding them to bargain collectively with school districts or other agencies.

Until recently, teachers also handicapped themselves in even more serious ways by their failure to speak with a single voice. Although they are united in support of pay raises and in opposition to publicly funded vouchers for private schools, the four main teachers' groups disagree among themselves with regard to the tactics they should pursue to achieve their goals. As Representative Bill Haley explained, "They each want to affect legislation differently, leaving all the members [of the legislature] totally confused."[15]

In addition to their disunity, teacher organizations damaged whatever political influence they might have had by their politically clumsy behavior during the 1980s. During the 1982 gubernatorial election, they had supported

15. Quoted in Connie Pryzant, "Teachers Groups' Philosophies Differ," *Dallas Morning News,* August 10, 1986, A51; see also by the same author in the same issue, "Teachers Taking a Stand," A47.

Democrat Mark White, who was victorious. White responded by persuading the legislature to raise teacher pay, but he also supported an educational reform bill that was bitterly opposed by teachers' groups.

Among other educational reforms, House Bill 72 required that teachers take periodic competency tests. Since most other people in the working world, especially in private business, must be occasionally evaluated to determine whether they are remaining productive, this was a sensible, indeed overdue, reform. The reform was especially justified in light of the fact that teachers are paid by taxpayers, who have a right to determine that they are not subsidizing incompetence. The teachers, however, viewed competency tests as demeaning, and they loudly protested. They thus belied the public image of self-sacrifice and public spirit that they tried to project and created an image as just another grasping, self-centered group.

Moreover, the bill contained a "no-pass, no-play" provision, mandating that students who failed courses would be unable to participate in extracurricular activities, including sports. Since by most measures, Texas students lag behind those in many other states (see Table 1–2 in Chapter 1), this was a reasonable way to attempt to induce the state's young people to take schoolwork more seriously. But coaches, who were members of the teachers' groups, worried that this provision would deny them some athletic talent, and persuaded their organizations to back their opinion. In the public mind, the teachers seemed to be willing to place athletic convenience ahead of educational values. Again, they stood exposed as a group whose claim to public-spiritedness rang hollow. House Bill 72 passed despite teacher opposition.

The teachers' greatest self-inflicted wound came in Mark White's 1986 reelection campaign. Despite the pay raise he had engineered for them, the largest teachers' group, the TSTA, refused to endorse his candidacy because of the competency test and no-pass, no-play provisions. White lost. Although it probably was the bad state economy, not teacher desertion of his cause, that caused his defeat; the public disloyalty of educators convinced other politicians that since the teachers were a treacherous ally, there was no profit in helping them. "The message politicians got from that was that teacher concerns are a losing issue because the education community won't rally around you," ruefully observed John Cole, president of the small Texas Federation of Teachers, which had supported White.[16]

And so the teachers were left without any powerful political allies. The 1993 legislative session illustrated their lack of clout. Lawmakers chipped away at some of the gains House Bill 72 had won for them, failing to reenact duty-free lunch periods, the forty-five-minute planning period allowed during the school day, and the requirement that every teacher have an employment contract. The 1995 and 1997 legislatures wee similarly resistant to teacher influence. And thus, still underpaid, overworked, and often abused, teachers face a serious challenge in winning back the political ground they lost in the 1980s.

Teachers may have begun to turn their political fortunes around in the last half of 1997. In the first half of that year, the legislature passed a law requiring that teachers renew their "lifetime" certificates every five years by enrolling in continuing education classes. Teachers were outraged that the state, having refused to pay them a comfortable wage, was now preparing to betray the promise that it had made to certify them for life.

This threat to their certification caused the quarelling teachers' groups to unite. At a series of eighteen hearings held around the state by the state Board of Education in the fall of 1997, representatives of the TSTA, ATPE, and TFT (see box) thronged the meeting room, expressing fierce opposition to the planned change.

Faced with unanimous and intense opposition to the implementation of the new law, the board decided to "grandfather" Texas's 250,000 working teachers. New educators would be subject to the five-year certification requirements, but people who already had certificates could regard them as permanent.

•If teachers can continue to present a united front to the state's policy makers, they may be able to overcome the legacy of their blunders in the 1980s and become a far more potent political force. Observers of education politics are curious to see what happens.

OTHER INTEREST GROUPS

The groups we have discussed are a small sample of the many interests and interest groups that influence Texas politics. Other important interests and their organizations include the following:

1. Banking and financial organizations, represented by the Texas Bankers Association and a number of others

2. The Texas Association of Realtors

---

16. Quoted in A. Phillips Brooks, "Teachers Losing Power in Legislature," *Austin American-Statesman,* July 24, 1994, B1.

3. Insurance groups, represented by nine associations

4. Health, medical, and drug-manufacturing groups, including the Texas Medical Association

5. Associations of local governments, such as the Texas Municipal League and the Texas Association of County Officials

6. Outdoor sporting groups, including Sportsmen Conservation, Texas Association of Bass Clubs, Texas Black Bass Unlimited, Gulf Coast Conservation Association, Texas Trophy Hunters Association, Texas Wildlife Association, and Lone Star Bowhunters

Regulation of Lobbying

Aside from laws of general application regarding such crimes as bribery and conspiracy, Texas makes little attempt to regulate the activities of interest groups except in the area of lobbying. Early attempts at regulation in 1947, 1973, and 1981 were weak and ineffective because no state agencies were empowered to enforce the laws.

In December 1990, however, Speaker Gib Lewis of the Texas House of Representatives was indicted by a Travis County grand jury for accepting and failing to report a gift. He was the third speaker in twenty years to be indicted for accepting money or gifts illegally. Public concern over the sorry state of ethics in the legislature was so great that it created an irresistible momentum for reform.

In 1991 the legislature passed a much-publicized "ethics bill" that limited the amount of food, gifts, and entertainment that lobbyists can furnish legislators and that required lobbyists to report the name of each legislator on whom they spent more than $50. Most importantly, it created an Ethics Commission that could hold hearings on complaints of improper behavior, levy fines, and refer violations to the Travis County district attorney for possible prosecution. Texas at last seemed to have a lobbyist-regulatory law with teeth.

The 1991 law did not have the teeth that it appeared to have, however. It failed to require legislators to disclose the sources of their income and also neglected to ban the use of campaign contributions for living expenses. A three-quarters majority on the Ethics Commission is required for some important actions, which handicaps its activities. Finally, although the members of the commission are appointed by the governor, lieutenant governor, speaker of the House, and chief justice of the Texas Supreme Court, those who are chosen must come from a list of candidates furnished by the legislature. Needless to say, legislators are unlikely to nominate candidates whose rectitude and zeal they fear. Reformers tried to pass revisions of this law in 1993 and 1997, but both attempts failed.

After passage of the 1991 bill, House Speaker Gib Lewis was quoted as saying that he doubted that the new provisions would change life at the capitol very much.[17] As reported in the earlier parts of this chapter, subsequent

---

17. Lewis quoted in Laylan Copelin, "New Ethics Bill Sneaks Up on Lawmakers," *Austin American-Statesman,* May 28, 1991, B1.

events have proven him to be a prophet. As long as legislators' salaries remain below the poverty line and as long as private money dominates public elections, the prospects for effective control of lobbying are poor.

The Texas Ethical Standards Task Force, a coalition of public interest and religious organizations, has created a list of "Seven Principles of Ethical Conduct" and asked lawmakers and public officials to sign, display, and follow them. They are:

1. I will treat my office as a public trust.
2. I will use campaign contributions only for expenses directly related to my campaign.
3. I will make myself, my office, and my staff equally accessible to all persons.
4. I will deem it an abuse of the power of my office to seek favors or special treatment for myself, my family, clients and business associates or my contributors.
5. I will not use my position to enrich myself upon leaving office.
6. I will conscientiously avoid conflicts of interest, both real and perceived.
7. I will conduct my affairs with honesty and truthfulness, respecting the spirit as well as the letter of the law.

Source: Denise Gamino, "Group Pushes Ethics Reform," *Austin American-Statesman,* November 27, 1996, B3.

Conclusion

Political interest groups present a dilemma to partisans of democratic government. By giving people a channel of input to government in addition to the one vote possessed by each citizen, such groups broaden and intensify the people's participation and are therefore good for democracy. But by creating a means by which some individuals can be much more influential than others, they often allow private perspectives to dominate public policy making. This is bad for democracy. In Texas, where interest groups are very powerful, this dilemma is acute.

There are ways to soften the dangerous aspects of interest groups while retaining some of their useful functions. Where parties are strong, groups are forced to work through them, and so their attempts at influence become part of the regular process of argument and coalition building. Where groups are forced to make many of their activities public, they must participate in the give-and-take of politics instead of relying on behind-the-scenes maneuvering and personal contacts. Where public financing is provided for candidates for office, they rely much less on private fund raising, and consequently are able to distance themselves from groups with special interests.

In Texas, however, the system is organized so as to enhance the impact of private influence. As will be explained in the next few chapters, Texas political parties are weak, and candidates for state offices rely entirely on private money. And as this chapter has detailed, regulation of lobbying in the state still leaves much to be desired.

In other words, Texas politics is organized so as to do nothing to stifle the bad parts of the interest-group system. The state is rife with private interests contaminating public policy. Over the past few years an outraged public has managed to slightly reform this system, but it still has a long way to go.

Summary

Interest groups are very influential in American and Texas politics because they provide two indispensable ingredients, money and information. Groups are active in every phase of politics: They engage in electioneering, lobby government officials, co-opt agencies, litigate in the courts, and attempt to persuade the public to support their point of view. Private interests thus frequently dominate the making of Texas public policy.

Although many efforts have been made to regulate lobbying, the results have not been encouraging. The Texas political system provides a nearly ideal setting for maximizing interest-group influence. The most powerful groups tend to be those that represent major economic interests.

Interest groups are good for democracy in that they enhance debate about public policy and encourage citizens to participate in politics. But they also damage democratic government by substituting private influence for public deliberation in the creation of government policy. In Texas, where interest groups are very powerful, the negative qualities of the interest-group system dominate.

Key Terms

Co-optation	Lobbyist	Political interest group
Lobby	Political action committee	Revolving door

Study Questions

1. What is meant by the terms *interest group, lobby,* and *lobbyist?* Are interest groups and lobbies the same thing? If you write a letter to your legislator, are you lobbying?

2. What is the difference between a political party and an interest group?

3. What functions do interest groups perform? How do they perform them?

4. What is good and what is bad about the power of interest groups in Texas?

5. What are the most important resources of interest groups? Why?

6. What interests tend to be organized? What is the difference in political influence between organized and unorganized groups?

7. How can an interest group attempt to influence public opinion? What is good and what is bad about such efforts?

8. How do industries co-opt regulatory agencies? If you were asked to reform the system to eliminate co-optation, what changes would you make?

9. From the perspective of Texas democracy, what are the advantages and disadvantages of explicitly religious groups participating in politics?

10. Can you think of any political issues in which there is clearly and absolutely a wrong and right side? Or are all issues only the result of differences of opinion among people?

11. Why are TSTA, LULAC, and organized labor generally ineffective in Texas politics of the 1990s? Why are the TGRTA and the oil and gas industry generally effective?

12. Do you think the 1991 ethics law will succeed in eliminating the advantage that wealthy private interests have in influencing public policy? Why or why not?

Internet Assignment

Internet site: http://.www.crp.org/

Go to the "Center for Responsive Politics" site. Click on "Incumbents" and type "Texas" into the search field. Find out where Texas senators and representatives get their money. From which PACs? In-state or out-of-state?

Chapter Five

Ideology and Political Parties

Here are photos of two prominent Texas party leaders. Garry Mauro (top) was first elected state land commissioner in 1982. In 1998 he was the Democratic candidate for governor. Republican United States Senator Kay Bailey Hutchison (bottom), shown at a news conference, was first elected in 1993.

Great leaders like Franklin Roosevelt and John Kennedy lift people above themselves. Great parties thrive by holding together disparate interests.

> Paul Samuelson
> Nobel prize–winning economist

A political party is an organization that takes money from the rich and votes from the poor under the pretext of protecting the one from the other.

> Anonymous

Introduction

Both Samuelson's favorable assessment of **political parties** and the anonymous cynical disparagement of their value are partly true. Parties are, indeed, the only organizations capable of holding together many fractious interests so that governing is possible. At the same time, in Texas and elsewhere, parties frequently serve democracy badly.

The first topic of this chapter will be ideology, the basis for much party conflict. That discussion will be followed by a brief history of the state's political parties, an examination of the major functions of parties, and an outline of party organization in Texas. The "three-faction" system that often makes the Texas two-party system confusing will then be explained, followed by a discussion of the state's occasional third-party efforts. At several points, the reality of Texas's party politics will be contrasted with the democratic ideal.

Ideology

In Texas as elsewhere, party rivalry is often based upon differences in **ideology.** By ideology is meant a system of beliefs and values about the nature of the good life and the good society, about the relationship of government and the economy, about moral values and the way they should be achieved, and about how government is to conduct itself. The two dominant, and contesting, systems of beliefs and values in American and Texas life today are usually referred to as "liberalism" and "conservatism."

CONSERVATISM

The basic principle underlying **conservatism,** at least in economic policy, is laissez-faire. In theory, conservatives prefer to allow free markets, not government, to regulate the economy. As we noted in Chapter 1, in practice, conservative governments often pursue pseudo laissez-faire, in that they claim to cherish free markets but actually endorse policies that deeply involve government in helping business to overcome problems in the marketplace. Nevertheless, at the level of ideology, and certainly at the level of their argument with liberals, conservatives believe that economies run best if governments leave them alone. When contemplating economic problems such as poverty, pollution, unemployment, or health care, conservatives argue that government has caused most of them through overregulation and that the best way to deal with them is for government to stop meddling and allow the market to work. For example, local land developers don't want a city to tell them how high a sign should be or what kind of landscaping is required to hide ugly buildings or old, junk cars. It is common to speak of conservatives as being on the "right wing" of the political continuum.[1]

LIBERALISM

Liberalism is the contrary ideology. Liberals are suspicious of the workings of unregulated markets, and place more faith in the ability of government to direct economic activity. When thinking about economic problems, they are apt to blame "market failure" and suggest government activity as the solution. To continue the development example used with conservatism, a liberal would want a city government to protect the environment and would work for sign ordinances and landscaping policies. It is common to speak of liberals as being on the "left wing" of the political spectrum.

All this is relatively clear. When dealing with issues of personal belief and behavior, such as religion, sexual activity, or drug use, however, liberals and conservatives switch sides. Conservatives are generally in favor of more government regulation; liberals are in favor of less. Liberals oppose prayer in school, while conservatives favor it; liberals oppose laws regulating sexual behavior, while conservatives endorse them; and so on.

As with many other things, there are gradations of ideology. Ideologues run from the moderate to the extreme. There is a tendency for people who are ideologically extreme to also be emotionally intense about their beliefs. Moderate beliefs tend to go with willingness to tolerate differences of opinion; extreme beliefs tend to go with intolerance.

U.S. Senator Phil Gramm understands the problem of extremism. In the ordinary world of American politics, Gramm is clearly a conservative. For example, the liberal group Americans for Democratic Action rated his Senate voting record zero in 1996, whereas the American Conservative Union scored that same record one hundred. You therefore might think that no one could possibly find fault with Gramm's conservatism.

You would be mistaken. The Associated Conservatives of Texas keeps a "Gramm file" in which they compile evidence of his alleged softness on liberalism. Among his offenses are a vote for the 1990 budget accord (in which President Bush broke his "Read my lips: no new taxes" pledge), support for the (now defunct) superconducting supercollider outside of Waxahatchie, and his friendliness to former Texas State Republican Chairman Fred Meyer, whom the ACT regards as sort of a "closet Democrat."

In politics, unfortunately, there is no pleasing some people.

Source: Michael Barone and Grant Ujifusa, *The Almanac of American Politics 1998* (Washington, D.C.: National Journal, Inc., 1997), 1341; William McKenzie, "Gramm Challenged by Texas GOP," *Dallas Morning News,* June 21, 1994, 11A.

---

1. The customary assignment of liberals to the left side of the political spectrum and conservatives to the right side derives from the seating of parties in the French parliament. Royalists, Gaullists, and others of a conservative persuasion always sit to the right of the center aisle, while Socialists, Communists, and others of a "progressive" persuasion sit to the left.

Thus, American ideological fights are confusing because liberals usually favor government activity in the economic sphere but oppose it in the personal sphere, while conservatives usually oppose government activity in the economic sphere but favor it in the personal sphere. This ideological split is the basis for a great deal of rhetorical argument and many intense struggles over public policy (see Table 5–1).

IDEOLOGY IN TEXAS

As discussed in Chapter 1, Texas has historically been dominated by political conservatism. The distribution of opinions in the present-day population suggests that this domination does not misrepresent the center of gravity of state ideology. A survey conducted in 1997 reported that only 19.4 percent of Texas adults were willing to label themselves liberals, while 27.2 percent called themselves moderates and 38.3 percent claimed the label conservative.[2] The meaning of these simple self-reports is not completely clear, since by calling themselves conservative, people might be referring to economic issues, social issues, or both. Moreover, national public opinion research over many years has shown that a significant percentage of American citizens will label themselves conservative in general, but endorse many specific liberal government programs. Still,

TABLE 5–1

Policy Differences between Liberals and Conservatives

Issue	Conservative Position	Liberal Position
Taxation	As little as possible, and when necessary, regressive taxes such as sales taxes*	More to cover government spending; progressive preferred*
Government spending	As little as possible, except for military	Acceptable to provide social services
Nature of government regulation	More in personal sphere; less in economic	Less in personal sphere; more in economic
Organized labor	Anti-union	Pro-union
Crime	Support more prisons and harsher sentences; oppose gun control	Support social spending to attack root causes; favor gun control
Environment	Favor development over environment	Favor environment over development
Affirmative action	Oppose	Support
Abortion	"Pro-life"	"Pro-choice"
Prayer in public schools	Support	Oppose
Military spending	Higher	Lower

*A progressive tax is one that increases proportionately with income or benefit derived, such as a progressive income tax. A regressive tax, such as the sales tax, places proportionately less burden on wealthy taxpayers and more burden on those with lower incomes.
Note: Two words of caution are in order. First, this table presents an extremely brief summary of complex issues, and thus some distortion is inevitable. Second, it would be inaccurate to assume that every liberal agrees with every liberal position or that every conservative agrees with every conservative position. Even the most devout ideologues have inconsistencies in their beliefs and hitches in their logic.

2. The Texas Poll, February 1997—thanks to Professor Daron Shaw of the Government Department of the University of Texas at Austin for supplying this information.

the self-report numbers are sufficiently dramatic to emphasize the weakness of the liberal ideological tradition in the Lone Star State.

In Texas as elsewhere, the contradictory nature of political ideologies often makes the arguments of politicians and journalists difficult to understand. Nevertheless, ideologies form the basis for much of the party battle. In general, the Democratic Party is controlled nationally by liberals, and the Republican Party is controlled by conservatives. In Texas, however, the picture is more complicated. Both common observation and scholarly research conclude that both the Democratic and Republican Parties in Texas are unusually conservative.[3] The Democrats are more liberal, because they, unlike the Republicans, harbor a large and active liberal minority. To understand how this situation has come about, we must have some knowledge of the way ideologies are learned, and of the history of Texas as a Southern state.

Political Socialization

As we saw in Chapter 1, the attitudes and values of the conservative political culture that dominates Texas include a basic hostility to government action, pseudo laissez-faire, social Darwinism, and the trickle-down theory of

---

3. Robert S. Erickson, Gerald C. Wright, Jr., and John McIver, "Political Parties, Public Opinion, and State Policy in the United States," *American Political Science Review* 83, no. 3 (September 1989): 729–50, especially 737.

economics. How is this ideology perpetuated? How is it transmitted from one generation to another?

The process by which we teach and learn our political knowledge, beliefs, attitudes, values, and habits of behavior is called **political socialization.** In this process, we are influenced by many things—peer groups, political leaders, and a variety of experiences—but the basic agents of political socialization seem to be family, schools, churches, and the media. An extensive discussion of the process of socialization is beyond the scope of this book, but some attention should be paid to these four agents, particularly as they operate in Texas.

FAMILY

The family is the most important agent of socialization. The first things a child learns are the basics: attitudes toward authority, others, oneself, and the community outside the family. Although scholarly studies of the process of political socialization in Texas are rare, it is fair to say that most parents in the state pass along their attitudes and philosophy to their children. Parents transfer political ideas along with religious beliefs and attitudes toward other people almost unconsciously as their children hear their conversation and observe their behavior throughout the many hours of association at home. Most often, these attitudes are conservative and antigovernment. By the time other social institutions begin to "teach" children consciously, they have already learned fundamental attitudes. For this reason, basic political orientations are difficult to alter, and the ideas of the population, in Texas as everywhere else, change only slowly.

SCHOOLS AND CHURCHES

The public school system, and in some cases the churches, can be very influential in shaping political attitudes and beliefs. Again, the influence is strongly conservative. Many Texans regularly attend religious services, and most houses of worship teach acceptance of religious theology, an acceptance that often spills over to include acceptance of prevailing social and political institutions as well. Among Whites, the religious establishment is probably more conservative than most, since the type of Protestantism that dominates Anglo religion in the state stresses the responsibility of individuals for their own fate rather than the communitarian (government) responsibility of everyone for everyone else.

Other religious traditions are also important in Texas, most notably Roman Catholicism among Mexican Americans. The Catholic Church has historically been more encouraging of government activity on behalf of society's underdogs than have Protestant churches. However, Protestantism, the dominant religion among the historically dominant social group, has been associated with attitudes that reinforce political conservatism.

The overall influence of churches, however, may not be as intense or pervasive as that of the public schools, where students spend six or more hours a day, five days a week, for up to twelve years. There is little indication that schools in Texas educate children about politics or encourage them to participate in the political process in any way other than voting.

The essence of politics is conflict, but Texas public education does not recognize this. Instead, the schoolchild is taught to value the free enterprise system but not to be aware of its potential deficiencies, to be patriotic, and to respect authority. The nature of politics is distorted. The child is educated to passivity rather than to democratic participation.

In the most thorough study of socialization by public schools in Texas, anthropologist Douglas Foley spent sixteen months in a small South Texas town (which he called "North Town") during 1973 and 1974, then returned during the summers and some weekends in 1977, 1985, 1986, and 1987. After interviewing students, teachers, administrators, politicians, and townspeople, and observing many activities, including sporting events, classroom teaching, social dating, and ethnic confrontations, Foley came to definite conclusions about the sorts of ideas passed along by North Town's schools:

> After a year in North Town . . . I came to see that the school simply reflected the general conservatism of the community. The town's social and political environment did not demand or encourage a highly open, imaginative, critical curriculum. North Towners did not want their children reading avant-garde literature or critiques of corporation polluters or revisionist accounts of President Johnson's political corruption. They wanted their schools to discipline and mold their children into hardworking, family-oriented, patriotic, mainstream citizens.[4]

North Town is only one small place in a big state, but Foley's conclusions are consistent with common observations about Texas schools in general. The conservatism he found in North Town, while it is not found in every classroom or every school district, is generally representative of Texas public education.

MEDIA

Like other institutions in the state, the mass media in Texas are conservative. Most newspapers and TV and radio stations are profitable businesses, dependent on other economic interests for their advertising revenues. Consequently, there is a tendency among the media to echo the business point of view on most issues. As Everett Collier, former editor of the *Houston Chronicle,* used to put it, "We are not here to rock the boat."[5]

In the last decade or so, a new media force has appeared on the political scene: talk radio. Its superstar, Rush Limbaugh, offers his listeners a mixture of energetic conservative argument, personal attack, misinformation, comedy, and egotism that has proved to be enormously popular. By the 1990s he was playing to an estimated radio audience of twenty million people each day and, according to surveys, was the main source of political news for 26 percent of the population, or almost seventy million.[6]

---

4. Douglas E. Foley, *Learning Capitalist Culture: Deep in the Heart of Texas* (Philadelphia: University of Pennsylvania Press, 1990), 110.
5. Quoted in Molly Ivins, "Political Writing—A State of Lazy Journalism," *Texas Humanist,* November–December 1984, 14–15.
6. Donna St. George, "Americans Are Using Talk Radio to Carry Their Voices to Congress," *Austin American-Statesman,* November 6, 1994, 1D.

Limbaugh's success spawned a host of imitators. The national airwaves are now full of talk-show hosts offering polemical analyses of public policy, almost all from the right-wing point of view. Limbaugh is popular in Texas, as he is everywhere. But in the state's local markets also, the airwaves are governed by talk-show hosts with conservative points of view. Austin supports John Doggett and Carl Wigglesworth on KVET, Houston listens to John Matthews on KPRC, Fort Worth is entertained by Mark Davis on WBAP, Dallas tunes in to David Gold on KLIF, and so on. It is possible to hear liberal opinions on the radio, but they must be searched for; conservative ideology is everywhere.

EVALUATION

After reviewing the socializing effects of families, schools, churches, and the media, one might wonder how any view other than the conservative ideology exists in Texas. It does exist, however, for several reasons: Some people adopt a personal point of view that is contrary to the opinion-molding forces around them; liberal families, churches, schoolteachers, and news outlets do exist in Texas, although they are in the minority; the national, as opposed to local, news media often display a liberal slant; and millions of non-Texans have moved to the state in the last few decades, bringing different political cultures with them. Political conservatism continues to dominate, but as the Texas population increases and becomes more diverse, the ideology is being challenged and modified by competing cultural values.

Ideology, however, is not the only basis for political party support. Equally important are people's interests, and the way parties attempt to recruit citizen loyalty by endorsing those interests.

Interests

An **interest** is something of value or some personal characteristic that people share and that is affected by government activity—their investments, their race, their jobs, and so on. When there is a question of public policy on which the two parties take differing positions, people often line up behind the party favoring their interests, whether or not their political ideology is in line with that party's. Moreover, parties often take positions that will attract the money and votes of citizens with clashing interests. Thus parties put together **coalitions** of interests in order to attract blocs of voters and campaign contributions. Party positions are therefore almost always much more ambiguous and confusing than they would be if they were simply based on ideology.

For example, in recent years, Republican Party candidates in Texas have tended to criticize the state's tort laws—the statutes that allow people who believe that they have been injured by someone else to sue for damages. Republicans have argued that the state makes it too easy to file "frivolous" lawsuits and allows juries to award damages to injured parties that are too large. They have supported "tort reform" by the state legislature. On the other hand, Democrats have tended to side with plaintiffs in lawsuits, arguing that injured people should have easy access to the courts and should be entitled to large amounts of money as compensation for injuries. They have usually opposed tort reform (see Chapter 12).

As a result, the types of people who tend to be the target of tort lawsuits (doctors and business owners, for example) have been inclined to support Republican candidates. Those who tend to benefit from such suits (plaintiff's attorneys, for example) have tended to side with Democrats. This has very little to do with ideology, and a great deal to do with who gets what from government.

Not all interests are economic. Mexican Americans, for example, have traditionally tended to support the Democratic Party because they have perceived the Republicans as being less tolerant of ethnic diversity. Whether an interest arranges people in a politically relevant manner depends on what sorts of questions become issues of public policy.

Interests and ideologies tend to combine in different ways in different people, sometimes opposing and sometimes reinforcing one another. For example, a Mexican American doctor in Texas would be drawn to the Republicans by her professional interest and drawn to the Democrats by her ethnic interest. She might have had trouble making up her mind about how to vote in the 1996 election. On the other hand, an Anglo oil company executive or an African American labor union president would probably have experienced no such conflict. In each case, the citizens's personal ideology may either reinforce or contradict one or more of his or her interests. The way interests and ideologies blend and conflict, and interact with candidates and parties, is one of the things that makes politics complicated and interesting to study.

Interests thus help to structure the party battle. They are politically important for other reasons as well. See Chapter 4 for a detailed discussion of the organizing and lobbying efforts of interest groups.

The partisan coalitions that have characterized recent Texas politics are summarized in Table 5–2. It is important to understand that not every person who has an interest agrees with every other person with the same interest, and so citizens who share interests are not unanimous in their partisan attachments. For example, although most of the people in the computer business who contributed large amounts to a political party in the 1990s gave to the Republicans, not all did. Similarly, although the great majority of African Americans who voted in 1994 and 1996 supported the Democrats, thousands

TABLE 5–2

Interests Generally Supporting the Two Major Parties

Type of Interest	Democrats	Republicans
Economic class	Poor Labor union	Middle; wealthy Management
Professions	Plaintiff's attorneys, public employees	Physicians, business entrepreneurs
Development vs. environment	Environmentalists	Developers, rural landowners
Industry	Entertainment	Oil and gas, computers
Ethnic	African American, Mexican American	Anglo
Religion	Catholic, Jewish	Protestant, especially evangelical

did not. The table describes how interests lean in general, not how every person with that interest behaves.

Politics would be fascinating enough if, once ideologies and interests had arranged themselves into a party coalition, they stayed that way. In fact, however, the party battle evolves as history changes the way people live. A hundred years ago, the Democratic Party was the more conservative party and dominated Texas almost completely. Today, the Republican Party is more conservative and has achieved parity with the Democrats. It is not too much of an exaggeration to say that the history of Texas is written in the story of the two major parties.

Texas Political Parties—A Brief History

Prior to joining the Union, Texas had no political parties. In the early days of settlement, the free spirits who came to Texas were happy to leave government and politics behind them. During the period of the Texas Republic (1836–1845), Texas politics was dominated by Sam Houston, the hero of the war for independence from Mexico. While there were no political parties, pro-Houston and anti-Houston factions provided some discussion of public policy.

Texas entered the United States in 1845 as a slave state. Nationally, the Democrats were proslavery, while the Whigs ignored the issue. Moreover, the Democrats had endorsed the admission of Texas to the Union in the 1844 election, whereas their opponents, the Whigs, had waffled. Thus, most Texans were Democrats.

Party divisions became intense when the Civil War ended in 1865. The Republican administration of Abraham Lincoln had defeated the Confederacy, of which Texas was a member, and freed the slaves. Reconstruction, or Union occupation, settled on all the Southern states. White Southerners found themselves under the rule of Northerners, the military, and African Americans. Rightly or wrongly, they believed themselves to be subject to tyranny by a foreign conqueror. They identified this despotic occupation with the Republican Party. In this emotionally searing experience, the Southern politics of the next century were forged. The Democratic Party became the vehicle of Southern resistance to Northern domination, and of White opposition to full citizenship for Blacks. As a result, when Reconstruction ended in 1874, Texas, like the other former members of the Confederacy, was a solid one-party Democratic state. It remained a **one-party state** until the 1970s, with telling effects on politics and public policy.

At the national level, the United States has a competitive two-party system. For example, between 1920 and 1996 the Republicans and Democrats each won ten presidential elections. Competitive party systems are characterized by a great deal of public dialogue between the parties. Although personal attacks are made and inaccurate statements are common, intelligent discussion and genuine debate also occur. Emerging groups of voters—African Americans, Latinos, and women, for example—and emerging issues such as the environment and abortion find receptive ears in one or more of the competitive parties. In this way, these concerns become known throughout the political system.

Citizens are relatively active in a two-party system, and voting turnouts are therefore fairly high. A one-party system is very different, and

Texas in the first three-quarters of this century furnishes a good example. Because there was no "loyal opposition," elections were decided in the Democratic primary, and nominees usually ran unopposed in the November general election. The party label is the most important guide the American voter has at election time, but in Texas it was of no value. Texas's voters usually had a choice of several candidates for each elective office, but they all ran as Democrats. There was some debate on public policy between liberal Democrats and conservative Democrats, but only a little.

A good example of a different way of organizing party competition is found in Great Britain, where the minority party—the party out of power—is referred to as "the loyal opposition." Its leader is on the government payroll, and his or her function is to *criticize* the ruling party! This institutionalized opposition voice provides the British with an alternative perspective, competing policy choices, and the robust debate that is essential in making democratic government work. The system does not guarantee that British democracy never produces foolish policies, but when bad policies arise, they stem from some cause other than inadequate discussion.

Without party competition to create debate and spur voter interest, most White citizens (in most areas of the state African Americans were prevented from voting) were apathetic, and voter turnout was very low. Candidates of all ideological persuasions, from Ku Klux Klansmen to liberals, ran as Democrats. Traditional party functions such as recruiting, financing, and conducting campaigns were performed not by the party but by informal, unofficial organizations, campaign committees, and other groups. Voters were uninformed about these groups and knew little, if anything, about who controlled them or what their goals were.

One result was that when voters elected Democrats to the offices of governor, lieutenant governor, attorney general, treasurer, and so on, they were not sending a Democratic "team" to Austin. They were sending independent officials who were frequently rivals and had little in common except personal ambition and a Democratic label. The parties acted to emphasize, not overcome, the fragmentation of power created by the state constitution (see Chapter 2).

Under these conditions of splintered power, because there was no unified team, there was no unified program. Each politician went his or her own way. The act of holding together disparate interests praised by Paul Samuelson at the beginning of the chapter was not performed.

In other words, one-party politics in Texas was really no-party politics. Instead of the vigorous debate and citizen involvement that characterize well-run democracies, confusion and apathy reigned.

The transition to two-party politics in Texas, as in most of the South, has been gradual. Beginning in 1928, Texans sometimes voted for Republican presidential candidates. In 1961, Republican John Tower cracked the Democratic monopoly at the state level by winning a special election for a U.S.

Senate seat. Republicans began to win a few local elections in Dallas and Houston soon thereafter, but conservative Democrats continued to dominate state politics into the 1970s. In 1978, Bill Clements beat John Hill for the governorship and became Texas's first Republican governor in 104 years. But Clements could not win reelection in 1982, in spite of spending a record $13.2 million during his campaign.

Republican President Ronald Reagan's landslide reelection in 1984 seemed to have finally broken the Democrats' hold on Texas. Dozens of Republican candidates rode Reagan's coattails to victory in local elections, as did Phil Gramm, the Republican candidate for U.S. senator. Some of the local officeholders subsequently lost their reelection bids, but by then Texas could no longer be considered a Democratic monopoly.

Seen against this historical background, the election of 1994 appears to be truly a watershed. Republicans defeated an incumbent Democratic governor, retained a second U.S. Senate seat, pulled almost even in the state Senate, and saw hundreds of local offices fall to their candidates (for more detail on this election, see Chapter 6).

By 1998 Texas was a two-party state that seemed to be moving toward domination by Republicans. The governor, both U.S. senators, a majority of state senators, the agriculture commissioner, all three railroad commissioners, and a majority of the state board of education belonged to the GOP ("Grand Old Party," a nickname from the post-Civil War era). Moreover, Texans gave decisive majorities of their major-party vote to Republican presidential candidates in both 1992 and 1996. Democrats were holding on to a majority of the delegation to the U.S. House of Representatives and another majority in the state House, and claimed the lieutenant governor, the attorney general, the speaker of the House, the land commissioner, and the comptroller as party members. Table 5–3 displays the growth in the number of Republican officeholders in Texas from 1974 to 1997.

Among the citizens, the story was somewhat more complicated. In a poll conducted in the summer of 1993, 30 percent of Texans identified them-

TABLE 5–3

Growth in the Number of Republican Officeholders in Texas

Year	Texas House	Texas Senate	Other Statewide	U.S. House	U.S. Senate	Other	Total
1974	16	3	0	2	1	53	75
1978	22	4	1	4	1	87	119
1982	35	7	0	5	1	166	214
1986	56	6	1	10	1	504	578
1990	57	8	6	8	1	722	802
1994	61	14	13	11	2	956	1,057
1997	68	17	27	13	2	1,232	1,359

SOURCES: *Austin American-Statesman*, November 13, 1994, 16A for figures for the years 1974 to 1990; Texas Republican Party Headquarters for the years 1994 and 1997.

selves as Republicans, 31 percent called themselves Democrats, and 32 percent claimed to be independents, with 7 percent having no opinion. Four years later, the percentage of Republicans in the population had climbed only a point, while the percentage of citizens claiming to be Democrats had shrunk by the same amount, which was within the margin of error of the survey.[7]

The Republicans are gaining government officials not only through election, but also through conversion. Former Democratic Governor John Connolly started the trend in 1973 when he jumped to the GOP, but party switching accelerated in the 1990s. From the election of President Bill Clinton in 1992 to late 1997, *ninety* Democratic officials changed their affiliation. They included officials as lowly as justice of the peace and as important as state Supreme Court justices.

Occasionally, a Republican will become a Democrat. Such a switch sets up interesting possibilities, as in the contest for agriculture commissioner in 1994. In that election, Rick Perry, a Democrat-turned-Republican, defeated Marvin Gregory, a Republican-turned-Democrat.

Source: Sam Attlesey, "A Switch in Texas Politics," *Dallas Morning News,* October 20, 1997, A1.

If Republicans are increasingly winning elections, therefore, the explanation cannot be that the GOP has a decisive edge in the number of Texans who identify with it. Either many people who consider themselves Democrats are voting Republican, or independents are supporting Republican candidates, or Republicans are going to the polls on election day while Democrats are staying home. No doubt each of these explanations contains some truth. However, Chapter 6 will argue that it is mainly the third explanation, different voter turnout rates, that holds the key to understanding the rise of Republicans in Texas.

In the 1990s, with Texas beginning to look like a two-party democracy, a new force complicated the picture. Ross Perot entered the 1992 presidential race, winning a very respectable 22 percent of the state's popular vote. Afterward, Perot's quasi-party, "United We Stand America," was putting money and energy into trying to organize citizen support around the country, including Texas. Exit polls in 1992 indicated that Perot's candidacy hurt Republican Bush more than Democrat Clinton in Texas.

If that trend had continued, then the further rise of United We Stand America might have meant the decline of the Republican Party just as it was about to achieve parity with the Democrats. But United We Stand America seemed to fizzle out in the mid-1990s, with Perot receiving only 7 percent of the state's vote in the 1996 presidential election. Thus the way seemed clear for the further ascent of the Republicans in Texas.

---

7. David Jackson, "Poll: Hispanics Not Flocking to GOP Banner," *Dallas Morning News,* August 1, 1993, A45; The Texas Poll, February 1997—thanks to Professor Daron Shaw of the Government Department of the University of Texas at Austin for supplying this information.

The growth of two-party competition in Texas has been good for democracy. Instead of the confused jumble that characterized Texas politics when Texas was a one-party state, there is now robust debate between the parties on many issues of importance to the citizens.

The public debate is so loud because policy differences between the parties are quite substantial. Table 5–4 displays some summary statements from the state Democratic and Republican Party platforms of 1996. As the table illustrates, the differences between the activists who write these platforms are of two kinds. First, on some issues—for instance, abortion, immigration, the minimum wage, labor unions, and homosexuality—party activists are clearly and firmly on opposing sides. Second, the parties are concerned about different issues, and therefore talk about different subjects. For example, the Republicans, but not the Democrats, mention the right to gun ownership, while the Democrats are the only party to mention health care, child care, and workers' safety and rights.

Functions of Political Parties

Following this summary of the history of the two parties in Texas and their ideological and interest bases, it would be helpful to list the useful functions the parties perform. The basic purpose of parties is to win elections and thus gain the opportunity to exercise control over public policy. While pursuing this goal, they perform several functions that make them valuable institutions in a democracy. These include:

★ Involving ordinary people in the political process, especially persuading them to vote and teaching them the formal and informal "rules of the game"

★ Recruiting political leaders and inducing them to restrain their individual ambitions so that the party can achieve its collective purposes

★ Communicating to the leaders the interests of individuals and groups

★ Adding factual information and persuasive argument to the public discussion of policy alternatives

★ Structuring the nature of political conflict and debate, including screening out the demands of certain people and groups (usually fringe individuals or minority groups that lack political clout)

★ Moderating differences between groups, both within the party and in the larger society

★ Partially overcoming the fragmented nature of the political system so that gridlock can be overcome and coherent policy made and implemented

Political parties in any democracy can be judged according to how well or badly they perform these functions. How do Texas parties measure up?

Party Organization

All parties are organizations, but they follow many different patterns of structure. In general, we can say that American parties, compared to those in for-

TABLE 5–4

1996 Texas Political Party Platforms

Issue	Republican	Democratic
Religion	"We believe in you! We believe you are a sacred being created in the image of God."	"No political party . . . holds an exclusive lock on religious belief."
Education	"Republicans encourage the Governor and Legislature to enact legislation which advocates school choice options, including a voucher system. . . . We . . . support the teaching of creation science in Texas public schools."	"Texas Democrats have led the fight to improve public education while others have sought to weaken or destroy it. . . . The state must provide adequate funding to educate all children to their potential."
Affirmative action	"The Republican Party of Texas strongly supports legislation that would clearly direct the State of Texas . . . not to use age, sex, race, color, ethnicity, or national origin as criteria for either discriminating against or granting preferential treatment to any individual or group."	"We pledge to support efforts of business, governmental bodies, and institutions of higher learning to reach and make available opportunities to a diverse and qualified pool of talent."
Homosexuality	"Homosexual behavior is contrary to the fundamental, unchanging truths that have been ordained by God. . . . Accordingly, homosexuality should not be presented as an acceptable "alternative" lifestyle in our public policy."	"We pledge to ensure that all Texans, without regard to . . . sexual orientation . . . are protected from discrimination."
Guns	"The Party fully recognizes the constitutional right of citizens to keep and bear arms."	Not mentioned.
Abortion	"The Party believes that the unborn child has a fundamental individual right to life which cannot be infringed. We affirm our support for a human life amendment to the Constitution."	"The Democratic Party trusts the women of Texas to make their own decisions about such personal matters as whether or when to bear children. . . . We will work to guarantee every woman the right to make personal decisions regarding . . . abortion."
Minimum wage	"The Party believes the minimum wage law should be repealed in order to expand employment opportunities."	"We support an increased federal minimum wage for all workers as well as an increase in the state minimum wage."
Labor unions	"The Party applauds the Right-To-Work Law and encourages our legislators to call for a referendum to make this law a constitutional amendment."	"We support the rights of all employees, public and private, to organize, collect dues, and negotiate freely with their employers through agents of employees' choosing."
Workers' safety and rights	Not mentioned.	"We support the right of every employee to work in a safe workplace [plus a long section on this topic]."
Health care	Not mentioned.	"We support a comprehensive health care financing and delivery system that provides high quality personal health care [plus a long section on this topic]."
Child care	Not mentioned, except to confirm that "the family is responsible for its own welfare, education, moral training, conduct, and property."	"The Texas Democratic Party supports public/private initiatives that promote safe and affordable child care and after-school care for working families."
Environment	"We . . . affirm that groundwater is an "absolute ownership" right of the landowner. . . . The Party encourages the US Congress to rewrite and reauthorize the Endangered Species Act to protect wildlife while supporting the rights of private property."	"Protecting our environment is a fundamental policy priority. We pledge to increase funding for state pollution prevention and enforcement [plus many more specific policy pledges on this topic]."

eign democracies, are weakly organized. They are not structured so that they can function easily as a cohesive team. The parties in Texas are especially weak. As a result, they do not perform the function of overcoming gridlock and making coherent policy very well, nor do they structure conflict to make it sensible to most ordinary citizens. A review of state party organization will suggest why this is so.

Figure 5–1 shows that in Texas, as in most states, parties are divided into a permanent organization and a temporary one. The **permanent party organization** consists of little more than a skeleton force of people who conduct the routine but essential business of the party. The party's primary purpose of winning elections requires far more people and much greater activity. The party comes alive in election years in the form of a **temporary party organization** geared to capturing power.

THE TEMPORARY PARTY ORGANIZATION

The temporary party organization is focused on the spring primary and the fall general election. It attempts to choose attractive candidates and to mobilize voters to support them.

In Texas, party membership is determined by the act of voting; there are no permanent political party rolls. When citizens vote in the Democratic Party primary, for example, they are considered to be "affiliated Democrats" until the end of the calendar year. They may vote only in the Democratic runoff, if there is one, and participate only in Democratic conventions. The next year, they may legally change their affiliation and participate in Republican Party activities.

PRECINCT AND COUNTY CONVENTIONS

In the 254 counties of Texas are more than 6,000 precincts, each having from 50 to as many as 3,500 voters. Each voter is entitled to have a voice in choosing the precinct chairperson and proposing and voting on resolutions that will establish party policy, but voter participation in party affairs is low. Normally only a small fraction of those who vote in the primaries—who are themselves only a fraction of the total number of registered voters, and a smaller fraction of the citizens of voting age—participate in conventions or other party affairs.

The main function of the precinct convention is to select delegates to the county convention, which is the next echelon of the temporary party organization.[8] The main function of the county convention is to select delegates to the state convention. Both precinct and county conventions can be either short or long, peaceful or filled with conflict, productive of resolutions or not.

THE STATE CONVENTION

Both major parties hold their state conventions on a weekend in June during even-numbered years. The party state executive committee (SEC) decides when and where the convention is to be held. Depending on the year of the election cycle in which it occurs, the June convention performs some or all of the following activities:

---

8. The four largest counties—Bexar, Dallas, Harris, and Tarrant—are so populous that they are entitled to more than one state senator. In these counties, each state senatorial district holds its own district convention rather than there being a countywide convention.

FIGURE 5–1
Major Party
Organization
in Texas

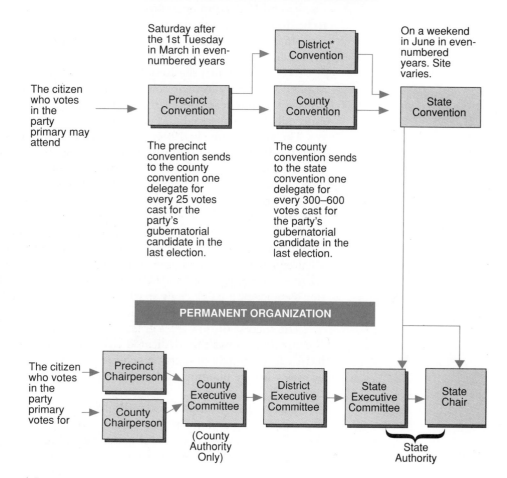

District conventions are held in counties with more than one senatorial district.

1. It certifies to the secretary of state the party nominees for the general election in November.

2. It writes the party platform.

3. It selects the members of the SEC.

4. It names the Texas committeeman and committeewoman to the national party committee.

5. It makes the final selection of delegates to the national party convention.

6. It selects a slate of presidential electors to serve in the electoral college in the event that the party's candidate for president and vice president win in Texas.

Party conventions have tended, over the past several decades, to travel in opposite directions—the Democrats from argument to harmony, and the

Republicans from agreement to disharmony. Until the 1980s, the liberal and conservative wings of the Democratic Party often fought viciously over party planks and leadership positions. In the 1990s, however, the party has come to be dominated more and more at the organizational level by the liberal faction. In conventions, the delegates now tend to adopt liberal platforms and save their criticisms for the Republicans.

In contrast, when the Republicans were a small minority, they rarely argued over policy in their conventions. As their influence in the state grew, however, Republicans generated greater and greater internal disagreement, especially between social and economic conservatives.

The climax came in 1994, when delegates from the Christian Right (see Chapter 4) dominated the convention. They easily elected Tom Pauken, their favored candidate, as state chair of the party, beating Joe Barton, the candidate of the business establishment, and Dolly Madison McKenna, who represented Republicans who were moderate on social issues. They adopted a party platform that was far more conservative, especially on social issues, than many of the party's candidates for public office wanted. Among other provisions, the Republicans supported federal and state initiatives to outlaw abortion under all circumstances, and recommended that the public schools teach "creation science" in biology classes. The socially conservative platform and the convention's choice of a party chair sparked vigorous but futile opposition from delegates who were economically conservative but more moderate on social issues.

The success of this 1994 grassroots takeover of the Republican Party organization shows that dedicated citizens who are willing to spend time can have a large impact on party machinery. There are probably many liberal groups who are planning to have a similar impact on the Democratic Party in the future.

Again in 1996, the Christian Right dominated the Republican state convention, writing a platform that began with the words, "We believe in you! We believe that you are a sacred being created in the image of God" (see Table 5–4). Again, the religious social conservatives elected their favored people to run the party, and again economic conservatives objected without effect.

The ideological gap between the two halves of the party was so wide, and the dominant social conservatives were in such an uncompromising mood, that several prominent state party members were not chosen as delegates to the Republican national convention because they were considered to be too moderate on the abortion issue. Fred Meyer of Dallas, the former chair of the party, and Brian Berry of Austin, who organized GOP presidential nominee Bob Dole's efforts at the state convention, were both denied national delegate status. Even U.S. Senator Kay Bailey Hutchison squeaked by as a delegate only after prominent Republican state officials, including Governor Bush, twisted arms on her behalf.

THE PERMANENT PARTY ORGANIZATION

PRECINCT CHAIRPEOPLE

The citizen who votes in the primary has an opportunity to participate in the selection of the precinct and county chairpeople of his or her party. The precinct chairperson is the lowest-ranking permanent party official. Elected for a two-year term, he or she is expected to be the party leader at the precinct level, recruiting candidates, arranging for the precinct convention, getting out the vote, and in general beating the drum for the party.

 Because they are matters of constant controversy, party rules are frequently changed and republished at least once every four years. The operating rules of the two major parties spell out in detail the organizations and activities covered in this section and include procedures for selection of delegates to the national convention. Under legislation passed in 1971, state party rules are enforceable in a court of law. Interested readers should contact their local Democratic or Republican Party headquarters for further information.

COUNTY EXECUTIVE COMMITTEES

Together the precinct chairs form the county executive committee, which is charged with two major responsibilities: (1) conducting the party primary elections and (2) conducting the county convention. It is presided over by the county chairperson, the most important official at the local level. Elected for two years to a demanding job, this official is unpaid, although some receive private donations. County chairs are compensated by the state for the expense of conducting their party's primary elections. After the primary election has been held, the county executive committee canvasses the vote and certifies the results to the state executive committee.

THE DISTRICT EXECUTIVE COMMITTEE

The Texas Election Code also provides for district executive committees. Their membership varies according to the number of counties and sections of counties that make up the senatorial district. These committees are supposed to perform party primary duties related to the district. In practice, however, few district executive committees are functional. Most district duties are performed by county executive committees.

THE STATE EXECUTIVE COMMITTEE

The highest permanent body in the state party is the state executive committee, and the highest state party official is the party chair. Both are elected by the state convention. If the party controls the governorship, the chair of this party works closely with the governor and is likely to be a friend and political ally of the governor. Normally, the governor and the party chair work together to advance the party campaign during an election year.

The Republicans in 1996 were a notable exception. The rancor between social conservatives, as represented by Tom Pauken, the party chair, and economic conservatives, as represented by Governor George Bush, caused a split in campaign duties. Bush ran the fund-raising and campaign efforts for GOP presidential candidate Bob Dole and congressional candidates, while Pauken oversaw money-raising efforts for "downballot" state candidates.

Like the chair of the party in power, the chair of the state committee of the party out of power usually has a close relationship with the party's top leaders. By law, the executive committee of each party is responsible for staging the state convention, for certifying the party's candidates, and for coordinating a general party campaign over and above the efforts made by each individual candidate.

THE (UN)IMPORTANCE OF PARTY ORGANIZATION

American political parties are not "responsible parties"—that is, they have neither centralized control over nominations and financing nor the power to impose the party platform on members. In Texas, parties are especially weak because it is, in fact, the primary election, not the party organization, that is important in determining who is nominated to office. Furthermore, candidates normally rely on their own fund-raising and organizing ability more than they rely on their party to help them get elected.

As a result, when candidates succeed in capturing an office, they mostly have themselves and the individuals and groups who contributed to their campaign fund to thank for their achievement. They therefore have very little loyalty to the party; they are more likely to feel beholden to some wealthy interest group. Officeholders are often ideologically friendly with others of the same party, but they are not obligated to cooperate with one another. The parties have no discipline over them.

Texas party organizations have some ability to fashion a "party attitude" on public policy because they are centers of information flow and personal interaction, but they are incapable of forging a disciplined governing team. Therefore, the party platforms summarized in Table 5–4 are in fact largely irrelevant to candidates' positions. They are a good indication of the sentiments of the party activists as a group, but they say little about the policy stands of candidates as individuals.

As previously discussed, in the 1990s Governor George Bush and Senator Kay Bailey Hutchison went their own way and pretty much ignored the official state party organization. In return, that organization showed no love for them. The unimportance of party organization in Texas is illustrated by the fact that the GOP was victorious in both 1994 and 1996 despite this internal squabble. In a similar fashion, the Democratic Party won elections in the Lone Star State in previous decades despite the fact that it was internally divided.

The consequence of their organizational weakness is that Texas parties fail to perform many of the functions that make parties elsewhere useful to democracy. By and large, they cannot recruit political leaders or overcome the fragmented nature of the political system by forming officials into disciplined organizations. Instead of thinking of parties in Texas as two stable, cohesive teams, therefore, it would be more realistic to imagine them as two (or, as discussed in the next section, three or even four) loose confederations of citizens, interest groups, and officeholders that sometimes cooperate because of occasional ideological agreement and temporary parallel interests.

Two Parties, Three Factions

REPUBLICANS

Ideologically, the Texas Republican Party tends to be strongly conservative, usually opposing government involvement in the economy but sometimes endorsing such involvement in personal life. The recent disagreements between Republicans who emphasize social conservatism and those who emphasize economic conservatism, while important during the election cycles of 1994 and 1996, have not persisted long enough for us to speak of two stable factions within the party. Moreover, although grassroots GOP activists are largely social conservatives, Republican elected officials are overwhelmingly economic conservatives. For the present, therefore, we will speak of the Texas Republican Party as being dominated by one outlook.

Republican opposition to government involvement in the economy ("laissez-faire"—see Chapter 1) occasionally slides into pseudo laissez-faire under the pressure of actual politics, and the need to maintain their interest coalitions sometimes induces Republican candidates to violate their professed ideology. Nevertheless, under most conditions, Republicans can be counted on to favor a cheaper, less active government than the Democrats. Both of Texas's U.S. senators, Phil Gramm and Kay Bailey Hutchison, are good representatives of this ideological position, as is Governor George Bush.

GEOGRAPHIC DISTRIBUTION

While the Republicans and Democrats are now approximately equal statewide in voter strength, their numbers are still very unevenly distributed. Republicans are found overwhelmingly in cities and suburbs, with Dallas and Harris County (Houston) containing about four out of every ten of the state's Republican voters. Other concentrations are found in the East and West Texas "oil patches," the German Hill Country north of San Antonio, several counties in the Panhandle, and two counties in South Texas.

SOCIOECONOMIC AND ETHNIC DISTRIBUTION

GOP activists come from a relatively narrow socioeconomic and ethnic base. Most candidates and party activists are Anglo, middle or upper class, businesspeople or professionals. Although a sprinkling of African Americans and Latinos can be found among active Republicans, the party has not appealed to significant numbers of minorities since the end of Reconstruction in 1874. Furthermore, the party's traditional opposition to policies such as welfare and job-training programs aimed at helping the poor has generally ensured that its activists and voters would be fairly wealthy.

CONSERVATIVE DEMOCRATS

Despite the fact that Texas has a "two-party system," it really offers its citizens three voting options, for the Democrats are split into two stable factions. This "three-faction system" has the advantage of making more choices available to the voters, and the disadvantage of making Texas politics more confusing and chaotic than it might otherwise be.

Conservative Democrats are the representatives of habits of thought and behavior that survive from when Texas was part of the Old South. This Old South culture is very conservative on social issues, but tends to be conflicted and indecisive on economic issues. Many Southerners are normally conservative economically, but can be aroused to a fervent belief in the ability of government to protect the little people of society from wealthy individuals and corporations—an attitude that has historically been known as *populism*. This populist streak makes the Old South part of Texas hard to predict on economic issues.

At the level of the party activists and officeholders, the conservative faction of the Democratic Party is slightly less devoted to laissez-faire than Republicans, but much more so than the liberal faction. It tends to be conservative on social issues, although conservative Democratic candidates have been known to bend to the left on social issues in order to attempt to persuade minority citizens to vote for them. Lloyd Bentsen, former U.S. senator and secretary of the Treasury, and Bob Bullock, the present, but retiring, lieutenant governor, are good examples of conservative Democrats.

GEOGRAPHIC DISTRIBUTION

Support for the conservative Democrats is more widespread than support for the Republicans, although there is considerable overlap. The traditional base is the piney woods of East Texas, where Old South traditions are strongest. This wing of the party can usually count on support from the Panhandle, from several counties in the Midland-Odessa area, from the German Hill Country north and west of San Antonio, and in Dallas, Lubbock, Midland, and Abilene. It is relatively weak in North Texas, in the sparsely settled counties of West Texas, and in larger urban areas other than those already noted. Small cities and rural areas generally remain conservative Democratic in their affiliation.

SOCIOECONOMIC AND ETHNIC DISTRIBUTION

Representing the historically dominant wing of the party, conservative Democrats draw support from all classes in Texas, although that pattern is changing as Republicans continue to increase their support among the wealthy. Like the Republicans, they have historically been popular among the Anglo middle and upper classes, business and professional people, and white-collar workers. Unlike the Republicans, they also draw substantial support from farmers, ranchers, and workers, especially those in rural areas and small cities. Again, this pattern may be changing as the Republicans grow in popularity.

Although African Americans, Mexican Americans, and other minorities have strongly favored liberal over conservative Democrats, they often end up furnishing support for the conservatives. The reasons are twofold. First, machine politics prevails in several South Texas counties. Mexican American leaders are able to deliver a substantial ethnic vote and frequently make deals to deliver it to conservative Democratic candidates. Second, many minority citizens vote a straight Democratic ticket, without regard to the ideology of the candidate. Thus, without catering to the wishes of ethnic minorities, conservative Democrats frequently win their votes in the general election. Today, facing serious competition from Republicans, conservative Democrats are paying more attention to minority groups and seeking their support.

WHY DID THEY ALWAYS WIN?

As we noted earlier, the Democratic Party, dominated by conservatives, won almost every public election in Texas from the mid-1870s until the mid-1970s. What accounted for its consistent success?

Part of the answer is that Republicans were extremely unpopular because of their identification with the abuses of Reconstruction. Other factors also bear on this question.

1. Since they represent the socioeconomic elite in the state, conservatives— Republicans as well as Democrats—have a pool of educated, interested people who have both the time and the money to devote to politics. This gives conservatives a great advantage over liberals, many of whom are less well off and lack the job flexibility necessary to devote daylight hours to political affairs.

2. As we will see in Chapter 6, voter turnout in support of liberals is lower than that in support of conservatives. The full strength of liberal sentiment is seldom reflected at the polls.

3. In former decades, conservative Democrats were usually in control within the party and frequently wrote its rules to their own advantage.

4. The open primary system in Texas has been a bonanza for conservative Democrats. As seen in Table 5–5, for many years thousands of Republicans ignored their own party primary and chose to vote in the Democratic primary. The combined votes of conservative Republicans and conservative Democrats frequently eliminated liberal candidates who otherwise might have won the Democratic nomination. This result left voters in the general election with a choice between a conservative Democrat and an even more conservative Republican. Conservative Democrats were happy with this situation because the liberal Democrats would usually "hold their nose" and vote for the conservative candidate of their party, thus ensuring his or her victory.

Until the 1980s, this system seemed to be self-perpetuating. Republicans appeared content with their own world of party politics. Liberal Democrats, trapped and frustrated, were unable to win within their party and unable to win without it. And conservative Democrats, knowing that they were well off, basked in the power of their position and did their utmost to retain it.

Today, however, Republicans contest almost every office at every level of government. Contested primary elections are now keeping the Republicans at

TABLE 5–5

Votes Cast in Primary and General Elections

Year	Office	Primaries		General Elections	
		Democratic	Republican	Democratic	Republican
1974	Governor	1,521,306	69,101	1,016,334	514,725
1976	President	1,529,168	356,307	2,199,956	1,636,370
1978	Governor	1,812,896	158,403	1,166,919	1,183,828
1980	President	No primaries held		1,881,147	2,510,705
1982	U.S. senator	1,264,438	262,865	1,818,223	1,256,759
1984	President	1,463,447	336,814	1,949,276	3,433,428
1986	Governor	1,096,552	544,719	1,584,515	1,813,779
1988	President	1,767,045	1,014,956	2,382,485	2,954,796
1990	Governor	1,466,869	852,121	1,921,895	1,825,148
1992	President	1,482,975	797,146	2,281,815	2,496,071
1994	Governor	1,036,944	557,340	2,016,928	2,350,994
1996	President	921,256	1,019,803	2,459,683	2,736,167

SOURCE: The Office of the Secretary of State.

home—voting in their own primary. In doing so, they are helping to build their party. Meanwhile, the advantage the conservative Democrats have historically held in the open primary system is disappearing. The emergence of the Republican Party in Texas has thus, paradoxically, strengthened the liberal wing of the Democratic Party.

LIBERAL DEMOCRATS

Liberals usually recommend policies that depend upon government's being active in economic affairs, especially on behalf of those who have less wealth and power. They tend, however, to oppose government intervention in personal life. Former Governor Ann Richards and former mayor of San Antonio (and also former U.S. secretary of housing and urban development) Henry Cisneros are good examples of Texas liberal Democrats.

The most famous and successful of all Texas Democratic politicians, Lyndon Johnson, was mainly, although somewhat inconsistently, a liberal. While a member of the U.S. House of Representatives, from 1937 to 1949, he tended to side with the left wing of the national party. While U.S. senator, from 1949 to 1961, he leaned more toward the conservative side. As president, from 1963 to 1969, however, he provided vigorous liberal leadership to the country.

GEOGRAPHIC DISTRIBUTION

Democratic voting strength in urban areas recently has been more or less equally divided between liberals and conservatives. Liberals are also strong where labor unions are a factor: in far East Texas, in East Central Texas, and in much of the Gulf Coast. Considerable support also comes from South

After tremendous statewide victories for Republican candidates in the 1994 and 1996 elections, Texas Democrats can be forgiven for wondering if they have become an endangered species.

Courtesy of Ben Sargent.

Texas, the South Plains, and parts of the Panhandle. Liberals can usually rely on doing well in Austin, the Beaumont–Port Arthur–Orange complex, Corpus Christi, Houston–Galveston, and Waco.

SOCIOECONOMIC AND ETHNIC DISTRIBUTION

Identifying the socioeconomic components of liberal Democratic strength in Texas is more complex than in the case of Republicans or conservative Democrats. Liberals form, at best, an uneasy coalition. White middle- and upper-class liberals can support African Americans and Mexican Americans in their quest for equal treatment, but labor unions have been noticeably cool in this area. African Americans and Mexican Americans usually give little support to reform legislation—of campaign spending and lobbying, for example—or to efforts to protect the natural environment, that energize Anglo liberals. Many Mexican Americans are reluctant to vote for African American candidates, and vice versa. While we can say, therefore, that liberal strength comes mostly from labor unions, African Americans, Mexican Americans, and certain educated Anglos, the mix is a volatile one that does not make for stable cooperation.

Liberal leadership comes largely, but not exclusively, from the legal, teaching, and other professions. In earlier years, union officials provided leadership for the liberal faction, and in some areas they still do. But officials of the state unions, like their national counterparts, have become more conservative in recent years. Leading the liberal Democrats is an uncertain business.

THE FUTURE OF THE THREE-FACTION SYSTEM

The future does not look bright for conservative Democrats in Texas. They are being drained from the right and squeezed from the left. As Republicans steadily draw away their voting support, they continuously lose power within the Democratic Party to liberals. It is possible to foresee a day in the not-too-distant future when Texas has only a conservative Republican Party and a liberal Democratic Party. Where will the conservative Democrats go? If they become Republicans, then that party will dominate Texas politics for a long time. If, however, they only become independents, casting their votes according to the candidates and issue stands offered by each party in each election, the future is much less predictable.

Third Parties in Texas

Texas has had its share of **third parties.** The Know-Nothing Party, representing those who objected to Roman Catholics and immigrants, made a brief appearance before the Civil War. After the Civil War, the Greenback Party, a cheap-money party, made an equally brief appearance. More important was the Populist, or People's, Party, which reflected widespread discontent among farmers and other "little people." The Populists advocated an extensive program of government regulation of big business and social welfare reform. The Populist candidate for president drew one hundred thousand votes in Texas in 1892—almost 20 percent of the votes cast. The major parties, especially the Democrats under Governor Jim Hogg, adopted some of the Populist positions, and the party ultimately disappeared.

The Populist Party may be long dead, but a group of 250 delegates from thirty-two states met in the Hill Country town of Hunt in November 1996 to try to resurrect its spirit. Complaining that corporate money has been dominating American (and Texas) politics, they discussed ways of reclaiming power for the common people. They decided to call themselves the Alliance for Democracy.

The theme of the gathering was nicely stated by former Texas Agriculture Commissioner Jim Hightower: "America doesn't need a third party. It needs a second one." The delegates discussed ways to limit business power over both major parties and advance the public interest: Create a means of yanking the charter of lawbreaking corporations, repeal the North American Free Trade Agreement, nationalize the oil companies, limit all political contributions to $100 or less, and other improbable actions.

The Alliance for Democracy may revitalize American politics, or it may quickly vanish like countless other fringe movements. In either case, it represents the ideal of democracy: citizens organizing to try to force their government to pursue their vision of the common good.

Sources: Sam Howe Verhovek, "Texas Meeting Seeks a Rebirth of Populism," *New York Times,* November 25, 1996, A8; Molly Ivins, "Populist Alliance: A Movement Reborn," *Austin American-Statesman,* November 27, 1996, A15.

The Populists were typical of third parties in America. Such parties tend not to achieve permanent status for themselves, but they can be important in influencing the major parties to adopt some of their positions and platforms. Since the Populist era, Texas has seen candidates who were Prohibitionists, Socialists, Socialist-Laborites, Communists, Progressives, Jacksonians, States

Righters, members of George Wallace's American Independence Party, members of the Citizen's Party, and Libertarians.

New parties cannot get on state ballots by simply announcing their intention to run candidates. To allow every splinter group to call itself a party and thereby grab a place on the ballot would make for confusing, chaotic elections with dozens of candidates running for each office. In addition, of course, the major parties are not eager to make it easy for upstart competitors to grab the attention of the voters. As a result, every democratic country, and every American state, has laws that discriminate in some manner against new parties.

Texas has some of the toughest ballot access laws in the nation. A person nominated for statewide office by one of the major parties is automatically accorded a spot on the ballot. But in the days following the April primary runoffs, an independent candidate must collect signatures totaling 1 percent of the total votes cast in the last gubernatorial election. These signatures must come from *registered* voters who *did not participate* in a primary or runoff that year. All signatures must be accompanied by the voter's registration identification number. The rules vary somewhat for candidates for federal offices and local offices, and for parties as opposed to individuals, but none of them are permissive. If a party manages to collect enough signatures to get its candidates on a ballot, it can ensure itself a place for the next election by garnering 5 percent of the vote for any statewide office or 2 percent of the gubernatorial vote.

Needless to say, these rules prevent most independent and third-party candidates from ever getting on the ballot. The difficulties facing hopeful candidates who are not members of the major parties is illustrated by the history of the Libertarian Party.

Libertarians represent the most consistent and extreme form of antigovernment ideology. They agree with the Republicans in opposing regulation of economic life, and with the Democrats in opposing regulation of personal life.

The Libertarian Party first gathered the required 1 percent of signatures in 1980. It failed to attract enough votes then, or in the next two elections, to ensure a ballot position for the subsequent election without again gathering signatures. In 1986, however, getting on the ballot once more by petition, the Libertarians fielded a candidate against Comptroller Bob Bullock. Because Bullock looked unbeatable that year, the Republicans did not bother to run a candidate for comptroller. This left Libertarian George Meeks as the only opposition. Meeks managed to attract 9.98 percent of the vote, enough to guarantee his party a line on the ballot in 1988.

Since then, the Libertarians have maintained their precarious hold, usually by running a candidate against some statewide officeholder who is otherwise unopposed. As Texas becomes a full-blooded two-party state, however, uncontested races have vanished, and this strategy is no longer available. If it wants to keep itself before the eyes of the voters, the Libertarian Party is going to have to start appealing to more of them.

African Americans have never established a separate political party in Texas, although their main interest group, the National Association for the Advancement of Colored People (NAACP), often functions as a subfaction of the liberal Democrats.

Mexican Americans have established several well-known political organizations aimed at improving the lot of Spanish-speaking Texans. In 1929 an interest group called the League of United Latin American Citizens (LULAC) was formed to try to overcome ethnic discrimination and to encourage Mexican American participation in civic affairs (see Chapter 4). The American GI Forum came into being to fight ethnic discrimination during World War II, and Viva Kennedy clubs and the Political Association of Spanish Speaking Organizations (PASO) were active in the 1960s.

In the 1970s, Mexican Americans formed a true political party called La Raza Unida (*la raza* means "the race"), which won some local elections—notably in Crystal City—and even ran candidates for governor and other state offices. But, infiltrated by the FBI for alleged radicalism and beset by personal and factional feuds, the party was out of existence by the early 1980s.

Mexican Americans in Texas are currently represented by a number of interest groups, including LULAC and the Mexican American Legal Defense and Educational Fund (MALDEF), and by two organizations within the Democratic Party, Mexican American Democrats (MAD) and Tejano Democrats. What organizational patterns future Mexican American politics will take is not clear, but it seems certain that Mexican Americans will be of growing importance in Texas politics, as they form an increasingly large percentage of the state's population.

Summary

Ideology is one of the most important bases for political parties everywhere, but in Texas, where parties have historically been weak, ideology has usually been more important than party affiliation. The major ideological conflict has been between conservatives and liberals.

Liberals tend to favor government regulation of the economy but oppose it in personal life, while conservatives tend to favor regulation of personal life but oppose it in the economy. These basic differences lead to differences in many areas of public policy, from taxation to abortion. The Texas Republican Party is consistently strongly conservative, but the Democratic Party is split into a conservative and a liberal faction.

Parties appeal to interests, as well as to ideology, to mobilize voter support and campaign contributions. In attempting to form winning coalitions by putting together groups of voters and contributors, they sometimes reinforce their ideological leanings and sometimes violate them.

From 1874 to the 1970s, Texas was a one-party Democratic state. One-party states are characterized by an absence of party competition, inadequate debate about public policy, low voter turnout, and usually conservative public policy. Today, Republicans and Democrats each have the affiliation of about a third of Texas's voters, although the Republican Party is growing in importance. In the early 1990s Ross Perot's third party, United We Stand America, seemed to have the potential to disrupt major party loyalties and become an important political force, but it is now apparently fading from the scene.

Texas's political parties have both temporary and permanent party organizations. Nominations are made in primaries, and party leaders have no control over candidates or officeholders, and so party organization is much less important than ideology and interests in explaining the politics of the state. This lack of organizational strength means that Texas's parties are not "responsible" and are incapable of fulfilling some of the functions that they would perform in an ideal democracy. Nevertheless, the present situation, featuring intense party competition, is far better for democracy than the one-party Democratic domination that prevailed from the end of Reconstruction to the 1970s. In today's political situation there is at least robust and spirited debate of public policy.

Texas has given birth to a number of third parties, none of which achieved permanency but several of which influenced public policy in the state.

Key Terms

Coalition

Conservatism

Ideology

Interest

Liberalism

One-party state

Permanent party organization

Political parties

Political socialization

Temporary party organization

Third parties

Study Questions

1. What is a political ideology?

2. What are the basic ideological differences between liberals and conservatives? What are the more important policy differences between them?

3. Are you a liberal or a conservative? Are there any policy areas in which you disagree with what would otherwise be your ideological tendency?

4. What were you taught about democracy and Texas politics in elementary and high school? Was your instruction adequate?

5. What are the similarities and differences between interest groups and political parties?

6. What major interests are associated with each party?

7. Can you think of any interests you have that are better represented by one party or the other? Do your interests tend to clash with or reinforce your ideology?

8. What are the functions of political parties? How well do Texas parties perform them?

9. What are the characteristics of a one-party state?

10. Describe briefly the temporary and permanent party organizations in Texas. What political institution renders both of them relatively unimportant in determining the activities of the parties?

11. The three party groups—Republicans, conservative Democrats, and liberal Democrats—draw their support from different geographical areas and sections of the population. Describe the support base of each group.

12. Describe the current status of the two major parties in Texas. Are these two parties threatened by any third parties?

13. Are you a Democrat, a Republican, or an independent? Why?

Internet Assignment

Internet site: http://isadore.tsl.state.tx.us/p/politics/#texas

Go to the "Texas State Electronic Library" page. Click on "Texas Politics and Political Science Resources." Visit the state Democratic, Republican, and Libertarian sites. How do these sites convey their ideological programs?

Chapter Six

Voters, Campaigns, and Elections

Newly elected Republican Governor George W. Bush talks to reporters after his victory over Democrat Ann Richards in November 1994.

Suppose they gave an election and nobody came?
  Bumper sticker from the 1960s

Politics has got so expensive that it takes lots of money to even get beat with.
  Will Rogers, American humorist, 1931

Introduction

Nothing is more basic to the concept of democratic government than the principle of elected representatives freely chosen by the majority of the people, with each person's vote counting equally. And few things are more disturbing to observers of democracy than elections in which a large percentage of the people do not vote, or in which control of wealth makes a few campaign contributors far more important than the great mass of their fellow citizens.

This chapter will begin with a consideration of the reasons that voting is important to democracy. The topics that follow will be the history of the suffrage (the right to vote) in Texas, the state's registration procedures, and its shockingly low voter turnout. The focus next goes to election campaigns, with special attention to the impact of money on the outcome. Afterward, the various types of public elections in Texas will be described. Next, the 1994, 1996, and 1998 election campaigns and voting results will be chronicled. Last comes a comparison of the reality of Texas elections with the democratic ideal, and an argument that there is much room for improvement.

Voters

WHY VOTE?

As is the case with many important questions, the answer to this one is, "It depends." It depends on whether voting is viewed from the perspective of the *individual voter,* of the *candidates,* or of the *political system.*

From the standpoint of the individual voter, there may seem to be no logic in voting, for public elections are almost never won by the margin of a single vote (but see the box). The individual voter has very little hope of affecting the outcome of an election. Why, then, do so many people bother to register and vote?

The main reason is that people do not think of voting in completely logical terms. Like other political behavior, voting is governed not only by reason but also by personal loyalties, ideological fervor, custom, and habit. Most people vote primarily because they have been taught that it is their duty as citizens (as, in fact, it is). And even though a single vote is unlikely to affect the outcome of an election, participation in the governing of the community is important to the self-development of each individual.

From the standpoint of the candidate, voting is extremely important. There is a saying among politicians that "votes are counted one by one by one." It expresses the insight that although citizens may seem to be part of a mass, it is a mass of individual personalities, each with his or her own motivations, ideology, and hopes for the future. Politicians who forget that each potential supporter is an individual soon find themselves forcibly retired.

 Occasionally, in small towns and in elections held in conjunction with special districts, a single vote is decisive. In one municipal utility district (MUD) election in the northern part of the state, a vote was held in 1986 to elect directors of the MUD. Only one qualified voter lived in the district, and thus one person decided the outcome of the election. A decade later in the same community, a single citizen moved his house trailer onto an industrial site and proceeded to cast the one vote to create an economic development district around the site. Suppose they gave *those* elections and nobody came?

From the standpoint of the political system, elections are crucial. In democratic theory, it is the *participation of the citizens* that makes government legitimate (that is, morally right and worthy of support). When large numbers of citizens neglect or refuse to vote, this raises questions about the most basic underpinnings of political authority.

Voting also performs other functions in a democratic society. The act of participating in an election decreases alienation and opposition by making people feel that they are part of the system. Further, the electorate *does* have some effect on public policy when it chooses one set of candidates who endorse one set of policies over another. While one vote is unlikely to swing an election, groups of like-minded citizens who vote the same way can be decisive. Finally, large-scale voting has the added virtue of helping to prevent corruption. It is relatively easy to rig an election when only a few people bother to go to the polls. One of the best guarantees of honest government is a large turnout on election day.

So, despite the fact that one vote almost never matters, democracy depends upon each citizen acting as if it does. When people take their right to vote seriously and act as responsible citizens, the system works. When they refuse to participate and stay home on election day, they abdicate control over government to the elites and special interests who are only too happy to run things. We can at least partly judge the extent to which a country or state has a decent government by the level of voter turnout among its citizens. How does Texas stack up?

This question will be addressed shortly. First, however, the legal context of the voting act must be explained. The most important parts of that context are suffrage and the system of registration.

SUFFRAGE

One of the most important historical developments in American politics has been the expansion of the **suffrage**—the right to vote. The writers of the U.S. Constitution delegated to the states the power to determine voter eligibility in both national and state elections. At the time the Constitution was written, laws varied from state to state—and they still do—but restrictions on voting were widespread. Generally, states restricted the suffrage to adult white male property owners who professed a certain religious belief, which varied with the state. As a result of these restrictions, only about 5 percent of the

3,939,214 persons counted in the first national census in 1790 were eligible to vote. An even lower percentage actually went to the polls.

In a democracy, voting is very important, but it is only one of the many forms of political participation. Other important ways that you can take part in the governmental process include:

1. Working in election campaigns—helping to operate a phone bank, contributing money, distributing literature in a neighborhood, even putting up signs and displaying bumper stickers.
2. Communicating your views to your national, state, and local representatives.
3. Calling in to a radio talk show to express your opinion.
4. Informing family and friends about political candidates and issues and urging them to participate.
5. Writing a letter to the editor of your newspaper.
6. Wearing political badges, buttons, etc.
7. Joining a political organization (see Chapter 4) or forming a new one.
8. Serving on committees such as zoning or planning commissions.
9. Participating in public demonstrations—parades and rallies, protests, picketing, and even civil disobedience. Caution: You may need a permit to organize an outdoor demonstration, and if you engage in civil disobedience, you may be arrested.

Since that era, a series of democratic reform movements has slowly expanded the suffrage. In the 1820s and 1830s church membership and property ownership were removed as qualifications for voting in most elections. After the Civil War, the Fourteenth and Fifteenth Amendments to the Constitution were enacted in an attempt to guarantee full political rights to the freed slaves. At first, African Americans voted in substantial numbers. But the Southern states, including Texas, retaliated with a series of legal and informal restrictions that succeeded in withdrawing the suffrage from Black citizens in most parts of the old Confederacy by 1900. It was not until 1965, when Congress passed the Voting Rights Act, that the federal government began to enforce the right of African Americans to vote. Women were enfranchised with the ratification of the Nineteenth Amendment in 1920, and in 1971 the Twenty-sixth Amendment lowered the minimum voting age to eighteen.

Several things stand out in this two-century evolution of the right to vote. First, it is not exclusively Texan but part of national, even a worldwide, movement toward expanded suffrage. Within the United States, suffrage has been substantially nationalized. States still enact laws, but they do so within guidelines set down by the Constitution, Congress, and the Supreme Court, and enforced by the federal Justice Department.

Second, an important part of the story of the struggle to include all citizens in the suffrage has been the fact that well into the 1970s, Texas and other Southern states attempted to evade and obstruct the post-Civil War amendments and, later, the Voting Rights Act. They came up with various gimmicks—poll taxes, White-only primaries, literacy tests, and more—to keep African Americans from exercising the franchise. These obstructions also successfully discouraged many Mexican Americans and poor Whites from voting. As a result, voter turnout in the South was far below the levels prevailing in the North.

Third, however, an equally important part of the story is that the federal government, supported by concerned citizens in both the North and South, gradually defeated these antidemocratic schemes, so that by the mid-1970s all adult Americans had the legal right to vote. As will be discussed shortly, not all of them exercised that right, but at least state governments were no longer preventing them from going to the polling booth. The legal battle for a democratic suffrage has been won.

REGISTRATION

Every democratic political system has a **voter registration** procedure to distinguish qualified voters from those who are ineligible because of immaturity, lack of citizenship, mental incapacity, or other reasons. In most countries, registration is easy; in some nations, the government goes to great lengths to make sure that all citizens are registered before every election.

Like the other former slaveholding states of the old Confederacy, however, for most of its history Texas used a series of legal devices to deliberately limit registration, and thus voting. The most effective and longest-lasting of the antiregistration schemes was the *poll tax*. This was a $1.50 fee that served as the state's system of registration during the first part of the twentieth century. Those who paid it by January 31 were registered to vote in that year's elections. It discouraged less affluent citizens from registering, for back before inflation had eroded the value of the dollar, the fee represented a substantial portion of a poor person's paycheck. Since people had to be registered in order to vote, this tax was a convenient way for the more affluent to ensure that they would not have to share power with their fellow citizens. Moreover, because minority citizens were usually poor, this device had the not accidental effect of keeping the ballot box a White preserve.

In 1964 the nation adopted the Twenty-fourth Amendment to the Constitution, outlawing the poll tax. Two years later, the U.S. Supreme Court threw out Texas's tax. The state legislature then devised a new system of voter registration. Although no tax had to be paid, the period of annual registration was identical: October 1 through January 31. Since most poor people (especially minorities) had little education, they were not apt to follow public affairs as closely as those with more education. By the time they became interested in an upcoming election, they had often missed their chance to register. The new law, then, was another ploy to reserve the ballot box for the White and wealthy.

In January 1971 a federal district court struck down this registration law as a violation of the **equal protection clause** of the Fourteenth Amendment to the U.S. Constitution.[1] Declaring two provisions of the law—the annual registration requirement and the very early deadline for registration—to be discriminatory, the court expressed the opinion that 1.2 million Texans were disenfranchised by them. Later that year, the legislature responded with a new law that made registration much easier. Its major provisions, as amended, are as follows:

1. Initial registration. The voter may register either in person or by mail. A parent, child, or spouse who is registered may register for the voter.

---

1. *Beare* v. *Smith*, 321 F.Supp., 1100 (1971).

2. **Permanency.** The voter remains registered as long as he or she remains qualified. A new voter registration card is issued every two years.

3. **Period of registration.** Voters may register at any time and may vote in any election, provided that they are registered thirty days prior to the election. To vote in Texas today, one must:

   a. Be a United States citizen eighteen years of age by election day.
   b. Be a resident of the state and county for thirty days immediately prior to election day.
   c. Be a resident of the election precinct on election day.
   d. Have registered to vote at least thirty days prior to election day.

 In 1994 the U.S. Congress passed and President Bill Clinton signed the "motor voter bill." This act mandates that states devise a registration system that allows an individual to register to vote whenever he or she renews a driver's license. The hope of those creating the law was that easier registration would result in more citizens being registered, which in turn would mean more people in the voting booths on election day. The law's advocates were disappointed, however, when voter turnout *declined* from 1992 levels in the 1996 election.

TEXAS TURNOUT—GOVERNMENT BY THE PEOPLE?

Despite the fact that registration has been relatively easy in Texas for over two decades, **voter turnout,** while climbing erratically, is still below national levels. *Voter turnout* means the proportion of the eligible citizens who actually cast ballots—not the proportion of those registered, but the proportion of adult citizens. Table 6–1 shows that the percentage of Texans voting in both presiden-

TABLE 6–1

Percentages of Voting-Age Population Voting in National Elections, 1972–1996

Presidential Elections							
	1972	**1976**	**1980**	**1984**	**1988**	**1992**	**1996**
United States	55.5	54.3	51.8	53.1	50.2	55.2	50.8
Texas	45.4	47.3	44.7	47.2	44.2	49.0	43.0

U.S. House of Representatives (Off-Year Elections)						
	1974	**1978**	**1982**	**1986**	**1990**	**1994**
United States	36.1	35.1	38.0	36.4	35.0	38.9
Texas	18.4	24.0	26.2	29.1	26.8	35.0

SOURCES: *Statistical Abstract of the United States,* 101st ed. (Washington, D.C.: U.S. Department of Commerce, Bureau of the Census, 1980), p. 517; 106th ed. (1985), p. 254; 109th ed. (1989), p. 259; Federal Election Commission, Washington, D.C.; "Political Intelligence," *Texas Observer,* November 27, 1992, 8; Walter Dean Burnham, Department of Government, University of Texas at Austin.

One of the ironies of American democracy in the twentieth century is that so few people take advantage of the opportunity to vote. This lack of voter turnout is especially serious in the Southern states, including Texas. In this cartoon, Ben Sargent satirizes our citizens' odd disinterest in participating in their government.

Courtesy of Ben Sargent.

tial and off-year congressional elections is considerably lower than the percentage voting nationally. An average of 45.9 percent of eligible Texans turned out for presidential balloting in the quarter-century since the new registration law went into effect, and an average of 26.6 percent turned out for off-year congressional elections. Other elections often attract even fewer voters; the June 1993 runoff between Kay Bailey Hutchison and Bob Krueger for U.S. Senate drew only 20.5 percent of the state's eligible electorate, for example.[2]

In other words, government in Texas is never "by the people." At best, it is by half the people; often it is by a quarter of the people or even fewer.

WHY DON'T TEXANS VOTE?

Americans in general are not known for high voter turnouts, but Texans seem to vote even less than the residents of many other states. Why?

POLITICAL SOCIALIZATION

People can be taught to vote, just as they can be trained to drive on the right-hand side of the road or sing "The Yellow Rose of Texas." The institutions of socialization in Texas—family, schools, churches, mass media, and others—do not encourage children to be politically active. As discussed in Chapter 5, Texans are taught to accept the political system, not to question or participate

---

2. "Political Intelligence," *Texas Observer,* June 18, 1993, 24.

in it. One answer, then, is that Texans don't vote because they are not trained to participate.

THE POLITICAL PARTY SYSTEM

A competitive party system is a major stimulant to political participation by citizens. Among the American states, voter turnout tends to be highest where the Republican and Democratic parties have historically been more or less evenly matched and fairly well organized. Participation seems to be lowest in the states of the Old South, where the Democrats dominated for more than a century and the parties are weakly organized. As the Republican Party in the South becomes more active and successful, political participation and voter turnout have been increasing. Nevertheless, parties in Texas, as in the rest of the South, remain weak, and voting levels are still below even the mediocre rates that prevail in the rest of the country.

National and Southern participation in general and Texas participation in particular remained low in 1996, despite easier registration (see box) and the achievement of two-party systems in most of the Southern states. Political scientists are not certain as to why voters were reluctant to go to the polls in 1996. Probably the best explanation, to be discussed shortly, is that neither of the major-party presidential candidates inspired much enthusiasm among the citizens.

SOCIOECONOMIC AND ETHNIC STATUS

Texas is a rather poor state with a very uneven distribution of wealth. The poverty rate is important because the poor and less educated, in the absence of strong parties to persuade them to go to the polls on election day, have a tendency to stay home. When the poor don't vote, the overall turnout rate is low.

The differences between rich and poor citizens are strongly related to differences between turnout rates for ethnic groups. Consider, for example, the turnout rates for the three dominant ethnic groups in the 1993 runoff for U.S. Senate:[3]

Anglo	African American	Hispanic
24%	13%	12%

Other studies confirm that Texas's low voter turnout rate is at least partly caused by the tendency of its Black and Hispanic citizens to stay home on election day. Thus, those who vote tend to be richer, better educated, and White; those who abstain tend to be poorer, uneducated, and minority.

These differences have major consequences for public policy. Minority citizens tend to have more liberal opinions on what government should be doing, at least partly because they are more likely to be poor than Anglos. When they fail to go to the polls, however, their views become irrelevant. Because the more conservative White citizens vote at higher rates, their preferences are usually the ones that determine which candidates win, and therefore which policies are pursued by government. Low minority turnout is one of the major explanations for conservative public policy in Texas.

---

3. *Ibid.*

TABLE 6–2

Anglo and African American Public Opinion, 1989–1997

	Issue	Percent Agreeing Among	
		Anglo	African American
1.	Think that government should do something to reduce differences between rich and poor (those most willing to redistribute); 1989	29	47
2.	Believe that government should help people pay doctor and hospital bills (those most supportive); 1989	29	49
3.	Feel that homosexuality should be considered an acceptable alternative lifestyle; 1992	37	50
4.	Favor more federal spending to help urban minorities; 1992	35	61
5.	Favor affirmative action in general; 1997	37	93
6.	Oppose preferential treatment for minorities in workplace; 1997	82	40

SOURCES: 1 and 2 from National Opinion Research Center, *An American Profile: Opinions and Behavior, 1972–1989* (New York: Gale Research, 1990), p. 572; 3 and 4 from Gallup polls of June 7, 1992, and June 12, 1992; 5 and 6 from Texas Poll, reported in Clay Robison, "Texas 2-Step: Preferences, No—Affirmative Action, Yes," *Houston Chronicle*, November 16, 1997, D2.

For example, minorities as a whole are far more Democratic than are Anglos. According to a survey released by the Texas Poll in 1997, 24 percent of Anglos, 34 percent of Hispanics, and 56 percent of African Americans identify as Democrats.[4] Nothing is permanent in politics, and rising incomes or some other circumstance may change the balance of party identification among ethnic groups in the near future. But for the present, when minorities don't vote, it hurts Democrats.

Furthermore, it is not just any Democrats who suffer from low minority turnout. The liberal wing of the party needs minority support to win. As Tables 6–2 and 6–3 illustrate, African Americans and Mexican Americans

TABLE 6–3

Anglo and Mexican American Public Opinion, 1990–1997

	Question	Anglo	Mexican American
1.	Government spending should increase on programs to help blacks (% agreeing); 1990	23.5	53.7
2.	Government spending should increase on programs for refugees and legal immigrants (% agreeing); 1990	16.4	41.1
3.	English should be the official language (strongly agree); 1990	45.6	13.7
4.	Favor affirmative action programs in general; 1997	37	75
5.	Oppose preferential treatment for minorities in workplace; 1997`	82	44

SOURCES: First three from Rodolfo O. de la Garza, Louis DeSipio, F. Chris Garcia, John Garcia, and Angelo Falcon, *Latino Voices: Mexican, Puerto Rican, and Cuban Perspectives on American Politics* (Boulder: Westview Press, 1992), pp. 91, 97, 110; 4 and 5 from Texas Poll, reported in Clay Robison, "Texas 2-Step: Preferences, No—Affirmative Action, Yes," *Houston Chronicle*, November 16, 1997, D2.

4. The Texas Poll, February 1997—thanks to Professor Daron Shaw of the Government Department of the University of Texas at Austin for making this information available.

often hold views on public policy that are clearly more liberal than the opinions of Anglos. Once again, the future may differ from the past and present. For now, however, it seems clear that if Black and Hispanic Texans had higher turnout rates, liberal Democrats would win elections much more often. Such an outcome would mean that government policy in Texas would be more liberal. As it is, the liberals rarely go to the polls, so state government remains conservative.

Election Campaigns

Democracies do not hold elections unannounced. There is a period of time before the voting day in which the candidates attempt to persuade potential voters to support them. This period is the **campaign.** In Texas, would-be officeholders run initially during the primary campaign. Those who win nomination in the primary then campaign to win the general election.

Many citizens simply vote their party affiliation, which is why the Democrats won most elections in Texas during the twentieth century. For those who identify with a party, the campaign serves as a reminder of their loyalties and an inspiration to go to the polls. A large and increasing percentage of the population, however, is only lightly anchored in party identification or is completely independent. Since people who "belong" to one party are unlikely to vote for the candidate of the other party, it is the independents who tend to decide elections by supporting one side or the other overwhelmingly. General election campaigns, therefore, are largely aimed at the undecided independents.

Government is vastly complex and obscure to everyone except those who make a hobby or a business out of following current events. Most citizens, most of the time, are relatively uninterested in and ignorant about most of the details of government activity. Ignorance and apathy are especially associated with independents, who are generally less involved in politics than strong partisans. They are quickly bored by long, technical discussions of present and proposed policy. As a result, candidates who follow two rules tend to be more successful:

1. The candidate's most important task is to get his or her name recognized in a favorable way by as many citizens as possible, and to get those citizens to the polls.

2. Most of the arguments used in a campaign must be simple and emotionally powerful, rather than complicated and rational.

Consequently, a great deal of the advertising during campaigns tends to consist of the endless presentation of the candidate's name on billboards and in newspaper ads and television spots. Further, the rest of the campaign effort, the part in which candidates actually discuss issues in public, tends to consist of the repetition of condensed, sloganlike statements ("I oppose a state income tax") or personal attacks on the other candidate ("My opponent is an illegal-drug user").

Even better, from the standpoint of candidates, are powerful **visual images** that can be broadcast on television. It is impossible for opponents to argue with an image, for it conveys a message that bypasses the head and goes straight to the heart.

A classic illustration of the impact of visual images is the campaign Clayton Williams used to capture the Republican nomination for governor in 1990. Williams, a West Texas millionaire oilman and rancher, purchased ads in the state's major media outlets that capitalized on the public's fear of crime. The spot showed a chain gang of criminals in a dusty yard breaking stones into pebbles with sledge hammers. While this image was on the screen, Williams was speaking in the background, promising in his best country drawl that he would solve the state's crime problem by making sure, as governor, that criminals would spend their time "bustin' rocks."

Williams's opponents attempted to counter this TV ad by pointing out that Texas already had a large proportion of its population in prison with no visible effect on the crime rate, that the governor did not have the power to reorganize the state's criminal justice system, and that making prison inmates break rocks would undoubtedly be forbidden by the federal courts on the ground that it was unconstitutional. But these arguments were futile because they tried to set reason against emotion. The "bustin' rocks" image was irrelevant to the problem of crime, but nevertheless was intensely appealing to a fearful and enraged public. Williams, a virtual unknown before 1990, won the Republican primary handily.

The reliance on images instead of discussion of real solutions to problems almost won Williams the general election as well. Coming out of the primary, he had a large lead in the polls over the Democratic candidate, Ann Richards. But during the general election campaign he made a series of blunders that offended many voters, especially women. In his most famous gaffe, he compared bad weather to rape, suggesting that "If it's inevitable, relax and enjoy it." With each offensive remark, he lost support, and on election day Richards beat him, 52 to 48 percent.

In other words, a reliance on television images, instead of honest discussion of the problems facing Texas, can put a candidate within striking distance of the highest office in the state. Even with such a strategy, however, a candidate cannot entirely escape the demand that he or she meet with the media at least sometimes and answer questions about public policy. Visual images are very powerful, but they are not the only things that voters use to make up their minds.

CAMPAIGN RESOURCES

Whatever their strategies, candidates must have two essential resources: people and money. The people who are needed are both professionals and volunteers. The professionals plan, organize, and manage the campaign; write the speeches; and raise the money. Volunteer workers are the active amateurs who distribute literature, register and canvass voters, and transport supporters to the polls on election day. No major election can be won without competent people who are brought together early enough to plan, organize, and conduct an effective campaign, or without a sufficient number of volunteers to make the personal contacts and get out the vote.

The act of volunteering to work on a campaign not only is useful to the candidate but also is of great importance to the volunteers and to the democratic process. People who work on a campaign learn about the stupendous

TABLE 6–4

Costs of Media in Major Markets, 1995

	Television		
City	**Station**	**Cost of 30-Second Spot**	**Cost of 10-Second Spot**
Houston	KHOU (CBS)	$3000–$6000	$1500–$3000
Dallas/Fort Worth	KDFW (CBS)	$3000–$7000	$1500–$3500
Austin	KVUE (ABC)	$1700	$850
Lubbock	KCBD (NBC)	$250–$400	$125–$200

	Newspapers		
City	**Paper**	**Cost of Full-Page, Black-and-White Ad**	**Full-Page, Color Ad**
Fort Worth	*Star-Telegram*	$17,418.87	$19,381.87
San Antonio	*Express-News*	$10,319.40	$11,289.40
El Paso	*Times*	$6,038.21	$6,923.21
Amarillo	*Daily News*	$4,226.04	$4,901.04

SOURCE: Compiled by the authors.

exertions, the difficult decisions, and the painful blunders that make up public life in a free society. They learn tolerance for other points of view, how to argue and evaluate the arguments of other people, and why the media are important. Finally, they learn that when they win, the faults of the republic are not all corrected, and that when they lose, civilization does not collapse. They learn, in other words, to be good citizens. In Texas as elsewhere, political campaigns are the most intense means of creating the truly participatory society.

Voluntary participation, the first major resource of campaigns, is thus entirely uncontroversial. Everyone endorses it. But about the second resource, money, there is great controversy.

Except in municipal elections, where volunteers are most important, money is the most important campaign resource. Politicians need money to publicize their candidacies, especially over television. Table 6–4 illustrates the costs of buying advertising in major media outlets in the mid-1990s. The need to buy campaign advertising in many such media repeatedly over a period of months makes the cost of running for office in Texas formidable. For example, George Bush and Ann Richards each spent about $13 million in the 1994 gubernatorial campaign.[5] In 1996, the seventy-four candidates attempting to win the thirty Texas seats in the U.S House of Representatives spent more than $35 million, not counting the runoffs.[6]

This money must come from somewhere. A very few candidates, such as Clayton Williams and H. Ross Perot, who tried to win the presidency as an independent in 1992 and 1996, are so rich that they are able to finance their

5. Laylin Copelin and David Elliot, "Small Group of Contributors Gives Large Share of Funds Raised," *Austin American-Statesman,* November 6, 1994, A15.
6. Christi Harlan, "Texas' House Races Prove Costly," *Austin American-Statesman,* January 11, 1997, B1.

own campaigns. The great majority of candidates, however, must get their money from somewhere other than their own pockets.

The United States is one of the few democracies that does not have **publicly funded campaigns.** In many other countries, the government gives the parties tax money to cover part of the expenses of campaigning. This means that the parties, if their candidates are successful, are relatively free of obligation to special interests. In the United States at every level except the presidency, however, we rely upon **privately funded campaigns.** Candidates and parties must persuade private citizens to part with checks, or their campaigns will fail.

The candidate with the most money does not win *every* election. In 1990, for example, Clayton Williams outspent Ann Richards two to one, and still lost.[7] But the best-financed candidate does win *most* of the time. And just because a victorious candidate spent less than the loser does not mean that money was unimportant in his or her campaign. Ann Richards spent over $10 million in the 1990 campaign, which is a large chunk of cash by anyone's accounting. Part of Richards's campaign treasury went to buy television ads that trumpeted Williams's gaffes, thus making sure that the public knew about them. If Richards had spent less, fewer people might have been offended by Williams, and he might have won. In other words, although money may not be the only resource that counts in campaigns, it is always crucial and sometimes decisive.

WHERE DOES THE MONEY COME FROM?

Most of the money given to candidates comes from wealthy donors who represent some sort of special interest. Individual contributions of $5,000 to $10,000 or more are common in campaigns for major state offices, and people and organizations with wealth or access to wealth are able to rent the gratitude of candidates by helping to fund their campaigns. In the 1994 gubernatorial race, for example, almost three-fourths of Ann Richards's contributions and nearly two-thirds of George Bush's came from donations of $1,000 or more.[8] In contrast, ordinary people who have to worry about paying their bills are not able to contribute nearly as much, and therefore cannot ensure candidates' attention to their concerns. Thus, private funding of campaigns skews public policy in favor of special interests.

Table 6–5 displays the major individual contributors to Bush and Richards during their contest for the governorship in 1994. The people and interests who supported the winner, Bush, have had more influence over public policy than the people and interests who supported Richards.

An example of the way election campaigns are partly a struggle among wealthy interest groups is the contest for U.S. Senate in 1993. Individuals and groups associated with the medical profession gave enthusiastically to Kay Bailey Hutchison, while individuals and groups associated with the legal profession contributed heavily to Bob Krueger. These groups differed on specific

---

7. Laylin Copelin and David Elliott, "Williams Outspending Richards 2–1," *Austin American-Statesman,* October 20, 1990, A1.
8. David Elliott, "Big Leagues, Silver Screen, and Politics," *Austin American-Statesman,* July 30, 1994, B1.

TABLE 6–5

Major Contributors to George Bush and Ann Richards, 1994

Bush

Name	Interest	Amount
Donald Carter	Business	$115,000
Dennis Berman	Business	108,092
Richard Rainwater	Investments	100,000
Nathan Crain	Computer software	97,092
Lonnie Pilgrim	Poultry	80,236
Bradford Freeman	Banking	79,188
Louis Beecherl	Oil, investments	65,000
Richard Heath	Cosmetics	64,949
Charles Wyly	Computer software	64,273
Walter Neuls	Insurance	58,736

Richards

Name	Interest	Amount
Arthur Schechter	Attorney	$138,000
John Moore	Computer software	135,000
Robert Bass	Oil	125,000
John O'Quinn	Attorney	110,000
Daniel Robinowitz	Real estate, gambling	108,000
Shelton Smith	Attorney	95,613
Walter Umphrey	Attorney	90,680
Stephen Spielberg	Movie producer	90,000
Lee Godfrey	Attorney	80,129
Edward Gaylord	Business	76,000

SOURCE: Wayne Slater, "Big Donors Fuel Governor's Race," *Dallas Morning News,* November 3, 1994, 21A.

questions of public policy. Among other controversies, doctors wished to see legislation that would limit medical malpractice suits; for obvious reasons, attorneys opposed such new laws. When Hutchison was elected, in effect doctors won and lawyers lost. Thus money helps to form public policy in Texas.

To repeat, it is not that the candidate with the most money always wins. In 1990, Clayton Williams outspent Ann Richards and lost. In 1994, both incumbent railroad commissioners, Jim Nugent and Mary Scott Nabors, were defeated by their underfunded challengers. Studies of congressional races by political scientist Gary Jacobson have shown that the relationship between money and victory is complex. There seems to be a threshold effect—a candidate needs a certain level of financing (which varies, of course, with the race) to have a chance at all. Beyond that, Jacobson found that the spending of challengers was much more important than the spending of incumbents. Although the challengers never had a very good chance to knock off an incumbent, the chance got better as they spent more. The level of spending by incumbents did not seem to matter much, probably because they always had enough money to get their message to the voters.[9]

It is not clear whether Jacobson's conclusions can be generalized to state politics. If they can, however, then the following summary seems to be justified: Money is very important in election campaigns, but it is not the only resource. Volunteers, imagination, ideology, partisanship, and personality also play a part, as do such things as the state of the economy and the presence or absence of a scandal. The 1994 elections demonstrated that on those unusual historical occasions when the voters are particularly angry at the incumbent party, money is relatively unimportant.

Nevertheless, because economic wealth is so unequally distributed, it seems particularly dangerous to democratic government. It gives a very few citizens access to a very large political resource. For that reason, journalists and textbook authors are always worrying about its potential power.

As a rule, politicians dislike the system of private campaign financing, finding it time-consuming and demeaning. Many retired officeholders have written in their autobiographies that they hated having to ask people for money, both because it made them feel humiliated and because they would rather have been working at crafting public policy. A survey of Texas candidates taken by Common Cause in 1990 revealed that 65 percent of them supported public financing of campaigns.[10] Yet the opposition of the special interests who benefit from the current system has thus far stymied efforts to introduce reform.

CONTROL OF MONEY IN CAMPAIGNS

The power of money in campaigns disturbs partisans of democracy because it seems to create an inequality of citizenship. Everyone has only one vote, but some people are millionaires. Those with more money to contribute seem to be "super citizens" who can wield influence denied to the rest. For this reason, many people have for decades been trying to control the impact of money in both state and national races. Their success at both levels is spotty at best.

In Texas, several laws have been passed to control the use and disclosure of the money collected by candidates. These laws have been made steadily tougher over the years, but they still allow wealthy individuals to purchase more political influence than is available to their fellow citizens.

THE REVENUE ACT OF 1971

This is a federal law intended to broaden the base of financial support and minimize the dependence of candidates on large donations from a few contributors. It provided that taxpayers may stipulate that one dollar of their U.S. income tax (two dollars on a joint return) be put in the Presidential Election Campaign Fund to provide for the partial public funding of these national campaigns. The amount that taxpayers can contribute has since been raised to three dollars for an individual and six dollars for a joint return.

9. Gary C. Jacobson, *The Politics of Congressional Elections,* 2d ed. (Boston: Little, Brown, 1987), 49–58; and Jacobson, *Money in Congressional Elections* (New Haven, Conn.: Yale University Press, 1980), 36–50.
10. Mike Ward, "65% of Politicians in Poll Favor Public Financing of Campaigns," *Austin American-Statesman,* March 11, 1990, B8.

THE FEDERAL ELECTION CAMPAIGN ACT OF 1972

This law applies only to campaigns for federal offices—president, vice president, and members of Congress. It establishes a Federal Election Commission, requires candidates to make periodic reports of contributions and expenses, and places certain limits on contributions. Individuals may donate up to $1,000 in each primary or general election and a maximum of $25,000 in a given year. Groups may contribute up to $5,000 per candidate.

THE TEXAS CAMPAIGN REPORTING AND DISCLOSURE ACT OF 1973

As amended, this act outlines procedures for campaign reporting and disclosure. It appears to strengthen the election code in several areas where previously it was deficient. As amended, the act's major provisions are:

1. Every candidate for political office and every political committee within the state must appoint a campaign treasurer before accepting contributions or making expenditures.

2. Contributions exceeding $500 by out-of-state political committees can be made only if the names of contributors of $100 or more are disclosed.

3. Detailed financial reports are required of candidates and managers of campaign committees. They must include a list of all contributions and expenditures over $50.

4. Violators face both civil action and criminal penalties.

The 1973 law sounds like a genuine attempt to force public disclosure of the financial sponsors of candidates. Its great flaw, however, is that it contains no provision for enforcement. Since laws do not enforce themselves, the public reporting of private contributions is at best a haphazard affair. Moreover, the law fails to impose any limits on the amount that individuals or organizations can contribute to campaigns; as long as they report the amount, they can attempt to buy as much influence as they can afford.

1991 ETHICS LAW

In 1991, the legislature passed another ethics bill designed to regulate and moderate the impact of private wealth on public policy in campaigns and at other levels of Texas politics. This law created an Ethics Commission that could hold hearings on public complaints, levy fines, and report severe violations to the Travis County (Austin) district attorney for possible prosecution.

Again, however, the law failed to place limits on campaign contributions. Furthermore, it required a "supermajority" of six out of eight commissioners for important actions, a provision that was practically guaranteed to prevent the vigorous investigation of violators. As John Steiner, the commission's executive director, stated publicly, "There's very little in the way of real enforcement . . . in most of the laws we administer. It's just an unenforced statute—except that if people don't [obey the law], it gets some bad press."[11]

---

11. Quoted in Jeff South and Jerry White, "Computer Network Tracks Politicians' Funds," *Austin American-Statesman,* August 16, 1993, B1.

There were attempts to toughen this law during the 1993 legislature, but they failed. In 1995, as discussed in Chapter 11, the legislature imposed some changes on the financing of judicial campaigns, but defeated proposals for broader reforms. Campaign finance reform was not addressed during the 1997 legislature.

In summary, there is virtually no control over, and very little effort to ensure the public disclosure of, the influence of money in Texas political campaigns. How badly this political laissez-faire damages the state's democracy is not clear, although it probably doesn't do it any good.

BUCKLEY v. VALEO

The Federal Election Campaign Act of 1972 originally set limits on the amount of money individual candidates could contribute to their own campaigns. But in the case of *Buckley* v. *Valeo* (424 U.S. 1, 1976), the U.S. Supreme Court held that these limits were unconstitutional suppressions of the freedom of speech guaranteed by the First Amendment. It is this decision that allowed Texas billionaire H. Ross Perot to spend millions of dollars of his own money to finance his independent candidacies for the presidency in 1992 and 1996.

Buckley v. *Valeo* also extended the right of free speech to political action committees (PACs) for "party building" at the state and local level. PACs are now permitted to spend unlimited amounts on political activities—such as get-out-the vote campaigns—as long as these are not directly coordinated with an individual candidate's election campaign.

In the jargon of campaign financing, contributions that go directly to a candidate are "hard money," while those that go to parties, and therefore presumably benefit candidates only indirectly, are "soft money." The line between direct and indirect campaign activities is hard to draw, however, and the Federal Elections Commission has been reluctant to act in this area. As a result, PACs contribute many hundreds of thousands of dollars of soft money to parties, and thus indirectly to candidates, during every election cycle.

The effect of *Buckley* v. *Valeo* was not limited to federal elections. Shortly after the case was decided, the attorney general of Texas ruled that the decision voided similar provisions in the state's 1973 campaign finance law as well (Texas Attorney General Opinion H864, 1976). As a result, Clayton Williams was able to spend $10 million of his own wealth in his run for governor in 1990, and corporate, labor, and trade association PACs may contribute whatever they please to state campaigns.

NEGATIVE CAMPAIGNING

In addition to the influence of money, another disturbing characteristic of contemporary campaigning is the use of personal attacks on candidates by their opponents. Candidates are accused of everything from drug addiction to mental illness to marital infidelity to financial dishonesty to Satanism. Mainly, they are simply accused of being liars.

People being the imperfect creatures they are, some of these charges are bound to be true. If anyone's past conduct is scrutinized closely, episodes of untruthfulness, unkindness, or sexual misbehavior can usually be uncovered.

Candidates can therefore almost always dig up some dirt on each other. Since politicians believe that such attacks are effective, they are placing more and more emphasis on the exposure of each other's personal flaws to the exclusion of other strategies. Their television advertising attempts to blow up ordinary human weaknesses into evidence of monstrous immorality, and to frighten citizens into believing that their opponents are not just mistaken, but hateful.

All over the country, 1994 and 1996 were particularly bad years for negative campaigning. The television airwaves were full of "attack ads" in which candidates accused each other of being sleazy, untrustworthy individuals. As journalist Charles Krauthammer observed in October 1994, "The basic theme of the 1994 campaign is that everyone running is a liar, a cheat, a crook, or a fraud. . . . Every state in the union will be sending to Congress some brutally excoriated campaign survivor. The 104th Congress is guaranteed to be an assembly of the most vilified persons in every community."[12]

Negative campaigning has a corrosive effect on democracy for four reasons. First, some elections are being decided on the basis of inaccurate or irrelevant charges. Second, discussions of public policy and how to solve national or state problems are shunted aside in everyone's eagerness to throw mud. Third, many good people may decide not to enter political life so that they can avoid being the targets of public attack. Fourth, negative campaigning disheartens citizens, who are thus more apt to stay home on election day. Research by political scientists has concluded that such campaigns may depress voter turnout by as much as 5 percent.[13]

Texas has had its share of negative campaigns. A large part of the gubernatorial race in 1990, during both the Democratic primary and the general election, consisted of accusations of illegal drug use by Ann Richards. As will be discussed shortly, the gubernatorial and U.S. Senate races in 1994 and the Senate race in 1996 were relatively clean, but some of the other contests were savage. Negative campaigning in Texas seems no worse than it is in most states, but that is bad enough.

CANDIDATES VERSUS PARTIES

One of the topics of Chapter 5 was a consideration of the fact that Texas political parties have almost no control over candidates. Although there are permanent and temporary party organizations, they do not have the power to nominate candidates, who are chosen in primaries. As a result, candidates accept whatever help the party organizations can give them, but feel little sense of obligation in return. In some countries, and in some areas of the United States, the party organization actually has some control over its candidates. In Texas, the parties are better thought of as service organizations for candidates. It is never a good idea to assume that a candidate will agree with party "leaders" on anything.

---

12. Charles Krauthammer, "Pols' TV Ads Make Voters Loathe Them," *Houston Chronicle*, October 31, 1994, A14.
13. Stephen Ansolabehere, Shanto Iyengar, Adam Simon, and Nicholas Valentino, "Does Attack Advertising Demobilize the Electorate?" *American Political Science Review,* 88, no. 4 (December 1994): 829–38.

The recent experience of the Republican Party illustrates this point. As discussed in Chapters 4 and 5, under the influence of the Christian Right, at its June 1994 convention the state party adopted a platform that took positions opposing abortion except to save the life of the mother, recommending that public schools teach "creation science" in biology classes, asserting that Americans have a constitutional right to own guns (see Chapter 12 on this point), and condemning homosexuality.

Republican gubernatorial candidate George Bush, however, distributed his own personal "platform." Although Bush supported requiring women under the age of eighteen to notify a parent before obtaining an abortion, and opposed public funding of abortions, he did not agree with the party's more uncompromisingly "pro-life" stance. He ignored the subjects of homosexuality, guns, and teaching creationism in public schools. While his list of campaign promises did agree with some of the party platform's policy recommendations on such issues as crime and welfare, he also emphasized lawsuit reform, which was not discussed in the platform. Therefore, while there was some overlap between what concerned the party and what concerned its most important candidate, the conjunction of positions was only partial, and the differences of emphasis were stark.

The lack of cooperation between Governor Bush and his own party organization was again emphasized during the 1997 legislative session. Bush proposed a major overhaul of the state's tax system that would have largely shifted the source of funding from the sales tax to corporations and service businesses. During the debate over Bush's proposal, Tom Pauken, the state Republican Party chair, purchased newspaper ads in East Texas urging citizens to "Say No to the Bush Tax Cut!"[14]

In other words, if you want to know what candidates plan to do if elected, you can pretty much ignore their party's platform and organizational leaders. Pay attention to the candidates themselves, not to the parties.

Public Elections

A public election is the only political activity in which large numbers of Texans (although, as we have seen, not a majority) are likely to participate. The state has three types of elections: primary, general, and special elections.

PRIMARY ELECTIONS

A **primary** is an election held within a party to nominate candidates for the general election or to choose delegates to a presidential nominating convention. It is because primaries are so important in Texas that parties are weak. (See Chapter 2 for a discussion of one of the consequences of Texas's strong-primary system: long voting ballots.) Because they do not control nominations, party "leaders" have no control over officeholders, and so, in reality, cannot lead.

Under procedures begun in 1988, the primary election in Texas occurs on the second Tuesday in March in even-numbered years, prior to the general

---

14. "Political Intelligence," *Texas Observer,* September 26, 1997, 16.

election. The Texas Election Code provides that any political party whose candidate for governor received 20 percent or more of the vote in the most recent general election must hold a primary to choose candidates for upcoming elections. Parties whose candidates polled less than 20 percent may either hold a primary or choose their candidates by the less expensive method of a nominating convention. In effect, Republicans and Democrats must hold primary elections, while smaller third parties may select their candidates in conventions.

Under Texas law, a candidate must win the nomination with a majority vote in the primary. If there is not a majority winner—as there frequently is not if there are more than two candidates—the two leading vote getters meet thirty days later in a general runoff election.

TEXAS'S "OPEN" PRIMARY

There are three types of primary election:

1. A **blanket primary,** used only in two states, is like a general election held before the general election. All candidates of all parties run on one list, and any registered voter can participate.

2. An **open primary** is one in which any registered voter may participate in any party primary.

3. A **closed primary** is one in which only registered members of a party may participate in that party's primary.

Technically, Texas laws provide for a closed primary. In practice, however, voters may participate in any primary so long as they have not already voted in the primary of another party during the same year. The only realistic sense in which Texas has a closed primary is that once voters have recorded their party affiliation by voting in one party's primary, they cannot participate in the affairs—the runoff primary or the convention—of another party during that year.

Aspiring candidates obtain a place on the primary ballot by applying to the state executive committee for statewide office or to the county chairperson for local office. Drawings are held for position on the ballot, and filing fees—discussed below—must be paid before the ballot is printed.

The requirement that a majority of the vote is needed to win the primary election is widespread in the Southern states. This practice was apparently adopted in former Confederate states because in the days when these states were dominated by the Democratic Party, it was not uncommon for six or more candidates to compete in the Democratic primary, with the winner garnering no more than 25 or 30 percent of the vote. Frequently, the winner would face no opposition in the general election. Such a candidate's claim to be the legitimate choice of the people would be quite weak. A majority, however, confers legitimacy.

SUPER TUESDAY

Several states with primary elections late in the year hold very early special primaries during presidential election years. New Hampshire, for example, has its regular primary elections in September but holds a presidential primary on March 1 every four years. Iowa holds special presidential party caucuses—similar to a primary—at the end of February. Presidential candidates target these early contests, hoping to make a strong showing and build enough early momentum to guarantee their nomination during the national party conventions in the summer.

For most of the century, Texas held its primary in May. As a result of the importance of the early contests in small Northern states, however, in recent decades the presidential nominating campaigns have often been nearly over by the time Southern primaries were held. In the Democratic Party, this could mean that candidates whom many Texas conservatives considered too liberal—George McGovern in 1972 and Walter Mondale in 1984, for example—had wrapped up the nomination before Texans had a chance to register their opinions.

For some years there was talk among conservative leaders about establishing an early presidential primary in Texas so that presidential candidates would be forced to cater more to the state's voters. In 1985, legislation providing for an early primary was introduced in the legislature but failed to win approval. Politicians of both parties and varying ideologies were unsure of its effects and refused to commit themselves, fearing that it might hurt rather than help.

By 1986, ten Southern states had moved to adopt a Southern regional "super primary," to he held the second week in March, beginning in 1988. In a surprise move, the Texas legislature adopted the new primary date during a special session in the summer of 1986. Texas primaries, both regular and presidential, are now held on the second Tuesday in March—**Super Tuesday**—with the primary runoff elections on the second Tuesday in April.

Like many other political reforms, the first Super Tuesday Democratic primary in 1988 had unanticipated results. Instead of being a vehicle for Southern and conservative candidates, the early election brought victory to Massachusetts Governor Michael Dukakis and strong support for African American candidate Jesse Jackson, both widely regarded as the two least conservative candidates in the race.

In 1992, moderate Governor Bill Clinton of Arkansas won the Democratic presidential primary in Texas, as well as his party's nomination later that year. The Super Tuesday system seemed to be working as its supporters had intended.

Nevertheless, in 1997 the chairs of both major parties and the secretary of state recommended that Texas's primary date be moved back to May. They argued that a March primary date made the campaign season too long and expensive. While the state House of Representatives endorsed this argument and voted for the change, the proposal failed in the Senate by one vote.

ADMINISTRATION AND FINANCE

In Texas, primary elections are administered entirely by political party officials, in accordance with the provisions of the Texas Election Code. The process is decentralized. Most of the responsibilities and work fall on the shoulders of the county chairperson and the members of the county executive committee. They must arrange for the polling places, provide the voting machines and other equipment, print the ballots, and determine the results.

The election is supervised by a presiding judge and an alternate appointed in each precinct by the county chairperson, subject to approval by the county committee. The presiding judge appoints two or more clerks to actually conduct the election—checking registration rolls, issuing ballots, and settling occasional disputes.

Conducting a primary election is expensive, especially in a state as large as Texas. Clerks are paid a salary, albeit a modest one. Polling places and voting machines must be rented, ballots printed, and other expenses paid. Prior to 1972, the costs were met by charging each aspiring candidate a filing fee. Texas was the only state in which primary elections were financed entirely by the candidate themselves.

In 1973, the sixty-third Legislature enacted a permanent primary election funding bill on the last day of the session. This law provides for a combination of state and private funding of primary elections. Filing fees are still in use, but the amounts are reasonable, ranging from $1,000 for statewide offices to $400 for state senator to $50 for minor local offices. Expenses beyond those are covered by the filing fees are paid by the state. County political party chairs pay the costs of the primary and are then reimbursed by the secretary of state.

GENERAL ELECTIONS

The purpose of a **general election** is to choose state and national executives and legislators, and state judges. General elections are held in even-numbered years on the Tuesday after the first Monday in November. In 1974, Texas joined the group of states that elect their governors and other state officials in the "off year," the even-numbered year between presidential election years. At the same time, the state adopted a constitutional amendment that extended the terms of office for the governor and other state officials from two to four years.

Unlike primary elections, general and special elections are the responsibility of the state. The secretary of state is the principal election officer, although the election organization is decentralized and most of the actual work is performed at the county level. The county commissioners court appoints election judges, chooses the method of voting—paper ballots or some type of voting machine—and pays the bills. The county clerk conducts absentee balloting and actually performs many of the functions charged to the commissioners court.

Nominees of established parties are placed on the ballot when they win a party primary or are chosen by a party convention. New parties and independent candidates get on the general election ballot by presenting a petition signed by a specified number of qualified voters who have not participated in the primary election of another party. The number of required signatures varies with the office. At the local level, it need not exceed five hundred; at the state level, it is 1 percent of the votes cast in the last gubernatorial election.

There is no standard election ballot in Texas. Primary ballots vary from party to party, and general election ballots vary from county to county. Paper ballots marked with a special pencil that can be scanned by computers are growing in popularity, because when the procedure works efficiently, it produces a faster count than other methods.

The ballot lists the offices that are to be filled, beginning with the president (in an appropriate year) and proceeding down to the lowliest local position. Candidates' political party affiliations are listed beside their names, and candidates of the party that polled the most votes in the most recent gubernatorial election are listed first. Other parties' candidates appear in descending order of that party's polling strength in the preceding election. A space is provided for write-in candidates. Constitutional amendments, if any, are listed separately, usually near the bottom of the ballot, followed by local referendum questions.

SPECIAL ELECTIONS

In Texas, a number of special elections are held in addition to primary and general elections. They may be called at the state level to fill vacancies in Congress or in the state legislature, or to vote on proposed constitutional amendments. At the local level, most cities choose their councils in special elections, with one important variation: The elections are nonpartisan. Party labels do not appear beside the candidates' names, and no party certification is needed to get on the ballot. It is custom abetted by city charter provisions, not state law, that prevents partisan politics at the local level. By denying the voters the guidance provided by a party label, nonpartisan elections are even more confusing for them than are general elections, and voter turnout tends to be even lower (see Chapter 3).

ABSENTEE OR EARLY VOTING

Texas citizens may vote absentee in any election. Voting may be done for a period of two weeks before the election, at the county clerk's office or at a variety of polling places throughout the county. In the past, one needed a reason to vote absentee, such as a planned trip from the county or illness. In 1987, the legislature removed the restrictions, and anyone can now vote early. A quarter to 40 percent of the voters cast early ballots.

Elections of 1994 and 1996

Both in the nation as a whole and in Texas in particular, the 1994 election was a great victory for the Republican Party. Nationally, this outcome seemed to be the result of Democratic President Clinton's unpopularity. Within Texas, it seemed to be the continuation of a long-term trend toward domination of the state by the GOP. Republicans won the governorship, successfully defended a U.S. Senate seat, picked up two seats in the U.S. House of Representatives, increased their representation in the Texas legislature, and garnered over nine hundred local offices. They won both vulnerable Railroad Commission seats, and captured majorities on the state Supreme Court and Board of Education.

The gubernatorial campaign of 1994 was relatively restrained and issue-oriented compared to the rude and personal contest of four years earlier. Among other disagreeable aspects of the 1990 campaign, Republican nominee Clayton Williams had made crude off-the-cuff remarks that offended many

Republican women, who then voted for Richards. In 1994, George W. Bush, Jr.'s emphasis on issues and his polite campaign drew alienated women back to the party.

Bush attacked incumbent Ann Richards's record on crime and education, and she attacked his record in business, but the accusations were not nearly as mean-spirited as those in the previous campaign. At one point, Richards labeled Bush a "jerk" for criticizing her education policies, but this was a comparatively mild accusation and was not repeated.[15] About the nastiest thing that Bush could think of to say about Richards was that she was a "liberal."[16]

The combination of Bush's restrained campaign style, Richards's association with President Clinton and liberalism, and Texas's bedrock conservatism, at least among those who go to the polls, was sufficient to overturn a sitting governor. Bush beat Richards with 54 percent of the statewide vote.[17]

Democratic strength continued to be concentrated among lower-income Anglos, Mexican Americans, and African Americans. As Table 6–6 illustrates, voting for governor in Houston precincts followed the familiar economic and ethnic lines. Middle- and upper-income Anglos supported Bush by large majorities, while he barely beat Richards in low-income Anglo neighborhoods. Richards won solid majorities in low-income, and middle-income African American and Mexican American precincts.

The trend of the vote compared to the results in 1990, however, was not uniform. As Figure 6–1 illustrates, Richards's support declined badly in urban and suburban Anglo-dominated counties in Central and East Texas, such as Williamson (north of Austin) and Jefferson (Port Arthur). Her voting percentages actually increased slightly from 1990 in heavily Mexican American counties, such as El Paso, Hidalgo (McAllen), and Cameron (Harlingen-Brownsville).

TABLE 6–6

Economic and Ethnic Voting in 1994 Gubernatorial Election, Selected Houston Precincts

Group	% Richards	% Bush	% Other
Low-income Anglo	48.3	50.6	1.1
Middle-income Anglo	35.9	63.7	0.4
Upper-income Anglo	27.7	71.9	0.3
Low-income African American	97.4	2.4	0.2
Middle-income African American	93.6	6.3	0.1
Mexican American	75.6	23.8	0.7

SOURCE: *Houston Chronicle,* November 11, 1994, 20A.

---

15. "Richards Labels Bush a 'Jerk' for Attacks on Administration," *Dallas Morning News,* August 17, 1994, A31.

16. R.G. Ratcliffe, "Bush Decries Richards as a 'Liberal,'" *Houston Chronicle,* August 18, 1994, A29.

17. "Gubernatorial Results," *Houston Chronicle,* November 10, 1994, A29.

FIGURE 6–1
County Support for Richards and Bush, 1994 Gubernatorial Election

Source: The Texas Secretary of State.

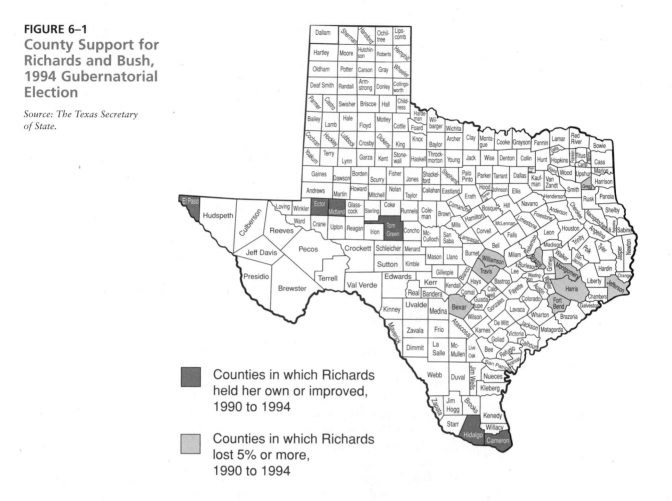

Counties in which Richards held her own or improved, 1990 to 1994

Counties in which Richards lost 5% or more, 1990 to 1994

What this suggests is that the Democratic strategy of attempting to put together a coalition of Mexican Americans, African Americans, and Anglo liberals is not sufficient in modern Texas. Given the low voter turnout of minority citizens, they are bound to be overwhelmed when party support splits along ethnic lines. Richards lost the White vote in 1994, and as a result lost the election.

Despite her defeat, Ann Richards did splendidly compared to the Democratic U.S. Senate candidate, Richard Fisher. After spending $1.7 million to overwhelm former Attorney General Jim Mattox in the Democratic primary, Fisher invested only $300,000 in the general election campaign. He never seemed to find a consistent theme with which to attack incumbent Republican Kay Bailey Hutchison, and she coasted to reelection with 60.8 percent of the statewide vote.[18] Fisher did manage to win the Mexican American counties, but his totals elsewhere were so dismal that it did not matter. He garnered only 18 percent of the vote in Midland County, 25 percent in Montgomery (Conroe), and 28 percent in Denton.

---

18. "Political Intelligence," *Texas Observer*, November 25, 1994, 24.

Not every Democratic candidate lost. Relatively conservative politicians such as Lieutenant Governor Bob Bullock and Attorney General Dan Morales were reelected. (As both Bullock and Morales announced in 1997 that they would not run again in 1998, Democratic prospects began to look desperate.) Democrats also managed to hold on to 19 of 30 U.S. House seats, despite the defeat of forty-two-year incumbent Jack Brooks in the ninth district (Galveston to Beaumont).

Republicans also failed to capture the Texas legislature. Although the Democrats lost ground, they retained their majorities, keeping 17 out of 31 seats in the Senate and 89 of 150 in the House.

It was perhaps at the level of the judiciary that the Republican Party made the most significant gains in 1994. GOP candidates won every seat they contested on the state Court of Criminal Appeals and Supreme Court, gaining their first majority on the latter since the days of Reconstruction. Republicans captured nineteen local judgeships from the Democrats in Harris County alone. "If Bozo the Clown had been running as a Republican against any Democrat, he would have had a chance," opined Gerald Treece, the dean of South Texas College of Law.[19] The major long-term result of the Republican court victories was to replace plaintiff-oriented, prolawsuit judges with business-oriented, antilawsuit judges. Regardless of what happens in the governor's mansion and the legislature, it will be harder to successfully sue anyone for damages in Texas in the future.

After the 1994 election, political observers wondered if it signaled a "realignment," with so many citizens moving over to the Republican side of the fence that the GOP would be the majority party in the nation's future. After the 1996 election, the answer for Texas appeared to be yes. The answer for the nation as a whole was much more ambiguous.

Nationally, President Clinton surprised almost everyone by outmaneuvering the Republican Congress in 1995 and 1996 and regaining his popularity. He accomplished this feat partly by moving in a conservative direction on social issues (endorsing welfare reform and opposing same-sex marriages, for example) and partly by thwarting the Republicans' determination to cut federal spending for such popular programs as environmental cleanup, school lunches, and Social Security. In the balloting in November, he defeated Republican challenger Robert Dole and independent candidate H. Ross Perot handily. At the congressional level, Democrats cut into the Republican majority in the House of Representatives, while the Republicans slightly increased their majority in the Senate from 53 to 55 seats. At the national level, therefore, the voters sent a confused and confusing message in 1996.

There was nothing confusing, however, about the voters' message in Texas. Texans gave victories to Republican candidates in all ten statewide races, bucked the national trend by supporting Dole for president, returned U.S. Senator Phil Gramm to Washington, awarded the GOP four more seats on the state Supreme Court and three on the Court of Criminal Appeals, and reelected a Republican railroad commissioner. Further, after some victories in runoffs a month later, they won majority control of the state Senate for the

19. Quoted in John Williams, "GOP Gains Majority in State Supreme Court," *Houston Chronicle*, November 10, 1994, A29.

first time since Reconstruction. Democrats managed to keep control of Texas's congressional delegation and of the state House of Representatives, but these were small consolations. Republicans seemed to be the party of the present and the future.

Always alert for new ways to get their message to potential voters, in the 1990s the parties and candidates moved into cyberspace. Despite the fact that by 1995 only about one in ten Texans (and Americans in general) had access to the World Wide Web, in 1996 politicians made sure that anyone with a computer, a modem, and a political interest could see plenty of free propaganda online. This form of electronic campaigning is sure to grow in importance as more citizens learn how to use computers.

If you wish to check out some of the partisan information available on the Web, here are some home page addresses:

Texas Republican Party:	http://www.texasgop.org/
Texas Democratic Party:	http://www.txdemocrats.org/
United We Stand, America, national headquarters:	http://www.uwsa.org/
Texas Libertarian Party:	http://www.tx.lp.org/

Sources: Jeffrey Weiss, "Electronic Handshaking," *Dallas Morning News,* November 20, 1995, A1; party headquarters.

The actual vote, however, was not quite the whole story. As is usually the case with Texas elections, differences in voter turnout provide much of the explanation for the results. Statewide turnout fell six percentage points from 1992 to 1996. The decline was not evenly distributed, however. Political scientists Richard Murray and Kent Tedin analyzed 149 precincts in Bexar (San Antonio), Harris (Houston), Tarrant (Fort Worth), Travis (Austin), and Dallas counties in both years. They concluded that turnout dropped off 28 percent in working-class white areas between the two elections, 24 percent in Hispanic areas, and 14 percent in African American areas. In other words, while the citizens who tend to favor Republicans were going to the polls, the citizens who tend to favor Democrats were staying home. The conservatives won because the liberals did not vote.[20]

In terms of a dramatic story line, the most interesting statewide race in 1996 was the contest between incumbent U.S. Senator Phil Gramm and his Democratic challenger, Victor Morales (no relation to Attorney General Dan Morales). Gramm had been one of the most outspoken and ideologically consistent conservatives in the Senate since his first election in 1984. His outspokenness had endeared him to wealthy contributors, who supplied him with a $20 million war chest for his Republican presidential nomination bid in 1996. The national Republican rank and file, however, were not so taken with Gramm, and they gave him so little support in the polls that he dropped out of the running early in the primary season. His abortive presidential bid, however, left Gramm with ample funds, and he ultimately spent over $5 million on television campaign ads in the Senate race.

---

20. Suzanne Gamboa, "Low Turnout of Democrats Led to GOP Sweep, Researchers Say," *Austin American-Statesman,* November 9, 1996, A10.

Ben Sargent illustrates the magnitude of the defeat of the Democrats in the 1994 elections. The name on the truck refers to Bob Slagle, chair of the state Democratic Party. The Republican victory was equally decisive in 1996.

Courtesy of Ben Sargent.

Gramm's opponent, forty-six-year-old Victor Morales, was a Mesquite high school civics teacher who ran for the Democratic nomination for the Senate on a dare from his students. Investing $8,000 of his $10,000 life savings in the campaign and traveling the state in an old white Nissan pickup truck, Morales appealed to ordinary people who were turned off by slick-talking, special-interest-courting professional politicians. He was especially popular among Mexican Americans. He astonished the professionals by beating two well-known, experienced Democrats in the March 1996 primary.

Morales was unstudied on the issues, often admitting, when asked, that he was not informed on this or that national problem. And he was utterly underfinanced, finally managing to raise and spend only about $300,000. But his honest, earnest personality charmed many citizens and much of the national and Texas media, which supplied him with millions of dollars of free publicity. He was profiled in *The New York Times,* the *Washington Post,* the *Los Angeles Times, USA Today,* and the *Miami Herald;* on the *Today* television program, *Dateline NBC* and CNN; and in *People* magazine. Reporters, harking back to a classic 1939 film called *Mr. Smith Goes to Washington,* about an ordinary, honest man who is elected to the Senate and is appalled by the corruption he finds in the national legislature, often referred to Morales as "Señor Smith."[21]

Despite his charm, however, Morales's low-information campaign annoyed people who like to have government officials who are familiar with public policy. Moreover, Morales blundered in September, referring to Mexican American Republican U.S. Representative Henry Bonilla as a "coconut." This was an intraethnic slur meaning "brown on the outside, white on the

21. Mimi Swartz, "Truckin'," *Texas Monthly,* June 1996, 98; John Jacobs, "Señor Smith Goes to Washington?" *The Sacramento Bee,* June 20, 1996, B6.

inside."[22] Not only was the slur inappropriate in itself, but it reinforced suspicions that Anglos might have had that Morales would, if elected, represent Mexican Americans rather than everybody.

Although Morales apologized, the damage was done, and his poverty made it impossible to counter, with his positive television advertising, the bad impression the "coconut" statement made among Anglos. In November, he received only about 30 percent of the Anglo vote. The 86 percent of the Hispanic vote that went to Morales was not enough to overbalance his lack of appeal among Anglos, and Gramm beat him, 55 to 44 percent.[23]

After the dust had settled on the 1996 balloting, the conventional wisdom among political observers was that so many Anglos had become habitual Republican voters that it was appropriate to speak of a realignment and expect Texas to be a Republican state under normal conditions in the future. The conventional wisdom is probably true, as far as it goes. It would not be true if the Democrats in general and minority Democrats in particular ever mobilized and went to the polls in percentages roughly comparable to Republicans. As long as the Democrats stay home on election day, however, Texas will continue to vote Republican.

The Elections of 1998

Nationally, voters again sent Washington an ambiguous message in the Congressional elections of 1998. Refusing to penalize Democratic candidates for President Clinton's personal troubles, citizens chose an extra five Democrats to take House seats in 1999, while defeating two Democratic and two Republican Senators. These choices left the Republicans with a small majority of twelve seats in the House, while they maintained their 55 to 45 margin in the Senate. Because the party that controls the White House usually loses Congressional seats in the sixth year of a President's term, these results were widely interpreted as a defeat for the Republicans, despite their continued majority in both houses.

In Texas, however, Republicans continued their march toward complete dominance of the state's politics, although they were halted just short of that goal. As in all previous state elections, the small voter turnout (not much over thirty percent), greatly skewed in favor of upper-income Anglos, gave a strongly conservative cast to the balloting.

Governor George W. Bush was never seriously threatened by his Democratic challenger, Garry Mauro, leading by roughly two-to-one margins in public-opinion polls all during the campaign. Bush received endorsements from the great majority of organizations that voiced opinions, including some, such as the Texas Association of School Administrators, that had never before taken sides in a gubernatorial contest. Outspending Mauro at a thirteen-to-one pace, he saturated the airwaves with polite, positive ads, while Mauro was reduced to trying to create support by walking door-to-door. Mauro attempted to offer his own alternative to Bush's education policies, and to criticize the governor for not attempting to squelch a proposed nuclear

---

22. Stuart Eskenazi, "Candidate Morales Issues Apology for Using Ethnic Slur," *Austin American-Statesman,* September 27, 1996, B3.
23. Dave McNeely, "GOP Ascends in Statewide Races," *Austin American-Statesman,* November 7, 1996, A15; Dave McNeely, "Election Shows Texas Democrats Must Muster More White Voters," *Austin American-Statesman,* November 26, 1996, A11.

waste dump near Sierra Blanca (the dump was eventually vetoed by the Texas Natural Resource Conservations Commission), but neither of these issues caught fire with the voters. A booming state economy, a falling crime rate, a record of success with the legislature, and a genial personality made Bush unbeatable. On election day, amid speculation about his plans to run for the Presidency in 2000, Bush garnered 69% of the vote.

Often appearing to ride Bush's coattails, Republicans swept into every other statewide office. Rick Perry and Carol Keeton Rylander squeaked by their Democratic opponents with an even 50% of the vote to become Lieutenant Governor and Comptroller, respectively, while John Cornyn became Attorney General, David Dewhurst Land Commissioner, Tony Garza Railroad Commissioner, and Susan Combs Agriculture Commissioner, by more substantial margins. Republicans also won every seat on the Supreme Court and Court of Criminal Appeals.

Democrats salvaged something from the wreckage by holding on to a 79 to 71 seat majority in the state house of representatives, and maintaining their margin of 17 to 13 in the United States House.

In campaigns during previous decades, Democratic candidates had advertised their party affiliation, while Republicans often downplayed theirs. By 1998, the roles were reversed. Republican billboards, for example, invariably trumpeted their candidates' party affiliation, while Democratic billboards neglected to remind the voters of the party of the candidate they were pushing. John Sharp, Democratic candidate for Lieutenant Governor, went to strenuous lengths to distance himself from his own party, attempting to portray himself as an "independent." His strategy almost worked, but on election day Sharp could not escape the fact that he was listed as a Democrat on the ballot. He managed to capture a respectable, but unsuccessful, 48% of the vote.

At the top of the tickets, Bush and Mauro generally maintained a tone of respectful disagreement in both their advertising and in their one face-to-face debate. Other races, however, were brutally negative. Republicans everywhere attempted to tar Democrats with the label "liberal," while Democrats sought to portray their opponents as anti-family, pro-crime, and untruthful.

Sharp ran a television ad claiming that Republican Rick Perry, if elected Lieutenant Governor, "would rob the public schools of hundreds of millions of dollars," and another suggesting that Perry, while a member of the legislature, had deliberately voted to release murderers from prison. In retaliation, Perry likened John Sharp to J. R. Ewing, the arch-villain of the 1978 to 1990 television series "Dallas."

Democratic Land Commissioner candidate Richard Raymond highlighted a legal dispute in which his opponent, David Dewhurst, had been sued by his former partners for fraud, and also accused Dewhurst of failing to pay taxes on his various business interests. Dewhurst charged that Raymond, while a member of the state legislature, had not actually lived in the house he claimed as his residence. Raymond's wife had a Dewhurst campaign worker arrested for trespass. So it went.

One of the lesser-known but more interesting aspects of the 1998 campaign was the latest attempt by the Christian Right (see Chapter Four) to win a majority on the State Board of Education. In the pivotal battle in District 1 (Far West Texas), Democrat Rene Nunez defeated Republican Donna Ballard, thus ensuring that Christian Conservatives would only control seven seats on the fifteen-member board.

Conclusion

All in all, a survey of voters, campaigns, and elections in Texas is not very encouraging to people who take democratic theory seriously. If the legitimacy of government in a democracy depends upon the participation of the citizens, then the very low voter turnout in state elections raises serious questions about the legitimacy of Texas government. Moreover, the great disparity in turnout between ethnic groups most certainly biases public policy away from the patterns that would prevail if all citizens voted. Looking beyond voting, the great impact of money on political campaigns and elections suggests the possibility, if not the certainty, that wealthy elites control the policy process, rendering whatever citizen participation exists irrelevant. A cynical view of democracy finds much support in Texas electoral politics.

There is, however, some cause for optimism. The old barriers to participation that kept people from exercising their citizenship are gone, and in fact voter turnout has been rising slowly and unsteadily in recent decades. It is possible that time and education will bring more people to fulfill their potential as citizens. Further, the gubernatorial campaign of 1990 proved that money is not the only thing that counts in Texas politics, and the Republican surge of 1994 demonstrated that the electorate is capable of making informed choices in the polling booth.

The system, then, is imperfect but not completely depraved. For anyone trying to make a better state, there are both many flaws to try to correct and some reason to hope that they may be correctable.

Summary

Voting, campaigning, and elections are important to study because in a democracy the legitimacy of the government depends upon the people's participation. Thus, despite the fact that single votes almost never determine the outcome of elections, voting is important to the individual, the candidate, and the political system.

Consistent with its Southern history and culture, Texas until recently attempted to suppress voting by all but wealthy Whites. Today, voter turnout is still below the national average, which is itself comparatively low. Turnout of African Americans and Mexican Americans is generally lower than the turnout of Anglos. This disparity makes public policy more conservative than it would otherwise be.

In campaigns, candidates attempt to persuade voters to support them. In order to do so, they are forced to spend large amounts of money, which means that they become dependent upon wealthy special interests that contribute to their cause. This has consequences for public policy. Money is not absolutely decisive in campaigns, however, and candidates who are outspent by their opponents sometimes win.

There are three kinds of elections in Texas. Primary elections are held to choose candidates for general elections. In general elections, the electorate determines who will serve in public office. Special elections are held when they are needed between general elections, often to either fill unexpected governmental vacancies or to ratify constitutional amendments.

One of the more disturbing trends in election campaigns is the prevalence of negative personal attacks in television advertising. Yet several of the most important state campaigns in 1994 and 1996 were fought cleanly, which gives some reason to hope that future elections may be more issue-oriented than those in the past.

The 1994 elections brought the Republican Party to full parity with the Democratic Party for the first time in the twentieth century in Texas, and the 1996 elections seemed to establish the GOP as the normal majority party. While many Democratic candidates were defeated, however, those who managed to convince the voters that they were conservative were able to survive. The future of Texas elections promises to be more volatile than the past.

A comparison of the reality of Texas electoral politics with the ideal of the democratic polity thus suggests that Texas falls very far below the ideal, but offers some reason for optimism.

Key Terms

Campaign

Closed primary

Equal protection clause

General elections

Open primary

Primary

Privately funded
  campaigns

Publicly funded
  campaigns

Suffrage

Super Tuesday

Visual images

Voter registration

Voter turnout

Study Questions

1. Why is the study of voters, campaigns, and elections important in a democracy?

2. In the days when Texas deliberately suppressed the voter turnout of everyone but wealthy Whites, was its government legitimate?

3. Since public elections are rarely won by the margin of a single vote, why should you, as an individual, bother to vote? Discuss the problem from the perspective of the voter, the candidate, and the political system.

4. What are the consequences of differences in turnout among ethnic groups in Texas?

5. What effects does money have on campaigns? Are these good or bad for democratic government?

6. Suppose Texas were to adopt a system of publicly funded electoral campaigns. What effects might this change have on candidates, political parties, campaigns, and public policy?

7. If there were no such thing as television, would money still play an important role in political campaigns in Texas? Why or why not?

8. Why have Texas's laws so far largely failed to curb abuses of private campaign financing?

9. If negative campaigns get results, why is there any concern about them?

10. What are the consequences for public policy of the importance of primary elections in Texas?

11. In what ways did the 1994 and 1996 general elections in Texas conform to the state's historical pattern of voting? In what ways did they depart from the state's historical pattern?

12. From the standpoint of democratic theory, what was encouraging and what was discouraging about the 1994 and 1996 general elections?

Internet Assignment

Internet sites: http://www.txdemocrats.org/

http://www.texasgop.org/

Visit the Democratic and Republican homepages. Find the links to those candidates who are running for state offices. Visit a few campaign sites. How do these candidates help you to understand their philosophies? What words are used to gain your trust? What sorts of objects are in the backgrounds of the photographs?

Chapter Seven

Organization of the Texas Legislature

The calm before the storm— workers are getting the House of Representatives chamber into tiptop shape before a legislative session begins. The laptops are ready, the carpet is clean, and the chairs are being moved into place.

Elementary school teachers, the medical profession, university professors, high school teachers, police officers, the FBI, the US Supreme Court, and the Texas Legislature [is the order in which Texans indicated their level of confidence in public institutions. The fourteen institutions falling below the legislature included local government, the U.S. Congress, newspaper reporters, the legal profession, and the National Rifle Association].
     The Texas Poll, August 3–15, 1995.

Introduction

Legislative bodies are meant to represent the people and to reflect the differing views of a community, state, or nation. At the same time, they are meant to enact public policy, to provide funds for government operations, and to perform a host of other functions on behalf of the people who elected them. The Texas state legislature is still not completely representative of the state as a whole, but, especially from the mid-1980s on, it has increased its diversity along party, ethnic, and gender lines. Achieving greater diversity helps the state more nearly to meet the most fundamental tests of democratic government, representation and fairness. The legislature is particularly important in democratic theory because it institutionalizes the people's choices and translates the people's wants into public policy.

Texas's **biennial** legislative sessions are the focal point of the state government. *Biennial* means that the regular legislative sessions occur every other year. In these sessions, legislators must wrestle with important economic and social issues, define public morality and provide methods to enforce it, and also attend to strictly political chores, such as redistricting. They are handicapped in these endeavors, however, by a number of structural weaknesses in the legislative system and by a historic lack of public confidence and support. As the Texas Poll cited above found in 1995, public support seems to be strengthening. One factor may be that the legislature accomplishes more than its structural weaknesses would lead one to think possible.

This chapter examines the functions of legislative bodies, characteristics of members of the Texas legislature, and legislative compensation. It describes the constitutional, statutory, and informal aspects of legislative structure and the politics of redistricting. It outlines the internal organization of the two houses, including presiding officers, committees, and staff. It then suggests reforms to improve the organizational aspects of the legislature. Chapter 8 reviews the legislature in action, making public policy.

Functions of Legislative Bodies

If asked what legislators do, most people would answer, "Make laws." The answer is correct, but incomplete. Legislative bodies have several other functions as well, most of which arise from the separation of political institutions and the system of checks and balances that underlie our system of government. Lawmaking, reapportionment/redistricting, and the constituent function of proposing constitutional amendments are all activities traditionally associated with legislative bodies. Americans also deem it appropriate for a legislature to help shape the political agenda.

In contrast, activities such as overseeing the administration or doing *casework*—favors— for constituents may at first blush seem to belong to the executive branch rather than to the legislative branch. Similarly, when the activity at hand is accusations and trial (impeachment), the details of court organization or procedures, or the settling of disputes such as those over elections, one may think first of the judiciary. Educating and informing the electorate may seem to be a function well suited to the schools or to private groups. In fact, the legislature is involved in all these functions.

FORMAL FUNCTIONS

LAWMAKING AND THE POLITICAL AGENDA

The most obvious legislative activities are those that involve the making of public policy through the passage of legislation. Although many other people—the governor, bureaucrats, the courts, lobbyists, and citizens—are involved in the process of making laws, the basic prerogative for writing, amending, and passing them belongs to members of the legislature. Legislators may gather facts and opinions through investigations and hearings. They also need to represent the views of their constituents—especially if their districts have a reasonable degree of consensus on an issue—in their proposals and their votes.

In the process of lawmaking, especially, legislators help to shape and fix the political agenda for Texas. That is, they have a major voice in determining what the state's policies will be in such important areas as education, welfare, and the environment. They set up priorities by how they appropriate money. Legislators also determine whether the political climate in Austin will be one of cooperation or competition with the executive branch. Will there be one *state* agenda for political action, or will there be two separate agendas, the legislature's and the governor's?

REAPPORTIONMENT/REDISTRICTING

Reapportionment and **redistricting** could be considered a part of the general lawmaking function, but they have occupied so much legislative time and attention in recent years that they deserve a separate listing. Every ten years, following completion of the federal census of population, the legislature must reapportion itself—that is, decide which parts of the state get more members of the legislature and which lose membership— by drawing boundary lines for the state senatorial and representative districts as well as for the Texas congressional districts. In between census reports, the legislature makes districting adjustments as needed or, more likely, as forced by litigation. *Redistricting*—the redrawing of the electoral lines—is a source of intense political activity.

THE CONSTITUENT/AMENDMENT FUNCTION

A body empowered to create or amend a constitution is described as having a **constituent function.** State legislatures are involved in the ratification of amendments to the national Constitution. They also propose amendments to state constitutions and pass statutes that "make do" until constitutional change can be brought about. As we saw in Chapter 2, Texas legislators are continuously engaged in this function.

THE JUDICIAL FUNCTION

Just as legislators are not the only people involved in lawmaking, judges are not the only ones involved in judicial matters. Whenever the House formally accuses—impeaches—a judge or executive branch official and the Senate tries the person accused, or whenever the legislature passes laws dealing with courts and court procedures, the judicial function comes into play. Legislative bodies also control the number, jurisdiction, and general organization of the judiciary through the lawmaking power.

THE ELECTORAL FUNCTION

Although it is infrequently exercised, the electoral function of the legislature is important. When necessary, election disputes are settled by the legislative body. In addition, the House makes the official declaration of the winners of the state executive offices after election results are tabulated.

THE ADMINISTRATIVE FUNCTION

Legislative bodies traditionally serve as executive bodies by supervising state administration—the process of **legislative oversight.** This supervision is exercised through the standing committees of each house, which hold hearings and request state agency administrators to testify and answer questions about their programs, rules, and expenditures. The oversight function of the Texas legislature was strengthened with the passage of the Sunset Act of 1977 and the establishment of the Sunset Advisory Commission to review administrative agencies and make recommendations to the legislature about their continuance or reorganization. (See Chapter 10 for details.) It was further strengthened in 1981 when a statute was passed that allowed the legislature to review rules and regulations of administrative agencies. Also included in the oversight function is the legislative audit of state expenditures, which serves to determine whether appropriated monies have been legally spent.

The relationship between state agency personnel and legislative supervisors, however, often is less that of the watched and the watchdogs than of program advocates and their supporters. When special interests and the press rally around a certain agency, that agency's so-called watchdogs generally become a friendly link to the larger assembly of legislators on the floor.

Approval of executive appointments, removal of state officials, and some aspects of budget preparation are other administrative duties of the legislature, as are those housekeeping activities designed to ensure its own smooth operation.

THE INVESTIGATORY FUNCTION

The relationship between state administrators and their overseers in the legislature is not always mutually beneficial. Legislators may perceive, sometimes with the assistance of representatives of special interests, that a state agency or set of state agencies is not doing its job properly or is not acting in the public interest. There may even be suspected malfeasance—illegal conduct—in office. An investigation may ensue by the committee that has jurisdiction over that agency, by the House General Investigating Committee, or by an ad hoc or interim committee created for the purpose; the committee may decide to recommend action to the appropriate house. The investigatory function is called into play less often in Texas than in other states where conflict-of-interest laws are stronger and special interests have less influence.

Today all public agencies undergo constant, intense scrutiny through the Texas Performance Review program of the comptroller's office (see Chapter 10) and through increased legislative demand for **privatizing** public functions—turning them over to private businesses or individuals. The beginning assumption is not illegal conduct but suspected inefficiencies.

INFORMAL FUNCTIONS

CASEWORK

One informal function performed by the legislature—that is, one that is not spelled out in law—is **casework:** troubleshooting or problem solving on behalf of a constituent. Casework stems directly from the formal function of representation. Being a state senator or representative does not just mean representing an abstract number of people living in a voting district, nor does it mean merely reflecting the views of the district when voting on legislation. Membership in the representative body also involves helping a constituent who is having difficulty getting a welfare check from the Department of Human Services or providing information for someone who wants to know how to apply for a job with the Department of Public Safety.

State legislators spend less time at this activity than do members of Congress, who serve on a full-time basis. Nevertheless, the attention of state legislators is often diverted from policy matters to the problems of their constituents. Lawmakers also spend virtually every weekend during the session in their districts, giving their constituents an opportunity to talk about pending legislation.[1]

---

1. In studies involving six other states, about one-third of the legislators indicated that casework is their most important function, and three-fourths of them reported spending at least one-quarter of their time on favors for constituents. See Patricia K. Freeman and Lilliard E. Richardson, Jr., "Casework in State Legislatures," *State and Local Government Review* 16 (Winter 1994): 21–26; and Richard Elling, "The Utility of State Legislative Casework as a Means of Oversight," *Legislative Studies Quarterly* 4, no. 3 (1979): 353–80.

EDUCATION AND INFORMATION

A second informal function of legislators is providing information to constituents and educating them on public issues of the day. This task may be performed in a low-key manner, such as by issuing a newsletter at regular intervals. It can be performed by giving speeches at meetings of the hometown Rotary, Kiwanis, or Business and Professional Women's Clubs. It includes interviews with media reporters.

Another source of information is the House Satellite News Service, which began in January 1995. The House provides video clips for statewide broadcast use to increase understanding of the legislative process and to perform a service for small and medium-size television stations that cannot afford to keep a crew stationed in Austin during the legislative session. Along the same lines, online computer access to bills and resolutions under consideration by the legislature was made available to the public beginning in 1995.

Structure of the Legislature

SIZE, ELECTIONS, AND TERMS

With the exception of Nebraska, which has a unicameral (single-house) legislature, the American states have patterned themselves on the **bicameral** model of the U.S. Congress. Article III of the Texas Constitution stipulates that the legislature is composed of a Senate and a House of Representatives.

The two houses have approximately equal power, but the Senate has more prestige and is considered the upper house. One reason is its smaller size. Another is that each senator represents nearly five times as many citizens as does a member of the House. Still another factor is the Senate's control over executive appointments. In addition, the Senate's presiding officer, the lieutenant governor, is elected by the entire state. The Senate's less formal procedures permit more extended—and sometimes highly publicized—debate than in the House, and a senator's term of office is longer than that of a member of the House. Traditionally, the Senate's national counterpart, the U.S. Senate, has been considered the more prestigious national legislative chamber. At both the state and the national level, when a member of the House seeks and wins a Senate seat, this achievement is regarded as a political promotion.

The average state senate has 40 members; the average lower house, 112. The Texas Constitution fixes the number of state senators at 31 and the maximum number of representatives at 150. The U.S. Congress has 100 senators and 435 representatives.[2] The number of senators is determined by the number of states; the number of members of the House, by statute (legislation).

---

2. The U.S. Constitution provides for a maximum of one representative for each 30,000 people. If no ceiling were statutorily set and this limit were actually attained, the U.S. House of Representatives would have about 8,833 members. The Texas Constitution sets a maximum membership of 150 in the House, although it allows one representative for each 15,000 citizens within that limit. If legislators represented only 15,000 constituents, the Texas House would have more than 1,295 members.

Among the fifty state legislatures, only the term *senate* is used consistently; the lower house is known variously as the assembly, house of representatives, and general assembly.[3] While the terms *House* and *Senate* are used by both national and state governments and the term *legislator* refers to a lawmaker at any level, *Congress* and *congressman/woman* are exclusively national.

Key features of the system for electing legislators include:

1. Selection in the November general election in even-numbered years

2. Election from **single-member districts**

3. Two-year terms for House members and four-year staggered terms for senators

4. A special election called by the governor to fill a vacancy caused by death, resignation, or expulsion from office

The issue of term limits is becoming increasingly important across the country. Republican members of Congress made term limits part of the campaign promises in their "Contract with America" in 1994, although in 1995 they failed to get enough votes to propose a constitutional amendment limiting their own terms. Twenty states had adopted some form of term limits by 1997. The U.S. Supreme Court in 1995 struck down efforts by states to limit the terms of members of the U.S. Congress.

The Texas legislature considered a variety of term limits bills but through 1997 had rejected all proposals. However, many municipal charters (see Chapter 3) have limits on the number of terms that can be served by the mayor and council.

Proponents of term limits see them as a way to try to regain public confidence in legislative bodies that increasingly have been regarded as remote and lacking in understanding of public wishes. Opponents are concerned about such matters as a possible lack of policy expertise on the part of legislative leaders and arbitrarily jettisoning a popular legislator because of artificial term limits. They contend that, "We have term limits now. Just ask any incumbent defeated in the last election." The greatest criticism of term limits, however, is that they are inherently undemocratic, since they rob voters of free choice in an election.

Newly elected legislators take office in January. Whenever reapportionment to establish districts of approximately equal population size occurs—at least every ten years—all senators are elected in the same year. They then draw lots to determine who will serve for two years and who will serve the full four-year term.

If a vacancy occurs because of death, resignation, or expulsion from office, the governor calls a special election to fill it. Expulsion is unusual because it requires a two-thirds majority vote in the legislator's house. Death is also rare among members of the legislature. The most common reason for a vacancy is resignation. A typical situation occurred in 1997, when Texas Sena-

---

3. Information on the legislatures of other states has been summarized from *The Book of the States,* 1996–97, vol. 31 (Lexington, Ky: Council of State Governments, 1996), 63–124.

tor Jim Turner was elected to Congress; he was then replaced in the Senate by Steve Ogden in a January special election.

SESSIONS

REGULAR SESSION

The constitution provides for regular biennial sessions, beginning on the second Tuesday in January of odd-numbered years. These sessions may run no longer than 140 calendar days. Six other states (all with considerably less population than Texas) also have biennial sessions; the rest have either annual or continuous sessions or the authority to divide a biennial session across two years.[4]

The truncated biennial legislative session accentuates all the formal and informal factors that influence legislation in Texas. For example, insufficient time for careful consideration of bills heightens the power of the presiding officers, the lobbyists, and the governor. Also, the short biennial session prevents issues from being raised in the first place, so that the state sometimes delays dealing with problems until a crisis occurs. Although there have been a number of changes in the specifics of the legislative sessions over the years, voters have consistently rejected amendments providing for annual sessions. They fear increased governmental power and spending, a reflection of the antigovernment attitude implicit in a conservative political culture.

One of the peculiarities of regular Texas legislative sessions is the constitutional provision for a "split session." The first thirty days are devoted to the introduction of bills and resolutions, emergency matters, and confirmation of recess appointments made by the governor; the next thirty days, to committee hearings (during this time, bills can still be introduced); and the next sixty days, to floor action on bills and resolutions. (The provision does not prescribe specific activities for the final twenty days of the session.) The governor, however, may declare that an emergency exists; this procedure allows the legislature to hold hearings and even vote on a bill more rapidly than the timetable ordinarily permits. The legislature, by the extraordinary vote of four-fifths, can allow introduction of a bill beyond the time limit.

CALLED SESSIONS

The governor can call the legislature into special session for a maximum of thirty days. The governor determines the agenda for this session. If a legislator wishes to add items to the agenda for a special session, the governor must agree. Thirty-one other state legislatures have mechanisms for calling

---

4. According to *The Book of the States, 1996–97*, 64–66, thirty-nine states have annual legislative sessions. Of these, thirteen have no limit on the number of days that the legislature can meet, thereby, in effect, creating continuous sessions. Most of the other very large states—California, New York, Ohio, Pennsylvania, and Illinois, for example—have continuous sessions. Four states technically have biennial sessions but may split the single session across two years. Besides Texas, the only states that have true biennial sessions are Arkansas, Kentucky, Montana, Nevada, North Dakota, and Oregon. The largest of these states is Kentucky, which has less than one-quarter the population of Texas.

themselves into special session. In Texas, only in the extraordinary situation that resulted in the impeachment of Governor Jim "Pa" Ferguson in 1917 has the legislature ever convened a special session on its own.

The governor may call one special session after another if necessary. However, since the voting public has rejected annual sessions several times, Texas governors usually try to avoid calling numerous special sessions that might appear to function as annual sessions. The average half-million-dollar price tag is another disincentive.

Nevertheless, governors sometimes have little choice about calling a special session because too much legislative business—often including the state budget—is unfinished. For example, Governor Bill Clements called two special sessions in 1989 and four in 1990 to deal with school finance and workers' compensation. Six weeks before the regular 1991 session ended, Governor Ann Richards had already called a special summer budget session. An additional budget session was needed in 1991, and public school finance was the subject of a 1992 session. No special sessions were called from 1993 through 1997.

LEGISLATIVE DISTRICTS

MECHANICS

Only one senator or representative may be elected from a particular district by the people living in that district. Although some districts are three hundred times larger than others in geographical size (see Figures 7–1 and 7–2), each senatorial district should have approximately 627,075 residents, and each House district, approximately 129,595.[5] Achieving equally populated districts does not come easily, however, since the task is a highly political one carried out by the legislature.

If the legislature fails to redistrict itself, the Legislative Redistricting Board (LRB) comes into play. The LRB is composed of five *ex officio* state officials; that is, they are members by virtue of their holding another office. These five are the lieutenant governor, the speaker of the House, the comptroller of public accounts, the general land commissioner, and the attorney general. Already powerful officeholders, once constituted as the LRB they control legislative redistricting in Texas.

HISTORY

Prior to the mid-1960s, legislative districts were a hodgepodge based partly on population, partly on geography, and largely on protecting rural interests. Members of the Senate have always been elected in single-member districts, but in the past those districts reflected land area, not population. Indeed, the Texas Constitution once prohibited a single county, regardless of population, from having more than one senator. House districts were constitutionally

---

5. According to the 1997 U.S. Bureau of the Census estimate, Texas has a population of at least 19,439,337. Dividing the official figure by 31 for senatorial seats gives the ideal district 627,075 people; dividing by 150 for representative districts gives 129,595. Obviously, citizens move into and out of districts, so the numbers are not exact, and they change as the population increases.

FIGURE 7–1
Typical Texas
Senate Districts

Source: Texas Senate *(Austin:
Senate Media Services and Senate
Publications and Printing,
January 1995).*

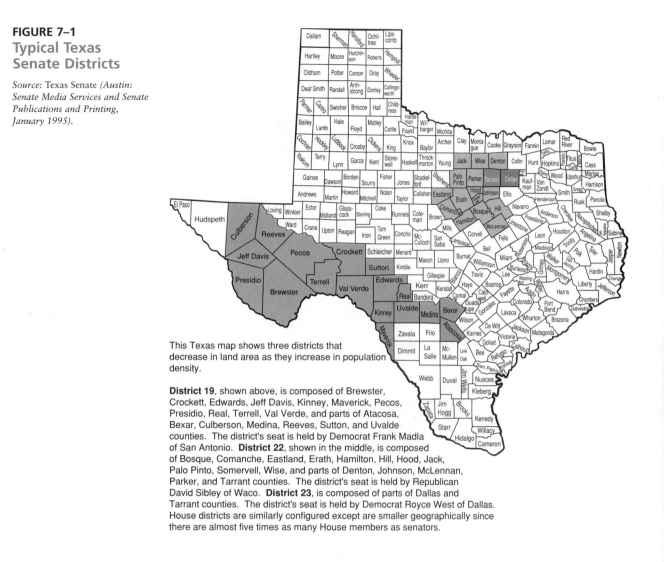

This Texas map shows three districts that
decrease in land area as they increase in population
density.

District 19, shown above, is composed of Brewster,
Crockett, Edwards, Jeff Davis, Kinney, Maverick, Pecos,
Presidio, Real, Terrell, Val Verde, and parts of Atacosa,
Bexar, Culberson, Medina, Reeves, Sutton, and Uvalde
counties. The district's seat is held by Democrat Frank Madla
of San Antonio. **District 22**, shown in the middle, is composed
of Bosque, Comanche, Eastland, Erath, Hamilton, Hill, Hood, Jack,
Palo Pinto, Somervell, Wise, and parts of Denton, McLennan,
Parker, and Tarrant counties. The district's seat is held by Republican
David Sibley of Waco. **District 23**, is composed of parts of Dallas and
Tarrant counties. The district's seat is held by Democrat Royce West of Dallas.
House districts are similarly configured except are smaller geographically since
there are almost five times as many House members as senators.

based on population, but with limitations that worked against urban counties.[6] In addition, *gerrymandering*—drawing district lines in such a way as to
give one faction or one party an advantage—was the norm.

The federal courts changed the ability of the state to artificially limit
representation from urban areas and forced the drawing of legislative districts according to population. In 1962, *Baker* v. *Carr*[7]—the one-person,
one-vote case—the U.S. Supreme Court overturned a legislative districting
system that gave one group substantial advantages over another. In 1964, in
Reynolds v. *Sims,*[8] the Court laid down its first guidelines on conditions
that would necessitate redrawing district lines, including a mandate that the

---

6. A county was entitled to a maximum of seven representatives unless its population exceeded
700,000; then one additional representative could be districted for each additional 100,000 in
population.
7. 369 U.S. 186 (1962).
8. 377 U.S. 533 (1964).

FIGURE 7–2
Typical Texas
House of
Representative
Districts

Source: Texas House of
Representatives
*(www.house.state.tx.us/house/
stmap/house.htm).*

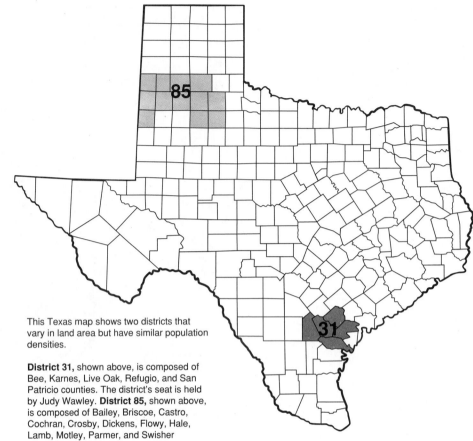

This Texas map shows two districts that
vary in land area but have similar population
densities.

District 31, shown above, is composed of
Bee, Karnes, Live Oak, Refugio, and San
Patricio counties. The district's seat is held
by Judy Wawley. **District 85,** shown above,
is composed of Bailey, Briscoe, Castro,
Cochran, Crosby, Dickens, Flowy, Hale,
Lamb, Motley, Parmer, and Swisher
counties. The district's seat is held by
Speaker of the House Pete Laney.

membership of both houses be based on population. The Texas House of Representatives continued to use multimember legislative districts[9] until the courts
forced some counties to abandon them in 1975 and others volunteered to do
so. The redistricting battles that arose after the 1980 census are reflected in the
Ben Sargent cartoon depicting a comedy of errors.[10]

Just as another state has to lose a congressional representative for Texas to gain one, Texas legislative districts must be changed, or even merged, to accommodate high-growth areas of the state.
After each redistricting, there are fewer rural districts in Texas and more urban and suburban ones.

9. A multimember district is one in which two or more representatives are elected by all of the
people in that district. All the representatives represent all the people of the district. Multimember
districts tend to reduce considerably the ability of ethnic minorities to win election, and the citizens tend not to be sure which representative is truly theirs.
10. See Steven Bickerstaff, "Legislative and Congressional Reapportionment in Texas: A Historical Perspective," *Public Affairs Comment* 37 (Winter 1991): 1–13, for a good review of redistricting developments.

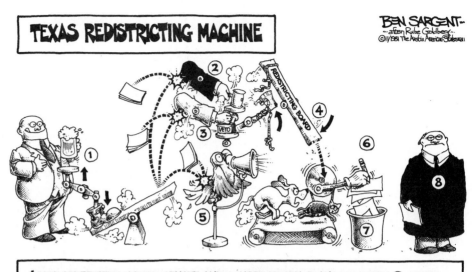

TEXAS REDISTRICTING MACHINE

BEN SARGENT—
~after Rube Goldberg~
©11/88 The Austin American-Statesman

LEGISLATURE SETS HOUSE, SENATE AND CONGRESSIONAL PLANS IN MOTION ①. HOUSE PLAN TRIPS JUDGE'S GAVEL ② AND SENATE PLAN TRIGGERS VETO STAMP ③, TOGETHER RELEASING REDISTRICTING BOARD ④, DROPPING CAT. CONGRESSIONAL PLAN CALLS LEGISLATURE INTO SESSION ⑤, WAKING DOG, CAUSING HAND TO DRAW DISTRICTS ⑥, WHICH IMMEDIATELY ROLL INTO TRASH CAN ⑦.
FEDERAL COURT ⑧ THEN DRAWS DISTRICTS FROM SCRATCH.

Citizens in urban areas, Republicans, and ethnic minority groups have all been prominent in redistricting suits. As Table 7–1 shows, the predominant ethnic minorities in Texas—African Americans and Hispanics—have made some gains through population-based districting. Ethnic minority groups made up 27 percent of the legislature in 1997. However, at that time, the non-Anglo population of the state was 42 percent, with Hispanics accounting for about 28 percent and African Americans, 12 percent.[11]

Table 7-2 shows the gains made by Republicans in the modern era, with most of these gains coming in urban areas. Republicans in Texas have bene-fited not only from reapportionment but also from the national trend toward conservative politics and from the steady evolution of the state's politics from one-party Democrat to two-party and perhaps to Republican dominance.

In addition to ethnic, party, and urban pressures, legislators also have to be concerned with the federal Voting Rights Act of 1965 and with pro-ducing redistricting plans that the governor will not veto. With all these competing demands, it is no wonder that the legislature usually fails to produce a plan that pleases everyone. For example, after the 1990 census, while executive-legislative friction was minimal, the judiciary, Republicans,

---

11. See Arturo Vega, "Gender and Ethnicity Effects on the Legislative Behavior and Substantive Representation of the Texas Legislature," *Texas Journal of Political Studies* 19 (Spring/Summer 1997): 1–21.

TABLE 7–1

Ethnicity in the Texas Legislature, 1987–1997, by Percentage*

Year	Anglo	Hispanic/Mexican American	African American
1987	78.5	13.3	8.3
1989	77.9	14.4	7.7
1991	78.5	13.3	8.3
1993	73.5	17.7	8.8
1995	72.4	18.8	8.8
1997	73.0	18.5	8.4

*Percentages do not always equal 100 due to rounding.

and ethnic minority groups all attacked the redistricting. The disputes centered on the Texas House and Texas Senate districts. Redrawing the congressional districts proved to be easy, since the state had gained three new U.S. House seats. The legislature redistricted in 1991 and made adjustments in 1993. The courts redrew the lines for thirteen Texas House districts in 1996.

PARTY AND FACTIONAL ORGANIZATION

Historically, Texas was a one-party—Democratic—state (see Chapter 5). In the legislature, unlike the situation in the U.S. Congress and many other state

TABLE 7–2

Political Party Membership in the Texas Legislature, 1977–1997, by Percentage

Year	Senate (N = 31)		House (N = 150)		Both Houses (N = 181)	
	Democrat	Republican	Democrat	Republican	Democrat	Republican
1977	90.3%	9.7%	87.3%	12.7%	87.9%	12.1%
1979	87.1	12.9	84.7	15.3	85.1	14.9
1981	77.4	22.6	74.7	25.3	75.0	25.0
1983	83.9	16.1	76.0	24.0	77.3	22.7
1985	83.9	16.1	65.3	34.7	68.5	31.5
1987	80.6	19.4	62.7	37.3	71.3	28.7
1989	74.2	25.8	62.0	38.0	63.9	36.1
1991	71.0	29.0	62.0	38.0	63.5	36.5
1993	58.1	41.9	61.3	38.7	60.8	39.2
1995	54.8	45.2	59.3	40.7	58.6	41.4
1997	45.2	54.8	54.7	45.3	53.0	47.0

legislatures, political party organization did not exist. As a one-party state, Texas saw factionalism within the Democratic Party replace the party differences that characterized other legislative bodies.

Political party affiliation and party organization have grown in importance as Texas has become a two-party state.[12] Table 7–2 shows, Republican representation in the legislature has grown from minuscule in 1977 to a majority in the Texas Senate in 1997 and possibly in the House by 1999. Beginning in 1983, party members in the House designated floor leaders. In the 1989 session, House Republicans formed a formal caucus for the first time since Reconstruction, and today they regularly select *party whips*—the persons designated to line up votes on behalf of the official party position. House members, particularly, reported more intensely partisan disagreements during the 1997 session.

However, in both houses, the presiding officers continue to deal with members on an individual basis, unlike the situation in the U.S. Congress, which is organized strictly along party lines. In the Seventy-fifth Legislature (1997–98), the Republicans held the Senate while Democrats constituted a majority in the House. Lieutenant Governor Bob Bullock, the Democratic presiding office of the Senate, appointed nine Democrats as committee chairs and eight Republicans as chairs of committees and the two permanent subcommittees. The very important Education and Finance committees were chaired by Republicans. Speaker of the House Pete Laney, also a Democrat, appointed twenty-two Democrats and fourteen Republicans as chairs. A Republican chaired the key Ways and Means Committee, which was very active during the session because it deals with taxation.

The liberalism or conservatism of a legislator is often more important than the party label. Liberals versus conservatives and urban versus rural/suburban interests are typical divisions. These differences cut across party lines and are most evident on issues such as taxation, spending, and social welfare programs.

COMPENSATION

Since 1975, members of the Texas legislature have received a salary of $7,200 each year; this figure was established by constitutional amendment. (Texas is one of only six states that set legislative salaries by constitution.) They also receive a $95 *per diem*—daily—allowance when the legislature is in regular or special session to cover lodging, meals, and other expenses. When they serve on a state board or council or conduct legislative business between sessions, legislators also are entitled to per diem expenses for up to twelve days a month. In addition, they receive a $0.28 mileage allowance. The presiding officers receive the same compensation but also are entitled to apartments furnished by the state.

As Figure 7–3 shows, as of 1995, California, the largest state in population, paid legislators $75,600, ten and a half times what Texas, the second

---

12. See Robert Harmel and Keith E. Hamm, "Development of a Party Role in a No-Party Legislature," *Western Political Quarterly* 39 (March 1986): 79–92, for a summary of party developments through the mid-1980s.

FIGURE 7–3
Legislative Salaries,
Per Diem in Ten
Largest States

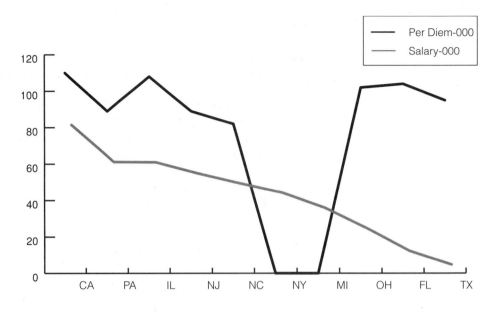

Source: "1997 State Legislators'
Compensation and Living
Expense Allowances during Ses-
sion," State Legislatures,
July/August 1997, 22.
*Note: Michigan allows $8,925
a year. The $89 figure is 1/100 of
that amount.

largest state, pays.[13] The Texas legislative stipend is not even half the federal minimum for a family of four to be above the poverty level! The low level of Texas salaries, which voters have repeatedly refused to change, makes legislators simultaneously more susceptible to lobbying tactics—at $7,200, a free lunch is important—and more likely to divert their attention to finding ways to earn a decent living. The latter task has become more difficult with the increase in committee work between legislative sessions and occasional special sessions. As the Ben Sargent cartoon shows, legislators haven't made much headway in gaining consideration for a raise.

Under a 1991 state constitutional amendment, the Ethics Commission can convene a citizen advisory board to recommend changes in legislative salary; the proposal must then be submitted to the voters. However, as of early 1998, no such board had been formed.

The bottom line on legislative compensation is that the low salary coupled with the generous per diem allowance results in an average payment of about $29,040 during a year when the legislature is in regular session. California legislators not only receive a much larger salary than do Texas lawmakers, but also receive a larger per diem, $110. Thus, the generous per diem allowance doesn't nudge Texas compensation very far toward that of California. However, some Texas legislators have manipulated salary, the per diem, and travel reimbursements to bring in as much as $70,000. The fundamentally undemocratic aspect of legislative compensation is that citizens have authorized only the $7,200 salary and might be surprised at the total compensation package.[14]

---

13. Karen Hansen, "Legislative Pay: Baseball It Ain't," *State Legislatures*, July/August 1997, 20–26.
14. Ben Wear, "Salaries Are Just the Start at Capitol," *Austin American-Statesman*, April 2, 1995, A1, A20.

Legislators also receive an allowance for operating an office both during the session and in the interim between sessions. Members of the Senate receive $25,000 a month for office expenses. Members of the House receive $8,500 a month. These allowances compare favorably with those granted by other states. Additionally, legislators are entitled to retirement benefits if they serve at least twelve years and pay $48 a month. Those benefits are generous because they are pegged to the salary of a district judge, which is about twelve times that of a legislator.

House members in particular are always seeking additional staff assistance because their office budgets are less than those of senators. Students often volunteer and frequently become very responsible members of a legislator's staff, either in Austin or in the home district. Some become paid staffers.

Membership Characteristics

FORMAL QUALIFICATIONS

The **formal qualifications** necessary to become a member of the Texas legislature are stipulated in Article III of the constitution. They are those commonly listed for elected officials: age, residency, U.S. citizenship, and voting status. Members of the Senate must be twenty-six years of age or older, qualified voters for five years, and residents of the senatorial district from which they are elected for one year. Members of the House must be at least twenty-one years old, qualified voters, legal residents of the state for two years, and residents of the district from which they are elected for one year.

PERSONAL CHARACTERISTICS

The formal qualifications are so broad as to make a substantial portion of the Texas citizenry eligible to run for legislative office. However, individuals with certain types of personal characteristics tend to get elected more readily than individuals who lack these characteristics. These characteristics reflect political, social, and economic realities and traditions and confirm the state's conservative political tradition. That they exist does not mean that they are desirable. Indeed, they indicate that certain groups may be underrepresented in the Texas legislature.

In general, Texas legislators are White male Protestant lawyers or businessmen in their late forties who are married, have college educations, belong to a number of civic organizations, have considerable personal money as well as access to campaign funds, and have the support of the local media. Not every legislator has all of these personal characteristics, but an individual elected without having any of them would be extraordinary indeed. Details of several of these characteristics are shown in Table 7–3.

WHITE, MALE

Race, ethnicity, and gender are all factors in politics. Both ethnic minorities and women are considerably underrepresented in the Texas legislature. Although Texas's total minority population was 42 percent in 1996 and reaches four-fifths of the population in some areas of the state, minority membership in the legislature is only 27 percent. No Native Americans or Asian Americans are members. Although there are about 100 women for every 97 men in society, only 18 percent of Texas legislators are women.[15]

LAWYERS AND BUSINESSPEOPLE

Legislators tend to be white-collar professionals and businesspeople. Other fields such as farming and ranching also have fairly strong representation, given their small numbers in the general population.

Law traditionally has been seen as preparation for politics. In fact, aspiring politicians often attend law school as a means of gaining entry into politics. The

---

15. See B. Drummond Ayres, "Many State Legislatures Fracturing Gender Gap," *Austin American-Statesman*, April 20, 1997, A28–A29. Lyn Kathlene, in "Power and Influence in State Legislative Policymaking: The Interaction of Gender and Position in Committee Hearing Debates," *American Political Science Review* 88 (September 1994): 560–76, reports that as the number of female legislators increases, the aggressiveness of their male colleagues also increases and seriously impedes the women's ability to participate on an equal basis.

Chapter One

The Context of Texas Politics

The Alamo in San Antonio symbolizes the state's colorful political history.

If I owned Hell and Texas, I'd rent out Texas and live in Hell.
General Philip H. Sheridan
Fort Clark, 1855

I wasn't born in Texas, but I got here as fast as I could.
On earth as it is in Texas.
Bumper stickers seen often on Texas roads in the 1990s

All government is bad, including good government.
Edward Abbey
The Journey Home, 1977

Introduction

Much has changed in Texas between the time General Sheridan made his oft-quoted evaluation of the state and the time the buyers of bumper stickers made theirs. In 1855 Texas was poor and sparsely settled, and offered few civilized comforts to a soldier assigned to garrison an outpost against Indian raids. Today, Texas is the nation's second most populous state, is 80 percent urban, and leads the country in consuming energy and producing semiconductors, among other distinctions. Yet, as we shall see, in some ways the state has changed little since Sheridan's time. Texas is a constantly evolving mix of old and new.

Old habits of thought and behavior evolved to meet the problems of the nineteenth century, when Texas was settled by Americans of western European background. They persist today, despite serious new problems created in the latter decades of the twentieth century. As Texans prepare themselves to meet the challenges of the twenty-first century, they have to ask themselves if the habits and institutions they have inherited are up to the job.

In this chapter, the first topic will be a summary of the history of Texas, with an emphasis on important political events and the development of the economy. Some of the most basic principles of democratic theory will then be discussed, along with an explanation of why it is vital to understand them. The focus will then shift to Texas's political culture and some historically crucial social and political attitudes. The next subject will be the economy of Texas and the way it interacts with the state's political system. As an introduction to some discussions later in the book, the origin and distribution of the state's population will then be a considered. Finally, there will be a brief outline of our agenda for the rest of the book.

Texas History: A Chronology

THE EARLIEST DAYS

The history of Texas is as exciting as that of any region in the nation, and our mythmakers have embellished it a little more than in most states. Texas has existed under six flags: those of Spain, France, Mexico, the Republic (and state) of Texas, the Southern Confederacy, and the United States. Texas has seen the administration of thirty-seven Spanish governors, fifteen Mexican governors, five presidents of the Republic, and forty-eight state governors.[1]

Humans have inhabited Texas for much longer than there has been such a thing as a state. Skull fragments found near Midland (dubbed "Midland Minnie") and a complete female skeleton discovered near Leander have been dated at ten thousand to thirteen thousand years old; a larger Clovis period (10,000–9,000 B.C.) site has been excavated in Denton County. At the time of the first European exploration in the sixteenth century, perhaps 30,000 to 40,000 Native Americans inhabited what is now Texas, and some estimates run as high as 130,000. Among the major groups were the Caddo tribes of North and East Texas, Tonkawas in Central Texas, Karankawas along the coast, Coahuiltecans from the Rio Grande river to what is now San Antonio, Lipan Apaches and Comanches in West Texas, and Jumanos in the Trans-Pecos region. Determined to keep their lands, they violently resisted European settlement. Westward advancement in Texas cost seventeen White lives per mile. We can only guess at the cost to the Native Americans, although it was probably much higher.

As early as 1519, just twenty-seven years after the European discovery of the New World and a century before the English pilgrims landed at Plymouth Rock, Spanish explorer Alonzo Alvarez de Pineda mapped the entire Gulf Coast. Several expeditions followed, but Spanish activity was not extensive until 1685, when the French explorer La Salle built a small fort in what is now South Texas. This threat of competition from their imperial rivals spurred the Spanish to establish a series of missions, beginning in 1690. The purposes of these missions were to extend the sphere of Spanish domination and civil law and to convert Native Americans to Christianity. Spanish influence extended across South Texas from Louisiana to New Mexico, and by the time of the American Revolution in 1776 about 2,300 Native Americans had been baptized.

But Spanish power was already waning as a result of economic and military factors. After one abortive attempt, Mexico achieved independence from Spain in 1821. What followed for Texas was a period of freebooters, privateers, and filibustering expeditions. Several American and Mexican adventurers led private invasions in unsuccessful attempts to establish control over Texas, and pirates—notably the Frenchman Jean Lafitte—operated out of Galveston Island, preying on Spanish shipping.

---

1. Much of this account draws on material in *The Texas Almanac, 1964–1965* (Dallas: A. H. Belo, 1963), 35–54; *The Texas Almanac, 1986–1987* (Dallas: A. H. Belo, 1985), 163–224; and *The Texas Almanac, 1992–1993* (Dallas: A. H. Belo, 1991), 27–54, 324; and other footnoted material.

For many years, Galveston permitted gambling and the sale of mixed drinks, despite state laws prohibiting these practices. State and local authorities looked the other way—probably because they were bribed—and pretended the practice did not exist until well into the 1950s. The common explanation in Texas was that "Galveston was discovered by pirates and has been run by them ever since."

Despite the centuries of Spanish influence, at the time of Mexican independence in 1821 there were only three permanent European settlements in Texas—San Antonio, Nacogdoches, and Goliad—and the European population had declined to 7,000 during the previous thirty years. Although their numbers were small, Spaniards and Mexicans left rich and indelible influences on Texas through their language and law, religion, and culture.

ANGLO-AMERICAN COLONIZATION

Colonization from the south did not succeed in Texas because of short-sighted economic policies. The Spanish government exploited the few settlers by paying poor prices for their cattle and other products and at the same time charging them high prices for trade goods. As a result, few moved to the giant province.

Texas was potentially much more attractive to settlers from the neighboring United States. There, frontier land was sold to would-be settlers, but in Texas, land was free if one could get a government grant. Since the Spanish government had failed to induce Mexican citizens to colonize the area, it was nervous about expansionist impulses in the United States. Spain decided to gamble that it could acculturate Anglo settlers and use them to protect Mexican interests against the growing, rambunctious democracy to the north.

Moses Austin, a native of Connecticut, abandoned his unsuccessful business activities in Missouri and turned his attention to Texas. Moses died after filing a formal application for settlement with the viceroy of Mexico in 1819. He was succeeded by his son Stephen F. Austin, who received a generous land grant as well as permission to bring in three hundred families for colonization.

The first settlements were at Columbus on the Colorado River and at Washington-on-the-Brazos. As **impresario,** or agent, Austin had wide powers over his colony to establish commercial activity, organize a militia, and dispense justice. Other colonies quickly followed, and the non-Indian population jumped from 7,000 to more than 35,000 between 1821 and 1836.

The great majority of the settlers came in good faith, intending to take the oath of allegiance to Mexico and be good Mexican citizens. But the cultural differences they encountered made this difficult. Not only was Spanish the official language, but the colonists, mostly Protestant, were required to accept Roman Catholicism. Some also continued to keep Black slaves, although this practice was illegal in Mexico. Furthermore, the new Mexican nation was suffering from violent political instability, and policy toward Texas was both inconsistent and being made eight hundred miles away in Mexico City by men who knew little about conditions in the area. Moreover, Anglos tended to regard themselves as culturally superior to Mexicans and vice versa. Alienation between Texas and Mexico grew, much as alienation between the colonists and the British had grown prior to the American Revolution two generations earlier.

REVOLUTION

The Mexican government now feared further Anglo-American settlement and acted to curtail it. The settlers responded with demands for concessions, including the right to use the English language in public business and the separation of Texas from the state of Coahuila. Austin was imprisoned in Mexico City for a time, and conditions degenerated. What followed is known to virtually every schoolchild in the state: Texas's war for independence. The most celebrated engagement was the battle in San Antonio in which a few Anglos and Texas-Mexicans held the Alamo against a much larger Mexican force for eleven days before being massacred.

During a skirmish with Mexican troops on April 19, 1836, a private named Mirabeau Lamar so impressed his officers with his bravery that General Sam Houston promoted him to colonel on the spot. (Lamar continued his meteoric rise and in December 1838 became Texas's third president.) Two days later, at the battle of San Jacinto, the Texans attacked in the afternoon while the Mexican general Santa Anna, who was also president of Mexico, and his troops were taking their siestas. So great was the element of surprise that the battle was over in eighteen minutes, and the war was ended. Santa Anna fled during the fighting, but was captured the next day; he was on his hands and knees hiding in a patch of tall grass, wearing the rough tunic of a Mexican private that did not quite conceal his white silk shirt. As captive of the Texans, Santa Anna was given an ultimatum: Agree to sign a treaty granting Texas independence and withdraw his troops south of the Rio Grande, or be executed. Santa Anna signed, but repudiated the treaty as soon as he was safely across the border. Texans, however, considered themselves independent, and the Republic of Texas was a reality.

Although Texans are certain that the men who gave their lives at the Alamo were heroes, no one is quite sure how many of them there were. For most of this century, the Daughters of the Republic of Texas maintained a roster of "Heroes of the Battle of the Alamo" that contained 183 names, mainly Anglos. Over the decades, a few Spanish-surnamed defenders were added, so that by the early 1990s the "official" number of heroes was 189.

Recent scholarly research, however, has suggested that the victorious Mexican army counted as many as 257 Texan bodies after the battle. Because of the incomplete nature of the Mexican records, it may be impossible to come up with a definitive number.

Source: David McLemore, "160 Years Later, Historians Ask: Who Died at the Alamo?" *Austin American-Statesman,* March 12, 1996, B6.

The history of the republic was eventful but short. Independence brought sudden growth, with the population rising rapidly to about 140,000. But the Mexicans twice invaded, capturing San Antonio, and Native Americans continued to cause severe problems. The new nation soon found itself in debt and with a depreciating currency. Sentiment for annexation by the United States had always been strong, and on December 29, 1845, the U.S. Congress voted to admit Texas into the Union as the twenty-eighth state. This was one of those rare events in history in which an independent nation gave up its sovereignty and became part of another nation.

Unlike other states, Texas retained the title to all of its public lands when it accepted statehood.

In the 1990s a tiny band of political eccentrics drew a great deal of media attention to themselves with the claim that the Lone Star State had not been constitutionally absorbed into the United States in 1845, and that therefore it was still an independent republic. The basis for the claim of this "Republic of Texas" group was the true observation that the United States admitted Texas under the authority of a joint resolution of Congress, rather than under a treaty ratified by the Senate, which would seem to be the method required by the U.S. Constitution.

Of more importance than the questionable way the federal government admitted Texas, however, is the unquestionable enthusiasm with which Texans embraced the union. In the 1845 referendum in which they were asked to approve their admission to the United States, they endorsed the change by the overwhelming vote of 4,254 to 257.

For over a century and a half, therefore, it has been official: Texas is one of the United States of America, not an independent republic.

Sources: Michele Kay, "Meet Your New President," *Austin American-Statesman,* February 25, 1996, A1; Paul Burka, "State of Mind," *Texas Monthly,* February 1996, 86.

EARLY STATEHOOD

A final peace treaty with Mexico had never been signed, and the Mexican government still considered Texas to be merely a rebellious province. Annexation of the area by the United States precipitated the Mexican War. This conflict was short and decisive. The first engagement took place at Palo Alto, near present-day Brownsville, on May 8, 1846, and Mexico City fell just four months later, on September 14. Under the Treaty of Guadalupe Hidalgo, the defeated nation relinquished all claim to Texas and, in return for $15 million, ceded all territory west of Texas and south of Oregon to the United States. One can only wonder what the value of this vast tract is today.

Acceptance of Texas into the Union was not without controversy. Since Texas permitted slavery, annexation was supported by the slave states and opposed by the states where slavery was illegal. The Whigs, soon to be succeeded by the Republicans, were generally opposed to slavery and to the admission of Texas. Democrats were generally in favor. Most Anglo-Texans had emigrated from the Southern states, where Jeffersonian Democrats dominated politics. Thomas Jefferson was a leader during the Revolution and president from 1801 to 1809. His philosophy can be summarized as, "That government is best which governs least."

No political parties, as such, existed in the Republic of Texas. Sam Houston, the hero of the battle of San Jacinto, was the dominant political figure, and political debate generally divided along pro-Houston and anti-Houston lines. But for the reasons outlined earlier, to the extent that Texans thought about national politics, most were Democrats.

By joining the United States, however, Texas plunged into the political controversy over slavery. That issue simmered at higher and higher temperatures until it boiled over with the election of an antislavery Republican, Abraham Lincoln, as president in 1860. Fearful that Republican control would mean a federal effort to emancipate their slaves, the Southern states withdrew from the Union. Texas seceded in February 1861 and joined the new Confederacy in March. Texans fought at home, on an expedition into New Mexico, and in large numbers in West Virginia, Tennessee, and elsewhere during the Civil War. Southern troops and Southern generals were usually superior to their Northern counterparts. The agricultural South, however, was outgunned, outmanned, and outsupplied by the industrial North, and Southern political leadership was inferior to Lincoln's. The U.S. president issued the Emancipation Proclamation, freeing the slaves, on January 1, 1863, an act that persuaded European powers not to enter the war on the South's behalf. As a consequence, the North ground down the South's ability to wage war over four years until the Confederacy fell apart in the spring of 1865. With the defeat of the rebellion, federal troops landed at Galveston on June 19, 1865, proclaiming the freedom of all slaves. "Juneteenth" is still celebrated by African American Texans as Emancipation Day.

POST-CIVIL WAR TEXAS

Confusion and bitterness followed the war. Despite President Lincoln's stated policy of "with malice toward none, with charity for all," the reaction in Texas, as in other parts of the South, was to continue to oppose national policy even though the war was over. Confederate officials and sympathizers were elected to state and local office; Black Codes that severely restricted the activities of the former slaves were passed by state legislatures. This defiance by the defeated South strengthened the position of the Radical Republicans in Congress and caused a hardening of policy, and Lincoln's assassination prevented him from moderating their desire to punish the states of the defunct Confederacy for their rebellion. Military government was imposed on the South, and former Confederate officials and soldiers were largely excluded from voting and from holding public office. These actions by the federal government intensified the bitterness with which most White Texans viewed the Republican Party.

African Americans, as one might expect, voted for the Republicans, giving White Texans even more reason to support the Democrats. Political activity by the freed slaves also gave rise to the Ku Klux Klan in Texas and throughout the South. Klan members met in secret, bound themselves by oath, and frequently wore hoods to conceal their identities. Their purpose was to keep African Americans in a position of great inferiority. Their methods included intimidation, violence, and sometimes murder.

The best remembered governorship of this Reconstruction period was that of E. J. Davis, one of a number of Texans who had fought for the Union during the war. A Republican, Davis held office from 1870 to 1874. Using the substantial powers granted by the Constitution of 1869, Davis acted like a true chief executive and implemented policies consistent with the philosophy of the Radical Republicans in Washington. To his credit, Davis reformed the penal system and greatly improved public education. To his discredit, during his tenure, state indebtedness increased considerably, and there were allegations of financial impropriety. But whatever the merits of his administration, to White Texans he was a traitorous agent of the hated Yankees.

In 1873, after political restrictions against former Confederate officials and soldiers were removed, a Democrat, Richard Coke, defeated Davis in his reelection bid by a two-to-one margin. Davis contested the election, and the pro-Republican state Supreme Court invalidated it on a technicality. The Democratic legislature, however, declared Coke the winner. For a time the capital city of Austin was a battleground. Coke and the legislature occupied one part of the capital, and Davis, surrounded by loyal state police, held another. Davis left office in 1874 only after President Grant refused his request for assistance. For years Texas Democrats used the Davis administration as a horrible example of what would happen if voters ever again strayed from the fold and voted Republican. Indeed, it was more than a century before another Republican governor was elected in Texas.

More important than the ouster of Davis, however, was the repudiation of the Constitution of 1869 and its replacement with Texas's current basic law, the Constitution of 1876. The adoption of this document represented the end of Reconstruction and a substantial return to the traditional principles of the Jeffersonian Democrats, including very limited government and low taxes.

THE LATE NINETEENTH CENTURY

Texas did not suffer the physical destruction that handicapped other Confederate states, and economic recovery and development came quickly after the Civil War. The Hollywood version of this era in Texas is one of cowboys, cattle drives, and range wars, and although these did exist and were important, the actual foundation of the state's economy was King Cotton. In East Texas, the fields were worked largely by African Americans, and in West Texas, by Mexican Americans. Cotton remained the cash crop and principal export well into the twentieth century.

Texas has few navigable rivers, and transportation was a major problem. Because of the size of the state, thousands of miles of railroad track were laid. In 1888 railroad construction in Texas exceeded the total for all of the other states and territories combined. In 1881 embarrassed officials discovered that the state legislature had given the railroads a million more acres of land for rights-of-way than were available, and the land-grant laws were repealed. In all, more than 32 million acres of land were given to the railroads, thus establishing early on the easy relationship between the state government and large corporations.

The railroads shipped commodities to market and in the process created new cities and industries. In 1880 the Texas and Pacific (T & P) Railroad alone purchased five hundred thousand wood crossties. Lumbering soon became the largest manufacturing activity in the state.

In 1882 Jay Gould, owner of the T & P Railroad, and Collis P. Huntington, owner of the Southern Pacific, entered into an agreement to eliminate competition and restrain trade. They secretly agreed to operate as a monopoly, purchasing all competing railroads, setting rates, dividing the market, and jointly using track. When the Texas legislature threatened to act against the monopoly, Gould made thinly disguised threats to withdraw capital from the state. The legislature did set maximum rates on freight, but the law was loosely enforced—a problem that still plagues many areas of state government.

After the mini-revolution that returned the Democrats to power in 1874, the Coke administration made drastic cuts in funding for public education and continued the tragic practice begun under Davis of leasing convicts to private contractors—pay-as-you-go penitentiaries. Despite this harsh policy, lawlessness was a problem, and Coke reestablished the Texas Rangers, which Governor Davis had changed into state police. The Rangers killed and captured many Indian raiders and outlaws, but they also treated Mexicans, Mexican Americans, and African Americans with great cruelty.

Race relations were difficult statewide, but particularly in East Texas. Jim Crow laws—a later version of the Black Codes—began to make their appearance, and in East Texas violence against the former slaves was common and often fatal. Between 1870 and 1900, an estimated 500 African Americans died as a result of mob violence, much of it led by the Ku Klux Klan. Many were lynched after being accused of crimes; sometimes the victim was later found to be innocent. Race relations and equality of treatment for all citizens continue to be problems today.

Throughout most of the final quarter of the nineteenth century, conservative Democrats maintained control of the state. Their rule was based on White supremacy and the violent emotional reaction to the Radical Republican Reconstruction era. But other political parties and interest groups rose to challenge them.

With the abuse of power by the railroads and the increase in manufacturing came organized labor. Most notable were the militant Knights of Labor, which struck the T & P Railroad in 1885 and won concessions. Another strike a year later, however, turned violent. Governor John Ireland used troops, ostensibly to protect railroad property, and the strike was broken. The union was severely criticized. In the optimistic and growing economy of the 1880s, labor unions were even less acceptable in the South than elsewhere. In Texas they were viewed as "Yankee innovations" and "abominations." Although an aggregation of capital was called a corporation and given approval by the state to operate under a charter, aggregations of labor, called unions, were frequently labeled restraints of trade by the courts and forbidden to operate. Laws and executive actions also restricted union activities. These biases in favor of capital and against organized labor are still common in Texas.

More important than early labor unions was the agrarian movement. By the 1870s and 1880s, many of those who worked the land in Texas—whether White, African American, or Mexican American—were tenant farmers. Having to borrow money for seed and supplies, they worked all year to pay back what they owed, and rarely broke even. Money and credit were scarce even for those who owned land, and railroad rates were artificially high.

The National Grange, or Patrons of Husbandry, was founded in Washington, D.C., in 1867 to try to defend farmers against this sort of economic hardship. The first chapter was established in Texas in 1872, and the organization quickly grew. Grangers were active in local politics, and the state organization lobbied the legislature on issues relevant to farmers. The Grange not only was influential in establishing Texas Agricultural & Mechanical College (now A&M University) and other educational endeavors, but also played a significant role in writing the Constitution of 1876. About half of the ninety delegates to the constitutional convention were Grangers, and they left their mark on the charter, writing provisions for a figurehead governor, restrictions on taxation and indebtedness, and provisions for the regulation of railroads. Despite hundreds of amendments, the constitution is still essentially the narrow, restrictive document created more than a century ago.

On the heels of the Grangers came the Greenback Party, which nationally supported such changes as women's suffrage and an income tax. It appealed to farmers because it championed an increase in the supply of money. In four gubernatorial elections between 1878 and 1884, the Greenback Party supplanted Republicans as runners-up to Democrats in total votes. However, it followed the pattern of most third parties in American politics: A major party—in this case, the Democrats—adopted much of its program and thus preempted its appeal and voter support.

James S. Hogg, representing a new breed of Texas politician, was elected governor in 1890 and 1892. The first native Texan to hold the state's highest office, Hogg was not a Confederate veteran. He presided over a brief period of reform that saw the establishment of the Railroad Commission, regulation of monopolies, limitations on alien ownership of land, and attempts to protect the public by regulating stocks and bonds. Unfortunately, it was also an era that saw the enactment of additional Jim Crow laws, including the requirement for segregation of African Americans from Whites on railroads.

Both major political parties were in turmoil, and in the 1890s opposition to the Democrats in Southern states was most effectively provided by the new People's, or Populist, Party. Populists advocated monetary reform, railroad regulation, control of corporations, and other programs aimed at making government responsible to the citizens. Populists reached their peak strength in Texas in 1894 and 1896, but failed to unseat the Democrats in statewide elections. The dominant party, as it had done with the Greenbackers, usurped some Populist programs, and most farmers returned to the Democratic fold. However, Populism, although not the dominant sentiment, is still influential in Texas.

Jim Hogg left the governorship in 1895, and the brief period of agrarian reform waned, due in large measure to changes in the membership of the legislature. In 1890 about half the representatives were farmers, but by 1901 two-thirds were lawyers and businessmen. The representation of these professions is even higher today (see Chapter 7).

THE EARLY TWENTIETH CENTURY

Seldom has a new century brought such sudden and important changes as the beginning of the twentieth century brought to Texas. On January 10, 1901, an oil well came in at Spindletop, near Beaumont. Oil had earlier been produced in Texas, but not on such a scale. In 1900 the state had supplied 836,000 barrels of oil—about 6 percent of the nation's production. The Spindletop field exceeded that total in a few weeks, and in its first year gushed out 3.2 million barrels.

At first Texas competed with Oklahoma and California for oil production leadership. But with the discovery of the huge (6 billion barrels) East Texas field in 1930, the Lone Star State became not only the nation's leading producer, but the world's. Oil's abundance and low price led steamship lines and railroads to abandon the burning of coal and convert to oil. Petroleum created secondary industries, such as petrochemicals and the well service business. Thousands of farm boys left home and took jobs as manual-labor "roughnecks." A few became wildcatters (independent explorers), and some of these earned fortunes. More large fields were discovered in every part of the state except the far western deserts and the central hill country. Oil, combined later with gas, replaced cotton and cattle as the state's most important industry. Severance (production) taxes became the foundation for state government revenue.

The year 1900 was noteworthy for one of the great natural disasters in American history: A hurricane that produced a tsunami ("tidal wave") and flood that killed 7,200 people in Galveston. In rebuilding from that disaster, the city's leaders devised the commission form of municipal government, which was widely copied in the early decades of the new century.

The agrarian movement had ended, but the spirit of progressivism was not completely dead. In 1903 the legislature passed the Terrell Election Law, which provided for a system of primary elections rather than the hodgepodge of practices then in use. The legislature also curtailed child labor by setting minimum ages for working in certain industries. National child labor legislation was not passed until thirteen years later. Antitrust laws were strengthened, and a pioneer pure food and drug law was enacted. Farm credit was eased, and the legislature approved a bank deposit insurance plan, a program not adopted by Washington until the 1930s.

Running counter to this progressive spirit, however, was the requirement that a poll tax be paid as a prerequisite for voting. Authorities differ as to whether African Americans, Mexican Americans, or poor Anglos were the primary target of the law, but the former were especially hard hit. African American voter turnout, estimated to be 100,000 in the 1890s, dropped to about 5,000 by 1906.

Early efforts to ensure conservation of the state's natural resources enjoyed little success. Few attempts were made to extract oil from the ground efficiently. A large majority of the oil in most reservoirs was never extracted, and some of the recovered oil was improperly stored so that it ran down the creeks or evaporated. Many improperly drilled wells polluted groundwater. The "flaring" (burning) of natural gas was commonplace into the 1940s. Fifteen million acres of virgin pine trees in East Texas were clear-cut, leading to severe soil erosion. By 1932, only a million acres of forest remained, and wood products had to be imported into the state. Conservation and environmental protection are still uphill battles in Texas.

FARMER JIM

One of the state's most colorful political figures was elected governor in 1914—James E. Ferguson, a small-town banker who identified himself as "Farmer Jim." By 1914, 62 percent of the state's farmers were tenants whose hard life and financial problems continued despite the efforts of the agrarian reformers, and despite general national prosperity. Farmer Jim, promising to limit tenant rents, was easily elected. The legislature adopted Ferguson's programs, increasing aid to rural schools and enacting a ceiling on tenant rent that was later ruled unconstitutional.

Governor Ferguson was popular and was easily reelected in 1916, despite increasing rumors of financial irregularities in his administration. He worked well with the legislature, which passed additional school legislation and created the state highway commission (later to become the Texas Department of Transportation). After the legislative session ended, Ferguson had a dispute with the Board of Regents of the University of Texas and took the drastic step of using his line-item veto power to delete from the appropriations bill all funding for the university. This generated an immediate response from the politically potent university alumni. The Travis County grand jury indicted Ferguson for misappropriation and embezzlement, and shortly thereafter the speaker of the House of Representatives called a special session of the legislature to consider impeaching Ferguson. The Texas Constitution provides that only the governor may call the legislature into special session, but the attorney general, in a critical decision, ruled that under the circumstances the speaker's action was appropriate.

The House voted twenty-one articles of impeachment, and the Senate voted for conviction on ten of these, including charges of using state funds for personal gain, depositing state funds in the Temple State Bank (which Ferguson owned), and tampering with state officials. Ferguson was removed from the governorship and barred from holding further state office. He was succeeded by the lieutenant governor, William P. Hobby.

WARS AND DEPRESSION

World War I brought major changes to Texas. The state became an important military training base, and almost 200,000 Texans volunteered for military service. Five thousand lost their lives, many dying from influenza rather than enemy action. Prohibition was a major issue, and in a special session in 1918 the legislature, to protect soldiers from alcohol and vice, passed an act prohibiting saloons within ten miles of military bases. One wit observed that that step alone would dry up 90 percent of the state. Shortly thereafter the Eighteenth Amendment to the U.S. Constitution (sponsored by Texas Senator Morris Shepherd) was ratified. Alcohol was made illegal everywhere. Texas and the nation lived under prohibition until the amendment was repealed in 1933.

With the war came nativism—hostility to immigrants and their children, especially those who were not from northwestern Europe and/or not Protestant—and superpatriotism. German-Americans were particularly suspect. A law was passed making it illegal to speak against the war effort, and Governor William Hobby vetoed the appropriation for the German Department at the University of Texas!

America's native terrorist organization, the Ku Klux Klan, flourished in the early 1920s. Originally founded to keep African Americans subjugated, after the war the Klan expanded its list of hated peoples to include immigrants and Catholics. Between 1922 and 1924 the Klan controlled every elective office in Dallas, in both city and county government. In 1922 the Klan's candidate, Earle Mayfield, was elected to the U.S. Senate. Hiram Evans of Dallas was elected imperial wizard of the national Klan, and Texas was the center of Klan power nationwide.

In 1924 disgraced former Governor Jim Ferguson attempted to run again for the governorship against a Klan-backed candidate, Judge Felix Robertson. The Texas Supreme Court ruled Ferguson ineligible, so Farmer Jim substituted his wife, Miriam, as the candidate. Mrs. Ferguson, dubbed "Ma," ran on a platform of "two governors for the price of one" and became Texas's first female chief executive. Voters also sent ninety-one new members to the

House of Representatives, ousting many Klan members, and the organization's power waned.

The administration of the governors Ferguson was filled with conflict. Jim was accused of gross favoritism in awarding highway construction contracts, and Miriam continued Jim's practice of granting clemency to criminals. In two years the governor released 3,595 convicted felons. Critics of the Fergusons claimed that "Ma pardons criminals before they're indicted."

When Alfred E. Smith, a New Yorker, a Roman Catholic, and an anti-prohibitionist, was nominated for the presidency by the Democrats in 1928, Texas party loyalty frayed for the first time since Reconstruction. Texans voted for the Republican candidate, Herbert Hoover, a Protestant and a prohibitionist. Partly because of such defections from the formerly Democratic "Solid South," Hoover won.

By the time Hoover took office in 1929, meat packing and cottonseed processing (largely for cattle feed), as well as various milling operations, had come to exceed oil in economic importance in Texas. The state annually grew more than a million bales of cotton, amounting to about 25 percent of world production.

Partly because the state was still substantially rural and agricultural, the Great Depression that began in 1929 was less severe in Texas than in more industrialized states. Further, a year after the stock market collapsed, C. M. "Dad" Joiner struck oil near Kilgore, discovering the supergiant East Texas oil field. This directly and indirectly created jobs for thousands of people. Houston became so prosperous because of the oil boom that it became known as "the city the Depression forgot."

The black gold gushing from the earth in East Texas, however, also created major problems. So much oil came from that one field so fast that it flooded the market, driving prices down. The price of oil in the middle part of the country dropped from $1.10 per barrel in 1930 to $0.25 a year later, and some lots sold for as little as a nickel a barrel. With their low overhead, the small independent producers who dominated the East Texas field could prosper under low prices by simply producing more. But the major companies, with their enormous investments in pipelines, refineries, and gas stations, faced bankruptcy if the low prices continued. The early 1930s was therefore a period of intense conflict between the large and small producers, with the former arguing for production control and the latter resisting it. The Railroad Commission attempted to force the independents to produce less, but they evaded its orders, and millions of barrels of "hot oil" flowed out of the East Texas field from 1931 to 1935.

There was much confusion and some violence before the state found a solution to the overproduction problem. In 1931 Governor Ross Sterling— a former president of the Humble Oil and Refining Company, which later became part of Exxon—declared martial law. Under the command of Jacob E. Wolters, who was also chief counsel for Texaco, National Guardsmen moved to East Texas to maintain order and enforce the production quota orders of the Railroad Commission. This move was strongly opposed by many independents and widely interpreted as a sign that the state administration was siding with the major companies. A federal court later declared Sterling's action illegal, and for a while chaos reigned in the Texas oil industry.

After much political and legal intrigue, the Railroad Commission devised a formula for "prorating" oil that limited each well to a percentage of its total production capacity. By restricting production, this regulation propped up prices, and the commodity was soon selling for over a dollar a barrel again. As part of this system of controlling production and prices, Texas Senator Tom Connally persuaded Congress to pass a "Hot Oil Act," which banned the sale in interstate commerce of oil produced in violation of state law. The major companies thus received the state-sanctioned production control upon which their survival depended. Meanwhile, the Railroad Commission was mollifying the independents by creating production regulations that favored small producers.

For four decades, the Railroad Commission was in effect the director of the Texas economy, setting production limits, and therefore price floors, for the most important industry in the state. Because Texas was such an important producer, the commission's regulations exerted a powerful effect on the world price of oil. The commission's nurturing of the state's major industry was a major reason that the Depression did not hit Texas as hard as it did many other states.

Most Texans were thus able to weather the Depression, but there were still many who were distressed. Unemployment figures for the period are incomplete, but in 1932 Governor Sterling estimated that 300,000 citizens were out of work. Private charities and local governments were unprepared to offer aid on this scale, and in Houston, African Americans and Hispanics were warned not to apply for relief, since there was only enough money to take care of Anglos. The state defaulted on interest payments on some of its bonds, and many Texas banks failed. A drought so severe as to create a dust bowl in the Southwest made matters even worse. Texans, with their long tradition of rugged individualism and their belief that "that government is best which governs least," were shaken and frustrated by these conditions.

Relief came not from state or local action but from the national administration of the new liberal Democratic president, Franklin D. Roosevelt. Texas Democrats played prominent roles in Roosevelt's New Deal (1933–1945). Vice President John Nance Garner presided over the Senate for eight years, six Texans chaired key committees in Congress, and Houston banker Jessie Jones, head of the Reconstruction Finance Corporation, was perhaps Roosevelt's most important financial adviser and administrator. The New Deal poured more than $1.5 billion into the state in programs ranging from emergency relief to rural electrification to the Civilian Conservation Corps.

In spite of the Depression, companies moved to Texas to take advantage of its cheap energy supplies, and manufacturing grew at a rate of more than 4 percent per year between 1919 and 1939. On the eve of World War II, Texas stood on the threshold of becoming one of the nation's major industrial states.

As it had during the first global conflict, Texas contributed greatly to the national effort during the Second World War from 1941 to 1945. The state was once again a major military training site; many bases and many out-of-state trainees remained after the war. More than 750,000 Texans served in the armed forces, and 32 received Congressional Medals of Honor.

Secretary of the Navy Frank Knox claimed that Texas contributed a higher percentage of its male population to military service than did any other state.

During the Depression an incident occurred that is of particular interest to students in Texas politics classes. Dr. D. C. Perry Patterson, chairman of the Department of Government at the University of Texas, was faced with the prospect of a greatly reduced budget and a consequent loss of teaching positions in the department that would force him to fire several of his colleagues. Patterson convinced the legislature to make the six semester-hour course in American Government a required class in all Texas colleges receiving public funds. He thus saved the jobs of his colleagues by imposing a degree requirement that accounts for many of you reading this book. The History Department was not able to convince the legislature to pass a similar requirement for the American history course until twenty years later, in 1956.

Audie Murphy was probably the most famous Texas soldier to serve in World War II. He was born on a farm in Hunt County, one of a poor sharecropper's nine children. His mother died when he was sixteen, and he never got past the fifth grade in school. When he enlisted in the Army at the age of eighteen in the early months of the war in 1942, he told his sister that he would "try to do his share of the fighting."

It was an understatement. Murphy won twenty-one medals in combat, making him the most decorated American fighting man in history. In January 1945, in the Alsace border region of France, he was wounded with a piece of shrapnel in the leg. Yet he stood on a burning "tank destroyer" vehicle that was loaded with gasoline and ammunition and ready to explode, holding off attacking Germans with the machine gun mounted on the vehicle. He killed so many infantrymen that the German tanks, deprived of their support, retreated. For this action he won the Congressional Medal of Honor, the nation's highest combat award.

After the war Murphy went to Hollywood and starred in several dozen movies, mostly Westerns. Probably his best role was in the 1955 film made of his own military autobiography, *To Hell and Back,* in which he played himself. He was killed in a plane crash in 1971, a few weeks before his forty-seventh birthday.

Source: Murphy's life story is told in the book *No Name on the Bullet,* by Don Graham.

SHIVERCRATS AND SEGREGATION

By 1950 profound changes had occurred in Texas society. The state's population had shifted from largely rural to 60 percent urban in the decade of the 1940s, the number of manufacturing workers had doubled, and Texas had continued to attract outside capital and new industry. Aluminum production, defense contracting, and high-technology activities were among the leaders. In 1959 Jack Kilby, an engineer employed by Texas Instruments, developed and patented the microchip, a tiny piece of technology that was to transform the world.

Texas politics continued to be colorful. In 1948, Congressman Lyndon B. Johnson opposed former Governor Coke Stevens for a vacant U.S. Senate seat.

The vote count was very close in the primary runoff, which, Texas still being dominated by the Democratic Party, was the only election that mattered. As one candidate would seem to pull ahead, another uncounted ballot box that gave the edge to his opponent would be conveniently discovered in South or East Texas. The suspense continued for three days, until Johnson finally won by a margin of eighty-seven votes. Historical research has left no doubt that the box that put Johnson over the top was the product of fraud on the part of the political machine that ruled Duval County. Among students of American politics this is probably the most famous dirty election in the history of the country. The circumstances surrounding the election have attracted so much attention because "Landslide Lyndon" Johnson went on to become majority leader of the U.S. Senate, vice president, and then in 1963 the first Texan to attain the office of president of the United States.

After the war the state's politics were increasingly controlled by conservative Democrats. The state legislature passed a so-called right-to-work law forbidding a closed shop—mandatory union membership—and in 1952 Governor Allan Shivers, a conservative Democrat, abandoned the party's presidential nominee Adlai Stevenson and led the "Shivercrats" in support of Republican Dwight Eisenhower. Part of the reason for the Democratic insurrection was ideological (Stevenson was a liberal) and part was economic. The economic dispute concerned Texas's tidelands. Valuable oil and gas fields were thought to lie under the coastal waters of the Gulf of Mexico. Texas, to gain additional revenue for the state, claimed jurisdiction twelve miles out into the gulf instead of the more widely accepted three-mile limit. The oil industry sided with the state because royalties paid to the state were lower than those paid to the federal government. After his election, Eisenhower signed a bill giving the tidelands to Texas. It was neither the first nor the last time that Texas would vote for Republican presidential candidates while under the control of conservative Democrats at home.

A former slave state, Texas was one of twenty-two states that had laws requiring racial segregation. The 1954 U.S. Supreme Court decision (*Brown* v. *Board of Education*, 347 U.S. 483) declaring segregated public schools unconstitutional caused an uproar in Texas. State leaders opposed integration, just as their predecessors had opposed Reconstruction ninety years earlier. Grade-a-year integration of the schools—a simple and effective solution—was rejected. Millions of dollars in school funds were spent in legal battles to delay the inevitable.

After World War II, Texas again experienced an influx of immigrants. Immigration in the nineteenth century had been primarily from adjacent states, Mexico, and west, central, and southern Europe. Today immigrants come not only from all fifty states but from all of Latin America and a variety of other countries, including those of the Middle East and Southeast Asia.

GRADUAL POLITICAL CHANGE

Since the 1950s, Texas has become increasingly diverse politically as well. Liberal, "progressive," or "populist" candidates such as U.S. Senator Ralph Yarborough (1957–1971), Commissioner of Agriculture Jim Hightower (1987–1991), and Governor Ann Richards (1991–1995) demonstrated that liberals could win statewide offices. Republicans also began winning, first with U.S. Senator John Tower (1961–1984) and later with Governor Bill Clements (1979–1983 and 1987–1991).

Furthermore, politicians from formerly excluded groups enjoyed increasing success, especially after the passage of the Voting Rights Act of 1965. Morris Overstreet was the first African American to be elected to statewide office, gaining a seat on the Court of Criminal Appeals in 1990. That same year, Mexican Americans Dan Morales and Raul Gonzalez were elected attorney general and justice of the supreme court, respectively. Kay Bailey Hutchison broke the gender barrier in elections to national office by being elected U.S. Senator in 1993.

CONTEMPORARY TEXAS

Texas entered a period of good times in the early 1970s. As worldwide consumption of petroleum increased fantastically, the demand for Texas oil outstripped the supply. The Railroad Commission removed market-demand production restrictions in 1972, permitting every well to produce any amount that would not damage ultimate recovery. The following year, the Organization of Petroleum Exporting Countries (OPEC) more than doubled world oil prices and boycotted the American market. Severe energy shortages developed, and the price of oil peaked at more than forty dollars per barrel. Consumers, especially those from the energy-poor Northeast, grumbled about long lines at gas stations and high prices, but the petroleum industry prospered and the state of Texas enjoyed billion-dollar treasury surpluses.

The 1980s, however, were as miserable for Texas as the previous decade had been agreeable. High oil prices stimulated a worldwide search for the black liquid, and by 1981 so many supplies had been found that the price began to fall. The slide was gradual at first, but the glut of oil was so great that in 1985 the price crashed, from its peak of over thirty dollars a barrel in the 1970s to under ten. As petroleum prices plunged, so did Texas's economy: For every one-dollar drop in world oil prices, 13,500 Texans became unemployed, the state government lost $100 million in revenue from severance taxes, and the gross state product contracted by $2.3 billion.[2] Northern consumers smiled as they filled the gas tanks of their cars, but the oil industry and the state of Texas went into shock.

The oil depression reverberated throughout the state. As its economy contracted, Texas found itself badly overbuilt in both residential and commercial construction. Since no one was buying land or buildings, developers went out of business, and the banks and savings and loans that had financed their projects died with them. In 1988, 113 banks failed, and by the spring of 1989 only one bank among the ten largest in the state had avoided being acquired by an out-of-state concern or being taken over by the national Federal Deposit Insurance Corporation. Property foreclosures set new state records in 1987 and 1988. Former Governor John Connally and former Lieutenant Governor Ben Barnes were among the thousands of Texans forced to declare bankruptcy.

---

2. "Texas a Net Loser from Falling Oil Prices, Economist Reports," *Energy Studies*, vol. 11, no. 5 (May/June 1986), 1 (newsletter of the Center for Energy Studies of the University of Texas at Austin).

Economic poverty was only one of the miseries that visited Texas in the 1980s. The state's crime rate shot up 29 percent.[3] Most of the crimes committed were related to property, and were probably a consequence of the demand for illegal drugs, which constantly increased despite intense public relations and interdiction efforts at the national level.

Texans insisted upon better law enforcement and longer sentences for convicted criminals just as the state's tax base was contracting. The combination of shrinking revenues and growing demand for services forced the political system to do the very thing it hated most: increase taxes. In 1984 the legislature raised Texas taxes by $4.8 billion. Then, faced with greatly reduced state income, it was forced to act again. First came an increase of almost $1 billion in 1986, and then in 1987 a boost of $5.7 billion, the largest state tax increase in the history of the United States up to that time. The system of raising revenue, relying even more heavily on the sales tax, became more regressive than ever. To make matters worse, the increase came just as Congress eliminated sales taxes as a deductible item on the federal income tax. By the end of the 1980s, Texans were battered, frazzled, and gloomy.

But the situation reversed itself again in the 1990s. As the petroleum industry declined, entrepreneurs created other types of businesses to take its place. Computer equipment, aerospace, industrial machinery, and scientific instruments became important parts of the economy. The state began to export more goods. Despite the fact that Texas oil production reached a fifty-year low in 1993, by the mid-1990s the economy was booming, even outperforming the nation as a whole. The boom continued through 1997, at which point the state had the eleventh largest economy in the world. The entry into a new economic era was underscored by the fact that by 1997 more Texans were employed in high-tech industries than by the oil industry.

One of the new, rising industries in Texas in the 1990s was motion-picture and television production. In 1996, forty-four projects, with budgets totaling $267.2 million, were filmed in the state. Of these, twelve were big-budget theatrical features, eighteen were made-for-television movies, miniseries, episodes, and pilots; and and fourteen were low-budget theatrical features.
Source: Ann Hornaday, "Disquiet on the Set," *Austin American-Statesman,* January 26, 1997, J1.

Even as the economy revived in the 1990s, the legislature continued to devise means of increasing the government's income. In 1991 it enacted thirty new revenue measures, including a major restructuring of the corporation franchise tax, and instituted a state lottery. The combination of these additional sources of income and the reviving economy caused government revenue to spurt upward. At the end of 1994 the comptroller (pronounced

---

3. Adapted from table on page 14 of *Crime in Texas 1992* (Austin: Texas Department of Public Safety, 1993).

"controller") reported that Texas enjoyed a $2.2 billion budget surplus. Surpluses continued through 1997.[4]

Prosperity brought another surge in immigration, and in 1994 the Lone Star State passed New York as the second most populous in the country, with 18.4 million residents.[5] Even the crime rate was down.

Texas had not suddenly turned into the promised land, however. With over 17 percent of its population living in poverty, the state still faced major economic challenges. Although the overall crime rate was lower, the tide of drugs into society showed no signs of abating. And, as will be discussed in this book, Texas still has major problems with its society and political system. But there is no doubt that its citizens are more comfortable and more optimistic now than they have been in the recent past. Whether that attitude will translate into political reform is a question that will be considered in the course of the discussion.

Texas as a Democracy

In this book, one of the major themes will be the concept of **democracy** and the extent to which Texas approaches the ideal of a democratic state. A democracy is a system of government based on the theory that political **legitimacy** is based on the people's participation. Legitimacy is the belief that people have that their government is based upon morally right principles, and that therefore they should obey its laws. According to the moral theory underlying a democratic system of government, because the people themselves (indirectly, through representatives) make the laws, they are morally obligated to obey them.

Complications of this theory abound, and a number of them will be explored later. Because some means to allow the people to participate in the government must exist, free elections, in which candidates or parties compete for the citizens' votes, are necessary. There must be some connection between what a majority of the people want and what the government actually does; how close the connection must be is a matter of some debate. Despite the importance of "majority rule" in a democracy, majorities must not be allowed to take away certain rights from minorities, such as the right to vote, the right to be treated equally under the law, and the right to freedom of speech. There is more to be said about the nature of democratic theory, and its details will be explored as specific institutions and practices are discussed over the course of the book.

Although most of them could not state it clearly, the great majority of Texans and other Americans believe in some version of the theory of democracy. That being so, it is possible to judge our state government (as it is also possible to judge our national government) according to the extent to which it approximates the ideal of a democratic society. In this book, the reality of Texas government will frequently be compared to the ideal of the democratic polity, and readers will be invited to judge whether they think Texas is a successful democracy. First, however, some more aspects of Texas society must be introduced.

---

4. "Back in the Black," *Fiscal Notes*, December 1994, (Austin: Office of the State Comptroller), 3; Peggy Fikac, "Comptroller's Revenue Estimate Exceeds Budget Proposal by Almost $2.6 Billion," *Dallas Morning News*, January 13, 1997, A8.

5. Robbie Morganfield, "Texas Passes NY," *Houston Chronicle*, December 28, 1994, 1A.

Texas and American Federalism

This book is about the politics of one state. Just as it would be impossible to describe the functions of one of the human body's organs without reference to the body as a whole, however, it would be misleading to try to analyze a state without reference to the nation. The United States has a **federal system.** This means that its governmental powers are shared among the national and state governments. A great many state responsibilities are strongly influenced by the actions of all three branches of the national government.

Education, for instance, is primarily a responsibility of state, not federal, government. Yet the national Congress influences Texas education policy through many laws that direct the state to govern the schools in a certain way, or that promise money in return for taking some action. The U.S. Supreme Court has often forced Texas schools to stop something they were doing—prayers in the classroom, for example. It has also made it necessary for them to do things they did not want to do—integrate racially, for example. Finally, the president makes many decisions that help or hinder the state in its pursuit of its own objectives. The areas in which the federal government makes an impact on Texas government are several:

1. A significant portion of state revenue each year comes from federal grants (see Chapter 13).

2. The U.S. Supreme Court oversees the actions of the state government, and, historically, has forced Texas to make many changes in its behavior, especially with regard to civil rights and liberties (see Chapter 12).

3. Congress allocates many of the "goodies" of government—military bases, veterans' hospitals, highways, etc.—which have a crucial impact on the state's economy.

4. Congress also mandates the state government to take actions, such as making public buildings accessible to handicapped people or instituting background checks on gun purchasers, that force the Texas legislature to raise and spend money.

5. When Congress declares war, or the president sends troops to a foreign conflict without a declaration of war, Texans fight and die.

6. The president has many discretionary powers, such as cutting tariffs on imported goods or releasing federal disaster-relief funds, that leave their mark, for good or ill, on the state's economy.

7. When the Federal Reserve Board raises or lowers interest rates, it constricts or stimulates Texas's economy along with the economies of the other forty-nine states. The changes thus created powerfully affect both the amount of money the state legislature has to spend and the demands on its allocation of resources.

Texas politics is thus both a whole subject unto itself and a part of a larger whole. While the focus of this book will be on Texas, there will be frequent references to actions by national institutions and politicians.

The Texas Political Culture

Like the other forty-nine states, Texas is part of a well-integrated American civil society. It is also a separate and distinctive society with its own history and present-day political system.

Culture is the product of the historical experience of a people in a particular area. Our political system is the product of our political culture. By **political culture** we mean a shared system of values, beliefs, and habits of behavior with regard to government and politics. Not everyone in a given political culture accepts all of that culture's assumptions, but everyone is affected by the beliefs and values of the dominant groups in society. Often, the culture of the majority group is imposed on members of a minority who would prefer not to live with it.

Texas's political culture is distinctive for a variety of reasons. Among the more important are the state's great size; its relative geographic isolation until the twentieth century; the fact that Texans were engaged almost continuously in warfare against Indians, Mexicans, or Yankees for the first decades of the state's history; and Texans' experience as citizens of an independent nation from 1836 to 1845. In addition, Texas shares with other Southern states its history as a society that formerly held slaves, and one that was defeated in a civil war and then occupied in a humiliating fashion by victorious Northern troops. Political culture reflects these and other aspects of our history and culture.

According to a public opinion survey conducted in the summer of 1997, if they had to choose, 23 percent of the residents of the Lone Star State would consider themselves Texans first rather than Americans first. Pollster Frank Luntz, while admitting that he has never asked this question in large surveys in other states, has employed it in smaller focus groups in those states. The results were unusable. "They just don't understand what I'm asking," he laughs.

Source: Michael Holmes, "Poll Shows Texans' Allegiance to State," *Austin American-Statesman,* July 24, 1997, B3.

There is one sense in which Texas has a well-earned reputation for uniqueness. All visitors to the state have testified to the intense state patriotism of Texans. Whatever their education, income, age, race, religion, gender, or political ideology, all Texans seem to love their state passionately. The bumper stickers that are quoted at the beginning of this chapter are examples of the public declaration of state patriotism that is common in Texas.

Whether this state patriotism is due to the myth of the Old West as peddled by novels, schools, and Hollywood, or to the state's size and geographic isolation, or to its unusual history, or to something in the water is impossible to say. This patriotism has little political relevance, since native Texans show no hostility to nonnatives, and have elected several governor. But woe to the politician who does not publicly embrace the myth that Texas is the most wonderful place to live that has ever existed on the planet! As scholars rather than politicians, the authors of this book intend to look at the state through a more realistic lens.

Not all Texans have shared the beliefs and attitudes that will be described here. In particular, as will be discussed in more detail in Chapter 5, African Americans and Mexican Americans have tended to be somewhat separate from the political culture of the dominant Anglo majority. Nevertheless, both history and present political institutions have imposed clear patterns on the assumptions that most Texans bring to politics.

Part of the larger American political tradition is a basic attitude toward government and politicians that was most famously expressed in a single sentence attributed to President Thomas Jefferson: "That government is best which governs least." As the quote from Edward Abbey at the beginning of this chapter attests, Jefferson's philosophy has a powerful presence in the United States today. The name usually given to that philosophy is *conservatism,* and it has dominated Texas politics in the twentieth century.

The term **conservatism** is complex, and its implications change with time and situation. In general, however, it refers to a general hostility to government activity, especially in the economic sphere. Most of the early White settlers came to Texas to seek their fortunes. They cared little about government and wanted no interference in their economic affairs. Their attitudes were consistent with the popular values of the Jeffersonian Democrats of the nineteenth century: The less government the better, local control of what little government there was, and freedom from economic regulation, or **laissez-faire.**

Texas conservatism minimizes the role of government in society in general and in the economy in particular. It stresses an individualism that maximizes the role of businesspeople in controlling the economy. To a Texas conservative, a good government is one that mainly keeps taxes low.

In practice, laissez-faire in Texas has often been *pseudo* (false) *laissez-faire.* Entrepreneurs don't want government to regulate or tax them, and they denounce policies to help society's less fortunate as "socialism." But when they encounter a problem that is too big for them to handle, they do not hesitate to accept government help. A good example is the city of Houston. Its leaders praise their city as the home of unrestrained, unaided free enterprise. In fact, however, Houston has historically relied upon government activity for its economic existence. The ship channel, which connects the city's port to the sea and thereby created it in an economic sense, was dredged and is maintained by government. Much of the oil industry, which was responsible for Houston's twentieth-century boom, was sustained either by state regulation through the Railroad Commission or by the federal government's selling facilities to the industry cheaply, as occurred with the Big Inch and Little Inch pipelines. Billions of dollars of federal tax money have flowed into the area to create jobs in the space industry (the Johnson Space Center and NASA).

Houston's business leaders have not resisted such government action on their behalf—quite the contrary. It is only when government tries to help ordinary people that the business community upholds the banner of laissez-faire.

Source: Joe R. Feagin, *Free Enterprise City: Houston in Political-Economic Perspective* (New Brunswick, N.Y.: Rutgers, 1988), passim.

Consistent with the emphasis on pseudo laissez-faire is a type of **social Darwinism**—the belief that individuals who prosper and rise to the top of the socioeconomic ladder are worthy and deserve their riches, while those who sink

Cartoonist Ben Sargent pokes fun at the political culture with its purportedly businesslike approach to government. Junior Mosbacher, a wealthy Republican businessman, was appointed Commissioner of the Department of Human Services. In 1990, he failed to stay within his department's budget and was then forced to substantially curtail services to the sick and the poor.

Courtesy of Ben Sargent.

to the bottom (or, having been born there, stay there) are unworthy and deserve their poverty. Social Darwinists argue that people become rich because they are intelligent, energetic, and self-disciplined, whereas those who become or remain poor do so because they are stupid, lazy, and/or given to indulgence in personal vices. Socioeconomic status, they argue, is the result of natural selection.

Of course, a person's success in life frequently *is* the result of his or her behavior and qualities of character. But it also depends on many other factors, such as education, race and ethnicity, proper diet and medical care, the wealth and education of the person's parents, and luck. Nonetheless, social Darwinism continues to dominate the thinking of many Texans.[6] They strongly resist the idea that government has an obligation to come to the aid of society's less fortunate. This resistance to government aid to the needy has resulted in many state policies that mark Texas as a state with an unusually stingy attitude toward the underprivileged. For example, among the fifty states, in the mid-1990s Texas ranked forty-eighth in its weekly payments to the mothers of poor children (AFDC), and forty-third in its average payment to poor people needing medical care (Medicaid).[7]

Pseudo laissez-faire economic doctrine and social Darwinism lead to a **trickle-down theory** of economic and social development. If business flourishes,

---

6. For a description and evaluation of social Darwinism in American culture, see Carl N. Degler, *In Search of Human Nature: The Decline and Revival of Darwinism in American Social Thought* (New York: Oxford University Press, 1991).
7. Jonathan Eig, "Economy's Climb Hasn't Aided Poor, Study Finds," *Dallas Morning News,* October 7, 1994, 1A.

so the theory goes, prosperity will follow and benefits will trickle down to the majority of Texans. In other words, if government caters to the needs of business rather than attempting to improve the lives of the poor, everyone's economic situation can be improved. To a degree, the trickle-down theory does work—but only to a degree, since about 17 percent of the state's citizens existed at or below the poverty level in the mid-1990s.[8]

There is another general attitude toward government, called **liberalism,** that accepts government activity as often a good thing. Although conservatives have dominated Texas politics through most of its history, liberals have occasionally been elected to public office, and liberal ideas have sometimes been adopted as state policy. The conflict between liberalism and conservatism underlies much political argument in the United States. We will explore the way these two ideologies have formed the basis for much of Texas politics in Chapter 5.

Economy, Taxes, and Services

When General Sheridan made his harsh evaluation of Texas in 1855, the state was poor, rural, and agricultural. As summarized earlier in this chapter, however, in the twentieth century its economy was transformed, first by the boom in the oil industry that began with the new century, then by its diversification into petrochemicals, aerospace, computers, and many other industries. Metropolitan areas boomed along with the economy, and the state became the second most populous in the nation.

The state's political culture, however, has not changed as rapidly as its population and its economy. Texas's basic conservatism is evident in the way the state government treats business and industry. In 1996, a private firm conducted a nationwide survey to determine how favorable a "business climate" each of the states had created. North Carolina was found to have the most favorable business climate, with Texas second.[9]

But while in the short run a "favorable business climate" consists of low taxes, weak labor unions, and an inactive government, in the long run these policies may create a fragile economy. In particular, the state's toleration of a terrible public education system is damaging its future. In its 1990 annual report, the Corporation for Enterprise Development (CED), a nonprofit group, gave Texas a very poor report card: D for economic performance, C for vitality, B for capacity, and F for state policy. Doug Ross, president of CED, was particularly critical of the educational system: "The quality of the work force and skill levels, both products of the school system, are still among the worst in the United States." Ross asserted that the most alarming condition was the inactivity of the state's policy makers in Austin.[10]

---

8. Bob Dart, "Texans' Income Up, Poverty Rate Down," *Austin American-Statesman,* September 27, 1996, A7.

9. Steve Brown, "Texas No. 2 on List of Best Business Sites," *Dallas Morning News,* October 2, 1996, D1.

10. Robert Dodge, "Texas Fails to Make Grades," *Dallas Morning News,* April 6, 1990, 1D. The topic of *economic performance* included employment, earnings, and equity; *vitality* referred to competitiveness, entrepreneurism, and diversity; *capacity* referred to human resources, technology, finance, and infrastructure and amenities; and *state policy* encompassed governance, tax and fiscal policy, education, capital, enterprises, and treatment of the disadvantaged.

TABLE 1–1

Texas Rank among States in Expenditure and Taxation

Category	Year	Rank
a. Per capita state government expenditure	1996	50
b. Teacher salaries	1996	36
c. Medicaid benefits	1994	43
d. Per-pupil expenditure	1993	37
e. Funding for mental health and retardation	1993	50
f. Tax rate on the poor	1996	6
g. Tax rate on the rich	1996	40

SOURCES: a: Jennifer Bradley, "Texas Offers Glimpse of Post-Welfare State," *Austin American-Statesman,* March 12, 1996, A9; b: Peggy Fikac, "Group: Better Pay Needed to Curtail Teacher Shortage," *Austin American-Statesman,* January 25, 1997, B10; c: *The American Almanac, 1996–1997* (Statistical Abstract of the United States) (Washington, D.C.: U.S. Bureau of the Census, 1996), Table 167, p. 117; d: Michelle Mittelstadt, "Study Says Big Jump in Funding Hasn't Paid Off for Texas Schools," *Dallas Morning News,* September 10, 1993, 23A; e: Jim Hightower, "Re-building the Democrats," *Texas Observer,* July 16, 1993, 7; f: Michael P. Ettinger, Robert S. McIntyre, Elizabeth A. Fray, John F. O'Hare, Julie King, and Neil Miransky, *Who Pays? A Distributional Analysis of the Tax System in All 50 States* (Washington, D.C.: Citizens for Tax Justice, Institute on Taxation and Economic Policy, 1996), p. 2 ("poor" here defined as the bottom 20 percent of the population); g: Ibid., Appendix I ("rich" here defined as the top 1 percent of the population).

By 1996, despite a great deal of public argument about education policy, Texas was still not doing an impressive job of educating its children. The state ranked thirty-ninth among the fifty states in the percentage of high school graduates and thirty-third in percentage of college graduates. A survey of 250 North Texas manufacturers conducted the previous year showed that their biggest concern was a lack of adequate skills in the workforce.[11]

For most of the twentieth century, Texas could rely upon its vast petroleum reserves to bring it prosperity. With seemingly endless gushers of oil supplying them with jobs and their government with revenue, Texans believed that they did not have to worry about policies to create a high-quality workforce, or the taxes necessary to pay for such policies. They have yet to come to terms with the implications of current economic trends, which suggest that states without an educated citizenry will inevitably decline into Third World status.

Just as Texas's Jeffersonian conservative government has a minimalist approach to education, it also does little, in comparison to the governments of other states, to improve the lives of its citizens. As Table 1–1 illustrates, on several measures of state services, Texas ranks near the bottom.

The philosophy that dominates Texas politics holds that if government will just keep taxes low and stay out of the way, society will take care of itself. The available evidence, however, suggests that Texas's laissez-faire ideology

---

11. Terrence Stutz, "State Board Targets Adult Illiteracy," *Dallas Morning News,* March 11, 1994, 23A; Bill Hobby, "Economically Robust Now, Texas Faces Uncertain Future," *Austin American-Statesman,* January 25, 1996, A11.

TABLE 1–2

Texas Rank in Measures of Quality of Life

Measure of Quality of Life	Year	Rank
a. Number of deaths on the job	1996	1
b. Percentage of children without health insurance	1996	1
c. High school graduation rate	1996	48
d. Toxic emissions	1995	1
e. Percentage of population in poverty	1995	5
f. Health of population	1994	32
g. Scholastic Aptitude Test scores	1993	42
h. Adult literacy	1993	47
i. Immunization of preschool children	1992	50

SOURCES: a: Matthew Cooper, "So Long 'Dallas,' Hello High Tech," *Newsweek,* April 21, 1997, 32; b: Chip Brown, "Texas Leads U.S. in Percentage of Uninsured Kids," *Austin American-Statesman,* March 29, 1997, B4; c: Jon M. Roberts, "Incentives for Development Shouldn't Compromise Future," *Austin American-Statesman,* August 9, 1996, A15; d: Jennifer Files, "Texas Tops List on Toxic Emissions," *Dallas Morning News,* January 29, 1996, 1D; e: Eleanor Baugher and Leatha Lamison-White, "Poverty in the United States: 1995" (Washington, D.C.: U.S. Bureau of the Census, 1996), Table B, p. IX; f: Harold A. Hovey, *State Fact Finder: Rankings across America* (Washington, D.C.: Congressional Quarterly, 1996), Table I–3; g: Michelle Mittelstadt, "Study Says Big Jump in Funding Hasn't Paid Off for Texas Schools," *Dallas Morning News,* September 10, 1993, 23A; h: Jim Hightower, "Rebuilding the Democrats," *Texas Observer,* July 16, 1993, 7; i: David Elliott, "Texas Child-Care Record 'Deplorable,'" *Austin American-Statesman,* December 25, 1992, A1.

may have had a pernicious effect on its quality of life. As Table 1–2 emphasizes, Texas ranks low not only in educational attainment, but in child immunization, efforts to control air pollution, and many other measures of civilized living. Texans as a group are so patriotic that it is difficult for them to believe that their state is a comparatively undesirable place to live. But the evidence is consistent: One study that evaluated all fifty states on such criteria as crime rate and the cost of living ranked Texas thirty-third on the list of "Most Livable States."[12]

Texas state government is therefore faced with serious problems in preparing its citizens and society for the future. So far, it has demonstrated little inclination to deal with them. The greatest accomplishment of Texas state government through the twentieth century has been to keep taxes low—although, when state and local taxes are added together, Texans' tax burden ranks about in the middle of the fifty states.[13] As Texans approach the twenty-first century, they have to wonder if low state taxes are enough of an achievement.

12. Reported in Diane Jennings, "Job-Seekers Making Tracks to Texas Again," *Dallas Morning News,* September 5, 1994, 1A.
13. Jane Seaberry, "Bursting the Myth," *Dallas Morning News,* April 29, 1997, D3.

The People of Texas

In many ways Texas is the classic American melting pot of different peoples, although it occasionally seems more like a boiling cauldron. The state was originally populated by various Indian tribes. In the sixteenth and seventeenth centuries the Spaniards conquered the land, and from the intermingling of the conquerors and the conquered came the "mestizos," persons of mixed Spanish and Indian blood. In the nineteenth century Anglo Saxons wrested the land from the heirs of the Spaniards. They often brought with them Black slaves. Soon waves of immigration arrived from Europe and Asia, and more mestizos came from Mexico. After a brief outflow of population as a result of the oil price depression of the late 1980s, the long-term pattern of immigration resumed and brought many more thousands to the state in the early 1990s.

THE 1990 CENSUS

At the end of each decade the national government takes a census of each state's population. The census itself is a hot political topic because it is the basis for distributing money from many federal programs, and also for allocating seats in both the U.S. House of Representatives and the state legislatures. Critics of the census charge that it misses millions of poor people, especially those for whom English is not the first language. Local authorities claimed that the population of Texas was undercounted by about 600,000 people in 1980.

The 1990 census was also the subject of political wrangling, and the final figures eventually had to be ratified by the courts. Table 1–3 shows the official 1980 and 1990 figures for Texas. The increase in population indicated in the table entitled Texas to three additional seats in the U.S. House, bringing the state's total to thirty.

The U.S. Census Bureau makes unofficial population estimates between the counts it makes at the end of each decade. By its 1996 estimate, the Texas population had soared past 19 million, making it the second largest state (after California at almost 32 million, and the fastest growing of all fifty. More than one-third of the present population consists of African Americans

TABLE 1–3

The Texas Population, 1980 and 1990

Ethnic Group	1980	1990	% of 1990 Population	% Increase
Anglo	9,350,297	10,291,680	60.6	10.1
Hispanic*	2,985,824	4,339,905	25.6	45.4
African American	1,692,542	1,976,360	11.6	16.8
Other	200,528	378,565	2.2	88.8
TOTAL	14,229,191	16,986,510		19.4

*The great majority of Hispanics in Texas are Mexican American.
SOURCE: *1992–93 Texas Almanac and State Industrial Guide* (Dallas: A. H. Belo Corp., 1991), 137.

FIGURE 1–1
**Texas's Hispanic
Population as a
Percentage of Total
Population by
Counties, 1990**

*Source: Texas Legislative Coun-
cil, based on 1990 census data.*

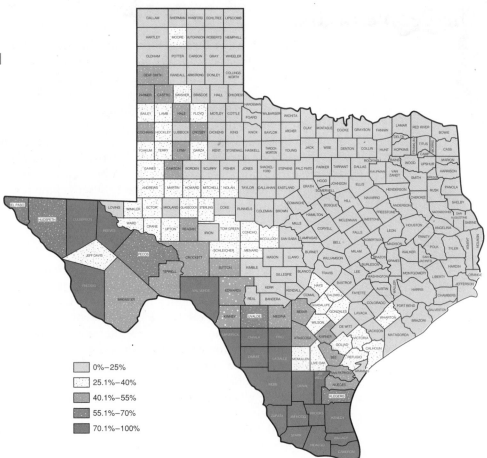

Legend:
- 0%–25%
- 25.1%–40%
- 40.1%–55%
- 55.1%–70%
- 70.1%–100%

(11.6 percent) or Mexican Americans (25.5 percent). By 2010, these minority groups are expected to account for one-half of the state's population, with most of the increase being among Mexican Americans.

THE DISTRIBUTION OF POPULATION

The distribution of population in Texas shows evidence of three things: the initial pattern of migration, the influence of geography and climate, and the location of the cities. The Hispanic migration came first, north from Mexico, and to this day is still concentrated in South and West Texas (Figure 1–1). Likewise, African Americans still live predominantly in the eastern half of the state (Figure 1–2).

As one moves from east to west across Texas, annual rainfall drops by about five inches per hundred miles. East Texas has a moist climate and supports intensive farming, whereas West Texas is dry and requires pumping from underground aquifers to maintain agriculture. The overall distribution of settlement reflects the food production capability of the local areas, with

FIGURE 1–2

Texas's African American Population as a Percentage of Total Population by Counties, 1990

Source: Texas Legislative Council, based on 1990 census data.

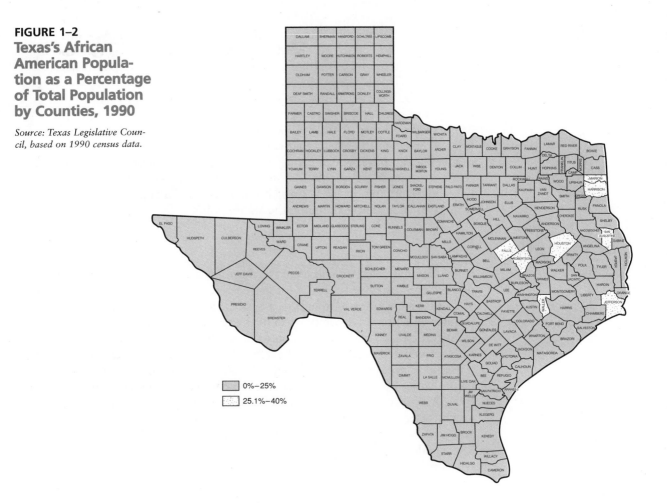

Legend:
- 0%–25%
- 25.1%–40%

East Texas remaining far more populous. Cities developed at strategic locations, usually on rivers or the seacoast, and the state's population is heavily concentrated in the urban areas.

THE POLITICAL RELEVANCE OF POPULATION

Dividing the Texas population into Anglos, Mexican Americans, and African Americans reflects political realities. Historically, both minority groups have been treated badly by the Anglo majority. Today, the members of both groups are, in general, less wealthy than Anglos. For example, according to the 1990 census, the mean household income of Anglos was about twice that for Mexican Americans. Foreign-born Mexicans, especially, were four times as likely to live below the poverty line as were Anglos.[14]

14. *Latinos in Texas: A Socio-Demographic Profile* (Austin: The Tomas Rivera Center, 1995), 66, 84, 111.

Political differences often accompany economic divisions. As will be discussed in Chapters 4, 5, and 6, Mexican Americans and African Americans tend to hold more liberal political opinions than do Anglos, and to vote accordingly. This is not to say that there are no conservative minority citizens and no liberal Anglos. There are tens of thousands of Texans who do not conform to statistical generalizations. Nevertheless, looked at as groups, Mexican Americans, African Americans, and Anglos do display general patterns of belief and behavior that can be discussed without being unfair to individual exceptions. As a result, as the minority population increases in size relative to the Anglo population, its greater liberalism is sure to make itself felt, sooner or later, in the voting booth. Texas's changing mix of population is therefore constantly changing the state's politics.

The Agenda

The following chapters will examine the ways Texas organizes and operates politically to attempt to deal with its social and economic problems. There will also be a cautious attempt to assess the state's future prospects. Every chapter will contain a comparison of the reality of Texas politics to the democratic ideal, and a discussion of how defensible the reality is. The topics to be considered are, in order, the Texas Constitution and local government, the state's important interest groups, the activities of political parties, and the individual voter within the context of campaigns and elections. Next, the focus will shift to the institutions of state government—the legislature, the executive branch, and the judiciary. A consideration of how the state raises and spends its money, and other important issues of public policy, will follow. Finally, an attempt will be made to suggest some challenges the state will face in the future.

Summary

This chapter began with a summary of the history of Texas, with emphasis upon important political events and the development of the economy. The discussion then shifted to the topic of democratic theory, which holds that the legitimacy of a government rests upon the citizens' participation, and to the topic of Texas's place in the American federal system.

The focus then moved to the state's conservative political culture. As a result of its political culture, ran the argument, there is a preference in Texas for the less-government-is-better approach, pseudo laissez-faire, social Darwinism, and the trickle-down theory of economic and social development. The twin results are an inactive government and a relatively poor quality of life, compared to that in many other states.

Texas has a large and diverse population that continues to grow and change. Insofar as the future can be predicted, it seems that the population will continue to grow, with an increasingly large non-Anglo, and especially Hispanic, component.

Key Terms

Conservatism   Laissez-faire   Pseudo laissez-faire

Democracy   Legitimacy   Social Darwinism

Federal system   Liberalism   Trickle-down theory

Impresario   Political culture

Study Questions

1. Can you see anything in Texas's history that might account for the fact that Texans tend to have an unusually intense state patriotism?

2. What habits of thought and behavior do you think the citizens must share in order for a country or state to sustain a democracy?

3. Could a king be legitimate? According to what theory?

4. Describe the basic features of a conservative political culture. Describe the basic features of a liberal political culture.

5. In your family and community, which political culture would you say dominates?

6. How do you think the Texas political culture differs from the political culture of the United States as a whole?

7. In general, what has been Texas's historical policy toward business (the economy)? Toward taxes? Toward education? Toward welfare? Toward environmental protection?

8. Would you say that the evidence supports the opinion that Texas is a better place to live than other states?

9. Why is the U.S. census so important to Texas politics? In another ten to twenty years, present-day minority groups will constitute a majority of the Texas population. What effects might this change have on the state's politics and government?

Internet Assignment

Internet site: http://www.lsjunction.com/

Go to the "Lone Star Junction" history site. Click on the "Scrapbook." Inside you will find historical facts about Texas (e.g., flags, Rangers, and Constitution). What sorts of facts and values are given? What sorts are not given?

Chapter Two

The Constitutional Setting

This faded tableau is the only pictorial record remaining of the ninety delegates who wrote the Texas Constitution. Three of the delegates were freed slaves. African Americans would not again participate in statewide politics for almost a century.

All political power is inherent in the people, and all free governments are founded on their authority, and instituted for their benefit.

> Article I, Texas Constitution

It is very doubtful whether man is enough of a political animal to produce a good, sensible, serious and efficient constitution. All the evidence is against it.

> George Bernard Shaw
> English dramatist

Introduction

Since its ratification in 1789, the Constitution of the United States frequently has been used as a model by emerging nations. State constitutions, however, seldom enjoy such admiration. Indeed, the constitution of the state of Texas is more often ridiculed than praised because of its length, its obscurity, and its outdated, unworkable provisions.

Such criticism of state constitutions is common. The political circumstances that surrounded the writing of the national Constitution differed considerably from those that existed at the times when many of the fifty states—especially those of the old Confederacy—were writing their constitutions. State constitutions tend to be very rigid and to include too many specific details. As a result, Texas and many other states must resort to frequent **constitutional amendments,** which are formal changes in the basic governing document.

In federal systems, which are systems of government that provide for a division and sharing of powers between a national government and state or regional governments, the constitutions of the states complement the national constitution. Article VI of the U.S. Constitution provides that the Constitution, laws, and treaties of the national government take precedence over the constitutions and laws of the states. This provision is known as the "supremacy of the laws" clause. Many states, including Texas, have constitutional and statutory provisions that conflict with federal laws, but these are unenforceable because of Article VI. Although the national Constitution is supreme, state constitutions are still important because state governments are responsible for many basic programs and services, such as education, that daily affect citizens. A major difference between the U.S. and Texas constitutions is the generality of the national document and the statutelike specificity of the state charter.

A **constitution** is the basic law of a state or nation that outlines the primary structure and functions of government; thus, the purposes of all constitutions are the same. This chapter will examine those purposes, as well as outline the development of the several Texas constitutions. It will elaborate the principal features of the state's current document, briefly trace the movement for constitutional reform in Texas, and provide an overview of constitutional politics.

Purposes of Constitutions

LEGITIMACY

The first purpose served by a constitution is to give legitimacy to the government. Legitimacy is the most abstract and ambiguous purpose served by constitutions. Legitimacy derives from agreed-upon purposes of government and from government keeping its actions within the guidelines of these purposes. The constitution contributes to this legitimacy by "putting it down on paper." A government has legitimacy when the governed accept its acts as moral, fair, and just, and thus believe that they should obey its laws. This acceptance cuts two ways. On the one hand, citizens will allow government to act in certain ways that are not permitted to private individuals. For example, citizens cannot legally drive down a city street at sixty miles an hour, but police officers may do so when in the act of pursuing wrongdoers. Proprietors of private schools cannot command local residents to make financial contributions to their schools, but these same residents pay taxes to support public schools.

Public regard for what is legal is dynamic. For example, traditionally Texans were unable to carry a concealed weapon legally, although police detectives could do so. However, the 1995 legislature passed a "right to carry" bill allowing ordinary citizens who had passed certain requirements and paid a fee to carry concealed weapons.

On the other hand, citizens also expect governments not to act arbitrarily; the concept of legitimacy is closely associated with limiting government. If the police officer sped down a city street at ninety miles an hour just for the thrill of doing so, or if citizens were burdened with confiscatory school taxes, these acts probably would fall outside the bounds of legitimacy.

What citizens are willing to accept is conditioned by their history and their political tradition. In Texas and the remainder of the United States, democratic practices including citizen participation in decision making and fair processes are a part of that history and culture. Even within that broad acceptance of democratic principles, legitimacy varies from nation to nation, and even from state to state. In England, for example, most police do not carry weapons; in California pedestrians have absolute right-of-way in crossing streets.

ORGANIZING GOVERNMENT

The second purpose of constitutions is to organize government. Governments must be organized in some way that clarifies who the major officials are, how they are selected, and what the relationships are among those charged with basic governmental functions. Again, to some extent, the American states have been guided by the national model. For example, both incorporate **separation** of powers with a system of **checks and balances** to ensure that each separate branch of government can be restrained by the others. In reality, separate institutions and defined lines of authority lead to a sharing of powers. For example, passing bills is thought of as a legislative function, but the governor can veto a bill.

Each state has an elected chief executive. Each state except Nebraska has a legislative body composed of two houses, usually a house of representatives and a senate. Each state has a judicial system with some sort of supreme court. Just as the U.S. Constitution includes many provisions that establish the relationship between the nation and the states, state constitutions include similar provisions with respect to local governments. The organizational provisions of state constitutions vary widely and invariably reflect the political attitudes prevalent at the time the constitutions were adopted.

PROVIDING POWER

Article I, Section 8, of the Constitution of the United States expressly grants certain powers to the national government and implies a broad range of additional powers through the "necessary and proper clause." This clause, also known as the "elastic clause," enables Congress to execute all its other powers by giving it broad authority to pass needed legislation. Thus, granting specific powers is the third purpose of constitutions. The Tenth Amendment reserves for the people or for the states powers not explicitly or implicitly granted to the national government. As the U.S. Constitution has been developed and interpreted, many powers exist concurrently for both the federal and the state levels of government—the power to assess taxes on gasoline, for example. Within this general framework, which continues to evolve, the Texas Constitution sets forth specific functions for which the state maintains primary or concurrent responsibility. Local government, criminal law, and regulation of intrastate commerce illustrate the diversity of the activities over which the state retains principal control.

A combination of factors has reduced the power of state officials, however. For example, the federal government's widespread use of its interstate commerce powers has limited the range of commercial activities still considered strictly intrastate. The application of the **Bill of Rights**—the first ten amendments to the U.S. Constitution—has compelled changes in the criminal justice systems of the states. In addition, many socioeconomic matters such as energy use, civil rights, and urbanism are now considered beyond the ability of individual states to deal with. Thus, they are increasingly viewed as a responsibility of government at the national level. Nevertheless, the fundamental law of the state spells out many areas for state and local action. Which, if any, of the broad problems the national government addresses depends on the prevailing Washington political philosophy, the party that controls Congress, the national administration, and who sits on the U.S. Supreme Court.

LIMITING GOVERNMENTAL POWER

American insistence on the fourth purpose of constitutions—limiting governmental power—reflects the influence of British political culture, our ancestors' dissatisfaction with colonial rule, and the extraordinary individualism that characterized national development during the eighteenth and nineteenth centuries. In Texas, the conservative political tradition resulted in a heavy emphasis on limiting government's ability to act. For example, the governor has very little power to remove members of state boards and commissions except by informal techniques such as an aggressive public relations campaign against a board member. This belief in limited government continues to wax strong as the millennium approaches. Citizens want less government regulation and more controls on spending.

Chief among the guarantees against arbitrary governmental action is the national Bill of Rights. It was quickly added to the original U.S. Constitution to ensure both adequate safeguards for the people and ratification of the Constitution. The Texas Bill of Rights, included as Article I in the Texas Constitution, resembles the national Bill of Rights. Later amendments to the national Constitution have extended guarantees in several areas, especially due process and equal protection of the laws, racial equality, and voting rights. In Texas, reactions to post-Civil War Reconstruction rule were so keen at the time the current constitution was written that the document contains many specific and picayune limitations. The creation of certain hospital districts and the payment of pensions to veterans of the war of independence from Mexico are examples. Such specificities have made frequent amendments necessary and have hamstrung legislative action in many areas.

Texas Constitutions

The United States has had two fundamental laws: the short-lived Articles of Confederation and the present Constitution. Texas is currently governed by its sixth constitution, ratified in 1876.[1] The fact that the 1876 constitution had five predecessors in only forty years illustrates the political turbulence of the mid-1800s. Table 2–1 lists the six Texas state charters.

Having been governed by Spain for 131 years and by Mexico for 15, Texans issued a declaration of independence on March 2, 1836. This declaration stated that "the people of Texas, do now constitute a Free, Sovereign, and Independent Republic, and are fully invested with all the rights and attributes which properly belong to independent nations." After a brief but bitter war with Mexico, Texas gained independence on April 21 after the Battle of San Jacinto. Independence was formalized when the two Treaties of Velasco were signed by Mexican President Antonio López de Santa Anna and Texas President David Burnet on May 14, 1836. By September, the Constitution of the Republic of Texas, drafted shortly after independence was declared, had been implemented. Major features of this charter paralleled those of the U.S. Constitution, including a president and a congress, but the document also guaranteed the continuation of slavery.

The United States had been sympathetic to the Texas struggle for independence. However, admission to the Union was postponed for a decade

---

1. Texas was governed by Mexico from 1821 to 1836. Beginning in 1824, the Mexican Congress, acting under the Mexican Constitution, joined Texas and Coahuila, with Saltillo as the capital. That arrangement prevailed until independence in 1836. Thus, Texas was also governed by a seventh constitution, albeit as a colony, not as an independent nation or a state.

TABLE 2–1

Constitutions of Texas

Constitution	Dates
Republic of Texas	1836–1845
Statehood	1845–1861
Civil War	1861–1866
Reconstruction	1866–1869
Radical Reconstruction	1869–1876
State of Texas	1876–present

because of Northern opposition to admission of a new slave state. After ten years of nationhood, Texas was finally admitted into the Union. The Constitution of 1845, the "statehood constitution," was modeled after the constitutions of other Southern states. It was regarded as one of the nation's best at the time. The Constitution of 1845 not only embraced democratic principles of participation but also included many elements later associated with the twentieth-century administrative reform movement and was a very brief, clear document.[2]

The Constitution of 1845 was influenced by Jacksonian democracy, named for President Andrew Jackson. Jacksonians believed in an expansion of participation in government, at least for White males.[3] Jackson's basic beliefs ultimately led to the spoils system of appointing to office those who had supported the winning candidates in the election ("to the victors belong the spoils"). Jacksonian democracy also produced long ballots, with almost every office up for popular vote, short terms of office, and the expansion of voting rights. Thus, while participatory, Jacksonianism was not flawless.

 Because Texas was an independent republic when the United States annexed it, the annexation agreement reflected compromises by both the state and the national governments. For example, Texas gave up its military property but kept its public lands. The national government refused to assume the state's $10 million debt. Texas, however, can carve four additional states out of its territory should the state want such a division.

When Texas joined the Confederate States of America in 1861, the constitution was modified again. This document, the Civil War Constitution of 1861, merely altered the Constitution of 1845 to ensure greater protection for the institution of slavery and to declare allegiance to the Confederacy.

---

2. See, for example, Fred Gantt, Jr., *The Chief Executive in Texas: A Study in Gubernatorial Leadership* (Austin: University of Texas Press, 1964), 24.
3. The Jacksonians supported slavery and the brutal treatment of Indians.

Texas was on the losing side of the Civil War and was occupied by federal troops (see Chapter 1). President Andrew Johnson ordered Texas to construct yet another constitution. The 1866 document declared secession illegal, repudiated the war debt to the Confederacy, and abolished slavery, although it did not provide for improving conditions for African Americans. In other words, the state made only those changes that were necessary to gain presidential support for readmission to the Union.

Radical postwar congressional leaders were not satisfied with these minimal changes in the constitutions of Southern states. They insisted on more punitive measures. In 1868–1869, a constitution that centralized power in the state government, provided generous salaries for officials, stipulated appointed judges, and called for annual legislative sessions was drafted. It contained many elements that present-day reformers would like to see in a revised state charter. Because the constitution was forced on the state by outsiders in Washington and by carpetbaggers—Northerners who came to Texas with their worldly goods in a suitcase made out of carpeting—White Southerners never regarded the document as acceptable. They especially resented the strong, centralized state government and the powerful office of governor that were imposed on them. However, because all former rebels were barred from voting, the Constitution of 1869 was adopted by Unionists and African Americans. Ironically, this constitution least accomplished the purpose of legitimacy—acceptance by the people—but was the most forward-looking in terms of power and organization.

The Present Texas Constitution

Traditionally Democratic as well as conservative, Texans began to chafe for **constitutional revision**—changes to reform or make better the basic document—when the Democrats regained legislative control in 1872. An 1874 reform effort passed in the Texas Senate but failed in the House. This constitution would have provided flexibility in such areas as how tax dollars could be spent and terms of office. It also would have facilitated elite control and a sellout to the powerful railroads, which were hated by ordinary citizens because of their pricing policies and corruption of state legislatures.[4] The legislature called a constitutional convention and ninety delegates were elected from all over the state. The convention members were overwhelmingly conservative and reflected the "retrenchment and reform" philosophy of the Grange, which was one of several organizations of farmers. This conservatism included a belief in White supremacy and a strong emphasis on the constitutional purpose of limiting government. As noted in Chapter 1, the Southern farmers were determined to prevent future state governments from oppressing them as they believed they had been oppressed under Reconstruction.

Accordingly, the new constitution, completed in 1875, curbed the powers of government. The governor's term was limited to two years. A state debt ceiling of $200,000 was established. Salaries of elected state officials were

---

4. Historical perspectives are based on remarks of John W. Mauer, "State Constitutions in a Time of Crisis: The Case of the Constitution of 1876," Symposium on the Texas Constitution, sponsored by the University of Texas Law School and the *Texas Law Review,* October 7, 1989.

fixed. The legislature was limited to biennial sessions, and the governor was allowed to make very few executive appointments.

When this document went to the people of Texas for a vote in February 1876, it was approved by a margin of 136,606 to 56,652; 130 of the 150 Texas counties registered approval. All the ratifying counties were rural areas that were committed to the Grange and would benefit from the new constitution. The 20 counties that did not favor the new charter were urban areas where newspaper criticism of the proposed document had been severe and heavily Republican areas.[5]

GENERAL FEATURES

The Texas Constitution of today is very much like the original 1876 document in spite of 377 amendments by the end of 1997 and some major changes in the executive article. It includes a preamble and sixteen articles, with each article divided into subsections (see Table 2–2).[6] When the Texas Constitution was drafted over a century ago, it incorporated protection for various private interests. It also included many details of policy and governmental organization to avoid abuse of government powers. The result is a

TABLE 2–2

Articles of the Texas Constitution

I.	Bill of Rights
II.	The Powers of Government
III.	Legislative Department
IV.	Executive Department
V.	Judicial Department
VI.	Suffrage
VII.	Education [and] the Free Public Schools
VIII.	Taxation and Revenue
IX.	Counties
X.	Railroads
XI.	Municipal Corporations
XII.	Private Corporations
{XIII.	Spanish and Mexican Land Titles—*deleted by amendment in 1969*}
XIV.	Public Lands and Land Office
XV.	Impeachment
XVI.	General Provisions
XVII.	Mode of Amending the Constitution of the State

5. Wilbourn E. Benton, *Texas Politics: Constraints and Opportunities* (Chicago: Nelson-Hall, 1984), 51.
6. Because of its length, the entire Texas Constitution is rarely reproduced. However, the *Texas Almanac and State Industrial Guide* (published every two years by the *Dallas Morning News*) always includes the complete text as well as a history of recent amendments.

very long, poorly organized document that does not draw clear lines of responsibility for government actions. As an example of details that might be contained better in legislation than in constitutional law, Article V, Section 18 spells out procedures for electing justices of the peace and constables. These provisions have been amended four times; one amendment allows Chambers County the flexibility to have between two and six justice of the peace precincts.

The Texas Constitution reflects the time of its writing, an era of strong conservative, agrarian interests. It was a reaction to the carpetbagger rule of Governor E. J. Davis, a former Union general. Changes in the national Constitution, both by amendment and by judicial interpretation, have required alterations of the state constitution, although provisions that conflict with federal law remain. These unenforceable provisions, along with other provisions that are so out of date that they will never again be enforced, are known as deadwood. The last systematic cleanup effort was in 1977, when the sixty-fifth Texas Legislature began, but did not complete, work on removing deadwood provisions through the formal amending process.

The public had voted on 548 proposed amendments by the end of 1997, resulting in the addition of 377 amendments. These amendments have produced a state charter that is poorly organized and difficult to read, much less interpret, even by the courts.[7] Yet, the amendments are necessary because of the restrictiveness of the constitution.

The Lone Star State can almost claim the record for the longest constitution in the nation. Only the constitution of Alabama contains more words than the 81,000-plus in the Texas charter.[8]

SPECIFIC FEATURES

The Texas Constitution is similar in many ways to the U.S. Constitution, particularly the way in which the purposes of organizing and limiting government and legitimacy are addressed. That is, the two governments are organized similarly: Each has executive, legislative, and judicial branches. Both are separation of powers systems; that is, they have separate institutions that share powers. Both include provisions against unequal or arbitrary government action, such as restricting freedom of religion. The two documents are less alike in terms of the purpose of providing power to government. The national Constitution is much more flexible in allowing government to act than is the state document. Texas legislators, for example, cannot set their own salaries.[9] Thus, George Bernard Shaw's assertion in the chapter-opening quotation was more nearly correct with regard to state constitutions than with regard to the U.S. national constitution.

---

7. A full discussion of poorly organized sections and provisions in conflict with federal law can be found in *Reorganized Texas Constitution without Substantive Change* (Austin: Texas Advisory Commission on Intergovernmental Relations, 1977).
8. The Alabama Constitution had approximately 220,000 words as of 1996. This and other comparative information can be found in *The Book of the States, 1996–97*, vol. 31 (Lexington, Ky.: Council of State Governments, 1996), 3.
9. The definitive study of the Texas constitution is Janice C. May, *The Texas State Constitution, A Reference Guide* (Westport, Conn.: Greenwood Publishing Group, 1996).

Cartoonist Ben Sargent pokes fun at the fact that the Texas Constitution had been amended 377 times by the end of 1997 and that in recent years voters have had to familiarize themselves with as many as twenty-eight amendments in a single election.

Courtesy of Ben Sargent.

BILL OF RIGHTS

Like the national Bill of Rights, Article I of the Texas Constitution provides for equality under the law; religious freedom, including separation of church and state;[10] due process for the criminally accused; and freedom of speech and of the press. Among its thirty protections, it further provides protection for the mentally incompetent and provides several specific guarantees, such as prohibition against outlawing an individual from the state.

---

10. Article I, Section 4, stipulates acknowledgment of the existence of a Supreme Being as a test for public office; however, this provision is not enforced because it violates the U.S. Constitution.

Citizens generally support the U.S. and Texas bills of rights. However, just as the public sometimes gets upset with the U.S. Bill of Rights when constitutional protections are afforded to someone the public wants to "throw the book at"—an accused child molester, for example—Texans sometimes balk at the protections provided in the state constitution. A 1992 Texas Poll revealed that, if given a chance to vote on the Bill of Rights today, "a signficant number of Texans would balk at several sweeping protections—including the rights to assemble and protest, to hold unpopular beliefs, and to bear arms."[11] Nevertheless, modern efforts toward constitutional revision have left them intact.[12] Chapter 12 discusses rights and liberties in greater detail, including interpretations of the right to keep and bear arms.

SEPARATION OF POWERS

Like the national Constitution, the state charter allocates governmental functions among three branches: the executive, the legislative, and the judicial. Article II outlines the separation of powers, including the "departments"— as the branches are labeled in the state constitution—of government. The national government divides power between the nation and the states as well as among the three branches. Providing for a sharing of power should keep any one branch from becoming too powerful. Article II outlines the separation of institutions, and the articles dealing with the individual departments develop a system of checks and balances similar to those found in the national Constitution. Often, the same checks found in the U.S. Constitution are established in the state constitution.

A check on power results from assigning a function commonly identified with one branch to another. For example, the House of Representatives may impeach and the Senate may try—a judicial function—elected executive officials and judges at the district court level and above.[13] The governor has a veto over acts of the legislature and an item veto over appropriation bills— a legislative proceeding. The Texas Supreme Court may issue a writ of mandamus ordering an executive official to act—an executive function. These examples are mostly applicable at the national as well as the state level and illustrate that powers are not truly separated but overlapping and shared.

LEGISLATIVE BRANCH

The Texas legislature, like the U.S. Congress, consists of a Senate and a House of Representatives. The legislative article (III) establishes a legislative body, determines its composition, sets the qualifications for membership, provides its basic organization, and fixes its meeting time. All these features are discussed in Chapter 7. The article also sets the salary of state legislators. A

---

11. Todd J. Gillman, "Bill of Rights Might Face Tough Ride Now," *Dallas Morning News*, August 22, 1992, 12F.
12. So long as citizens were legally perceived to be citizens of the state first and of the nation second, state guarantees were vital. In recent years state courts have begun to reassert themselves as protectors of rights because the federal courts have begun to be less assertive in their own decisions (see Chapter 12).
13. Article XV specifies the grounds for impeachment of judges but not for the impeachment of executive officers; only the *power* to impeach the latter is given.

1991 constitutional amendment created an Ethics Commission whose powers include recommending legislative salaries, but the recommendation still must be approved by the voters. The Ethics Commission has made no such recommendations. In the interim, a $7,200 salary prevails.

Rather than emphasizing the positive powers of the legislature, the article spells out the specific actions that the legislature cannot take, reflecting reaction to the strong government imposed during Reconstruction. For example, the U.S. Constitution gives Congress broad powers to make any laws that are "necessary and proper." In contrast, rather than allowing lawmaking to be handled through the regular legislative process, the Texas Constitution forces state government to resort to the constitutional amendment process. For example, an amendment is needed to add to the fund maintained by the state to help veterans adjust to civilian life by giving them good deals on the purchase of land. Another example is the need for an amendment to change the percentage of the state budget that can be spent on public welfare.

The state constitution also provides the following limitations on legislative procedure.

1. The legislature may meet in regular session only every two years.

2. The number of days for introduction of bills, committee work, and floor action is specified. To permit early floor action, the governor can declare an emergency.

3. Salaries and the per diem reimbursement rate are described. Historically, this degree of specificity made an amendment necessary for every change in these figures. Some flexibility may exist once the Ethics Commission begins to recommend future salaries.

4. The legislature cannot authorize the state to borrow money. Yet, Section 23-A provides for a $75,000 payment to settle a debt to a contractor for a building constructed at the John Tarleton Agricultural College (now State University) in 1937.

5. The legislative article, not the municipal corporations article, includes provisions for municipal employees to participate in Social Security programs.

6. In spite of a stipulation that the legislature cannot grant public monies to individuals, exceptions are made for Confederate soldiers and sailors and their widows.

These examples are taken only from the legislative article. A list of all similar idiosyncratic provisions in the constitution would be massive because limitations on legislative action are scattered throughout the constitution, especially in the General Provisions. Such detailed restrictions tie the hands of legislators and make it necessary for them to take many issues to the voters that are seemingly of little significance. Restrictive provisions of this sort have caused the Texas Constitution to be evaluated as a rigid document compared to the U.S. Constitution. Still, the legislature is the dominant institution in the state.

EXECUTIVE BRANCH

Little similarity exists between the provisions for the executive branch in the state charter and those in the national Constitution. The U.S. Constitution provides for a very strong chief executive, the president, and creates only one other elected official, the vice president, who runs on a ticket with and, since 1804, has been chosen by the presidential candidate. Article IV provides that the governor is the "chief executive" of the state. However, the state constitution requires that the following individuals also be elected statewide, just as the governor is:

1. The lieutenant governor, who presides over the Texas Senate

2. The comptroller (pronounced con-TROL-ler) of public accounts, who collects the state's taxes and determines who keeps the state's money

3. The commissioner of the General Land Office, who protects the state's environment and administers its vast public lands

4. The attorney general, who is the state's lawyer

5. Members of the Texas Railroad Commission, who regulate intrastate transportation and the oil and gas industry

Furthermore, statutory laws require that the commissioner of agriculture and members of the State Board of Education be elected. Thus, quite unlike President Bill Clinton, who appoints most other key federal executives, Governor George Bush finds himself saddled with five other elected executives and two key elected policy-making boards. He has no formal control over these individuals.

The result is that Texas has a "disintegrated" or "fragmented" executive branch—that is, the governor has little or no control over other officials. The governor must contend with more than 250 state agencies, most of which receive policy direction from an administrative board or commission. The governor also has little power to reorganize executive agencies.

Thus, the executive article, like the legislative one, is overly specific and creates roadblocks to expeditious governmental action. Government cannot act when faced with too many restrictions, even when citizens need a fast response. More than the other articles, Article IV reflects the period of its writing—the extreme reaction in the 1870s to the excesses of Reconstruction Governor E. J. Davis. Scholars who have compared all the states' governorships rate the Texas governorship as one of the six weakest in the country.[14]

Nevertheless, through control of special sessions and through veto power, the governor retains significant legislative power. There is also no restriction on the number of terms that a governor may serve. Additionally, two modern amendments have strengthened the governor's position. In 1972 the governor's term of office was lengthened from two years to four years. In 1980 gubernatorial removal powers were strengthened by an amendment to Article XV. This amendment allows governors to remove, with the advice and consent of the Senate, individuals they have appointed. Legislation approved in 1993 further strengthened the office by giving the governor greater control over major policy boards such as those dealing with insurance regulation and public education. (See Chapter 9 for greater detail.)

14. Thad L. Beyle, "Governors," in Virginia Gray, Herbert Jacob, and Kenneth N. Vines, *Politics in the American States*, 4th ed. (Boston: Little, Brown, 1993), 202.

JUDICIAL BRANCH

The national judicial system is clear-cut—district courts, appeals courts, the U.S. Supreme Court—but the Texas judicial system is not at all clear. Like so many other articles in the constitution, the judicial article has various specific sections. These range from the requirement for an elected sheriff in each county to the restricted right of the state to appeal in criminal cases.[15]

Article V, the judicial article of the state constitution, has three distinctive features. First, the constitution establishes a rather confusing pattern of six different types of courts. Further complicating the picture is the fact that Texas has two supreme courts, one each for civil (Supreme Court) and criminal (Court of Criminal Appeals) matters.

Second, each level of trial courts has concurrent, or overlapping, jurisdiction with another level; that is, either level of court may hear the case. Additionally, trial courts established by statute have different jurisdiction from those established by the constitution. For example, in civil matters, constitutional county courts have concurrent jurisdiction with justice of the peace courts in civil cases involving $200 to $5,000. County courts at law overlap district courts in civil matters involving up to $100,000. Although the legislature can adjust the jurisdiction of statutory courts, the authority of constitutional courts can be altered only by constitutional amendment. Furthermore, the minimum dollar amounts stated in the constitution reflect economic values of the previous century. In an area of multimillion-dollar lawsuits, having a district court—the chief trial court of the state—hear a case in which the disputed amount is $1,000 or less hampers the more significant trial work of that court. The courts are fully discussed in Chapter 11.

Third, qualifications for Texas judges are so stated as to allow those with no legal training to be eligible for a trial court bench.[16] The resulting confusion increases the likelihood that someone without legal experience will be elected as a justice of the peace or county judge. The problem of judicial qualifications is aggravated by the fact that judges are elected in Texas, so that, on occasion, vote-getting ability may be more important than the ability to render judgments.[17] The tradition of elected judges reflects the nineteenth-century passion for long ballots. In the national government, the president appoints all judges.

LOCAL GOVERNMENT

Local governments in Texas fall into three categories: counties, municipalities (cities and towns), and special districts. The state constitution, through Articles III, IX, and XI, gives these governmental units varying degrees of flexibility.

---

15. Even with all the modern cases dealing with the rights of the criminally accused, no national prohibition exists on the state's right to appeal in criminal cases. See *Palko* v. *Connecticut* (302 U.S. 319, 1937) for the Supreme Court's position on the issue. Texas allowed no appeal by the state until 1987.

16. Contrary to popular opinion, a justice of the peace without legal training cannot become a judge on a superior (appeals) court. Qualifications for these courts include ten years as a practicing lawyer or a combination of ten years of legal practice and judicial service.

17. According to *Forbes* magazine, Texas and Alabama have the most expensive judicial elections in the country. With major amounts of money—as much as $2 million for a Texas Supreme Court seat—on the line, vote-getting skills become especially important. See Laura Castaneda, "D.C. Worst, Utah Best on Litigious List," *Dallas Morning News*, January 3, 1994, 1D, 4D.

An important consequence of elected judgeships stems from straight-party voting when voters consider the nominees of only one party. In 1994, for example, the Republican Party dominated national elections and made some important gains in Texas. Some of those gains came through the election of inexperienced Republican judges at the expense of experienced Democratic jurists.

Counties, which are administrative and judicial arms of the state, are most restricted. They are saddled with a commission form of government that combines executive and legislative authority and is headed by a judge. The power vested in the county governments and the services they offer are fragmented. An amendment of some two thousand words was passed in 1933 to allow larger counties to adopt a home-rule charter, but the provisions were so restrictive as to be inoperable. **Home rule** allows a government to write its own charter and make changes in it without legislative approval. Had it been workable, this provision would have allowed counties to choose their own form of government and have more flexibility in day-to-day operations. The provision was deleted in 1969.

On the other hand, cities enjoy a workable home-rule provision. Those with populations of more than 5,000 may become home-rule units of government. General-law cities, which are those without home-rule charters, must operate under statewide statutes. Cities, towns, and villages, whether operating under a home-rule charter or general law, are fairly free to provide whatever services and create whatever policies the citizens and governing bodies want as long as there is no conflict with constitutional or statutory law. The major constitutional handicaps for cities are the ceilings imposed on tax rates and debt, and limitations on the frequency of charter amendments.

Special districts are limited-purpose local governments that have taxing authority. The legislature generally authorizes the creation of special districts, although constitutional amendments have created some water and hospital districts. School districts are the best-known type of special district, but there are literally dozens of varieties. Because these types of government provide a way around the tax and debt limits imposed on cities and counties, they continue to proliferate.[18] (Chapter 3 discusses local government in detail.)

SUFFRAGE

The provisions on voting and the apportionment of legislative bodies are interesting because many of them clearly conflict with federal law, which itself continues to evolve as the legal/political philosophy of federal judges changes. For example, Article VII of the Texas Constitution still contains references to twenty-one as the minimum voting age. Such provisions are known as "deadwood" because they cannot be made operational. In some cases, legislative acts have been passed as stopgap measures to attain compliance with federal

18. In spite of numerous consolidations of small school districts in the past twenty years, Texas for many years has ranked in the top five states in the nation in the number of total special districts and nonschool special districts. There were 3,494 special districts in the state when the census of governments was conducted in 1992, almost three times the number of municipalities.

One of the thorniest constitutional problems was the determination by state courts that the Texas public education system did not provide "efficient and effective" education for all students. From 1989 to 1993, the legislature struggled to produce a funding scheme to equalize public education that was acceptable to the courts. Tax schemes in 1997 put such funding in the spotlight again.

Courtesy of Ben Sargent.

law, but the retention of the constitutional provisions has been confusing. (See Chapter 6 for details about voting in Texas.) The most glaring conflicts between national law and the state constitution are in the following areas:

★ Minimum voting age

★ Residency requirements

★ Voter registration

★ Property ownership as a requirement for voting in bond elections

★ Population as a basis of election to both legislative houses

AMENDMENTS

The framers of a constitution cannot possibly anticipate every provision that should be included. Consequently, all constitutions specify a procedure for amendment. Unlike eighteen other states—most notably California—which allow citizens to initiate constitutional amendment proposals by petition, Texas has only one way to propose an amendment. In Texas, proposals for amendments may be initiated during a regular or special session of the legislature, and an absolute two-thirds majority—that is, one hundred House and twenty-one Senate members—must vote to submit the proposed changes to the voters. The legislature also specifies the date of the election at which an amendment is voted on by the public. At least three months before the election, a proposed amendment must be published once a week for four weeks in a newspaper in each county. Whenever possible, amendments are placed on the ballot in general elections to avoid the expense of a separate, called election. Only a simple majority—that is, half plus one—of those citizens who choose to vote is needed for ratification, making it rather easy to add amendments. The governor officially proclaims the passage or rejection of amendments.

Texas's 377 constitutional amendments are vivid proof that the amendment process in the state has occupied considerable legislative time and that citizens have frequently confronted constitutional propositions at the polls. Table 2–3 points out the relentlessness of the amendment phenomenon and the increasing reliance on amendments as a way to get something done in government. Over one-third of the amendments were added in the seventeen years between 1980 and 1997. Some streamlining of the state charter should ensue from a constitutional amendment passed in November 1997 that called for an elimination of duplicate numbers in the Texas constitution and of obsolete provisions. However, most observers thought that the amendment did not provide sufficient clout to take care of all the needed cleanup.

Constitutional Revision

OVERVIEW OF THE NEED FOR REFORM

The framers of the U.S. Constitution were wise enough to provide only the essential structure of national government and to consign broad powers to governmental agents. The flexibility inherent in this approach has made possible our country's transition from a nation whose government was mainly concerned with fending off hostile Native Americans and delivering the mail to one whose government now shoulders the burdens of world leadership and

---

TABLE 2–3

Texas Constitutional Amendments, 1879* to Present

Decade(s)	Proposed	Adopted	Cumulative Total
1870s–1880s	16	5	5
1890s	15	11	16
1900s	20	10	26
1910s	35	9	35
1920s	26	12	47
1930s	45	34	81
1940s	35	25	106
1950s	43	33	139
1960s	84	55	194
1970s	67	44	238
1980s	99	88	326
1990s (through 1997)	63	51	377
Total through 1997	548	377	377

*The first amendment to the 1876 Texas Constitution was adopted in 1879.
SOURCE: Compiled by C. Neal Tate and Charldean Newell.

myriad socioeconomic policies. State constitutions, on the other hand, tend to reflect the concerns of vested interests. These interests prefer the "security blanket" of constitutional inclusion to being left at the mercy of legislatures with changing party alignments, political persuasions, and political concerns.

 One Texas example of a security blanket is the provision authorizing workers' compensation insurance for state and local government employees. Another example is the section that benefits veterans by providing funds for land purchases. A third benefits homeowners, who receive a partial tax exemption for their primary residence (homestead).

During the bicentennial celebration of the U.S. Constitution (1987–1989), Americans were proud that their fundamental law had been amended only twenty-six times (twenty-seven by 1995) and that ten of the amendments—the Bill of Rights—were added almost immediately after ratification. In contrast, the average state constitution has almost five times this number of amendments. State legislatures across the country devote much of their time to debating and deliberating on further constitutional amendments.

The continuing efforts to improve on imperfect documents reflect a fact of constitutional life. A constitution can create a structure of government that provides a tolerable degree of citizen input and, in an ultimate sense, allows citizens control of public policy. Nevertheless, that structure still may be cumbersome, inefficient, and expensive and impede the quest for justice and prosperity rather than facilitating it.

The ratification dates of state constitutions tell us much about what to expect in the way of content. The two newest states, for example—Alaska and Hawaii—have workable, sound constitutions that were modeled in part on the ideal document proposed by the National League of Cities[19] and have clearly profited by the mistakes of others. Some of the oldest states—Connecticut, New Jersey, and Virginia—have undergone total constitutional revision and now have flexible, operational charters. In general, however, state constitutions are long, restrictive, inclusive, and confusing and need frequent amending to permit the provision of necessary services as well as to keep pace with contemporary needs.[20]

Like all law, the state charter is a product of its time. When the Texas Constitution was drafted over a century ago, it incorporated protection for various private interests. It also included many details of policy and governmental organization to avoid abuse of governmental power. From the perspective of the 1990s, the 1876 constitution is too long and complex, yet not clear

---

19. The National League of Cities Committee on State Government periodically revises its *Model State Constitution*. The most recent version is the seventh edition (Washington, D.C.: National League of Cities, 1968).
20. The Texas Constitution specifies a ceiling on funds to be expended for assistance to the needy aged, needy children, and the needy blind. If funds are inadequate—for example, when the number of people requiring assistance or the amount of assistance needed has grown—an amendment must be passed.

enough to permit effective government. Results of the confusion and ambiguity are readily found—in the provisions for levying school taxes, the procedures for administering the Teacher Retirement System, and the hodgepodge of constitutionally created executive officers and regulatory boards that undermine gubernatorial authority.

Texas is not the only state with a proliferation of constitutional amendments. At the beginning of 1996, the average state constitution had been amended 134 times. The champions of amendments are Alabama (with 582) and California (with 491). In contrast, four state constitutions revised in the modern era—those of Illinois (1971), Michigan (1964), Pennsylvania (1968), and Montana (1973)—have only 10, 20, 21, and 21 amendments, respectively. The Texas Constitution allows only legislative proposal of amendments, although eighteen other states permit citizens to initiate amendments. Both methods of proposing amendments (legislative proposal and citizen initiative) can result in few or many charter changes depending on how good the basic document is.[21]

The Texas document well illustrates the problem of having to legislate by constitutional amendment. Public policy matters (such as education, which is spelled out in Article VII) are included in the constitution, as are other details more appropriate to statutes. For example, in recent years amendments have included everything from legalizing bingo for church and fraternal organizations to allowing an East Texas farmer to keep the land he had bought almost fifty years earlier in spite of a technical defect in the title to the property.

Such clumsy governance has spawned many calls for constitutional revision. But constitutions, like all laws, are political. What one group advocates may be strongly opposed by other interests. Nevertheless, the advocates of reform, although not always agreeing on what the change should be, tend to focus on the following provisions of the current constitution:

1. The biennial legislative session: As state politics and finance become more complex, the short legislative sessions held only every other year become more of a handicap to developing long-range public policy.

2. The judicial system: The Texas judicial system, as previously discussed, is characterized by multiple layers of courts with overlapping jurisdictions. Many reform advocates would like to see the establishment of a streamlined, unified judicial system.

3. The fragmented executive branch: The executive branch has many elected officials and a policy-making board. Reformers suggest an executive branch modeled on the national executive—that is, a single elected official and a series of executive departments responsible to that official.

4. County government: Especially in urban counties, the structure of county government and its lack of power to pass ordinances (local laws) mean that the counties cannot respond readily to urban problems. Reform advocates suggest that county government be streamlined and given at least limited ordinance power.

21. For example, Alabama, like Texas, does not have a provision allowing citizens to initiate legislation. California, Illinois, Michigan, and Montana all provide for the citizen initiative. See *The Book of the States*, 3–7.

TABLE 7–3

Selected Characteristics of Members of the Seventy-Fifth Legislature, 1997–98, by House, by Percentages*

Characteristics	Senate (N = 31)	House (N = 150)
Ethnicity		
Anglo/White	71.0%	73.5%
Hispanic/Mexican American	22.6	17.7
Black/African American	6.4	8.8
Gender		
Male	90.3%	80.0%
Female	9.7	20.0
Age		
Average age	50	47.5
Oldest/youngest member	64/31	72/24
Education		
Graduate or professional degree	51.6%	54.0%
Some college up to bachelor's degree	45.2	41.3
No college or no answer	3.2	4.7
Marital Status		
Married	96.8%	72.7%
Not married or not reporting	3.2	27.3
Religious Preference		
Protestantism†	67.7%	No information
Roman Catholicism	29.0	
Judaism	3.2	

*Percentages do not always equal 100.0 due to rounding.
†Protestantism includes nine Methodists, five Baptists, three Episcopalians, one Christian Scientist, and three undesignated Christians.

result is that attorneys, who make up less than 1 percent of the state's population, hold almost one-third of Texas legislative seats. Their numbers have been waning in recent years, reflecting a national trend away from lawyers as legislators. The quotation at the beginning of this chapter from the Texas Poll may indicate why the trend is waning: The public ranks the legal profession only slightly above the National Rifle Association as a public institution. The most frequent business fields are real estate, insurance, and investments. Table 7–4 shows the wide variety of occupations represented in the Seventy-fifth Legislature.

FIFTYISH

The average age of members of the Texas legislature has been creeping up from the middle forties to the late forties in the House and fifty in the Senate. The growing numbers of citizens over sixty and single persons are not proportionately represented.

OTHER FACTORS

Education, marital status, religion, organization, money, and *the media* are additional factors in legislative elections. Since the late 1970s, virtually all

TABLE 7–4

Occupations and Professions Represented in the Texas Legislature

Accounting	Firefighting
Advertising	Insurance
Aviation	Investments
Business	Law
Chiropractic	Manufacturing
Civics	Medicine
Communications	Ministry
Construction	Oil and gas
Consulting	Public finance
Customs brokering	Public relations
Dentistry	Publishing
Education	Ranching
Electronics	Real estate
Engineering	Sales and marketing
Farming	Transportation

members of the legislature are college-educated, and slightly over half hold more than one degree—especially in law or business.

The preponderance of legislators are married, although the reporting system tends to make it appear that the House has a large number of single members. In 1991, the legislature had its first acknowledged gay man as a member.

The last year for which religion information on the House is available is 1991, when 54 percent of the members were Protestant, 26 percent were Roman Catholic, 4 percent were Jewish, and 16 percent did not respond. In 1997, the Senate included 68 percent Protestants, 29 percent Roman Catholics, and 3 percent Jews (one member). That the preponderance of legislators are Protestants merely reflects the religious composition of Texas society. The religious affiliations of the state's population are approximately: Roman Catholic, 25 percent; Protestant, 67 percent; Jewish, 0.4 percent; other religions and those without religious beliefs make up the rest.[16]

Legislators also tend to be members of the "right" groups. Membership in civic associations, business and professional groups, and social clubs all help convince voters that the candidate is a solid citizen.

Campaigning for office is expensive. In highly competitive urban districts, members of both houses have spent more than $500,000 to win an election. In a noncompetitive rural race, a candidate may spend as little as $20,000.[17] Can-

16. Helen Parmley, "Question of Faith," *Dallas Morning News,* June 9, 1990, 1A, 14A. A later survey just of Dallas-area residents differs little: Roman Catholic, 29 percent; Protestant, 57 percent; Jewish, 4 percent; other, primarily Native American and Eastern religions, 10 percent; see "Religious Groups in Dallas Area," *Dallas Morning News,* November 4, 1995, 11C. Statewide, a smaller proportion of individuals outside the Judeo-Christian tradition can be expected outside the large cities.
17. In 1988 House candidates averaged $11,000 in campaign expenses for the primary election and $14,517 in the general election. These costs have surely gone up, and the costs in the much larger Senate districts obviously would be higher. See Robert E. Hogan, "Expenditure Patterns in State Legislative Campaigns," paper presented at the Southern Political Science Association annual meeting, November 2–4, 1994, as cited by Samuel C. Patterson, "Legislative Politics in the States," in Virginia Gray and Herbert Jacob, *Politics in the American States,* 6th ed. (Washington, D.C.: CQ Press, 1996), 168.

didates with some personal money are better able to attract financial support than those of ordinary means, in part because they move in "money" circles.

Favorable media exposure—news coverage and editorial endorsements by newspapers, magazines, radio, and especially television—is of tremendous importance during a campaign. The media decide who the leading candidates are and then give them the lion's share of free news space. Texas media tend to be conservative and to endorse business-oriented candidates.

EXPERIENCE AND TURNOVER

Seniority has long been of great importance in the committee structure of the U.S. Congress, and Texas voters in many districts are accustomed to reelecting members of the Texas congressional delegation. However, rapid **turnover** of 20 percent to 25 percent has traditionally characterized the Texas legislature, with the result that state legislators have been accused of being inexperienced and amateurish. In recent years, the turnover rate has been less—only 18 percent in 1997. Moreover, a typical freshman senator is likely to have had prior governmental experience in the House, and a typical freshman House member may have served on a county commissioners court, city council, or school board.

What causes legislative turnover? Running for higher office, retirement, moving into the more profitable private sector, and reapportionment/redistricting are among the causes. So also are tough urban reelection races, changing party alignments, and voter perception—correct—that seniority is not so important in the state legislature as it is in the U.S. Congress. Nevertheless, seniority is important. Not only does it increase the probability that a legislator will be knowledgeable about policy issues, but also it means that the legislator will understand how the system works. In the Senate, especially, the most senior members tend to chair committees.

What will the Seventy-sixth Legislature in 1999 look like? One senator and fifteen House members from the Seventy-fifth Legislature chose not to run for reelection. The senator and four House members sought higher offices. Seven of the nonreturning House members were committee chairs in 1997–98. Nine senators and eighty House members had no opponents. Seven senators and fifty-nine House members had opponents. Thus, as usual, some turnover will occur.

Internal Organization of the Legislature

THE PRESIDING OFFICERS

The presiding officers of any legislative assembly have more power and prestige than do ordinary members. In Texas, however, the lieutenant governor and the speaker of the House have such sweeping procedural, organizational, administrative, and planning authority that they truly dominate the legislative scene.

Although most state legislatures have partisan leadership positions analogous to the majority and minority leaders in the U.S. Congress, this is not yet the case in Texas because of the historical one-party tradition. The committee chairs hold the secondary positions of power, after the presiding officers. Chairs are appointed by the presiding officers and thus do not offer any threat to the power of either the speaker or the lieutenant governor.

THE LIEUTENANT GOVERNOR

The lieutenant governor is elected independently by the citizenry, serves as president of the Senate but is not a member of it, and does not run on the ticket with the gubernatorial candidate. The lieutenant governor rarely performs any executive functions and is chiefly a legislative official. The term of the office is four years.

Twenty-seven other states use the lieutenant governor as the presiding officer of the upper house. But these states (usually) also look to the governor for policy recommendations; their chamber rules are such that the lieutenant governor, far from exercising any real power, is generally in a position similar to that of the vice president of the United States—neither an important executive nor a legislative force. Such is not the case in Texas, where the lieutenant governor is regarded as a major force in state politics and the dominant figure during legislative sessions. The lieutenant governor orchestrates the flow of legislation in the upper house.

What an Ending!

The Seventy-fifth Legislature ended on a surprising note in 1997 when Lieutenant Governor Bob Bullock announced that he would not run for reelection in 1998. That news produced an immediate scramble among both Democrats and Republicans, who saw an opportunity to contend for what is probably the most powerful office in the state. It also brought about considerable speculation as to whether the immense powers of the presiding officer—which are granted through Senate rules adopted by the members—might be curtailed beginning in 1999, especially if a Republican Senate once again were to be led by a Democratic presiding officer. Bullock, with forty years in various public offices, was able to convince the members to do his bidding in most cases. A newcomer might prove less potent.

Agricultural Commissioner Rick Perry, a Republican, was elected lieutenant governor in November 1998.

Bob Bullock, who gained his political experience as the state comptroller of public accounts, became lieutenant governor in 1991, succeeding Bill Hobby, who retired after eighteen years in the office. Bullock had been in state politics since 1957 and in elective office since 1975. A colorful figure with considerable expertise in state finance, Bullock's personal history includes five marriages and continuing recovery from alcoholism. Bullock is very much a Democrat, but the increasing conservatism of the Senate caused him in 1993 to switch positions from his long-time advocacy of a state income tax to ramrodding through a constitutional amendment that makes such a tax virtually impossible to enact.[18] In late 1997 he endorsed Governor George Bush for reelection rather than one of his own protégés, Democratic Land Commissioner Garry Mauro.

SPEAKER OF THE HOUSE

The speaker of the Texas House of Representatives is an elected member of the House who is formally chosen as speaker by a majority vote of the House membership at the opening of the legislative session. The results of the election are rarely a surprise; by the time the session opens, everyone knows who the speaker will be. Candidates for speaker begin maneuvering for support long before the previous session has ended. And during the interim between sessions, they not only campaign for election to the House in their home districts, but also try to secure from fellow House members written pledges of support in the race for speaker. If an incumbent speaker is seeking reelection, usually no other candidates run.

Until 1951, speakers traditionally served for one term; between 1951 and 1975, they served either one or two. The House seems to have abandoned the limited-term tradition, however. Billy Clayton served four terms as speaker (1975–1983), and his successor, Gib Lewis, served five (1983–1993). James E. (Pete) Laney, a West Texas cotton farmer, bested eight other House members to become speaker in 1993 and was elected to a third term in 1997. He campaigned for the leadership on the promises of reforming the rules and creating higher ethical standards.

The Democrats held onto their majority in the House by the narrow margin of 79–71. Thus, Pete Laney is expected to be re-elected as speaker.

Laney's style is very different from that of his predecessor or of Bob Bullock. A quiet individual with an equally quiet personal life, Laney has been a member of the House since 1973. He is known among House members as being dedicated to making the legislative process work.

It is important for legislators to know whether the speaker is seeking reelection because they must decide whether to back the incumbent or take a chance on supporting a challenger. The decision is crucial: The speaker rewards supporters by giving them key committee assignments—perhaps even the opportunity to chair a committee—and by helping them campaign for reelection to the legislature. A House member who throws support in the wrong direction risks legislative oblivion.

18. See Robert Bruce, "The Last Don," *Texas Observer,* January 31, 1997, 8–15; Dave McNeely, "Bullock U," *Austin American-Statesman,* September 17, 1995, E1, E4–E5; and Sam Howe Verhovek, "Texan Turns His Flaws into Capital," *New York Times,* March 23, 1997, 17.

Following the 1972 Sharpstown bank scandal, which involved prominent politicians receiving special favors in exchange for banking legislation, Speaker Price Daniel, Jr., dedicated the 1973 session to reform, emphasizing financial disclosure, restricting campaign contributions, and trying to eliminate some of the behind-closed-doors deals of former speakers. More recently, Speaker Pete Laney quickly moved to clean up the House after the Gib Lewis regime, which ended with the lodging of ethics charges. Laney cut lobbyists' access to members inside the House chamber and prohibited his staff from taking lobbying jobs after they left state government. He pushed for reform of the House rules on everything from early filing of bills to getting bills out of committee.

This push included stopping the legislative freight train that traditionally occurred in the last three days of the session when almost one-quarter of the bills would be voted on. Laney insisted on earlier, more rational debate and voting. He made the ethical conduct of the speaker and the members a matter of high priority. He exercised his right to vote only five times and did not introduce bills. At the close of the session, lobbyists complained of how hard they had to work, and members praised him for refusing to dominate the legislative process. He remained equally aboveboard in 1995 and 1997.

PRO TEMPORE POSITIONS

Pro tempore ("for the time being") positions are largely honorific in Texas. At the beginning of the session, the Senate elects one member to serve as president pro tempore to preside when the lieutenant governor is absent or if the lieutenant governor's office becomes vacant. At the end of the session, another individual is elected to serve as president pro tempore during the legislative interim; this person is usually one of the senior members. House rules also provide for the speaker to appoint someone to preside over the House temporarily or to appoint a speaker pro tempore to serve permanently. Whether to select anyone at all and who the individual will be are options left to the speaker.

LEGISLATIVE COMMITTEES

Legislative bodies in the United States have long relied on committees to expedite their work because the alternative is trying to accomplish detailed legislation, planning, and investigation by the whole house. These committees are critical to the legislative process. We offer here only a general outline of Texas legislative committees; a more detailed discussion of their powers will be found in Chapter 8. The presiding officers appoint committee members. The five basic types of committees in the state legislature are listed here. Note that these categories are not mutually exclusive.

1. Standing committees are established by the rules of the two houses as permanent committees. They deal with designated areas of public policy.

2. Subcommittees are subdivisions of standing committees. They consider specialized areas of their standing committees' general jurisdiction.

3. Conference committees are formed for the purpose of arriving at acceptable compromises on bills that have passed both houses but in different

forms. These temporary committees include members from both houses; a selected number of members of the standing committees that originally had jurisdiction over the bills in question are usually members of the conference committee.

4. Ad hoc committees are temporary and are appointed to consider specific issues or problems; they resemble special and select committees in the U.S. Congress. In fact, in 1995, the Texas Senate designated three such committees as "special." Conference committees are a type of ad hoc committee.

5. Interim committees continue the work of the legislature after the session ends, to study a particular problem and/or to make recommendations to the next legislature. Interim committees are frequently joint committees—that is, they have members from both houses.

STANDING COMMITTEES

Before Speaker Daniels's reform legislation of 1973, Texas lawmakers had to contend with forty-six House committees and twenty-seven Senate committees. All legislators served on at least four committees. The lines of committee jurisdiction were hazy; determining which committee had jurisdiction over a bill was much like trying to fit together a jigsaw puzzle. In 1973, however, the number of standing committees was reduced to nine in the Senate and twenty-one in the House. By 1997 the number of Senate committees had grown to fifteen and the number of House committees to thirty-six. One Senate committee was designated as "special" and one as a committee of the whole (all thirty-one senators). Five of the House committees are procedural, that is, they deal with House procedures rather than substantive bills (see Table 7–5). Senators usually serve on three committees and House members, on two.

In 1973 a modified seniority system was introduced in the Texas House of Representatives. Under this system, a representative may ask for appointment to a desired committee slot on the basis of seniority—that is, the number of terms the legislator has served in the House.[19] If less than half the committee's membership has been selected according to seniority, the member's request is granted. The speaker then appoints the remainder of the committee members, including the committee chairperson and vice chairperson.

During his years as speaker, Lewis concentrated power in the hands of the presiding officer. He created a budget officer for each committee to enhance his control over committee leadership; he gained the power to dismiss committee chairpersons and staff at will, and he declared eight powerful committees to have only speaker appointees. Laney, the reform speaker, dismantled this centralized control.

---

19. In the U.S. Congress, seniority is more narrowly defined as continuous service on a committee. The congressional reforms of the 1970s modified the selection of committee chairpersons to allow some departure from the practice that the most senior member of the committee who is a member of the majority party always serves as chair. While seniority remains the usual basis for the selection of congressional committee chairs, Speaker Newt Gingrich succeeded in bypassing the most senior members of the powerful Appropriations Committee in 1995 to get his choice of chair selected.

TABLE 7–5

Committees of the Seventy-Fifth Legislature, 1997

Fifteen Senate Committees (thirteen standing, one special, one of the whole)	Thirty-Six House Committees (all standing)
Committee of the Whole	Agriculture and Livestock
Criminal Justice	Appropriations
Economic Development	Business and Industry
Education	Calendars*
Finance	Civil Practices
Health and Human Services	Corrections
Intergovernmental Relations	County Affairs
International Relations, Trade, and Technology	Criminal Jurisprudence
Jurisprudence	Economic Development
Natural Resources	Elections
Subcommittee on Agriculture	Energy Resources
Subcommittee on Water	Environmental Regulation
State Affairs	Financial Institutions
Senate Committee on Administration	General Investigating
Senate Committee on Nominations	Higher Education
General Investigating	House Administration*
Veteran Affairs and Military Installations (special)	Human Services
	Insurance
	Judicial Affairs
	Juvenile Justice and Family Issues
	Land and Resource Management
	Licensing and Administrative Procedures
	Local and Consent Calendars*
	Natural Resources
	Pensions and Investments
	Public Education
	Public Health
	Public Safety
	Redistricting*
	Rules and Resolutions*
	State Affairs
	State, Federal, and International Relations
	State Recreational Resources
	Transportation
	Urban Affairs
	Ways and Means

*These committees are procedural.
SOURCE: Official records of the Seventy-fifth Legislature, compiled by House and Senate staff members.

In the Senate, the lieutenant governor appoints all committee members and the committee chairpersons and vice chairpersons. A modified seniority rule applies as follows: For committees of ten or fewer members, three must be persons who have served on that committee in the last session; for committees of more than ten members, four must have served on that committee during the last session. A senator may serve as chairperson of only one standing committee during any one session. Ironically, while reformers at the federal government level have worked hard and with some success to gain a relaxation of the seniority rule in Congress, reformers at the state level have sought to introduce seniority into the Texas legislature. The reason proposed for introducing seniority into the Texas system is the same as that for originally instituting the system in Congress: to mitigate some of the power concentrated in the hands of the presiding officers.

Although seniority can discourage capable young legislators, it does assure that those who play a significant part in conducting legislative business have experience and possibly some degree of expertise. Given the turnover rate of the Texas legislature, the experience factor is important. Legislative committees control the flow of legislation in both houses, and the method by which their members are selected generally influences the outcome of public policy in the state.

OTHER COMMITTEES

The two standing subcommittees in the Senate are appointed by the lieutenant governor. Other subcommittees in both houses are named by the committee chairpersons, who are unlikely to act contrary to the wishes of the presiding officers. Ad hoc and conference committees are creatures of the speaker and lieutenant governor.

Interim committees are somewhat different. Their members may include a combination of appointees of the presiding officers and the governor, including citizen (nonlegislative) members. The 1961 Legislative Reorganization Act directed standing committees to study matters under their jurisdiction during the legislative interim, but in many cases special interim committees are appointed instead. Often these committees are support-building devices for legislation that failed during the previous session. Such committees are not mandated to deliver a report back to the legislature. Of course, if the speaker or lieutenant governor is interested in the study, the likelihood of a full report substantially increases. Although legislative staff is available to assist either standing or special committees between legislative sessions, interim committees often are created without a staff and/or funds. A modern device is the select committee, which includes legislators and governor's appointees. The Select Committee on Public Education created by the Sixty-eighth Legislature (1983–84) had the support of the leadership and the governor; consequently, it is an example of a well-funded, highly publicized study committee. Another example is the Select Committee on Tax Equity in 1987–88, created by the Seventieth Legislature.

LEGISLATIVE STAFF

Although Texas legislators enjoy better office budgets and staff allowances than their counterparts in many other states, they still must rely on information furnished by outside groups. For example, the Texas Research League, a private business-oriented group, performs numerous studies and makes recommendations to the legislature. The Legislative Budget Board (LBB), an internal agency of the legislature, makes recommendations on the same appropriations bills that it helps to prepare. The Legislative Reference Library, while a valuable tool, is limited to maintaining a history of legislation in Texas and furnishing information on comparable legislation in other states.

Legislative committees also have limited budgets and professional staff. Accordingly, committees often must rely on assistance from the institutional staff of the legislature, such as the LBB, and from other state agencies, such as the attorney general's office or the comptroller's office. In addition, from time to time, legislators with compatible views form study groups to work on issues.

The lack of adequate staffing is of major importance to Texans. It means that legislators, in committee or individually, cannot easily obtain impartial, accurate information concerning public policy. Nonetheless, citizen interest in supporting larger budgets for legislative operations seems to be nil. Indeed, some Texans see any move on the part of legislators to eliminate their dependence on private groups and state administrators for information as a ploy to "waste" more tax money. This attitude, fully encouraged by lobbyists, keeps staffing low. This situation also gives even greater clout to the comptroller of public accounts when he makes recommendations based on the Texas Performance Review (see Chapter 10).

The creation of the Texas Legislative Council (TLC) in 1949 was a major step toward providing research and technical services to Texas legislators. But the TLC has never been adequately funded to provide full-time bill-drafting and research services, and its small staff receives more requests for information than it can handle. The LBB, composed of the presiding officers and other legislators, prepares the legislative budget (see Chapter 13). Its staff, heavily influenced by the presiding officers, is in an awkward position to make independent recommendations. And the other auxiliary organization of the legislature, the Legislative Audit Committee, is composed of the presiding officers and certain ex officio legislators. Its professional staff, headed by the state auditor, who serves at the pleasure of the committee, also is heavily influenced by the presiding officers.

There are other political appointees who assist members individually but whose major responsibilities are to the House or Senate as a body. These include the secretary of the Senate, the chief clerk of the House, their assistants, the sergeants-at-arms, the pages, and clerical staff.

General Criticism and Suggested Reforms

CRITICISM

Extensive efforts to revamp state legislative structures have been made by organizations such as the National Legislative Conference, the Council of State Governments, the Citizens Conference on State Legislatures, and the National Municipal League. This last organization even produced a Model State Constitution as a "companion piece" for its Model City Charter. But state legislatures have been universally noninnovative. As Alexander Heard observes, "State legislatures may be our most extreme example of institutional lag. In their formal qualities, they are largely 19th-century organizations, and they must, or should, address themselves to 20th-century problems."[20]

The Texas legislature seems caught in the proverbial vicious circle. Low salaries and short terms force legislators to maintain other sources of income, a necessity that leads to inattentiveness to legislative business, especially between sessions. On salary alone, a legislator would be far below the federal poverty line. However, the generous $95 a day allowance when the legislature is in session helps to raise the total compensation to almost $30,000 for the average legislator during a legislative year.

The electorate, on the other hand, views the legislature as a group whose members work only 140 days every two years, but get paid every month.

---

20. Alexander Heard, ed., *State Legislatures in American Politics* (Englewood Cliffs, N.J.: Prentice-Hall, 1966), 3.

Most citizens probably do not realize—and may not care—that legislators make only $600 a month in salary. They would probably care more if they realized that most of a legislator's compensation comes from the per diem allowance. In 1984, voters explicitly refused to allow legislators more than $30 a day in expense money. The $95 figure came about through the discovery of a loophole in the statute setting per diem payments.

Yet citizens are not very consistent in their views. While they are reluctant to vote for decent legislative salaries, they seem to find little difficulty in entrusting a *multibillion*-dollar budget to an inexperienced and poorly paid group of legislators whom they view as amateurs at best and scalawags at worst.[21] Furthermore, they seem oblivious to the detrimental effect on legislation caused by inadequate salaries for both legislators and their staffs and the resulting dependence on special interests or on "gamesmanship" to maximize the per diem payments.

SUGGESTED REFORMS

SESSIONS

The institution of annual legislative sessions has been a major reform proposal in all recent constitutional revision efforts. Annual sessions would allow legislators time to familiarize themselves with complex legislation, permitting them, for example, to bring a little more knowledge to the chaotic guessing game that produces the state's biennial budget. Annual sessions would virtually eliminate the need for special sessions when a crisis arises between regular sessions. They would allow the continual introduction of all those special resolutions (described in Chapter 8), such as declaring chili the official state dish, that have negligible importance for the general public but take up so much valuable legislative time. They also would provide an opportunity for legislative oversight of the state bureaucracy. Coupled with adequate staff support, annual sessions would allow legislators to engage in more long-range planning of public policy.

The legislature also needs to be empowered to call itself into special session. At present, if legislative leaders see the need for a special session and the governor is reluctant to call it, the legislature is helpless. In thirty-one other states, legislators can initiate a special session either independently or in conjunction with the governor.[22] At a minimum, legislators need more freedom to add to the agenda of special sessions. Even though a session is called for a

---

21. Christopher Z. Mooney concludes that Texas defies the national pattern that states with large populations and a high degree of heterogeneity tend to be more professionalized than small, more homogeneous states. See "The Political Economy of State Legislative Professionalism," paper presented at the annual meeting of the Southwestern Political Science Association, March 19–21, 1992, Austin. Mooney examined thirty years of measurements of the professionalism of legislative bodies in "Measuring U.S. State Legislative Professionalism: An Evaluation of Five Indices," *State and Local Government Review* 26 (Spring 1994): 70–78. This article is a methodological note, but a table showing the fifty states indicates that Texas does not fare well on professionalism measures.
22. *The Book of the States, 1996–97,* 64–66.

specific purpose, other significant items could be entered on the agenda and dispensed with, thus lessening the clutter of the next regular session's agenda.

The restrictions on both regular and special legislative sessions result in a high concentration of political power. The presiding officers dictate the flow of business during regular sessions, and the governor dominates special sessions. The next chapter more fully examines this concentration of power and its effects.

SIZE AND SALARIES

Some advocates of reform have recommended that the Texas House be reduced in size to one hundred members. Others have suggested that, since both houses are now elected on the basis of population distribution, one house should be eliminated altogether and a unicameral legislature adopted. But tradition strongly militates against such a change. The physical size of the state poses another risk to reducing the size of the legislature. As population and thus district size continue to grow, citizens will increasingly lose contact with their representatives. A reduction in the number of legislators would be a trade-off between legislative efficiency and representativeness. Although efficiency is important to citizens, so is being represented by someone from a small enough geographic and population area to understand the needs of the people in the district.

More serious are recommendations for salary increases. The $7,200 salary is insufficient to allow legislators to devote their full energies to state business. A salary in the range of the average among the nine other largest states— $45,077—would not, of course, guarantee that legislators would be honest and conscientious and devote all of their working time to the business of the state. A decent salary level, however, would ensure that those who wished to could spend most of their time on state business. Moreover, it might also eliminate the retainer fees, consultant fees, and legal fees now paid to many legislators. Also, it would guard against only the rich being able to run for public office.

TERMS OF OFFICE

If Senate members had staggered six-year terms and House members staggered four-year terms, legislators could be assured of having time to develop expertise in both procedures and substantive policy. Moreover, the virtually continuous campaigning that is required of legislators who represent highly competitive urban districts would be greatly reduced, leaving them more time to spend on legislative functions. Less campaigning also might serve to weaken the tie between legislators and the lobbyists who furnish both financial support for campaigning and bill-drafting services.

A new aspect of terms that is emerging in many states is term limitations.[23] In one proposed new Texas constitution (see Chapter 2), a limit of two consecutive six-year Senate terms and three consecutive four-year House

---

23. See B. Drummond Ayres, Jr., "Term Limit Laws Are Transforming More Legislatures," *New York Times*, April 28, 1997, A1, A14; and Karen Hansen, "The Third Revolution," *State Legislatures*, September 1997, 20–28.

terms was included. Term limits have a chance of finding legislative acceptance and probably voter approval in a constitutional amendment in the future. The term limit battle, both in Texas and nationally, is an irony. In an effort to place restrictions on legislators, enthusiasts are robbing voters of the right to choose at the ballot box whether to reelect or replace an incumbent in the future. Thus, democracy today is seeking to limit democracy tomorrow.

Summary

In many ways, the Texas legislature is typical of state lawmaking bodies: its large size (181 members), its domination by Anglo males, its somewhat limited professional staff, its relatively short terms of office for its members (two years in the House and four in the Senate), and its reliance on legislative committees as the workhorses of the legislative process. Nevertheless, the following distinctive features of the Texas legislature are atypical, especially when it is compared with the legislatures of other large urban states:

1. The legislature is restricted to one regular session of 140 days every two years.

2. Legislators are paid only $7,200 a year, although they receive a generous per diem payment for expenses.

3. The presiding officers—the speaker of the House and the lieutenant governor in the Senate—are preeminent in the legislative process. If either presiding officer is inclined to be arbitrary, democracy suffers.

4. A frequently high turnover rate and the shifting memberships of the large number of committees—fifteen in the Senate, thirty-six in the House in 1997—make it difficult for legislators to develop expertise in specific areas of legislation.

5. Special interests have an extraordinary influence on both the election and the performance of legislators. This dominance raises the issue of when and how constituent voices are heard.

Texas legislators face the biennial task of developing sound public policy for a major state without jeopardizing the support of the presiding officers or the special interests crucial to their reelection. Moreover, they operate in the highly constrained environment of both structural handicaps and lack of public confidence. They must spend much of their time tending to casework, sitting in committee meetings, or running for office. As Chapter 8 will show, they succeed better than one might expect given the many handicaps they face. Nevertheless, changes in legislative organization would help promote legislative independence and allow more time for planning and policy development. Recommendations for reform include the following:

1. Annual sessions

2. Higher salaries, in the $45,000 range

3. Four-year terms for House members and six-year terms for senators

4. Reduction in the number of legislative committees

Were these reforms to be implemented, the Texas legislature might be better prepared to govern the second-largest state in the nation.

Key Terms

Bicameral
Biennial
Casework
Constituent function
Formal qualifications

Legislative oversight
Privatizing
Reapportionment
Redistricting

Seniority
Single-member districts
Turnover

Study Questions

1. What are the differences between a regular and a called legislative session?

2. What does "one person, one vote" mean? What have been its implications for Texas? Do you think this concept is responsible for the increases in ethnic minority representation in the legislature? Why or why not?

3. What are the characteristics of the average Texas state legislator? Is it significant that the legislature is in fact likely to underrepresent important groups in the state's population? Why?

4. What are the problems caused by a biennial legislative session?

5. Do you think Texas legislators should be paid more? Why or why not?

6. Besides making laws, what other functions do legislators perform?

7. Do you think the number of terms that a legislator can serve should be limited? Why or why not? If you support term limitation, indicate how many terms you would have senators and representatives serve. Also, would you keep the terms at their present length? Discuss.

8. Do you prefer that the Texas legislature remain as it is, or that it be more like the legislatures of other big urban states such as California and New York? Discuss.

Internet Assignment

Internet site: www.capitol.state.tx.us/

Click on either the House or the Senate; then click on "committees." Select one committee; then, after finding out who the chair of that committee is, click on the name of that representative or senator and read about the chair and his or her district. Repeat this exercise for two other committee chairs. What party dominates the committee chairmanships? Do the legislative districts seem to have anything in common?

Chapter Eight

The Legislative Process

Speaker of the House Pete Laney (top, left) gavels the Texas House of Representatives to order. Former Lieutenant Governor Bob Bullock, who presided over the Texas Senate until his retirement in 1999, emphasizes a point during his final inauguration (bottom, right).

There wasn't enough money for people—the elderly, the poor, handicapped, children, education, teachers. I would have voted for horse racing, dog racing . . . a state lottery . . . another seven-eighths of a penny sales tax.

Senator Gonzalo Barrientos of Austin

What lobbyists can dream, lobbyists can do.

Representative Steve Wolens of Dallas

Legislative bodies seldom live up to what the public expects of them.

Texas Monthly

Introduction

Each January of odd-numbered years, 31 senators and 150 representatives gather in Austin to try to work their way through more than five thousand legislative proposals. Texans can predict that prisons, education, utilities, and tax reform will be headlined in the state's newspapers, but the process by which these and other issues are resolved can be a confused jumble to the layperson. If they think of it at all, citizens often consider the legislative session a biennial free-for-all.

One reason for this seeming confusion is that complex rules are a basic part of the legislative process. The larger the assembly, the more necessary are the parliamentary procedures that facilitate working through the agenda.

Another reason is that the legislative process consists of several stages. To judge the fate of a particular proposed piece of legislation known as a bill, one must know which stage the bill is in. Is it in committee? On the floor for debate? In a conference committee? In the governor's hands? Discussion, changes, votes, approvals, and disapprovals occur at various stages. Those who wish to follow the process of a piece of legislation through newspaper accounts must read carefully to determine whether votes taken are on the bill itself, an amendment to an amendment, a substitute motion, or a motion to table the bill or return it to committee. Indeed, to the uninitiated, it may seem that the same bill is being voted on over and over again.

A third reason is the growing complexity of the issues that legislators face. As the Gonzalo Barrientos quote made at the close of the 1985 session still reflects, juggling the need for services with revenue sources is a frequent source of dismay.

Although their powers were somewhat limited by the modest seniority rules adopted by both houses in 1973, the presiding officers basically control the flow of legislation in Texas. Their power over public policy in Texas is tremendous. However, many who are not legislators—a supporting cast that includes the governor, the lobbyists, the state bureaucrats, legislative staffers, and sometimes the public—are also involved in making legislative policy. Representative Wolens's comment at the opening of the chapter expresses his frustration at the brazenness of the business lobby during the 1995 session.

This chapter describes the important influences on legislation, how a bill becomes a law in Texas, and lawmaking outside the legislature.

Power of the Presiding Officers

By constitutional mandate, the presiding officer in the Senate is the lieutenant governor, and the presiding officer in the House of Representatives is the speaker of the House. The powers that the holder of each of these positions enjoys are derived from the rules of the legislative body over which he presides and are of two basic sorts. The first has to do with the organization of the legislature and legislative procedure. In varying degrees, all presiding officers exercise this power of the chair. The second sort of power is institutional, and it has to do with the maintenance of the legislature as a vital organ of government.

A reform-oriented House or Senate can limit the powers of the presiding officers. In 1973, for example, the House provided for a limited number of seniority appointments to standing committees, the Senate provided for some experience on committees, and both reorganized the committee structure. Politics can also dictate a change, as may be the case in 1999, depending on whether Agriculture Commissioner Rick Perry or Comptroller John Sharp replaces Bob Bullock as lieutenant governor. However, tradition and the realities of politics militate against any real overthrow of the powerful legislative leadership. So also does the legislative amateurism that results from short sessions, low pay, and high turnover in membership.

From time to time, the leaders themselves have a reform bent. One reason for the introduction of modified seniority in 1973 was that one-term reform Speaker Price Daniel, Jr., insisted on some controls over lobbyists. In 1993, Speaker Pete Laney blunted the power of the speaker and made the House more democratic.

Often, though, powerful leaders are a convenience, albeit sometimes a tiresome or costly one. The significance of some of the specific procedural and institutional powers of the lieutenant governor and speaker of the House is discussed in the following sections.

PROCEDURAL POWERS

Legislative committees have life-or-death power over a **bill,** which is the way in which legislation is introduced. Legislators' appointments to major committees, especially as chairperson or vice chairperson, largely determine their influence with the legislature as a whole. Presiding officers can thus use their powers of appointment to reward friends and supporters with key positions on important committees and to punish opponents with nonleadership positions on minor committees.

COMMITTEE MEMBERSHIP

Although seniority does play a role in the formation of House committees, the speaker still effectively determines their composition. The seniority appointments are made after the speaker appoints the chairpersons and vice chairpersons of the committees. The speaker always has some choice because several representatives often have the same amount of seniority in the House.

Senate rules stipulate only that a minority of members must have prior service on a particular committee. Thus, the lieutenant governor, as presiding officer of the Senate, dominates those committee selections.

Special-interest representatives, as well as legislators, are frequently involved in the bargaining that eventually determines who will fill committee slots. Members of interest groups, wanting friends on committees, frequently make suggestions to the presiding officers about member selection. The only committee appointments not made by the presiding officers are those few appointments to special-interest study committees that the governor might make. And even in these cases, the legislature has the power to approve or disapprove nonlegislative appointments to the interim committee.

CONFERENCE COMMITTEES

A major bill seldom passes both houses in identical form. Each time one fails to do so, a conference committee may be appointed to resolve the differences. Before 1973, conference committees could, and frequently did, produce virtually new bills. Beginning in 1973, the House adopted a rule effective at the beginning of each session limiting the conference committee to ironing out differences in the two versions of a bill. Resolving these differences often means adding new material to the bill at the conference stage. Five members from each house are appointed to conference committees by their respective presiding officers. Each house has one vote on the conference committee report—in other words, three members on each house's team of five must agree on the conference version of the bill before the bill can be reported back to the House and Senate. The conference report must be accepted or rejected, without change, by each house. This procedure makes conference committee members key figures in the legislative process. Most conference reports, or versions of the bill, are accepted because of time limitations.

Appointees to conference committees usually share the viewpoints of the presiding officers on what should be done with the bill in question. Representatives of special interests often become involved in conference committee deliberations in an attempt to arrange trade-offs, or bargains, with the presiding officers, making one concession in exchange for another.

COMMITTEE CHAIRPERSONS

The standing committees control legislation, and their chairpersons not only specify the committee agenda, subcommittee jurisdiction, and assignments, but also control the committees. Lobbyists for special-interest groups work hard to influence the selection of chairpersons and vice chairpersons of committees. A lobbyist's year is generally successful if his or her choice is appointed to chair a committee crucial to the lobbyist's special interests. However, if a lobbyist must deal with an unfriendly chairperson, the session may seem long and trying.

The reward-and-punishment aspect of committee appointments is especially evident in the appointment of chairpersons, for it is through them that the presiding officers control legislation. True seniority is relatively unimportant in determining chairmanships, but some experience is useful. Obviously, political enemies of the lieutenant governor or the speaker are not likely to chair standing committees. Speaker Gib Lewis increased his control of standing committees by creating a new position on House committees, that of chairperson for budget and oversight (CBO). The speaker appointed the CBOs.

As noted in Chapter 7, Democrats and Republicans are increasingly sharing power in the legislature. Through 1997 the presiding officers preferred to operate on a nonpartisan basis by ignoring party labels, and they have blessed the members of both parties with committee chairmanships. This approach avoids the gridlock that is common in Congress, where each party has traditionally put up roadblocks against the favored legislation of the other party. It thus allows the Texas legislature to set public policy in spite of a very short legislative session (see Chapter 7). Taking a nonpartisan approach to legislation has worked well as the partisan alignment in the legislature has gone from Democratic domination to Republican ascendancy. It remains to be seen whether this tactic will be continued if the Republicans come to hold a majority in both houses and the lieutenant governor's position. That situation last occurred shortly after the Civil War.

REFERRAL

Because of the large number of committees, which committee has jurisdiction over a particular legislative proposal is ill defined by the Texas legislature. Unlike the U.S. Congress, where committee jurisdictions are relatively clear, jurisdictional ambiguities are pervasive in the Texas committee system. The large number of committees—thirty-six in 1997—in the House and the absolute silence of Senate rules on committee jurisdiction create these ambiguities. The committee system in Texas thus allows the presiding officers to use their referral power to determine the outcome of a bill. In other words, if the speaker or lieutenant governor favors a bill, the bill will be referred to a committee that will act favorably toward it. If the presiding officer opposes the proposed legislation, it will be assigned to an unfriendly committee. However, the referral powers of the Senate's presiding officer were curtailed somewhat by the 1973 reform of the committee system and by Senate rules that can force a change in referral. An unprecedented use of the referral power occurred in the second special session of 1986. When the House Ways and Means Committee stalled the bill to increase taxes to help meet the state's revenue problems, Speaker Gib Lewis removed the bill from that committee and assigned it to the State Affairs Committee.

Some of the factors considered by the presiding officers when assigning bills to committees include (1) the positions of their own financial supporters and political backers on the bill; (2) the effect of the bill on other legislation, especially the availability of funding for other programs; (3) their own ideological commitment to the bill; (4) the past record of support or nonsupport of the bill's backers, both legislators and special interests; and (5) the bargaining in which the bill's backers are willing to engage, including promises of desired support of, or opposition to, other bills on which the presiding officers have strong positions as well as a willingness to modify the bill itself.

SCHEDULING/THE CALENDAR

In all legislative bodies, bills are assigned a time for debate. This scheduling—placing the bill on a legislative calendar—determines the order of the bill's debate and vote. In Congress, the majority leader controls the two Senate calendars, although the informality of the Senate reduces the importance of the calendars; the Rules Committee of the House assigns bills to one of five calendars. In Texas, power is concentrated in the hands of the presiding officers, who determine to which calendar, and where on that calendar, a bill will be assigned.

Scheduling is more important in Texas than in some other states or in Congress because of the short biennial legislative session. A bill placed far down on the schedule may not come to the floor before the session reaches its 140-day mandatory adjournment. In addition, items on the calendars are called in order, and some calendars do not allow debate. For example, in the House, it is highly advantageous to have a bill placed on the Consent Calendar, which is used for uncontested legislation. The timing of debate may well determine the outcome of the vote. Legislative strategies include trying either to delay the call of a bill until negative votes can be lined up or to rush a bill through before opposition can materialize. Another factor to be considered in Senate scheduling is the possibility of a **filibuster.** It is much easier to shut off attempts to "talk a bill to death" early in the session than when only a few days are left for action. (The filibuster is discussed under "Floor Action" later in this chapter.)

In the House, the powerful Calendars Committee and, to a lesser extent, the Local and Consent Calendars Committee control the placement of bills on one of the House calendars. The speaker's powers are indirect through the appointment of the committees and their chairpersons and vice chairpersons. A member essentially goes "hat in hand" to one of these gatekeeper committees—usually the Calendars Committee, since it deals with major legislation—to try to get her or his bill on the calendar. However, if any committee member objects to the bill, the bill is never scheduled. Moreover, these committees meet in secret. House members can challenge a ruling by the committee, but since a two-thirds vote is required to pry the bill from committee and other members fear reprisals as they try to get their own bills out of committee, attempts to force a scheduling of debate are very rare.

The names of the House calendar committees (see Table 8–1) are largely self-explanatory. Well-publicized bills will find their way to the Major State Calendar unless an emergency exists (such as authorizing repairs to the capitol after a fire); other general legislation is slated to the General State Calendar. The Local Calendar deals with business involving one part of the state (for example, the creation of a new special district in a single county). Placement of a bill on the Consent Calendar signifies no opposition, although the bill can be withdrawn from the Consent Calendar if opposition develops later. The other calendars are restricted to proposed constitutional amendments and other resolutions.

No calendars committee exists in the Senate, and technically the main calendar—the Senate Calendar—is simply called in numerical order. However, bills virtually never come up in order because of motions to take up other bills out of order. A motion to take up a bill out of order requires a two-thirds vote. Moreover, if a senator intends to ask for consideration of a bill out of order, he or she must file an intention to do so with the clerk, stipulating the date on which the motion will be made and asking for a place on the Intent Calendar. When Bill Hobby was lieutenant governor, he formalized the Intent

TABLE 8–1

A Comparison of the Legislative Calenders in the Texas Legislature and the U.S. Congress

Texas Legislative Calendars

Senate	House
Senate	Emergency
Intent	Major State
	Constitutional Amendments
	General State
	Local
	Consent
	Resolutions

Congressional Calendars

Senate	House
Senate	House
Executive	Union
	Consent
	Private
	Discharge

Calendar as a way of forcing the members to reveal their plans in advance to avoid surprising the presiding officer. All other business, not on the Intent Calendar, can then be placed on the Senate Calendar.

Two Ways to Block a Bill

The Filibuster

Former Senator Bill Meier, who talked for forty-three hours straight in 1977, holds the Texas and world records for filibustering. More recently, in 1993, Senator Gonzalo Barrientos stopped just short of eighteen hours in an unsuccessful effort to protect Barton Creek and its popular swimming hole.

The Technicality

One of the most bizarre events in the history of the Texas legislature occurred in 1997, when conservative Representative Arlene Wohlgemuth, angry at the blockage of a bill regarding parental notification before girls under eighteen could get an abortion, raised a point of order about the calendar for May 26. The effect was to kill fifty-two bills that were scheduled for debate because the point of order concerned the calendar itself. Her fellow legislators referred to the incident as the "Memorial Day Massacre," and were irate that months of work, including the delicate negotiations between House and Senate members to achieve compromise bills, apparently had been for nought. After tempers cooled, legislators found ways to resurrect some of the bills, by tacking them onto other bills that had not been on the calendar for Memorial Day and by using resolutions.

A legislator has two ways to improve the chances that a bill will be placed high enough on a calendar to ensure floor debate on it. First, members may prefile bills as soon as the November elections are completed. Early filing does not ensure that the presiding officer or the chair to whose committee the bill is referred will be favorably disposed toward the proposed legislation, but obtaining a low number because of quick filing may at least ensure that the bill is referred to committee early in the session. Second, if the bill is one in which the governor has a keen interest, the governor can declare an emergency to force speedy consideration of the proposal.

RECOGNITION

One of the prerogatives of the presiding officer of any assembly is the recognition of individuals who wish to speak. In legislative bodies, with the occasional exception of presiding officers who are simply arbitrary, the recognition power is traditionally invoked in a fair and judicious manner. Speaker Laney and Lieutenant Governor Bullock have followed this tradition. In Texas, the Senate procedures for scheduling legislation—that is, the Intent Calendar—give the presiding officer extraordinary power. The lieutenant governor must recognize a bill's sponsor before the sponsor can move the bill for consideration, and the sponsor needs the presiding officer's support to achieve the necessary two-thirds vote of the legislation. Effectively, eleven senators who oppose a bill can block it, since the sponsor cannot hope to achieve a two-thirds majority.

PROCEDURES

At the beginning of each regular session of the Texas legislature, each house adopts the rules of procedure that will govern that session's legislative process. Although procedures can change considerably—as was evidenced by the 1973 reforms and the 1983 House changes giving the speaker more control over appropriations, members' office budgets, and committee jurisdictions—many rules are carried over from one session to another or are only slightly modified.[1] Numerous precedents determine how the rules will be applied, and, of course, all parliamentary rules are subject to interpretation by the chair. Thus, the presiding officers greatly influence the outcome of policy deliberations by their acceptance or rejection of points of order, their decisions as to whether a proposed amendment is germane, their announcement of vote counts, and so forth.

In summary, procedural interpretation, recognition of those wishing to speak, determination of the timetable for debate, referral of bills, and the appointment of committees and their chairpersons all combine to make the presiding officers truly powerful. While none of these powers is unusual for a club president, they take on greater significance when we realize that they are used to determine the outcome of policy struggles within the government of a major state.

---

1. Like constitutional revision, major rules changes seldom take precedence at the beginning of a busy legislative session. Representative Kent Grusendorf made an effort at introducing major rules changes for the 1997 session through his "Fair Rules for an Open House: A Call for Comprehensive Rules Reforms of the Texas House" but found little interest among his fellow legislators.

Vote Early and Vote Often

The presiding officer of the Senate has limited voting powers, since the lieutenant governor is not a member of the Senate. He can vote when a tie on a bill occurs and during debate when the Senate sits as a committee of the whole.

The speaker is a member of the House and can vote. One of the most extraordinary uses of speaker power occurred in 1967 when Speaker Ben Barnes voted to make a tie, then voted again to break the tie on a bill he favored. He thus cast two votes on the same bill.

INSTITUTIONAL POWERS

The presiding officers also appoint the members of three important arms of the legislature: the Legislative Budget Board, the Texas Legislative Council, and the Legislative Audit Committee. Each of these bodies exists to serve the legislature as a whole, providing policy guidelines at the board level and technical assistance at the staff level. Not only do the presiding officers control these three policy-setting and policy-recommending bodies, but for all three, the president of the Senate also serves as chairperson and the speaker of the House as vice chairperson.

THE LEGISLATIVE BUDGET BOARD

At the national level, in most states, and even in most cities, the chief executive bears the responsibility for preparing the budget. In Texas, both the governor and the legislature prepare a budget, and state agencies must submit their financial requests to each. The legislative budget is prepared by the Legislative Budget Board (LBB), a ten-member Senate-House joint committee that operates continually, whether the legislature is in session or not. In addition to the presiding officers, there are four members from each house appointed by the presiding officers. By tradition, these include the chairpersons of the committees responsible for appropriations and finance. Because of the importance of these "money" committees, their chairpersons sometimes develop power bases within the legislature that are independent of the presiding officers.

A professional staff assists the board in making its budget recommendations, then often helps defend those recommendations during the session. The staff recommendations on state agency requests are crucial to an agency's appropriations. Executives in administrative agencies therefore work closely with LBB staff in an effort to justify their spending requests.

Additionally, the staff assists the legislature in its watchdog function by overseeing state agency expenditures. This function increased in importance during the long period of budget "crunches" from 1985 through 1995, so that the LBB and the Governor's Office of Budget and Planning now oversee agency planning and monitor agency performance in meeting state goals and objectives.

THE TEXAS LEGISLATIVE COUNCIL

The seventeen-member Texas Legislative Council includes the presiding officers and five senators and ten representatives appointed by their respective presiding officer. The council oversees the work of the director and professional staff. During the session, the council provides bill-drafting services for legislators; between sessions, it investigates the operations of state agencies, conducts studies on problems subject to legislative consideration, and drafts recommendations for action in the next session. In short, it is the legislature's research office, similar to the Congressional Research Service.

LEGISLATIVE AUDIT COMMITTEE

In addition to the presiding officers, the other four members of the Legislative Audit Committee are the chairpersons of the Senate Finance, House Ways and Means, House Appropriations, and Senate State Affairs committees. The state auditor, appointed by the committee for a two-year term subject to two-thirds confirmation of the Senate, heads the professional staff. This committee oversees a very important function of all legislative bodies, that of the postaudit by the auditor and the auditor's staff of expenditures of state agencies to ensure their legality. The auditor's staff also checks into the quality of services and duplication in services and programs provided by state agencies. The highly detailed work of the professional staff involves a review of the records of financial transactions. In fact, the larger state agencies have an auditor or team of auditors assigned to them practically year-round.

Presiding Officers' Powers of the Chair: A Summary

Procedural Powers

1. Appointing half or more of the members of substantive committees and all members of procedural and conference committees (the House reserves half of the positions for seniority appointments; the Senate requires only that some members have prior experience)
2. Appointing the chairs and vice chairs of all committees
3. Determining the jurisdiction of committees through the referral of bills
4. Interpreting procedural rules when conflict arises
5. Scheduling legislation for floor action (especially important in the Senate, which lacks a complex calendar system)
6. Recognizing members who wish to speak, or not recognizing them and thus preventing them from speaking

Institutional Powers

1. Appointing the members of the Legislative Budget Board and serving as the chair and vice chair thereof
2. Appointing the members of the Texas Legislative Council and serving as the chair and vice chair thereof
3. Appointing the members of the Legislative Audit Committee and serving as chair and vice chair thereof

Limits on Presiding Officers

It may seem as if the presiding officers are nearly unrestrained in their exercise of power. There are several personal and political factors, however, that prevent absolute power on the part of the speaker of the House and the lieutenant governor.

PERSONALITY AND AMBITION

Although there is always the danger that presiding officers may become arbitrary or vindictive and thus abuse their office, they usually are so powerful that they do not need to search for ways to gain influence other than through persuasion, compromise, and accommodation. Arbitrariness is a function of personality, not of the office. Former Lieutenant Governor Bill Hobby of Houston, who served eighteen years and seemed content to play a statesmanlike role rather than seeking higher office, was the epitome of fair play.

Also, speakers or lieutenant governors with political ambitions—at least five have become governor—generally avoid angering special interests and thus cutting themselves off from potential financial campaign support or business credit. And they prefer not to anger other state officials who may be instrumental in furthering their political plans. Not making enemies is also the rule for presiding officers contemplating lucrative business positions when they leave office.

LEGISLATORS

State senators and representatives have their own power bases, without which they probably would not have been elected. Long-time members not only have supporters across the state, including influential special interests, but also have the advantage that seniority brings within the legislature itself. If they have served as the chairperson of a major committee for more than one session, legislators are especially likely to have their own power bases as well as the support of the presiding officers. For example, in 1997 Senator Bill Ratliff single-handedly rewrote the formula by which higher educational institutions are funded, while Representative Ron Wilson won the day by insisting that if minorities could not be given preferential treatment in admissions (see Chapters 11 and 14), athletes should not receive preferential treatment.

Furthermore, the presiding officers are limited in their leadership responsibilities to legislators. The speaker of the House, especially, spends considerable time trying to organize and manage his 149 colleagues, their pet bills, and their requests. The lieutenant governor is more of a statewide public figure. He is elected independently of the governor and is in demand as a speaker and goodwill ambassador. In addition, the House has more complicated legislative procedures than does the Senate. The president of the Senate can frequently bring about consensus behind the scenes and prevent disruption on the Senate floor.

It may appear that the membership always follows the lead of the presiding officers. In many cases, basic agreement on ideological positions already exists, since the leadership and most legislators are usually conservative. In other instances, members will go along with the leadership in the hope of later being able to act independently on matters of importance to them or to their districts. Finally, the powers of the presiding officers are largely granted by House and Senate rules. A totally arbitrary leader whose abuse of the system became intolerable could be stripped of much of his power by changes in those rules. Such action is highly unlikely.

Sometimes, individual legislators show independence but little leadership. Some weeks after the close of the 1997 legislative session, Senator Drew Nixon was arrested for solicitation of prostitution and carrying an illegal weapon.

INTEREST GROUPS AND STATE ADMINISTRATION

Over the past fifty years, as the number of state governmental agencies and bureaucrats has increased (see Chapter 10), an alliance has developed between private and public interests. These coalitions and the presiding officers often share the same political viewpoint, making confrontations unlikely.

The public is seldom considered by these alliances, especially when some of the more powerful special interests of the state, such as oil and gas, insurance, banking, and real estate, are involved. An example of a bureaucracy–private interest alliance is the Texas Department of Transportation and the Texas Good Roads and Transportation Association, which was discussed in Chapter 4.

THE GOVERNOR

Constitutionally, the governor is a weak chief administrator; hence the alliance is between state bureaucrats and the lobbyists, not the chief executive. Even so, the governor is by no means a weak chief legislator. The governor's veto power is almost absolute because the legislature often adjourns before the governor has had time to act on a bill.

A governor who wants a particular piece of legislation enacted can threaten the legislature with a special session if the legislation seems to be in jeopardy. Because special sessions are costly to state legislators in terms of both time and money, such a threat can be a powerful tool for the governor. The governor must be prepared to make good such a threat, as, for example, Bill Clements did when he called a special session on tort reform—that is, changes in the basis of civil lawsuits—in 1987 after failing to get action from the 1987 legislature. Such threats, however, do not always work.

Another of the governor's strengths lies in the strong ties a conservative (usually the political orientation of the Texas governor) has to the same interest groups as the legislators. These ties often make it possible for the governor to call on these interests to support a position that is in conflict with that of the legislature. Ann Richards, an avowed populist who tackled some powerful special interests, often sought ties to the voters to bolster her influence on the legislature.

THE ELECTORATE

Legislative bodies were created to be the people's voice in government, although only about one-third of the eligible voters bother to vote in legislative elections. Citizens are likely to find it challenging and perhaps difficult to exert as much influence over the leadership and members of the Texas legislature as do state officials and private interests. One reason for this situation is the strength of special interests. Another is the lack of knowledge on the part

The Seventy-Fourth Legislature in 1995 proved to be a great boon for business interests, with consumers losing a number of traditional protections against bad products, shoddy service, malpractice, and environmental pollution.

Courtesy of Ben Sargent.

of most citizens in Texas and other states about what goes on in the state capital. Citizens focus on issues affecting them directly, such as drunken driving, but the ordinary day-to-day legislative events do not stir the interest of most Texans. Furthermore, powerful special interests work hard to avoid stirring up the citizens. One exception in 1995 involved an impressive show of solidarity by women who suffered from symptoms resulting from breast implants as the legislature was debating a measure that would make it difficult to sue for such problems. They were a vocal lobby.

How a Bill Becomes a Law in Texas

The Texas Constitution specifies that a bill be used to introduce a law or a change in a law. Bills that pass both houses successfully become acts and are sent to the governor for his signature or veto. In addition to bills, there are three types of resolutions in each house:

1. Simple resolutions are used in each house to take care of housekeeping matters, details of business, and trivia. Examples include procedural rules adopted by each house—serious business, indeed—and trivia such as birthday greetings to a member.

2. Concurrent resolutions are similar to simple resolutions but require the action of both houses. An example would be their use for adjournment.

3. Joint resolutions are of major interest to the public because they are the means of introducing proposed constitutional amendments.

Each bill or resolution is designated by an abbreviation that indicates the house of origin, the nature of the legislation, and a number. For example, S.B. 1 is Senate Bill 1; S.J.R. indicates a joint resolution that originated in the Senate.

Bills may originate in either house or in both simultaneously, with the exception of revenue bills. They must originate in the House, according to the Texas Constitution. During a typical session, legislators introduce five thousand or more bills and resolutions, of which only 30 percent are passed. When the legislature must also deal with reapportionment and redistricting, the number is reduced by several hundred as a concession to the time redistricting will take. Because lawmakers must consider so many proposals in such a limited time, originators of a bill often mark a bill "By Request" and drop it in the hopper—the traditional legislative "in-basket." This is their way of indicating that they were asked to introduce the legislation but do not expect it to receive serious consideration.

The major differences in the procedures of the two houses are:

1. The House has more than twice as many committees as the Senate; therefore, the speaker has a greater choice in determining where to refer a bill.

2. The calendars are different (as explained earlier in this chapter).

3. Debate is unlimited in the Senate, whereas House debate is usually limited to ten minutes per member and twenty minutes for the bill's sponsor.

To be enacted into law, a bill must survive as many as four legislative steps and a fifth step in the governor's office (see Figure 8–1). Because the smaller size of the Senate enables it to operate with less formality than the House, we will use the Senate to trace the path of a bill through the legislative process.

STEP ONE: INTRODUCTION AND REFERRAL

Every bill must be introduced by a member of the legislature, who is considered the sponsor. If a bill has several sponsors, so much the better—its chances of survival will be greatly enhanced. There are two ways to introduce bills: (1) the member, after being recognized by the lieutenant governor as president of the Senate, may introduce it from the floor, or (2) the member may deposit copies of the bill with the secretary of the Senate (in the House, with the clerk), including prefiling a bill in November. The secretary assigns a number to the bill that reflects the order of submission. The reading clerk then gives the bill the first of the three readings required by the constitution. The first time, only a caption is read, which is a brief summary of the bill's contents. The second method of introducing bills is the one more commonly used.

The lieutenant governor (in the House, the speaker) then refers the bill to a committee. If the bill is to survive, it must be assigned to a friendly committee. The bill's sponsor will have been on "good behavior" in the hope that the lieutenant governor will give the bill a favorable referral.

FIGURE 8–1
How a Bill Becomes a Law in Texas

This figure traces the passage of a bill that originated in the Senate. Steps 1 to 3 for the Senate and House would be reversed if the bill originated in the House. The example presumes the need for a conference committee.

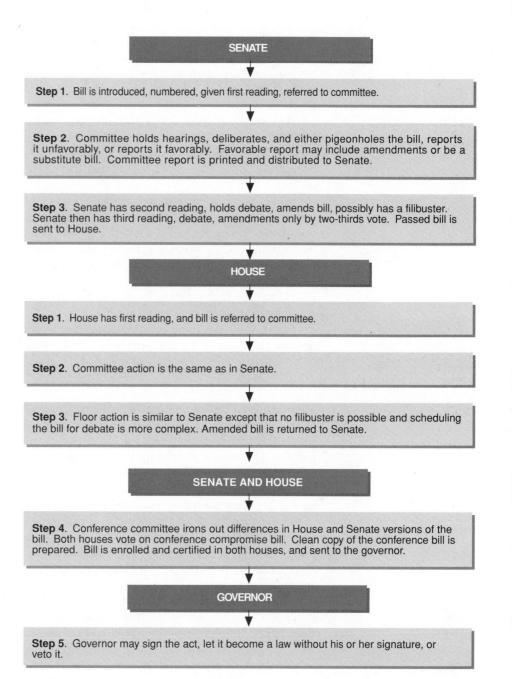

SENATE

Step 1. Bill is introduced, numbered, given first reading, referred to committee.

Step 2. Committee holds hearings, deliberates, and either pigeonholes the bill, reports it unfavorably, or reports it favorably. Favorable report may include amendments or be a substitute bill. Committee report is printed and distributed to Senate.

Step 3. Senate has second reading, holds debate, amends bill, possibly has a filibuster. Senate then has third reading, debate, amendments only by two-thirds vote. Passed bill is sent to House.

HOUSE

Step 1. House has first reading, and bill is referred to committee.

Step 2. Committee action is the same as in Senate.

Step 3. Floor action is similar to Senate except that no filibuster is possible and scheduling the bill for debate is more complex. Amended bill is returned to Senate.

SENATE AND HOUSE

Step 4. Conference committee irons out differences in House and Senate versions of the bill. Both houses vote on conference compromise bill. Clean copy of the conference bill is prepared. Bill is enrolled and certified in both houses, and sent to the governor.

GOVERNOR

Step 5. Governor may sign the act, let it become a law without his or her signature, or veto it.

STEP TWO: COMMITTEE ACTION

Standing committees are really miniature legislatures in which the nitty-gritty of legislation takes place. Legislators are so busy—particularly in Texas, with the short, infrequent sessions—that they seldom have time to study bills in detail and so must rely heavily on the committee reports. A bill's sponsor, well aware of the committee's role, will do everything possible to ensure that the committee's report is favorable. It is particularly important to avoid having the bill *pigeonholed* (put on the bottom of the committee's agenda, never to be seen again) or totally rewritten, either by the committee or, if the bill is referred to a subcommittee, by the subcommittee. If the bill can escape being pigeonholed, its sponsor will have a chance to bargain with the committee in an effort to avoid too many changes in the bill.

The standing committees hold hearings on proposed legislation. Major bills will generate considerable public, media, and lobbyist interest. The large number of committees—especially in the House—and the volume of proposed legislation sometimes means that these hearings are held at odd hours, such as 11:00 P.M.

A senator, but not a representative, can **tag** a bill, indicating that the lawmaker must get forty-eight hour's written notice of the hearing. If the senator does not receive notice or if the bill was not posted publicly seventy-two hours in advance, a senator can use a tag to object to the bill and delay the committee hearing. Tagging is sometimes an effective practice to defeat a bill late in the legislative session.

The committee may report the bill favorably, unfavorably, or not at all. An unfavorable report or none at all will kill it. Unless there is a strong minority report, however, there is little reason for the committee to report a bill unfavorably; it is easier to pigeonhole it and avoid floor action completely.

STEP THREE: FLOOR ACTION

Once reported out of committee, a bill must be scheduled for debate. The Senate Calendar is rarely followed; instead, senators list their bills on the Intent Calendar, which in essence is a declaration of intent to ask for a suspension of the rules to take up a bill out of order. As with any motion to suspend the rules, two-thirds of those present and voting must vote yes on the suspension. Before filing an intent to ask for a suspension, the bill's sponsors generally get an assurance from the presiding officer that they will be recognized and thus given an opportunity to make the motion. When the bill receives the necessary two-thirds vote, it can proceed to its second reading and debate.[2] The sponsor is relieved because only a simple majority of votes is required for passage. (In the House, the Calendars Committee establishes a schedule for debate.)

Senators have unlimited privileges of debate: They may speak as long as they wish about a bill on the floor. Sometimes senators use this privilege to filibuster—that is, to try to kill a bill by talking at length about it and anything else that will use up time. By tying up the floor and preventing other bills from being considered, the senator or group of senators hopes to pressure enough of the membership to lay aside the controversial bill so that other matters can be debated. The filibuster is most effective at the end of the legislative session when time is short and many bills have yet to be debated. Shutting off debate, however, requires a simple majority vote. Despite their potential effectiveness, filibusters do not occur frequently because so much Senate business is conducted off the Senate floor in bargaining sessions. The

---

2. If the second reading has not occurred by the time the legislature is within seventy-two hours of adjournment, the bill dies.

presiding officer, incidentally, has the power to ask the intention of a member when the member is recognized for debate and thus knows when a filibuster will occur. Tradition also dictates that a member who plans to filibuster notify the press of the forthcoming event.

If a bill is fortunate enough not to become entangled in a filibuster, debate proceeds. During the course of debate, there may be proposed amendments, amendments to amendments, motions to table, or even motions to send the bill back to committee. However, if a bill has succeeded in actually reaching the floor for discussion, it is usually passed in one form or another. A vote is taken after the third reading, again by caption, of the bill. At this stage, amendments require a two-thirds vote. It is more or less routine for four-fifths of the Senate to vote to suspend the rules and proceed immediately to the third reading.

IN THE HOUSE: STEPS ONE THROUGH THREE REPEATED

If it was not introduced in both houses simultaneously, a bill passed in the Senate must proceed to the House. There, under its original designation (for example, S.B. 341), it must repeat the same three steps, with the exceptions noted earlier. It has little chance of passing if a representative does not shepherd it through. (This situation is true in reverse also, when a bill passes the House and is then sent to the Senate.) In addition, the Laney reforms of 1993 included a series of deadlines concerning the final seventeen days of a legislative session, and a bill must comply with those House rules. For example, after 135 days of a regular session, the House cannot consider a Senate bill except to adopt a conference report, reconsider the bill to remove Senate amendments, or override a veto; the deadlines for various types of House bills are earlier.[3] To facilitate our explanation, the assumption here is that the bill passes the House, but with one amendment added that was not part of the Senate's version.

STEP FOUR: CONFERENCE COMMITTEE

Because the Senate and House versions of the bill differ, it must go to a **conference committee,** which consists of ten members: five appointed from each house by the presiding officers. If the House and Senate versions of the bill exhibit substantial differences, the conference committee may attach several amendments or rewrite portions of it. It may even be pigeonholed. On a bill with only one difference between the versions passed by the two houses, the single vote of the committee members from the Senate and the single vote of those from the House may be obtained without too much wrangling.

The bill is then reported back to the Senate and the House for action in each chamber. The report of the conference committee must be voted on as it stands; neither house can amend it. It must be accepted, rejected, or sent back to the conference committee. If it fails at this stage—or indeed at any stage—it is automatically dead. No bill can be introduced twice during the same session, although a bill can be rewritten and introduced as a new piece of legislation.

If the bill receives a majority of the votes in each house, the engrossing and enrolling clerk prepares a correct copy of it, first for the house where the bill originated, then for the other house. Its caption is read a final time, and it is signed by the presiding officers, the House chief clerk, and the Senate secretary. The vote of passage is certified, and the engrossed (officially printed) bill, now an act, is sent to the governor for action. A record of these steps is printed in the journal of each house.

STEP FIVE: THE GOVERNOR

The governor has 10 days (excluding Sundays) to dispose of enacted legislation. If the legislature adjourns, the 10-day period is extended to 20 days. The governor has three options available to deal with an act. The first is to sign it, thus making it law.

The second is to allow the act to become law without signing it. If the governor does not sign it, an act becomes law in 10 days if the legislature is in session and in 20 days if it is not. By choosing this rather weak course of action, the governor signifies both opposition to the legislation and an unwillingness to risk a veto that could be overridden by a two-thirds vote of both houses or that would incur the disfavor of special interests supporting the bill.

Third, the governor may veto the act. Although it is possible for the legislature to override a veto, the governor often receives legislation so late in the session that the act of vetoing or signing it can be deferred until the session has ended. A veto then is absolute, since it must be overridden during the same legislative session in which the act was passed and the legislature cannot call itself into special session. At any time, the legislature may have difficulty

3. House Research Organization, *How a Bill Becomes a Law,* u.d., 24.

mustering the two-thirds vote necessary to override a veto. Because recent legislative sessions have been faced with one crisis after another and have had too little time to deal with issues, the governor's powers have been strengthened through use of the veto and threats of a veto.

If the governor chooses to veto, the veto applies to the entire act, except in the case of appropriations bills. On an appropriations act, the governor has the power of **item veto;** that is, specific items may be vetoed. This is a powerful gubernatorial tool for limiting state spending, but in recent years the legislature has blunted this tool by making lump-sum appropriations to agencies such as colleges and universities.

When the governor signs an act, it becomes one of the few proposals that manage to survive. It is entered in the statute books by the secretary of state. If it contains an emergency clause, it becomes effective as law either immediately or whenever designated in the bill. If it does not, it becomes effective 90 days after the session ends. Again, there are special circumstances for appropriations acts. They always become effective September 1 because the state's **fiscal year** (its budget period) is from September 1 through August 31 of the following year.

Legislative Dynamics

The public often thinks that the legislature accomplishes very little, as the chapter-opening quotation from *Texas Monthly* notes. It is, in fact, amazing that the legislature accomplishes as much as it does, given the limitations under which the institution must labor. The forces influencing legislation are complex and varied: interest groups, the powers of the presiding officers, the governor, constitutional limitations, political parties, the role of committees, short and infrequent sessions, inadequate salaries, and the prerogatives of individual members.

HANDICAPS

Each legislator must face five thousand or so bills and resolutions during every regular session. Thus the legislative workload is very heavy. Very few of these five thousand are substantively important, and many are trivial matters that could more easily be left to administrative agencies. Only about 30 percent of them are passed. Nevertheless, in the short 140-day session, legislators must acquaint themselves with the proposals, try to push their own legislative programs, attend to a heavy burden of casework, spend countless hours in committee work, meet with hometown and interest-group representatives, and hear the professional views of state administrators who implement programs. Although many legislators are personally wealthy, those who are not must also try to avoid going into debt because their salaries are inadequate and their personal businesses or professions cannot be attended to when the legislature is in session.

Lenient lobbying laws, lack of public support for adequate information services for legislators, and the need for continuous campaigning make the average legislator easy prey for special interests. On many issues, the interests of a legislator's district and of special-interest groups often overlap and are difficult to distinguish. Even when the interests are not so closely aligned, legislators may have to depend on lobbyists for much of their information. Certainly, they depend on them for campaign help.

During the regular session of the Seventy-fifth Legislature (1997), bills and resolutions accomplished the following:

★ An accolade to actor Ed Asner for his work in the *Mary Tyler Moore* television show
★ Naming the Pleurocoelus the official state dinosaur
★ Naming the chiltepin the official pepper; the sweet onion the official vegetable; and the guitar the official musical instrument
★ Designating the following "capitals": Waxahachie, crape myrtle; Weslaco, citrus; and Knox City, seedless watermelon

Source: Charles Mantesian, "The Official Waste of Time," *Governing,* September 1997, 18. The legislature also designated rodeo as the official sport.

Whose Bill Is It, Anyhow?

An Austin lawyer-lobbyist remarked on his 20 years as a legislator by noting, "Here at the legislature, if you ask the question, 'Whose bill is it?' what you mean is, which lobby wrote it. If you want to know which legislator is sponsoring the bill, you ask, 'Who's carrying the bill?' That'll give you some idea of how influential lobbyists are."

The legislators' frustrations are especially evident when the biennial budget is considered. Appropriations are the major battleground of legislative sessions. There are always more programs seeking support than there is money available to support them. Power struggles over money continue because each individual who promotes a program—be it for highways, public schools, higher education, utilities rates, environmental protection, lending rates, or welfare administration—believes in either its moral rightness or its economic justification. Who wins the struggles is determined not only by the power and effectiveness of the groups backing a program but also by the political preferences of the legislators. Furthermore, the winners largely determine public policy for the state, since few government programs can operate without substantial amounts of money. Chapter 13 examines the politics of the budgetary process in detail.

Lack of public understanding and support is another handicap for legislators. The public often criticizes politicians for being unprincipled and always willing to compromise. But the role of compromise in the political system, and especially in legislative bodies, is undervalued by the citizens. Caught in all the cross-pressures of the legislative system, members rarely have the opportunity to adhere rigidly to their principles. Those who watch closely what happens in the legislature are not the electorate back home but campaign supporters, lobbyists, and influential citizens. Members must satisfy these people if they are to have any chance of getting their own proposals through the legislature or, in fact, of being reelected for another term.[4]

The Texas legislature provides up-to-the-minute information on its Web page (www.capitol.state.tx.us).

Legislators may have to vote for new highways that they view as superfluous in order to get votes for issues important to them and their home districts. They may have to vote in favor of high interest rates on credit cards to gain support for tighter regulation of nursing homes. They may have to give up a home-district highway patrol office to obtain funds for needy children. Just as legislators who hope to be successful must quickly learn the procedural rules, they must also learn the art of legislative compromise.

CHANGING ALIGNMENTS

Recent sessions of the legislature have been especially interesting because of the shifting alliances within it. The transitional nature of the state, and thus of the legislature, serves to substantiate the adage that "politics makes strange bedfellows." Thus, an additional difficulty legislators face is adjusting to the shifting trends within the legislature. Long dominated by rural, Democratic conservatives, in recent years the legislature has become more urban and more Republican. When urban issues are at stake, temporary bipartisan alliances among big-city legislators are frequently formed. Compounding the problem of party and geographic transition is the fact that the two houses have not changed in the same way. The Senate was heavily Democratic and politically progressive during the 1985 and 1987 sessions; it became more Republican in 1989 and 1991 but still was more progressive than the House. In 1993, the Senate had eighteen Democrats and thirteen Republicans; in 1995, seventeen Democrats and fourteen Republicans. In 1997, the Senate became Republican, with seventeen GOP members and fourteen Democrats. Even Bob Bullock, the presiding officer, backed away from some of his favorite positions, such as favoring an income tax, to align himself more closely with the Senate membership. Since any eleven senators can block legislation through parliamentary procedures, the upper chamber ran the constant risk of being paralyzed into inaction.

The House retained a Democratic majority of 82 to 68 during the 1997 session, but the alliance of conservative Democrats and Republicans gave the

---

4. The lack of public support for the legislature is not unique to Texas. See "The Poor Public Attitude toward the Legislature," *State Legislatures,* April 1995, 5.

The 1997 legislature passed 1,487 bills, but failed to produce tax reform legislation other than a proposed constitutional amendment to increase the amount of the homestead exemption from property taxes.

Courtesy of Ben Sargent.

SARGENT 6/4/97

House a distinctly conservative flavor beginning in the mid-1980s. The Texas House of Representatives seemed to draw strength from the Laney reforms, which brought a higher sense of ethics as well as fairer procedures to the lower chamber. Thus, since 1993 it has been somewhat more progressive than the Senate. However, liberal-conservative skirmishes were plentiful in 1997 and promise to continue in 1999 regardless of which party is in the majority.

Evaluation and Reform

ASSESSING THE LEGISLATURE

At the close of each legislative session, a number of organizations assess the session and evaluate the membership. Many of these rankings merely reflect how closely the members adhered to the position favored by the organization, so it is difficult to use those lists except as measures of, say, probusiness or prolabor votes. The press also joins in the rating game but reflects publishers' viewpoints—for example, the liberal viewpoint of the *Texas Observer*'s annual legislative assessment. One effort to judge legislators on grounds other than political philosophy, however, is that of *Texas Monthly,* which includes both liberals and conservatives of both urban and rural persuasions in its biennial list of ten best and ten worst legislators.[5] The criteria used by *Texas Monthly* are also suitable for use by the public in its evaluation:

---

5. The *Texas Observer* analysis is published each June and the *Texas Monthly* rankings each July following the legislative session.

A good legislator is intelligent, well prepared, and accessible to reason; because of these qualities, he is respected by his colleagues and effective in his work. He uses power skillfully and to its maximum without abusing it, and without exception his integrity is beyond reproach. On issues of statewide importance, he wears no parochial blinders; he is both faithful to, and broader than, his district.

Source: "The Ten Best and the Ten Worst Legislators," *Texas Monthly,* July 1977, Copyright 1977 by Mediatex Communications Corporation. Used by permission.

The session as a whole is even more difficult to evaluate. One's own political viewpoint and interest in specific issues can bias one's view of the actions of legislators. It is necessary to consider the bills and the votes as well as the people. A sample of general criteria for such an assessment would include these questions:

1. Did the legislature deal with major issues facing the state or mainly with trivial issues?

2. Did the appropriations bill reflect genuine statewide concerns or only the interests of the large lobbies?

3. Did the leadership operate effectively, forcing the legislature to give attention to major issues and arranging compromises on stalled bills, or did it cater to the lobbyists?

4. Was the effect of current legislation on future social, economic, and physical resources considered, or did the legislature live for today?

Legislative Scorecard: A 1997 Sampler

The most significant event in the 1997 legislature was what lawmakers did not do: pass a significant tax reform bill. House members and senators could not agree on a strategy. The second most significant event was that after "giving away the store" to business interests in 1995, the legislature approved very little of the 1997 business agenda and approved several decidedly antibusiness measures. The legislature did pass bills and resolutions intended to:

★ Improve safety regulations for school buses
★ Provide women access to an obstetrician-gynecologist without going through a primary-care physician
★ Allow patients to sue health maintenance organizations (HMOs) for malpractice
★ Permit astronauts who are up in space during an election to cast their ballots from there
★ Require more monitoring of the attorney general's office with regard to efforts to collect child support
★ Crack down on teenage smoking and drinking
★ Curb election fraud
★ Allow Texans to borrow against the equity in their homes for general purposes (approved by the voters as a constitutional amendment)
★ Provide some tax relief through a budget surplus by increasing the amount of the mandatory tax exemption given homeowners (approved by the voters as a constitutional amendment)

The Sixty-ninth Legislature (1985–86) was a legislature of goodwill that attended to some social problems but mainly put off problems for the Seventieth to deal with. The Seventieth Legislature (1987–88) had to pass the largest tax bill that any state had ever had. The Seventy-first Legislature (1989–90) lacked distinction in the bills it passed and showed an inability to grapple with reform legislation in such areas as workers' compensation, ethics, and the judiciary. The Seventy-second Legislature (1991–92) was characterized by rancorous debates over issues such as redistricting and the quest for new revenues while avoiding the "I" word (income tax). The Seventy-third Legislature (1993–94) streamlined the penal code and began the withdrawal of support for state regulation of business that characterized the Seventy-fourth Legislature in 1995–96. See the scorecard for a more detailed view of the work of the Seventy-fifth Legislature in 1997.

SUGGESTED REFORMS

In the previous chapter, ways to improve the formal structure for the legislature were suggested. Improvements are also needed in legislative organization and procedures, especially in the areas of committees, the leadership, and ties to lobbyists.

COMMITTEES

The twenty-one House committees of 1973 had grown to thirty-six for the 1989 through 1997 sessions. The Senate managed to operate with only nine committees from 1973 until 1985 but moved to twelve in 1985 and fifteen, including special committees, in 1997. Thus both houses need to be wary of further committee expansion. The U.S. Advisory Commission on Intergovernmental Relations recommends no more than ten to fifteen committees in each house.

Having substantially fewer committees would result in less ambiguity over committee jurisdiction. In addition, both houses could make more use of joint committees instead of submitting every issue for separate study and hearings. A joint budget committee is particularly needed. Fewer committee meetings would give legislators more time to familiarize themselves with the issues and the contents of specific bills.

Fewer committees might also increase the chance for adoption of uniform committee rules throughout the two houses. Better meeting facilities for committees and more professional committee staff are also needed. Currently, chairs can hire staff or elect to use their own, so that independence is also a political issue.

THE LOBBY

Until legislators are able to declare their independence from lobbyists and state administrators, it will be impossible for the legislature to be truly independent of all interests but the public interest. Such a change depends on many factors: citizen attitudes such as public willingness to allow adequate legislative sessions, pay, and staff support for legislators; public financing of election campaigns; and a commitment on the part of legislators to give up the social and economic advantages of strong ties to the lobby. The likelihood of total independence from the lobby is not high: All legislative groups everywhere have some ties to special interests. At a minimum, however, Texas needs to abandon such blatant practices as allowing lawyer-legislators to accept retainer fees from corporations that subsequently send lobbyists to Austin to influence these same legislators. A starting point in reform was Speaker Laney's rule prohibiting members of his own staff from accepting a job as a lobbyist for a year after leaving the speaker's office.

CONCLUSION

The Texas legislature is becoming more representative with each election. Moreover, unlike the U.S. Congress, where fragmentation of power makes coherent public policy virtually impossible, the powerful presiding officers in Texas make coherent public policy highly likely. Thus, for all its problems, the Texas legislature can be highly effective. Since the Texas legislature is centralized, it is capable of translating public preferences into policy. Because so few Texans vote, however, it often translates the preferences of the richer and better-educated minority into policy. Although liberals then criticize the content of public policy, they cannot deny that the policy is effective and that it is rational from the standpoint of most Texas voters, if not of all citizens.

Nonlegislative Lawmaking

The responsibility for lawmaking was intended to rest with the legislature; however, executive, administrative, and judicial officials also make public policy that has the force of law. This overlap of functions, rather than being described as a separation of powers, should more correctly be defined as a separation of roles and institutions, with a sharing of powers.

LAWMAKING BY THE GOVERNOR

The governor is involved in lawmaking in two ways. First, by presenting messages to the legislature giving actual recommendations on legislation, the governor influences its outcome. The governor may also rally the support of political cronies and lobbyists for or against a bill. Besides actually vetoing bills, the governor can threaten to veto and so force changes in appropriations and other bills.

Second, the governor can indirectly influence how, or even if, legislation will be administered through appointments to state boards and commissions. Because the bureaucracy interprets general legislation and thus determines how it is to be applied in specific instances, gubernatorial appointees may have tremendous influence on how the public does (or does not) benefit from state laws. Often, though, the ties between an agency's permanent bureaucracy and legislators are so strong that the board members appointed by the governor have only limited influence.

The governor also influences legislation indirectly by being the major liaison between Texas and other states, and between Texas and the federal executive establishment. In this capacity, the governor can affect interstate and federal-state relationships and policies.

LAWMAKING BY THE ADMINISTRATION

In addition to the governor, the state executive branch includes five other elected executives and two elected state boards. There also are dozens of policy-making boards and their staffs. As noted earlier, the administration (or bureaucracy) has a tremendous effect on how legislation is carried out. Because statutes are written in rather general terms to avoid unnecessary rigidity and specificity, administrative policies, rules, and regulations are a must. Each board policy made and each staff rule or regulation written supplements the statutes enacted by the legislature and constitutes lawmaking.

Individual administrators also interpret statutes, an action that is a type of lawmaking. In addition, by functioning as expert advisers to members of the legislature during the session, administrators can directly influence the outcome of bills. Indeed, they often use their bureaucratic skills in conjunction with special-interest groups that are concerned with similar issues. Perhaps no executive agency is as influential as the attorney general's office, which can issue opinions on the constitutionality of legislation. These opinions have the force of law unless they are successfully challenged in court (see Chapter 11).

LAWMAKING BY THE COURTS

The judiciary, too, has a role in lawmaking. The courts are frequently asked to determine whether a statute is in conflict with higher law. Both federal and state courts can review legislative acts that have been challenged on the grounds of unconstitutionality. Federal and state judges also spend considerable time hearing challenges to administrative interpretations of laws. In fact, most of the civil dockets of the courts are taken up with administrative matters—for example, whether an agency has jurisdiction over the matter at hand or whether an administrative interpretation is correct.

Summary

Understanding the legislative process in Texas involves some knowledge of parliamentary procedure and an appreciation for the role of the presiding officers. To become a law, a bill must survive numerous parliamentary and political obstacles. Most bills never become laws. Important features of the Texas system are:

1. The presiding officers control both the composition of legislative committees and the appointment of committee chairpersons.

2. The speaker of the House and the lieutenant governor in the Senate—the presiding officers—decide whether a friendly or unfriendly committee will consider a bill.

3. The presiding officers indirectly determine when and if a bill will be debated.

4. The presiding officers decide who will speak for and against a bill once it reaches the floor, and the lieutenant governor can even use this power of recognition to allow a filibuster to develop.

5. The staff agencies designed to assist the legislature have relatively low budgets and are dominated by the presiding officers.

6. Even if a bill passes both houses, it may still be killed by a conference committee or a governor's veto.

Legislators face many pressures, and evaluating their work is more difficult than it might seem. Sometimes they are blamed for lawmaking that is really the handiwork of the governor, the state bureaucracy, or the courts. Changes in legislative organization and procedure would help improve legislative efficiency and independence. Recommendations for reform include the following:

1. Reducing the number of committees, especially in the House, then, in turn, providing funds for a professional and independent committee staff

2. Evaluating continually the method of selecting committee chairpersons

3. Lessening the influence of the lobby

Reforms in the day-to-day operation of the legislature are unlikely to be made, however, unless some of the changes suggested in the previous chapter, such as higher pay, better staff support, and annual sessions, are instituted.

Nevertheless, we can note that, despite its handicaps, the Texas legislature is able to produce laws that are in keeping with the political sentiments of a majority of Texas voters. Legislative bodies are the manifestation of representative government. While elected executives must represent the whole, diverse state of Texas, individual legislators represent smaller and presumably more homogeneous districts. Thus, they more easily can discern the wishes of their constituents and try to enact those wishes into law. Although any given individual may not like the public policy developed by the legislature, we must admire the legislature's ability to conduct business under the pressure of a short session. The gridlock for which the U.S. Congress has been criticized traditionally has not been a problem in Texas. We can conclude that the Texas legislature serves its democratic purpose of enacting the public will into statutory law. We now turn to an examination of the executive branch. Chapter 9 deals specifically with the Texas governor.

Key Terms

Bill	Filibuster	Item veto
Conference committee	Fiscal year	Tag

Study Questions

1. In what ways are the presiding officers extremely powerful? Why do you think this situation exists?

2. Trace the process by which a bill becomes a law in Texas.

3. You are a member of the Texas House of Representatives and are sponsoring a bill. What kind of people—inside and outside the legislature—would you hope to line up in support of the bill? Why?

4. You are a member of the Texas Senate and are opposed to a bill that has been introduced. What strategies are available to you to defeat the bill at various stages in the legislative process?

5. Reexamine the Seventy-fifth Legislature's scorecard. Think also of what you know about political beliefs and political processes in Texas. Why do you think the Seventy-fifth Legislature was better known for what it didn't do than for what it did?

6. If you could change any one aspect of the Texas legislative process, what would you change? How would you change it? Why do you think this reform is the most important?

7. Legislators are supported by the LBB, the State Auditor's Office, and the Texas Legislative Council but still also depend on lobbyists. Why? What do you think should be the minimum ground rules for the behavior of a lobbyist? How does this dependence detract from democratic principles?

8. In Texas, the legislature dominates state politics. As a student of democratic political theory, discuss whether this domination results in the most democratic government the state could have.

9. Having studied how the Texas legislature is organized and how it functions, do you think you would ever want to run for the legislature? Why or why not?

Internet Assignment

Internet site: www.capitol.state.tx.us/

Click on either the speaker of the House or the lieutenant governor and read about the office; then click on the other one. Next, go to the "visitors center" and read about the legislative process.

Chapter Nine

The Governor

After his election in 1994, George W. Bush set about mending legislative-executive fences and pushing for action on the issues that were the cornerstone of his campaign.

Why does anyone want to be governor of Texas? The governorship is like the super-super gift in the Neiman-Marcus Christmas catalog—something for the man who has everything and absolutely unique!
    Anonymous political scientist

He's [George W. Bush] a deal maker. He came out of the oil and gas business, from the front end—drilling—where you need acumen in deal making. He focuses on that and doesn't get involved in something that is not part of his agenda.
    Texas Business, *1996*

Governors as a group are riding higher and exerting more authority and influence than at any time since some of their predecessors led the Progressive movement of the early 1900s.
    New York Times, *1989*

Introduction

Democratic theory pays much more attention to the legislature than to the executive. Nevertheless, because chief executives and administrative agencies are important components of government, they too deserve to be measured against the ideal of democracy. In Texas, the legislature has been the dominant branch of state government through most of the state's history. Indeed, Texas is often cited for the weaknesses associated with the governor's office. However, a Texas governor with ideas and boldness can capture the support of the public and greatly enhance the limited constitutional and statutory powers of the office. Bargaining skills and persuasive ability rather than the formal powers of the governorship are the keys to gubernatorial leadership.

This chapter first examines the basic structure of the governor's office, the formal qualifications for the office and personal characteristics of those who are typically elected to it, the roles that the governor plays, and the limitations on those roles. It is a portrait of a well-paid, prestigious state office hampered by a restrictive state constitution, a legislature that seldom is willing to augment gubernatorial powers, and a state administration that is largely independent of the governor's control. It is also a portrait of individuals who have overcome the constitutional weaknesses of the office through their political skills and personal magnetism.

Basic Structure of the Governor's Office

ELECTION, TERM OF OFFICE, AND TENURE

ELECTION

In Texas the governor is chosen in a statewide election held during "off years"—that is, even-numbered years when there is no presidential election. The candidates are selected in party primaries held earlier the same year (see Chapter 6). Gubernatorial elections are held in the off year so that national issues won't overshadow state ones. However, election contests for the Texas governor's office often focus on personalities, not issues, so that the importance of the off year is lost, and its main effect is that fewer people vote because they don't have the presidential election as a drawing card. In fact, voter turnout reached a modern low of 16 percent of registered voters (roughly 10 percent of eligible citizens) during the 1994 primaries. The lieutenant governor is selected in the same manner but runs independently of the governor.

TERM

In 1974, when a 1972 constitutional amendment went into effect, the governor's term of office was extended from two to four years. There is no constitutional limit on the number of terms a governor may serve in Texas.

TENURE

Until World War II, Texas governors were routinely elected for two terms.[1] During and after the war, this precedent was supplanted by a trend to three terms, as indicated in Table 9–1. The precedent was broken when Governor Preston Smith, trying for a third term in 1972, was among the many state politicians who were swept out of office on the wave of public reaction to the Sharpstown Bank scandal.

Modern governors serving four-year terms have had difficulty being reelected. Bill Clements lost to Mark White in 1982, but White lost to Clements in 1986. Ann Richards then served a single term after her 1990 election. On the other hand, George W. Bush's reelection campaign in 1998 seemed to be on track. In fact, Governor Bush won a second term by an overwhelming majority. The long-term likelihood is that governors will serve no more than two terms. The rise of the two-party system and the difficult and controversial problems governors face both suggest shorter service. In addition, because Texas is the second most populous state in the Union, Texas governors will often be in the spotlight as future presidential or vice presidential candidates.

---

1. Two exceptions to this tradition were (1) Richard Coke, the first governor under the 1876 Constitution, who served only one term, and (2) Ross S. Sterling, who was not reelected in 1932. James E. Ferguson was reelected in 1916 but was impeached and removed from office in 1917. His wife, Miriam A. Ferguson, was later elected twice to nonconsecutive terms.

TABLE 9–1

Texas Governors and Their Terms of Office, under 1876 Constitution

Richard Coke*	1874–1876	Ross S. Sterling	1931–1933
Richard B. Hubbard	1876–1879	Miriam A. Ferguson	1933–1935
Oran M. Roberts	1879–1883	James V. Allred	1935–1939
John Ireland	1883–1887	W. Lee O'Daniel*	1939–1941
Lawrence S. Ross	1887–1891	Coke R. Stevenson	1941–1947
James S. Hogg	1891–1895	Beauford H. Jester*	1947–1949
Charles A. Culberson	1895–1899	Allan Shivers	1949–1957
Joseph D. Sayers	1899–1903	Price Daniel	1957–1963
S. W. T. Lanham	1903–1907	John Connally	1963–1969
Thomas M. Campbell	1907–1911	Preston Smith	1969–1973
Oscar B. Colquitt	1911–1915	Dolph Briscoe	1973–1979
James E. Ferguson†	1915–1917	William (Bill) Clements	1979–1983
William P. Hobby	1917–1921	Mark White	1983–1987
Pat M. Neff	1921–1925	William (Bill) Clements	1987–1991
Miriam A. Ferguson	1925–1927	Ann Richards	1991–1995
Dan Moody	1927–1931	George W. Bush	1995–

*Coke and O'Daniel resigned from the governorship to enter the U.S. Senate. Jester died in office.
†Ferguson was impeached and convicted.
SOURCE: Adapted from the *Texas Almanac and State Industrial Guide, 1978–1979* (Dallas: A. H. Belo, 1977), 623.

IMPEACHMENT AND SUCCESSION

IMPEACHMENT

In Texas a governor may be removed from office only through an **impeachment** proceeding. Impeachment is similar to a grand jury indictment; that is, it is a formal accusation. The state constitution is silent on what impeachable offenses are.[2] By implication and by the precedents set in the impeachment of Governor James E. Ferguson in 1917, however, the grounds are malfeasance, misfeasance, and nonfeasance in office—in other words, official misconduct, incompetence, or failure to perform.[3]

The impeachment procedure in Texas is similar to that at the national level. The House of Representatives, by a majority vote of those present, must first impeach the executive. Once the formal accusation is made, the Senate acts as a trial court; a two-thirds vote of the senators present is necessary to convict. Penalties for conviction are removal from office and disqualification from holding future governmental offices in the state. If there are criminal charges, they must be brought in a regular court of law.

---

2. The constitution does spell out the grounds for removing judges, however. Other officials subject to impeachment include the lieutenant governor, the attorney general, the commissioner of the General Land Office, the comptroller, and appellate court judges. The grounds stipulated for impeachment of judges include partiality, oppression, official misconduct, incompetence, negligence, and failure to conduct the business of the court. See Fred Gantt, Jr., *The Chief Executive in Texas* (Austin: University of Texas Press, 1964), 123.
3. Ferguson was impeached and convicted for mishandling public funds, conduct brought to light because funds for the University of Texas were involved.

SUCCESSION

If a governor is removed from office by impeachment and conviction, dies in office or before taking office, or resigns, the constitution provides that the lieutenant governor shall become governor. A supplementary statute stipulates that, should no lieutenant governor be available to serve, the president pro tempore of the Senate and the speaker of the House must call a special legislative session to elect a governor and lieutenant governor to serve until the next general election. Governor Beauford Jester died in office in 1949 and was succeeded by Lieutenant Governor Allan Shivers.

COMPENSATION

A 1954 amendment allows the legislature to determine the salary of the governor and other elected executives. The legislature provided generous increments for many years, raising the governor's salary from $12,000 in 1954 to $99,122 in 1992–93. Then the state budget allowed no raises for state employees for five years. In 1997–98, other state employees received a $100 per month raise and state executives received a 15 percent increase. Governor George Bush and Railroad Commissioner Carole Rylander turned down the raises. Bush commented through a spokesperson that he "does not believe he should accept the additional money because he feels he signed on for four years at" $99,122.[4] The salary of other elected executives, including the other two railroad commissioners, was raised to $92,217 through 1998–99.

Show Me the Money

Although well paid, particularly in comparison to legislators with their $7,200 salaries, the Texas governor is by no means the best-paid executive on the state payroll. Top-dollar honors belong to the larger universities in the state—University of Texas at Austin, Texas A&M University, the University of Houston/Main Campus, the University of North Texas, and Texas Tech University, all of which are the hub institutions of systems. The chancellors of the university systems and the presidents of the largest institutions receive base salaries of $200,000 or more. Beyond that, they get all sorts of perquisites, such as houses and cars. Some large institutions pay bonuses for successful fundraising, and some chancellors receive supplemental pay from individual institutions in the system—particularly medical schools. Money raised from local funds are used to supplement rather modest state-appropriated salaries. These large salaries often are matters of contention when university appropriations are discussed—and for that matter, among faculty when the president gets a raise but faculty members do not.

Coaches of major sports at the larger institutions do even better than any chief executive in the state. When Mack Brown was hired as the head football coach of the Texas Longhorns in late 1997, his base salary was set at $600,000, and his total compensation package—including extras such as television shows—was $750,000.

4. Wayne Slater, "Bush, Railroad Commissioner Reject Pay Raises," *Dallas Morning News*, June 2, 1997, 17A–18A.

Once second only to that of the governor of New York, the Texas governor's salary has slipped to fourteenth—although the governors of California and Washington have taken voluntary reductions from the amount designated by statute.[5] The lieutenant governor is supposedly paid at the governor's rate when acting as governor—for example, when the chief executive is out of the state. The amount budgeted to pay the lieutenant governor for these duties has been $20,000 a year through several bienniums.

The governor also receives numerous fringe benefits. The constitution provides an official mansion, and other benefits include a travel and operating budget, a car, the use of state-owned aircraft, bodyguards furnished by the Texas Department of Public Safety, and offices and professional staff, including an executive assistant. How do these benefits compare with those of other governors? A comparison several years ago showed that the Texas governor drives a Ford Crown Victoria while Lincolns seem to be the car of choice among the nation's governors. The official mansion is "middle-sized" in comparison to those in other states, but the operating budget for it is the second highest in the country.[6]

In 1997 the budget for the governor's office was over $85 million; however, this amount fluctuates from year to year depending on the number of programs (see the following discussion) housed in the office at any given time. The perks, or fringe benefits, described above take only about 5 percent of that amount. The remainder is spent on planning, programs, grants, compliance activities, economic development, and providing an **ombudsman** (grievance) function on behalf of citizens.

STAFF AND ORGANIZATION

Like other chief executives, the governor alone is unable to perform all the functional and ceremonial tasks assigned to the governor's office. Assistance in fulfilling these obligations comes from a personal staff and from the professional staffs of the divisions that make up the Office of the Governor. Certain staff members are assigned to act as legislative liaisons—in effect, to lobby for the governor's programs—and often it is through them that the governor makes known an impending threat to veto a particular piece of legislation. Other staff members are involved in recommending candidates for the hundreds of appointments the governor must make to state boards, commissions, and executive agencies. The governor's aides also prepare the executive budget, coordinate the various departments and activities of the governor's office, and schedule appointments and activities. Overall, in addition to handling routine duties and occasional emergency situations, the governor's staff must provide assistance in performing the specific tasks assigned to the office by law and in formulating political moves to promote the enactment of the governor's programs.

5. "The Governors: Compensation," *The Book of the States, 1996–97,* vol. 31 (Lexington, Ky.: Council of State Governments, 1996), 20–21.
6. See Walter L. Updegrave, "Stately Splendor: How Our Governors Live It Up," *Money,* October 1993, 114–128.

Governor Ann Richards (1991–1995) found herself in some political difficulty after she preached to state agencies the need to prune their budgets, then let her staff grow from the usual 225 or so to almost 400. She responded in 1994, an election year, by cutting back on personnel. Governor George Bush pruned the size of the staff even more, to 190 by 1996. Even so, only New York (203) and Florida (264) had more gubernatorial staffers.[7]

The comparison between Richards and Bush is somewhat deceiving, since the payroll changed very little between the two administrations. Richards followed a traditional **populist** approach of creating many jobs for "the people"—a populist appeals to ordinary citizens—although the jobs didn't pay well. Bush followed a traditional businesslike approach of appointing fewer people but at much higher salaries.

Each governor organizes the office somewhat differently. Commonly, new program initiatives begin under the governor's auspices, then become independent or move to other agencies. More than anything else, the configuration of programs makes the difference in organization. As of 1998, the governor's office consisted of the following elements:[8]

★ The Appointments Office, which assists the governor in making nominations for boards, commissions, and advisory committees

★ The Office of Budget and Planning, which prepares the executive budget, including coordination of requests from state agencies and cooperation with the Legislative Budget Board to prepare a state strategic plan and monitor the development and implementation of the plans of individual agencies

★ The Legislative Office, which keeps the governor apprised of legislative matters and works with the governor to develop legislative initiatives, and the related Policy Office, which provides analytical services and helps solve citizen complaints

★ The State Grants Team, which alerts state, local, and nonprofit agencies to funding opportunities

★ Administrative offices, including the Executive Office, the Office of Administration, the Communications Office, the Office of General Counsel, the Office of the First Lady, and the Governor's Mansion, all of which support the governor's (and first lady's) activities

★ Programmatic divisions, including the Criminal Justice Division, the Governor's Commission for Women, the Governor's Committee on People with Disabilities, the Film/Music/Multimedia Offices, the Division of Emergency Management, and the Texas Council on Work Force & Economic Competitiveness, each of which administers executive programs

---

7. *The Book of the States, 1996–97,* p. 20.
8. The World Wide Web site of the Texas governor (www.governor.state.tx.us/) provides an up-to-date list of the various divisions of the governor's office.

One of the surprising consequences of the end of the Cold War between the United States and the former Soviet Union has been the assertion of American state activity in international affairs. Although Article I, section 10 of the U.S. Constitution forbids the states to "enter into any Agreement or Compact with . . . a foreign power," both California and Texas seem to have been pursuing their own foreign policies for several years. California has opened ten trade offices in foreign capitals, including Mexico City, London, and Tokyo. In Texas there is an Office of Border Affairs within the Texas Natural Resource Conservation Commission, a Mexico trade liaison office within the governor's office, and a Texas-Mexico Border Task Force within the attorney general's office. People in these agencies are working to craft agreements with Mexico dealing with trade, environmental management of the Rio Grande, and immigration.

Sources: Julie Blase, "The Evolution of State Influence on U.S. Foreign Policy as Illustrated by Texas-Mexico Relations," unpublished paper, Department of Government, University of Texas at Austin, December 1, 1997; Dave Lesher, "Golden and Global California," *Los Angeles Times,* January 8, 1998, A1.

Qualifications for Governor

FORMAL QUALIFICATIONS

As is true of the qualifications for members of the legislature, the formal qualifications for governor are so broad that several million Texans could legally run for the office. Article IV of the constitution stipulates that the governor must be at least 30 years old, be a citizen of the United States, and have been a resident of Texas for the five years immediately preceding the election. These qualifications also pertain to the lieutenant governor. Article IV also mandates that the governor "shall be installed on the first Tuesday after the organization of the Legislature, or as soon thereafter as practicable." Article III gives the legislature the responsibility for settling any election disputes that might arise concerning the governor.

PERSONAL CHARACTERISTICS

Formally qualifying for the governorship and actually having a chance at being considered seriously as a candidate are two very different matters. The social, political, and economic realities of the state dictate that personal characteristics, not stated in law, help to determine who will be the victors in gubernatorial elections. Some of these personal characteristics are based on accomplishments, or at least positive involvement, of the gubernatorial aspirant. Others are innate traits that are beyond the control of the individual.

These characteristics are similar to but even more stringent than those for members of the legislature. In short, *unless something unusual occurs in the campaign,* tradition dictates that the successful candidate for governor will be a White Anglo-Saxon Protestant (WASP) male who is politically conservative, involved in civic affairs, and a millionaire. More than likely, but less inevitably, this individual will have held some other office, often attorney general or lieutenant governor, although being a professional politician is fast becoming a liability among voters with a penchant for electing "good ol' boys."

The most atypical governor in more than a half century was Ann Richards, 1991–1995, a populist Democratic female (see Chapter 5 for a discussion of populism in Texas). Richards took strong stands against concealed weapons, environmental destruction, and selected state agencies, such as the Insurance Commission and Department of Commerce, that had strong ties to business.

George W. Bush, a Republican, is very much in the mainstream of Texas political belief but defied tradition by not having any previous experience in elective office when he was elected in 1994. His inaugural speech reflected his thinking when he said,

> You and I know that people have become cynical. It has happened partly because government has tried to do too much. It has also happened because people run for office saying one thing and then do another. I intend to keep my word.

Source: "These Are Texas Values," *Dallas Morning News,* February 8, 1995, 13A.

CONSERVATIVE

Traditionally, a gubernatorial candidate had to be a conservative Democrat. E. J. Davis, a much-maligned Republican governor during Reconstruction, was the only Republican governor until Bill Clements was elected in 1978. Today, because of the growth of the Republican Party, the key label is "conservative" rather than the party tag.

The evolution of the state from one-party Democrat to two-party was traced in Chapters 5 and 6. In the 1990 Ann Richards–Clayton Williams race, Richards's self-proclaimed Democratic populism did not win the race for her. Rather, Clayton Williams's "open-mouth-put-foot-in" rhetoric lost the election for him. He seemed particularly adept at insulting women and ordinary tax-payers. In the first instance, he opined that rape was like bad weather, so that "If it's inevitable, [a woman should] just relax and enjoy it." In the second, Williams, a multimillionaire who financed much of his own campaign, bragged about not paying federal income taxes.

Ann Richards wanted to ensure that Texans understood the difference between her people's campaign (populism) and run-of-the-mill liberalism. She went to some lengths to look like a "good ol' girl," including joining the "boys" for the opening of bird-hunting season. She also posed for the cover of *Texas Monthly* wearing a black leather jacket and sitting on a Harley-Davidson motorcycle.

In the previous race, between Clements and Mark White in 1986, White—the conservative Democrat—lost because of a faltering economy that he neither caused nor could fix and because of the education funding issue. White had taken a strong stand for school reform and the tax increase necessary to finance it, noting at the time that he probably had forfeited his own second term. Indeed, during the 1986 campaign, White was portrayed as a high-tax, free-spending liberal.

George W. Bush entered the race in 1994 as a mainstream Republican, concerned with state control over state policy, the integrity of the family, the quality of education, and the rising incidence of juvenile crime. He and Richards differed little on those issues. He reflected more of a national Republican position in wanting to cut welfare and in openly advocating a freer operating climate for business, especially by placing many restrictions on lawsuits for such activities as professional malpractice and faulty products. Significantly, however, he talked about his conservatism, not his party affiliation.

Most state officeholders in Texas are conservative, and a candidate for governor needs not only their support but also access to the big campaign money waiting in the pockets of conservative businesspeople, bankers, and attorneys (these last often have state agencies as customers and clients). While unanimity does not exist in either party, and while urban-rural differences increase yearly, the nominee generally can count on all factions of the party for support in the general election.

WASP, MIDDLE-AGED MALE

Texas has never had a non-Anglo governor since it became independent of Spain and Mexico.[9] Only one Roman Catholic—Frances (Sissy) Farenthold in the 1972 Democratic primary—and no Jew has even been a really serious contender for the office. The religious preferences of the governors elected in the Lone Star State have been confined to the mainstream Protestant churches, such as Methodist and Baptist. The average age of governors at the time of

---

9. The Raza Unida Party made serious, but unsuccessful, bids for the nomination. Because of internal factionalism and a poor financial base, the party no longer exists. (See Chapter 5.)

their inauguration is 50.3 years, and of the twenty-nine individuals who have served as governor under the 1876 Constitution, only two—Ann Richards and Miriam A. Ferguson—were female. However, that number is still greater than that of any other state. During Richards's tenure, her only fellow female governors were in Kansas and Oregon.

ATTORNEY/BUSINESSPERSON, COMMUNITY PILLAR

Governors, as well as legislators, are often attorneys. Since 1876, sixteen of the thirty Texas governors have been lawyers. However, of the four most recent governors in the state, only Mark White was a lawyer. Bill Clements and George Bush were businesspeople. Ann Richards, although she had been a public school teacher, was essentially a professional politician who went to work as a lobbyist for a Washington-based law firm when she left office.

The final personal characteristic that candidates must have is being a "pillar of the community." Governors are members of civic, social, fraternal, and business organizations and seem to be the epitome of stable family life. Richards, being divorced, was something of an exception but was frequently photographed with her children and grandchildren.

Roles of the Governor and Limits on Those Roles

The office of governor consists of a repertoire of at least seven roles that the incumbent must play. Five are formal; that is, they are prescribed by the constitution and supplementing statutes. Two are informal and symbolic; that is, they derive from the Texas political setting (see Table 9–2). Governors of all states play similar roles, as does the president, who also has added responsibilities in the areas of diplomacy and economics.

TABLE 9-2

Roles of the Governor

Constitutional and Statutory Roles	Informal and Symbolic Roles
Chief Executive	Chief of Party
Chief Legislator	Leader of the People
Commander in Chief/Top Cop	
Chief of State	
Chief Intergovernmental Diplomat	

The personality of the governor and the political and economic circumstances that prevail during a governor's administration largely determine which roles are emphasized. As the first opening quotation in this chapter indicates, the governorship is a unique office, with its distinctive qualities further highlighted by the varied approaches taken by different governors.[10] How a governor goes about trying to get policy preferences enacted by the legislature and implemented by the bureaucracy constitutes *leadership style*. Leadership style is crucial to Texas because the governor so often has to depend on persuasive skills to offset the many handicaps of the office. Democratic theory dictates that the elected executive be accountable for the executive branch. In Texas, the governor has to rely heavily on informal means to gain the expected control over the state bureaucracy and to achieve his or her policy agenda.

To view the governor in action, we will briefly look at the gubernatorial styles of the governors of the state during the 1980s and 1990s. We hope these brief biographical sketches will help the reader to understand the diverse personalities and operating styles of recent Texas governors.

Preston Smith (1969–1973) was an aggressive legislative leader who "called in his IOUs" from his days as lieutenant governor/presiding officer of the Texas Senate. Dolph Briscoe (1973–1979) was so low-profile that *Texas Monthly* pictured him on the cover as an empty chair, in reference to his spending more time at his Uvalde ranch than at his Austin desk. He personified the quest for the office just to acquire something more for the man who has almost everything. Mark White (1983–1987) inherited a deteriorating economy and emphasized education and economic development as ways to shore up the state financial picture. However, he was accused of being all style and no substance. Bill Clements (1979–1983, 1987–1991) emphasized tax reform, a war on drugs and crime, long-range planning, and better ties to neighboring states and Mexico during his first term. During his second, of necessity he emphasized economic diversification. Clements had a reputation as an obstructionist, making it difficult for public policy to be developed.

The governor acknowledged to be atypical, Ann Richards (1991–1995), was grounded in Travis County politics and got high marks for the quality and diversity of her appointments;[11] for forcing changes in the controversial boards governing some state agencies, especially the State Insurance Board and the Board of Pardons and Paroles; and for exerting executive control over other agencies, such as the Texas Department of Commerce. Richards insisted on high ethical standards, although some of her staff members stumbled later on. She also worked hard at economic diversification. However, Richards's approach to legislative relations was partisan and heavy-handed, and she was not particularly popular among legislators. Her 1994 bid for

---

10. Thad L. Beyle, "Being Governor," *The State of the States* (Washington, D.C.: Congressional Quarterly Press, 1996), 77–107, discusses how governors might be evaluated, including the index developed by the National Governors Association.

11. According to a September 1993 analysis published by the governor's office, the Richards appointees were 63 percent Anglo, 20 percent Hispanic, 15 percent African American, and 2 percent other; they were 45 percent female. The Richards appointees were considerably more diverse than even those of her Democratic predecessors. She more nearly followed tradition on another score—heavily drawing her appointments from big contributors. See Wayne Slater, "Richards Financial Backers Get Majority of Board Posts," *Dallas Morning News*, March 28, 1993, 1A. Also, she favored the Central Texas region as a source of appointments, much to the dismay of North Texans, especially. See Wayne Slater, "Area of Influence," *Dallas Morning News*, September 2, 1993, 1A, 24A.

reelection was inept, and she also faced the national Republican sweep. Richards lost handily to George W. Bush.

Bush, son of a former president,[12] operated very differently from Richards. The George Bush approach to legislators was nonpartisan, low-key, and consensus-building. As the second chapter-opening quotation indicates, Bush saw himself as a deal maker. He campaigned on four issues: reform of the juvenile justice system, setting limits on civil lawsuits *(tort reform)*, more flexible and better public education, and restrictions on welfare. These issues were common throughout the country in 1994. Once elected, Bush stuck with those issues and pushed each through the 1995 legislature. While he was successful in further expanding public school flexibility in the 1997 legislative session, his push for major changes in the Texas tax system was rebuffed. He had to settle for a proposed constitutional amendment to increase the tax exemptions for homesteads. Speculation was keen during the Seventy-fifth Legislature that Bush was trying to stage a platform from which to launch a presidential bid in the year 2000.

How a Governor Can Get Things Done

George W. Bush, elected in 1994, observed that "the way to forge good public policy amongst the leadership of the legislative branch and executive branch is to air our differences in private meetings that happen all the time. . . . The way to ruin a relationship is to leak things and to be disrespectful of meeting in private."

Source: R. G. Ratcliffe, "Away from the Spotlight, Governor Makes His Mark," *Houston Chronicle,* April 15, 1995, 10A.

Formal Roles and Limitations

The Texas Constitution was written at a time when concentrated power in the hands of a single state official was viewed with great apprehension. E. J. Davis, the last Republican governor before Clements, held office from 1870 to 1874, and his administration was characterized by corruption and repression. Consequently, when the 1876 Constitution was drafted, the framers reacted against the Davis administration by creating a constitutionally weak governor's office (see Chapter 2).

Today the governor must still cope with a highly fragmented executive branch that includes five other elected executives, two elected boards, and a complex system of powerful policy-making boards and commissions. The Texas governorship has been judged one of the weakest in the country in terms of executive branch control and general institutional power.[13]

---

12. Texas claims three former U.S. presidents: Dwight Eisenhower, who was born in the state; Lyndon Johnson, who was a lifelong resident; and George Bush, who moved to Texas during an oil boom when he was a businessman, not a politician.

13. See, for example, Thad Beyle, "Governors," in Virginia Gray and Herbert Jacob, *Politics in the American States,* 6th ed. (Washington, D.C.: CQ Press, 1996), particularly pp. 228–40. Beyle ranks the Texas governorship in the next-to-lowest category on institutional power but accords Texas governors greater power for their personal influence.

News stories frequently describe the governor as the "chief executive," referring to gubernatorial control over the state bureaucracy and **appointment and removal,** budgeting, planning, supervisory, and clemency powers. Although this is one of the governor's most time-consuming roles, it also is one of the weakest, as the following discussion will illustrate.

APPOINTMENT

Texas is said to have a long ballot because a large number of state officials are elected by the people rather than appointed by the governor. The list of officials elected on a statewide basis includes the lieutenant governor, whose major role is legislative; the attorney general; the comptroller of public accounts; the commissioner of the General Land Office; and the agriculture commissioner. In addition, members of the Texas Railroad Commission and the State Board of Education are elected. Since they are elected independently, they feel no obligation to the governor, and since they may want the governor's job, they may even wish to make the incumbent look bad. Absent direct influence on these elected officeholders, the governor must be highly skilled in the art of persuasion.

The most visible executive appointments that the governor makes are those of secretary of state, commissioner of education, commissioner of insurance, commissioner of health and human services, and executive director of the Commerce Department. The governor also appoints the director of the Office of State-Federal Relations and the adjutant general, who heads the state militia. He or she also fills any vacancy that occurs in one of the major elected executive positions, such as railroad commissioner. In the event of a vacancy, the governor appoints someone to fill the office until the next election. She or he also appoints all or some of the members of about two dozen advisory councils and committees that coordinate the work of two or more state agencies.

Most state agencies are not headed up by a single executive making policy decisions. The result is a highly fragmented executive branch; power is divided among both elected executives and appointed boards. Nevertheless, the governor has a major effect on state policy through appointments to approximately 125 policy-making, multimember boards and commissions. Examples include the University of Texas System board of regents, the Public Utility Commission, and the Insurance Board. The members of these boards are usually appointed for a six-year term, but with the following limitations:

1. The terms of board and commission members are overlapping and staggered to prevent the governor from appointing a majority of the members until late in his or her first term of office.

2. The statutes establishing the various boards and commissions are highly prescriptive and often specify both a certain geographic representation and occupational or other background characteristics of the members.[14]

---

14. For example, three members (half of the total) of the Commission on Alcoholism and Drug Abuse must be recovering substance abusers.

3. Appointments to some boards and commissions must be made from lists supplied by members of professional organizations and associations.[15]

One other important use of the appointment power is filling vacancies in the judiciary. Although Texas has an elected judiciary (see Chapters 2 and 11), every legislature creates some new courts, and vacancies occur in other courts. The governor makes appointments to these benches until the next election. Indeed, more than half of the district court judges in the state are first appointed, subsequently standing for election.

The governor must obtain a two-thirds confirmation vote from the Senate for appointments; the president needs only a simple majority from the U.S. Senate. And, as in national politics, there is the practice of "senatorial courtesy": The Senate will usually honor the objection of a senator from the same district as the nominee for appointment by refusing to approve confirmation.

Texas's short biennial legislative session, however, permits the governor to make many interim appointments when the legislature is not in session. This practice gives these appointees a "free ride" for a period as long as 19 months. These recess appointments must be presented to the Senate within the first 10 days of the next session, whether regular or called.

Another aid to the governor is incumbency. If a governor is reelected, he will be able to appoint all members of the board or commission by early in his second term. The governor will then have considerable influence over policy development within the agency.

REMOVAL

The governor has only limited removal power in Texas. The governor can remove political appointees whom he has appointed, with the consent of the Senate, a power in effect only since a 1980 constitutional amendment. He also can remove personal staff members and a few executive directors, such as the one in the Department of Housing and Community Affairs. However, the governor cannot remove members of boards and commissions whom he did not appoint. This lack of removal power deprives the governor of significant control over the bureaucrats who make and administer policy on a day-to-day basis. In turn, the governor has difficulty implementing policies through the state bureaucracy.

The three general methods for removing state officeholders are:

1. Impeachment, which involves a formal accusation—the impeachment— by a House majority and requires a two-thirds vote for conviction by the Senate

2. Address, a procedure whereby the legislature requests the governor to remove a district or appellate judge from office (a two-thirds vote of both houses is required)

3. Quo warranto proceedings, a legal procedure whereby an official may be removed by a court

---

15. This practice is most common with the licensing and examining boards in various health-care fields.

Because Article XV of the Texas Constitution stipulates the right to a trial before removal from office, impeachment is likely to remain the chief formal removal procedure, since it does involve a trial by the Senate. However, even its use is quite rare.

BUDGETING

By law, the governor must submit a biennial budget message to the legislature within five days after that body convenes in regular session. This budget is prepared by the governor's Office of Budget and Planning. The Legislative Budget Board (LBB), however, also prepares a budget for the legislature to consider, and, traditionally, the legislature is guided more by the legislative budget than by the governor's. The executive budget indicates to the legislature the governor's priorities and signals items likely to be vetoed. With the exception of the item veto, the Texas governor lacks the strong budgetary powers not only of the president but also of many state executives (see Chapter 13). The governor has one additional financial power, that of approving deficiency warrants of no more than $200,000 for the biennium for agencies that encounter emergencies and/or run out of funds.

PLANNING

Both modern management and the requirements of many federal grants-in-aid emphasize substate regional planning, and the governor directs planning efforts for the state through the Office of Budget and Planning. When combined with budgeting, the governor's planning power allows a stronger gubernatorial hand in the development of new programs and policy alternatives. Though still without adequate control over the programs of the state, the governor has had a greater voice in suggesting future programs over the past two decades, mainly because many federal statutes designated the governor as having approval power for federal grants.

Especially in his first term, Bill Clements approached the governor's office from the planning perspective, including the development of the Texas State Government Effectiveness Program to make state agency management more efficient and the creation of the Texas 2000 Commission to look at issues that will become increasingly more pressing as the next century nears. During the Richards administration, Comptroller John Sharp—in part at the request of the governor to allow a more rational appropriations act for fiscal years 1992–93—developed an elaborate system for monitoring the performance of state agencies. This system, known as the Texas Performance Review, requires state agencies to engage in strategic planning.

SUPERVISING

The state constitution charges the governor with the responsibility for seeing that the laws of the state are "faithfully executed" but provides few tools for fulfilling this function. The governor's greatest supervisory and directive powers occur in the role of commander in chief (described below). Governors can request reports from state agencies, remove their own appointees, and use

George W. Bush hammered at the need for a stronger justice system, especially to control juvenile crime. Ben Sargent's gentle gibe raises the question of where to put more convicted felons and suggests that the answer may be the Texas Rangers ballpark, given the prolonged baseball strike of 1994–95.

Courtesy of Ben Sargent.

political influence to force hiring reductions or other economies. But lack of appointment power over the professional staffs of state agencies and lack of removal power over a predecessor's appointees limit the governor's ability to ensure that the state bureaucracy performs its job.

The governor thus must fall back on informal tactics to exercise any control over the administration. In this respect, the governor's staff is of supreme importance: If staff members can establish good rapport with state agencies, they may extend the governor's influence to areas where the governor does not have formal authority. They are aided in this task by two factors of which agency personnel are well aware: the governor's leadership of the party and veto powers (both discussed below).

CLEMENCY

The governor's power with regard to acts of clemency (mercy) is restricted to one 30-day reprieve for an individual sentenced to death. In cases of treason against the state (a rare crime), the governor may grant pardons, reprieves, and commutations of sentences with legislative consent. The governor also may remit fines or bond forfeitures and restore driver's licenses and hunting privileges. In addition, the governor has the discretionary right to revoke a parole or conditional pardon. Beyond these limited acts, the state's chief executive officer must make recommendations to the Board of Pardons and Paroles, which is part of the Department of Criminal Justice. Although empowered to refuse an act of clemency recommended by the board, the governor cannot act without its recommendation in such matters as full and conditional pardons, commutations, reprieves, and emergency reprieves.

Although the legislature tends to dominate Texas politics, the governor is a strong chief legislator who relies on three formal powers in carrying out this role: **message power, session power,** and **veto power.**

MESSAGE POWER

The governor may give messages to the legislature at any time, but the constitution requires a gubernatorial message when legislative sessions open[16] and when a governor retires. By statute, the governor must also deliver a biennial budget message. Other messages the governor may choose to send or deliver in person are often "emergency" messages when the legislature is in session; these messages are a formal means of expressing policy preferences. They also attract the attention of the media and set the agenda for state government. Coupled with able staff work, message power can be an effective and persuasive tool. Examples of gubernatorial messages during the 1997 legislative session were a call for an overhaul of the state tax system and the need for more *charter schools,* which are publicly funded schools that do not have to follow all the rules of the Texas Education Agency. A governor also often delivers "informal" messages at meetings and social gatherings or through the media.

SESSION POWER

As discussed in Chapter 7, the legislature is constitutionally forbidden to call itself into special session; only the governor may do this. Called sessions are limited to a maximum duration of 30 days, but a governor who wants to force consideration of an issue can continue calling one special session after another. The governor also sets the agenda for these sessions, although the legislature, once called, may consider other matters on a limited basis, such as impeachment or approval of executive appointments. As the complexity of state government has grown, legislators sometimes have been unable to complete their work in the short biennial regular sessions. When they fail to complete enough of the agenda, they know they can expect a special session. However, any governor contemplating a special session must consider whether she or he has the votes lined up to accomplish the purpose of the session.

Special sessions offer a way around the restricted biennial legislative session of 140 days. The eight governors before Bush called a total of thirty-four special sessions. Bill Clements called six; Ann Richards called only two. Through 1997, Bush had called none, a reflection on the one hand of his ability to get along with the legislative leadership, and on the other hand of budget surpluses.[17]

---

16. George C. Kiser and Alan D. Monroe provide a national comparison of "State of the State" addresses in "State of the State Speeches as Political Documents," a paper presented at the Southwestern Political Science Association meeting, Austin, Texas, March 18–21, 1992.
17. E. Lee Bernick, in "Special Sessions: What Manner of Gubernatorial Power?" *State and Local Government Review* 26 (Spring 1994): 79–88, reports that special sessions tend to be cyclical and somewhat responsive to national events that force the states to enact new legislation. Bernick studied special sessions in all fifty states for 1959 through 1989.

VETO POWER

The governor's strongest legislative power is the veto. Every bill that passes
both houses of the legislature in regular and special sessions is sent to the
governor, who has the option of signing it, letting it become law without signing it, or vetoing it.[18]

If the legislature is still in session, the governor has 10 days—Sundays
excluded—in which to act. If the bill is sent to the governor in the last 10
days of a session or after the legislature has adjourned, the governor has 20
days—including Sundays—in which to act. If the governor vetoes a bill while
the legislature is still in session, that body may override the veto by a two-
thirds vote of both houses.

Because of the short legislative session, many important bills are often
sent to the governor so late that the legislature has adjourned before the governor has had to act on them. In such instances, the veto power is absolute.
The legislature cannot override if it is not in session, and consideration of the
same bill cannot be carried over into the next session. Short biennial sessions
thus make the governor's threat of a veto an extremely powerful political
tool. Also, the override of a veto takes a two-thirds vote in both houses of the
legislature, a majority that is not easy to get. As an indication of how rare an

---

18. Unlike the president, the governor does not have a "pocket veto." The governor must send a
veto message to block a bill; laying a bill aside without a signature results in the bill's becoming
law, even if the legislature adjourns.

override is, 38 years separated the last two: W. Lee O'Daniel had twelve vetoes overridden in 1939–1941, and Bill Clements had a veto of a local bill overridden in 1979.

The governor has one other check over appropriations bills, the item veto.[19] The governors in forty-two other states have this same power. This device permits the governor to delete individual items from a bill without having to veto it in its entirety. The item veto may be used only to strike a particular line of funding, however; it cannot be used to reduce or increase an appropriation.

The governor's veto power was an important issue in the 1990 campaign between Clayton Williams and Ann Richards. Some supporters were drawn to Richards because she promised to veto antiabortion legislation, while Williams picked up support from those who were comforted by his announced intent to veto any new taxes.

The item veto illustrates a reality of gubernatorial power in Texas. The governor's power over legislation is largely negative—he or she often finds it easier to say no than to get his or her own legislative agenda adopted. This truism particularly describes the budget process. Yet, the timing of the appropriations act and the number of items that the legislature can cram into one line item are factors that affect the governor's use of the item veto as a fiscal tool to control spending.[20] One illustration occurred in the term of Governor Clements, when the legislature, dismayed by his veto of special appropriations for higher education in 1985, began in 1987 to appropriate one large lump sum for each institution.

COMMANDER IN CHIEF/TOP COP

The state of Texas does not independently engage in warfare with other nations and thus would seem to have no need for a commander in chief. However, the governor does have the power to declare martial law—that is, to suspend civil government temporarily and replace it with government by the state militia and/or law enforcement agencies. Although seldom used, this power was invoked to quell an oil field riot in East Texas in 1931 and to gain control of explosive racial situations in East Texas in 1919 and on the Gulf Coast in 1943.

Additionally, the governor is commander in chief of the military forces of the state (Army and Air National Guard) except when they have been called into service by the national government. The head of these forces, the adjutant general, is one of the governor's important appointees. The governor also

---

19. Congress granted the U.S. president the item veto in 1996; the president used the power 82 times before the U.S. Supreme Court nullified it in 1998.
20. Pat Thompson and Steven R. Boyd, "Use of the Item Veto in Texas, 1940–1990," *State and Local Government Review* 26 (Winter 1994): 38–45.

has the power to assume command of the Texas Rangers and the Department of Public Safety to maintain law and order. These powers become important during disasters such as floods or tornadoes, when danger from the aftermath of the storm or from unscrupulous individuals such as looters may be present.

Governor Mark White used the commander in chief powers in a controversial way in 1985. First, he authorized the state militia to participate in a military training exercise in Honduras, which borders on the politically volatile countries of Nicaragua and El Salvador. Then White joined the troops and oversaw the delivery of Texas barbecue to the militia over the Easter weekend—just as the legislature began to discuss the state budget.

In routine situations, the governor is almost wholly dependent on local law enforcement and prosecuting agencies to see that the laws of the state are faithfully executed. When there is evidence of wrongdoing, the state's chief executive often brings the informal powers of the gubernatorial office to bear on the problem, appealing to the media to focus public attention on errant agencies and officeholders. Such was the case in 1992, when Governor Richards received considerable media coverage for joining nursing home inspectors in on-site visits to both poorly run and well-run nursing homes.

CHIEF OF STATE

Pomp and circumstance are a part of being the top elected official of the state. Just as presidents use their ceremonial role to augment other roles, so also do governors. Whether cutting a ribbon to open a new highway, leading a parade, or serving as host for a visiting dignitary, the governor's performance as chief of state yields visibility and the appearance of leadership, which enhance the more important executive and legislative roles of the office. In the modern era, the governor is often the chief television personality of the state and sets the policy agenda through publicity. Ann Richards, for example, was a national TV celebrity, sometimes more popular outside the state than inside. George Bush is a possible presidential candidate and in demand outside the state, too.

More and more, Texas governors are using the ceremonial role of chief of state, sometimes coupled with the role of chief intergovernmental diplomat, to become actively involved in economic negotiations such as plant locations. Efforts are directed toward both foreign and domestic investments and finding new markets for Texas goods. In such negotiations, the governor uses the power and prestige of the office to become the state's salesperson. Mark White and Bill Clements both made significant use of this role to attract businesses to the state. Ann Richards strongly pushed for U.S. Senate approval of the North American Free Trade Agreement (NAFTA) because of the likelihood of expanded Texas-Mexico trade. One irony is the historic chief of state function of tossing out the first ball at the opening baseball game; in George Bush's case, he was one of the team owners until the beginning of 1998.

Before George W. Bush ran for public office, he was the managing owner of the Texas Rangers baseball team. When he was sworn in as governor, he became the commander of the Texas Rangers state police force. He is thus the only human being in history to go from being the head of the Texas Rangers to being the head of the Texas Rangers.

CHIEF INTERGOVERNMENTAL DIPLOMAT

The Texas Constitution provides that the governor, or someone designated by the governor, will be the state's representative in all dealings with other states and with the national government. This role of intergovernmental representative has increased in importance for three reasons. First, federal statutes now designate the governor as the official who has the planning and grant-approval authority for the state. This has given the governor's budgeting, planning, and supervising powers much more clout in recent years, and federal budget philosophy (see Chapter 13) further enhances the governor's role.

Second, some state problems, such as water and energy development, often require the cooperation of several states. For example, in 1981–1982, Governor Clements and five other governors tried to plan solutions for the water problems of the High Plains area. Additionally, although the U.S. Constitution precludes a governor from conducting diplomatic relations with other nations, Texas's location as a border state gives rise to occasional social and economic exchanges with the governors of Mexican border states on matters such as immigration and energy. The box earlier in this chapter outlines the aggressive international role of the two largest American states, California and Texas.

Third, acquiring federal funds is always important, since they relieve the pressure on state and local government revenue sources. Often, the governor works in concert with other governors to try to secure favorable national legislation, including both funding and limits on unfunded federal mandates (see Chapter 3). Thus, Governor George Bush is an active member of the National Governors Association and participant in the National Governors Conference. He also is active in regional and Republican Party groups. He takes his place among the proactive governors described in the chapter-opening quotation from the *New York Times*.

A more traditional use of the governor's intergovernmental role is mandated by Article IV of the U.S. Constitution, which provides for the rendition (surrender) of fugitives from justice who flee across state lines. The Texas governor, like other governors, signs the rendition papers and transmits them to the appropriate law enforcement officials. Law officers are then in charge of picking up the fugitives and returning them to the appropriate state.

Informal Roles and Limitations

In addition to the five "hats" described here, there are at least two others that the governor must wear. They have no basis in law, but they are nevertheless important to the job. The degree of success with which the governor handles these informal roles can greatly affect the execution of the formal ones.

CHIEF OF PARTY

As the symbolic head of the Democratic or Republican Party in the state, the governor is a key figure at the state party conventions and usually is the leader of the party's delegation to national conventions. A governor may, however, have to compete with his party's U.S. senator. Governors are able to use their influence with the party's state executive committee and at party conventions to gain a subsidiary influence over candidates seeking other state offices. An active, skilled governor can thus create a power relationship with state legislators and bureaucrats that the more formal roles of the office do not permit. The governor also wins some political influence by campaigning for other party candidates who are seeking state or national offices.

Governor Bill Clements, the first modern Republican governor of Texas, used the party role extensively to extend Republican influence through the appointment power. He appointed enough Democrats to maintain the good will of the majority leadership at the time. Governor Ann Richards also made key executive and judicial appointments from her Democratic Party colleagues. While generally supporting the party position on redistricting, she also showed some willingness to deal with the Republicans in exchange for GOP support for legislation that she and the Democrats wanted, such as a state lottery.

Governor George Bush is the most interesting "study" of the three. In 1995 he operated on a nonpartisan basis and secured the support of both members and leaders of the Democratic-majority legislature for his legislative program. He also made his own Republican Party angry by cooperating with the Democrats and by having a moderate position on a number of issues. For example, Governor Bush and Speaker of the House Pete Laney worked especially well together, and Bush told the state party bigwigs to back off from trying to defeat Laney in his 1996 reelection bid. Consequently, Bush was not included in the Republican delegation to the presidential nominating convention in 1996. In 1997, he fared somewhat less well with the legislature even though the Senate had become Republican, in part because of resistance to his tax plan by conservative members of the GOP.

LEADER OF THE PEOPLE

Most Texans, unaware of the limitations on formal gubernatorial powers, look to the chief executive of the state for the leadership necessary to solve the state's problems and to serve as their principal spokesperson on major issues. A skilled governor can turn this role to substantial advantage when bargaining with other key figures in the policy-making process, such as the presiding officers, legislators, and top bureaucrats in the state's administration. For example, through the media, the governor can rally public support for programs and policies. Choosing to accept invitations to speak is another way a governor can gain public exposure and thus support for programs and plans, including the budget. Public appearances usually also serve as occasions for emphasizing gubernatorial accomplishments. They also allow a governor to show concern for ordinary citizens with extraordinary problems, such as visits to areas damaged by tornadoes or floods. In keeping with the traditionalistic tenor of the state, some governors use this role to show that they are "active conservatives." Coupled with the strong legislative role, this informal role is critical to a governor's success. Leadership has been depicted as consisting of two parts: the ability to "transact" (that is, to make things happen) and the ability to "transform" (that is, to decide what things should happen).[21] The successful Texas governor is one who can both make things happen and decide what policies ought to happen.

A populist approach is consistent with the values of democracy. So also is a more conservative approach that addresses issues that the public reiterates with each opinion poll. Thus, although they held different positions—except that both wanted to improve public education—and used different styles, Ann Richards and George Bush both demonstrated leadership.

Summary

The governor of Texas shares many of the characteristics attributed to members of the legislature in Chapter 7. Generally, the governor is a conservative White male attorney or businessman. Since 1974 the Texas governor has had the advantage of a four-year term and is fairly well paid. Nevertheless, the office is constitutionally weak, and the approval and successful implementation of gubernatorial budgetary and programmatic policies depend more on the governor's adroitness in developing leadership skills than on formal powers.

The Texas governor has many important functions to perform, which are embodied in the various roles that make up the office of chief executive for the state. These roles, however, are restricted in the following major ways:

1. There are five other elected executives, an elected state policy board, and an elected regulatory commission.

2. The state bureaucracy is largely controlled by multimember boards and commissions, with the result that the state administration is fragmented.

3. Not only do statutes limit what appointments to boards and commissions the governor may make, but also senatorial confirmation of appointees requires a two-thirds vote.

4. The governor's power to remove appointed officials other than personal staff is still restricted in spite of recent statutory increases in the removal power.

5. The state has both a legislative and an executive budget.

On the other hand, the governor does have some constitutional and statutory strengths, and gubernatorial powers have increased substantially with the New Federalism concept of federal funding for state programs and the subsequent prominence of the governor's role in planning and interstate problem solving. The major strengths of the governor's office are the following:

1. Effective control over regional planning and federal grant applications

2. An item veto over appropriations and a general veto over legislation that, because of timing, is often absolute

---

21. James McGregor Burns, *Leadership* (New York: Harper & Row, 1978), 42–45.

3. Command over the militia and law-enforcement agencies in time of crisis

4. Party, personal, and ceremonial leadership opportunities

The description of state bureaucracy in the next chapter should help the reader to gain a greater understanding of the governor's handicaps when trying to control state agencies.

Key Terms

Appointment and removal powers	Message power	Session power
Impeachment	Ombudsman	Veto power
	Populist	

Study Questions

1. What are the formal qualifications to be governor of Texas? What personal characteristics do governors tend to have? Which of the personal characteristics do you think is most likely to change, and why?

2. What powers does the governor have in the chief executive's role? What are the limitations?

3. Why do you think many analysts regard the role of chief legislator as the governor's most significant role?

4. What formal and informal roles other than chief executive and chief legislator does the governor perform? What does the governor do in these other roles? Which one(s) do you see as growing most in importance?

5. From your reading of this chapter, how important do you think the personality and "style" of a governor are? Why?

6. Do you think the governor should have more power than the constitution currently allows? Why or why not?

7. Would you like to work in the governor's office? In which part? What specifically would you like to do?

Internet Assignment

Internet site: www.governor.state.tx.us/

Click on "news releases and speeches" and read two of them. What do these public statements of the governor seem to say about the governor's political preferences?

Chapter Ten

The Administrative State

The seemingly serene and dignified Texas capitol is the focal point for the state's frequently noisy and sometimes undignified political conflicts. Administrative agencies are housed in office buildings surrounding the capitol.

Many people consider the things which government does for them to be social progress, but they consider the things government does for others to be socialism.

Earl Warren
Chief justice of the United States, 1953–1969

Don't forget the customer. Don't forget the mission.

John Sharp
Texas comptroller of public accounts

Introduction

Few of us need an introduction to the administrative state because public administration is part of our daily lives. Traffic police, public school principals, highway workers, college registrars, clerks in state and federal offices—we all have seen, or been involved with, public employees who apply and enforce public policy.

All of us have also heard considerable criticism of government policies and administration. Earl Warren's observation in the opening quote summarizes the dilemma of democratic government. As citizens seek more programs, any given individual's preferred program is social progress, but a contrary preference by someone else is suspect. Given the conservative mood of the United States during the last decade of the twentieth century, calling attention to this dilemma is particularly appropriate. We simultaneously want less government but more programs that benefit us.

This chapter begins with a description of the state administrative agencies. To help the reader gain a clearer understanding of the complexities of modern **bureaucracy** and how our state public administration works, this chapter then will discuss why and how "big government"—the administrative state—became so big. Bureaucracy is a type of organization associated with red tape, specialization, and **hierarchy.** Hierarchy refers to an arrangement that puts few people but maximum power at the top of the organization, and many people with little power at the bottom of the organization. Finally, Chapter 10 will examine efforts to control the bureaucracy and ensure that it performs as the public and elected officials intend.

A few definitions are in order at the outset. *Public policy* usually refers to the results of decisions arrived at by the three branches of government. These decisions come to us in forms such as laws, judicial rulings, and federal and state programs. Public policies are carried out, or implemented, by public administrators. Legislators determine what is to be done in general. Bureaucrats determine what is to be done specifically. Thus, some bureaucratic decisions are in themselves public policy—for example, determining the student activities fee on a campus.

Public administration has several different but related meanings. It refers not only to the activities necessary to carry out public policy but also to the various agencies, boards, commissions, bureaus, and departments that are responsible for these activities and collectively to the employees who work in the various agencies. The term *agency* itself refers to any department, agency, commission, board, bureau, or other public administrative organization. Both *administrator* and *executive* refer to top-level individuals in public administration. Any state employee may be a *bureaucrat,* but the term most commonly is limited to administrators, executives, and lower-echelon white-collar office employees who are appointed politically or, especially, selected because of some test of their merit. Members of the traditional professions and also of the professions peculiar to government are more usually referred to by their professional titles, such as teacher, nurse, attorney, or game warden.

Implementing or executing the law is formally the responsibility of the executive branch of government; and thus the bureaucracy is nominally headed by the chief executive—in Texas, the governor. We shall see, however, that the bureaucracy permeates all branches and that its interests and powers crisscross the entire fabric of governmental structure. Furthermore, as discussed in Chapter 9, the governor is a constitutionally weak chief executive who lacks anything approaching the formidable power required to control the bureaucracy. In fact, many politicians and political scientists consider the administrative state so powerful as to constitute a fourth branch of government.

State Administrative Agencies

Although we must concede that a state bureaucracy is necessary to carry out government policy, we might be happier if the Texas administration were easier to understand. Even for the experienced observer, state administration in Texas is confusing; for the novice, it is perplexing indeed. There are three essential characteristics of the state administration that cause this confusion:

1. There is no single, uniform organizational pattern.

2. There are numerous exceptions to the traditional bureaucratic characteristic of hierarchy.

3. The number of state agencies depends upon one's method of counting.

There are at least five different types of top policy makers in state agencies: (1) elected executives, (2) appointed executives, (3) an elected commission and an elected board, (4) ex officio boards and commissions, and (5) appointed boards and commissions (see Table 10–1). Agencies headed by an elected or appointed executive follow traditional hierarchical principles in that a single individual clearly is "the boss" and thus is ultimately responsible for the operation of a particular department or office. But the agencies that are headed by a multimember board or commission have three or six or even nineteen bosses—whatever the number of the members on the board. Although there also is a hierarchical organization in these agencies, it begins with the professional staff of the agency, the level below that of the policy-setting board.

Another complication is that one office, board, or commission may be responsible for the general policies of a number of separate agencies. For example, the Board of Regents of the University of Texas is the policy-making board for the entire University of Texas System, which includes 15 agencies that are separately funded. Another example is the state Department of Mental Health and Mental Retardation, which has overall policy responsibility for more than 30 programs and agencies. As of fiscal year 1998, at least 254

TABLE 10–1

Types of Administrative Agencies in Texas

Agencies Headed by Elected Executives

Office of the Attorney General
Department of Agriculture
Office of the Comptroller of Public Accounts
General Land Office

Agencies Headed by Appointed Executives

Examples: Office of the Secretary of State, Texas
Department of Commerce

Multimember Boards and Commissions

Elected Board and Commission: State Board of
Education, Texas Railroad Commission
Example of Ex Officio Board: Bond Review Board
Examples of Appointed Boards and Commissions:
Department of Mental Health and Mental
Retardation, Texas Higher Education Coordinating
Board, Public Utility Commission

agencies, institutions, and independent programs are funded by general appropriations.[1] This list is not all-inclusive, however, because not all agencies are budgeted, especially ex officio ones and regulatory commissions that derive their revenues from fines and fees, such as the Alcoholic Beverage Commission. A rough count of just the policy-making boards, commissions, departments, and offices—excluding the courts and related agencies, the legislature and its staff agencies, and the offices of elected executives—yields a count of about 115 agencies. Community/junior colleges are excluded from the 115 because they have locally appointed boards. Perhaps the reader is beginning to see why the number of state agencies is usually expressed in approximate terms. In the space allotted here, there is no way to name, much less describe, even those agencies with which the authors are very familiar. A few of the most important state agencies are used to illustrate the various bureaucratic arrangements in the state.

AGENCIES WITH ELECTED EXECUTIVES

Five state officials, in addition to the governor, are elected on partisan ballots for four-year terms. They are, in theory at least, directly accountable to the citizenry for their performance and their integrity in office. One of these, the lieutenant governor, presides over the Texas Senate and does not head any executive office. The lieutenant governor performs as an executive only when the governor is away from the state or upon succession to the governorship.

---

1. *Fiscal Size Up: 1998-99 Biennium Texas States Services* (Austin: Legislative Budget Board, 1998), A-1–A-9. The figure 254 includes 90 executive and administrative departments, but excludes another 30 to 40 authorities, councils, and committees that do not receive general appropriations. The 254 also includes 121 educational institutions; among these are 35 general academic universities and 50 community college systems. Finally, 8 legislative, 22 judicial, and 13 health and human services agencies round out the total. The list would be longer if each state hospital and each corrections institution were separately listed.

The other four are department heads. The incumbents named here were those *prior* to the 1998 elections, which promised the possibility of changes in both the elected executives and elective boards.

ATTORNEY GENERAL

Along with the governor, the lieutenant governor, and the speaker of the House, the attorney general is one of the most powerful officers in Texas government. Although candidates for the position often run on an anticrime platform, the work of the office is primarily civil. As the attorney for the state, the attorney general and staff represent the state and its agencies in court when the state is a party to a case. The Office of the Attorney General also is responsible for such varied legal matters as consumer protection, antitrust litigation, workers' compensation insurance, organized-crime control, and environmental protection. During 1996–1997 the efficiency of the attorney general in collecting child support payments was called into question, and the legislature placed this function under tighter scrutiny beginning in 1997.

The attorney general's greatest power, however, is that of issuing opinions on questions concerning the constitutionality or legality of existing or proposed legislation and administrative actions. These opinions are not legally binding, but they are rarely challenged in court, and thus they effectively have the same importance as a ruling by the state's Supreme Court (see Chapter 11). Because the attorney general's opinions often make the headlines, and because the attorney general works with all state agencies, the office is second only to the governor's office in the public recognition it receives. Because the position is regarded as one of the stepping-stones to the governor's office, attorneys general often encourage publicity about themselves, their agency, and their support groups with an eye to possible future election campaigns. Democrat Dan Morales, a former House member and district attorney, was first elected attorney general in 1990 and is the first Mexican American to hold statewide executive office. He announced in 1997 that he would not run for reelection. Seven individuals representing the Republican, Democratic, and Libertarian Parties declared their candidacy. The most likely successor was either Democrat Jim Mattox, a former attorney general, or Republican John Cornyn, a former Supreme Court justice.

COMPTROLLER OF PUBLIC ACCOUNTS

The comptroller (pronounced "controller") is responsible for the administration of the state tax system and for performing preaudits of expenditures by state agencies. In addition, as part of the budget process, the comptroller certifies to the legislature the approximate biennial income for the state. The Texas Constitution precludes the legislature from appropriating more funds than are anticipated in state revenues for any biennial period. Texas, like most other states, must have a balanced budget. Since the phaseout of the treasurer's office in 1996, the comptroller is also the state's banker. As such, the comptroller is the custodian of all public monies and of the securities that the state invests in or holds in trust. The comptroller's office also issues the excise tax stamps used to indicate the collection of taxes on the sale of alcoholic beverages and cigarettes in the state. In short, the comptroller takes in the state's revenues, safeguards them, and invests them. The merger of the comptroller's and the treasurer's offices made the comptroller's position even more powerful than it already was.

John Sharp, a former Democratic House, Senate, and Railroad Commission member, was first elected in 1990. Sharp led the Texas Performance Review study of ways to save state money. Sharp was the first person to announce his candidacy for lieutenant governor in 1998 after Bob Bullock indicated that he would not run for reelection. The November ballot featured Republican Carol Keeton Rylander, member of the Railroad Commission, and Democrat businessman Paul Hobby.

COMMISSIONER OF THE GENERAL LAND OFFICE

Only Texas and Alaska entered the Union with large amounts of public lands, and only they have land offices. About 20.6 million Texas acres are administered by the commissioner of the General Land Office. This acreage includes 4 million acres of bays, inlets, and other submerged land from the shore line to the three-league marine limit (10.36 miles out). The land commissioner's land-management responsibilities include

1. Supervising the leasing of all state-owned lands for such purposes as oil and gas production, mineral development, and grazing (over 11,500 leases)

2. Administering the veterans' land program, by which veterans may buy land with loans that are backed by state bonds

3. Maintaining the environmental quality of public lands and waters, especially coastal lands

Democrat Garry Mauro was first elected as commissioner in 1982. Like all land commissioners, he had to try to balance environmental interests with land and mineral interests. Mauro was the Democratic nominee for governor in 1998. Democrat Richard Raymond, a House member, squared off against Republican businessman David Dewhurst in November.

COMMISSIONER OF AGRICULTURE

Farming and ranching are still important industries in the state, even though only about 1 percent of the population is engaged in agriculture. The Department of Agriculture, like its national counterpart, is responsible both for the regulation and promotion (through research and education) of the agribusiness industry and for consumer protection, even though these functions may sometimes be in conflict. Departmental activities are diverse—for example, enforcing weights and measures standards, licensing egg handlers, determining the relative safety of pesticides, and locating export markets for Texas agricultural products. Pesticides illustrate the conflicting nature of the roles assigned to this office: Requiring that pesticides be safe for workers, consumers, and the environment may be detrimental to the profits of farmers. Election to this office is specified by statute rather than by the state constitution. Republican Rick Perry was first elected in 1990. He was the Republican nominee against Sharp in the lieutenant governor's race in 1998. The likely

Land Commissioner Garry Mauro ran against incumbent Governor George Bush in 1998. When his old mentor, Lieutenant Governor Bob Bullock, endorsed Bush, Mauro no doubt wondered who would desert him next.

Courtesy of Ben Sargent.

successor is Democrat Pete Patterson or Republican Susan Combs, both former ranchers.

The November election results were as follows:

Attorney General	John Cornyn
Comptroller of Public Accounts	Carol Keeton Rylander*
Commissioner of the General Land Office	David Dewhurst
Commissioner of Agriculture	Susan Combs
Texas Railroad Commission	Tony Garza

*Her Texas Railroad Commission seat will be filled in a special election.

AGENCIES WITH APPOINTED EXECUTIVES

One example of an agency headed by an appointed executive is the Office of the Secretary of State. The state constitution stipulates that the governor shall appoint the secretary of state, whose functions include safeguarding the great seal of the state of Texas and affixing it to the governor's signature on proclamations, commissions, and certificates. In addition to this somewhat ceremonial duty, the duties of the secretary include certifying elections (verifying the validity of the returns), maintaining records on campaign expenditures, keeping the list of lobbyists who register with the state, administering the Uniform Commercial Code, issuing corporate charters, and publishing the Texas Register—the official record of administrative decisions, rules, regulations, and announcements of hearings and pending actions. Governor George Bush appointed his top legal counsel, Al Gonzales, to the job in late 1997.

The secretary of state's office, though appointive, can sometimes be a springboard to elective office. Lieutenant Governor Bob Bullock and former Governor Mark White both held the position, as did Mayor Ron Kirk of Dallas. Antonio (Tony) Garza, the Bush secretary of state from 1995 through most of 1997, hopes to continue in their footsteps, since he resigned to run for railroad commissioner.

BOARDS AND COMMISSIONS

Multimember boards or commissions head most state administrative agencies and make overall policy for them. These boards appoint chief administrators to handle the day-to-day responsibilities of the agencies, including the budget, personnel, and the administration of state laws and those federal laws that are carried out through state governments. Two of these boards and commissions have elected members. The others have appointed or ex officio members.

ELECTED BOARD AND COMMISSION

As previously mentioned, the Texas Railroad Commission is one of the most influential agencies in the state, and its three members are powerful indeed. The commission has tremendous political clout in the state because of its regulation of all mining and extractive industries, including oil, gas, coal, and uranium. Of growing importance is its control of intrastate road transportation—buses, moving vans, and trucks, including tow trucks—because of the importance of trucking rates to economic development. (Trucking is the number one method by which goods are conveyed to market.) The TRC also regulates intrastate railroads. Its members are chosen in statewide elections for staggered six-year terms. In 1994, the TRC became all-Republican for the first time, with Commissioners Barry Williamson, Carol Keeton Rylander, and Charles Matthews. The first two ran for other offices in 1998.

The State Board of Education was originally created as an elected body. As part of the public school reforms of 1984, it was made an appointive board. In 1987 the voters overwhelmingly approved returning it to elective status. Its fifteen members are chosen by the voters from districts across the state. A majority of the board's members are conservative Republicans, a fact that has reintroduced a long-standing controversy about the board's selection of textbooks for public schools.

EX OFFICIO BOARDS AND COMMISSIONS

There are many boards in the state administration whose members are all *ex officio;* that is, they are members because of another office they hold in the administration. When these boards were created, two purposes were served by ex officio memberships: The members usually were already in Austin (no small matter in prefreeway days), and they were assumed to have some expertise in the subject at hand. An example is the Bond Review Board, which includes the governor, lieutenant governor, comptroller, and speaker of the

House and oversees all bonds and installment sales or lease-purchases over $250,000 by state agencies.

APPOINTED BOARDS AND COMMISSIONS

Administration of most of the state's laws is carried out by boards and commissions whose members are appointed rather than elected and by the administrators the boards then appoint. The members of many boards are appointed by the governor, but some other boards have a combination of gubernatorial appointees, appointees of other state officials, and/or ex officio members. These boards vary in size and, as a rule, have general policy authority for their agencies. Members serve six-year overlapping terms, without pay.

There are three broad categories of appointed boards and commissions: (1) health, welfare, and rehabilitation; (2) education; and (3) general executive and administrative departments. Examples of each category are (1) the Department of Mental Health and Mental Retardation, (2) the Texas Higher Education Coordinating Board, and (3) the Parks and Wildlife Department and the Public Utility Commission, respectively.

APPOINTED BOARDS AND YOU: THE CASE OF THE STATE BOARD OF INSURANCE

How do the 115 or so policy-making boards affect you? One example is the State Board of Insurance, which regulates insurance companies (see Chapter 4) and sets rates for auto, property, title, and workers' compensation insurance. The State Board of Insurance has long been perceived as a captive of the insurance industry. Governor Ann Richards had some success in turning the insurance board toward consumer interests early in her term. Her successor, Governor George Bush, helped the insurance industry by pushing for limitations on lawsuits, but in 1995 also demanded responsible rate behavior. By 1997, the board had approved hefty increases in property insurance rates to cover a series of weather-related disasters in the 1990s. If you own a car, you'll worry a little each year when the board meets to set rates.

THE CASE OF THE COLLEGE GOVERNING BOARD

Whether you are in a public community college, a private university, or a public university, that institution has a board of trustees or a board of regents. These board members set policy for the college and appoint the president. At a typical board of regents meeting, the board members (1) renewed the president's contract, (2) approved a resolution increasing the amount of fees for most courses, (3) granted tenure to twenty faculty members, (4) approved the hiring of a new dean of business, and (5) approved a contract for construction of additional classrooms in the social sciences building. Each of these actions affected students—directly in the case of fee increases and classroom space, and indirectly in the case of the three types of personnel actions.

THE CASE OF THE PARKS AND WILDLIFE BOARD

If you are an outdoors person who likes to camp, fish, or hunt, the annual decisions of the Parks and Wildlife Board on what fees will be levied for each

Sometimes the State Board of Insurance is criticized for allowing too much leniency in the regulation of even fly-by-night companies. Alternatively, it is criticized by the industry as having a stranglehold that jeopardizes company profits. Whatever the prevailing mood, insurance regulation is almost sure to be on the agenda for each new legislative session.

Courtesy of Ben Sargent.

of these activities will be of interest to you. Texas traditionally has had very low parks and wildlife fees compared with other states. If that fishing license suddenly cost you $100 instead of $12, you might have second thoughts about this form of recreation. You also are affected by decisions of this board as to what type of fish it will release into the lakes of the state.

Big Government: How Did It Happen?

Our country changed from an individualistic society that depended on government for very little to an urban, interdependent nation supporting a massive governmental structure. How did this change come about? And why?

The many, and complex, answers to these questions involve the Industrial Revolution, the mechanization of farms and ranches, and the technological revolution. When workers followed job opportunities from farms to factories, much of the nation's population shifted from rural to urban areas. The American business philosophy was pseudo laissez-faire—that is, that commerce and industry should be allowed to develop without government restraint but with governmental aid and that government's responsibility for the well-being of its citizens was minimal. The American social philosophy was social Darwinism, which holds that the poor are poor because they are "supposed" to be that way because of their "naturally" inferior abilities and that the rich are rich because of their "naturally" superior abilities (see Chapter 1). American barons of industry—individuals earlier in our history and now usually corporate owners—grew rich and powerful, controlling not only the economy but also the politics of the nation.

Eventually, the conditions resulting from these two philosophies, principally an unpredictable boom-and-bust economy and widespread poverty, caused a number of political developments. The expansion of voting rights, big-city ward politics, and a Populist movement that insisted on protection for workers and farmers are only a few examples (see Chapters 5 and 6). The outcry against the economic conditions brought about by pseudo laissez-faire finally became so great that the national government stepped in to curb the worst excesses of big business and to attempt to protect those citizens who could not protect themselves. For example, the railroads so controlled state legislatures in the last quarter of the nineteenth century that state governments were powerless to protect their citizens. The Interstate Commerce Commission (ICC) was created in 1887 to regulate the railroads, which had been pricing small farmers out of business by charging exorbitant freight rates.

The creation of the ICC illustrates the first major thrust of governmental activity, which took place during the thirty years just before and just after the turn of the twentieth century. The second came in response to the Great Depression of the 1930s, with the expansion of both government services and the administration necessary to implement them. For example, the Social Security, farm price support, and rural electrification programs all began in the 1930s. This expansion represented a major shift in political ideology from a conservatism that held, in the words attributed to Thomas Jefferson, that "that government is best which governs the least, because its people discipline themselves," to a liberalism that held government intervention to be the best route to the betterment of the individual.

POSTWAR GROWTH

After World War II, government continued to expand in scope. There were social concerns such as civil rights, newly recognized industrial problems such as environmental pollution, and technologies such as nuclear power that required oversight. The federal government not only entered areas that traditionally had been left to state and local governments—education and health care, for example—but also fostered social change through such policies as equal opportunity and affirmative-action employment. By channeling funds for new programs at the state and local levels through state agencies, the federal government has served as the major catalyst for the increased role of the public sector.

The scope of government grew for two basic reasons. First, once politics ceased to be solely the domain of the social and political elite, newly enfranchised and politically active citizens demanded government intervention to improve the quality of their lives. The elderly wanted security when they retired from the workforce. Veterans returning from World War II wanted an education and jobs. Minority groups wanted better housing, economic opportunity, and political rights. In an urbanized, interdependent society, neither the church and charities nor individuals themselves could provide a better quality of life. Only government, with its resources and its power, could do so.

Second, the complex society created a need for governmental expansion. How could the private sector deal with chemical wastes that forced the closing of a whole town or with the Three Mile Island nuclear accident? How could individuals or businesses cope with unemployment created by complicated forces such as spiraling production costs, interest rates, and world oil markets? How could private citizens and business corporations tackle issues such as immigration, right-to-life/abortion, or the chronic cycle of poor education/limited job possibilities/poverty? Modern issues simply transcend both private-sector and limited-government solutions.

The national government continued to expand its programs and their associated costs throughout the 1970s. From the end of World War II until 1980, state and local governments grew rapidly. This growth occurred to take advantage of available federal dollars for new programs, to respond to mandatory federal initiatives, to promote economic expansion, and to develop new programs and services brought about by citizens' demands for an improvement in the quality of life. Each new service increased the number of people necessary to keep the wheels of government turning. In a state such as Texas, with a high population growth rate, it is inevitable that the combination of more programs and increased population would cause an increase in the size and scope of state and local governments.

1980 ON

However, the election of Ronald Reagan to the presidency in 1980 signaled a shift away from liberal ideology and a new stress on the role of the states in the American federal system. It also brought about cuts in funding for federal programs, forcing reductions in state and local social programs that had previously been funded by the national government. Poor economic conditions in both the Midwestern industrial states and "oil belt" states such as Texas also brought about a reduction in programs and services.

Moreover, citizens across the nation were beginning to doubt what liberal ideology had wrought. In the 1970s, states like California and Massachusetts experienced a citizens' revolt against high taxes as the voters questioned whether the vast array of government services was worth the costs, namely giant national, state, and local bureaucracies. Soon, the taxpayers' revolt became a national phenomenon. Throughout the 1980s, citizens and elected officials demanded more accountability from the administrative state. At the national level, programs such as education and social welfare were cut back or capped, and "tax reform" meant lower income taxes, particularly for the affluent. At the same time, defense spending went up significantly. The gap between government spending and government revenue was filled by borrowing. By the end of the decade, the United States had become the world's largest debtor nation while its domestic programs largely fell into disarray.

During the early 1990s, the economy faltered all across the country. The largely Anglo middle class was more concerned about the economy and its role in it than about social issues. Economic and political distance between the mainly white suburbanites and the basically minority lower economic class in the central cities increased. Because the lower class tends not to vote, governments at all levels tended to listen to the suburbanites, a phenomenon that meant even more emphasis on accountability, greater demands for tax ceilings and spending cutbacks, and more emphasis on economic development and less on the welfare state. However, major problems that only government could address remained—crime, environmental pollution, and the educational system, for example. Moreover, the national government began

FIGURE 10–1
State and Local Government Employment in Texas, 1980–1996

Source: Adapted from Texas Almanac, 1982–83 *through* 1998–99 (Dallas: A. H. Belo Corporation, 1982–83–85–87–89–91–93–95–97), 410, 421, 597, 427, 502, 608, 467, 556, 548, *respectively.*

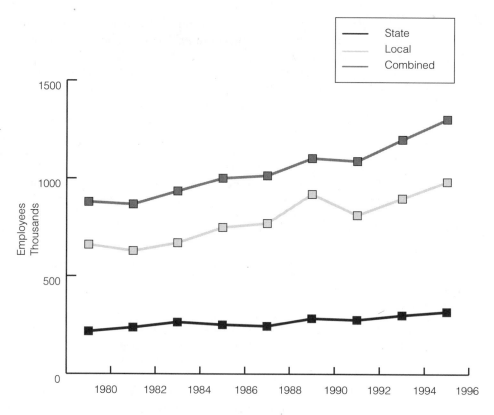

to impose requirements, known as mandates, such as clean air and water upon the states. The states then passed problems and mandates such as the need for better education to the local governments. Therefore, state and local governments began to grow in size, programs, and expenditures, much to the regret of many taxpayers, who preferred less government and an end to state and local tax increases. Figure 10–1 shows relatively steady growth since 1980. Even when the economy is in the doldrums, government employment often holds steady or even grows as government responds to the needs of the people. The best example was the Great Depression of the 1930s.

In Texas and many other states, a review of bureaucratic performance was begun, especially on the criterion of efficiency—the least expenditure of dollars and other resources per unit of output. President Bill Clinton assigned Vice President Al Gore to begin a similar initiative in the national government based on the models set by Texas and a half-dozen other states. These activities are known as reinventing or reengineering government.

Citizen dissatisfaction was nowhere more evident than in the election of 1994 (see Chapter 6), with the national sweep of elections by conservative Republicans. Candidates for the U.S. Congress, especially the House of Representatives, had campaigned on a "Contract with America" platform that included major federal governmental cutbacks among its many provisions.

Although federal program cutbacks and efforts to balance the budget were applauded in many quarters, state and local governments now must either increase revenues to pay for services that have been decentralized or cut back on popular programs or both. Chapters 3, 13, and 14 explore these issues further.

An example of what happens when a higher-level government begins to retrench is the case of Graham, a city of about 9,000 people located west of Fort Worth and south of Wichita Falls. For fiscal years 1990 through 1994, the citizens of Graham paid almost $400 each to bring local water, sewer, and solid waste facilities up to federal standards. Graham ships much of its trash to Fort Worth because federal regulations make it very difficult for smaller communities to maintain a sanitary landfill. While the higher-level government can boast of budget slashing and program reduction, citizens don't pay any less—they just transfer their dollars from one government to another.

Source: "A Small Town Pays the Price," *Fiscal Notes,* April 1995, 4.

Characteristics of Bureaucracy

Of the many ways to organize human activities—committees, commissions, task forces, and so forth—the form most often used is bureaucracy, not only in government but also in businesses, clubs, churches, and many other organizations. The bureaucratic structure is traditionally viewed as the most efficient way to organize human endeavor so as to assure competent, quick, and expert problem solving. As so often happens, however, the ideal differs considerably from the reality. Indeed, experts on governmental organization and management frequently suggest alternatives to a strict bureaucratic organization.[2]

TRADITIONAL CHARACTERISTICS

Early in this century, Max Weber, considered the father of modern sociology, listed the main characteristics of a bureaucratic organization as part of his examination of the phenomenon of authority. Weber's list is important because it has been the starting point for subsequent discussions of bureaucratic structures.

1. Authority is hierarchical; that is, the levels of power in an organization begin with maximum authority at the top, or peak, and have the least authority at the bottom. An organization chart of a bureaucracy looks like a pyramid.

2. Individuals are assigned specific tasks to perform, and a combination of training and the continual performance of these tasks results in expertise in the specific area.

---

2. See, for example, Grover Starling, *Managing the Public Sector,* 4th ed. (Homewood, Ill.: Dorsey Press, 1993), chapter 7.

3. Bureaucracies have defined jurisdictions; that is, they are created to accomplish definite and limited goals.

4. There are extensive rules and regulations to ensure that policy is implemented uniformly and consistently.

5. Bureaucrats, because they follow comprehensive and detailed rules that depersonalize administration, are politically neutral.[3]

MODERN CHARACTERISTICS

Today's American bureaucracies deviate considerably from the classic European organizations that Weber observed. Boards and commissions, rather than a single chief executive, are often at the power peak of agencies; authority (and accountability) is thus diffused. Jurisdictions are so broadly defined (as in the national Department of Health and Human Services) that limits on goals and authority are obscured; confusion and competition result from overlapping jurisdictions and authority. Agency staffers, especially executives and sometimes minor bureaucrats, far from being politically neutral, are very much involved in political processes. The public interest sometimes becomes lost in the shuffle. We seemingly are overwhelmed by the administrative state, which Emmette Redford defines as a society in which "we are affected intimately and extensively by decisions in numerous organizations, public and private, allocating advantages and disadvantages to us."[4]

The rules designed to ensure consistency and fairness sometimes contradict one another. Equal opportunity requires absolutely equal treatment of all candidates for a job, for example, but affirmative action requires special measures for protected classes of citizens. Other rules create problems while trying to solve them. For example, regulations of the federal Office of Safety and Health Administration (OSHA) require roofers to be tethered to the roof to avoid falling, but roofers contend that many injuries can occur because of tethering. However, rules or "red tape" have always been a nuisance to citizens. In fact, the term *red tape* goes back to the days of a powerful British monarchy when orders from the king were bound in packets by red ribbons.

Today we also are unsure of what the role of the expert should be. Traditionally, the expert was to carry out detailed functions—whether issuing a driver's license or testing water purity in the city's laboratory. But increasingly, experts, who often disagree with one another or have narrow views, dominate our organizations. Lawyers and accountants are prime examples in both business and government.

Another characteristic of modern bureaucracies is their reliance on managers not only to oversee policy implementation but also to serve as brokers between citizens and elected officials. In both business and government, layers of management isolate the citizen-customer from key decision makers.

In the United States, size also is of concern, especially the relationship between the number of government employees and the numbers of citizens served. The number of federal employees—about 185,000 of whom work in

---

3. See "Bureaucracy" in *From Max Weber: Essays in Sociology,* translated, edited, and with an introduction by H. H. Gerth and C. Wright Mills (New York: Oxford, 1946), 196–244.
4. Emmette S. Redford, *Democracy in the Administrative State* (New York: Oxford, 1969), 3.

Texas—changed little from the 1960s to the 1990s because state and local governments along with contract employees and consultants administered many of the national programs. Major shifts in the numbers of federal government personnel occurred only when the military was engaged in a buildup or in a downsizing. In the 1990s government reorganization and the quest for a balanced budget have resulted in the elimination of about three hundred thousand federal jobs.

Economic Development, Texas Style

An Arizona grocery store chain found that it needed fifteen permits, licenses, or registrations from eight different state agencies to open a single new store in San Antonio.

Source: John Sharp, *Fiscal Notes* (Austin: Comptroller of Public Accounts, December 1994), special section.

An economy of scale exists in the states. Generally, the larger the state, the lower the ratio of state employees to citizens. As Figure 10–2 shows, this relationship is approximate. California, the most populous state, has the lowest number of employees per 10,000 population and is ranked fiftieth. However, Texas and New York, the second and third largest states, respectively, seem to have some inefficiencies, since they rank only forty-fifth and thirty-seventh. Still, they look very efficient indeed when compared with the 439 and 413 employees per 10,000 population of Hawaii and Alaska, respectively. Hawaii is a series of islands and Alaska is huge in land mass but sparsely populated, making service delivery difficult. Texas may appear slightly inefficient because it has a similar problem in the western part of the state.

A final characteristic of modern bureaucracy is reorganization. In trying to find the most efficient means of carrying out policies and at the same time coping with increased numbers of employees and the proliferation of programs, governments keep shuffling their internal organization. President Jimmy Carter drew up a major reorganization plan for the federal bureaucracy that was approved by Congress in 1978. In the 1990s, President Bill Clinton assigned Vice President Al Gore the task of government reorganization. Many states, Texas among them, have enacted legislation that calls for periodic evaluations of state agencies. The Sunset Law, for example, is discussed later in this chapter. Some major agencies in Texas, such as those dealing with health, welfare, and water, have been reorganized, with an emphasis on consolidating fragmented services. Other agencies have initiated their own reorganizations. For example, many students have probably seen examples on their campuses of departments being combined or moved from one dean to another.

Bureaucratic Survival Techniques

Bureaucratic agencies have one characteristic in common with the rest of us: They need money. In the push and scramble of overlapping jurisdictions, authorities, and programs, agency staffers must fight for funds if they want

FIGURE 10–2

Number of Full-Time Equivalent State Employees per 10,000 Population; Ten Largest States

Source: Adapted from "Texas Among the States," Tables 1 and 20, Fiscal Size Up: 1996–97 Biennium, Texas State Services (Austin: Texas Legislative Budget Board), 3–1, 3–15.

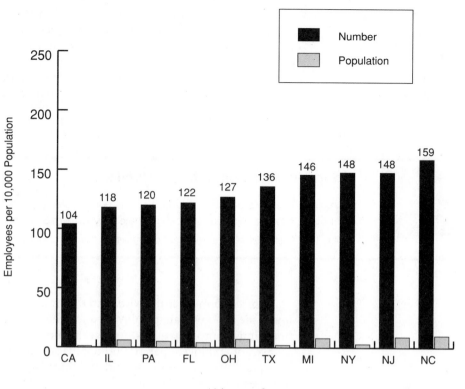

their agency to continue. There are three principal reasons why agency people seek first survival and then growth: (1) personal—their jobs; (2) programmatic—a genuine commitment to the program administered by the organization; and (3) clientele—a sincere concern for the people who benefit from the agency's programs. Because the administrators operate in the arena of political activities, they use political tactics to achieve their goals, just as state legislators and the governor do. Administrators must develop their own sources of political power if they want policies favorable to them enacted into law, and they have done so.[5]

SOURCES OF BUREAUCRATIC POWER

CLIENTELE GROUPS

The cornerstone of an agency's political clout is its relationship with its **clientele** (interest) **group** or groups. This relationship is mutually beneficial. The agency and its clientele have similar goals, are interested in the same programs, and work together in a number of ways, including sharing personnel,

---

5. An excellent study of bureaucratic power at the national level is Francis Rourke, *Bureaucracy, Politics, and Public Policy,* 4th ed. (Boston: Little, Brown, 1986). Rourke's framework is adopted here.

information, and lobbying strategies. The greater the economic power of the clientele groups, the stronger are the political ties between them and "their" agencies—so strong, in fact, that "regulation" often becomes promotion of the clientele group's interests. Among the better-known agency–clientele relationships are those between the oil, gas, and transportation industries and the Texas Railroad Commission; the Texas Good Roads and Transportation Association (an interest group) and the Texas Department of Transportation; and the banking industry and the State Banking and State Depository Boards. The ties are not always economically motivated, however, as for example, in the case of the support given to the Parks and Wildlife Department by local chapters of the National Rifle Association or to Texas A&M University by its alumni. During a legislative session, the competition for as large a share as possible of the state's financial resources can be fierce indeed, with phalanxes of agency–clientele-group coalitions lined up against one another.

THE LEGISLATURE

Agencies' relationships with legislators are of two types, direct and indirect. First, agencies directly attempt to influence legislation and their budgets by furnishing information in writing and through testimony to legislative committees. In addition, agency executives work hard to get to know the speaker of the House, the lieutenant governor, and the members of the Legislative Budget Board and the Legislative Council, all of whom operate year-round, even when committee chairs and other legislators have gone home. Second, agencies use their clientele groups to try to influence legislation, budgets, and the selection of legislative leaders. Because of the frequent budget shortfalls in recent years, a number of state agencies—including higher education—have become adept at finding powerful groups such as chambers of commerce and specially formed support groups to try to ward off agency budget cuts.

One example occurred in 1997 when first the largest universities, then the entire higher education establishment—supported by their alumni and by groups representing ethnic minorities, public schools, and employers concerned about the state's lagging number of college graduates—joined together for a "Back to Basics" initiative. This effort is detailed in Chapter 14, but higher education ended up with an extra $600 million.

THE CHIEF EXECUTIVE

As we saw in Chapter 9, the governor's power over state agencies is weak, but bureaucrats nonetheless want gubernatorial support. The governor usually appoints the agency head or members of the board or commission that oversees the agency. A governor who is a skillful chief legislator can help an agency get its budget increased or add a new program. The chief executive can also referee when an agency does not have the support of its clientele group and give an agency visibility when it might otherwise languish in obscurity. The governor's legislative and party roles can be used to influence neutral legislators to look favorably on an agency, and the governor can greatly affect an agency's success or failure through appointments to the policy board or commission that oversees it. To state administrators, the chief executive is more powerful than the formal roles of the gubernatorial office would suggest. For example, in 1991, Governor Ann Richards forced the reorganization of the Texas Department of Commerce, ending its practice of making expensive foreign "economic development" trips. In 1995, Governor George Bush pushed legislation that would benefit insurance companies by making it harder to sue and to gain large dollar amounts from a suit. He then put the Insurance Commission on notice to begin looking at lowering insurance rates since the companies would be more profitable in the absence of big settlements against them.

THE PUBLIC

Some bureaucratic agencies enjoy considerable public recognition and support. Among these are the Texas Rangers (perhaps the most romanticized bureaucracy in the state), the Texas Department of Transportation, and the Parks and Wildlife Department. The Rangers are well known, of course, because of many dramatic incidents in the early days of bringing "law and order" to the state. The latter two agencies use the technique of news and information for gaining public attention: road maps, carefully labeled highway projects, mapped-out camping tours, and colorful signs.

Usually, however, agencies have little, if any, public support to help them gain legislative or gubernatorial cooperation. The public, diverse and unorganized, often is unaware of the very existence of many agencies, much less able to give them the concerted support necessary to influence top-level elected administrators. Such support, when forthcoming, depends largely on the public's awareness of the importance of the agency's programs to the general welfare.

EXPERTISE AND INFORMATION

Expert information is a political commodity peculiar to bureaucrats, who enjoy a unique position in state government through their control of the technical information that the governor and legislators must have in order to develop statewide policies. Although all bureaucracies have this advantage, it is particularly strong in Texas because the state's legislative committee system does not produce the same degree of legislative expertise as do the seniority system and continuous sessions of the U.S. Congress. Usually the only alternative source for the legislator who does not want to use the information from an agency is the agency's clientele group. For example, if the legislature is trying to determine whether the state is producing enough physicians, the Board of Medical Examiners and the Department of Health, as well as the Texas Medical Association and the Texas Osteopathic Medical Association, are all ready to furnish the information. The public's ideas on the subject are seldom considered. The more technical an agency's specialty, the greater is that agency's advantage in controlling vital information.

LEADERSHIP

Another factor that determines the political power of bureaucracies is the caliber of leadership within the agency. Agency heads must be able to spark enthusiasm in their employees, encourage them toward a high level of performance, and convince elected officials and clientele groups that their agencies are performing effectively. A competent chief administrator will usually be retained by the members of the agency's governing board or commission, even though the board or commission membership changes over the years. The department benefits from continuity and stability at the top, and there is minimal disruption in the agency's relationship with clientele groups and legislators.

INTERNAL ORGANIZATION

Some agencies have a **civil service system** that protects agency workers from outside influence. In a civil service system, workers are hired on merit—that is, their performance on written tests and other forms of examination—and are evaluated on job performance. Agencies with a merit-based personnel system can resist the influence of, for example, a legislator trying to get his nephew hired for the summer or an aide to the governor who wants an agency employee fired because the two had a disagreement.

BUREAUCRATIC INVOLVEMENT IN THE POLICY-MAKING PROCESS

IMPLEMENTATION OF THE LAWS

The primary task of state bureaucrats is to implement the laws of Texas. In carrying out this task, however, they have considerable **administrative discretion;** that is, they are relatively free to use their own judgment as to just how the laws will be carried out. Regulatory boards illustrate most clearly the power of administrative agencies. When the Texas Railroad Commission determines the monthly oil allowable (the number of barrels of oil that can be pumped during a particular month), it is making (administrative) rules that, like legislative statutes, have the force of law. It is, therefore, performing a quasi-legislative function. When the Alcoholic Beverage Commission decides who will be issued a license to sell beer, wine, and distilled spirits, it is performing a quasi-judicial function by determining whether a person has the right to go into business. The Texas Aeronautics Commission makes quasi-judicial judgments when it decides which of two competing airlines may fly a certain route within the state.

Often, a statute passed by the legislature creates a general framework for implementing a service or regulatory program, but state agencies have considerable discretion in interpreting statutes. Consequently, the 115 or so policy-making boards, commissions, and authorities are very important in determining what government actually does. Especially in a state like Texas, which lacks a cabinet system and an integrated executive branch, the average citizen is affected on a daily basis by what these boards do, but that citizen may have little understanding of how they work or how to approach them.

Compounding the problem is the fact that the chair is basically an equal member of the board, so that no single readily identifiable person is in charge. As Chapter 3 noted, the board and commission structure makes public participation more difficult. Moreover, these boards usually appoint an executive director or college president to carry out their policies, and that executive officer has considerable influence over board policies.

For example, a college student may wish to protest the abolition of a popular major. Who made the decision? The college's board of regents? The Texas Higher Education Coordinating Board? Were the students consulted before the decision was made? However, administrative discretion can be a positive factor in effective government. A common example is the decision of a Department of Public Safety law enforcement officer to allow one suspect to go free in the hope that he will lead criminal-intelligence agents to a more important suspect. Thus, by interpreting laws, making rules, and making judgments, administrators make public policy.

INFLUENCING LEGISLATION

Bureaucrats directly influence the content and meaning of statutes that are passed by the legislature, and they do so in three principal ways: by drafting bills, by furnishing information to legislators, and by lobbying.

During its short session, the Texas legislature is under great pressure to draft, consider, and dispose of needed legislation (see Chapters 7 and 8). State bureaucrats are eager to aid the lawmakers, and two ways in which they do so are mutually beneficial: furnishing specialized information to legislative committees and drafting bills that individual legislators may then present as their own. Legislators thus gain needed assistance, and administrators are able to protect their agencies by helping to write their own budgets and develop their own programs.

Bureaucrats also influence legislation by lobbying legislators for or against proposed bills. Agencies usually work closely with their clientele group or groups in this endeavor. The governor is also lobbied not only for support of legislation that is favored by agencies and their clients, but also for agency appointments that are acceptable to them and their clients. If successful, both these lobbying activities can greatly influence the decisions of legislators as well as the policies set by boards and commissions. Moreover, over 300,000 state employees, through such organizations as the Texas Public Employees Association, are an active lobby at budget time on matters of salary and fringe benefits.

What Happens to the Public Interest?

Public administration originally was created to serve and protect the public interest. John Sharp's quotation at the opening of the chapter reminds us that we must keep that public interest and the mission of the agency in mind.

Earlier, this chapter showed how the public interest can be forgotten in the shifting, complex kaleidoscope of hundreds of agencies, bureaus, departments, and commissions constantly striving for more money, more personnel, more programs, and more power. Bureaucrats are no more evil, incompetent, or venal than employees of privately owned companies. However, the bureaucracy is funded with public money—tax dollars—so people naturally are a little more concerned with the honesty and efficiency of the state's administration than with that of Texas Instruments or Tenneco, for example.

Administrative scandals such as the mistreatment of mentally retarded people at state schools that has been reported since 1985 heighten that interest. Almost forty years ago, Paul Appleby drew the distinction between government and private administration by noting that the public administrator is continually subject to "public scrutiny and outcry" by "press and public interest in every detail of his life, personality, and conduct."[6] In short, public administrators live in the proverbial goldfish bowl.

BUREAUCRATIC ORIENTATION

It is a fact of organizational life that the longer one remains in one agency or company, the more one's perspectives narrow to those of the organization. Moreover, after a while, one begins to support that organization's way of doing things. In a public agency, this orientation often leads to a loss of concern for more general public goals and an inability to see different points of view. This shifting of bureaucratic orientation is known as *goal displacement,* that is, the replacement of one goal by another. In this case, the public interest is forgotten and the agencies' interests and those of their clientele groups become paramount. Many complex factors are involved in the displacement of publicly stated goals in agency priorities: (1) the rapid, piecemeal creation of new agencies that have overlapping jurisdictions and authorities; (2) the co-optation of regulatory agencies by their clientele groups; (3) the fact that most top-level administrators are appointed by an executive who has no power to remove them from office and that most career bureaucrats are protected in their jobs by tenure; (4) the fact that the public is generally bewildered about which government official or body is responsible for what governmental action or program; and (5) the fact that the publicly stated goals may not have been the "real" goals to begin with.

The vast majority of public managers and bureaucrats are conscientious, and many of them have a keen sense of public interest. Nevertheless, the authors share with democratic theorists a concern about reconciling bureaucracy and democracy. The growth in the size and scope of government brings with it a need for adequate controls. Even if the controls are not needed all the time, citizen participation in government requires their presence.

OVERSTEPPING THE LAW

In addition to the bureaucratic orientation that develops over time, some state administrators are further tempted toward inappropriate bureaucratic activities. In Texas, these temptations are due to (1) extremely strong special-interest groups, (2) the weak governor, and (3) the handicapped legislature. State agencies and bureaucrats have run afoul of the law in a variety of ways, from using state funds for personal travel to letting contracts without bids, and from awarding six-figure consulting contracts as a means of hiring "unseen" staff to causing injuries and deaths through failure to enforce safety regulations. These incidents involved irregularities, not simply inefficiencies.

---

6. Paul Appleby, *Big Democracy* (New York: Alfred A. Knopf, 1945), 7.

How, then, do we go about the job of ensuring that the state bureaucracy performs honestly, efficiently, and effectively? How do we ensure that public trust is warranted and that legislative intent is satisfied? In short, how do we ensure accountability on the part of the state administration?

Harnessing the Administrative State

As part of the state's system of checks and balances, the governor has a veto over legislative acts, and the legislature can impeach a governor or refuse to confirm gubernatorial appointments. As well as controlling various offices and agencies that report directly to them, all three traditional branches of government—executive, legislative, and judicial—have means of holding the bureaucracy, sometimes called the "fourth branch" of government, in check. Democratic theory posits that government should be elected by the people, but most administrators are not. The governor and other elected officials have legitimacy. State administrators must derive as much legitimacy (popular acceptance) as they can from these elected officials.

During the 1980s, the issue of bureaucratic accountability to the people through their elected representatives became increasingly important at both the state and the national levels because of tight budgets, public desire to maximize each tax dollar, and a strong, conservative, antigovernment trend. The importance of accountability was brought home in 1991 when the governor and the legislature agreed that a budget would not be forthcoming for the 1992–93 biennium until all state functions were audited to determine if money was being wasted. From that agreement sprang the nationally recognized Texas Performance Review (TPR) system administered by Comptroller John Sharp. Since 1993, before agencies can submit their budget proposals, they must prepare strategic plans that emphasize quality of service, access to programs, and measures of agency performance. Citizen demand for accountability and government's response to it illustrate that both citizens and elective officials play a role in harnessing the administrative state.

The Budget Is Made Up of a Lot of Little Things . . .

In the Texas Performance Review prior to the 1995 legislative session, the comptroller's office discovered that the state had spent $70,000 in tax money over the previous three years just to provide copies of the mileage chart to state agencies. The mileage chart is the official table of how many miles a state employee can claim when traveling from one city to another on state business. As a result, the Seventy-fourth Legislature in 1995 mandated that this information be transmitted electronically.

HOW MUCH ACCOUNTABILITY TO THE CHIEF EXECUTIVE?

It would seem logical to make the bureaucracy accountable to the governor, the chief executive and nominal head of the state administration. But as Chapter 9 discussed, the governor's powers were limited intentionally to avoid centralizing government power in any one office. For example,

1. Appointment powers are restricted and removal powers are limited.

2. There is no true executive budget.

3. The executive is fragmented: Four departments, a major commission, and a major board are headed by elected officials, and many separate agencies deal with related functional areas—more than 30 policy-making boards are involved in the area of education alone. Instead of single-headed agencies, about 115 multimember boards and commissions officially make policy for their agencies. In reality, the executive director of the agency, who administers the affairs of the agency, is usually the most powerful person connected with the organization—and is partially insulated from elected officials by the board.

Even if there were to be a complete reorganization of the executive branch, including consolidated departments headed by officials who constituted a governor's cabinet, the sheer size and diversity of the bureaucracy, coupled with other demands on the governor's time and staff, would make executive control loose and indirect. Just as it is difficult to hold a president responsible for the actions of a Social Security clerk in Laramie, Wyoming, it would be difficult to hold a governor responsible for the actions of a college professor in Canyon or a welfare caseworker in El Paso. However, in 1993, the governor adopted the use of an ombudsman—grievance person—to hear public complaints against administrative agencies in an effort to increase executive responsiveness to citizen problems.

Stronger supervisory control would allow the governor to exercise greater influence over major policy decisions. With a consolidated executive branch, unencumbered by other elected administrators, and with managerial control over the state budget, the chief executive would have more hope of implementing policy. The advantage of having a strong chief executive as the head of a more truly hierarchical administration would be having overall responsibility vested in a highly visible elected official who could not so easily be dominated by special interests. Currently, the governor relies mainly on the roles of chief legislator, chief of state, and leader of the people (all discussed in Chapter 9) to influence state agencies. However, all the modern governors have succeeded in adding some clout to their chief executive role—more removal power, the performance review, more appointments to the executive director positions in state agencies, and mandatory strategic planning.

HOW MUCH ACCOUNTABILITY TO THE LEGISLATURE?

LEGISLATIVE OVERSIGHT

Legislatures traditionally have been guardians of the public interest, with powers to oversee administrative agencies. These powers include budgetary control, the postaudit of agency expenditures to ensure legality, programmatic control through the statutes, investigation of alleged wrongdoing, and impeachment of officials. Although traditional legislative oversight is somewhat effective in Texas, several factors militate against its total success. One is the tripartite relationship among legislators, bureaucrats, and special-interest groups. Another is the high turnover of legislative committee personnel. A third is the lack of ongoing supervision because legislators are on the job only part-time as a result of Texas's short biennial legislative sessions. Much of the burden of oversight falls on the Legislative Budget Board, the Legislative Council, and the Legislative Audit Committee, although none of these has adequate staff or time for a thorough job, and none is well known to the general public.

A substitute for direct legislative oversight is legislation that micromanages an agency or set of agencies and requires some other agency to be the control force. A good example is the highly specific legislation passed in the 1997 session that dictates the core curriculum, the admission standards, and the maximum number of credit hours at publicly assisted colleges and universities. The Texas Higher Education Coordinating Board was put in charge of enforcing these statutes.

SUNSET ACT

With the passage of the Sunset Law by the Sixty-fifth Legislature in 1977, Texas established a procedure for reviewing the existence of all statutory boards, commissions, and departments—except colleges and universities—on a periodic basis. More than 200 agencies and advisory committees are included, and new ones are added as they are created. These **sunset reviews** are conducted by a 10-member Sunset Advisory Commission composed of four senators and four representatives appointed by their respective presiding officers, who also appoint two citizen members. The chairmanship rotates between the House and the Senate every two years. The sunset commission can determine the list of agencies to be reviewed before the beginning of each regular legislative session as long as all agencies are evaluated within a twelve-year period. The agencies must submit self-evaluation reports, and the sunset commission coordinates its information gathering with other agencies that monitor state agencies on a regular basis, such as the Legislative Budget Board, legislative committees, and the offices of the state auditor, governor, and comptroller. Following sunset review, the legislature must explicitly vote to continue an agency and may reorganize it or force it to modify its administrative rules and procedures.

By 1998, the sunset process had resulted in the following:

★ Public membership on most state boards and more public participation

★ Stronger prohibitions against conflicts of interest

★ Improved enforcement processes

★ Elimination of overlap and duplication

★ Abolition of 28 agencies

★ Abolition of 12 additional agencies, with functions transferred to other agencies

★ Merger of 7 agencies

★ More than $581 million in savings and increased revenues to the state[7]

7. See the Sunset Advisory Commission's Web site, www.sunset.state.tx.us, for information on both previous legislative sessions and upcoming ones.

The Sunset Commission's 1999 agenda includes agencies of general government, health and human services, public safety, and criminal justice.

Landon Curry summarized the first twelve years (1977–1989) of Texas sunset review by noting that the procedure has resulted in greater uniformity in agency procedures and practices, better coordination of interagency and oversight activities, and strengthened reporting requirements. Furthermore, "Fifteen percent of agencies under review were abolished and another 10 percent were significantly modified."[8] Nevertheless, some agencies are able to fend off negative sunset recommendations: "Those agencies with more clout and constituency support are better able to resist pressure for administrative change."[9]

 Although most of the agencies abolished through the sunset process had outlived their usefulness, such as the Pink Bollworm Commission, the State Board of Dental Examiners was eliminated in 1993 when the legislature failed to pass the statute authorizing its renewal. Its function of testing and licensing dentists and other dental personnel was taken over by the Texas Department of Health for two years until the board was re-created.

In 1993 the sunset process itself was almost "sunsetted." Of great concern was the influence of the lobby on the sunset process, seen particularly during 1993 when review of the Public Utility Commission bought out every electric and telephone company in the state. Also, the lobby enjoyed great success in undoing some Sunset Advisory Commission recommendations once they went to the full legislature. However, the legislature backed off from doing away with the sunset process because of consumer demand.

A continuing issue is the several dozen quasi-state entities such as the Texas High Speed Rail Authority, various river authorities such as the Lower Colorado River Authority, task forces, councils, and special districts. The concern is that they enjoy citizen support as public agencies but act with the independence of private organizations because they do not depend on general appropriations revenue. There is some support for including these entities in sunset review, in general state financial and performance audits, or in both.

HOW MUCH ACCOUNTABILITY TO THE PUBLIC?

ELECTIVE ACCOUNTABILITY

American government is based on the premise that it will be accountable to the people it governs. If accountability cannot be achieved directly—all

8. Landon Curry, "Politics of Sunset Review in Texas," *Public Administration Review* 50 (January/February 1990): 62.
9. Cynthia Slaughter, "Sunset and Occupational Regulation: A Case Study," *Public Administration Review* 46 (May/June 1986): 241.

citizens of a political division meeting to vote directly on laws and policies—theoretically it can be achieved through elected representatives who meet in government and report back to their citizen-constituents. But voters encounter difficulty when they try to make intelligent decisions regarding the multitude of names on the long ballot in Texas. Long ballots tend to lead to confusion, not accountability. Additionally, the vastness of the bureaucracy and the reality that incumbents can usually count on being reelected simply because the voters recognize their names mean that the elective process has become an unsatisfactory method of ensuring responsible administrative action.

In view of these problems, Texas citizens need some way to check on the activities of particular administrators and agencies on which public attention, for whatever reason, is focused. Until recently, however, there has been no easy way to do this.

OPEN RECORDS AND MEETINGS

Under the *Texas Open Records Act*, originally passed in 1973, the public, including the media, has access to a wide variety of official records and to most public meetings of state and local agencies. Sometimes called the **"Sunshine Law"** because it forces agencies to shed light on their deliberations and procedures, this act is seen as a way to prevent or expose bureaucratic ineptitude, corruption, and unnecessary secrecy. An agency that denies access to information that is listed as an open record in the statute may have to defend its actions to the attorney general and even in court.

The 1987 *Open Meetings Act* strengthened public access to information by requiring government bodies to certify that discussions held in executive sessions were legal or to tape-record closed meetings. Closed meetings are permitted when sensitive issues such as real estate transactions or personnel actions are under consideration, but the agency must post an agenda in advance and submit it to the secretary of state, including what items will be discussed in closed session. Since 1981 the legislature has also required state agencies to write rules and regulations in understandable language.

In recent years, the Texas Open Records Act has been frequently amended to permit exceptions. For example, many search committees looking for city managers, executive directors of agencies, and college presidents were being foiled by premature disclosure of the names of individuals under consideration and sought some protection from the act.

WHISTLE-BLOWER PROTECTION

The 1983 legislature passed an act affording job security to state employees who spot illegal or unethical conduct in their agencies and report it to appropriate officials. The national government established the precedent for "whistle-blower" legislation in 1978. The term *whistle-blower* comes from the fact that employees who report illegal acts are "blowing the whistle" on someone. The implementation of this act has not been promising, as the situation described in the box indicates.

In 1991, George Green, a former Department of Human Services architect, was awarded $13.6 million under the Texas whistle-blowing protection legislation. Green had repeatedly complained to supervisors that the state welfare department was being cheated by building contractors. Ultimately, the department fired Green and tried to prosecute him on the petty charge of making a $0.13 telephone call to his father.

In 1995, legislators finally voted to pay the judgment—the Senate at the full value, the House at less. No compromise was reached, and Green had to wait until November to receive a $13.7 million payment.

Source: "Fired Whistle-blower Wins $13.6 million in DHS Suit," *Dallas Times Herald,* September 25, 1991, 1–18; and Christy Hoppe, "Senate Backs Payment to Fired Whistle-blower," *Dallas Morning News,* May 25, 1995, 20A.

IS THERE ACCOUNTABILITY?

The passage of sunshine and sunset laws in recent years has enabled the public, the press, and the legislature to harness the worst excesses of bureaucracy more successfully. In addition, routine audits often turn up minor violations, a forceful governor or attorney general can "shake up" a state agency, and the state budget can be a means of putting a damper on any agency that seems to be getting out of hand. Top-level officials also have to file financial disclosure forms as a check on potential conflicts of interest. These devices help to guard against serious wrongdoing on the part of state officials and help to ensure accountability.

But serious wrongdoing is not usually the problem. Much more frequently, we see indifference or occasional incompetence. How can we minimize the indifference and incompetence that citizens sometimes encounter in state, federal, or local agencies? How can we reduce the amount of time-consuming red tape? There seem to be few formal means of ensuring that bureaucratic dealings with citizens are competent, polite, and thorough—until citizen reaction demands them. What little political attention is given to the administrative state is aimed primarily at the federal bureaucracy rather than at state or local bureaucracies. Yet, public managers may have come up with their own solution: the "Citizens as Customers Movement." This approach requires that public employees treat citizens as customers in the same way that a business treats its customers as valuable resources.

Thus, we find that elected officials, with the assistance of the media, can ensure a fair measure of bureaucratic accountability and that they continue to seek ways to control the appointed bureaucracy. The current emphasis on government performance is merely the latest of these ways.

Suggested Reforms

The Texas administrative structure is difficult for the average individual to understand. Overhauling it would not be easy because a major package of constitutional amendments and statutes would be required. Perhaps the most important suggestion is also the most obvious: to create a cabinet-type government. The 250-plus total agencies could be consolidated into a series of executive departments reporting to the governor. The only elected executives would be the governor and the lieutenant governor. The new departments might include the following:

★ Public and Higher Education

★ Health and Human Services

★ Natural Resources

★ Highways and Public Transportation

★ Public Safety and Criminal Justice

★ Commerce and Economic Development

★ Administrative Services

★ Professional and Occupational Licensing

This scheme, similar to the organization of the national government, would still leave the biggest regulatory commissions as independent agencies—the Texas Railroad Commission and the Public Utilities Commission, for example.

The likelihood of such a sweeping change is almost zero. However, minor steps toward consolidation have occurred, most noticeably in the creation of a single office to oversee health and human service activities.

Summary

A combination of the Industrial Revolution, public reaction against a pseudo laissez-faire philosophy and social Darwinism, urbanization and the development of a mass society, and the enormous amount of federal funds that have been made available to the states in the past few decades contributed to the rise of big government. Big government means big bureaucracy: the administrative state.

The Texas bureaucracy, like administrations everywhere, has had to develop its own sources of political support and power. Having done so, it influences the development of state policy not only in the day-to-day execution of the state's laws but also through providing information and influencing legislation. A major problem, then, is to harness the powerful state administration, a task that is far from easy. Two measures, however—the Open Records Act and the Sunset Law—have made strides in the direction of giving Texas citizens a responsible bureaucracy. Since 1991, the combined efforts of the governor, the comptroller, and the legislative leadership to insist on a budget based on planning and on quantitative measures of agency performance—the Texas Performance Review—have been another important step. Traditional controls such as the legislative audit and the legislature's power to investigate agency activities also help to promote accountability on the part of the administration.

Nevertheless, major problems continue. The fragmented structure of the state's administration—more than 250 agencies, including five department heads and a commission and a board that are completely independent of the governor—permits the bureaucracy considerable flexibility in carrying out legislative mandates according to its own priorities.

For the present, the growth of government—prompted by public demand for services, business demands for programs, and bureaucratic survival tactics—

seems destined to continue in a hodgepodge fashion. On the one hand, such a system means that citizens can gain access to their government through many points of access. On the other hand, it means that it is very difficult to tell "who's in charge here" and to place responsibility. To some extent, then, the state's bureaucracy represents the proverbial twin horns of a dilemma. The goal of representativeness may be achieved by the administrative state in Texas; the goal of responsiveness may not be. Yet democratic theory demands that government not only represent its many constituents but also respond to their needs.

Chapters 13 and 14 cover the state budget and major policy issues in Texas. Together they provide a picture of state elected officials and state administration in action.

Key Terms

Administrative discretion	Civil service system	Sunset review
Bureaucracy	Hierarchy	Sunshine Law
Clientele groups		

Study Questions

1. What were the two key factors in the growth of the administrative state?

2. What are the sources of bureaucratic power?

3. How are bureaucrats involved in the policy process?

4. What devices are available to both elected officials and the public to keep the bureaucracy in check?

5. What are the five types of policy makers in Texas administrative agencies? What do each of the elected executives do? What do the Texas Railroad Commission and State Board of Education do?

6. Can you think of state agencies other than the State Board of Insurance, the Higher Education Coordinating Board, and the Parks and Wildlife Department that regularly affect you? In what way does each agency you considered impinge on your life?

7. What changes do you think should be made in the Texas executive branch? Why? What would you hope to accomplish?

8. Have you had an especially bad experience with a state agency? What was it? Have you had an especially good experience? What was it? What factors do you think may have caused the differences between the two experiences?

Internet Assignment

Internet site: www.sunset.state.tx.us/sunset/outline.htm

First read about the sunset process in general; then find the schedule for the next round of sunset reviews. What topic or topics seem to be covered? In what year will education next be reviewed?

Chapter Eleven

The Judiciary

Many of the activities of the Texas system of justice take place in the county courthouses, such as this one in Gonzales County.

It would take gods to give men laws.
> Jean Jacques Rousseau, French philosopher
> The Social Contract, 1750

If I asked you to design a criminal justice system and you came up with one like we have here in Texas, we'd have to commit you to Austin State Hospital because you'd be a danger to yourself and society.
> Jim Mattox
> Attorney General of Texas, 1988

Tell God the truth, but give the judge money.
> Russian proverb

May your life be filled with lawyers.
> Mexican curse

May you have a lawsuit in which you know you are right.
> Spanish gypsy curse[1]

Introduction

All over the United States, courts and the system of justice they administer are in a state of crisis. Texas's problems are among the more acute. In addition to many other ills, the state suffers from a high crime rate, a system of financing judicial campaigns that invites corruption, long delays in court proceedings, unequal treatment of richer and poorer citizens, and a prison system that is inadequate to handle the state's criminals. Judges have made some progressive decisions in recent years, especially in regard to school finance, but overall the system in which they must work does not function well. The state has also improved its prison system, although problems with it remain.

In part, these problems are caused by the high levels of criminality in American society (especially the traffic in illegal drugs) and are not the fault of Texas government. In part, however, they are the result of a state judicial system that is chaotically organized and lacks the resources necessary to deliver as much justice to the poor as to the rich. In recent years, both judges and the legislature have made partially successful efforts to improve this system, but it remains the most troubled institution of Texas democracy.

In this chapter the myth of the nonpolitical nature of judges will be the first topic, followed by a discussion of the organization of the judiciary, and then a look at the reasons it is in crisis. Finally, some of the players in the judicial system will be briefly identified. A discussion of the substance of justice will be saved until the next chapter. As the discussion proceeds, the reality of the Texas judicial system will be compared to the ideal of democratic theory.

---

1. These foreign sayings are taken from Jonathan Roth and Andrew Roth (eds.), *Poetic Justice: The Funniest, Meanest Things Ever Said about Lawyers* (Berkeley, Calif.: Nolo Press, 1988), 112, 57, 88.

The Myth of the Nonpolitical Judiciary

"There ought to be a law . . ."

This expression is heard frequently in America and reflects the faith many of our citizens have in laws as solutions to social problems. When a law is enacted, Americans tend to believe that the problem has been solved, and promptly forget about it. The fact that the many laws already on the books have not solved our society's problems does not seem to shake our faith that a few more will do the trick.

Hand in hand with this faith goes the American perception of judges as men and women who are "larger than life." Professor Geoffrey C. Hazard, Jr., of Yale Law School describes this perception:

> Scratch the average person's idea of what a judge should be and it's basically Solomon. If you had a benign father, that's probably what you envision. We demand more from them, we look for miracles from them. . . . It's romantic, emotional, unexamined, unadmitted, and almost undiscussable.[2]

Judges themselves have perpetuated this unrealistic vision. Templelike courthouses, altarlike benches, black robes, and solemn judicial ritual all have a mystical and religious quality designed to instill a sense of awe in ordinary citizens. Americans believe that politics, at bottom, is a rather seamy enterprise. Since judges are father (and, more and more frequently, mother) figures with perfect integrity, it follows that judges are nonpolitical. Judges encourage this misleading impression because it helps them to induce cooperation, not only from the citizenry, but also from other institutions of government.

The popular view of the judicial process is as unrealistic as the popular image of judges, and, again, judges themselves have done much to maintain the myth. The symbolic image of blind Justice holding the balance scales aloft as she measures out reward and punishment without fear or favor is well known. Unfortunately, however, legal cases are often not decided entirely on their own merits. Most of us also have seen the illustration of Justice peeking out from under her blindfold. Politics enters into the process of interpreting laws and constitutions just as it enters into the processes of making and administering them.

Over the centuries, great jurists in England and the United States have developed—and are developing—neutral, impersonal criteria to use in making decisions. The ideal is that a judge is like a surgeon operating on a patient, or a scientist examining evidence to support or contradict a hypothesis: impartial and incorruptible, above passion and prejudice. The ideal judge will rule on evidence and procedure purely on the basis of fairness and established principles. Common observation suggests that this ideal has some basis in reality, and that judges are less moved by personal idiosyncrasy and outside influence than are legislators or governors. The best judges probably are the superior human beings of myth.

The worst judges, however, are unattractive politicians wearing black robes. And the system in which judges operate can either encourage them to

---

2. Quoted in Donald Dale Jackson, *Judges* (New York: Atheneum, 1974), 7.

be at their best, by providing for training and independence, or guarantee that many of them will be at their worst, by choosing them badly and then subjecting them to intense pressure from outside. As we shall see, many observers believe that the system Texas has chosen does not permit the state's judges to be the best they can be.

The misleading nature of the image of the nonpolitical judiciary does not rest only on the reality that some judges are less than judicious. It is also based on the fact that judges do not just interpret laws; they also make them. Theoretically, legislatures create laws and judges apply them. But in truth, the act of "applying" a law almost always involves interpreting it, and the process of interpretation often involves creativity and personal ideology. In other words, judges often fashion laws while interpreting them. Even more, members of the Texas Supreme Court and Court of Criminal Appeals, in particular, become crucial components of the state political system whenever they interpret the state constitution.

The task of "interpreting" laws may seem grand and noble, and often it is. But laws, like all works of humanity, are sometimes nonsensical or absurd. Imagine what you would do if you were asked to judge someone accused of breaking one of the following laws, which have actually existed in Texas in the twentieth century:

1. At one time it was illegal to own a copy of the *Encyclopedia Britannica* in the state—because that publication contained a formula for making liquor.
2. There was a law that prescribed that when two trains met at a railroad crossing, each had to come to a full stop, and neither could proceed until the other had gone.
3. The town of Princeton outlawed onion throwing.
4. In Clarendon, it was forbidden to dust any public building with a feather duster.
5. El Paso made it a crime to throw a faded bouquet into a trash can.
6. A law in Madisonville required persons to own at least two cows before they were permitted to tuck their trouser legs into their boot tops.

Source: Dick Hyman, *The Trenton Pickle Ordinance and Other Bonehead Legislation* (Lexington, Mass.: Stephen Green Press, 1976), 2, 34, 44, 52, 80, 106).

Former Texas Judge W. A. Morrison, a justice of the Texas Court of Criminal Appeals, made no bones about his personal contribution to the state's system of laws. "I have engrafted into the law of this great state my own personal philosophy," he stated. Claiming that every appellate judge does much the same thing, he explained that during his first day on the bench as a young man, the other two judges—both of whom were "at least seventy years old"— could not agree on more than a dozen cases, and so Morrison cast the deciding vote in each one. He attributed his having "engrafted" his personal philosophy into the state's law to a greater degree than most other judges to the fact that he came to the bench early in life and remained longer than most.[3]

3. "Gin 'Barbed' Cases Make Morrison Fun," University of Texas *Daily Texan*, February 19, 1964, 1.

Another Texas judge acknowledged even more clearly the political aspects of the judiciary:

> This job is more politics than law; there's no two ways about it. Hell, you can have all kinds of dandy ideas, but if you don't get yourself elected, you can sell your ideas on a corner somewhere. Politics isn't a dirty word in my mouth.[4]

The question to be considered, therefore, is not whether Texas judges perform political functions. They do. The question is whether the way the institution of the judiciary is set up is conducive to fair, honest decision making according to defensible principles. As the next two chapters will discuss, the Texas judical system often deviates very far from the ideal, but there are also instances in which it performs admirably.

The problem of Texas judges begins with the organization of the state's judicial system.

The Judiciary

Judiciary is a collective term that refers to both courts and judges. The judiciary interprets and applies all statutory law, settles disputes between individuals and institutions, sentences criminals to punishment, and awards damages in civil cases. It also serves—and here its political position is clearest—as final arbiter of the meaning and application of federal and state constitutions.

THE COURTS

In 1972 the Texas Chief Justice's Task Force for Court Improvement wrote:

> The Texas Constitution prescribes the basic organizational structure of the Texas court system. That structure is essentially the same today as it was under the republic of Texas. The rigidity of the constitutional structure has led to the development, of necessity, of *one of the most complex and fragmented judicial systems of all the states.*[5]

Nineteen years later, the Texas Research League opened its study of the state's court system with the words,

> The Texas judiciary is in disarray with the courts in varying parts of the state going their own way at their own pace. . . . Texas does not have a *court system* in the real sense of the word.[6]

These are not the only reformers' panels to have been dismayed by the Texas court system. As the quotation from former Attorney General Jim Mattox suggests, almost anyone who has looked closely at the state judicial system has concluded that its tangled organization prevents it from functioning efficiently. Critics complain about the duplication of jurisdiction between

---

4. Jackson, *Judges,* 98.
5. *Justice at the Crossroads: Court Improvements in Texas* (Austin: Chief Justice's Task Force for Court Improvement, 1972), 11.
6. *Texas Courts: A Study by the Texas Research League,* Report Two: "The Texas Judiciary: A Proposal for Structural-Functional Reform" (Austin: Texas Research League, 1991), xi.

types of courts, about the fact that not all courts keep records of their proceedings, and about the fact that a single court may both try cases and hear appeals.

Whether it functions well or badly, however, the court system does function. The following sections present a brief description of the activities of Texas's system of 2,553 courts and almost 3,000 judges from its lowest to its highest levels (see Figure 11–1).[7]

MUNICIPAL COURTS

City courts are authorized by the state constitution and by state laws to handle minor criminal matters involving a fine of $500 or less with no possibility of imprisonment (Class C misdemeanors), where they have **concurrent jurisdiction** with justice of the peace courts. They also have **exclusive jurisdiction** regarding municipal ordinances and can impose fines of up to $2,000. Municipal courts have no **civil jurisdiction** and deal mainly with violations of traffic laws. They generally do not keep records of trials. In fiscal 1997 there were 1,186 municipal court judges, who disposed of 5,949,622 cases.

Most municipal judges are appointed by the governing body of the city, although in a few cities they are chosen in nonpartisan elections. Terms of office are usually two years. Their salaries are paid entirely by the city and are highly variable.

JUSTICE OF THE PEACE (JP) COURTS

These are **original trial courts** with both civil and **criminal jurisdiction.** JP courts deal with misdemeanor criminal cases when the potential punishment is only a fine. They have exclusive jurisdiction over civil cases where the amount in controversy is $200 or less and concurrent jurisdiction with both county and district courts when the amount in controversy is $5,000 or less. JPs also act as judges of small claims courts and as notaries public, and, like other Texas judges, are authorized to perform marriages. In all but the largest counties they may function as coroners, and in this role they may be required to certify cause of death, despite the fact that few if any JPs have any medical training.

Justices of the peace are elected by the voters of the precinct and, like other county officials, serve for four years. Salaries range from practically nothing to over $60,000 per year, depending on the size of the precinct, the volume of activity, and the generosity of the county commissioners. Texas JP courts disposed of 1,940,802 criminal cases and 199,511 civil cases in the fiscal year ending August 31, 1997.

COUNTY COURTS

The Texas Constitution requires each county to have a *court of record,* that is, a court where a complete transcript is made of each case. Judges of these

---

7. The following information on the Texas courts, their jurisdictions, salaries, etc., is taken from *Texas Judicial System Annual Report for Fiscal Year 1997* (Austin: Office of Court Administration, 1998).

FIGURE 11–1
Court Structure of Texas

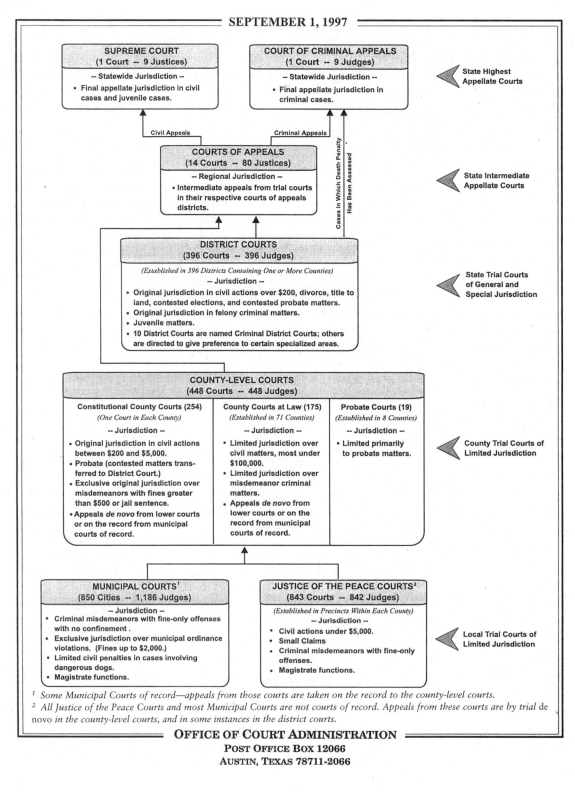

SEPTEMBER 1, 1997

SUPREME COURT
(1 Court -- 9 Justices)

-- Statewide Jurisdiction --
• Final appellate jurisdiction in civil cases and juvenile cases.

COURT OF CRIMINAL APPEALS
(1 Court -- 9 Judges)

-- Statewide Jurisdiction --
• Final appellate jurisdiction in criminal cases.

> State Highest Appellate Courts

Civil Appeals   Criminal Appeals

Cases in Which Death Penalty Has Been Assessed

COURTS OF APPEALS
(14 Courts -- 80 Justices)

-- Regional Jurisdiction --
• Intermediate appeals from trial courts in their respective courts of appeals districts.

> State Intermediate Appellate Courts

DISTRICT COURTS
(396 Courts -- 396 Judges)

(Established in 396 Districts Containing One or More Counties)
-- Jurisdiction --
• Original jurisdiction in civil actions over $200, divorce, title to land, contested elections, and contested probate matters.
• Original jurisdiction in felony criminal matters.
• Juvenile matters.
• 10 District Courts are named Criminal District Courts; others are directed to give preference to certain specialized areas.

> State Trial Courts of General and Special Jurisdiction

COUNTY-LEVEL COURTS
(448 Courts -- 448 Judges)

Constitutional County Courts (254)	County Courts at Law (175)	Probate Courts (19)
(One Court in Each County)	*(Established in 71 Counties)*	*(Established in 8 Counties)*
-- Jurisdiction --	-- Jurisdiction --	-- Jurisdiction --
• Original jurisdiction in civil actions between $200 and $5,000. • Probate (contested matters transferred to District Court.) • Exclusive original jurisdiction over misdemeanors with fines greater than $500 or jail sentence. • Appeals *de novo* from lower courts or on the record from municipal courts of record.	• Limited jurisdiction over civil matters, most under $100,000. • Limited jurisdiction over misdemeanor criminal matters. • Appeals *de novo* from lower courts or on the record from municipal courts of record.	• Limited primarily to probate matters.

> County Trial Courts of Limited Jurisdiction

MUNICIPAL COURTS[1]
(850 Cities -- 1,186 Judges)

-- Jurisdiction --
• Criminal misdemeanors with fine-only offenses with no confinement .
• Exclusive jurisdiction over municipal ordinance violations. (Fines up to $2,000.)
• Limited civil penalties in cases involving dangerous dogs.
• Magistrate functions.

JUSTICE OF THE PEACE COURTS[2]
(843 Courts -- 842 Judges)

(Established in Precincts Within Each County)
-- Jurisdiction --
• Civil actions under $5,000.
• Small Claims
• Criminal misdemeanors with fine-only offenses.
• Magistrate functions.

> Local Trial Courts of Limited Jurisdiction

[1] *Some Municipal Courts of record—appeals from those courts are taken on the record to the county-level courts.*
[2] *All Justice of the Peace Courts and most Municipal Courts are not courts of record. Appeals from these courts are by trial de novo in the county-level courts, and in some instances in the district courts.*

OFFICE OF COURT ADMINISTRATION
POST OFFICE BOX 12066
AUSTIN, TEXAS 78711-2066

254 "constitutional" courts need not be lawyers but only "well-informed in the law of the state." They are elected for four-year terms, and their salaries are paid by the counties and are highly variable. In 1996 Harris was the most generous county, paying its judge $100,716 per year. At the other end of the scale, the judge in Motley County was compensated at the rate of only $10,392. Vacancies are filled by appointments made by the county commissioners court.

Not all constitutional county courts exercise judicial functions. In large counties, the constitutional county judge may devote full time to the administration of county government.

When county courts do exercise judicial functions, they have both **original** and **appellate jurisdiction** in civil and criminal cases. Their original jurisdiction extends to all criminal misdemeanors where the fine allowed exceeds $500 or a jail term may be imposed. County courts also hear appeals in criminal cases from JP and municipal courts. In civil matters, constitutional county courts have concurrent jurisdiction with JP courts when the amount in controversy is between $200 and $5,000.

The volume of cases in approximately thirty of the state's larger counties has moved the legislature to establish a number of specialized county courts, with jurisdiction that varies according to the statute under which they were created. Some exercise jurisdiction in only civil, criminal, probate, or appellate matters, while others are in effect extra, generalist county courts. Judges for these "statutory county courts" must be attorneys. They are paid the same amount as the judges in the constitutional county courts.

Appellate jurisdiction from the decisions of county courts rests with the courts of appeals. County courts disposed of 104,167 civil, 547,092 criminal, and 6,736 juvenile cases in fiscal year 1997.

STATE TRIAL COURTS: THE DISTRICT COURTS

In Texas, district trial courts are the principal trial courts. There were 396 of these busy courts as of 1997. Each has a numerical designation—for example, the 353rd District Court—and each court has one judge. Most district courts have both criminal and civil jurisdiction, but in the metropolitan areas there is a tendency for each court to specialize in either criminal, civil, or family law cases.

District court judges must be attorneys who are licensed to practice in the state and who have at least four years' experience as lawyers or judges prior to being elected to the district court bench. The basic salary of $98,100 paid by the state is supplemented by an additional sum in most counties. Terms are for four years, with all midterm vacancies being filled by gubernatorial appointment.

Cases handled by district court judges are varied. The district courts usually have jurisdiction over felony criminal trials, divorce cases, suits over titles to land, election contests, and civil suits in which the amount in controversy is at least $200. They share some of their civil jurisdiction with county courts, depending on the relevant state statute and the amount of money at issue.

District court cases are appealed to a court of appeals, except for death-penalty criminal cases, where appeal is made directly to the Court of Criminal Appeals. In fiscal year 1997 district courts disposed of 477,217 civil, 209,355 criminal, and 34,656 juvenile cases.

INTERMEDIATE STATE APPELLATE COURTS: THE COURTS OF APPEALS

The courts of appeals have intermediate civil and criminal appellate jurisdiction. Unlike the lower courts, appellate courts—the courts of appeals, the Court of Criminal Appeals, and the Supreme Court—are multijudge courts that operate without juries. Appellate courts consider only the written records of lower-court proceedings and the arguments of counsel representing the parties involved.

Texas's fourteen courts of appeals, each of which is responsible for a geographical district, have from three to fourteen justices per court, for a total of eighty justices statewide. In each court the justices may hear cases *en banc* (together) or in panels of three. All decisions are by majority vote. Justices are elected for staggered six-year terms and must have the same qualifications as justices of the state's Supreme Court: Each must be at least thirty-five years of age and have ten years' legal experience either as a practicing attorney or as a practicing attorney and judge of a court of record. Associate justices receive an annual salary of $103,550, and the chief justice, elected as such, receives $104,050. Within each district, counties are authorized to supplement the basic salary up to $1,000 less than the salary of judges of the highest state appellate courts.

Jurisdiction of the courts of appeals consists of civil cases appealed from district courts, county courts, and county courts at law and of criminal cases, except for capital murder, appealed from lower courts. They both review the decisions of lower-court judges and evaluate the constitutionality of the statute or ordinance on which the conviction is based. Decisions of the courts of appeals are usually final, but some may be reviewed by the Court of Criminal Appeals or the Texas Supreme Court. The courts of appeals disposed of 4,517 civil and 6,732 criminal cases in fiscal year 1997.

HIGHEST STATE APPELLATE COURTS

Texas and Oklahoma are the only states to have split their highest appellate jurisdiction between two courts: a *Supreme Court* that hears only civil cases and a *Court of Criminal Appeals* for criminal cases. Each has responsibility not only for reviewing the decisions made by lower-court trial judges, but also for interpreting and applying the state constitution. It is this last power of constitutional interpretation that makes these courts of vital political importance.

The Court of Criminal Appeals. This is the state's final appeals court in criminal matters, although in rare instances its decisions may be appealed to the U.S. Supreme Court. It considers *writs of error,* filed by losing attorneys who contend that their trial judge made a mistake in applying Texas law and who wish to have the verdict overturned, and *writs of habeus corpus,* in which attorneys claim that a certain person has been unlawfully detained and should be released. In fiscal year 1997, this court disposed of 447 cases, in the process writing 747 opinions.

Qualifications for judges of the Court of Criminal Appeals and the justices of the Supreme Court are the same as those for justices of the courts of appeals. The nine judges of the Court of Criminal Appeals are elected on a statewide basis for six-year staggered terms, and the presiding judge runs as such. Vacancies are filled by gubernatorial appointment. Cases are normally heard by a three-judge panel. The salary is $104,263 per year, with the presiding judge receiving $105,247.

The Supreme Court. Like its counterpart at the national level, the Texas Supreme Court is the most prestigious court in the system. Unlike its national counterpart, it hears only appeals from civil and juvenile cases.

Qualifications for Supreme Court justices are the same as those for the judges of the courts of appeals and Court of Criminal Appeals. There are nine justices on the bench, including a chief justice who campaigns for election as such. All are elected for six-year staggered terms, with three justices elected every two years. Salaries are the same as those for the Court of Criminal Appeals.

The Supreme Court has no authority in criminal cases. Its original jurisdiction is limited, and most cases that it hears are on appeal from the courts of appeals. Its caseload is somewhat lighter than the caseloads of other state courts; it disposed of only 121 cases in fiscal 1997.

However, the Supreme Court also performs other important functions. It is empowered to issue *writs of mandamus*—orders to corporations or persons, including judges and state officials other than the governor, to perform certain acts. Like the Court of Criminal Appeals, it spends much of its time considering applications for *writs of error,* which allege that the courts of appeals have ruled wrongfully on a point of law. It conducts proceedings for removal of judges and makes administrative rules for all civil courts in the state.

The Supreme Court also plays a unique role for the legal profession in Texas. It holds the power of approval for new schools of law; it appoints the Board of Law Examiners, which prepares the bar examination; it determines who has passed the examination; and it certifies the successful applicants as being entitled to practice law in Texas.

The Courts in Crisis

There is a common perception among observers of Texas government that its courts are in crisis, that they have lost the confidence of the population and are on the brink of functional breakdown. In part, this perception is caused by the fact that the complex, ambiguous, inefficient court structure does not make for swift and sure arbitration of society's conflicts. Even more important, however, are two other factors: the overwhelming caseload in the criminal justice system, and the shortcomings of a judicial selection system based upon partisan elections.

TOO MUCH CRIME, TOO MANY CRIMINALS

Even if the Texas court system were perfectly organized, it would still be having major problems. There are simply too many accused criminals being arrested for any system to handle. From 1982 to 1992 the state's crime rate increased 12 percent, so that its citizens suffered 44,583 reported robberies, 9,424 reported rapes, 86,196 reported aggravated assaults, and 2,239 reported murders in the last of those years.[8] In the middle 1990s, however, the crime rate declined. By 1996, despite an overall increase in population, the state's total number of murders had dropped 34 percent in four years, its number of robberies 26 percent, its number of rapes 11 percent, and its number of aggravated assaults 6 percent.[9] Nevertheless, even with the dramatically lowered crime rate, the police still made 1,124,861 arrests.[10]

Further, while the crime rate as a whole was moderating, the number of offenses by juveniles—especially of a violent nature—remained dismayingly high. All the states discovered that a larger and larger proportion of their criminals were young people. In Texas, arrests of those between the ages of ten and sixteen for violent crime increased 282 percent from 1984 to 1993. Although the growth in juvenile violence leveled off after that, the long-term trend was still alarming. Whereas only 3 percent of those arrested for murder in 1977 had been juveniles, by 1996 juveniles were contributing 12 percent of the murderers in Texas.[11]

Outrage and anguish at the apparently uncontrollable criminality of young people was undoubtedly a major reason for the increase in concern about crime among members of the public in the early and mid-1990s. Furthermore, the decline in adult crime did not mean that Texans were now safe—the state still endured the second highest crime *rate* of all the states (after Louisiana). The common feeling in Texas cities that "you can't walk the streets in safety at night," while something of an exaggeration, does express the realistic awareness that ordinary citizens are often at risk in their daily lives.

The high levels of street crime, leading to large numbers of arrests, have swamped the courts, making Texas's 2,985 judges, the most of any state, still not enough. In Harris County (Houston), for example, in October 1993 there were 219 capital murder cases pending for trial, up from 180 for the same period the previous year. Since there are twenty-two felony courts in Harris County and each capital murder trial lasts about six weeks, it would take over a year to clear the county's docket, assuming that no new murders were committed in the meantime. Also, of course, while a murder trial is proceeding, the courtroom cannot be used for anything else, so the backlog of non-murder felony trials would grow huge while the county waited for the murder trials to end.[12]

Not only are the courts dangerously overcrowded, but so also are the prisons. Late in 1997 state prisons in Texas held over 140,000 inmates, far more than in any other state. Of every 100,000 Texas residents, 677 were incarcerated, and a total of 5 percent of the state's population was under criminal justice supervision of some kind, either in prison or jail, or on parole or probation. Despite having spent $1.5 billion in the previous four years to build new prison facilities, the state's leaders discovered in 1997 that they

---

8. *Crime in Texas 1992* (Austin: Department of Public Safety, Crime Records Division, 1993), 14.
9. *Crime in Texas 1996* (Austin: Department of Public Safety, Crime Records Division, 1997), 10.
10. Ibid., 15.
11. Michael Graczyk, "Juvenile Arrests Rise 282% over Ten Years, Study Says," *Austin American-Statesman,* March 22, 1995, B4; *Crime in Texas 1996,* 69.
12. "Capital Murder Cases Swamp Harris County Courts," *Dallas Morning News,* October 25, 1993, A12.

were running out of places to put sentenced criminals; they planned to spend an additional $107.4 million to create space for another forty-one hundred prison beds.[13]

Members of the public, justifiably outraged over the threat of murder, rape, assault, robbery, and drug dealing in their neighborhoods, demand that officials "lock 'em up and throw away the key." But the truth is that there are few places to put today's criminals, let alone tomorrow's.

Given this impossible situation, judges do what they can to keep the system functioning by accepting **plea bargains.** A defendent pleads guilty to a lesser charge—say, manslaughter instead of murder—and receives a lesser penalty (less time in prison, or a probated sentence), and a trial is avoided. More than nine out of ten criminal trials in Texas end in a plea bargain.[14]

Frustrated by their seeming inability to control crime, many citizens call for harsher punishments for criminals. Their representatives hear them, and often respond by writing laws that mandate longer prison terms for convicted felons. Sometimes the desire to punish sparks disturbing schemes. For example, Representative Al Edwards of Houston has several times introduced a bill in the Texas House to punish habitual thieves by cutting off their fingers. Edwards's bill has not passed, and is unlikely to pass in the future, partly because the federal courts would undoubtedly toss it out as constituting "cruel and unusual punishment," which is prohibited by the Eighth Amendment to the U.S. Constitution. Nevertheless, Edwards's bill reminds us that the response to the primitive emotions created by crime is sometimes to demand a primitive punishment.

Since a plea bargain puts the criminal back on the streets quickly, it does almost nothing to make society safer. Ordinary citizens are often appalled at the swiftness with which violent criminals are recycled into their neighborhoods, but the courts cannot handle the twin problems of a crushing caseload and overstuffed prisons any other way. A 1994 report from the state comptroller's office expressed public exasperation with the situation like this:

> Congestion in the correctional system has forced the return of thousands of criminals to the streets of Texas after serving a fraction of their time. There is no "truth in sentencing" when "life" equals 15 years, and a ten-year prison sentence can be completed in ten months.[15]

Texas officials have not sat by wringing their hands while the prison population expanded to unsustainable levels. The state has begun programs to cut the recidivism rate (that is, the proportion of inmates who, once they have served their time and are released, commit other crimes and are returned to prison). At least one out of every five of the people in prison are there for

---

13. "Prison Giant Growing," *Austin American-Statesman,* November 20, 1997, A14; Mike Ward, "State Officials Want More Prison Beds," *Austin American-Statesman,* September 5, 1997, A1.
14. *Texas Crime, Texas Justice* (Austin: Comptroller's Office, 1994), 51.
15. Quoted in ibid., 119.

drug-related offenses.[16] In 1993 the legislature appropriated money to set up substance-abuse programs within the prisons. By 1996 the state correctional system ran the largest substance-abuse prevention program in the world, with twelve thousand beds. If this program works, it will greatly cut the number of people who continue their illegal activities after being released from prison.[17]

As public anger over criminality has escalated, legislators have passed harsher laws to deal with criminals. Since the public is particularly outraged by sex offenders, politicians have given them special attention. In 1997, the legislature passed several laws making punishment of such criminals more rigorous.

Most prominently, there is now a "two strikes and you're out" law. People convicted of certain sex offenses twice must be automatically sentenced to life in prison.

In addition, a new law requires anyone convicted of a sex offense as far back as 1970 to register with local law enforcement agencies. At the time the law was passed, Texas already had 22,000 sex offenders behind bars and 17,000 more who were out in the community but registered.

A third law allows extension of probation from a maximum of ten years to a maximum of twenty, and mandates more extensive supervision of parolees.

These new laws may make the community safer. They will certainly require state government to spend much more money.

Source: "Plethora of New Laws Take Effect," *Denton Record Chronicle,* September 1, 1997, A11.

Fewer crimes would mean less pressure on the court system. Nevertheless, unless and until the new programs dramatically lower the state's crime rate, Texas's prisons will remain overstuffed and expanding, and its judicial system will continue to be overwhelmed.

JUDICIAL SELECTION

In the United States, six methods are used to select judges:

1. Partisan elections. Judges are chosen in elections in which their party affiliation is listed on the ballot. This is the system employed in Texas.

2. Election by legislatures. The state legislature chooses the judges, although the governor often influences its choices.

3. Appointment by the governor. The chief executive appoints judges, sometimes with the consent of the legislature. Various interest groups—legal, political, and economic—attempt to influence the governor's choice.

4. Merit plan. The governor makes the appointments from a list submitted by a nominating commission. At regular intervals, judges must be

---

16. Ibid., ix.
17. Lieutenant Governor Bob Bullock, "Campaign to Combat Violence Has Begun," *Austin American-Statesman,* October 5, 1992, A11; Stefanie Asin, "Drug Program's Popularity Keeps a Backlog in Jail," *Houston Chronicle,* December 13, 1997, A37.

approved by the voters in a referendum. If they fail to win a majority of the votes, they must leave office, and the governor appoints someone else.

5. Nonpartisan election. Judges are chosen in elections, but no party labels appear on the ballot.

6. Combination. There are various combinations of the first five methods.

In Texas, all judges except municipal judges are popularly elected in a partisan contest. Trial court judges serve for four years before having to face the voters again, while appellate judges benefit from a six-year term.

Until recently, most Texas judges enjoyed substantial job security once they reached the bench; vacancies were usually created only by the death, retirement, or resignation of the incumbent. Unexpired terms were filled by appointment, with state judges being appointed by the governor, county judges by county commissioners, and municipal judges in accordance with individual city charters or the general municipal laws. Once he or she had been elevated to the bench, the typical judge could exercise substantial independence.

The election of 1994 changed all that. Voters pulling straight-ticket levers removed Democratic judges all over the state. Republicans won every race they contested for the Court of Criminal Appeals and the Supreme Court, capturing their first majority on the latter since Reconstruction. In Harris County alone, nineteen Democratic jurists were unseated.[18] Republican victories continued in 1996 (see Chapter 6).

As Texas acquired a competitive two-party election system, judges lost their security of tenure. The era of a judiciary that was confident of its employment, and therefore mostly independent in its decision making, was over.

The across-the-board nature of the Republican triumph in 1994 led many Democrats to question the state's method of judicial selection for the first time. But many Republicans, including the chief justice of the state's Supreme Court, also called for a reform of the selection process. Complaints against the status quo were of three kinds. Critics argued that the courts were being damaged because judges' reliance on campaign contributions compromised their independence, because partisan elections created a divided and nonneutral judiciary, and because at-large elections discriminated against minorities. These criticisms will be discussed in turn.

IS JUSTICE FOR SALE?

The first criticism of the judicial selection process is the charge that it permits judges to be corrupted by campaign contributions. Texas retains its traditional means of selecting judges in elections, as it does with all other politicians. This practice is in line with democratic theory. Like legislators and executives, judges are government officials, and like them, they presumably serve the people. However, when judges have to run for office like other politicians, they also have to raise money like other politicians. When lawyers who practice in judges' courtrooms or others with a direct interest in the

---

18. John Williams, "GOP Gains Majority in State Supreme Court," *Houston Chronicle*, November 10, 1994, A29; Alan Bernstein, "Judge Elections Debated Anew," *Houston Chronicle*, November 10, 1994, A1.

outcome of legal cases give judges campaign contributions, it raises the uncomfortable suspicion that those judges' court rulings might be affected by the money. Wealthy special interests may taint the administration of justice just as they deform the public policy made by other institutions.

The possible corruption of justice is not only a theoretical possibility. Texas and Alabama have the most expensive judicial races in the country.[19] Some individual law firms have contributed more than $100,000 to a single judicial candidate.[20] And some examples raise the strong suspicion that such donations have induced judges to commit improprieties.

Perhaps the most famous instance involved a mammoth suit filed by Pennzoil in 1986 against Texaco. Claiming that Texaco had interfered with its takeover of Getty Oil, Pennzoil went to court, demanding $11 billion in compensation.

The trial lawyer hired by Pennzoil, Joe Jamail, gave District Judge Anthony Farris a $10,000 campaign contribution *after* Farris had been assigned to the case, and Farris then enlisted Jamail to raise $50,000 more. Farris subsequently ruled several times during the trial in favor of Jamail and Pennzoil, and they won the case, being awarded the largest judgment for damages in history. Texaco appealed, but the Texas Supreme Court refused to hear the case. Attorneys for both oil firms had contributed to members of the Supreme Court, but Jamail and Pennzoil's corporate lawyers had been much more generous, giving them a total of more than $300,000 in 1986 alone. "The appearance," observed State Senator Frank Tejada, then chair of the Jurisprudence Committee, "is that perhaps justice is for sale." Indeed, the appearance was strong enough to bring critical attention from the national press, including a segment on the television program *60 Minutes*.

Responding to the public perception that justice might be for sale, in 1995 the legislature passed the Judicial Campaign Fairness Act (JCFA). This legislation limited individual contributions to statewide judicial candidates to $5,000 each election and prohibited law firms from contributing more than $30,000 to individual Supreme Court candidates. Judicial candidates were also forbidden to accept more than a total of $300,000 from all political action committees.

Although the intent of the JCFA was clearly to stop the contamination of the Texas judiciary by money, events almost immediately proved it to be ineffective. In 1996, Justice James A. Baker of the Supreme Court allowed an attorney with a case pending before him to participate in his fundraising efforts.[21] When journalists reported this obvious conflict of interest, the bad publicity forced Baker to withdraw from the case. His withdrawal solved the immediate concern about one questionable case, but it did not address the basic problem. As long as attorneys are allowed to raise campaign funds for judges and to contribute money themselves, there will be public doubts about the impartiality of the judiciary. The JCFA, while it was well intentioned, does not address this fundamental problem.

---

19. Laura Castaneda, "D.C. Worst, Utah Best on Litigious List," *Dallas Morning News*, January 3, 1994, D1.
20. Lloyd Doggett, "Judicial Campaign Fairness Act Essential," *Austin American-Statesman*, May 26, 1993, A17.
21. Mike Ward, "High Court Justice Leaves Case Involving Campaign Solicitor," *Austin American-Statesman*, April 13, 1996, B6.

As this cartoon by Ben Sargent attests, the Texas public is skeptical that judges who take large campaign contributions from lawyers can render impartial verdicts.

Courtesy of Ben Sargent.

PARTISAN ELECTIONS?

Closely allied to the problem of the dependence of elected judges on campaign contributions are the difficulties created by partisan elections. The consequence of the state's system is that judges are like other politicians in that, although they do not campaign all the time, they must always be thinking about the next election. Like other politicians, they are aware that what they do or say today may affect their chances for reelection tomorrow. Unlike other politicians, however, judges are supposed to be fair and impartial when trying cases, and pay no attention to the possible partisan consequences of their decisions.

This task is too difficult for imperfect humans. With the next election always just over the horizon, partisanship comes to permeate a courthouse, and the struggle for advantage may taint the quest for impartial decisions. After her defeat in the 1994 Republican landslide, Democratic District Judge Eileen O'Neill wrote a sad analysis of the impact of Texas's judicial electoral processes on its justice system:

> As the campaign season approaches at the courthouse, lines get drawn. Sitting judges join in the search for contenders for open, and sometimes occupied, benches. Judges become guarded in their comments to colleagues and suspicious of their staffs. . . . By November, most everyone belongs to a side, willingly or otherwise, with some perceived stake in the outcome.[22]

---

22. Judge Eileen F. O'Neill, "Judicial Lottery Snake-Eyes for Texans," *Houston Chronicle,* November 20, 1994, C1.

Obviously, it would be placing too much faith in human self-restraint to expect justice to be blind under such circumstances.

Partisanship also creates another difficulty: judicial qualifications. Ideally, in a democracy the citizens learn something about the candidates before they vote. In reality, most people are relatively ignorant about the candidates and issues when they cast their ballots, and the overwhelming majority are ignorant about such low-profile races as judgeships. Often this mass ignorance has no greater consequence than that most incumbents are returned to their benches. But in partisan landslide elections such as those of 1982, 1984, 1994, and 1996, when the candidates of one party benefit overwhelmingly from a surge in voter sentiment, straight-ticket voting can sweep out a host of experienced judges and sweep in a group whose members may have qualifications that are at best marginal.

A classic case of the straight-ticket problem occurred in 1994. Among the many Republican candidates defeating Democratic incumbent judges was a previously unknown lawyer named Steve Mansfield. Mansfield did not win just any seat on the bench by receiving more votes than Charles Campbell; he captured a place on the Court of Criminal Appeals, one of Texas's two highest tribunals. There is no doubt that Mansfield won entirely because he was a Republican. It is entirely possible that not a single voter in the state, with the exception of Mansfield himself, had any knowledge about the candidate's past life. Shortly after the election, however, some journalists began to investigate Mansfield's credentials. Eventually, various inquiries turned up these facts about the new judge:

1. He had claimed in campaign literature that his "background is primarily in criminal defense," only to admit after the election that his career had been spent almost entirely as in-house counsel for insurance and pension companies. It is unclear whether Mansfield has ever acted as a lawyer in a single criminal case.

2. Mansfield had been arrested for possession of marijuana in Boston and paid a fine after being arrested for practicing law without a license in Florida.

3. Although he told a Houston newspaper that he had no previous political experience, it later came out that he had run unsuccessfully for Congress in New Hampshire in 1978 and 1980.

4. He wrote on his 1992 application for a Texas law license that he had never been late on or missed a child support payment for his three children. His ex-wife claimed in a 1990 bankruptcy filing, however, that he was $10,000 behind.

5. When he registered to vote in Texas, he swore that he had been born in Houston. During the campaign, he repeated this statement to reporters. Later, when it became known that he had actually been born in Brookline, Massachusetts, he amended his story by saying that he had moved to Houston with his family when he was a toddler and had lived there for several years as a child. Upon being pressed, he admitted that this, also, was untrue, and that he had never been in the city until adulthood.

6. Also, when he first registered to vote and when he changed his registration address four years later, he misstated his birthdate by two years.

When these facts began receiving publicity in November, 1994, the state Board of Law Examiners began an investigation to see if Mansfield had done anything that would justify removing him from the bench. Eventually, the board decided that Mansfield's mistatements of fact did not justify his removal. As a result, he still sits on the state's highest court of criminal jurisdiction.

In 1988 the New York State Commission on Government Integrity made a thorough survey of methods of selecting state and local judges. It concluded that:

1. There is "no persuasive evidence correlating systems of judicial selection with the quality and integrity of judges."
2. An appointive system does not "necessarily produce more qualified judges nor fewer corrupt ones."

In short, there is no proof that the way Texas chooses its judges is an unusually bad way, or that some other way would be better.

Source: Frank D. O'Connor, "New York Should Continue to Elect Its Judges," *New York Times*, June 11, 1988, p. 14.

People who want to change the way Texas chooses its judges point to Mansfield as an illustration of what is wrong with the system. One journalist called him a "Poster Boy for Reform."[23] But others are less eager to see in one evident mistake a reason to throw out the system. All systems have flaws, and the democratic appeal of partisan elections is strong. As David Willis, an adjunct law professor at the University of Houston, wrote in a defense of partisan elections:

> Judicial candidates, like everyone, have philosophical preferences. Choosing a partisan label suggests a whole cluster of attitudes toward the role of government in addressing social challenges. It is an inexact science, but why deprive us of this crucial information about a candidate?[24]

Moreover, as the box detailing the findings of a New York state study illustrates, there is no good evidence that a different system of choosing judges would produce a more honest system than the one Texas has now. An appointive or nonpartisan system might not create a better judiciary, and would be less democratic.

AT-LARGE OR SINGLE-MEMBER DISTRICT ELECTIONS?

State district judges in Texas are selected in **at-large elections.** All candidates receive their votes from the whole district, which in a metropolitan area is typically a county. Such elections tend to make it difficult for minorities to be elected. If, for example, a quarter of the population of a county is Hispanic, and there is more-or-less bloc voting by each ethnic group, then Hispanic

---

23. Louis Dubose, "A Poster Boy for Reform," *Texas Observer*, December 9, 1994, 3.
24. David J. Willis, "Separate Myth, Fact on Texas Judicial System," *Houston Chronicle*, February 5, 1995, C1.

candidates will be outvoted three-to-one every time. Although Hispanics represent 25 percent of the population, they will have 0 percent of the judges.

The solution to such a problem is to institute **single-member district elections.** If the county is carved into a number of single-member districts, with each single-member district electing a single judge, then (assuming that people of different ethnic groups tend to live in different areas) the proportion of judges from each group should be roughly proportional to that group's representation in the population. If Hispanics have a quarter of the total population of the county, and a quarter of the single-member districts are largely Hispanic in population, then probably about a quarter of the elected judges will be Hispanic. Consequently, minority representatives almost always prefer single-member district election systems over at-large systems.

In 1988 the League of United Latin American Citizens (see Chapter 4 for a discussion of the history and recent situation of LULAC) filed suit in federal court, charging that Texas's at-large system of electing district judges discriminated against minorities, and thereby violated a section of the 1965 Voting Rights Act that attempted to ensure fair access to the electoral system by minorities. This case (*Houston Lawyer's Association et al.* v. *Attorney General of Texas et al.,* 501 U.S. 419, 1994) climbed step by step through the federal court system, with each level tending to reverse the ruling of the previous level. In August 1993, the Fifth U.S. Circuit Court of Appeals held that at-large elections were not discriminatory, and that therefore Texas's system could continue. In January 1994, the U.S. Supreme Court refused to hear an appeal of this ruling, thereby allowing it to stand.

Unlike voting cases earlier in the twentieth century, in which a white majority was undoubtedly rigging the system so as to prevent minorities from participating, the rights and wrongs of this case are not so clear. The issue was not whether black and Hispanic citizens were allowed to vote—they were. The issue was whether a side effect of the electoral system was to reduce the ability of African Americans and Mexican Americans to be elected, which is a far more obscure problem.

Attorneys for LULAC could point to unarguable evidence that the proportion of minority judges does not begin to approach minority strength in a county. In Dallas County, for example, at the time the lawsuit was filed, only five of thirty-seven state district judges were minority (13.5 percent), although 41 percent of the county's population was African American or Hispanic. In Harris County (Houston), five of fifty-nine judges were minority (8 percent), although 42 percent of the population was minority.[25]

Yet lack of *representation* is not necessarily evidence of *discrimination.* As the Fifth Circuit Court pointed out in its opinion, there is a very small pool of experienced minority lawyers available to become judges. For example, in Travis County (Austin) in the late 1980s, Hispanics made up 7.7 percent of the population but only 2.7 percent of the attorneys eligible to be elected to the bench.[26] Given that fact, it is not surprising that the number of Hispanic judges was not proportional to the number of Hispanics in the county. In other words, a strong argument can be made that minorities hold relatively

---

25. James Cullen, "Judges Protect Their Own," *Texas Observer,* September 17, 1993, 4.
26. Suzanne Gamboa, "Judicial Elections Proposal Rejected," *Austin American-Statesman,* August 25, 1993, A1.

few judgeships because there are relatively few minority citizens qualified to be judges. If that is so, then there is no illegal discrimination to be overturned.

The issue became even more tangled after the 1994 election. Since almost all African American and Mexican American judges are Democrats, they stand or fall with that party's electoral fortunes. In 1994 (and again in 1996), they fell. Almost every minority judge in the state was eliminated in the Republican landslide. Minority advocates immediately charged that racist voting explained the defeats. This accusation was mistaken, for Anglo Republican voters did not spare Anglo Democratic judges. Minority judges lost because of their party, not their ethnicity. Still, if judges had run from single-member districts instead of at-large, the heavy Democratic voting in minority areas would undoubtedly have reelected many Democrats, including judges. Clearly, the way to protect minority jurists in Republican election years in Texas would be to change to a single-member district judicial election system. Since the preservation of minority judges under these circumstances would also mean the preservation of Democrats, however, Republicans wonder why they should be expected to endorse a "reform" that would be, in effect, a protection scheme for the other party.

The rights and wrongs of single-member judicial districts are therefore highly ambiguous. The politics is somewhat clearer. In the national Democratic Party and in the liberal faction of the Texas party, African Americans and Hispanics make up a significant part of the coalition (see Chapter 5). As a consequence, Democrats tend to favor single-member judicial systems, and Republicans tend to favor at-large systems.

Dissatisfaction with the troubles caused by campaign contributions, partisan elections, and the at-large election system grew throughout the 1980s and into the 1990s, so that the movement for judicial reform seemed to have an irresistible momentum as the 1995 legislative session opened. In late 1994 a bipartisan commission chaired by Democratic Lieutenant Governor Bob Bullock recommended a reform plan in which judges would first be appointed by the governor, then have to be retained by the voters in the next election. This change was endorsed by former Governor Bill Clements and Chief Justice Tom Phillips of the Texas Supreme Court, both Republicans.

Despite an apparently favorable bipartisan climate for reform, however, the 1995 legislature made few changes in the state's system of electing judges. Having slightly modified the laws regulating campaign contributions to judicial candidates, it rejected the plan to change the selection system from elective to appointive, and ignored requests to create single-member districts as opposed to at-large elections. Among the several reasons for the demise of reform efforts was Governor Bush's expressed preference for partisan elections. In the 1997 legislature, also, various suggested changes in the manner of selecting judges failed.

For the foreseeable future, therefore, Texas's method of selecting judges will remain unchanged, and for the foreseeable future, a significant percentage of political actors will be unhappy with it.

EQUAL JUSTICE?

Before people are put in prison, they must be tried and convicted. Since one of the most important ideals of democracy is that everyone is equal before the law, Texans would like to think that all accused persons are treated fairly and impartially in this process. A well-functioning democracy features a judiciary that rigorously but fairly judges the guilt of everyone brought to trial.

Unfortunately, however, the Texas judicial system does not affect all citizens equally. It inevitably discriminates against less wealthy defendants. Legal fees are expensive—well over $100 per hour for most lawyers working on a case—and the system is so complex (see box) that accused people cannot defend themselves without extensive and expensive legal help. The result is that the prisons, and death row, are full of poor people. Wealthier, white-collar defendants can afford to hire attorneys to help them try to "beat the rap" and, in any case, are often offered plea bargains that allow them to stay out of prison. Texas, however, lacks a system of state-employed public defenders whose job is to defend accused criminals who cannot afford private counsel, except in the case of people convicted of capital murder who have been sentenced to death. The county, not the state, recruits and compensates lawyers to defend accused persons who cannot hire their own counsel. When defendants are indigent, the judges in their cases appoint private attorneys to represent them, but frequently these attorneys are inexperienced or already busy with paying clients.

Here is a brief summary of how the Texas criminal justice system would typically handle a person accused of committing a felony (serious crime):

1. *Investigation/arrest.* If the police think that they have "probable cause" to arrest a suspect, they take him or her into custody.
2. *Initial appearance.* The accused is informed of the charges lodged, provided counsel if indigent, and informed of the right to a preliminary hearing. At this time, the judge also sets bail.
3. *Preliminary hearing.* While constitutionally guaranteed, this hearing is usually waived by the defendant. If a hearing is requested, the state must demonstrate probable cause, both that a crime was committed and that the defendant committed it.
4. *Motions of discovery and inspection.* Both prosecution and defense file motions to be furnished the evidence available to the other side.
5. *Grand jury.* This jury examines the evidence to determine if it is sufficient to justify trying the defendant.
6. *Arraignment.* The charges against the accused are again specified, and the accused's plea (guilty or not) is accepted by the court.
7. *Plea bargaining.* The prosecutor and the defense attorney may negotiate a reduction in sentence in return for a guilty plea.
8. *Selection of the trial jury.*
9. *Trial.* The prosecutor attempts to prove that a crime was committed and that the accused committed it, beyond a reasonable doubt; the defense attorney attempts to rebut the evidence.
10. *Sentence.* If the defendant is found guilty, the judge prescribes the punishment. A conviction for capital murder requires a separate hearing.
11. *Appeals.* Losing defense attorneys may file one or more appeals, claiming that the trial judge made one or more mistaken rulings as to the law or courtroom procedures. Such appeals frequently take years to resolve.

Source: Raymond H. C. Teske, Jr., *Crime and Justice in Texas* (Huntsville: Sam Houston State University Press, 1995), 88.

In 1993 the Texas Bar Foundation sponsored a study of the state's system of appointing attorneys for indigents accused of murder by the Spangenberg Group of Massachusetts. The group's conclusions about Texas justice were consistent and unambiguous:

> In almost every county, the rate of compensation provided to court-appointed attorneys in capital cases is absurdly low . . . the quality of representation in these cases is uneven and . . . in some cases, the performance of counsel is extremely poor.[27]

If such poor legal representation is common for citizens accused of murder, which is a high-profile crime, then the representation afforded people accused of lesser crimes must be even worse. Although there are no scholarly studies to prove it, it stands to reason that defendants who receive inferior public legal representation would be convicted more often, and be given harsher sentences, than defendants who can afford to hire private attorneys. Reformers argue that if justice is to be done, Texas should have a system of public defenders equal in number and experience to the public prosecutors. For now, however, the ironic question posed by the judge in the cartoon, "How much justice can you afford?" is a challenge to the democratic legitimacy of the Texas judicial system.

The problem of unequal justice is especially acute because Texas is a state with the death penalty. From the year 1982, when Texas began to again execute people convicted of capital murder after a hiatus ordered by the U.S. Supreme Court, through 1997, the state executed 144 murderers, including 37 in 1997. (The state that was the second most active in administering capital punishment, Virginia, executed only 46 criminals in the same period.)[28]

In Chapter 12 the issue of whether capital punishment is defensible will be examined. Whether or not the death penalty is defensible, however, it would seem to be inflicted unequally on poorer and wealthier defendants. The implication of the findings of the Spangenberg report must be that indigents charged with murder and defended by a court-appointed attorney are more likely to be sentenced to death than are defendants who can afford private counsel.

The fact that poor defendants probably have a greater chance of being incarcerated, and executed, would not be so worrisome if there were reason to have confidence in the fact that they were all guilty. However, as Jean Jacques Rousseau points out in the quotation at the beginning of this chapter, only gods could be perfect enough to give human beings perfect justice. Since the Texas courts are not staffed with gods, they sometimes make mistakes.

Recent history affords several instances in which people were convicted of crimes and sentenced to prison, only to have later advances in investigative science prove them innocent. In 1997, Governor Bush pardoned Ben Salazar, who had spent five years in prison, and Kevin Byrd, who had been incarcerated for twelve years, both for rape. DNA tests, unavailable when they were first tried, had established the innocence of both men.

Even more unsettling is the case of David Wayne Spence.[29] In 1982, three teenagers were tied to trees and stabbed to death in a park near Lake Waco.

27. The Spangenberg Group, *A Study of Representation in Capital Murder Cases in Texas* (Austin: State Bar of Texas, Committee on Legal Representation for Those on Death Row, 1993), 157, 163.
28. Texas Department of Criminal Justice, December 4, 1997, and subsequent news programs.
29. This discussion is based on Bob Herbert, "The Wrong Man," *New York Times*, July 25, 1997, A15.

In most Texas cities, a person charged with felony DWI or possession of drugs can expect to pay $5,000 or more for representation by a good attorney.

Courtesy of Ben Sargent.

Mr. Spence was tried twice for the murders. Two juries agreed that he had been hired by a convenience store owner to kill a girl, and had mistaken another teenager for his target. He had killed her, and he had also killed another girl and a boy who were with her because they were witnesses. The girls had been raped. Spence was sentenced to die and went through the state appeals process.

For people who support justice, whether they advocate the death penalty or not, the case of David Wayne Spence must be disturbing. There was never any direct evidence that Spence had been at the scene of the 1982 crime—neither eyewitnesses nor physical evidence. Although hairs that presumably came from the murderer were found on the female victims, the FBI crime lab concluded that they were not from Spence. He was convicted on the basis of testimony from inmates who had served time in jail with him while he waited for trial; in return for relating self-incriminating statements that he had allegedly made to them in the cell, they were granted many favors. Court papers showed, among other irregularities, that some were given the opportunity to have sex with their wives or girlfriends in the district attorney's office as a reward for their cooperation. One of the men who thus testified later stated, "We all fabricated our accounts of Spence confessing in order to try to get a break from the state on our cases."

After Spence's second conviction and while his case was being appealed, the police detective who actually conducted the investigation and the lieutenant who supervised it made public statements to the effect that they believed that he was innocent and was being railroaded. A Waco businessman who subsidized a private investigation of the case concluded that all the evidence contradicted Spence's guilt; none supported it.

It didn't matter. Spence's final appeal was turned down an hour before he was executed on April 3, 1997.

Such examples of possible miscarriages of justice must make observers wonder how many other people are in prison or on death row in Texas because they were too poor to pay a lawyer, or were in the wrong place at the wrong time, or made an enemy of some county prosecutor, or happened to be assigned an indifferent or incompetent defense attorney. Once someone is executed, of course, it is too late to prove him or her innocent.

The System of Justice

The judiciary is part of an entire system that attempts to interpret and apply society's laws. The parts of this system, and some of its subject matter, will be briefly examined here.

THE ATTORNEY GENERAL (AG)

Over the years the attorney general has developed an unusual and highly significant power, the authority to issue **advisory opinions**. The state constitution establishes the attorney general as Texas's chief legal officer and as legal adviser to the governor and other state officials. The legislature later expanded the scope of the AG's advisory activity. Out of this expansion has arisen the now firmly established practice of the legislature, as well as the agencies of the executive branch, seeking advice as to the constitutionality of legislative proposals, rules, procedures, and statutes.

In the period from 1935 to 1975, more than 400 bills and legislative proposals were declared invalid by the attorney general, and the volume of decisions continues to grow. In 1996 the AG handed down 210 "Letter Opinions" dealing with the constitutionality of proposed government laws or actions, 14 signed interpretations of the Open Records Act, and 2,477 unsigned opinions (issued by the AG's office without his actual signature) as to the application of the same act.[30]

By going to the attorney general rather than filing a court action, which is expensive and time-consuming, state officials obtain a ruling on disputed constitutional and legal issues in a relatively brief period of time and at almost no expense. Rarely, someone takes the attorney general to court over one of these opinions; more rarely still, the courts reverse one of them. In

---

30. Texas Attorney General's Office, April 1, 1997.

general, however, the Texas judiciary and virtually everyone else in the state have come to accept the AG's rulings without challenge.

The most publicized attorney general's ruling of recent years, and perhaps in history, dealt with the divisive subject of "affirmative action." For some years prior to 1996 the University of Texas Law School had been favoring African American and Latino applicants in its admissions process. That is, minority applicants were judged by a lower set of standards than were Anglo applicants. An Anglo woman, Cheryl Hopwood, was turned down for admission to the law school, despite the fact that her qualifications (grades and Law School Aptitude Test scores) were superior to those of some minority applicants who had been admitted. Hopwood sued in federal court. In 1996 the federal Court of Appeals for the Fifth Circuit ruled in Hopwood's favor, deciding that such "reverse discrimination" against Anglos was unconstitutional (*Hopwood* v. *State of Texas,* 78 F.3d 932[5th Cir. 1996]).

The circuit court's decision was significant as it stood, because it applied to the state's premier law school. Nevertheless, its scope did not extend to other schools. On February 5, 1997, however, Attorney General Dan Morales dismayed Texas's university community by issuing Letter Opinion 97-001, in which he decreed that the federal court's ruling had outlawed race as a consideration in any admissions process at any public school. Affirmative action is now forbidden in all Texas public colleges.[31] Such is the judicial power of the Texas attorney general.

LAWYERS

As in the rest of the country, the legal profession is a growth industry in Texas. In early 1997 the state was home to 56,447 attorneys, or one lawyer for every 332 people.[32] Lawyers represent clients, be they the state, a corporation, or a private individual, in both criminal prosecutions and civil suits (see Chapter 12).

THE STATE BAR OF TEXAS

All lawyers who practice within the state are required to maintain membership in the State Bar and pay annual dues. The State Bar occupies a unique position: It is an agency of government, a professional organization, and an influential interest group, active in state politics.

JUDGES

Judges preside over civil and criminal trials. The number, activities, and organization of Texas judges have been discussed earlier in this chapter.

REMOVAL AND REPRIMAND OF LAWYERS AND JUDGES

The Texas State Bar is authorized by the legislature to reprimand or disbar any practicing attorney in the state for fraudulent, dishonest, or unethical

---

31. Attorney General's Letter Opinion 97–001, February 5, 1997.
32. "How Many Texans Are There for Each Lawyer?" *Austin American-Statesman,* December 1, 1997, B3.

conduct. Grievance committees have been established in each congressional district to hear complaints and to act against offending attorneys. In practice, however, reprimand and disbarment are uncommon and usually occur only after the offending lawyer has been convicted on some serious charge.

District and appellate court judges may be removed from the bench by impeachment after a vote of two-thirds majority of the legislature. District judges may also be removed by the Supreme Court, and lower court judges may be removed by action of a district court.

A 1965 constitutional amendment established a twelve-member Texas State Commission on Judicial Conduct that is authorized to hear complaints against any judge in the state and to censure, reprimand, or recommend removal by the Texas Supreme Court. But again, like the disbarment of lawyers, punishment of judges is a rare occurrence and takes place only after some flagrant violation of ethical standards has been committed.

 Initially the State Commission on Judicial Conduct was called the Judicial Qualifications Commission. It changed its name in 1977, however, after receiving many communications from ordinary citizens citing their qualifications and urging that they be appointed judges.

JURIES

As with so many other features of our judicial system, the use of **grand juries** and **trial juries** is part of our English heritage. In medieval England, charges could be brought against a person in secret and without verification. Trials were then conducted by the king's judges, who often reached their verdicts using their personal and political biases rather than the evidence at hand. The grand jury was developed to determine whether sufficient evidence existed to justify formal charges—to prevent "persecution through prosecution." The trial jury came into use in an attempt to ensure a fair verdict. Judgment by a "jury of one's peers" came to be regarded as the fairest way of determining guilt or innocence. Interestingly, in the England of today, grand juries have all but disappeared, and trial juries are used in only a minority of cases.

Although grand and trial jurors in Texas are selected by different processes, the basic qualifications for both are the same. Jurors must be citizens of the county and qualified voters, they must be able to read and write, and they must not either have been convicted of or be under indictment for a felony. In earlier years, many classes of persons were exempted by law from jury duty. Today, legal exemptions are limited to women having legal custody of a child under ten years of age, full-time students, and persons sixty-five years of age or older. Judges are empowered to excuse or postpone potential jurors for other reasons and occasionally do so.

GRAND JURIES

Grand juries meet in the county seat of each county and are convened as needed. Jurors are chosen from a list prepared by a panel of jury commissioners—three to five persons appointed by the district judge. From this list, the judge selects twelve persons who sit for a term, usually of three months' duration.

Grand jurors consider the evidence submitted by prosecutors to determine whether there is sufficient evidence to issue a formal indictment. Normally, the cases considered are alleged felonies (serious crimes). Occasionally persons are indicted for misdemeanors (minor crimes). In Texas, grand juries are also frequently used to investigate such problems as drug traffic within the community, increasing crime rates, and related matters.

TRIAL JURIES

Trial juries actually make decisions about truth and falsehood, guilt and innocence. Under Texas law, defendants in civil cases and anyone charged with a crime may demand a jury trial. While this right is frequently waived, thousands of such trials take place within the state every year. Lower-court juries consist of six people, while district court juries have twelve members. The call to duty on a trial jury is determined through the use of a jury wheel, a list generated by combining names from the county voter registration rolls with driver's license records.

Conclusion

From one point of view, the Texas judiciary is a model of democratic accountability. Because state judges must run in partisan elections, they are theoretically responsive to the citizens. From another point of view, however, the dependence upon private campaign contributions that distorts other areas of the state's government has an even more alarming effect on the neutrality of the judiciary. In terms of democracy, simply having elections is not enough. Some provision must be made for candidates to depend upon the support of the voters as a whole rather than upon campaign contributors, so that officeholders are free to place the public interest, not private interests, foremost. The problem of dependence upon special-interest campaign contributions is acute in Texas.

From the standpoint of democratic theory, the other serious problem with the Texas judiciary is its evident discrimination against poor defendants. The fact that people who are not wealthy are less able to defend themselves when accused of crimes contradicts the democratic notion that all citizens should be equal before the law. The fact that Texas is a state that executes people convicted of capital murder makes the problem of unequal justice more acute.

In other words, the judiciary is so deeply flawed that many people feel that the word *crisis* is justified. Nevertheless, after considering a package of reforms endorsed by important state politicians of both parties, the 1995 legislature chose not to change the judicial system. Its members evidently thought that a highly democratic system, with all its evident problems, was superior to other possible arrangements.

Summary

The judiciary is an uncomfortable part of the political system. There is a sense in which what judges do is neutral and nonpolitical, and jurists play up this aspect of their job. It is a myth, however, that the judiciary handles every problem in a nonpolitical manner. Especially in the higher appellate courts, which are responsible for interpreting the state constitution, the act of judging is an intensely political process. The conflict between functioning as neutral arbiters and functioning as political adjudicators creates problems for all judges, and it especially does so in Texas where judges are part of the partisan system of state governance.

The state's judicial system is inadequately organized, which makes its other problems worse.

Over the last quarter century, many observers have concluded that the Texas judiciary does not function well. Besides its inefficient organization, its problems are caused, first, by the fact that there is simply too much crime for the system to process effectively. Second, the system forces judges to rely on campaign contributions from people affected by judicial decisions, which creates many opportunities for impropriety. Third, the system of partisan elections, when coupled with the occasional partisan landslide, runs the risk of placing many unqualified judges in office. Fourth, at-large districts have the effect of making the election of minority judges less likely. The 1995 legislature rejected a reform plan to change the system so that judges would first be appointed, then have to be approved by the voters in order to keep their seats.

Key Terms

Advisory opinions	Criminal jurisdiction	Original trial courts
Appellate jurisdiction	Exclusive jurisdiction	Plea bargain
At-large elections	Grand jury	Single-member district elections
Civil jurisdiction	Judiciary	
Concurrent jurisdiction	Original jurisdiction	Trial jury

Study Questions

1. Are elected judges politicians in the same way that legislators and members of the executive branch are? Explain.

2. Describe *briefly* the organization and jurisdiction of the Texas judiciary.

3. How many "supreme courts" does Texas have? What is the jurisdiction of each?

4. Why do so many people object to the fact that judges must accept campaign contributions from attorneys who practice in their courtrooms? Do you agree with the criticism?

5. What are the advantages and disadvantages of filling judgeships by partisan elections?

6. Why do minorities generally object to at-large judicial elections? What are the advantages of such a system? What are the disadvantages?

7. Do you think that all Texans receive equal treatment from the judicial system? On what evidence do you base your opinion?

8. Why is the attorney general such an important component of the state's judicial system?

Internet Assignment

Internet site: http://www.courts.state.tx.us/

Go to "The Texas Judicial Server" page. Familiarize yourself with the over-all judicial structure and then explore its various parts. Where are the many political aspects of the Court noted in this chapter? (for example: Biographies)

Chapter Twelve

The Substance of Justice

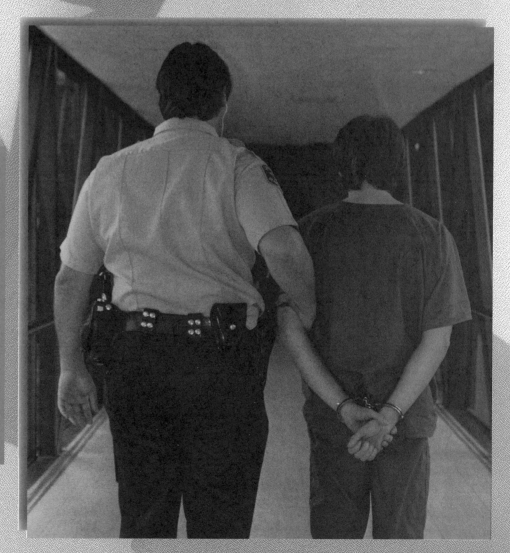

A Travis County deputy sheriff escorts a manacled prisoner from the courthouse over an elevated walkway—The Bridge of Sighs—to the new county jail. Jail and prison overcrowding are serious problems throughout the state.

The majority, in that country [the United States] . . . exercise a prodigious actual authority, and a power of opinion which is nearly as great; no obstacles exist which can impede or even retard its progress, so as to make it heed the complaints of those whom it crushes in its path. . . . I know of no country in which there is so little independence of mind and real freedom of discussion as in America.

Alexis de Tocqueville, French visitor to the United States
Democracy in America, 1835

The law, in its majestic impartiality, forbids the rich as well as the poor to sleep under bridges, to beg in the streets, and to steal bread.

Anatole France (Jacques Thibault)
French Nobel Prize–Winning Writer
Le Lys Rouge, 1894

Introduction

The output of the judicial system is extraordinarily important to all of us. The system protects—or fails to protect—our rights in a democratic society and processes our case in the event that we are accused of a crime. It also allocates large amounts of money and power by arbitrating between various conflicting interests, especially those of a business nature.

The subject of the previous chapter was the structure and behavior of the Texas judiciary. On the whole, it earned rather low marks for democratic virtue. That being so, it might be expected that the products of the system—the substance of justice—would similarly fail to stand up under scrutiny. Somewhat surprisingly, however, close examination reveals that justice in Texas is a good deal more complicated, and in some cases more admirable, than a knowledge of the judiciary's institutional weaknesses might lead us to believe.

The first topic of this chapter will be an examination of the Texas judiciary's record on civil liberties and civil rights, followed by an evaluation of the manner in which it deals with accused criminals, and then a discussion of some of the issues surrounding the cry for "tort reform" in the area of lawsuits against business. The conclusion will be that the system's record is uneven. In some areas, particularly the area of criminal law, it is disheartingly backward. In other areas, especially the manner in which it has been forcing the state to equalize education, it is surprisingly progressive. When measured against the standards of democratic theory, Texas justice provides cause for both pessimism and optimism.

Civil Liberties

The phrase **civil liberties** refers to the basic *individual freedom from government interference* that is crucial to sustaining a democratic government. Democracy requires that citizens be free to speak, read, and assemble, so that they may choose in an independent and informed manner among competing ideas, candidates, and parties. In addition, since a democratic society must respect individual autonomy of thought and conscience, government must not be allowed to interfere with freedom of religious choice.

The First Amendment to the U.S. Constitution declares that Congress may not abridge the people's freedom of speech or of the press, nor their right to assemble peaceably, nor to petition the government for a redress of grievances. It also forbids Congress to "establish" religion—that is, support it with money and coercive laws—or prohibit its free exercise. The Fourteenth Amendment, passed after the Civil War in the 1860s, has gradually been held by the U.S. Supreme Court to apply most of these protections to the states.

In addition, the states have similar guarantees in their constitutions. Article I, Section 8 of the Texas Constitution assures us that "no law shall ever be passed curtailing the liberty of speech or of the press," and Section 27 promises that the state's citizens may assemble "in a peaceable manner" and petition the government "for redress of grievances or other purposes." Individual liberties are thus acknowledged in Texas, as in the federal government, to be of fundamental importance to a democratic society. Given this apparent unanimity, we might think that there would be little disagreement about how these freedoms were to be protected. If so, we would be mistaken.

The words in both constitutions seem clear enough in their protection of individual freedoms, but the history of the documents makes it clear that the meaning of any political guarantee must be fought over. In the South, especially, the political culture has never been eager to grant the individual freedoms promised by constitutions. It has been especially resistant to the idea that African Americans and Mexican Americans should enjoy the same personal liberties as Anglos. For most of the twentieth century, Texas was quite reluctant to give its citizens the freedom its constitution guarantees.

In the last two decades, however, the opening up of the Texas judiciary to new ideas and new people has caused a different spirit to pervade the courts, and they have become more activist in this area. For example, the Texas Civil Liberties Union has successfully sued in state courts to secure a number of new rights, including workers' compensation benefits for migratory workers and protection of state employees against mandatory lie detector testing.[1] On this subject it would seem to be a new era for the Texas judicial system, in which the rules of the past no longer apply.

Nevertheless, there are always politicians and private citizens who either do not understand the importance of civil liberties or do not value them. Individual rights are therefore frequently under siege somewhere, in Texas or

---

1. The workers' compensation case is *Guadalupe Delgado* v. *State of Texas,* 356, 714 (District of Travis County, 147th Judicial District of Texas, modified May 22, 1985); the lie-detector case is *Texas State Employees Union* v. *Department of Mental Health and Mental Retardation,* 746 S.W.2d 203 (Texas, 1987).

other states. Sometimes the battle over civil liberties is fought in the legislature. More often, however, the struggle takes place in court.

FREEDOM OF EXPRESSION

Although "freedom of speech and press" seems to be an unambiguous phrase, only a little thought can create a variety of difficult problems of interpretation. Do constitutional guarantees of freedom of speech protect those who would incite a mob to lynch a prisoner? Teach terrorist recruits to make bombs? Tell malicious lies about public officials? Wear a T-shirt lettered with obscenities to high school? Spout racist propaganda on a local cable TV access program? Fake a television demonstration of an exploding pickup truck? Publicly burn an American flag? Falsely advertise a patent medicine? These questions and others like them have sparked intense political and intellectual conflict.

In 1925, in *Gitlow* v. *New York,* the U.S. Supreme Court, for the first time, held that the freedom of speech and press guarantees of the First Amendment of the federal Constitution were binding on state and local governments through the "due process of law" clause of the Fourteenth Amendment.[2] In the seven decades since the *Gitlow* decision, the Court's interpretation of the meaning of "freedom of speech and press" has constantly evolved, so that American liberties are never quite the same from year to year. Since the 1960s the First Amendment has come to contain protection for a "freedom of expression" that is larger than mere speech and press. Citizens may engage in nonspeech acts that are intended to convey a political communication.

For example, at the 1984 Republican National Convention in Dallas, Gregory Lee Johnson and others protested the Reagan administration's policies by burning an American flag while chanting, "America the red, white, and blue, we spit on you."[3] Johnson was arrested and charged with violating a Texas law against flag desecration. Johnson's attorneys argued that his act was "symbolic speech" protected by the First Amendment.

The U.S. Supreme Court agreed. In its 1989 decision in *Texas* v. *Johnson,* the majority held that "Johnson's burning of the flag was conduct sufficiently imbued with elements of communication to implicate the First Amendment,"[4] thus overturning the Texas law and freeing Johnson from the threat of jail time.

This decision caused a national furor. A large majority of Americans, while they supported freedom of expression in the abstract, were not willing to grant it to someone whose ideas they found so obnoxious. In this they showed the inconsistency that people sometimes display when they discover that they dislike the specific consequences of general principles they otherwise endorse.

It is despised expressions of opinion such as Johnson's that most require First Amendment protection. Democracy requires not only majority rule, but also minority rights. Fashionable opinion does not need protection—its very

---

2. *Gitlow* v. New York, 268 U.S. 652 (1925).
3. This account of the flag-burning incident is taken from Thomas R. Dye, *Politics in America* (Englewood Cliffs, N.J.: Prentice-Hall, 1994), 546–547.
4. *Texas* v. *Johnson,* 491 U.S. 397 (1989).

popularity renders it immune from suppression. But the expression of a political idea that the great majority finds agreeable is not "freedom of expression" at all. Freedom comes into play only when there is some danger to the speaker for expressing his or her thought—that is, when the thought is disagreeable to the majority. The American—and Texas—public missed this point. The clamor to outlaw flag burning was an example of the "tyranny of the majority" that Alexis de Tocqueville, quoted at the beginning of this chapter, warned would be the dark side of American democracy.

Crucial issues such as freedom of speech can sometimes get lost in the absurdities of politics. For example, in 1995 the Texas legislature passed the so-called veggie libel law, which established that people or groups who stated or implied that the state's agricultural products were not safe could be sued for damages.

Although this law clearly violates the rights of people to express their opinions, that fact has not stopped it from being enforced. In 1997 TV talk show host Oprah Winfrey and Humane Society activist Howard Lyman were taken to court for slandering Texas beef. While a guest on Winfrey's program, Lyman had criticized the practice, common in Texas, of feeding ground-up dead cows to live cattle, and suggested that this practice could lead to the spread of "mad cow disease," an affliction that has devastated British livestock, in the United States. Upon hearing his opinion, Winfrey had stated that she would not eat any more hamburgers.

A group of Panhandle ranchers filed suit under the 1995 Texas law, claiming that Lyman and Winfrey had caused the price of beef to drop.

Jurors found Winfrey and Lyman not guilty. Even if the ranchers had won, however, the veggie libel law would almost certainly have been declared unconstitutional on appeal.

Sources: "'Beef Slander' Lawsuit against Oprah Gets Trial," *Austin American-Statesman,* January 7, 1998, B2; Molly Ivins, "Ranchers and the Veggie Libel Law: Where's Their Beef?" *Austin American-Statesman,* January 10, 1998, A13.

The public being so aroused, the U.S. Congress was not about to stand in its way. Congress quickly passed the Flag Protection Act of 1989, mandating a one-year jail sentence and $1,000 fine for anyone who "knowingly mutilates, defaces, physically defiles, burns, maintains on the floor or ground, or tramples upon, any flag of the United States." A federal court quickly struck down this law for the same reason that the Supreme Court had invalidated the Texas statute.

The Texas legislature still insisted on having its say, however. February 1995 saw the fiftieth anniversary of the battle for the island of Iwo Jima in World War II. That particular clash is memorable in the popular imagination because of a stirring photograph, taken just after the American victory over the Japanese, of five Marines raising the Stars and Stripes on the top of the mountain in the center of the island. It is perhaps the most reproduced war photograph ever taken, and is often used to evoke feelings of American patriotism.

On February 23, the Texas House and Senate chose to commemorate the battle by voting to ask the U.S. Congress to pass a constitutional amendment to exempt flag desecration from First Amendment protection. Legislators thus decided to honor a famous moment in the flag's history by contradicting the

principle of personal liberty the flag stands for. The vote was a graphic
reminder that freedom of expression is sometimes better protected by judges
than by legislators.

While expressions of political opinion thus require, and are given, very
great protection by the courts, other types of expression are less free. Graphic
sexual expression, for example, is irrelevant to citizen debate about public
policy alternatives. It therefore receives much less protection from government
regulation than does political speech. But when does actual obscenity shade
over into the expression of a political opinion? Is a book such as D. H.
Lawrence's *Lady Chatterly's Lover,* which contains many explicit sexual
scenes but uses those scenes to make criticisms of the British political system,
to be suppressed because of its sexuality or protected because of its political
expression? Someone has to decide.

It has fallen to the U.S. Supreme Court to define obscenity and pornography and to determine whether state antipornography laws violate the First
Amendment. In attempting to do so, the Court has trapped itself in a quag-
mire of contradiction and incoherence from which it shows no sign of
escaping.

In 1964 U.S. Supreme Court Justice Potter Stewart famously illustrated
the extreme difficulty of dealing with human sexuality in a judicial setting. He
wrote that although he could not define pornography, he knew it when he
saw it.[5] His admission was charmingly candid, but it did not help the Court
give the country clear guidelines about what might be legal and what forbidden when it came to sexual expression.

---

5. *Jacobellis* v. *Ohio,* 387 U.S. 184 (1964).

The controlling decision in this area, *Miller* v. *California,* is universally admitted to be more confusing than helpful. The Court offered three tests for whether a written work was merely erotic, and therefore legal, or pornographic, and therefore subject to government suppression:

1. " . . . the average person, applying contemporary community standards," would find that the work taken as a whole appeals to "prurient interest;"

2. the work depicts or describes in a "patently offensive" way sexual conduct specifically defined by the applicable state law;

3. the work taken as a whole lacks serious literary, artistic, political, or scientific value.[6]

In fashioning these tests, the Court substituted a variety of unknowns—especially contemporary community standards and artistic value—for the previous single unknown, pornography. Further, the Court held that a work must both please (prurient interest) and displease (patently offensive) a judge at the same time to be held pornographic. In other words, although the justices still could not define pornography, they hoped that other judges would know it when they saw it.

In the spring of 1992, charges were brought against an "adult" store in Denton County for selling, among other things, allegedly pornographic films. The defense attorney was given permission to show a number of the films in court, and did so. The trial was then delayed because the county judge required hospitalization and treatment for high blood pressure.

Very little clarity has come out of this area in the two decades since the *Miller* ruling. Local governments in Texas and other states continue to pass laws that attempt to suppress pornography—whatever it is—and sometimes these laws are upheld. Occasionally the Texas legislature discusses new, restrictive legislation aimed at businesses that sell allegedly pornographic material, although they are uncertain whether these laws, if passed, would be acceptable to the courts. The area continues to be litigated. Meanwhile, everybody knows pornography when they see it, although nobody can define it.

The few cases discussed here in no way exhaust either the number of court rulings on freedom of expression or the complexities of the problem. In general, it can be said that the U.S. Supreme Court attempts to balance competing interests: the value to the democratic community of the free flow of information versus the harm that may come to it through the unrestricted production of certain types of information. The choices are often very difficult, but the Court usually follows the philosophy that it is better to have too much expression, some of which may be harmful, than not to have enough.

6. *Miller* v. *California,* 413 U.S. 15 (1973).

The First Amendment provision that forbids Congress to pass laws "respecting an establishment of religion" has been interpreted to mean both (1) that there should be a "wall of separation" between church and state, and that government may not help or even acknowledge religion in any way, and (2) that government may aid religion, at least indirectly, as long as it shows "no preference" among the various religious beliefs. Although the U.S. Supreme Court frequently talks "wall of separation," in practice it has allowed the states to provide a variety of aids to religion—for example, school lunches and public facilities for church-run schools and tuition grants for church-run colleges—as long as government agencies do not show a preference for one church over another.

A First Amendment provision regarding religion that is frequently misunderstood forbids Congress to prohibit the "free exercise" of faith. The freedom to believe in a supreme being necessarily involves the freedom to disbelieve. The freedom to worship requires the freedom not to worship. Under the U.S. Constitution, therefore, the atheist and the believer are equally protected. Thus, the provision of the Texas constitution—Article I, Section 4—that requires persons holding public office to "acknowledge the existence of a Supreme Being" is in conflict with the nation's fundamental law and is no longer enforced.

Because of the passion and prejudice that surround the subject of faith, government officials sometimes follow momentary convenience rather than timeless principles when making decisions about religious questions. As a result, the politics of religious freedom is often characterized by inconsistency and hypocrisy. Nevertheless, courts have devised some tests with which to bring a measure of rationality to their decisions.

On the one hand, the courts usually do not permit a general law protecting the public welfare to be violated in the name of religious freedom. For example, early in this century Texas courts ruled that parents could not refuse to have their children vaccinated against smallpox on the grounds that it was contrary to their religious convictions.[7] In a similar vein, Texas courts ruled that members of a church were not denied their freedom of religion by a zoning ordinance that restricted use of property surrounding the church to single-family dwellings.[8]

On the other hand, laws conflicting with religious beliefs may sometimes be overturned if the public interest is not seriously threatened. For example, in 1938 a Texas appellate court, anticipating a similar U.S. Supreme Court ruling five years later, held that a parent who refused to salute the flag as a matter of religious conviction could not be deprived of custody of his or her child.[9]

In Texas as in other states, religious belief can be intense, and religious people can sometimes be intolerant of others who do not share their particular doctrinal enthusiasm. Politicians responding to their constituencies sometimes take actions that threaten the religious rights of people whose views happen to

---

7. *New Braunfels* v. *Waldschmidt*, 109 Texas 302 (1918).
8. *Ireland* v. *Bible Baptist Church*, 480 S.W.2d 467 (1972).
9. *Reynolds* v. *Rayborn*, 116 S.W.2d 836 (1938).

be in the minority. When they do so, they come into conflict with the federal Constitution, and religious fervor is translated into political tension.

A major issue of this sort is the question of religious recitation in public schools. In 1962 and 1963, the U.S. Supreme Court ruled that a nondenominational prayer used in public schools[10] and the reading of the Bible and the recitation of the Lord's Prayer[11] were unconstitutional. The basis of the decisions was that the prayer was a Christian ritual imposed upon all children of a school, many of whom may be non-Christian. Since the prayer takes place in a public school, it is an example of the "establishment" of religion outlawed by the First Amendment.

Although the reasoning of these decisions is difficult to refute, they nevertheless caused a great public outcry, and even today many Americans would support a constitutional amendment to permit prayer in the schools. In the absence of such an amendment, local politicians and school boards in many areas try to evade the Court's pronouncements by sneaking in prayer under some other name. As a result, the courts still deal with school prayer cases.

For example, in 1982 the Lubbock school board instituted a program of "voluntary" school prayer, in which a student read a daily prayer over the public-address system. There is, however, nothing voluntary about being held in a room while someone reads something over a loudspeaker. Imagine how the parents of the students in Lubbock would have reacted if their children had been forced to listen to passages from the Koran or *The Communist Manifesto* over the school's public-address system! The Lubbock Civil Liberties Union filed suit, and a federal district court judge forbade the practice to continue.[12]

The judge also ruled, however, that the use of classrooms by students before and after school was not unconstitutional. Thus, neither side won a complete victory, and both appealed. The Fifth U.S. Circuit Court of Appeals found that since the school district had not offered its facilities to other groups, it was creating a preferred position for religion, and ruled in favor of the Civil Liberties Union. The school board, with the cooperation of fundamentalist religious groups, appealed to the U.S. Supreme Court. This Court refused to grant *certiorari* (declined to hear the case), meaning that the appeals court's decision was final.

Because many Americans continue to believe that public schools should be allowed to sponsor official prayers, the courts can expect to see more cases like the one in Lubbock.

A RIGHT TO KEEP AND BEAR ARMS?

Crime has become one of the most important political issues in the United States in general, and Texas in particular, and arguments about how to control it are part of contemporary political discussion. One of the suggested ways of reducing the number of homicides is to restrict access to guns. Since firearms are employed in about eight hundred thousand violent crimes each

---

10. *Engel v. Vitale*, 370 U.S. 421 (1962).
11. *Abington School District v. Schempp* and *Murray v. Catlett*, 374 U.S. 203 (1963).
12. *Lubbock Civil Liberties Union v. Lubbock Independent School District*, 50 L.W. 2557 (1982).

year in the United States, and are used to murder about 18,000 Americans
annually, including over 70 percent of those murdered in Texas, it is not
implausable to argue that crime would be less of a problem if fewer people
had guns.[13]

On the other hand, since there are about 14 million hunters in the country, and millions more who own firearms for target practice or self-defense,
there is also a great resistance to the idea of gun control. Many people agree
with the opposite of the gun-control argument—they believe that law-abiding
citizens would be safer from crime if they were allowed to carry concealed
weapons. In 1995 this armed-citizen attitude carried the day in the state legislature, which passed a law allowing citizens who have undergone ten hours of
training to carry concealed handguns.

This is a topic on which reasonable people can disagree. For example,
one of the authors of this textbook holds a concealed weapons license and
occasionally carries a pistol; the other two would never contemplate such
behavior for themselves.

It is not the purpose of this chapter to examine the entire political issue
of whether government should attempt stricter control over firearms. As part
of a discussion of civil rights and liberties, however, it will be useful to evaluate one important part of the argument: the claim that Americans have a personal right, guaranteed by the Second Amendment to the U.S. Constitution,
to own guns. The Amendment reads in its entirety, "A well regulated Militia,

---

13. This discussion of the argument over the Second Amendment is based on information in
Robert J. Spitzer, *The Politics of Gun Control* (Chatham, N.J.: Chatham House, 1995); and
Raymond H. C. Teske, Jr., *Crime and Justice in Texas* (Huntsville: Sam Houston State University
Press, 1995), 19.

being necessary to the security of a free State, the right of the people to keep and bear Arms, shall not be infringed."

Millions of Americans believe that this part of the Bill of Rights prohibits government from interfering with their gun ownership. The National Rifle Association, an organization with a membership in the mid-1990s of about 3.3 million and an annual budget of roughly $90 million, is particularly tireless in arguing this position. Any issue of the NRA's magazine, *The American Rifleman,* contains numerous assertions of an individual "right to keep and bear arms" as promised by the Second Amendment. Although public opinion surveys consistently show that two-thirds of the American people favor stricter gun control, many politicians echo the claim that the Second Amendment prohibits all regulation of firearms. A significant proportion of Texans evidently believe that they have a constitutional guarantee to own anything from a purse pistol to an assault rifle, and that government does not have the legitimate authority to do anything about it.

Citizens can, of course, interpret the Constitution as they see fit. There is no magic person or institution that can say for certain what the document "means." If some people want to argue that the Second Amendment gives them a right to own guns, that is their right under the First Amendment.

Nevertheless, a consultation of both the judicial and historical records makes it clear that, under the normal rules of logic and language, the Second Amendment does not create an *individual* right to keep and bear arms. The amendment was created in 1789 to protect state militias—that is, official state military organizations, not private clubs or vigilante groups—from being disbanded by the federal government. It was not intended to guarantee the right to firearm ownership to private citizens. Beginning in the nineteenth century, the courts have been consistent in applying this historical understanding to gun control laws whenever these have been challenged. In the most important case, decided in 1939, the U.S. Supreme Court held that the "obvious purpose" of the Second Amendment was to protect militias, not individuals.[14] In fifteen decisions since 1939, the Court has been consistent in this interpretation.

The notion that Americans have a constitutional right to bear arms individually, as private citizens, thus has no historical or legal support. Nevertheless, since millions of people continue to believe the opposite, the argument over government's right to regulate firearms will not be soon resolved, in the United States in general or in Texas in particular.

ABORTION

Today, in Texas and in the United States as a whole, abortion joins race at the top of the list of divisive and inflammatory political issues. People do not even agree on what they are arguing about. Supporters of legal abortion maintain that the issue is whether a woman should have the right to control her own body. Opponents insist that the issue is whether the born should be allowed to kill the unborn. Because those on each side feel so deeply, discussion of the issue never produces agreement; it only creates division and anger. Sometimes it results in violence.

---

14. *United States* v. *Miller,* 307 U.S. 174 (1939).

In general, in the early nineteenth century, abortions were legal in the United States up to the moment of "quickening"—the time when the mother felt the fetus move within her—or about three months into the pregnancy. Then, between 1860 and 1890, almost all states enacted laws discouraging or forbidding the practice. Nevertheless, women continued to go to doctors to have pregnancies terminated, although the procedure had been made more expensive and dangerous by being forced underground. By the early 1960s, police experts called abortion the third largest criminal activity in the country—after narcotics and gambling—and several hundred thousand were performed in the country every year.[15]

Through the 1960s and early 1970s, however, there was a strong movement, associated with feminism, to liberalize state antiabortion laws. By 1973, many non-Southern states, including California and New York, had in effect legalized the practice, although some restrictions remained. In that year, however, the situation was radically changed by the U.S. Supreme Court's decision in the case of *Roe* v. *Wade,* a case arising from the Texas courts.[16] Building on the notion of a right to personal privacy that it had been expanding since the mid-1960s, the Court wrote that the Bill of Rights protected sexual privacy, including the right to have an abortion. All state antiabortion laws were overturned.

Roe v. *Wade* ignited an intense national political debate that continues today. People who support the Court, who call themselves "pro-choice," argue that the decision as to whether to terminate a pregnancy should be made by the woman and her doctor; government has no business interfering. Those who disagree, styling themselves "pro-life," argue that to terminate a pregnancy is to commit homicide, and that government has every obligation to prevent such a crime. Pro-lifers have blocked entrances to abortion clinics, set them afire, and even murdered doctors and clinic workers in their determination to bring abortion to an end. The great majority of pro-life activity, however, is lawful and intended to create a political climate in which *Roe* v. *Wade* can be overturned and abortion prohibited.

The abortion debate is as fierce in Texas as it is in any other state. The Christian Right, in particular, is fervently antiabortion. In 1994 it captured the state's Republican Party and wrote an uncompromising antiabortion plank into the platform at the state convention. (The 1996 state Republican platform repeated this call for a "Human Rights Amendment" to the U.S. Constitution—see Chapters 4 and 6.) Statewide Republican candidates have generally tried to distance themselves from the party's official position on this issue. For example, in 1994, Governor George W. Bush and U.S. Senator Kay Bailey Hutchison offered their own moderate positions on abortion and ignored the party's position during their campaigns. Meanwhile, the liberal wing of the state Democratic Party, as exemplified by former Governor Ann Richards, is staunchly pro-choice. The party as a whole, however, contains many different views on the issue.

Despite the passions aroused by the abortion debate, the 1995 legislature mostly ignored the conflict. The 1997 legislature considered a "parental noti-

15. John D'Emilio and Estelle B. Freedman, *Intimate Matters: A History of Sexuality in America* (New York: Harper and Row, 1988), 253.
16. *Roe* v. *Wade,* 410 U.S. 113 (1973).

fication law," which would require that, before a girl under the age of eighteen could get an abortion, her physician must inform her parents. Although the parents could not stop the operation, they would have forty-eight hours to counsel the girl about her choices. A public opinion poll showed that 73 percent of Texans supported this law. It passed in the House and was on the verge of passing in the Senate when it was derailed at the last moment by a parliamentary maneuver (see Chapter 8).[17] Although the last two legislative sessions have thus failed to pass legislation dealing with abortion, the issue remains one of the most emotional in the state.

If there is a single lesson to be learned from the history of the abortion debate, it is that conflicting opinions that rest on strongly held, clashing moral convictions cannot be resolved by judges. Perhaps they cannot be resolved at all. Whether it is pro-life or pro-choice positions that dominate Texas government during the next few years, the abortion issue will not go away.

Civil Rights

Broadly speaking, *civil liberties* refers to citizens' rights to be free of government regulation of their personal conduct, whereas **civil rights** refers to the claims the members of all groups have to be treated equally with the members of other groups. Generally, if government harasses people because of something they have said or done, it may have taken away a civil liberty. If government oppresses people because of some ethnic, gender, or other group to which they belong, it has violated their civil rights.

---

17. Suzanne Gamboa, "Most Favor Abortion Notice Bill," *Austin American-Statesman,* March 3, 1997, B1; Ken Herman and Suzanne Gamboa, "Abortion Bill Lost in Parliamentary Battling," *Austin American-Statesman,* May 28, 1997, B1.

> Civil liberties refer to those actions that government cannot take. Civil rights refer to those actions that government must take to ensure equal citizenship for everyone.

Historically, the domination of Texas by the Old South political culture inhibited state courts from actively protecting the civil rights of African Americans and Mexican Americans. Jim Crow laws, Black Codes, poll taxes, and other infringements on rights and liberties existed undisturbed by the state judicial system for decades. These blights on democracy were overturned by federal, not state, courts (see Chapter 1).

VOTING RIGHTS

Along with its suppression of civil liberties, Texas, along with the other Southern states, denied voting rights to large parts of its population for much of the twentieth century. At first, the extension of voting rights came at the initiative of the national government, with state and local governments fighting rearguard actions. Attempts by states to keep African Americans from voting were slowly defeated by the tireless efforts of the National Association for the Advancement of Colored People (NAACP) in bringing suits in federal courts.

Two Texas cases were important in this fight to open the polls to all citizens. In 1944, in *Smith* v. *Allwright,* the federal courts struck down Texas's "White primary" laws, which prevented African Americans from voting in primary elections. In 1971, in *Beare* v. *Smith,* highly discriminatory registration procedures were declared unconstitutional, making much more open procedures possible (see Chapter 6).[18]

After such flagrant suppressions of minority voting rights were ended, the struggle over voting rights turned toward more ambiguous forms of discrimination. One of the most contentious of these involved the system of electing state judges, which was discussed in Chapter 11. In general, it can be said that except for occasional relapses into racism in backwaters of the Old South—relapses that are quickly stifled by the federal government—the fight for equal voting rights has been won.

SCHOOL SEGREGATION

In 1954 the U.S. Supreme Court rendered one of the landmark decisions of its history. In a unanimous verdict, the Court ruled that public schools that were segregated on the basis of race were in violation of the "equal protection of the laws" clause of the Fourteenth Amendment.[19] This decision was intensely disagreeable to the ruling Anglos in Texas and the sixteen other states that had segregated schools. It was condemned as a violation of "states' rights,"

---

18. *Smith* v. *Allwright,* 321 U.S. 649 (1944); *Beare* v. *Smith,* 321 F.Supp. 1100 (1971).
19. *Brown* v. *Board of Education of Topeka,* 347 U.S. 483 (1954).

and some Texas politicians talked defiantly of "interposition," a theory that allegedly allows states to interpose their own statutes against national laws when the national laws are locally unpopular.

Opposition to integration diminished greatly over the next forty years, but never quite disappeared. Some school boards continued a kind of interposition policy, deliberately failing to comply with court-ordered desegregation. The Dallas school district, for instance, was in almost continuous litigation for three decades, spending millions of tax dollars to draw up unsatisfactory desegregation plans and then contest the adverse rulings of the courts. In 1976, to take another example, a federal district court ruled against the El Paso School Board, holding that building a school of a certain size at a certain location with conscious knowledge that it will be segregated showed "discriminatory intent on the part of the school board."[20]

As with school prayers and Bible reading, school boards occasionally still attempt to get away with segregating their students by ethnicity. Nevertheless, the great majority of school districts, the great majority of the time, are now legally integrated. The major problem today is not that school districts deliberately separate students, but that economic class separates them. Because poor people and middle-class people tend to live in different areas, and especially because the poorer tend to make their homes in the cities while the wealthier often live in the suburbs, citizens of different economic classes are served by different school districts. And because poorer districts cannot afford to supply adequate schooling, economic disparity is turned into educational inequality. This is one of the major civil rights problems of the 1990s.

EDUCATION—A BASIC RIGHT?

In 1987 Texas District Judge Harley Clark shocked and outraged the Texas political establishment by ruling in the case of *Edgewood* v. *Kirby* that the state's system of financing its public schools violated its own constitution and laws. Clark's ruling referred to Article VII, Section 1, which requires the "Legislature of the state to establish . . . an efficient system of public free schools," and part of Article 1, which asserts that "All free men . . . have equal rights." Additionally, Section 16.001 of the Texas Education Code states that "public education is a state responsibility," that "a thorough and efficient system [is to] be provided," and that "each student enrolled in the public school system shall have access to programs and services that are appropriate to his or her needs and that are substantially equal to those available to any similar student, notwithstanding varying local economic factors."

The state's educational system, however, did not begin to offer equal services to every child. During the 1985–86 school year, when the *Edgewood* case was being prepared, the wealthiest school district in Texas had $14 million in taxable property per student, and the poorest district had $20,000. The Whiteface Independent School District in the Texas Panhandle taxed its property owners at $0.30 per $100 of value and spent $9,646 per student. The Morton I.S.D., just north of Whiteface, taxed its property owners at $0.96 per $100 evaluation, but because of the lesser value of its property was able to spend only $3,959 per student. Gross disparities such as these made a

---

20. *Alvarado* v. *El Paso Independent School District,* 426 F.Supp. 575 (1976).

mockery of the constitutional and statutory requirements for equal educational funding. An estimated one million of the state's three million school children were receiving inadequate instruction because their local districts could not afford to educate them.

The obvious remedy was to transfer some revenue from wealthy to poorer districts. But given the distribution of power in the state, and especially the way it is represented in the legislature, this strategy was nearly impossible. As explained in Chapters 4, 5, and 6, the state's poorer citizens are less likely to vote and because of the high cost of campaigning, wealthier citizens are overrepresented in the legislature. Taxpayers in wealthier districts were reluctant to give up their money to educate the children of the poor in some other district. Their representatives refused to vote for any sort of revenue distribution, regardless of what the court had said.

In October 1989, the Texas Supreme Court unanimously upheld Clark's ruling that the system was unconstitutional and gave the legislature until May 1, 1990, to fix it.[21] Then-Governor Clements called four consecutive special sessions of the legislature in the spring of 1990 to deal with the issue. His leadership was negative, however, consisting largely of threats to veto any plan that called for increased taxes. The legislators, caught between the court's mandate that they equalize funding and their constituents' command that they not equalize it, complained, blustered, and repeatedly refused to act. Finally, in June 1990, the legislature passed, and the governor signed, a bill calling for somewhat increased funding, to be phased in over a five-year period.

Poor districts immediately protested, and in September 1990, Judge Scott McCown, Clark's successor on the district court bench, found the new law to be unconstitutional because it perpetuated the inequities of the old system. In January 1991 the Supreme Court agreed with him, again unanimously, and it was back to the drawing board.

In April 1991 the legislature passed another makeshift school finance bill, and in January 1992 the Supreme Court tossed that out also. The legislature, in a special session, then tried a different tack. It passed a plan that would allow the state to redistribute property tax revenue from richer to poorer districts. Legislators ducked responsibility for their work, however, by passing the new law in the form of a proposed constitutional amendment, thus making it contingent upon voter approval in a statewide election. When, in May 1993, in a typically small turnout, 63 percent of the voters defeated the amendment, chaos loomed.

Judge McCown threatened the 1993 legislature, then in session, with a court takeover of the schools. It responded with a law that would take about $450 million in property taxes from ninety-eight high-wealth districts and give them to poor districts. (This law was instantly dubbed the "Robin Hood Plan" by the media.) In December 1993 the judge accepted this effort as constitutional. But both many wealthy districts (which objected to being forced to give up their tax money) and some poor districts (which complained that funding was still too unequal) vowed to appeal this ruling to the Supreme Court. In January 1995, however, the Supreme Court upheld the new law with a bare 5 to 4 majority.

---

21. *Edgewood Independent School District v. Kirby,* 777 S.W.2d 391 (Tex. 1989).

Although the number of dissenters on the court, plus the qualms evident in the majority opinion, suggested that the issue might not be over, one thing had become clear in eight years of litigation: The Texas judiciary, at least in this one area, had become the champion of the underdog. As explained in Chapter 11, the legal system sometimes discriminates against the poor because there are not enough resources available to give them adequate justice. In the area of education, however, the Texas courts are attempting to force the political system to ensure equal access to education. They may not succeed in this crusade, but at least they have given us some cause for optimism regarding the future.

CIVIL RIGHTS IN THE 1990S: VIDOR

Although the civil rights atmosphere in Texas is very different from what it was a few decades ago, there are still problems to overcome before everyone is treated equally. One of the most interesting recent confrontations between the attitudes of the Old South and progressive racial policies occurred in the East Texas town of Vidor in 1993 and 1994.

Vidor, a small, obscure suburb north of Beaumont, had a long history of Anglo racism.[22] Among other things, its public housing projects had no minority residents. In 1988, however, Federal Judge William Wayne Justice ordered projects owned by seventy housing authorities in thirty-six East Texas counties to integrate. After some stalling, in August 1992 the coordinator of the Orange County Housing Authority, which operated the Vidor project, announced plans to move several African American families to the project.

Immediately, two rival Ku Klux Klan factions came to Vidor to protest. Threats of violence were reported in the newspapers. Nevertheless, in the spring of 1993, four African American tenants moved into the housing project. By August, all had moved out, claiming that they had been harassed and threatened by Anglo project residents and townspeople. Less than twelve hours after he moved, one of the tenants, Bill Simpson, was murdered on the street in Beaumont. There was immediately a national outcry, with many accusations that Simpson had been targeted by the Klan or some similarly motivated individuals. In May 1994, however, police arrested four Beaumont teenagers for the killing. The four young men were convicted and are now serving time. Apparently, Simpson's death had been merely the outcome of a botched robbery attempt.

Despite the evident lack of a racial motive in Simpson's murder, the events in Vidor were tragic and dispiriting, and suggested that Texas had not grown out of the bad old days of unequal citizenship. Nevertheless, what happened next showed how times have changed in the state. In September 1993, federal Department of Housing and Urban Development (HUD) Secretary Henry Cisneros announced that his bureau was taking over the Orange County housing agency. In January 1994, HUD moved four African American families into the same housing project, accompanied by armed police and federal marshalls. The urban decor of the Vidor project now includes a bullet-proof guard shack, twelve security cameras, a wrought-iron fence with

---

22. For example, see Norma McLemore, "Growing Up in Hate City," *Texas Monthly*, December 1993, 137.

motion detectors, and twenty-four-hour police patrols. There were soon several African American families living in the Vidor projects. Meanwhile, the U.S. Justice Department was investigating the Ku Klux Klan in the area, and its leaders were kept busy answering subpoenas to appear in court. Moreover, HUD has pressured the remaining nine segregated housing projects to admit African American residents.

From the standpoint of democracy in Texas, the story of Vidor is both saddening and encouraging. The denial of equality that was standard in many small communities had to be attacked by federal, not state, government. A federal judge issued the order to integrate the Vidor housing project, and a federal agency, HUD, finally enforced the order.

One of the weirder aspects of the Vidor episode is that the attorney representing Michael Lowe, the Grand Dragon of the Texas Knights of the Ku Klux Klan, was an African American. When the state attorney general filed suit to force the Klan to release its membership lists, the organization did not have enough money to hire legal representation to defend itself. Since government snooping into membership lists may well violate the First Amendment guarantees of freedom of speech and assembly, the Klan appealed to the American Civil Liberties Union (ACLU) to provide it with an attorney. The ACLU complied, but, with a delicious sense of irony, asked Anthony Griffin, an African American lawyer, to take the case.

By assigning Griffin, the ACLU made sure that the Klan's defeat would be larger than a mere legal setback. In the months after the beginning of the suit, photographs of Griffin and Lowe together in the courtroom graced most of the newspapers of the state. The pictures made it unnecessary to repeat the appropriate lessons about human equality in words.

Yet despite this similarity to events in the pre-civil rights days of institutional racism, the Vidor episode also demonstrates how far Texas has progressed. Although the state government was late in moving to protect African Americans in Vidor, at least it moved. In October 1994, the state attorney general's office sued nine individuals and two Klan organizations (see box), accusing them of violating state fair-housing laws by intimidating African Americans in the Vidor housing projects. By late 1997 the organizations had agreed to keep their members at least twenty-two feet from the projects, and to limit their demonstrations. There were then eighteen African American families living in government housing in Vidor.[23]

Moreover, a few decades ago, such actions by federal institutions would have been met by determined opposition from Texas politicians. Local authorities would have been vocally or tacitly on the side of the Ku Klux Klan. Not so in the 1990s. No important person, whether politician, sports celebrity, entertainment idol, or anyone else who counted in modern Texas, had stood up for the racists. The members of the Klan, when they dared to show themselves publicly, were clearly few, poor, uneducated, and on the margins of society. Vidor made clear that those who would deny others their civil rights are on the losing side of Texas history.

---

23. Consumer Protection Division of the Texas Attorney General's Office, January 15, 1998.

Criminal Law

A crime is whatever a legislative body—usually a state legislature or a city council—defines as an act offensive to society. Crimes are broadly classified as either misdemeanors (minor crimes) or felonies (major crimes). Table 12–1 shows how both categories are scaled according to severity.

How much crime is there is Texas? Information is not available on all types, but the Texas Department of Public Safety does maintain data on offenses that are categorized as "index crimes"—murder, rape, robbery, aggravated assault, burglary, larceny-theft, and motor vehicle theft. The bad news is that in 1996 there was an estimated total of 1,091,878 index crimes *reported* in Texas. One offense occurred every twenty-nine seconds, and there was a murder every five hours, eleven minutes. The good news is that the violent crime rate was down 2.9 percent from 1995.[24]

Does crime pay? It depends. Murder is a pretty risky business. The DPS reported that 71 percent of reported murders were "cleared"—that is, an arrest was made. But for robbery the chance of being arrested was less than one in three, and for arson, only 17 percent.

WHO ARE THE CRIMINALS?

By definition, criminals are those who have been convicted of a crime. From the data on those who have been arrested, we can say that crime is largely a young man's activity, although women are catching up in this area, as in others. About one out of every six males will be arrested and tried for a crime before he reaches the age of eighteen. Juveniles (under the age of seventeen) accounted for 16.5 percent of those arrested for crimes in 1996, including 11.3 percent of those arrested for murder. Young African American and Mexican American males are arrested at a rate higher than their proportions of the population, although in 1996 Anglos constituted the largest proportion of the total arrested, 50 percent.[25]

Crime is overwhelmingly an urban phenomenon and is more likely to be committed by someone who has already been convicted of a crime. Authorities estimate the recidivism rate at around 60 percent.

Finally, the criminal is defined by the number and types of acts the legislature declares to be illegal. Police officers have literally thousands of laws to enforce. For example, 8 percent of the arrests made by the DPS in 1996 were for drug offenses. If drug use were decriminalized, therefore, crime rates would fall.

THE COLOR OF THE COLLAR MAKES A DIFFERENCE

Blue-collar crime (often called "street crime")—the personal, often violent felonies discussed above—is what law enforcement agencies keep statistics on. This is the kind of crime that people are afraid of. But there is another

---

24. Texas Department of Public Safety, *Crime in Texas 1996* (Austin: Department of Public Safety, 1997), 10–36, 69.
25. Ibid., 76–77.

TABLE 12–1

Classification of Crimes in Texas, 1998

Crime	Maximum Fine or Other Penalty	Example of Offense
Class C Misdemeanor	Up to $500	Public intoxication
Class B Misdemeanor	Up to $2,000—Up to 180 days confinement	Prostitution
Class A Misdemeanor	Up to $4,000—Up to one year confinement	Breach of computer security
State jail felony	Up to $10,000—180 days to 2 years confinement	Credit card abuse
Third-degree felony	Up to $10,000—2 to 10 years confinement	Tampering with consumer products
Second-degree felony	Up to $10,000—2 to 20 years confinement	Aggravated assault
First-degree felony	Up to $10,000—life imprisonment, or 5 to 99 years	Murder
Capital felony	Life sentence or execution	Murder of a peace officer

SOURCE: *Texas Law for Law Enforcement Officers* (Bulverde, Tex.: Omni Publishers, Inc., 1998), 173–174, 177, 196, 204, 224, 236.

type of crime that, because of its low visibility, we hear relatively little about: **white-collar crime.** Consisting of such impersonal offenses as embezzlement, misappropriation of funds, bribery, and fraud, it is usually nonviolent and is frequently committed against an institution, such as the government, a bank, or a corporation. White-collar criminals are usually older, middle class, and in some cases pillars of the community until they are discovered.

In 1996 the U.S. Justice Department estimated that blue-collar crime cost the country about $450 billion a year. This is a huge sum, but it is smaller than the scholarly estimates of the costs of white-collar crime. In the mid-1990s one study concluded that people steal about $450 billion a year from their employers, another estimated that companies lose an additional $400 billion annually through embezzlement, and still another concluded that financial fraud costs the country a similar amount.[26] The greater monetary costs of white-collar crime, of course, cannot be compared to the emotional costs of street crime. They do not take into account the physical pain caused by blue-collar violence, nor the lingering emotional effects it frequently has on its victims, nor the way it damages community morale.

Nevertheless, the costs of white-collar crime are paid, if only indirectly, by all of us in the form of higher taxes (to cover losses to government agencies) and higher prices (to allow victimized businesses to stay afloat). Yet because they do not elicit the revulsion brought forth by violent criminals, and because there is often not enough room for them in prisons, white-collar criminals often are punished lightly, perhaps with a fine and a period of probation. If they are confined, they spend fewer than fifteen months, on the average, in a minimum-security prison.

---

26. Fox Butterworth, "Survey Finds that Crimes Cost $450 Billion a Year," *New York Times*, April 22, 1996, A5; Lori Hawkins, "Employees Steal Billions, Study Says," *Austin American-Statesman*, October 3, 1995, E1; Bob Banta, "U.S. Cost of Embezzling: $400 Billion," *Austin American-Statesman*, December 27, 1995, A1; Earl Golz, "Fraud Expert: Losses in Billions," *Austin American-Statesman*, December 9, 1997, D1.

1995 CHANGES IN CRIMINAL LAW

With the public intensely interested in the control of blue-collar crime, the 1995 legislature made this issue one of its main arenas of action. Among the more prominent items passed into law in 1995 were the following:

1. A measure limiting the number of appeals available to death row inmates, but also requiring the state to appoint lawyers to represent them in their appeals

2. An overhaul of the juvenile justice system that made it easier to try as adults juveniles accused of serious crimes, created a habitual-offender provision that would allow a juvenile to receive a forty-year sentence if convicted of a third felony, expanded counseling services, and made parents liable for the conduct of their children

3. A package of sex-crimes legislation that provided for more efficient sharing of information on sex offenders among state agencies, increased the penalty for some crimes, and aided victims and victims-rights organizations

With crime already dropping, the impact of this new legislation on the problem it is addressing will be difficult to determine.

CIVIL RIGHTS FOR THOSE IN CUSTODY

People convicted of crimes are still citizens, and, although they lose many of their civil rights, they retain others. The Eighth Amendment to the U.S. Constitution forbids "cruel and unusual punishments," and most people, upon reflection, would probably agree that, however much we may fear and dislike criminals, there is something unseemly about subjecting them to torture or bestial conditions while they are incarcerated.

For most of the twentieth century, however, state prison systems, especially in the South, were places where criminals were subjected to treatment that, if not unusual, was certainly cruel. A number of states even passed laws declaring the inmates of correctional institutions to be legally dead during their confinement. They might sue the state for violation of their rights after being released—being returned to life—but the chances of receiving justice months or years after the fact were remote.[27]

In the 1960s, however, as courts became more receptive to civil rights cases, literally hundreds of suits were brought in areas such as access to courts, mail censorship, medical care, solitary confinement, racial discrimination, work programs, staff standards and training, and a host of other aspects of a prisoner's existence. A glance at the legal record indicates that more cases were being filed against Texas jails and prisons than against those of any other state.[28]

In an important and well-publicized case, in 1971 Federal Judge William Wayne Justice found that the Texas Youth Council was guilty of cruel and

---

27. *Legal Responsibility and Authority of Correctional Officers* (College Park, Md.: American Correctional Association, 1975), 5.
28. See, for example, Frank S. Merritt, *Correctional Law Digest 1977* (Toledo, Ohio: University of Toledo, 1978).

unusual punishment against the children and young people in its custody. Investigation disclosed that guards had not only beaten the youthful prisoners and assaulted them sexually, but had forced inmates to beat other inmates.[29]

The most important case of this type, and one that attracted national attention, began in 1972. An inmate brought suit against the Texas Department of Corrections (TDC), alleging cruel and unusual punishment. In *Ruiz* v. *Estelle,* David Ruiz charged the TDC with violating prisoners' constitutional rights in five areas:

1. The physical security of prisoners

2. Living and working conditions

3. Medical care

4. Internal punishment administered by TDC

5. Access to courts of law

Testimony in the case revealed shocking differences between the ideal system portrayed by top TDC officials and the actual conditions that existed within the prisons. Among the more chilling revelations was the fact that guards rarely entered the prisoners' cell blocks. Internal security was maintained by "building tenders"—privileged prisoners—who maintained order by terrorizing other inmates with lead pipes and other weapons.

Judge Justice ruled in favor of Ruiz, finding the TDC guilty of violating the Eighth Amendment. He ordered the organization to make a series of changes in its housing and treatment of prisoners. State officials reacted by "stonewalling"—denying that poor conditions existed, criticizing Judge Justice's "interference," and stalling on reform. The case dragged on for years before Governor Clements and other officials finally agreed to spend the money to make an effort to bring the TDC up to minimum standards.[30] In 1992 Judge Justice approved a partial settlement of the Ruiz case, and the state was put back in charge of most of its prison functions. Texas had been put on notice, however, that the federal government would be monitoring its treatment of prisoners. Indeed, in 1997 Judge Justice rejected a court action brought by two state lawmakers to have him withdraw from exercising authority over the prisons entirely.

As with any social change, the recognition that prisoners and others in state custody are human beings and have constitutional rights came about only with difficulty. But much progress has been made. Official attitudes and programs today are far more enlightened than those of two decades ago. (See Chapter 11 for a discussion of the prison expansion and improvement program Texas has undertaken in the 1990s.)

---

29. *Morales* v. *Turman,* 326 F.Supp. 577 (1971); Frank R. Kemmerer, *William Wayne Justice* (Austin: University of Texas Press, 1991), 145–49.
30. *Ruiz* v. *Estelle,* 666 F.2d 854 (1982). One of the authors of this text made several visits to TDC units during the period of litigation and can personally attest to the accuracy of many of Ruiz's charges. See also Steve J. Martin and Sheldon Ekland-Olson, *Texas Prisons: The Walls Came Tumbling Down* (Austin: Texas Monthly Press, 1987), and "Inside America's Toughest Prison," *Newsweek,* October 6, 1986, 48–61.

THE DEATH PENALTY

The great majority of Texans approve of the capital punishment—the death penalty—for criminals who have been convicted of "capital felony," or murder (see Table 12–2). An ancient Greek definition of *justice* is "getting what one deserves." The majority of citizens believe that some people have committed crimes so terrible that they "deserve to die." Yet many scholars and people of conscience argue that the death penalty does not deter crime and only adds a public, official murder to the private, unauthorized murder committed by the criminal. Both sides in the debate feel very strongly. As with other emotional social issues such as abortion, the courts are not able to resolve the dispute.

In 1972, the U.S. Supreme Court stopped the states from carrying out capital punishment, because, it said, the death penalty was capriciously applied and, especially, racially biased.[31] In 1976, after the states had taken steps to meet the Court's objections, it allowed executions again, subject to a number of rather stringent rules. The state must ensure that whoever imposes the penalty—judge or jury—does so after careful consideration of the character and record of the defendant and the circumstances of the particular crime. States are not allowed to automatically impose capital punishment upon conviction of certain crimes—murder of a peace officer, for example. The capital sentencing decision must allow for consideration of whatever mitigating circumstances may be relevant. Capital punishment may be imposed only for crimes resulting in the death of the victim, so no one may be executed, for example, for rape.[32]

Texas resumed executions in 1982. Of the thirty-eight states that now allow capital punishment, it has been the most enthusiastic in killing criminals. The Lone Star State executed 144 murderers from 1982 through 1997, far more than its share of those who were put to death nationally. It executed 37 in 1997.[33]

 On February 3, 1998, Texas executed Karla Faye Tucker by lethal injection. In 1983, while she and her boyfriend were robbing an apartment, Tucker had helped her boyfriend hack two people to death with a pickax. She was the first woman to be officially put to death in the Lone Star State since 1863, and only the second woman executed in the country since the U.S. Supreme Court restored the death penalty in 1976.

Despite the great popularity of the death penalty, it draws persistent criticism from many intellectuals and some politicians. There are three practical and one moral argument against state executions. Practically, opponents first contend that executions are extremely expensive. It costs as much as $2 million

---

31. *Furman* v. *Georgia,* 408 U.S. 238 (1972).
32. *Gardner* v. *Florida,* 430 U.S. 349 (1977); *Woodson* v. *North Carolina,* 428 U.S. 289 (1976); our summary of these death penalty rules is based on J. W. Peltason, *Understanding the Constitution,* 8th ed. (New York: Holt, Rinehart and Winston, 1979), 185.
33. Texas Department of Criminal Justice, December 4, 1997, and subsequent news reports.

more to put an inmate to death than to keep him—women are rarely executed—in prison for forty years.[34]

Supporters of the death penalty counter by saying that the reason it costs so much is that condemned criminals keep the system tied up with appeals for an average of twelve years before their sentence is finally carried out. Eliminate frivolous appeals and streamline the process, they insist, and the cost will come down. In 1995, the legislature enacted a series of reforms to cut down on the number of appeals and shorten the interval between the time a convict is sentenced and the time he is killed. In December 1996, the Texas Court of Criminal Appeals upheld this law, and the state immediately began to execute the more than 450 convicted murderers waiting on death row.

The second practical argument is that no matter how careful the judicial system is to safeguard due process and the rights of the accused, it will always make mistakes. Some innocent people will be convicted of murder either through bungling by their defense counsel or—as in the case of David Wayne Spence, discussed in Chapter 11—because of misbehavior by police and/or district attorneys. If all convicts are kept alive in prison, there is a chance that new evidence may be discovered, or that the judicial system will discover its error and free them. If they are killed, the error has been turned into a tragedy.

Proponents of the death penalty counter that the system is now so full of procedural safeguards that a wrongful execution is extremely unlikely. They dispute the assertion that people such as David Wayne Spence are "really" innocent.

---

34. Jim Mattox, "Texas' Death Penalty Dilemma," *Dallas Morning News,* August 25, 1993, A23.

TABLE 12–2

Texas Public Opinion about Capital Punishment

Question	% Yes	% No	% DK
In general, do you feel that Texas should have the death penalty for some crimes?	84	11	5
	Favor	**Oppose**	**DK**
What about the death penalty for murder— would you favor or oppose it?	82	10	8
What about the death penalty for major drug dealers— would you favor or oppose it?	55	36	9
What about the death penalty for rape— would you favor or oppose it?	48	37	15

SOURCE: Harte-Hanks *Texas Poll,* Fall 1994.

The third practical argument against the death penalty is that it does not deter crime. Murderers are generally stupid, impulsive people who give little thought to the possible consequences of their actions. Studies of the fifty states generally show that the presence or absence of capital punishment does not affect a state's murder rate. If the death penalty does not deter, its opponents ask, how can it be justified?

Supporters of capital punishment have a ready answer. "I believe in the death penalty not because it's a deterrent but for retribution, plain and simple," states Harris County District Attorney John B. Holmes.[35] In Holmes's view, which is clearly shared by most citizens, not only in Texas but in the country as a whole, a murderer deserves to die for his or her crime.

The moral argument against capital punishment is that "two wrongs do not make a right." Some people believe that states simply should not be able to carry out official homicide, whatever the alleged crimes of the convict. This view, however, is held by only a small minority. The opinion of the great majority of Texans is much better represented by John Holmes than by Ben Sargent, whose cartoon in this book make his opposition to capital punishment clear.

Whatever its moral or practical shortcomings, therefore, capital punishment is going to continue in Texas. The only way it might conceivably be ended would be by another U.S. Supreme Court decision. In recent years, however, the Court has been becoming more, not less, permissive in allowing states to have their way in matters of criminal law. So Texas will continue to execute people convicted of murder, and some Texans will continue to abhor the practice.

Torts and Tort Reform

A **tort** is a private or civil wrong or injury resulting from a breach of a legal duty that exists by reason of society's expectations about appropriate behavior, rather than a contract. The allegedly injured party sues the alleged wrongdoer

---

35. Holmes quoted in Audrey Duff, "The Deadly D.A.," *Texas Monthly,* February 1994, 38.

in order to receive compensation for his or her losses. Because tort actions are civil, not criminal, the losing party does not go to jail, but must pay money to the injured party. The loser may also sometimes have to pay "punitive damages," compensation in excess of the actual damages. These are awarded in the case of willful and malicious misconduct. A doctor whose negligence causes health problems to a patient may be the object of a tort action, as may a company whose defective product causes injury to its customers, a business whose unsafe premises cause an accident among its shoppers, and so on.

Tort lawsuits became more common in American courts in the 1980s and early 1990s. In 1984, there were 258,028 damage suits filed nationwide. The total was 318,338 in 1993, an increase of 23 percent.[36] Moreover, large sums of money have been awarded to some people whose suits have seemed, to the public, to be rather frivolous. An Alabama jury, for example, awarded a doctor $4 million in punitive damages in a case involving a paint job on his $40,000 luxury automobile. This and other, similar cases have created a public perception that the tort system is out of control and needs reform.

Business has been claiming for years that it is being stifled by unjustified litigation. The Kwik Wash laundromat chain, for example, reports that it is drastically cutting back its business because of lawsuits. A woman who had done her laundry at a Kwik Wash took her laundry back to her car, then visited a bar nearby. When the bar closed two and a half hours later, she left with the bar manager. As the two walked to her car, they were accosted by a criminal, who robbed the manager. The woman sued Kwik Wash, charging that the lights in the strip mall outside its laundromat were not bright enough. The proliferation of this type of suit has caused Kwik Wash to either sell or close sixty laundromats in Texas in recent years.[37]

In the early 1990s, business interests in Texas and elsewhere launched a major offensive to rewrite some of the tort laws. They enlisted the Republican Party in this crusade. In particular, the "tort reform" movement in Texas wanted to change four aspects of the state's civil liability laws:

1. Punitive damages. Reformers wanted to change the law to make a litigant prove that not just "gross negligence"—the wording under the state's statute—but actual malice was involved before punitive damages could be awarded. Also, they wanted to limit the amount of punitive damages.

2. Joint and several liability. Under the law prevailing to 1995, anyone who participated in as little as 11 percent of the cause of the injury could be held liable for the actions of others. This meant that if company A was found to be 11 percent at fault, and the other companies were bankrupt or otherwise unreachable, company A had to pay 100 percent of the award to the plaintiff. Reformers hoped to eliminate this responsibility of the richest, most available company.

3. Venue. Attorneys filing tort cases had been able to "shop around" for a judge who was known to be sympathetic to plaintiffs. Reformers wanted to restrict filings to the geographical area where the injury occurred.

---

36. Aaron Epstein, "Litigants Ready to Fight over Tort Award Limits," *Houston Chronicle,* March 4, 1995, A4.

37. Robert Howden, "Texas Sue-Happy Culture Hurts Small Business," *Houston Chronicle,* January 25, 1995, 23A.

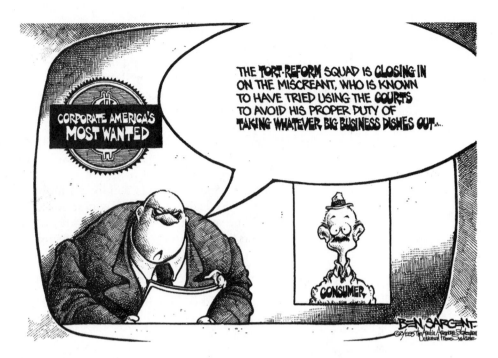

4. **Deceptive Trade Practices Act.** Texas's consumer protection act provided triple damages for things such as deceptive real estate or stock deals. Reformers wanted to make a consumer prove that a deceptive act occurred knowingly.

Tort reform was a hot topic in the 1994 campaign and the 1995 legislative session. During his election campaign, Governor George W. Bush charged, "One punitive damage award can destroy almost any small business. Companies are moving from Texas or putting their new plants and facilities in other states because of this situation."[38] The legislature was lobbied hard by the Texas Civil Justice League, Texans for Lawsuit Reform, Texans Against Lawsuit Abuse, and the Texas Medical Association to radically change the state's laws.

There were, however, powerful forces arrayed on the other side. A great many attorneys, for example, make their living from torts. They disputed the argument that there were too many lawsuits in Texas. "The business community and industry groups are selling the American public a bogus bill of goods about frivolous lawsuits and a litigation explosion," charged Larry Stewart, president of the Association of Trial Lawyers of America.[39]

Consumers' organizations also opposed changes in tort laws. They viewed lawsuits as one of the few ways in which ordinary, unrich, unpowerful people could force rich, powerful corporations to treat them decently. Tim Curtis, executive director of Texas Citizen Action, based in Austin, argued,

---

38. Bush quoted in Bruce Hight, "Questioning Tort Reform," *Austin American-Statesman,* January 8, 1995, J1.
39. Stewart quoted in Epstein, "Litigants."

"Remember that these defendants include: insurance companies who cheat their policyholders; manufacturers of dangerous and defective products that have killed and maimed children; inexperienced, careless, or drug impaired doctors who commit medical malpractice on trusting patients; even unscrupulous lawyers. . . . Legal concepts like joint and several liability and punitive damages have removed countless dangerous products from store shelves. Professionals who abuse their trust have been forced to change their practices or leave the profession."[40] Citizen Action was joined by Consumers Union, Public Citizen, and the Texas Trial Lawyers Association in lobbying against tort reform in the 1995 legislature.

With both good arguments and lots of lobbying clout on both sides, the result in the 1995 legislature was a compromise. Although they did not get everything they wanted, the reformers did force important changes. Some of the highlights of new laws passed in 1995 were:

1. Punitive damages were limited to the greater of $200,000 or the sum of two times economic damages, plus $750,000.

2. The joint and several liability rule was changed so that a defendant would have to be more than 50 percent responsible to be held liable for all damages.

3. To eliminate venue shopping, the legislature decreed that a business can be sued only in the county in which an injury occurred or in a county in which it has a principal office.

4. Judges were given more power to punish plaintiffs who file frivolous suits.

5. Plaintiffs who sue doctors or hospitals were required to post a $5,000 bond; if the claim proves baseless, the plaintiff forfeits the bond.

Predictably, business representatives praised the reforms while consumer spokespersons criticized them. In the 1997 legislature, pro-reform advocates argued for more changes in the tort laws, but were rebuffed. The attitude of most legislators was that they should be allowed to wait a few years and evaluate how the 1995 laws were working before being asked to pass another batch of reforms. For writers of textbooks, also, it is too soon after the reforms to be able to evaluate them.

Conclusion

Overall, a survey of the state court system suggests that it works better than its chaotic organization and controversial system of judicial selection might lead us to expect. Although Texas courts are not perfect examples of democracy in action, they have often been ahead of the rest of the state's political system in dealing with the substance of justice. The state's judicial system, troubled as it is, gives some hope that it will be able to cope with the challenges of the future.

Meanwhile, courts will continue to be asked to resolve the unresolvable social conflicts of our time.

---

40. Tim Curtis, "Tort 'Reforms' Trying to Take Away Your Rights," *Houston Chronicle*, January 19, 1995, A29.

Summary

The output of the Texas system of justice has improved in some ways in recent years. Whereas Texas courts used to be inhospitable to claims that people's civil rights and liberties had been violated, they are now more open to such claims. As the town of Vidor illustrates, Texas still contains hard-core racism, but both the federal and state governments are working hard to mitigate its effects.

The Texas courts have courageously taken on the rest of the political establishment, including especially the legislature, in ordering a more equitable distribution of school revenues. They have not completely succeeded in introducing educational equality into Texas public schools, but they have forced the legislature to make the educational system at least somewhat more equitable.

Arguments are ongoing over some questions of rights and liberties. Although the national and state courts participate in social struggles over abortion, gun possession, prayer in the schools, and pornography, these issues provoke so much disagreement that they cannot be settled judicially.

In one area, however, the rights of criminals in Texas prisons, the federal courts have been very active over the past quarter century in forcing the reform of the system.

In recent years, many businesses became convinced that the outcome of Texas's tort laws were damaging the state's economy. They complained that the courts were too tolerant of frivolous suits that sometimes cost businesses so much money that they were forced to close down. In 1995 the legislature, at the urging of Governor Bush, reformed many of the tort laws. This made consumer representatives unhappy, however, and the future will probably see more efforts to revise the state law of torts.

Key Terms

Blue-collar crime	Civil rights	White-collar crime
Civil liberties	Tort	

Study Questions

1. What is the difference between civil rights and civil liberties?

2. Why is freedom of expression important in a democracy? How well has the Texas legislature seemed to understand these arguments? The Texas judiciary?

3. What is the general history of freedom of religion in Texas?

4. Is the right to keep and bear arms guaranteed by the U.S. Constitution? To whom?

5. Why do you think the issue of abortion is so divisive? Could you imagine a way to resolve it, either legislatively or judicially?

6. Discuss the facts and issues in *Edgewood* v. *Kirby*. Do you agree with the way the courts handled the problem of school funding, or do you agree

with the legislature? Since the Texas Constitution was written in 1876, why do you think it took until 1989 for the state Supreme Court to declare the system of school funding unconstitutional?

7. Do you think it matters whether people arrested for committing crimes have rights? What is the recent record of Texas in granting such rights?

8. Do you support the death penalty? Why or why not?

9. Should the tort laws of Texas matter to its citizens? What recent changes have been made in those laws? Who wanted the changes, and why? Who opposed the changes, and why?

Internet Assignment

Internet site: http://oyez.nwu.edu/

Go to the "Oyez Oyez Oyez: Supreme Court Database" page. Click on "Cases." Type the names of several of the cases mentioned in this chapter (e.g., *Gitlow* v. *New York, Texas* v. *Johnson, Smith* v. *Allwright, Edgewood* v. *Kirby*). Read the brief provided (click on "Written Opinions of the Court" for the full case). How does the brief differ from the full opinion?

Chapter Thirteen

The State Economy and the Financing of State Government

Traditionally conservative Texans generally dislike taxes, and they particularly dislike the thought of a state income tax. These demonstrators wanted their state officials to understand their antipathy to new state taxes.

People want JUST taxes more than they want LOWER taxes. They want to know that every man is paying his proportionate share according to his wealth.

> Will Rogers,
> legendary American humorist

Texans are like the tea bags of life. They perform when the water's hot.

> Carolyn Pesce,
> reporter, USA Today

Texas was second only to North Carolina in the business beauty pageant.

> Steve Brown,
> real estate editor, Dallas Morning News

Introduction

The ability of any government to generate the revenues needed to provide the programs and services that citizens want is directly tied to the economy. Are most people working? Are wages good? Are profits high? Is money available for loans to finance business expansion and home ownership? This chapter begins by sketching the robust economy of the late 1990s that emerged from the troubled economy that began in 1983, when plummeting oil prices wreaked havoc on the Texas economy and on state finance. In 1997 Texas had a sizable surplus at the beginning of the legislative session, causing long-time observers of the Texas political scene to recall fondly the 1970s, when every year brought with it a surplus.

A major issue concerning the revenue system is its fairness. As Will Rogers noted in the quotation above, citizens always seek fairness. Yet, as we shall see, the poor in Texas pay a higher proportion of their incomes in taxes than do the wealthy. This fact raises questions about how democratic the state revenue system is and constitutes a major theme of this chapter.

The chapter also looks at how the state spends its money, including how elected officials struggle to agree on what the budget will be. Because the budget is the best guide to policy priorities, it is a practical test of how well citizens' interests are accommodated in state spending.

Texas has grown from 15.3 million people in 1982 to an estimated 19.1 million people at the beginning of 1997—an increase of 28.8 percent in just fifteen years. During that same period, the state budget has increased from $28.5 billion for **fiscal (budget) years** (FY) 1983–1984 to $87.1 billion for FY 1998–1999—an increase of 213 percent. However, when adjusted for population growth (more people require more services) and for **inflation** (that is, increases in what things cost), the Texas budget was relatively flat across this period, as Figure 13–1 shows. Budget growth has been only about 2.4 percent a year, less than the inflation rate for the period as a whole.[1]

---

1. *Fiscal Size Up: Texas State Services 1982–83 Biennium* and *Fiscal Size Up: Texas State Services 1998–99 Biennium* (Austin: Legislative Budget Board, 1982, 1998), 5 and 1–9, respectively.

FIGURE 13–1
Trends in Texas
State Expenditures,
1983–1999

Source: Fiscal Size Up: Texas State
Services 1998–99 *(Austin: Legislative Budget Board, 1998), 1–9.*
Estimated expenditures.

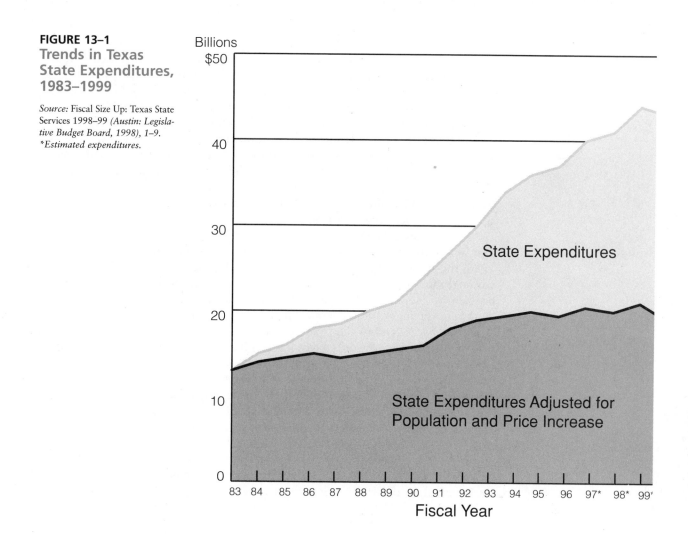

The Texas Economy

THE PAST

Historically, the Texas economy has been based on natural resources, chiefly oil, land, and water. Indeed, Texas has been characterized as the state where "money gushes from the ground in the oil fields and grows on the citrus trees in the irrigated orchards."[2] Texas and Alaska vie for fourth position—after Saudi Arabia, Iran, and Iraq[3]—in oil production. Chemicals, cotton, and cattle also contribute their share of wealth. In fact, the economy is robust and complex enough that the *Wall Street Journal* noted in 1998 that the state could not identify its largest industry.

2. Wayne King, "Despite Success, Sun Belt Oil Patch Is Finding It's Not Immune to Recession," *New York Times,* June 9, 1981, 11.
3. Anne Reifenberg, "Playing to OPEC's Power," *Dallas Morning News,* June 7, 1989, 1D, 2D.

The state's natural resources are finite—that is, once used, they cannot be replaced. Furthermore, the global economy is shifting from one based on natural resources to one based on information and technology. In 1997, the overall Texas economy was $776 billion a year. Of that, $8.8 billion—slightly over 1 percent—came from agriculture, forestry, and fisheries. Although the percentage of the state economy derived from agriculture has declined, only California has a larger agribusiness economy. By 1997, oil and gas production—once 27 percent of the state's economy—had shrunk to less than 6 percent. Both of these figures are somewhat misleading because the manufacturing (25 percent of the economy) and construction (another 3 percent) segments of the economy included projects such as petrochemical plants, drill sites, and agricultural processing factories.[4]

Nevertheless, the erosion of the natural resource–based economy meant that hundreds of thousands of Texans found themselves out of work. In June 1986, the state unemployment rate reached 9.6 percent, compared with a national rate of 7.3 percent. The collapse of financial institutions made the problem worse. From 1988 to 1990, Texas led the nation in the number of banks and savings and loans that failed. Then, the defense industry was depressed by the end of the Cold War in the early 1990s.

State government worked to shore up the shaky economy by consolidating economic development programs, developing aggressive marketing campaigns for farm and ranch products, and selling the high-technology capability of the state through industry-university partnerships. Nevertheless, in 1991 Texas was given a grade of D by the nonprofit Corporation for Enterprise Development, with the educational system, economic performance, international marketing, and state policies cited as particular weaknesses.[5]

However, Texas got high marks on technology, and the state comptroller frequently noted that the state should outperform the nation economically during much of the 1990s.[6] State leaders talked about the history of the state and the ability of Texans to overcome adversity—"perform when the water's hot," as one of the chapter-opening quotations says.[7] In 1994 state leaders strongly supported passage of the North American Free Trade Agreement (NAFTA), which economically links all of North America, because Texas will be a major gateway for trade with Mexico. National analysts also saw a bright future for the state.[8]

---

4. Anne Reifenberg, "Biggest Industry in Texas? You'll Be Sorry You Asked," *Wall Street Journal,* January 28, 1998, T1.

5. Mark Tatge, "Texas Fails to Make the Grade," *Dallas Morning News,* April 24, 1991, 1D, 4D. This rating measures public policies promoting economic development.

6. See, for example, "The Texas Economic Outlook," *Texas Economic Quarterly,* a publication of the Comptroller of Public Accounts, March 1994, 1–4; and John Sharp, *The Changing Face of Texas: Texas through the Year 2026: Economic Growth, Cultural Diversity* (Austin: Comptroller of Public Accounts, August 1992).

7. See Diane Jennings, "Extracting a Lesson: Texas Emerges from Economic Bust Wary, Wiser," *Dallas Morning News,* August 8, 1993, 1A, 34A, 35A, and the four-part series, "Texas in the Last Decade: From Boom to Bust—and Back Again," *Dallas Morning News,* March 17–20, 1996, for in-depth looks at economic recovery in the state.

8. "Forbes Survey Finds Texas in Top 6 for Jobs Outlook," *Dallas Morning News,* January 17, 1994, 1D, 4D.

THE PRESENT

The optimism proved to be well founded. By 1996 Texas had regained its place as one of the top places to locate a business, running second only to North Carolina in the "business beauty pageant," as the third chapter-opening quotation muses. This ranking by Development Counsellors International was based on a poll of 173 executives in top firms concerning sites they would consider for relocation.[9] Texas was one of nine states with a job growth rate of 6 percent or more from 1994 to 1996, and it added another two hundred thousand new jobs in 1997.[10] In December 1997 unemployment statewide was 4.8 percent—a level not seen since 1977. High-technology centers such as Austin, Dallas, and Bryan–College Station had virtually full employment, with only 2 to 4 percent of workers unable to find work. Petrochemical centers and border cities were less fortunate; unemployment in McAllen-Edinburg-Mission stood at 17.7 percent.[11] New and expanded corporate facilities in 1994 to 1996 numbered 1,968, second only to Ohio.[12] High technology, financial services, manufacturing, and communications were the economic engines for the job growth. As we shall see, one reflection of the newly booming economy was the $87.1 billion budget approved by the legislature in 1997.

ANALYSIS

At least six factors help explain the ups and downs of the Texas economy and the growth in the state budget over the past quarter-century. First, the domination of the world oil market by Middle Eastern countries led to the bust in the oil business. Although the industry has had something of a recent resurgence, oil prices were slipping in 1998 as a result of a world oversupply. Second, federal assistance to the states has waxed and waned over the past twenty years and is likely to decline again as a result of changes in federal social programs that took effect in the fall of 1997. Third, Texans responded to the challenges posed by the economic doldrums of the 1980s and diversified the economy. Fourth, at times during the 1970s, double-digit inflation prevailed; both public and private spending increased in proportion to the inflation rate. During the 1980s and 1990s, the nation continued to experience some inflation, but the rate was much lower. Fifth, the Texas revenue system, particularly its tax structure, lacks **elasticity;** that is, it does not easily adjust to ups and downs in the economy. In the mid to late 1990s, the most important factor is the booming economy, but only cautious optimism should prevail, since the inelastic revenue structure coupled with spending demands and federal cutbacks could be a problem if the economy should sag. Sixth,

---

9. Steve Brown, "Texas No. 2 on List of Best Business Sites," *Dallas Morning News,* October 2, 1996, 1D, 10D.
10. John Greenwald, "Where the Jobs Are," *Time,* January 20, 1997, 54–61; eight of the nine were Western states, with only Georgia being located east of the Mississippi River. See also "Growing the Economy," *Fiscal Notes* (Texas Comptroller of Public Accounts), October 1997, 1.
11. Jane Seaberry, "Unemployment Hits Lowest Level since Oil Boom," *Dallas Morning News,* January 28, 1998, 1D, 2D.
12. "Expanding in Texas," *Fiscal Notes,* May 1997, 16.

when state government did enjoy a surplus in 1997, it chose to rebate the money to taxpayers in the form of reduced local school taxes. This action was in line with strong conservative trends to reduce taxes rather than increase spending.

Where Does the Money Come From?

State finance consists of raising and spending money. For most of those who are involved in government, the budget is the bottom line, as it is for the rest of us. Policy decisions regarding state financing are made in the glaring light of political reality—what political scientist Harold Laswell called "Politics: Who Gets What, When, and How" back in 1911. Whenever money is raised, it comes from someone; whenever it is spent, someone gets it. Struggles over who will pay for the government and who will receive dollars from it are at the heart of politics in Texas, as elsewhere.

Figure 13–2 gives an approximate idea of the sources of state revenue for FY 1998–99. It shows that 49.9 percent of all revenues come from taxes; 29.1 percent from federal grants; 4.4 percent from interest and dividends, fees, and the surplus; and 16.7 percent from other receipts.

Table 13–1 provides a view of the changing revenue picture in the state during the period in which the flattened state economy began to turn around. This table shows several trends: the steady decline in revenues generated by the oil and gas industries, the increase in nontax sources of revenues, and the instability of federal funding. The table reflects the decline of the oil industry both in the relentless loss of revenues from the severance tax—the tax on the production of oil, gas, and other minerals—and in the downward trend of leases, interest, and investment income. As the oil business slacked off, interest in leasing state land to explore for oil or gas also declined. Texans historically enjoyed low taxes because of the oil and gas revenue, which was an especially appealing tax source because out-of-state purchasers paid for much of it. Other revenues paid directly by individuals—for example, licenses and fees—showed steady increases in the twelve-year period, in an effort to offset the

TABLE 13–1

Texas State Revenue Sources, FY 1988–89 to FY 1998–99, in Percentages*

Source	1988–89	1990–91	1992–93	1994–95	1996–97	1998–99
Taxes	61.4	60.0	51.8	50.9	49.9	49.9
General sales	30.8	33.5	27.9	27.7	27.7	27.6
Severance	5.4	4.9	3.4	3.2	2.1	2.0
Other	25.2	21.6	20.5	20.0	20.1	20.3
Federal funds	22.2	24.6	28.8	30.1	30.1	29.1
Licenses, fines, fees, other receipts	9.5	9.1	10.1	10.9	11.4	11.5
Leases, interest, investments	6.9	6.3	7.1	5.7	4.1	4.4
Lottery	—	—	2.2	2.3	4.5	5.1

*Percentages do no always equal 100.0 due to rounding.
SOURCE: *Fiscal Size Up* (Austin: Legislative Budget Board, 1988, 1990, 1992, 1994, 1996, 1998), Chapter II, revenue.

FIGURE 13–2
Estimated Texas State Revenues by Source, 1998–99 Biennium, in Percentages

Source: Office of the State Comptroller as reported in Fiscal Size Up: 1998–99 Biennium, 2–3.

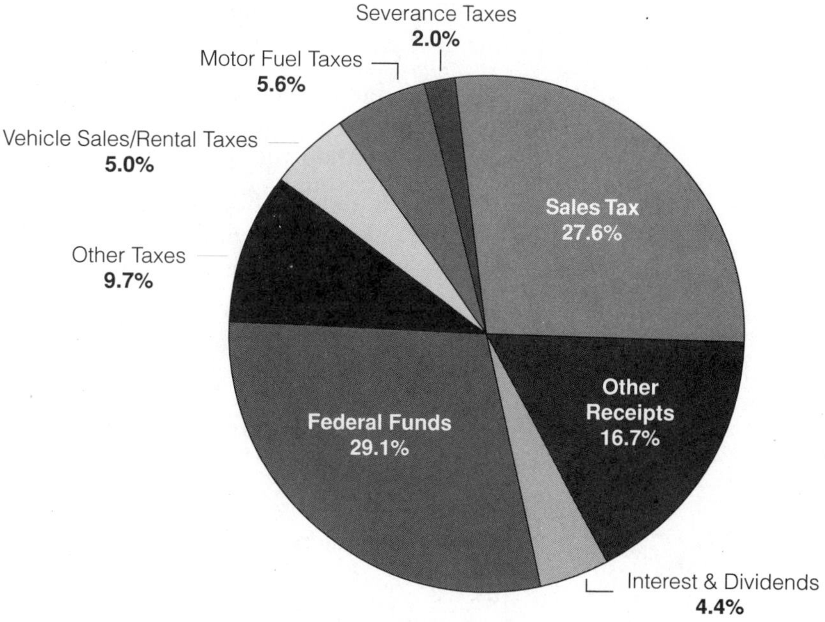

loss of severance tax dollars. Seeking to avoid tax increases, the legislature has frequently turned to charges such as the fee paid for a professional license or charges such as college tuition to augment the state treasury. The percentage of revenues from the lottery is shown as steadily increasing during the FY 1988–1999 period, but lottery revenue had begun to decline in the latter part of calendar 1997.

Always of importance is the proportion of state revenues generated by the general sales tax—the added cents you pay on every hamburger and notebook you buy—because this tax tends to hit the poor the hardest (see the discussion on ability to pay later in this chapter). The sales tax actually has declined in percentage of revenues generated, although not in dollars, over the period from FY 1988–89 to FY 1998–99 because of the increase in nontax revenues. This chapter examines each major source of state income.

COLLECTION AND ADMINISTRATION

State revenues are collected in many ways by many people. Monies from federal grants may be sent directly to the state agency responsible for administering the program being funded. The general retail sales tax is collected by retail merchants and then forwarded to the state comptroller. Other taxes, such as the inheritance tax, may be forwarded directly from the individual to the state comptroller. The two officials who are most concerned with state financial administration are the comptroller, who is responsible for tax collection, investments, and the safeguarding of public funds, and the auditor, who oversees state agencies to ensure the legality of their expenditures.

Once collected, state revenues are channeled into various funds, some of which are designated to supply monies for the general operation of government, while others are dedicated to (reserved for) specific services. The five major funds in Texas are:

1. The General Revenue Fund, which supports the majority of state programs

2. The Omnibus Tax Clearance Fund, which is allocated in part to two other funds, the General Revenue Fund and Available School Fund, and in part to such specific functions as the construction of farm-to-market roads, parks, and teachers' retirement

3. The Available School Fund, which underwrites public school textbooks and part of the Foundation School Program, the major source of state aid for local school districts

4. The Highway Motor Fuel Fund, one-fourth of which is allocated to the Available School Fund and the remainder to highways and roads

5. The State Highway Fund, which is used for highway and road construction and maintenance, right-of-way acquisition, and related purposes

Other funds set aside for particular purposes include those dedicated to parks and wildlife, county and district roads, teachers' retirement, and the Department of Commerce.

NONTAX SOURCES OF REVENUE

The state has sources of revenue other than the checks oil producers write to the state comptroller and the pennies, nickels, and dimes that citizens dig out of their pockets to satisfy the sales tax. These revenues include federal grants, borrowing, and several other sources, including fees such as college tuition. Together these sources account for about 50.1 percent of state revenues.

FEDERAL GRANTS

The largest nontax source of money is federal grants. Beginning in the 1960s, state and local governments became heavily dependent on national budgetary policies that distributed monies to the treasuries of states, cities, and other local governments. Originally these dollars came to states in the form of **categorical grants-in-aid** that could be used only for specific programs such as community-health centers. Under President Richard Nixon, **general revenue sharing** was enacted. Distributed by formula, general revenue-sharing funds could be used by state and local governments for whatever projects these governments wanted—police salaries, playground equipment, home care for the elderly. In addition, the federal government began to fund **block grants,** which provide money for general use in broad programs such as community development. However, federal funding of state and local programs reached a peak in 1978; after that, President Jimmy Carter's administration began to phase the national government out of some programs. General revenue sharing for states ended in 1979 and that for cities, in 1986.

When President Ronald Reagan was elected, he emphasized the concept of block grants even more. State and local governments gained considerable flexibility under Reagan's "New Federalism" because more and more categorical grants were consolidated into block grants. The state gained more control because many funds were no longer channeled directly to local governments, but rather "passed through" a state agency. This flexibility came at a price, however, as the amount of funding for many programs, especially those affecting the poor and urban development, was reduced. For the first time in a third of a century, states had a dollar drop in federal aid in 1982[13] as a result of Carter-Reagan fiscal federalism.

Recent increases in federal funding have been attributable to interstate highway construction and maintenance spending following the increase in the national motor fuels tax in 1983. In the early 1990s, additional federal funds were forthcoming as a result of the state's aggressive pursuit of Medicaid funds to assist with hospital care for the needy and the school lunch program. However, critics of state policy processes have continued to cite Texas officials for not taking full advantage of national programs. Although expressing sympathy for the nation's cities and their problems, President Bill Clinton had to contend with the need for budget balancing. The "implication of this budget-balance strategy is that by 2002 grants to state and local governments will need to be about 25 percent less."[14] National welfare reform legislation signed shortly before the 1996 presidential election has resulted in the states' being asked to take over new responsibilities for health benefits for the poor and to emphasize job placements instead of cash assistance as the focus of welfare programs (see Chapter 14).[15]

Texas fared well in *pork-barrel spending*—funding for specific local projects that was gained by a U.S. representative's or senator's making a deal with a colleague. Citizens Against Government Waste issued a report in 1995 called the *Pig Book*, which indicated that Texas garnered $130.3 million for 1994–95 for such projects as dairy goat research, research on the effects of drought on crops, and an air base equipment shop.

Sources: Catalina Camia, "Group Says Texas No. 2 Hog at Pork-Barrel Trough," *Dallas Morning News*, February 16, 1995, 34A.

BORROWING

Governments, like private citizens, borrow money. The reasons are varied. Political expediency is one. Borrowing allows new programs to be implemented and existing ones to be extended without increasing taxes. A second reason is that borrowing allows future beneficiaries of a state service to pay for that service. Students who live in residence halls, for example, help pay off the bonds used to finance those halls through their room fees.

13. *The Book of the States, 1984-85*, vol. 25 (Lexington, Ky.: Council of State Governments, 1984), 315.

14. Andrew Reschovsky, "A Balanced Federal Budget: The Effect on States," *The LaFollette Policy Report*, 8, no. 1 (Winter 1997): 8.

15. See, for example, Carl Tubbesing and Sheri Steisel, "Answers to Your Welfare Worries," *State Legislatures*, January 1997, 12–19; Rob Gurwitt, "Cracking the Casework Culture," *Governing*, March 1997, 27–30; and William McKenzie, "Texas Tries to Pick Up the Federal Burden," *Dallas Morning News*, May 20, 1997, 13A.

State government indebtedness is highly restricted in Texas, however. The framers of the state constitution strongly believed in "pay-as-you-go" government. A four-fifths vote of the legislature is needed to approve emergency borrowing, and the state's debt ceiling originally was limited to $200,000. A series of amendments has altered the constitution to allow the issuance of state bonds for specific programs, particularly land for veterans, university buildings, student loans, parks, prisons, and water development. In FY 1995, *authorized* state indebtedness was almost $8.3 billion, but slightly less than $5 billion in bonds had been issued. About half of the bonds that are outstanding are for prison construction. Although both the authorized and the issued figures may seem high, only Kansas had a lower level of indebtedness than Texas on a per-person basis.[16]

OTHER NONTAX SOURCES

Because taxes are unpopular in Texas and elsewhere, government inevitably looks to nontax revenue sources whenever possible. The prospective budget deficits that began in 1985 have resulted in a pattern of raising money by increasing fees for almost everything, looking to gambling as a source of public revenue, and even manipulating state pension funds. An excellent example is senior college tuition, a type of **user fee**—that is, a sum paid in direct exchange for service. Senior college tuition tripled, from $4 per credit hour to $12 in 1985, and has continued to increase, with $32 set as the base rate for 1997. Institutions can and do charge more for graduate and professional education. The $4 rate is the minimum tuition at community colleges, with each district setting its own rate. What college students have really noticed is the great increase in fees, with universities in particular charging a separate fee for almost everything—for each course, for publications, for building use, and so on—in their desperate attempt to overcome inadequate state funding and deal with the privatization of higher education—that is, the steady erosion of public support. Beginning in FY 1998–99, the biggest of these fees was incorporated into tuition. Some undergraduates will be paying more than $60 per credit hour in larger institutions.

Another revenue measure that you as a college student will notice is that a driver's license will cost more beginning in fall 1997—$24 for six years. Other fees—for everything from car inspections to water permits, from personal automobile tags to day-care center operator licenses—have also been increased. Fines for various legal infractions have risen. Even the cost of fishing licenses has gone up.

Other nontax sources of state revenue include the interest on bank deposits, proceeds from investments, and sales and leases of public lands. Having a surplus increases investment income. The doldrums of the oil industry decrease income from land leases.

The 1987 legislature proposed a constitutional amendment, approved by the voters in November of that year, that permitted pari-mutuel betting on

---

16. See "State Indebtedness" at www.lbb.state.tx.us for information as of February 11, 1998, and *The Book of the States, 1996–97*, vol. 31 (Lexington, Ky.: Council of State Governments, 1996), 256.

One of the arguments against establishing a state lottery was that the people who could least afford to wager in a lottery would be the most enticed to do so. Nevertheless, a lottery was approved by the voters and began in 1992. It has proved to be the most successful state lottery in the country. In 1997, the issue was dedictation of all lottery proceeds to the public schools.

Courtesy of Ben Sargent.

horse races and, in three counties, on dog races on a local-option basis. By 1991, however, track betting had contributed virtually nothing to state coffers because the state's share of the proceeds—5 percent—was so high that track developers declined the opportunity to invest. Even though the 1991 legislature lowered the state's share to a graduated rate beginning at 1 percent, first-class tracks have been slow in coming.

A state lottery also was debated in 1987, 1989, and 1991 but was not approved by the legislature. Ann Richards and her Democratic primary opponent Jim Mattox had both campaigned on a prolottery platform in 1990. Governor Richards apparently was able to work out a deal with enough legislators—allegedly supporting their redistricting concerns—to get a lottery on the November 1991 ballot. Voters approved the lottery, which began in summer 1992. Since then, whether the revenues were to be dedicated to education has been an issue. The 1997 legislature did dedicate the revenues, but moved other funds that had previously been earmarked for education back to the general fund. For the FY 1998–99 biennium, the lottery was budgeted to account for at least 5.1 percent of the state's revenues. Administrative scandals and some fall-off in betting may result in the lottery's not meeting expectations.

TAXATION

Taxes are the most familiar sources of governmental revenue and the most controversial. Since colonial days and James Otis's stirring phrase "no taxation without representation," citizens have sought justice in the tax system. The conservative heritage of Texas has not always made justice easy to find.

Taxes are collected for two principal reasons. *Revenue taxes*—for example, the general sales tax—are the major source of government income. They make it possible for government to carry out its programs. *Regulatory taxes*—for example, the taxes on tobacco and alcohol—are designed primarily to control those individuals and/or organizations that are subject to them and to either punish undesired behavior or reward desired behavior.

Both individuals and businesses pay taxes. Certain taxes, such as the retail sales tax, are paid directly by the citizens, while others, such as the tax on insurance transactions, are paid directly by businesses. Some would contend, however, that in the final analysis private citizens pay both types of taxes because business passes its tax expenses on to the consumer. Only a tax on profits works to slow or stop this pass-through of tax costs.

Although our discussion focuses on **tax equity** (fairness), another great concern with the Texas tax system is the lack of elasticity, which was discussed earlier in this chapter as one of the key factors resulting in a restricted state budget for more than a decade. A system based so heavily on sales and excise taxes runs into problems when the economy sours because the lower and middle classes, on whom such taxes depend, curtail their spending. With that curtailment comes a tailing off of tax revenues tied to consumer spending.

The tax policies of individual states reflect their economic resources, their political climates, and their dominant interest groups. Forty-three of the fifty states levy a personal income tax, although in two, the income tax is limited to interest and dividends. Forty-five states levy a corporate income tax. Texas levies a business franchise tax of 4.5 percent of earned surplus (profit); Michigan, a rather complicated business activities tax.[17] While neither of these taxes is technically a corporate income tax, both are tied to business revenues.

Texas relies heavily on the general sales tax and other forms of sales taxes, such as the one paid at the pump for motor fuels. Even official state documents have begun to recognize the equity problems inherent in a system based heavily on sales taxes: "Both the SCOTE [Select Committee on Tax Equity] and Governor's Task Force reports note that the current system places a disproportionately high taxpaying burden on poor and middle-income taxpayers, and that the taxpaying burden is not spread equally among different types of businesses."[18] Governor George W. Bush pushed very hard for tax reform in the 1997 legislative session, although his concern was mainly high local property taxes.

Discussions about taxation, whether at the national, state, or local level, are seldom objective. One's own political philosophy and tax status inevitably color one's comments on the subject. Indeed, when government talks about taxes, its noble-sounding phrases such as "the public interest" do not always ring true. Today's citizens are sophisticated enough to realize that extensive campaigning, heated debates, and vigorous lobbying have formed our tax policies, and that the public interest usually has been construed so as to benefit the influential. One of the least successful aspects of American democracy is the tax system, which at both the national and state levels tends to favor

---

17. *The Book of the States, 1996–1997*, 263, 266–67.
18. "A Proposal to Implement Tax Equity Notes," a working paper used during Legislative Budget Board discussion in the spring of 1992.

those who are better off. Modern-day proposals to eliminate the federal income tax and move to a system of a very large (over 20 percent) national sales tax exemplify how tax systems can be made to benefit the wealthy, since such schemes include taxes on clothing, cars, and washing machines but not on the purchase of stocks, bonds, or real estate investment trusts.

Texas professes fiscal conservatism and practices that philosophy by limiting state and local debt and by operating on a "pay-as-you-go" basis. The state budget reflects the political conservatism of Texas in its taxing and spending practices. An analysis of who pays, who does not pay, and who benefits from Texas taxes reveals not only the political and economic philosophy behind taxation in the state but also which special-interest groups most influence the legislature.

WHO PAYS?

The question of who pays which taxes raises two issues. The first is ability to pay, and the second is whether individuals and businesses both really pay.

Ability to Pay. A matter of some importance to taxpayers is whether the tax system is progressive or regressive. **Progressive taxation** is characterized by a rate that increases as the object taxed—property, income, or goods purchased—grows larger or gains in value. Progressive taxation is based on ability to pay. The best-known example is the federal income tax, which progresses from relatively low rates for those with the least income to increasingly higher rates for those with larger incomes. Note, however, that loopholes in the federal tax laws and ceilings on special taxes such as Social Security still result in a proportionately heavier tax burden for the middle class than for the wealthy.

Although technically a tax system that involves a higher rate with a declining base, **regressive taxation** has come to refer to a system in which lower-income earners spend larger percentages of their incomes on commodities subject to flat tax rates. The best example of Texas's reliance on regressive taxes is the general retail sales tax, which provides more than one-quarter of total state revenue and over half of all tax money. The general sales tax is assessed at 6.25 percent on a wide variety of goods and services at the time of sale, regardless of the income or wealth of the purchaser. Municipalities also can levy a 1 percent additional tax, as can mass transit districts and county economic development districts. Municipalities can also add additional sales tax percentages of a half percent each for economic development and in lieu of reduced property taxes.

The additional selective sales (excise) taxes—those levied on tobacco products, alcoholic beverages, and motor fuels, for example—also are regressive. The $16,000-a-year secretary and the $100,000-a-year executive who drive the same distance to work pay the same 20-cent-a-gallon tax on gasoline, but who is better able to bear the tax burden? Figure 13–3 shows the major taxes in Texas.

Citizens for Tax Justice, a Washington, D.C.–based research and lobbying group, examined the tax structures in all fifty states. Ten states, including Texas, were dubbed "the terrible 10" for the regressivity of their tax structures. Only Washington and Florida have higher tax rates for their poorest

FIGURE 13–3
**Estimated State
Tax Collections by
Major Tax, 1998–99
Biennium, in
Millions**

Source: Adopted from Fiscal Size
Up: 1998–99, 2–2.

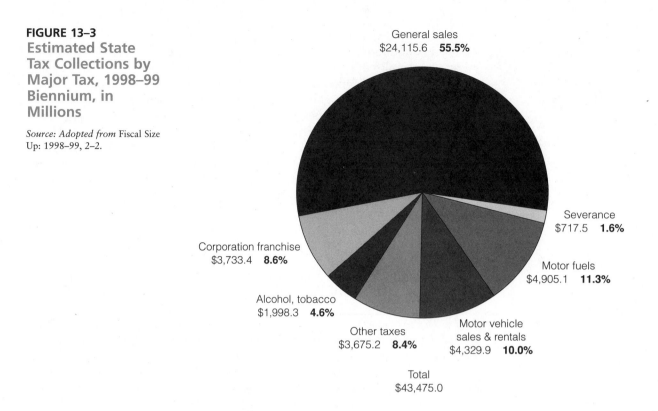

General sales
$24,115.6 **55.5%**

Severance
$717.5 **1.6%**

Corporation franchise
$3,733.4 **8.6%**

Motor fuels
$4,905.1 **11.3%**

Alcohol, tobacco
$1,998.3 **4.6%**

Other taxes
$3,675.2 **8.4%**

Motor vehicle
sales & rentals
$4,329.9 **10.0%**

Total
$43,475.0

citizens than does Texas, and only Washington, Florida, South Dakota, and Tennessee tax their richest citizens as lightly as does Texas. Figure 13–4 shows the sharp drop in percentage of income paid in sales and excise taxes in Texas and nationally as income itself increases. The poorest Texans pay 13.8 percent, while the richest pay only 4.4 percent.[19] One positive sign, and evidence of growing democratic fairness, is the fact that this spread from poorest to richest has grown narrower in the years since the tax group began studying state taxes. The spread was once 17.1 to 3.1.[20] Also, Texas, unlike some states, does not tax food purchased at a grocery store, prescription medicines, or work clothes.

At this stage, Texas cannot claim to have a progressive tax system. The restructuring of the corporation franchise tax did produce greater equity in business taxes, but the state has also passed a constitutional amendment making institution of a personal income tax very difficult. Yet a fair tax system is a value associated with democratic government. Many observers believe that a progressive income tax would be fairer than the general sales tax and could

19. Michael P. Ettlinger, *Who Pays? A Distributional Analysis of the Tax Systems in All 50 States* (Washington, D.C.: Citizens for Tax Justice, 1996), 2–3. All these states rely on sales taxes rather than a personal income tax.
20. Jennifer Dixon, "Texas Taxes Burden Middle Class," *Denton Record-Chronicle,* April 22, 1991, 1A, 5A, summarizing the 1991 report of the Washington, D.C.–based Citizens for Tax Justice. See also *Nickels and Dimes: How Sales & Excise Taxes Add Up in the 50 States* (Washington, D.C.: Citizens for Tax Justice, in cooperation with the Institute on Taxation and Economic Policy, March 1988), 28–35.

FIGURE 13–4
Percentage of Income Paid in Sales and Excise Taxes by Selected Economic Groups

Source: Michael Ettlinger et al., Who Pays? A Distributional Analysis of the Tax Systems in All 50 States (Washington, D.C.: Citizens for Justice, June 1996), 1–2.

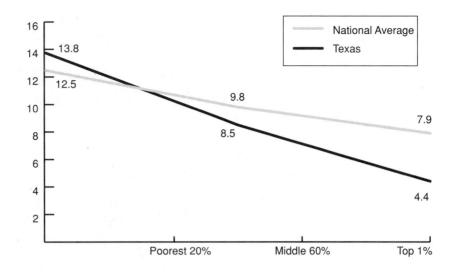

replace all or part of it. But the state's conservatism and the dominance of business lobbies in the state government have thus far precluded the adoption of a progressive tax policy. Moreover, as the twentieth century draws to a close, resentment against the U.S. Internal Revenue Service and the federal income tax is carried over into state politics and makes tax reform virtually impossible.

Taxes Paid by Individuals. A number of taxes are levied directly against individuals, for example, the *inheritance tax,* collected at the time beneficiaries inherit estates; the *motor fuels tax,* paid each time a motorist buys gasoline; and the *ad valorem property tax,* collected on real property, buildings, and land by local governments.[21] Businesses also pay the motor fuels tax and local property taxes, of course, but by increasing prices they let their customers pick up the tab.

Most authorities also would include all sales taxes in the category of taxes paid by individuals on the assumption that businesses pass them on to the consumer just as they do local ad valorem and state vehicle registration taxes—whether that is the intention of the law or not. There are two types of individual sales taxes:

1. The general sales tax is a broadly based tax that is collected on most goods and services and must be paid by the consumer. It is illegal for a business to absorb the tax—for example, as a promotional device. This familiar tax was first adopted in Texas in 1961, with a 2 percent rate. Nationally, Mississippi was the first state to have a sales tax, but twenty-nine other states adopted the tax during the Great Depression of the 1930s. Some basics such as prescription medicine, food purchased at grocery stores, and work clothes are exempt from the Texas tax. Originally, many exemptions existed, but these become fewer and fewer with each legislative session.

---

21. The state ad valorem (property) tax was abolished by a 1982 constitutional amendment.

2. Selective sales taxes (excise taxes) are levied on only a few items, comparatively speaking, and consumers are often unaware that they are paying them. These taxes are included in the price of the item and may not even be computed separately. Tobacco products, alcoholic beverages—tobacco and alcohol taxes are sometimes called "sin taxes"— automobiles, gasoline, rental of hotel rooms, and the admission price for amusements (movies, plays, nightclubs, sporting events) are among the items taxed in this category.

Taxes paid by individuals account for 37 percent of the state's revenue, almost three times what taxes paid by businesses account for.

Taxes Levied on Businesses. Taxes levied on businesses in Texas produce considerable revenue for the state but are often regulatory in nature. One example is the *severance taxes* levied on natural resources, such as crude oil, natural gas, and sulfur, that are severed (removed) from the earth. Their removal, of course, depletes irreplaceable resources, and part of the tax revenue is dedicated to conservation programs and to the regulation of production; thirty other states have similar taxes. Severance taxes once were the backbone of the state's revenue system, but the steady decline in the oil business for more than a decade has resulted in these taxes contributing less than 2 percent of current revenues.

The major Texas business tax today is the *corporation franchise tax,* which is assessed against corporations as the price of doing business in the state. Some people regard it as a type of corporate income tax because the business pays tax on whichever amount is greater, invested assets (capital) or income. This tax was overhauled substantially in 1991 to make it fairer, since it originally emphasized taxes only on capital-intensive businesses such as manufacturing and collected little from labor-intensive businesses such as computer software firms, financial institutions, and even the big downtown law firms. The tax is expected to provide at least 8.6 percent of the revenue for FY 1998–99.

Gross receipts taxes are levied on the total gross revenues (sales) of certain businesses: cement production and gas, electric, and water companies are two major examples. Among other taxes levied directly on businesses in Texas is the *insurance premium tax,* levied on gross premiums collected by insurance companies. Miscellaneous *special taxes and fees* for such varied activities as chartering a corporation, brewing alcoholic beverages, and selling real estate also exist. Whenever possible, businesses pass these taxes along to consumers in the form of higher prices. Together they account for about 2.7 percent of the state's revenue.

All business taxes together account for 12.9 percent of the state's revenues. Thus, we have seen that nontax sources account for 50.1 percent; individual taxes, for 37 percent; and business taxes, for 12.9 percent.

WHO BENEFITS?

To address the question of who benefits from tax policies, we must consider the kinds of services the government provides. Nothing would seem to be more equitable than a tax structure resulting in an exact ratio between taxes paid and benefits received, and in Texas some taxes are levied with exactly that philosophy in mind. The motor fuels tax, 20 cents per gallon on gasoline and diesel fuel, is paid by those who use motor vehicles, and three-fourths of the revenues from this tax are spent on maintaining and building highways and roads. The remainder goes to public schools. However, the motor fuels tax also points up a problem with the "benefit theory" of taxation. People who do not own automobiles and do not buy gasoline also benefit from those big trucks hauling goods to market over state highways. The owners of an ambulance that transports an accident victim to a hospital buy the gasoline but may benefit far less from it than do the victim and her or his family and friends.

One of the "sin" taxes collected by the state is on tobacco. This tax is based on the philosophy that those who subject their bodies to the damaging effects of tobacco may be discouraged from doing so and thus benefit if they have to pay more money for the privilege. This tax has not stopped people from smoking, of course, and has become, in effect, a use tax. Those who smoke receive no special benefits from revenues from this tax, which are used for schools, parks, and general government functions. To conform to the benefit theory of taxation, the revenue from the tobacco tax would need to be spent for cancer research, the treatment of lung diseases, and other programs related to the effects of smoking.

Where There's Smoke . . .

In 1997 and 1998 individual states sued tobacco companies in an effort to recover the huge costs of treating smoking-related illnesses and conducting research on those ailments. Just before the case was to be heard in federal court in early 1998, the state and the tobacco industry settled the Texas case for a payment of $15.3 billion over twenty-five years. Two big controversies broke out immediately: paying the private attorneys the 15 percent of the settlement they had been guaranteed ($2.3 billion), and whether the legislative appropriations power included spending the money for programs totally unrelated to those included in the suit.

A strict benefit philosophy would have a disastrous effect on low-income citizens. For example, if all taxes were assessed on a pay–benefit basis, then the poorest citizens could not afford to educate their children, a situation that would only entrap them further in the cycle of minimal education, low-paying jobs, and marginal incomes. The extremely wealthy, on the other hand, could have their own police forces, four-lane roads to their weekend farms, and college classrooms with five-to-one student-teacher ratios. Society would hardly benefit from such a situation. Clearly, trying to apply a benefit theory of taxation, like all issues in taxation, is very difficult.

THE TAX BURDEN IN TEXAS

Texas has prided itself on being a low-tax state, but, in large measure, the state is misleading itself and the citizens by making this claim. While the *state* ranks forty-fourth in tax burden,[22] analysis in conjunction with the 1997 tax

---

22. Mary I. Sprouse and Teresa Tritch, "Stop Paying 50% in Taxes," *Money*, January 1995, 92–93.

debate (see below) made it clear that in terms of *combined state and local taxes,* the state was "just average." Figures from the Tax Foundation, a Washington think tank, and the U.S. Census Bureau revealed that the national median was 11.5 percent; the combined Texas state and local rate prior to the 1997 session was 11.1 percent, putting the state in thirtieth place.[23] These numbers imply that the state provides less aid to localities than do other states, forcing the local governments to rely heavily on regressive sales and property taxes. In other states, particularly those with an income tax, the state pays a greater portion of the cost of local government, especially schools.

One irony of the Texas tax situation is that the state does not fare well under many federal grant formulas, which include tax effort—the tax burden already borne by citizens—as a criterion. The state does least well on matching grants for social services and welfare. Although the state is third in total federal receipts, mainly from defense spending at military bases and with military contractors (see the earlier boxed item about pork barrel spending), only nine states have less *per capita* federal expenditure than Texas.[24] Typically, Texans contribute more in federal taxes to get back a dollar in federal grants than residents of other states. Moreover, because of the way deductions work in the federal income tax system, the Texas tax system costs Texans an estimated $331 million a year in extra federal taxes that would not have to be paid if the state relied on an income tax rather than sales taxes.[25] New Mexico is at the top of the list in terms of getting more money back than it paid in. New Jersey is at the bottom.[26]

LOOKING TOWARD 2000

PERSPECTIVES FROM THE PAST

For a half-century, Texas relied on oil and gas production taxes as the major source of state revenue, with most of these being paid by out-of-state purchasers. How good were the good old days? "Texas went from 1971 to 1984 . . . without an increase in state tax rates, or new taxes" while the population was growing 42 percent.[27] After the world oil market crashed, Texans were ill prepared to develop a responsible and responsive revenue policy to provide funds for state services. As the boxed item shows, the state got better at revenue measures, then benefited subsequently from a booming economy and some additional federal funds.

WHAT'S NEXT?

Texas will be no different from other governments in its need to find adequate *and* equitable revenue sources to support the services needed by a

23. Jane Seaberry, "Bursting the Myth," *Dallas Morning News,* April 29, 1997, 1D, 3D.
24. "Texas Is 3rd in Receipt of Federal Money," *Austin American-Statesman,* April 3, 1997, A10.
25. Dave McNeely, "No Texas Income Tax Means More for Feds," *Austin American-Statesman,* April 15, 1997, A11.
26. "Do You Subsidize New Mexico?" *Money,* January 1998, 23.
27. "Bullock's Tax Speech Serves as a Warning for State," *Austin American-Statesman,* January 27, 1991, A8.

rapidly growing citizenry and to make up for federal funding cuts that will have a major effect on the states. One strategy that the state will pursue is *cutbacks*, particularly funding cutbacks that are recommended in the biennial Texas Performance Review. The importance of the Texas Performance Review can only grow. For FY 1998–99, Comptroller John Sharp published his fourth annual "Disturbing the Peace" study, giving 428 proposals designed to improve services and to save $3.5 billion in state expenditures. In his words, "We hope to shake up the culture of complacency, expediency and indifference that tends to crop up when times are good. The main gains enacted since TPR began its work won't be consolidated if we lower our sights now."[28] The performance evaluation/cutback approach is grounded in a national movement to "reinvent government."[29] This demand emerged from strategic planning and quality management movements in the private sector as sluggish industries had to downsize—or, in the new terminology, "rightsize."

A Summary of Revenue and Spending Measures in the FY 1984–85 to FY 1997–98 Period

FY 1984–85—broad-based $4.8 billion revenue package to provide additional funding for highways and public schools; major increases in user fees

FY 1986–87—$512 million in budget cuts, $872 million in new taxes

FY 1988–89—$5.7 billion in new taxes; intensive study by a Select Committee on Tax Equity, whose recommendations were subsequently ignored

FY 1990–91—legislative authorization of a 12 percent *spending* increase by fiscal sleight-of-hand tricks such as using the money reserved to settle lawsuits against the state; another tax study that was ignored

FY 1992–93—initiation of the governor's Texas Performance Review (TPR) spearheaded by Comptroller John Sharp, leading to $382 million in budget cuts—not all of which materialized, leading to other cuts in agency budgets for FY 1993; thirty new revenue measures, including a major restructuring of the corporation franchise tax, totaling $2.6 billion; voter approval of a state lottery

FY 1994–95—$2 billion in increased revenues without any tax increase as a result of measures such as TPR savings on Medicaid and changes in tax collection schedules; voter approval of a constitutional amendment limiting the possibility of an income tax to simultaneous local property tax relief

FY 1996–97—$9.8 billion in increased revenues without any tax increase as a result of an improved economy, more federal contributions, more lottery revenues

FY 1998–99—constitutional amendment to triple the homestead tax allowance for school districts; more than a $7 billion *spending* increase as a result of a strong economy, federal funds, and a big surplus; failure to produce a bill incorporating recommendations from the governor's tax study

28. John Sharp, "Disturbing the Peace," *Fiscal Notes*, January 1997, 10 (online version: www.window.state.tx.us). See also Jan Jarboe, "John the Knife," *Texas Monthly*, March 1994, 106–16.

29. See for example, David Osborne and Ted Gaebler, *Reinventing Government* (Reading, Mass.: Addison-Wesley, 1992), especially Chapter 5, "Results-Oriented Government"; Jonathan Walters, "The Cult of Total Quality," *Governing*, May 1992, 38–41; and the many reports stemming from the Texas Performance Review and the National Performance Review. See also Julia Melkers and Katherine Willoughby, "The State of the States: Performance-based Budgeting Requirements in 47 out of 50," *Public Administration Review*, 58 (January/February 1998): 66–73.

The legislature struggled in 1997 to produce tax relief, but the only "fish" it landed was to use the $1 billion budget surplus for property tax relief.

Courtesy of Ben Sargent.

Another strategy is *privatization*. The state's big experiment in partially privatizing the welfare system and its struggles with Washington for approval are chronicled in Chapter 14. Another example is the private prisons that now serve the state.

A third strategy is to *change the revenue structure* in order to avert the **revenue shortfalls**—insufficient funds to cover spending needs—that plagued the state in the 1980s. At the same time, public demand for local property tax reduction and greater equity might be achieved by such changes.[30] The dominant issue of the 1997 legislative session was, in fact, revenue restructuring.

Democratic theory recognizes the equality of the citizenry, and many people think that a tax system that extracts more from people the poorer they are seriously compromises equality. Since 1991, business has paid a greater share of taxes, but, as we have noted, the tax system in Texas is still regressive, placing a proportionately heavier burden on those with the lowest incomes. The reality is that without an income tax, the state will always have difficulty meeting its revenue needs in anything other than a booming economy. Historically, Texas attracted businesses because they found a favorable tax structure in the state. However, the experience of other states with economic development indicates that many modern industries are also concerned about the stability of state services. Such stability is difficult in the absence of a flexible tax structure.

Another aspect of revenue structure is the competition among governments for tax sources. National and state governments both tax motor fuels, tobacco, and alcohol, for example, and both levels of government keep increasing tax rates. Both the state and local governments have general sales

30. See *Report of the Staff Work Group on Property Tax Relief, Part I* (Austin: Governor's Office of Budget and Planning, March 1996).

taxes. The upshot is that the combined tax rates begin to vex citizens after a while. Ironically, federal income tax rates were cut in the 1980s, enhancing the income tax as a logical new source of state revenue.

The work of the Seventy-fifth Legislature in 1997 illustrates the difficulty of tax restructuring. The governor made reduction of the local school property tax and elimination of the Robin Hood system of rich school districts making financial contributions to poor ones his number one concern. He proposed that the state pick up the slack for the schools by imposing a business property tax for school maintenance and operations, expanding the franchise tax to include all partnerships, eliminating exemptions from the sales tax, and increasing the motor fuels tax .

Although political observers claimed that the governor's plan was dead on arrival (DOA), both the House and the Senate produced tax bills. The bills varied significantly in the amount of local property tax reductions, the amount of the increase in sin taxes, whether to include new motor fuels taxes, and the amount of special business fees. The business lobbies went to work and effectively prevented the emergence of a compromise bill.

In the end, all that happened in the 1997 session was a proposed constitutional amendment that would increase from $5,000 to $15,000 the amount of valuation of a homestead that could be protected from taxation. The resulting revenue deficit for school districts was covered by a budget surplus (and perhaps by future taxes in years when there is no surplus). Legislators themselves were frustrated by the huge amount of work they had done with such a small result.

Sources: See, for example, Wayne Slater and Richard A. Oppel, Jr., "Legislature Abandons Tax Efforts: Bush Turns Focus toward Raising Homestead Break," *Dallas Morning News,* May 25, 1997, 1A, 32A; Shannon Noble, "Countdown to June 2," *Legislative Newsletter of the League of Women Voters of Texas,* May 29, 1997, 1–2; and Michele Kay, "Tax Overhaul Is Dead, Bush Declares," *Austin American-Statesman,* May 25, 1997, A1, A14–15.

For tax restructuring to occur, state politics will have to change. Businesses, including partnerships, are going to have to accept some sort of business activity tax that functions as an income tax, whatever it is called. Ultimately, private citizens are going to have to be willing to accept a personal income tax. Businesses accepted major changes in the corporation franchise tax in 1991, but the 1997 tax reform efforts ran into buzz saws wielded by groups such as law partnerships that escape the present system and by large corporations, which wanted to exempt dividends and interest that they received from out of state from the franchise tax. Only about one-third of private citizens now file an itemized federal tax return, so that one argument that traditionally favored an income tax—the ability to deduct state income taxes but not sales taxes from one's federal income tax return—may be dead, too. Changes in public attitude are critical to legislative action, since in the past mere advocacy of an income tax was a sure ticket out of office. As Jared Hazleton, former director of the Texas Research League stated: "The more the sales tax is broadened, the more it looks like an income tax in drag."[31] Thus, the state might just as well consider a real income tax on personal income, corporate net profits, or both.

---

31. Robert Reinhold, "For Texans, the Unthinkable: State Income Tax on the Horizon," *New York Times,* April 6, 1987, 1.

Former Lieutenant Governor Bill Hobby was fond of saying that "the [legislative] session is all about the budget; the rest is poetry." The budget is not just spending, but also revenues. In 1988, 1991, and 1996, high-level special committees studied the state's revenue system. Although Governor George W. Bush made tax reform his number one legislative issue in 1997, only minor tinkering resulted.

Courtesy of Ben Sargent.

Where Does the Money Go?

Occasionally an argument is heard in the state's legislative chambers that reflects serious concern about budgeting a particular program—who will benefit from it, whether it is needed by society, and how it will be financed. More generally, however, whether funds are allocated for a proposed program depends on which interests favor it and how powerful they are, who and how powerful the opposition is, and what the results are of compromises and coalitions between these and "swing vote" groups. The political viewpoints of the legislators, the governor, and the state bureaucracy also have an impact on budgetary decisions. In short, decisions about spending public money, like decisions about whom and what to tax, are not made objectively. Rather, they are the result of the complex relationships among the hundreds of political actors who participate in the state's governmental system. The biases of the political system are thus reflected in the biases of state spending.

This section outlines the stages in the budgetary process, then describes the state's major expenditures.

PLANNING AND PREPARATION

The budgetary process consists of three stages: planning and preparation, authorization and appropriation, and execution (spending). Budget planning and the preparation of the proposed budget is a function of the chief executive in the national government and in forty-four states, but Texas has a **dual-budgeting system.** The constitution makes the legislature responsible for the state budget. The legislature is aided in this task by the Legislative Budget

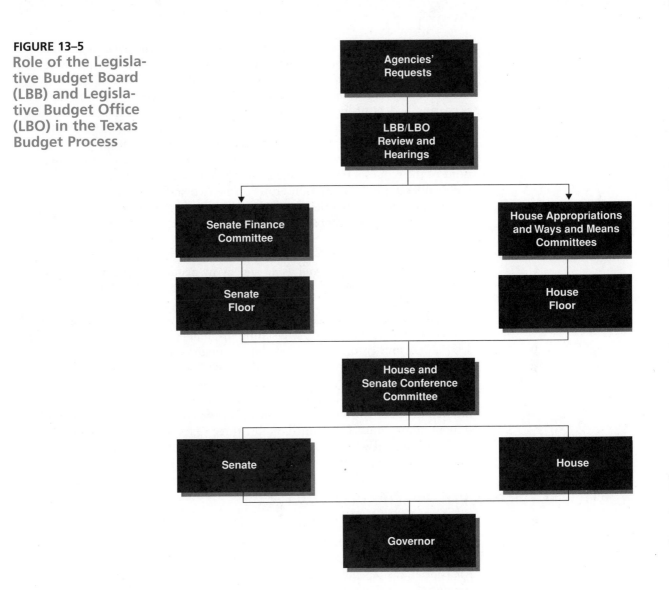

Board (LBB) and its staff, which prepare a draft budget. Four senators and four representatives compose the LBB, which is chaired by the lieutenant governor; the speaker of the House serves as the vice chair. Figure 13–5 depicts the workings of the LBB.

Modern governors have understood the importance of the budget as a political tool, and so, with the aid of the Office of Budget and Planning, the governor also prepares a budget. This duplicate effort is wasteful, but it does allow different political perspectives on state spending to be heard.

The two budgets agree in one respect: Both tend to be *incremental*—that is, both propose percentage increases or decreases for existing programs and the addition of new programs by way of feasibility studies and pilot programs. The recent emphasis on performance may at least give lawmakers a better picture of the real priorities of state agencies and how costs relate to benefits to the state.

Budget planning ordinarily begins in the spring of the even-numbered year before the year in which the legislature meets in regular session. Since 1992, strategic planning has been integrated with budgeting so that the LBB, the governor's office, and the agencies had a compressed time period for preparing budget proposals. State agencies submit their requests for the next biennium on forms prepared jointly by the governor's and the LBB's staffs. Then, at joint hearings, the two staffs try to obtain sufficient information from agency representatives about agency needs to make adequate evaluations of the requests from the agencies. These hearings are usually held in the early fall and are the final joint effort of the two staffs. At this time, individuals and outside groups—the state's dominant interest groups—also provide input. Each staff then prepares a budget that reflects the priorities of its office.

When completed, each document is almost two inches thick and provides summary information, as well as an agency-by-agency breakdown by specific budget categories. Both are submitted to the appropriate legislative committees for consideration.

Both budgets outline state expenditures for a two-year period. Completed in time for the opening of the legislature in January of one year (for example, 1999), they must project state spending through August two years later (2001), regardless of any changes in the economic outlook that may take place during that thirty-two-month period. Consequently, shifts in the funding of state programs may be needed. Certainly, when we realize that the constitutional directive for biennial legislative sessions means that the funding of state programs must be planned almost three years in advance, we more easily understand why the state budget planners lean toward incrementalism rather than rationalism.

AUTHORIZATION AND APPROPRIATIONS

The authorization and appropriation stage consists of the authorization of programs to be provided by the state and the passage of a bill appropriating money—the state budget. The House Ways and Means (revenues), House Appropriations (spending), and Senate Finance (both revenues and spending) committees are the key legislative players. Agency representatives, the governor's staff, interest-group representatives, and private citizens testify on behalf of the particular agency or program of concern to them. There is considerable forming and re-forming of coalitions as legislators, lobbyists, and committee members bargain, compromise, trade votes, and generally endeavor to obtain as much for "their side" as possible. Past campaign contributions begin to pay off at this stage, and the relative power of different interest groups is reflected in the state budget. For example, political campaigns frequently include a call to "get tough on crime" and to build more prisons; in turn, prisons are typically well funded. The four main teachers' groups in the state expend considerable effort in trying to influence legislators, and schoolteachers usually get raises, albeit often small ones. The success of the business lobby is the most problematic. In 1995, business got virtually everything it wanted. In 1997, business buried the tax bill it did not want, but also found itself on the receiving end of a lot of negative legislation.

The authorization and appropriation stage is a lengthy one, and the Appropriations and Finance committees submit their reports—the two versions of the appropriations bill—near the end of the session. Speaker Pete Laney and Lieutenant Governor Bob Bullock improved the process considerably, beginning in 1993, when they insisted on adequate time for review of the proposed state spending plan. The two versions never agree, so a ten-member conference committee composed of an equal number of senators and representatives carefully selected by the presiding officers must develop a single conference report on the budget, including adequate revenue measures to fund the proposed spending, since Texas has a balanced-budget requirement. The two houses must accept or reject the report as it stands.

The approved appropriations bill then goes to the governor for signature. The governor has a very powerful weapon, the line-item veto, this allows him to strike individual items from the appropriations bill if he disagrees with the spending provision. However, the governor cannot add to the budget or restore funding for a pet project that the legislature rejected.

EXECUTION/SPENDING

The actual disbursement of the state's income is rather technical and less interesting as a political process. It includes such details as shifting money into various funds, issuing state warrants and paychecks, internal auditing of expenditures by agency accountants, and external auditing by the state auditor's staff to ensure the legality of expenditures.

The major political issue involving budget execution has been efforts by several governors to gain greater control over spending between legislative sessions. In 1980 and 1981, voters defeated constitutional amendments that would have increased the governor's authority. The 1987 special legislative session resulted in some increase in the governor's authority to slow down expenditures. In 1991 the legislature not only empowered the LBB to move money from one agency to another agency based on performance, but also created a new tripartite body—the governor, the lieutenant governor, and the speaker—to deal with spending and reallocation.

A second political issue in budget execution concerns auditing. The state auditor, a legislative appointee, monitors state agencies and for many years has issued management letters directing agencies both to abandon and to implement different management practices. In 1988 Attorney General Jim Mattox issued an attorney general's advisory opinion that a legislative appointee could not constitutionally tell an executive agency head how to run the agency. However, with new powers granted in the tidal wave of performance-oriented reforms in 1991, the state auditor is now mandated to perform management audits.

Because the services delivered through state budget expenditures are of more interest to the average citizen than the technicalities of how the budget is executed, this section emphasizes a summary of spending on major state services. Figure 13–6 shows how Texas spends its money. Some of the program areas discussed here as objects of expenditure are discussed in Chapter 14 and throughout the book as significant political issues.

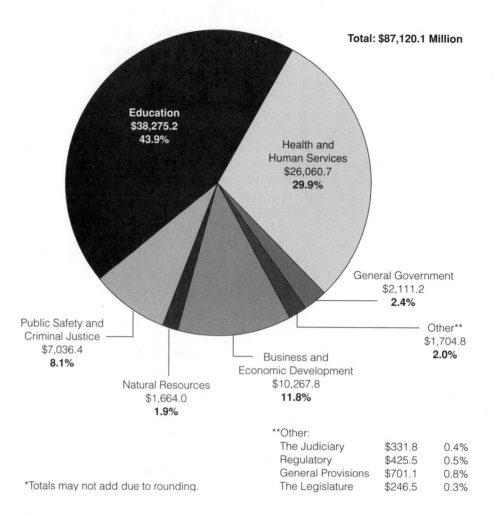

FIGURE 13–6
Texas State Spending by Function, 1998–99 Biennium, in Millions

Source: Fiscal Size Up: 1998-99, 1–2.

Total: $87,120.1 Million

Education
$38,275.2
43.9%

Health and Human Services
$26,060.7
29.9%

General Government
$2,111.2
2.4%

Other**
$1,704.8
2.0%

Business and Economic Development
$10,267.8
11.8%

Public Safety and Criminal Justice
$7,036.4
8.1%

Natural Resources
$1,664.0
1.9%

**Other:		
The Judiciary	$331.8	0.4%
Regulatory	$425.5	0.5%
General Provisions	$701.1	0.8%
The Legislature	$246.5	0.3%

*Totals may not add due to rounding.

EDUCATION

For FY 1998–99, 43.9 percent of the state budget was slated for public schools and higher education. More than three-fifths of the $38.3[32] billion education budget—$26.2 billion—was for elementary and secondary schools in the state's 1,044 independent school districts.[33] The state provides textbooks as well as special services such as programs for disabled children and vocational courses, the Texas Assessment of Basic Skills (TABS) achievement tests, school buses, operating costs, and teacher salaries. The state does not pay the total costs of public education, however. Local school districts share the cost and also are responsible for buildings and other school facilities. Those that can afford it provide supplements to attract the best teachers, buy additional library books, develop athletic programs, and offer students enrich-

32. Figures are rounded in this discussion.
33. The number of independent school districts as of 1997 was 1,044 plus 6 common districts, less than the number in the most recent Census of Governments. School districts continue to consolidate over time, but population growth and new communities have led to the creation of a few new districts.

ment opportunities. The state budget includes $1 billion to cover local revenue losses due to the mandatory increase in homestead tax exemptions approved by the voters in 1997. As we saw in Chapter 12, financial equality is the dominant issue affecting public schools.

The other big slice of the education-dollar pie—$11.9 billion—supports higher education: the operation of thirty-five general academic institutions, including six upper-level institutions and a marine science institute, three lower division centers, fifty community/junior college districts, a technical institute with three campuses and four extension centers, ten medical and dental schools plus related programs, and such services as agricultural and engineering extension programs. Higher education did not fare well in the state funding game for more than a decade, but in 1997, with the state treasury rebounding, the legislature paid attention to higher education. For both junior and senior colleges, a formula system based on such factors as semester credit hours determines the basic level of state support, with the formula funding supplemented by special program funding and affected by performance norms originally adopted in 1992. One positive piece of legislation in 1997 was creation of a greatly simplified funding formula. The community/junior colleges also are supported by local districts.

As we shall see in Chapter 14, higher-education funding is a continuing issue in Texas. Texas ranked thirty-ninth among the states in higher education funding, although it may have improved its ranking somewhat with the attention paid to higher education in 1997. New initiatives funded by the Seventy-fifth Texas Legislature included a "Back to Basics" program to assist the institutions in recruiting and retaining students, especially ethnic minorities.

The remainder of the education budget—less than $200 million—pays for such items as telecommunications improvement and state schools for the deaf and visually impaired. As of 1996, Texas ranked thirty-eighth among the states in per capita spending for all education programs combined.[34]

HEALTH AND HUMAN SERVICES

Over $26 billion—29.9 percent of the budget—is allocated for human services programs, including welfare, unemployment compensation, employment services, workers' compensation, services for special groups such as the blind and the elderly, and health programs such as mental health and retardation, substance abuse, contagious-disease control, and treatment for catastrophic illnesses such as AIDS, cancer, and kidney failure. Of the $26.1 billion total, about 58.4 percent of the funding comes from the national government. In Chapter 14, we will discuss changes in the health and welfare systems that have resulted in a reduction in the proportion of these costs paid with federal funds.

Although expenditures for health and human services are the second largest segment of the state budget, Texas ranked thirty-seventh among the fifty states in per capita expenditures for welfare services and twenty-third in hospital services. A major factor in the state's low ranking is the fact that the majority of the funding for these programs comes from federal grants, not

---

34. *Fiscal Size Up: 1998–99*, 3–10.

from the general revenues of the state. However, the state has moved from forty-seventh and thirty-sixth in these two service areas since FY 1990–91.

BUSINESS AND ECONOMIC DEVELOPMENT

Texas's expenditures for FY 1998–99 for business and economic development are almost $10.3 billion, 11.8 percent of the total budget. This category includes transportation; the Department of Commerce, which promotes the state's economy; the efforts of the Housing and Community Affairs Department on behalf of local governments; and employment and training services. Slightly more than one-quarter of the expenditures in this category come from federal highway matching funds to maintain and upgrade the 3,233 miles of federal interstate highways in Texas. In 1977 the legislature capped highway expenditures, with the result that the transportation portion of the state budget has declined from 21 percent to about 8 percent. Texas ranks forty-fifth among the states in per capita spending on highways. Rankings are not available for other services in this category.

OTHER MAJOR EXPENDITURES

The next largest category of expenditures is public safety at slightly over $7 billion, or 8.1 percent of the total budget. This category includes law enforcement, prisons, and related programs. Texas has the largest prison population in the country and employs 147 percent more corrections personnel than the national average.

The remainder of the budget, $5.5 billion, accounts for 6.3 percent of the expenditures in the state. Services, programs, and agencies in this category include general government—the legislature, the judiciary, the governor, and various management offices—as well as parks, natural resources, and regulatory agencies. For all of the general expenditures together, Texas ranked fiftieth among the states on a per capita basis.

Summary

Economic conditions, the political climate, and power plays are all part of the game of generating revenues for state government and determining how that income will be spent. Both taxing and spending are usually incremental, with major changes rarely occurring. However, the state's poor economic health through much of the 1980s and early 1990s meant more tax and fee increases than usual and less budget growth. That "downer" scenario clearly reversed itself for FY 1998–99, when both revenue and spending decisions were attributable to a robust economy.

In comparing Texas with other states, we find that the state tax burden is low while the local tax burden is relatively high, leaving the state in the middle of the ranking for combined state and local taxes. We also note the significant absence of any personal or corporate income tax, although business has been asked to pay a larger share of the tax burden through the corporation franchise tax. Another difference from most other states is the dual-budgeting system, coupled with the extraordinary dominance of the presiding officers in the appropriations process and the virtually absolute veto power of the governor as a result of the short legislative session. Important aspects of state finance in Texas are:

1. The reliance on taxes paid directly or indirectly by the individual

2. The reliance on regressive taxes such as the sales tax as a major revenue source for the state

3. The restrictions on borrowing

4. The importance of federal funds in the state budget

5. The extent to which the budgetary process is dominated by the legislature and the legislature, in turn, is dominated by the presiding officers

6. The obvious need for diversified revenue sources

The largest expenditure category is education, followed by health and human services, business and economic development, public safety and criminal justice, and "other," which includes everything else. Critical issues affecting some of these state service areas are discussed in the next chapter.

Key Terms

Block grants	Fiscal years	Regressive taxation
Categorical grants-in-aid	General revenue sharing	Revenue shortfalls
Dual-budgeting system	Inflation	Tax equity
Elasticity	Progressive taxation	User fee

Study Questions

1. What are the different sources of nontax revenue in Texas? How have these changed in recent years?

2. Give two reasons why Texas should adopt a personal income tax. Then, give two reasons against the state's adopting an income tax. With which side do you agree? Why?

3. Now think about a corporate net profits tax or a corporate income tax. Offer at least one reason favoring this kind of tax and one against offering this kind of tax. Do you think Texas will adopt either type of business tax in your lifetime?

4. This chapter has criticized both the regressiveness and the lack of elasticity in the Texas tax system. What does each of those terms mean? Give and discuss an example of each; then indicate what some of the revenue considerations are as we prepare to enter the twenty-first century.

5. What pitfalls do you think exist because of the dual-budgeting system? Do you think there are any advantages to such a system?

6. Throughout this chapter, the authors have made comparisons with other states. What similarities and differences can you identify?

7. If you could increase spending in any one of the six categories shown in Figure 13–6, which would it be? What if the total amount available had to remain the same? Would you still increase spending in that category? If so, in what category would you decrease expenditures to offset this increase? Discuss the likely effects on services in both the increased and the decreased categories of expenditure.

Internet Assignment

Internet site: www.window.state.tx.us/

Click on "The Texas Economy." Then read about the Texas economic outlook or the revenue forecast for the legislative session. What are the comptroller's projections for the Texas economy? Good times or bad times?

Chapter Fourteen

Issues in
Public Policy

Welfare lines in the midst of a boom symbolize one of the policy dilemmas facing Texas. Although the overall state economy is strong, and millions of citizens are prosperous, other millions, including the ones photographed here, remain mired in poverty.

The new federal welfare law gives states wide flexibility to create solutions for getting people into jobs. It also sets parameters, prescribes standards and penalizes states if they don't comply.
    Carl Tubbesing and Sheri Steisel, State Legislatures, 1997

There's no great secret that discrimination was—and is—alive and well. We have to confront it head on.
    Texas State Senator Royce West, Dallas, 1997

Water is like sex. Everybody thinks that there's more of it around than there really is and that everybody else is getting more than his fair share.
    Old Wyoming Saying

Introduction

Texas, like all other states, has an agenda of programs and services that it needs to address. These constitute the policy agenda for the state. When elected officials develop **public policy,** they are establishing priorities for programs that provide services and benefits to the public. However, agreement on what those priorities should be rarely exists. People even argue, sometimes intensely, about whether government should address some problems at all. Consequently, many controversial issues confront state policy makers. This disagreement and debate are part of a democratic society. Also, even when people agree on a particular issue, they may disagree about *how* to resolve the issue. Too, the fiscal health of the state (see the previous chapter) can complicate the policy agenda considerably. There is rarely enough money to fund all the desired programs, and so state finance itself becomes a major policy issue.

The development of public policy begins with the emergence of an issue that needs to be addressed. When someone in government recognizes the need to deal with a problem, it is placed on the policy agenda. One way in which a prospective program or service makes its way onto the policy agenda is through the efforts of the governor and key legislators (see Chapters 7 to 9). Often the gubernatorial and legislative viewpoints conflict, as was the case in 1997 when the governor could not get his tax reform bill passed by the legislature. Other times, these viewpoints coincide. For example, Governor George W. Bush campaigned on four issues—juvenile justice, education reform, tort reform, and welfare reform—and pushed all four through the 1995 legislature. Tax reform was discussed in Chapter 10; welfare reform is discussed in this chapter.

A second way in which a prospective program or service gets onto the policy agenda is through the political processes described in Chapter 4. Interest groups and lobbyists make known the priorities they think the state should set. These individuals and groups work through both elected officials and the bureaucracy, but they are especially vigorous in pursuing legislative support for their priorities (see Chapters 7 and 8). The water policy discussed in this chapter is an example of the coming together of legislative, bureaucratic, and interest-group concerns.

Another avenue for setting the policy agenda is through the *intergovernmental* system—the complex relationships among federal, state, and local governments—and through the *intragovernmental* system, the relationships that cut across the different branches of government. Often these relationships result in a **mandate,** a term that refers to an action of one government or branch of government that requires another government to act in a certain way. National clean air standards that must be implemented by state and local governments are an example.

Intergovernmental and intragovernmental mandates help policy makers to identify and define issues even when they would prefer to ignore them. Mandates are often burdensome to the lower level of government, which is required to act but receives no funding to help implement the new programs.[1]

Mandates can come about in several ways. These include the courts, administrative regulations, legislation, and/or highly publicized shifts in national priorities. For example, changes in Texas public school finance began in 1973 with a federal court order and continued with a 1987 state court order to provide a more equitable and "efficient" system of funding public schools.[2] Similarly, the state prison system was tied up in a long-running court suit from 1971 until 1993, when the suit was dismissed, as the state seemed headed in the right direction to correct historic problems such as overcrowding, abuse of prisoners, and poor health facilities.[3] Both of these issues are discussed in Chapter 12.

The welfare system in Texas is a product of the state's emphasis on efficiency, national budget cutting and changing national priorities, and state efforts to gain administrative approval from the federal bureaucracy. All states are struggling to provide adequate welfare services in the midst of federal changes. The transition from welfare to workfare is discussed in this chapter.

An example of intergovernmental influence through administrative regulations is environmental standards. Across the country, states are trying to deal with provisions of the Clean Water Act, the Safe Drinking Water Act, and the Clean Air Act. As we shall see in this chapter, Texas is one of the states that is furthest from meeting the national standards. Texas has problems in meeting federal standards because, despite improvements in its pollution of the ground and streams, it still ranks first among the fifty states in the quantity of toxic **pollutants** released into the air. One price the state pays for housing the largest petrochemical industry in the country is a large volume of

---

1. Marcella Ridlen Ray and Timothy J. Conlon discuss the high price of unfunded mandates on the American states in "At What Price? Costs of Federal Mandates since the 1980s," *State and Local Government Review* 28 (Winter 1996): 7–16. Janet Kelly, in "Institutional Solutions to Political Problems: The Federal and State Mandate Cost Estimation Process," *State and Local Government Review* 29 (Spring 1997): 90–97, looks at the problem of determining costs in order to comply with PL 104-4, the Unfunded Mandates Reform Act.

2. See *San Antonio Independent School District et al.* v. *Rodriguez,* 411 U.S. 1 (1973) for the appeal. The case was originally styled *Rodriguez* v. *San Antonio ISD,* since Rodriguez instituted the suit. Then see *William Kirby et al.* v. *Edgewood Independent School District et al.,* 777 S.W.2d 391 (1989) for the state case on appeal. Originally, the Edgewood ISD sued Kirby, who was commissioner of education.

3. *Ruiz* v. *Estelle* (666 F.2d 854, 1982, and 650 F.2d 555, 5th Cir., 1981). Ruiz was a prisoner and Estelle was the head of the prison system.

toxic wastes. Other industries produce different toxic wastes, such as those polluting the Ogallala aquifer from the Pantex weapons plant in the Panhandle and agricultural use of pesticides and fertilizers.

Highway construction also shows a sensitivity to changing national priorities. For example, the state's spending on highways was intentionally decreased in 1977 but rose temporarily in the 1980s because of federal funds that were made available to refurbish and to complete the interstate highway system. Federal funding was held back for years, although a reliable transportation system is fundamental to economic development. As we shall see, the Texas Department of Transportation (TX-DOT) can address only a fraction of the need for new roads and highway improvements. Local governments are thus challenged to find other funding for costly surface transportation without adequate state or national government help.

Another example of how public policy gets set is the intragovernmental example of state-assisted higher education in Texas. A public university is a state agency, just as is the Department of Human Services or the Department of Parks and Wildlife. As will be discussed later in this chapter, the 1997 legislature, after years of ignoring higher education, enacted rules governing a number of procedures that had previously been regarded as local business for the institutions. In doing so, the legislature was giving explicit instructions to executive branch agencies.

Although the mandates may be difficult to implement, they are not the causes of society's problems. Urbanization, industrialization, inflation, depletion of natural resources, the world oil market, citizen demand, and the curtailment of federal funds to state and local governments are among the causes. Because new and different problems constantly emerge, we cannot even conceive of all the problems that are on the Texas policy agenda.

Nor can this chapter explore even all the major items on that agenda. Some issues—the state budget, local government politics and finance, campaign finance, redistricting, civil liberties, education reform, and tort reform, for example—have been discussed elsewhere in this book. Other issues that are not discussed here include the need for deinstitutionalization of the mentally retarded, child care and child abuse, care of the elderly, illegal aliens, substance abuse, and acquired immune deficiency syndrome (AIDS). Simply put, the chapter discusses a sample of the diverse issues on the agenda—economic development (the business of business), poverty and welfare, saving the environment, higher education, and transportation—to illustrate policy making in the nation's second largest state.

Some of these issues, such as poverty and welfare, are favorites of progressives and liberals. Others, such as economic development, have traditionally been of greater interest to conservatives but are becoming more important for everyone. Others, such as education, create widespread concern. The reader who keeps track of what the governor requests and what the legislature does every two years can get an idea of which political forces are dominant at any given time. Certainly, state policy makers find it more to their liking to deal with economic issues, which fit the conservative culture of the state, than with social issues, which they often address only by trying to "reform" current policies and practices that deal with social problems.

Readers are also reminded that, through the early 1990s, the Senate was more progressive than the House and kept issues such as education, the environment, and social programs on the agenda. Since 1992, the Senate has grown much more conservative, and the two houses are more nearly alike. Also, the House has become prone to bickering as it has grown more partisan. For all the issues, the cast of characters is constantly changing. It includes elected officials—the governor and other state executives, legislators, and judges, as well as their national counterparts—plus bureaucrats, representatives of various general and special-interest groups, the media, local governments, business, and industry. In addition, public opinion changes as interpretations of any given situation become known.

The issues the state chooses to address and how state policy makers attempt to solve public problems permit another examination of how democratic the Texas political system is. Do policy makers try to deal with a wide variety of issues affecting all citizens? Or do they mainly look at issues placed on the agenda by political elites? Can they solve contemporary problems in the context of a conservative political culture when many of the issues stem from the needs of the "have-nots" of society, who traditionally have been supported by liberals? Do they consider alternative viewpoints? Can their policies be implemented effectively, or are they merely "smoke and mirrors" that seem to address the problem?

Overall, state policy makers have coped reasonably well. It is true that Texas, when compared with other states, tends to rank toward the bottom in many service areas. It is equally true that the state is sometimes slow to respond to emerging issues. However, state officials cannot proceed at a pace faster than that at which the public is willing to move and to fund. One of the awkward aspects of democracy is that following majority opinion does not always lead to wise or swift policy decisions.

The Business of Business

Chapter 13 reviewed the Texas economy since the mid-1980s and its effect on state finance. The state slid from boom to bust, in part because of depressed oil and agricultural prices and of fluctuations in the American dollar that heavily influenced the state's ability to market its agricultural products abroad. All of these factors were beyond the state's control. Once oil and agriculture weakened, spin-off effects included sharp declines in banking, the savings and loan industry, real estate, and construction. While the national focus shifted away from the oil states in the early 1990s as the troubled economy in New England and on the West Coast became more evident, Texas was still struggling to right the economic ship that had capsized in the 1980s. However, by the late 1990s, the Texas economy was booming again.

When Texas or any other state attempts to rebuild its economy, two basic strategies are available: recruiting major new industries or government installations and retaining and even expanding existing businesses, particularly small businesses. Sometimes, relying on major new industries or government installations can create problems. For example, after partially completing the superconducting supercollider in Ellis County, Congress killed the project in 1995. Ann Richards, when campaigning in 1990 and later through her tenure as governor, stressed jobs, jobs, and more jobs. George W. Bush made it clear in his 1994 campaign that he thought that the once-hospitable Texas business climate (see Chapter 13) had become much too inhospitable and that the state must correct the problem. Policies enacted by the 1995 legislature addressed Bush's concerns, but, as this chapter later discusses, for all its seeming robustness as 1997 drew to a close, the future growth of the Texas economy was still regarded as problematic in a major national ranking.

Economic prosperity is an issue for everyone in the state. It is supported by ethnic minorities and Anglos, by men and women, by Republicans and Democrats, by urbanites and rural interests. If the number of jobs is insufficient, if the markets for manufacturing and agricultural products are inadequate, if businesspeople cannot secure loans that enable them to expand, we are all affected. As is so often the case, however, tactics for achieving prosperity are open to debate. Conservatives think that government's role should be to create conditions that allow business and industry to grow, and that if business is healthy, prosperity will "trickle down" to the ordinary citizen. Liberals think that government should intervene more directly and ensure that ordinary workers are aided by such policies as a minimum wage, mandatory benefits, and health and safety programs.

A DECADE OF POLICY INITIATIVES

Texas developed a number of policy initiatives to promote the return to prosperity, and then to continue economic vitality. The measures described below are policies that pertain directly to business. However, equally important are measures described elsewhere in this chapter and this book to improve education, provide more adequate transportation, and improve the quality of life of Texans.

DEPARTMENT OF COMMERCE

The state began to rebuild the economy in 1987 when the legislature created a Texas Department of Commerce (TDC) to integrate most of the twenty-one separate programs, funds, offices, and commissions dedicated to economic development and related activities. TDC activities include workforce development and job training grants, block grants made for community development, tourism development, loans for exporters, small and minority-owned business programs, general business development, business expansion services, fine arts programs, advanced technology funds, and international trade and foreign office representation.

The TDC developed a reputation for spending money in ways that mainly benefited the governing board and key administrators and not the state of Texas. One of Governor Ann Richards's first acts after she was inaugurated in January 1991 was to tackle the reorganization of the commerce department. Ultimately, she gained control of the executive director's position.

WORKERS' COMPENSATION

A second major policy initiative was the revamping of the **workers' compensation** program in 1991. Workers' compensation is a program that provides income assurance for a worker injured on the job. The procedures and especially the costs of the program affect businesses of all sizes, from the local "Making the Cut" lawn-mowing service to the J. C. Penney Corporation, which is headquartered in Plano. The 1991 reforms were designed to move Texas away from a system that resulted in the state's having simultaneously the highest costs and the lowest benefits of any U.S. state. The complex 1991 legislation covered such diverse issues as mandatory safety programs, fraud, self-insurance, and a source of revenue for the insurance fund. Yet evolving a workable "workers' comp" program has not been an easy task.

By 1994, the state had returned to a situation of high costs and low benefits—it had the third highest costs to employers in the country and among the lowest weekly benefits, according to a national actuarial firm.[4] However, the costs were still lower than in 1991. Texas was not unique in its workers' compensation problems,[5] and the state took further steps to lower the costs to industry. Organized labor then brought a court challenge to the system, complaining that the lowered costs were directly at the expense of workers and their benefits. In 1995 the Texas Supreme Court ruled against the workers. By late 1996, not only was the system solvent, but also the workers' compensation fund had become a big money-maker. Even after the payouts to workers, the fund rebated $600 million to insurance companies.[6]

LEGISLATIVE BOON OF 1995

In 1995 the legislature addressed numerous business issues—so many that we could almost say that the business of the state is business. The thrust of the actions was to try to protect and develop Texas businesses—even at the expense of the environment and the consumer—and to increase their profitability. The legislation reflected a belief that helping business would result in a healthier economy and more jobs for Texans. The 1995 probusiness legislation included the following:

★ Tort reform to limit frivolous lawsuits and the amount of damages corporations might have to pay (see Chapter 12)

★ The "Southwestern Bell/GTE bill," a law restricting access to local phone lines by big, national long-distance carriers desiring to move into local phone service that is a huge boon to the two largest local phone companies

★ Reversal of previous legislation requiring the state to convert its vehicles to propane or natural gas—a victory for oil companies

★ Continuation of the "phantom tax" on utilities that allows power and telephone companies to pass along "taxes" that are really nothing more than devices for helping to defray the operating costs of the companies and maximize their profits

★ Reduction of insurance rates due to expected increases in insurance profits because of the limits on lawsuits

---

4. "State Seeks Savings in Workers' Comp," *Austin American-Statesman,* June 5, 1994, B2.
5. Brenda Trolin, in "Can Workers' Comp Work," *State Legislatures,* May 1992, 33–37, examines the problems and attempted solutions in various states, with Texas being prominently mentioned in the report.
6. Richard A. Oppel, Jr., "Workers' Comp Facility Goes on the Sales Block," *Dallas Morning News,* October 27, 1996, 1H, 8H.

★ Restrictions on the City of Austin's ability to regulate its environment in favor of high-powered developers (see the environmental discussion later in this chapter)

One area of activity that the legislature was not in a mood to support was historically underutilized businesses (HUBs), typically owned by minorities and women. Only through riders to the appropriations act did any HUB provisions survive.

Legislative generosity worked in part. Even the rural economy began to recover, at least as much as the weather would allow.[7] Texas outproduced all other states in cattle, crude oil, natural gas, and exports to Mexico,[8] according to a report produced by the state comptroller in 1997.

1997 ACTIONS

Although the 1997 legislature was more Republican—and thus presumably more probusiness—than in the past, legislators did not have a big agenda for business interests. The only tax cut measure that survived the session helped homeowners but not businesses. Bankers got a long-sought chance to lend people money based on the equity (amount of principal invested) in their homes, but with numerous restrictions. (Both of these measures required constitutional amendments, which passed.) Business failed to get further relief from lawsuits, health maintenance organizations were made liable for malpractice, deregulation of the electric industry died aborning, and new regulations to control teenage smoking and drinking placed the enforcement burden on business proprietors.[9]

ONGOING CONCERNS

Texas moved from the economic doldrums to economic prosperity in the 1987–1997 decade. Yet the state still has problems. Two separate rankings of the business climate illustrate those problems. The Corporation for Enterprise Development, a Washington, D.C., research firm, gave Texas these marks at the end of 1996:

★ Economic Performance: D. This category included earnings and job quality, equity (the gap between rich and poor), and employment. Many jobs are low-paying and foster a widening of the gap between rich and poor citizens.

★ Business Vitality: A. This category included business competitiveness, entrepreneurial energy, and structural diversity. The number of business starts and job growth in new companies helped the state earn the high grade.

---

7. Patrick Barta, "As the Economy Hums Along, Rural Population Recovers, Too," *Wall Street Journal*, November 5, 1997, T1, T3.
8. "Texas Rankings," *Fiscal Notes* (Texas Comptroller of Public Accounts), August 1997, 2.
9. Richard A. Oppel, Jr., "Business Laments Setbacks," *Dallas Morning News*, June 5, 1997, 1D, 12D.

★ Development Capacity: C. This category included human resources, technology resources, financial resources, **infrastructure** (roads, water systems, and other expensive public installations), and amenity resources. A major factor in the mediocre rating was the quality of the educational system.[10]

The in-state publication *Texas Business* was not much kinder in mid-1997.[11] The workforce climate earned a B−, with a note that the grade was rapidly slipping to a C− because of a lack of the skilled workers and college graduates needed to attract industry to the state. The regulatory environment also was graded B−, but slipping, because of the paperwork requirements of the major state regulators—the Texas Railroad Commission, the Texas Natural Resources and Conservation Commission, and the Secretary of State's Office—as well as city and county regulations. One should keep in mind that the magazine is published to meet the needs of business in the state.

The weakness of the state's educational system and problems with its job training programs are negative factors in the recruitment of new business and industry. The average per capita income in Texas is only 91 percent of the national average—a sign that job growth is more than likely in low-paying service industries. Some problems such as the cost/benefits ratio of workers' compensation will continue to resurface. Finally, the issue of equitable taxes will resurface, not only from the standpoint of individuals but also from the perspective of the fairness of business taxes. Several provisions in the corporate

10. Michael Totty, "It May Be Time for Texas to Rethink Business Plan," *Wall Street Journal,* September 24, 1997, T1.
11. Richard Seline, "Grade Deflation," *Texas Business,* July 1997, 20–21.

franchise tax, revamped in 1991, have proved to be nettlesome, particularly to the state's financial community.

The official state forecast is much brighter. The monthly publication of the state comptroller, *Fiscal Notes,* covers a different aspect of the economy each month. Taken collectively for 1997, the comptroller's forecast is for increasing diversity in industry, continued job growth, slow but steady improvement in the ratio of Texans'average annual income to that of the nation, and expansion of manufacturing capacity. However, the comptroller also warns of the need to improve the infrastructure, particularly highways and bridges, and the educational system.[12]

Poverty and Welfare

Conservative agendas have been dominating national and state politics in the 1990s. Texas politics has long been characterized this way. In short, for reasons that were discussed in Chapters 4, 5, and 6, the viewpoints of individuals in upper-income brackets often dominate public policy. This political fact of life is particularly important when we examine the issues of poverty and welfare. Whenever the government attempts to improve the quality of life for the poor, it is producing **redistributive public policy**[13]—that is, policy that redistributes wealth from those who have the most to those who have the least. Inevitably, then, poverty and welfare politics produces strong emotions and sharp political divisions. In Texas, with its conservative political tradition, feelings run especially high because much of the public, and some policy makers, believes that people are poor because they deserve to be. That philosophy was graphically expressed by nineteenth-century philosopher William Graham Sumner as "A drunkard in the gutter is where he ought to be, according to the fitness and tendency of things."[14] Other policy makers, more compassionate in their beliefs, see the problems as caused, at least in part, by society, and think that government must address social problems. These two positions represent irreconcilable differences in philosophy and lead to vigorous debate whenever poverty is on the political agenda.

Any state's role in combating poverty and seeing to the welfare of its citizens is a mix of both state policy and federal programs. As this section shows, because of changes in national policy, Texas, which has traditionally relied on federal funds for its welfare programs, has had to make changes in its own welfare system.

POVERTY IN TEXAS

The **poverty threshold** for a family of three was $13,716 for fiscal year (FY) 1998 and is estimated at $14,090 for FY 1999. Typically, the threshold for a

---

12. See especially Dan Hoyte, Fran Sawyer, and Michelle Spoonemore, "Economic Destiny," *Fiscal Notes,* October 1997, 10–12.

13. See, for example, the policy discussion of Randall B. Ripley and Grace A. Franklin, *Congress, the Bureaucracy, and Public Policy,* 5th ed. (Monterey, Calif.: Brooks/Cole, 1991), Chapters 1 and 6.

14. William Graham Sumner, *What Social Classes Owe to Each Other* (Caldwell, Idaho: Caxton Printers, 1970, originally published in 1883), 114.

family of four is about 25 to 28 percent higher than for a family of three.[15] Twenty percent of all Texans fell below this line, which demarcates the truly poor from the almost poor. Texas and Kentucky were tied for fifth in the percentage of the state population living in poverty, with only Mississippi, Louisiana, New Mexico, and West Virginia ranked higher.[16] As noted in the previous discussion, even though Texas led the country in the number of new jobs created, many of those jobs were low-paying. As a result, the average income per person in Texas was $2,200 less than the national average.[17] Ten of the forty-nine poorest counties in the country are in Texas. One-fourth of Texas children live in poverty, and almost half are eligible for the free/reduced-rate school lunch program. Half of these poor children live in families that have at least one working parent. Over a million children rely on Medicaid and on food stamps.[18] The reality is that the very young and the very old, especially females, are the most likely to be poor. Rural south and southwest Texas and the ghettos and *barrios* of the largest cities have the highest number of poor people.[19]

A special issue in Texas and in the nation is homeless people. The Dallas City Council embarrassed itself and the city in 1994 by first announcing that it would provide some minimal services—port-a-potties, running water, and trash cans—to the homeless people encamped under an interstate highway overpass, then indicating that the homeless people would be forced out of the location in less than a month, many months before a proposed new shelter would be built. Later the city delayed the evictions until June, when the weather warmed up. The city was being threatened by the federal government with a shutdown of the interstate for fear that it was being structurally damaged by fires that were built under it. Additionally, some analysts thought that the city was trying to clean up the downtown area before the World Cup soccer matches began.

THE PLAYERS AND THE PROGRAMS THROUGH EARLY 1998

The key players in delivering services to the needy in Texas are twelve administrative agencies that provide health, welfare, and social services—Department of Human Services (DHS); Department of Health; Department of Mental Health and Mental Retardation; Department on Aging; Commission on Alcohol and Drug Abuse; Commission for the Blind; Commission for the Deaf and Hard of Hearing; Interagency Council on Early Childhood Intervention Services;

15. *Fiscal Size Up: Texas State Services 1998–99 Biennium* (Austin: Legislative Budget Board, 1998), 5–20.

16. Diane Jennings, "Texas' Poverty Rate Up, Report Finds," *Dallas Morning News*, March 30, 1997, 13A.

17. *Fiscal Size Up: 1998–99 Biennium*, 3–3.

18. Bill Minutaglio, "Study Says Number of Texas Children in Poverty Could Rise if Social Services Are Cut," *Dallas Morning News*, April 27, 1997, 26A.

19. See David McLemore, "Child Poverty Soars," *Dallas Morning News*, October 10, 1993, 17A, 40A; Barbara Kessler, "Child Poverty at 25%," *Dallas Morning News*, November 12, 1996, 1A, 22A; "White Females Get Most Food Aid, Study Says," *Dallas Morning News*, March 10, 1998, 3A.

The two fastest-growing homeless groups are families with children and the deinstitutionalized mentally ill. The "hidden homeless" are so difficult to count that the national estimate of homeless people ranges from 300,000 to 3,000,000.

Courtesy of Ben Sargent.

Children's Trust Fund of Texas Council; Texas Rehabilitation Commission; Department of Protective and Regulatory Services; and Cancer Council. The Juvenile Probation Commission may also be involved. Overall policy is set by the Health and Human Services Commission, which acts through a commissioner appointed by the governor. Employment services and benefits are handled through the Texas Workforce Commission.

In Texas, programs to help needy citizens have long been funded primarily with federal dollars, supplemented by whatever additional funds the state was obligated to provide in order to be eligible for the federal dollars. The Texas Constitution places a ceiling on welfare expenditures. Since a 1982 amendment, that ceiling has been 1 percent of the state budget for general public assistance, so long as the state ceiling did not conflict with federal welfare program requirements. However, this provision is more flexible than the previous one, which was expressed in dollar amounts.

The national Social Security Administration provides direct case assistance for aged, disabled, and blind Texans through the Supplemental Security Income (SSI) program and channels funds to the DHS for the Temporary Assistance to Needy Families (TANF) program, which replaced the old Aid to Families with Dependent Children (AFDC) program. TANF, which is discussed further later in this chapter, is a program for families with needy children under age eighteen who have been deprived of financial support because of the absence, disability, unemployment, or underemployment of both parents. The U.S. Department of Agriculture administers the food-stamp program, passing dollars through the DHS. In Texas, eligibility for food stamps is the same as for TANF: an annual income below the federal poverty level. Medicaid, a program of medical assistance for the needy, is a joint federal-

FIGURE 14–1

Cash Value of Monthly Benefits and Services for a Typical TANF Family of Three,* FY 1998

*The typical TANF family in Texas consists of a single female caregiver and two children who receive no child support.

Source: Fiscal Size Up: 1998–99 Biennium, *based on data from the Department of Human Services, 5–22.*

Federal Poverty Level = $1,143

Total: $819

Medicaid
$316

Food Stamps
$315

TANF
$188

state program administered through the DHS. In Texas, the largest number of Medicaid recipients are children and their caregivers, but the greatest expense is for elderly and disabled recipients. TANF, food stamps, and Medicaid are the largest welfare programs. These programs all work in conjunction with one another, so that a person who is eligible to receive help from one program is usually eligible to receive help from one or more of the others. Although most states supplement these programs, Texas historically has chosen to provide "bare-bones" programs. Figure 14–1 illustrates the assistance that a typical welfare family received for fiscal year 1998: $316 for Medicaid, $315 for food stamps, and $188 for TANF. This typical family consisted of a mother and two children who receive no child support. At the time, maximum Texas payments amounted to $819 a month, while the federal poverty level was $1,143 a month. Thus, the Texas payments were still more than $300 below the amount needed to push recipients above the poverty line.

Table 14–1 shows the decreasing dependence of many Texans on food stamps and AFDC/TANF during the 1990s. Since food stamps can go to families or individuals with incomes below the poverty level who do not have minor children, the numbers for the two programs are not the same. Also, a TANF family receives a slightly higher allotment of food stamps. Many food-stamp recipients are the working poor. As Figure 14–1 indicated, the average was $315 for TANF families; for all families, food stamp assistance in FY 1998 averaged $229 a month for a household of three.

In addition to the two largest welfare programs—TANF and food stamps—other social services include day care, foster homes, energy assistance for low-income persons (to help with heating bills), and job training. As the discussion later in the chapter will verify, a particularly important part of these services is job training, since the conversion from AFDC to TANF is predicated on the assumption that most welfare recipients can be put to work. In all these programs, operationally the state gets most of its funding from the federal government, then, in turn, passes that funding along to local governments to administer the programs.

Health care is, of course, a problem affecting everyone, and problems shared by persons from all social classes tend to have a higher degree of

TABLE 14–1

Texas AFDC/TANF and Food-Stamp Households, FY 1994*–1999—Average Number of Monthly Recipients and Average Monthly Payment for a Family of Three

Program	1994	1995	1996	1997[†]	1998[†]	1999[†]
AFDC/TANF households	282,944 $181.64	274,458 $183.17	256,871 $183.51	219,863[‡] $183.51	177,058 $183.51	188,375 $183.51
Food-stamp households	1,033,985 $221	981,107 $228	921,010 $233	786,747 $229	685,252 $229	649,669 $229

*The peak year for number of recipients was FY 1994.
[†]Figures are not final.
[‡]AFDC became TANF in FY 1997.
SOURCE: *Fiscal Size Up: 1998–99 Biennium*, 5–23.

political support.[20] The Texas Department of Health and the Texas Department of Mental Health and Mental Retardation are the two largest agencies providing for the health needs of Texas citizens. State services range from programs for crippled children and for individuals with devastating diseases, such as cancer and tuberculosis, to rehabilitation of trainable people with mental impairments and the control of rabies in skunks. Although such programs are not restricted to the poor, their existence eases the burden of medical costs for less-well-off Texans. Additionally, a joint state-county system of indigent health care has existed since 1985. Medicaid, though often associated only with the financially needy, serves many constituencies and has income requirements that are very different—and much more complex—than those for food stamps or TANF. The lion's share—81.7 percent, or $10.45 billion—of Department of Health appropriations is spent on Medicaid clients.

Another related service is unemployment compensation—that is, payments to unemployed workers, administered by the Texas Workers' Compensation Commission. The TWCC is assisted by the Texas Workforce Commission, which not only supplies wage data but also assists individuals in finding jobs and keeps records of employment in the state. Unemployment compensation is a joint federal-state effort. The basic funding method is a tax on wages paid by employers, plus any surcharge needed to make the system fiscally sound, and reimbursements from governmental units for any unemployment benefits drawn by their former employees. If a state has its own unemployment compensation program and an agency to administer it, the employers can charge off most of the tax on their federal tax returns. If the federal government administers the program directly, employers cannot take advantage of the tax write-off. In Texas, unemployment benefits vary according to previous wage and disability status. In 1994, the range was $41 to $245, with an average of only $185 a week (the disabled unemployed receive about double the highest

---

20. For an excellent discussion of the importance of middle-class attitudes in the development of social programs, see Robert Morris, *Social Policy of the American Welfare State* (New York: Harper & Row, 1979), Chapters 1 and 2.

amount available to the able-bodied). A rough estimate of the maximum benefit in 1997 was $296 a week.[21] Benefits are payable for a period of up to twenty-six weeks except when the federal government extends the period.

RECENT LEGISLATION

TEXAS, 1995

Both as a reflection of the increasing conservative influence in the legislature and in anticipation of federal legislation, the state took a hard look at welfare in 1995. The Seventy-fourth Texas Legislature closely followed Comptroller John Sharp's plan for making welfare more cost-effective (see Chapter 10 for the performance review role of the comptroller). Legislation emphasized welfare recipients' responsibilities, chiefly an obligation to get training and find work and an obligation to sign an agreement with the state that stipulates agreement with these responsibilities. The legislation further required mothers of children receiving AFDC payments to identify the father and cooperate with efforts to get the father to pay child support. The Texas welfare reform act also restricted welfare payments to one to three years, depending on education and work experience, but did allow someone to return to the welfare rolls after being off for five years. The Texas approach to welfare reform also relied on technology, including fingerprint identification, electronic benefits transfer, and more use of the Lone Star debit card to deliver benefits. The state also went after "deadbeat dads" and "misanthrope moms" by passing very stringent legislation on child support that could result in forfeiture of professional, occupational, and recreational licenses for nonpayment of support by the noncustodial parent. The legislation even included a savings plan for the poor and recognized that the disabled did not belong in the welfare system but should be in the secure employment system.[22]

NATIONAL, 1996

In 1996 the U.S. Congress passed its own welfare reform bill, which was billed as an "experiment" until the year 2002. The massive bill was over five hundred pages in length and began to take effect in late 1996, with various parts being phased in later, especially during 1997. With Congress dominated by conservative Republicans, the national changes were similar to those made by the conservative state legislature in 1995—more rules and regulations, time limits to get people off welfare, and ways to save government money. Coupled with a devolution of responsibility to the states, these features explain the opening chapter quotation about the new federal welfare law.[23] The federal

---

21. *Statistical Abstract of the United States, 1996* (Washington, D.C.: U.S. Department of Commerce, Bureau of the Census, 1996), 378; *Fiscal Size Up: 1996–97*, 10–4; *Fiscal Size Up: 1998–99*, 3–3; and http://twcc.state.tx.us/408.html#408.061.
22. "New Laws of the Land," *Fiscal Notes*, September 1995, 1, 8.
23. For an excellent explanation of the new federal legislation and its consequences, see Carl Tubbesing and Sheri Steisel, "Answers to Your Welfare Worries," *State Legislatures*, January 1997, 12–19.

reform allowed five years of welfare support, but the time clock begins to tick from the first date a recipient receives a check, even if the person has extensive training to undergo. The federal requirement is that the individual be working within two years. The Texas requirement is for immediate participation in a work plan, but job training, parenting or life skills training, and education or literacy training are included within the definition of work.[24]

In their concern for changing a welfare system that clearly did not work well, politicians sometimes failed to address the fundamental reality of welfare reform, namely that the legislation forces single mothers of dependent children to go to work. "Workfare" means that these children will either be left alone all day or placed in day care, and this consequence would seem to contradict the conservatives' professed devotion to "family values." Less parental care is also likely to have the further consequences of more juvenile crime, poorer school performance, and thus, paradoxically, even more welfare dependency. Welfare reform legislation did not carry with it additional day-care funding.

The federal bill created a "cafeteria-style" welfare system for the states, with each state slated to receive a block grant for welfare support that the state could apportion among programs that the state judged as having the highest priority. AFDC was transformed into Temporary Assistance to Needy Families (TANF) in 1997, and the new program emphasized that individuals have no automatic entitlement to welfare support.[25] States had until July 1, 1997, to file a plan for TANF, with block grant funding to begin on that date or six months after submission of the plan, whichever was later. Proportionately less money will flow from Washington, and the states are allowed under the national legislation to slash their welfare payments by 20 percent with no loss of federal funds.

An especially troublesome feature of the national law for Texans was the end of benefits for *legal* aliens, as 20 percent of those in the nation live in Texas. Estimates released by the Texas Health and Human Services Commission a few days after the federal bill passed indicated a probable state loss of $153 million in food-stamp support for 186,572 legal immigrants; a drop in SSI payments of $178 million a year to 53,160 elderly and disabled legal immigrants; and the potential to end $441 million in Medicaid payments to legal immigrants, saving the state's $166 million share.[26]

 Conservatives in the U.S. Congress restricted payments to legal aliens both to save money and to emphasize the importance of U.S. citizenship. Should the state also refuse to support legal aliens who are poor? They have all the necessary and proper approvals for permanent residence in the United States and were at one point encouraged to emigrate here. They pay taxes. They contribute in many other ways to society. They deserve humane consideration.

24. "Welfare Reform, Part Two: A Kinder, Gentler Plan for Texas," *Texas Government News,* September 23, 1996, 2.
25. Mary Jo Bane, "Stand By for Casualties," *New York Times,* November 10, 1996, 13.
26. George Rodrigue, "Welfare Cuts May Hit Legal Immigrants Hard," *Dallas Morning News,* August 28, 1996, 1A, 16A.

Moreover, the principal welfare agencies in the state were concerned about far more than the legal immigrants, since 2.8 million Texans were receiving some form of public assistance when the federal law was passed. Some 12,500 disabled Texas children—about 10 percent of the national total—were destined for removal from the disability rolls under the new federal standards for SSI payments.[27] Also of grave concern was the long-term poverty concentrated in the counties bordering Mexico. In ten of those counties, more than one-third of all residents received food stamps and about one-tenth received welfare. In Zavala County, for example, the average wage is only $281 a week, so that a fully employed individual still lives in poverty. Even with enhanced job training, not enough new jobs were being created to handle the demand.[28] But the big cities also were the home of many poor people. In Harris County, which includes Houston, more than 400,000 people received food stamps, and almost one-quarter of the Dallas County population received them. In Harris, Dallas, Bexar, El Paso, and Tarrant Counties combined, well over 70,000 people received AFDC in 1996.[29] Both the Rio Grande Valley and the big cities of the state were hard hit by the federal changes that began in FY 1997. The number of legal immigrants receiving food stamps dropped from 168,517 to 47,582 statewide, for example, and to less than 39,000 in the five large counties previously mentioned.[30] The poor got poorer. They did not go away.

Governors across the land began to pressure Congress to back off from some of the more stringent provisions of federal welfare reform, especially the restrictions on assistance to legal immigrants.[31] Their greatest concern was elderly persons confined to nursing homes and disabled children. Even conservative Republican Senator Alfonse D. Amato of New York acknowledged the problem, saying, "What do we say to them? . . . Go out into the streets and become homeless?"[32] The U.S. Senate seemed disposed to provide stopgap coverage until the issue could be further addressed in the fiscal year 1998 federal budget. That "help" was questionable, since the proposed formula resulted in such disparities as payments of $8,333 each for the 30 legal immigrants in Wyoming and an average of only $281 a month for two months for the 32,410 Texas elderly and disabled immigrants.[33] Problems with the bill had not been dealt with when the legislation took full effect on October 1, 1997.

TEXAS, 1997

Texas in 1997 was not only trying to implement the welfare reform bill that the state had passed in 1995 but also trying to be prepared for the implementation

27. "12,500 Kids May Lose Benefits," *Austin American-Statesman*, August 17, 1997, B2.
28. Michael Totty and Patrick Barta, "Welfare Rolls in Rio Grande Valley Pose Dangerous Problem to the State," *Wall Street Journal*, October 22, 1997, T1, T3.
29. Diane Jennings, "Bracing for Welfare Change," *Dallas Morning News*, November 12, 1996, 1A, 12A.
30. Bill Minutaglio, "Food-Stamp Loss Strains Immigrants," *Dallas Morning News*, October 5, 1997, 1A, 16A.
31. Robert Pear, "Governors Limit Revisions Sought in Welfare Law," *New York Times*, February 3, 1997, A1, A10.
32. George Rodrigue, "Legal Immigrants' Fear of Losing Aid Grows as Deadline Closes In," *Dallas Morning News*, April 23, 1997, 1A, 9A.
33. Christi Harlan, "Texans Complain Formula Shortchanges Immigrants," *Austin American-Statesman*, May 2, 1997, A1.

of federal welfare reform. In an effort to save money, Texas had devised a plan to turn over administration of welfare to the private sector, with a potential savings of $120 million a year from laying off as many as 13,000 state workers. The governor promised to plow the savings back into programs for the needy.[34] After waiting since 1995 for the U.S. Department of Health and Human Services to approve the plan, the state was turned down on May 2, 1997, on the basis of a legal technicality that food-stamp eligibility decisions must be handled by government employees. The federal government said that Texas could privatize other aspects of the welfare system. The *New York Times* editorialized that the Clinton administration had focused on preventing a "policy triumph" by Texas Governor George Bush, who may be the opponent of Vice President Al Gore in the 2000 presidential race, rather than on the plan itself.[35] Advocates for the needy in Texas disputed the interpretation of the *Times* and pointed out that state as well as national welfare advocates opposed the plan because of concerns about accountability and using welfare as a profit-making service.[36] At the end of February 1998, Texas still had no plan approved by the federal government, but the national government up to that point was forgiving the possible fines that could be assessed for lack of compliance.

On the legislative front, the Seventy-fifth Texas Legislature included in the budget package $83 million in new Medicaid dollars for legal immigrants to take care of the elderly and disabled children.[37] Another $18 million was made available for food stamps for 28,000 disabled and elderly legal immigrants, although 93,000 more were not covered.[38] The state further created an "exceptions" provisions to the stringent new policy to allow benefits for persons who individually or whose parents had paid forty quarters of Federal Deposit Insurance Corporation (social security) taxes or who were in the U.S. military or married to someone serving in the military. Executive and legislative leaders were putting together a plan to reorganize government workers— "reorganize" means cutting out jobs, five thousand of them in this case—and make welfare "high tech" with a $200 million computer system.[39] The result was a bill permitting more parts of the state's welfare system to be parceled out to private business. Another bill provided incentives for business to hire welfare recipients. In 1996, Texas ranked twenty-second in the country in the percentage of adults on welfare receiving a newly created job.[40]

---

34. Judith Havemann, "Giving Welfare the Business," *Washington Post Weekly Edition,* March 17, 1997, 29.
35. "Another Bush Irks Clinton," *New York Times,* May 24, 1997, reprinted in the *Austin American-Statesman,* May 28, 1997, A19.
36. Patrick Bresette and Marcia Kinsey, "Welfare-Industrial Complex(ity)," *Austin American-Statesman,* May 30, 1997, A15.
37. William McKenzie, "Texas Tries to Pick Up Federal Burden," *Dallas Morning News,* May 20, 1997, 13A.
38. Bill Minutaglio, "Texas to Provide Food Aid to Some Legal Immigrants," *Dallas Morning News,* October 9, 1997, 1A, 27A.
39. Bill Minutaglio and George Rodrigue, "Texas Officials Revise Welfare-Overhaul Plan," *Dallas Morning News,* May 13, 1997, 1A, 10A.
40. Andy Dworkin, "Working to End Welfare," *Dallas Morning News,* June 12, 1997, 1D, 15D, and Wayne Slater, "Legislators End Session Dominated by Tax Issue," *Dallas Morning News,* June 3, 1997, 1A, 18A.

The signals sent during the 1995–1997 period were not entirely clear. One reading is that, despite the election of a set of officials who were even more conservative than those elected in the past, the state had developed a social conscience with regard to the needy. Indeed, if one looks at the legislation passed in other states—including lifetime ceilings on benefits, family caps, and lower benefits for new state residents—Texas has been rather liberal.[41] An alternative interpretation is that the state was mainly interested in money—finding ways not to spend state dollars on the poor and to get a bigger piece of the federal welfare pie. Beyond dispute is the fact that the welfare problem in Texas is tied to social divisions that rest on ethnic conflicts and struggles between the haves and the have-nots. Texas's border status ensures that its doors will be open to poor Mexicans seeking a better life in the United States. Its booming economy has blunted the effect of the federal welfare reform—by 1997, Texas had seen a 19 percent decline in its welfare caseload since 1994,[42] although the state still had one of the highest poverty rates in the country and still responded in only a limited way. Welfare is an issue that will be heard again in 1999 and beyond.

Higher Education

Higher education, more than any other policy area, seems to ride a roller coaster in Texas. In the 1970s and early 1980s, when the state was flush with funds from oil and gas taxes, a sort of national joke about "locking up the faculty so a Texas school won't get them" was told. When the state's budget surpluses turned to revenue shortfalls in the mid-1980s, higher education was the first program area to suffer, and it continued to suffer for a decade. Simply put, higher education represented the largest pool of budgeted funds available for reallocation. Public education, prisons, and mental health and retardation were all under court mandates to improve services. Welfare and highway programs were dominated by federal funding, not state dollars. Essentially, except as a source of funds for other programs, higher education was ignored until 1997.[43]

1984 TO 1997

There were some "pluses" during the "dark decade." A 1984 constitutional amendment provided a wider distribution of Permanent University Funds (PUF) to satellite campuses of the University of Texas System and the Texas A&M System and established a Higher Education Assistance Fund (HEAF) for capital expenditures for non-UT and non-A&M institutions. These expenditures

---

41. Jack Tweedie, "Building a Foundation for Change in Welfare," *State Legislatures,* January 1998, 26–33.
42. George Rodrigue, "Welfare Windfalls Examined," *Dallas Morning News,* February 19, 1997, 1A, 14A.
43. Higher education, K–12 education, Medicaid, and corrections are the "big four" of spending for state governments in the United States. See Ronald K. Snell, "The Budget Wonderland," *State Legislatures,* February 1998, 14.

include equipment, library materials, land, rehabilitation of older buildings, and new construction. In 1985 legislators created a science and high-technology research fund linked to the state's interest in attracting high-technology industries as a means of moving away from an economy dominated by oil.

The legislature also created a **Select Committee on Higher Education** with a wide-sweeping agenda to review higher education. That agenda encompassed educational quality, core curriculum, remedial education, teacher education, financial aid, management, accounting practices, research funding, the relationship between higher education and economic development, reorganization including mergers, and whether institutions should be organized into "tiers" of research institutions, general education institutions, and community colleges. The select committee report took the form of a Texas Charter for Public Higher Education, which was adopted by the Seventieth Legislature in 1987. In practical terms, the major impact of the charter was increased funding for both operations and research and, in exchange, increased state control. Community/junior colleges received little benefit from the charter.

From 1989 through the 1995 legislative session, higher education got modest increases that allowed it to stay more or less even with 1985 operations—but 1985 and 1986 were the primary budget-slashing years. The legislature seemed particularly willing to give small increases if the colleges and universities supported tuition increases.

To keep pace with enrollment growth, inflation, and other factors resulting in cost increases, the institutions began to raise dollars wherever possible. Particularly at the universities, students found themselves paying fees for almost everything as the institutions sought adequate operating funds, and graduate students on most campuses were asked to pay tuition rates above the state minimum.[44]

Although Texas institutions were hardly flush at the end of the 1980s and the beginning of the 1990s, they were often better off than their counterparts in other states. Some—Oregon, Virginia, and North Carolina, for example—had made major cuts in higher education.[45] The fact that higher education funding was troubled in a majority of the states by the early 1990s also prevented another faculty drain like the one Texas experienced in the mid-1980s.

In 1992, higher education had its own constitutional dilemma, parallel to the *Edgewood* decision on public school finance described in Chapter 12. The League of United Latin American Citizens (LULAC) filed suit against state officials, the Coordinating Board, and the officials of predominately Anglo universities, claiming that South Texas institutions were discriminated against in the allocation of graduate and professional programs in the state (the *LULAC* case). Ten days before the Texas Supreme Court's final ruling in the *Edgewood* case, District Judge Benjamin Euresti, Jr., of Brownsville ruled that the Texas system of higher education discriminated against the predominately Mexican-American border area of Texas and gave the state until May 1, 1993, to solve the problem or risk an order barring all higher education fund-

---

44. "Finance 101: Who's Footing the Bill for College Education," *Fiscal Notes*, May 1992, 1, 8–13.
45. Ellen Perlman, "Universities Receive Brunt of Cutting Ax," *City & State*, February 24–March 8, 1992, 1, 17; Richard Jones, "29 States Slash College Budgets," *U: The National College Newspaper*, September 21, 1991, 17.

ing.[46] Judge Euresti's ruling followed the logic of the *Edgewood* case, namely using the language of the Texas Constitution to determine that the educational system was unconstitutional because it was not efficient.

Additional higher education funds for FY 1992–93 went to address the problems spelled out in *LULAC*. The case merely made an already precarious funding situation worse. In 1992, the state ranked forty-fourth among all states in its funding per full-time student: $3,210 a year, about $1,100 below the national average. It ranked ninth among the ten most populous states in faculty salaries.[47]

As the state economy improved, higher education did receive increased funding for FY 1994–95 and FY 1996–97, although much of the money went to continue the South Texas initiatives mandated by the court. However, the HEAF program was reauthorized, and increasing enrollments were covered by the funding.

THE STATUS AFTER THE 1995 SESSION

At the end of the 1995 legislative session, four issues concerning higher education were obvious. First, higher education has an *image problem* that plagues it during legislative sessions. Elected officials often see higher education as composed of a group of affluent institutions that salt away their private contributions and revenues from auxiliary enterprises such as student unions, bookstores, and athletics while constantly seeking more state dollars. Governor Ann Richards was widely quoted as saying, "The average Texan is far more concerned about taking care of the kids and their elderly parents and the bills than they are about research on cold fusion."[48] By implication, she was saying that universities are best known for esoteric, impractical research and not much that is useful.

A second issue is *continued marginal funding.* Enrollments grew by 35 percent in the fourteen-year period from 1977 through 1991[49] before finally slowing down. Faculty and staff did not grow as rapidly. Thus, many institutions came to rely increasingly on part-time faculty and graduate assistants, a development that made the image problem worse. Other problems also resulted from inadequate funding, such as larger classes, fewer book and journal purchases by the libraries, and some buildings that were still in poor repair in spite of PUF and HEAF expenditures. Community colleges have an additional problem in that their districts often coincide with those of public schools; given the massive reorganization of public school finance, the college

---

46. See *LULAC et al.* v. *Clements et al.*, Cause No. 12-87-5242-A, in the District Court of Cameron County, 107th Judicial District; *Clements et al.* v. *LULAC et al.* (Appellees), Cause No. 13-90-146-CV, in the Court of Appeals, 13th Supreme Judicial District, Corpus Christi, Texas; and Final Judgment, *LULAC* v. *Richards*, January 20, 1992. (The style of the case changed when Ann Richards succeeded Bill Clements as governor.)

47. "Notes from the Joint Select Committee," January 28, 1992, prepared by Wanda Mills for the Council of Public University Presidents and Chancellors.

48. See, for example, Katherine S. Managan, "College Officials Are on the Defensive in Texas as They Lobby against a Budget They Say Will Devastate Higher Education," *Chronicle of Higher Education,* July 31, 1991, A15.

49. "Finance 101," 8.

boards are likely to be reluctant to seek a tax increase to generate more funds for the local two-year colleges. In short, while public and higher education are both vital to the state's economic recovery, higher education's consistent underfunding means that achieving the needed quality is almost impossible.[50]

A side effect with serious implications is disgruntled faculty members across the state. Faculty and professional staff members are recruited in a national market, and noncompetitive salaries make the larger research and comprehensive institutions vulnerable to "raiding" by institutions in other states.

Former Lieutenant Governor Bill Hobby, when he was interim president of the University of Houston System, noted at the beginning of the 1995 legislative session that Texas ranks forty-ninth in appropriations plus tuition, almost $1,000 per student below the national average ($5,084 versus $6,019). He also remarked that higher education's share of the state budget had shrunk from 18 percent in 1985 to 12 percent in 1995. He applauded the legislative leadership for preventing out-and-out cuts but pointed out that higher education funding had "remained flat compared to criminal justice, health and human services, and public schools."[51]

Third, *higher education is being privatized* steadily. This phenomenon is occurring in several ways. Institutions are being encouraged to sell long-standing university operations such as bookstores and residence halls to private companies. They are developing partnerships with private corporations to build parking garages, hotels, and residence halls. Depending on the spending patterns of the institution, the state may pay less than a third of the actual costs for some institutions; however, it pays more than half for most. Finally, students are constantly being asked for more dollars—that is, to support their state institutions with private funds.

The fourth issue is that *higher education is rarely high on the policy agenda.* Although higher education is clearly linked to economic development, since it provides valuable human resources trained to conduct the business of business, the legislature has not paid much attention to it since the *Edgewood* ruling invalidated public school funding. At the end of the 1995 legislative session, some key senators indicated that higher education might begin to receive attention in 1997. They proved to be prophetic.

1997

When the Seventy-fifth Legislature convened in January 1997, higher education clearly had a place on the policy agenda. The political fact of life that placed it there was the difficulty of coping with an increasingly diverse state. As the chapter-opening quote notes, Texas has a history of discrimination and has not overcome that history. The racial and ethnic diversity issues that confronted higher education were twofold: (1) a court case that struck down an *affirmative action* admissions program—that is, a program that gives advan-

---

50. Harry Reasoner, "Texas Is Underfunding Higher Education," *Dallas Morning News,* May 12, 1991, 8J. Reasoner was chair of the Texas Higher Education Coordinating Board at the time, but was removed by Governor Ann Richards because he was so ardent in support of the institutions.
51. Bill Hobby, "Stealth Budget Cuts Hurt Higher Education," *Austin American-Statesman,* February 9, 1995, A15.

tages to certain classes of people, including ethnic minorities, because of historic discrimination against them—and (2) a concern on the part of the universities that enrollments would plummet unless ways to attract more students, including ethnic minorities, to higher education were identified. In turn, Texas would lag even farther behind in creating a well-educated populace.

HOPWOOD

Four white students sued the University of Texas law school alleging reverse discrimination after they were denied admission in 1992. When the suit was filed, the UT law school reserved some admissions slots for minorities and, like virtually all law schools, had a maximum enrollment. The law school's affirmative action admission policy was based on the premise that it should be preparing attorneys who represented the ethnic diversity of the state. A formula score made up of grade point average, Law School Admissions Test score, and class ranking was used for admission, but the "automatic admission" score for ethnic minorities was lower than the "automatic rejection" score for Anglos. Therefore, some Anglo students who might otherwise have been admitted were denied entry. If such a preferential policy had discriminated in favor of Anglos, its constitutionality would probably have been challenged earlier.

Although the UT law school admission procedure was eliminated in 1993, *Hopwood* v. *State,* like many complex legal cases, took almost three years to clear the courts. The decision of the Fifth Circuit Court of Appeals that the race-based admission policy was unconstitutional was allowed to stand by the U.S. Supreme Court in July 1996.[52]

---

52. *Hopwood* v. *State,* 78 F.3d 932 (5th Cir. 1996), rehearing en banc denied, 84 F. 3d 720 (5th Cir. 1996), certiorari denied, 116 S.Ct. 2581 (1996).

Attorney General Dan Morales issued guidelines in August 1996 advising all Texas educational institutions to use "race-neutral" criteria. In February 1997, in response to a University of Houston query about the legality of race-based financial assistance, Morales issued a 24-page attorney general's opinion[53] on *Hopwood,* the essence of which was that the only situation in which an educational institution could take race into consideration was to demonstrate past discrimination with ongoing effects and to develop specific remedies to address that particular discrimination (see Chapters 9 and 11 on the role of the attorney general's opinion in Texas government). Morales specifically ordered the universities to stop making financial aid decisions based on ethnicity and race and cited the possible loss of $1.8 billion in federal funding if state institutions violated the federal court decision. The potential funding loss had been suggested by a former federal deputy solicitor general who was an attorney for the *Hopwood* plaintiffs.

The universities were unhappy: None wished to admit to past discrimination, and all—especially the urban ones—saw a future of sliding enrollments and an inability to serve their clientele. Former Lieutenant Governor Bill Hobby, the University of Houston chancellor at the time, publicly stated that the University of Houston would ignore the opinion, taking the position that the *Hopwood* case referred to one admission policy fixed in time at one law school.[54] The ethnic minority communities were unhappy: They saw fewer opportunities for admission and fewer opportunities for scholarship assistance. And the U.S. Department of Education was unhappy: Norma Cantú, assistant secretary for civil rights in the DoE, notified the state in March 1997 that she thought other federal court rulings upholding affirmative action allowed race still to be considered as a factor.

Morales was infuriated and sent an angry letter to U.S. Secretary of Education Richard Riley. Morales stated, "As the state's attorney, I simply do not have the luxury of putting aside the Fifth Circuit's decision, even in the pursuit of the very worthy goal of diversity."[55] Morales was saying that the federal executive branch could not tell a state to ignore a federal court opinion. Cantú's response had been at the request of forty-three members of the state legislature.

Whatever the reasons for the controversy, the results were plain to see. Between 1996 and 1997, in all Texas public medical schools, Black enrollment was down 38 percent, and Hispanic enrollment was off 22 percent. In public law schools, the enrollment drop among African Americans was 23 percent, and that among Hispanics, 19 percent.[56] In some cases, the students simply sought an environment in which they felt more comfortable, often out of state. In others, the students sought admission to schools where scholarship opportunities were greater. In still other cases, their place was taken by students with stronger admission credentials.

What was the attitude of the public concerning the *Hopwood* decision and its apparent consequences? The majority of Texans approved of the decision

---

53. *Attorney General's Letter Opinion No. 97-001,* February 6, 1997.
54. "Hoppin' Mad about Hopwood: A.G. "Opinion" Question," *Texas Government News,* January 27, 1997, 1.
55. Letter from Texas Attorney General Dan Morales to U.S. Secretary of Education Richard W. Riley, April 2, 1997, 2.
56. A. Phillips Brooks, "Law, Medical Schools Hurting for Minorities," *Austin American-Statesman,* October 17, 1997, B1, B7.

and its implication that race was no longer a valid criterion for university admission or financial assistance. Among all participants in a survey administered by the University of Texas Office of Survey Research in the fall of 1997, 58 percent backed the *Hopwood* ruling. However, only 39 percent of African Americans and 46 percent of Hispanics were in favor of the decision.[57]

The *Hopwood* decision is merely symbolic of American struggles with the concept of affirmative action (AA). At its simplest, AA merely calls for ensuring that all individuals have an opportunity to be part of the "pool"— whether the pool of talent is for work or admission. At its most complex, AA results in quotas for hiring or admitting on the basis of one of the protected categories—race, ethnicity, gender, disability, age, or veterans' status, for example, with the most common categories being ethnicity and race. When finite numbers are involved—there are only a certain number of allowable admissions or people to be hired or promotions to be handed out—those who are not part of the protected class feel that they have been discriminated against. Some people argue that such unequal treatment is justified to remedy past discrimination against minorities and women and, to a lesser extent, the other protected classes. Other people argue that "reverse discrimination" is not justified because it substitutes less qualified students (or employees) for more qualified ones and because "two wrongs don't make a right." Issues such as affirmative action illustrate why democracy, however desirable, can be such a difficult form of government.

BACK TO BASICS

The other major issue confronting the 1997 legislature was the need to address pent-up funding needs in higher education. Begun as an initiative of the chancellors of the six public university systems (University of Houston, University of Texas, Texas A&M, Texas Tech, University of North Texas, and Texas State University), who called themselves The Coalition, the "Back to Basics" movement became a theme that united higher education.[58] The Back to Basics proposals laid out a strategy to achieve a competitive edge for the state by:

★ Increasing partnerships between higher education and public schools

★ Increasing efforts to help "at risk" students who are most likely to drop out or "stop out" (interrupt their education)

★ Reversing the trend of less experienced faculty members teaching lower-division courses

★ Providing more state financial assistance

The information provided to legislators called their attention to the need to have a more educated workforce if Texas was to continue to prosper

---

57. Jayne Noble Suhler, "58% Back Ruling on Race, College Entrance," *Dallas Morning News,* November 16, 1997, 45A, 50A.
58. This section relies heavily on *Back to Basics: The Role of Higher Education in the Economic Future of Texas,* a set of proposals for the Seventy-fifth Texas Legislature prepared by The Coalition (of public university chancellors), January 1997.

economically. It pointed out that the state's college graduation rate was 16 percent below the national average and that this problem would get worse if corrective measures were not taken because the fastest-growing populations are those with low educational attainment historically. The report pointed out the below-average income of the state, the growing number of unskilled workers, and the importance of a highly productive workforce to provide the state with adequate public revenues.

What did The Coalition ask for? It wanted $1 billion to fund full professors teaching lower-division courses, to provide student financial aid, to boost health-related institutions, to improve reading in primary grades and develop preparatory programs for secondary students, and to develop workforce skills programs and fund research. Texas A&M Chancellor Barry Thompson summed up the request by saying, "If we do not do something, the problems will become irreversible."[59]

WHAT THE LEGISLATURE DID

The legislators were spurred by thoughts of economic decline, the consequences of not accommodating a growing segment of the population, and having more money to spend than usual. As a consequence, more than a thousand bills dealing with higher education were introduced during the 1997 session. Some addressed *Hopwood*. Some addressed Back to Basics. Some addressed pent-up needs of institutions. Overshadowing all the measures was a legislative desire to gain more control over the institutions, to treat them more like other state agencies. The result was typical politics—give a little, get a little.

The following list includes most of the better-known measures passed in 1997. The Seventy-fifth Legislature voted to:

★ Mandate a performance review system for tenured faculty members in each institution

★ Place a cap of 100 hours on the number of credit hours that would be funded by the state for a doctoral student

★ Place a cap of 170 hours on the number of credit hours that would be funded for an undergraduate degree student

★ Revise the formula by which universities are funded, both simplifying it and providing greater rewards for institutions already achieving efficiencies

★ Combine certain fees with tuition

★ Mandate a new core curriculum, more or less common to all institutions, to make transfers easier

★ Simplify admissions applications for individuals wishing to apply to multiple institutions

★ Create a new admission system that requires an institution to accept any student in the top 10 percent of his or her graduating class and encourages accepting the top 25 percent and that mandates that eighteen race-

---

59. Todd Ackerman, "Back to Basics," *Houston Chronicle,* January 10, 1997, 1A.

neutral criteria be considered for other admissions, including, for example, academic record, whether the individual was in the first generation of a family to attend college, the applicant's extracurricular activities, and whether the individual is bilingual

★ Force universities to eliminate the double standard of admitting athletes on one standard and denying other students with the same credentials

★ Give staff raises for the first time in five years and tell universities to find the money to give faculty raises

★ Fund more than half of the Back to Basics program—$593 million

THE HIGHER EDUCATION INITIATIVE

After the legislative session, both houses of the Texas legislature formed interim committees to deal with diversity recommendations before the 1999 session. The Higher Education Coalition that had been formed for the 1997 legislative session created a Commission on a Representative Student Body that sought ways to further diversify faculty, staff, and students and strategies to create a private endowment to support scholarships that would increase diversity—and enrollments—on Texas campuses. Increasing enrollments, while in part self-serving, is also a necessity because Texas produces about 15,000 fewer college graduates each year than a state its size should. Coalition presidents appointed citizen members to the commission. Other important committees, with responsibilities as diverse as developing a statewide core curriculum and making modifications in the funding formula, were formed under the auspices of the Texas Higher Education Coordinating Board (THECB). Diversity issues dominated the higher education scene as 1998 began.

ANALYSIS

State policy makers finally paid attention to higher education in 1997. The institutions got new money and a mandate to form partnerships with the public schools. They were told to diversify the factors they considered in admissions, to get rid of some of the bureaucracy that plagues almost all students, and to discourage "professional students." They got money—lots of it—and many new controls. In 1999 legislators will want an accounting of what that new money has bought and practical initiatives designed to achieve diversity.

Saving the Environment

The 1990s dawned with the return of Earth Day, initially celebrated in 1970. For many people, the return of Earth Day was a symbol that the 1990s would be a decade of environmental consciousness and renewed activism, just as 1970 had seen the original clean air and clean water legislation. For Texans, environmental issues are particularly important. The state lived off the environment—land, water, air, and minerals—for much of its history but increasingly finds that environment to be deteriorating (land, water, and air) or being used up (minerals). Too, Texas is a place where nature is often hostile—tornadoes, flash floods, hurricanes, and even occasional earthquakes confront its citizens, not to mention rattlesnakes, killer bees, and fire ants. Moreover, Texans, as the proud inheritors of a frontier past, remain unclear as to whether to nurture the environment or conquer it.

Furthermore, the national government has required a cleanup of the environment. Texas, like other states, is finding environmental cleanliness to be another of those well-intentioned but costly federal programs. Three key pieces of national legislation are the Safe Drinking Water Act of 1996, the Clean Water Act of 1972, and the Clean Air Act of 1996. These laws include standards that are expensive to implement. Federal funding adequate to assist state and local governments in meeting the new criteria was not forthcoming, although these laws are examples of the mandates discussed earlier in the chapter.

IS THERE ANY WATER? IS IT SAFE TO DRINK?

Texas has three basic kinds of water problems: water quality, water supply, and water damage. All are perennial contenders for the policy agenda, but water supply seems to come first in Texas. Moreover, the creation of dams and reservoirs to create water supply also helps to divert water runoff from destructive flooding to constructive water conservation.

WATER SUPPLY

Under normal rain conditions, the rule of thumb is that for every twenty miles one moves westward in the state, average annual rainfall diminishes by an inch. Since Texas is a very wide state indeed, by the time one reaches El Paso, the average rainfall is only eight inches a year, compared with fifty-five inches in the southeastern part of the state. Consequently, West Texas politicians have kept the issue of water supply at the forefront for thirty years. They made water a critical issue in the 1969, 1981, 1983, 1985, and 1993 legislative sessions, and the state produced various schemes and plans for providing water and engaged in extensive water planning.[60] Texans are very conscious of the old Wyoming saying that opens this chapter.

Drought plagued the state in 1996. Of Texas's 254 counties, 208 were judged severely drought-stricken, and the other 46 had moderate drought.[61] Agriculture was imperiled, small towns without good water resources found themselves without water, and images of a repeat of the seven-year drought of the 1950s began to loom.[62] Consequently, supply was the focus of water issues in the 1997 legislative session although 1997 proved to be an extraordinarily wet year, with severe spring floods.

---

60. See *Water for Texas Today and Tomorrow—1990* and *Water for Texas Today and Tomorrow—1992* (Austin: Texas Water Development Board, 1990 and 1992, respectively). The 1990 volume focuses on a detailed analysis of each water basin and aquifer, with emphasis on specific plans to meet water resource needs in the state. The 1992 volume focuses on legislative issues, progress toward meeting the state water plan, and recommended amendments to that plan.
61. Julie Crimmins et al., "Beyond the Drought," *Fiscal Notes,* July 1996, 1, 6–10.
62. Ralph K. M. Haurwitz, "In Drought, Towns Left Out to Dry," *Austin American-Statesman,* February 16, 1997, A1, A10, dramatically points out how drought can affect an area that is usually considered to be water-rich.

The old adage "When it rains, it pours" certainly holds true in Texas. In one week in June 1997, the area around Austin saw more than twenty-one inches of rain. Texas's infamous thunderstorms and the deluges that come from them are the reason that Texas ranked far higher than any other state in the number of deaths from flash floods in the 1960–1995 period. Texas had 610 deaths. California followed with 255, then came South Dakota with 248.

Source: "Texas Leads in Flash-Flood Deaths," *USA Today,* June 23, 1997, 14A.

In 1997, lawmakers came prepared to deal with water, and they produced a comprehensive, 220-page bill covering most aspects of water in the state. The exception was a failure to address the four hundred or so inadequate dams in the state—dams that could give way during any heavy rain.[63] Lawmakers agreed to the following:[64]

★ Requiring local, regional, and statewide planning for water supply, conservation, and drought management

★ Requiring economic and environmental studies before water can be transferred out of a river basin and discouraging such transfers

★ Streamlining procedures for creating groundwater districts, *but*

★ Leaving intact traditional Texas law that allows unlimited pumping of groundwater that is not part of a water district

★ Exempting water-conservation equipment from the sales tax

★ Creating an electronic mapping system for natural resources

★ Consolidating water management dollars, subject to voter approval since previously approved bonds are involved, in order to maximize their effect and garner federal funds

★ Increasing fines for illegal water usage

Toward the end of 1997, the adequacy of water supplies varied from one part of the state to another. The best-prepared areas seemed to be Dallas–Fort Worth in North Central Texas and Central and South Texas so long as the Edwards Aquifer remained at a high water level. Among the worst was the Trans-Pecos area, which includes El Paso. The estimated cost of maintaining an adequate water-related infrastructure for the period ending in 2050 was $65 billion in 1997 dollars.[65] The 1997 legislation addressed many water problems but also was fraught with implementation roadblocks, key among

63. Ralph K. M. Haurwitz, "Hazards of Dams Continue to Loom," *Austin American-Statesman,* June 3, 1997, B1, B5, and "Dams Need Help, Legislators Told," *Austin American-Statesman,* February 21, 1998, B1, B9.
64. The summary of legislation relies heavily on Ralph K. M. Haurwitz, "Legislature Takes Stand for Water Planning," *Austin American-Statesman,* A1, A4, and "Watershed Legislation," *Fiscal Notes,* September 1997, 1, 7–9.
65. "Watershed Legislation: Texas Enacts First Statewide Water Management Plan," *Grassroots, the Newsletter of Keep Texas Beautiful,* Winter 1998, 14–15.

which was the drawing of new water districts that determine access to existing water supplies.[66]

Much of the precious supply of Texas water goes into the ground. Slightly less than two-thirds of all water usage is for agriculture. For the average residence, the largest single category of use—35 percent—is for watering lawns.

WATER QUALITY

Another 1990s issue is water quality. The oft-cited "bottom line" for water and air quality in Texas is that since 1988, Texas has ranked either number-one or number-two in the country in the millions of tons of toxic pollutants it spewed into the air, let seep into the ground, and dumped into the water.[67] Pollutants are substances that are harmful to the environment or to human and/or animal life. The 1997 water act addressed quality issues such as downstream pollution and water treatment plants.

When it comes to the environment, sometimes the state is its own worst enemy. In 1991 the legislature was set on encouraging an insurance company to develop a large resort on environmentally sensitive Padre Island despite a 14½-hour filibuster from Senator Carlos Truan, who represented that area. The bill finally died at the last minute, but, had it been needed, Governor Ann Richards had promised a veto. In 1995 a similar situation occurred when the legislature overrode Austin's strict environmental regulations to allow the Freeport McMoRan corporation to develop the Circle C area in spite of potential degradation of the Barton Creek watershed. Austin Senator Gilberto Barrientos's 21-hour filibuster went for nought, and Governor George Bush did not veto the law.

The Texas Natural Resource Conservation Commission (TNRCC, pronounced "Ten-Rack"), created in 1993 as the result of a merger between the Texas Water Commission (TWC) and the Texas Air Control Board,[68] oversees

66. See Patrick Barta, "Surf and Turf: Battle Is Brewing over Water District Realignment," *Wall Street Journal,* October 8, 1997, T1, T4. This article indicates that if enough municipalities, special districts, and utilities dislike the redistricting plan, the 1997 legislation could be overturned by the 1999 legislature.

67. See, for example, Jennifer Files, "Texas Tops List on Toxic Emissions," *Dallas Morning News,* June 27, 1996, 1D, 10D; Michelle Mittelstadt, "Toxic Chemicals: Texas Near Top of List," an Associated Press story appearing in the *Denton Record-Chronicle,* May 27, 1993, 9A; "Texas Again among Worst U.S. Polluters," *Dallas Morning News,* May 28, 1992, 21A; and "Texas Ranks Second in Toxic Emissions, Survey Shows," *Austin American-Statesman,* June 5, 1990, B4. Louisiana was ranked second until 1996, when Tennessee took over that spot.

68. The creation of the Texas Natural Resource Conservation Commission was the final step in a series of steps to consolidate the variety of agencies dealing with water and wastewater and with air quality beginning in 1991.

quality concerns. TNRCC adopts regulations to ensure that Texas communities comply with the standards of the Environmental Protection Agency, which administers national policies. Taking the necessary steps to avoid toxic pollutants such as pesticides, heavy metals, and raw sewage is up to communities. The estimated cost of compliance with water quality standards for the 1997–2017 period exceeds $10 billion each for Texas, California, and New York.[69] TNRCC itself has had very mixed reviews: plaudits from industry and pans from environmentalists.

IS THE AIR SAFE TO BREATHE?

The Texas Natural Resource Conservation Commission sets standards and emission limits for the abatement and control of air pollution. This agency is responsible for state compliance with the national Clean Air Act. The national legislation, passed in December 1990, regulates emissions that cause acid rain and affect the quality of the air in metropolitan areas, and also controls the release of toxic pollutants into the air.

To repeat, Texas is the nation's number-one polluter. Consequently, much work must be done to clean up the state's air, particularly in large metropolitan areas, where motor vehicles emit a large volume of toxic gases, and in areas where the petrochemical industry operates. Sixteen counties failed to attain the national clean air requirements specified by the 1990 Clear Air Act, through most of the 1990s. Counties designated by the U.S. Environmental Protection Agency (EPA) as being "moderately" in nonattainment of federal standards were Collin, Dallas, Denton, Hardin, Jefferson, Orange, and Tarrant. El Paso County was designated as having a "serious" nonattainment problem. Brazoria, Chambers, Fort Bend, Galveston, Harris, Liberty, Montgomery, and Waller counties were designated as having a "severe" nonattainment problem.[70] The four North Texas counties—Collin, Dallas, Denton, and Tarrant—are the core of a metropolitan area with a population of almost 5 million. El Paso has the typical inversion problems of any city that sits in a valley that acts as a catch basin for whatever is in the area. The other counties are in Southeast Texas, where the petrochemical industry prevails. Under the reenacted 1996 Clean Air Act, the Dallas–Fort Worth area was predicted to be in the severe category by 1999 or 2000. The metropolitan areas of Austin, San Antonio, Longview-Marshall, and Tyler joined the list of potential nonattainment areas if new federal standards announced by President Clinton in 1997 are finalized in 1998.[71] The National Resources Defense Council, at the beginning of the 1990s, stated that "If Texas were an independent nation, it would rank seventh among the world's biggest sources of carbon-dioxide emissions."[72] In addition, Texas, like everywhere else in the world, faces the various effects of global climate change, holes in the ozone

---

69. Tom Arrandale, "The Price of Potability," *Governing*, December 1997, 78.
70. "EPA Clean Air Standards Threaten Texas Communities," *The Texas Nurseryman*, November 1997, 16–17, and Julie Crimmins et al., "Clearing the Air," *Fiscal Notes*, June 1997, 10–13.
71. "Counties vs. Pollution," *USA Today*, November 29, 1996, 9A, and Kathy Lewis and Catalina Camia, "President Announces Tougher Pollution Rules," *Dallas Morning News*, June 26, 1996, 1A, 11A.
72. Jeff Nesmith, "Texas Ranks No. 7 in Greenhouse Gases," *Austin American-Statesman*, July 27, 1990, E3.

layer, and the "greenhouse" effect in general. (The greenhouse effect is the buildup of gases that retain heat reflected from the earth's surface; the heat retention then causes climatic changes.)[73]

The 1995 legislature, one of the least environmentally sensitive on record, did its part for clean air by revoking the state's auto emissions testing program. This failure to comply with federal environmental standards not only may be costly in the allocation of future federal dollars, but also immediately led to a $160 million lawsuit by the firm that held the contract for emissions testing.[74] Texas political leaders, however, were perceptive in reading a lack of national impetus to enforce some of the aspects of the Clean Air Act, including emissions testing, and decided to spend the state's money elsewhere regardless of any long-term consequences. In 1996 Texas was one of only five states listed as making "no progress" with regard to clean-air compliance.[75]

THE LAND: IS IT SAFE TO WALK HERE? IS THERE ROOM?

Where does one put solid waste, whether that waste is toxic chemicals, radioactive byproducts, or simply the paper, plastic, bottles, and cans that are the residue of everyday living? Four possible solutions are recycling, composting, incineration, and landfill disposal.[76] In Texas, landfills are by far the most common solution. Consequently, the municipalities of the state are facing major problems because of both the amount of land needed to dispose of wastes—and the resistance of citizens to having a landfill in their part of town—and the need to meet stringent new federal regulations as of 1991. The federal regulations evolved from the Resource Conservation and Recovery Act. The TNRCC has jurisdiction over solid-waste disposal in the state.

One of the reasons that Texas has such a problem with wastes is that the state has so many "dirty" industries. For example, Texas is a major producer of petrochemical products such as fertilizers, paints, and motor fuels, all of which have hazardous byproducts. It is a big mining state, with the slag from mineral production a danger in itself. These industries also intensify the water pollution problem because of the runoff of toxic materials into the storm drains and waterways of the state.

With two nuclear power plants on line—Commanche Peak south of Dallas and South Texas near Houston—and other radioactive materials such as those from medical facilities and defense plants, the state must always be concerned about the disposal of radioactive materials. Furthermore, the national government periodically has looked to the state as a potential national storage site for radioactive wastes. Texas—along with Maine, Massachusetts, and New York—for years took a "Lone Ranger" approach to radioactive wastes

73. Judith Clarkson and Jurgen Schmandt, "Global Climate Change and Its Potential Implications for Texas," *Public Affairs Comment* 38, no. 2 (1992): 1–10.
74. Steve Scheibal, "Emissions Case Costs Texas $160 Million," *Austin American-Statesman,* April 5, 1997, A1, A10.
75. Gary Lee, "The Clean Air Act Evaporates, One Program at a Time," *Washington Post Weekly Edition,* March 11–17, 1996, 11.
76. John McNurney, "Solid Waste Disposal Options: The Pros and Cons," *Texas Town & City* February 1990, 6, 23.

in that it was not a member of any interstate compact seeking a multistate solution to the disposal problem.[77] However, faced with the possible shutdown of existing national sites for disposal of low-grade nuclear wastes, all states faced federal government pressures to make alternative arrangements. Texas formed a compact with Vermont and Maine, with Texas clearly the dominant member, since the proposed site was in Hudspeth County, Texas. The prospective arrangement was criticized by Hispanics because of the heavy Hispanic population in Hudspeth County.[78] The topic of environmental justice sometimes is a hotly debated one.[79]

ANALYSIS

Operating dirty industries and dirty municipal waste facilities is cheaper than operating clean ones. Sometimes it is even cheaper to bribe regulators than to comply with stringent rules. The conservative culture of the state celebrates industry and ignores waste products. However, more progressive attitudes that reflect a concern for a clean environment also exist. Consequently, environmental policy making often tends to produce diametrically opposed views and make compromise difficult. Environmental policy making is a great issue in which to explore democracy. In Texas, the politics of special interests often dominate land, water, and air policy, to the detriment of society as a whole. Thus, Texas state environmental policy does not meet the test of democratic theory.

Nevertheless, Texas is still spending considerable money on environmental matters—an apparent reflection of its size and the magnitude of its problems. In 1993, it ranked in the top ten for expenditures for air-pollution controls (fourth), wetlands protection (ninth), and support for solid-waste programs (sixth). It was not a top-ten state in helping local governments with recycling.[80] More recently, the 1998–99 state budget includes $1.7 billion for natural resources programs.

Highways and Byways

As has been stated repeatedly throughout this book, Texas is a large state, both in land area and in population, and the number of people in the state continues to grow. As a big, urban state, Texas needs jobs for its citizens, and it needs to be able to transport people and goods on its highways and roads. Those highways and roads were once a source of immense pride to Texans— smooth, wide roads traversing the terrain of Texas. Today, besides their general popularity, one reason why trucks and sports utility vehicles dominate even city traffic may be the fear that a smaller vehicle could disappear into

77. "Mounting Radioactive Waste but No Place to Put It," *City and State,* November 19, 1990, 36.
78. "Shipping Yankee Radioactive Waste to Texas," *Texas Government Newsletter,* Thomas L. Whatley, editor, November 1, 1993, 2; Nate Blakeslee, "The West Texas Waste Wars," *Texas Observer,* March 28, 1997, 8–13.
79. See the "Social and Policy Issues Forum" dedicated to environmental justice in *Social Science Quarterly* 77 (September 1997): 477–527.
80. Todd Sloane, "Environmental Survey of the States: Survey Finds States Still Going Green," *City and State,* July 5, 1993, 9.

the chuckholes that mar federal and state highways as well as local streets. Nowhere is the plight of the state's highways and byways more evident than on Interstate 35 (I-35), which begins in Laredo and goes to the Canadian border—the state's NAFTA highway. A ride on I-35, which is always under repair and often being expanded, too often includes stop-start traffic and bumpy pavement, particularly around the biggest cities along its path. Altogether, Texas has 31,000 miles of substandard highways.

The other graphic example of the problem is the 11,480 (24.3 percent) of the state's 47,196 bridges that are in dangerous condition.[81] Bridges, like roads, have a life span, and without major work, they cease to be safe or even usable after their lifetime has passed. The national average was 31.4 percent of the bridges being deficient, so that Texas does not have the worst problem.

Why are the state's highways (and bridges) no longer a matter of pride? First, population growth has been accompanied by increased use of the roadways. Second, the erratic Texas weather—drought and flood, warm winters followed by icy ones—takes a tremendous toll on highways. Third, road construction once consumed 21 percent of the state's budget; now, only 8 percent of the budget is dedicated to highways, roads, and bridges. Texas is forty-fifth among all states in its per capita expenditures for highways, having chosen to spend more of its funds on other programs. Fourth, although the motor fuels taxes at both the national and the state level were hiked in 1983 and 1984, respectively, highway funding is insufficient to meet needs.

One problem is that the federal government chose to put the national highway trust fund *"on budget."* That term means that monies in the trust fund can be used for general expenditures, and the increase in federal funds for highways and bridges was far less than anticipated. At the 1998 meeting of the National Governors' Association, state chief executives of both political parties called for Washington to turn loose highway trust money and return it to the states. One proposal that stalled in Congress in 1997 was to send back to the states at least 95 percent of what they send to Washington from the gasoline tax. Texas, for example, receives back only 77 cents of every dollar it sends to Washington. Pennsylvania, on the other hand, receives 130 cents.[82] Congress finally passed a generous highway measure for FY 1999.

Texas highway expenditures have been capped since 1977. Combined with the federal policy of diverting highway trust funds to cover other programs, this cap means that the Texas Department of Transportation can fund only a fraction of the projects that TX-DOT itself has evaluated as worthwhile. Officials of general-purpose local governments—cities and counties—talk more about roads than anything else, recognizing that clogged traffic arteries mean an inability to attract new industry, ineffective movement of people to their places of work and play, and, because of the greater air pollution created by cars idling in traffic, more difficulty in meeting air-quality standards.

Motor vehicles traveling on highways and roads obviously are not the only way of getting from place to place. Texas has other transportation issues, too. While the largest cities have done well under airline deregulation,

81. "Almost One-third of U.S. Bridges Need Repair Work, Analysis Shows," *Dallas Morning News*, November 3, 1997, 6A.
82. Kay Granger, member of Congress from the 12th District of Texas, February 27, 1997, in a speech to public administrators and public administration students in Denton.

smaller communities had their air service reduced or terminated. The state tried to encourage a high-speed rail system and authorized private development in 1989, but the company could not develop the line without public support. Meanwhile, two other railroads serving the state have run into problems as well. Union Pacific suffered one rail accident after another in 1997, and Amtrak planned to kill the Texas Eagle train until the legislature came up with a $5.6 million subsidy to keep it alive. The development of mass transit systems, whether bus or light rail, has been slow in the major cities because of both local political squabbles and a lack of the federal funding that once supported mass transit.

Texas must find a way to meet its transportation needs, both to keep its formidable economic engine running smoothly and to meet its obligations to clean up the air. The state has yet to find the right combination, although better highway funding is a beginning.

Conclusions

The state has shown stinginess in trying to mitigate poverty, a cavalier approach toward the environment, a neglect of higher education, and even an inconsistent policy toward business, fostering big business but not always considering smaller businesses or the importance of infrastructure such as highways. In each of the issues examined in this chapter, powerful interests dominate the outcome, and the average citizen's perspective is not always considered. As we have argued elsewhere in this book, when judged by standards of democratic theory, Texas often falters. However, there are signs of improvement—creating a consolidated environmental agency with real clout, for example, and the large number of measures designed to blunt the effects of the *Hopwood* decision—and public policy can only be improved by the further democratization of the state. Moreover, solutions to major state problems are often compounded and confounded by the intergovernmental and intragovernmental nature of public policy.

The resolution of each issue is important to the future of Texas, and each is linked not only to the others discussed here, but also to other significant issues that are not outlined in this chapter. Without addressing the considerable poverty of the state, Texas may find it difficult to resolve other policy issues such as economic diversification and sound public education. But without economic growth and the infrastructure to support it, finding jobs for those with limited skills will be impossible. Moreover, abject poverty tends to foster crime. Education has long been seen as the key to the proverbial better future. However, Texas has allowed its higher education system to lag behind that of the nation as a whole, and its economic future depends on catching up. Everyone needs clean water, air, and land, and environmental quality also is tied to the need for economic diversity to avoid further expansion of high-pollution industries. None of these issues is new. All are costly to deal with—so much so that solving one problem may worsen another.

Summary

Texas policy makers have dealt with all the issues described in this chapter to some extent, but problems remain on the public policy agenda:

1. Texas appears on the surface to be wildly successful in creating new jobs and fostering a boom economy. However, many of those jobs pay low wages, and the state has a problem finding places for job seekers with no skills.

2. The transformation of the welfare system into workfare is a national priority with which Texans can agree. However, the change in philosophy and the reduction in federal social spending are both boon and bane to Texas. Texas will have greater flexibility in making decisions on what programs to offer its neediest citizens. It will not enjoy having to spend more state money to pay for those programs. In addition, the state will continue to have one of the highest proportions of poor people in the country.

3. Higher education in Texas continues to be plagued by a bad image, underfunding, privatization, and, in most years, an inability to rank high on the policy agenda. The 1997 legislature did pay attention to higher education, providing it with not only improved funding but also a bundle of new regulations. However, improving the state's degree production is heavily tied to the ability to recruit, admit, and provide financial assistance for ethnic minority students.

4. Texas has always been proud of its resources, but it has materially damaged those resources. Now the state must find an integrated, comprehensive approach to environmental quality. It keeps trying to find a workable solution and has emphasized clean industry in its economic development efforts. In 1997, the state once again legislated a comprehensive water act (the *sixth* such effort in slightly less than thirty years).

5. Texas, both by itself and in concert with other states, must find a solution to the problems with its highways, roads, and bridges. Transportation is an element not only in economic development but also in air quality and even in education, with regard to moving students from home to school and back again.

The issues discussed in this chapter affect all citizens, albeit in different ways. They bring to mind the "haves" and "have-nots" of our society, disparities among ethnic groups, and even problems of mortgaging our children's future by failing to address current problems.

Key Terms

Hopwood v. *State*	Pollutants	Select Committee on Higher Education
Infrastructure	Poverty threshold	
Mandate	Redistributive public policy	Workers' compensation
Public policy		

Study Questions

1. This book argues that Texas public policy has long been dominated by special interests. Do you agree or disagree with this notion? Why? What

effect would domination by upper-income groups have on state policy toward the poor? On state policy toward economic development? What effects do you think the conservative political culture has?

2. What effects of the *Hopwood* decision have you seen on your own campus? Are there fewer ethnic minority students? Have you noticed administrators talking a lot about student recruitment or financial aid? How do you personally feel about the *Hopwood* decision? Why?

3. A former governor of Texas, Mark White, once said, "Education is the oil and gas of the future." What do you think he meant by this statement? What do you think is the link between economic development and education?

4. How do you think Texas political conservatism has affected Texans' attitudes toward the environment? What evidence have you personally seen that reflects an attitude that the environment is something to conquer or subdue? What evidence have you seen that reflects an attitude that the environment is something to be treasured and preserved?

5. Think back to what you have learned about the revenue system and revenue shortfalls in Texas. Given the revenue problems of the state, which of the issues discussed in this chapter—economic growth, poverty and welfare, higher education, the environment, and highways—would you address first? Should the state find new revenue sources to solve all the problems?

6. Consider any one of the five major issues discussed in this chapter. How well do you think democratic ideals such as participation, diversity, and concern for the general welfare are reflected in state policy?

7. How have *other* governments helped to shape the public policy agenda of Texas?

8. What do you think about the legislation to end the practice of some people's being "professional students"? Can you think of circumstances in which an undergraduate student might be justified in taking more than 170 hours to get a bachelor's degree?

9. What role do you think that you as a student should play in the performance review of a tenured faculty member? What role(s) would be inappropriate?

10. Do you agree or disagree with the arguments made about highways and bridges in Texas? What has been your personal experience? Has that experience changed as you moved from home to campus?

Internet Assignment

Internet site: www.state.tx.us/agency/agencies.html

Go to the list of state agencies. Find three agencies that are mentioned in Chapter 14. Click on each one and go to the agency's home page. What did you learn about the agency from its home page?

Chapter Fifteen

The Future of Texas Politics

Cowboys and cattle on the dusty range of west Texas symbolize the Texas of the past (top). College students celebrating their graduation (bottom) symbolize the Texas of the future.

The outstanding fact of history is that it is a succession of events that nobody anticipated before they occurred.

Ludwig von Mises
Austrian economist
Theory and History, 1969

It's the end of the world as we know it (and I feel fine)

R. E. M. band (William T. Berry
Peter Buck, Mike Mills, and
J. Michael Stipe, 1987)

Introduction

Most readers of this book are in their late teens or early twenties. Many, perhaps most, will spend the next half-century or so living in Texas. What will Texas and the Texas political system be like in the waning years of the twentieth century and the early years of the twenty-first?

Any attempt to anticipate the next several decades of Texas politics requires great caution. As Ludwig von Mises points out, people do not have a good track record when it comes to forecasting the future. Nevertheless, it is possible to call attention to conditions and trends that are likely to be important in shaping the next few decades of the state's history. Indeed, the attempt to foresee is important in itself. One of the purposes of knowledge is to help citizens anticipate and react intelligently to the changing world in which they live.

Prediction of the future can be based only on knowledge of the past and present. This final chapter will summarize the reality of the Texas political system as it currently exists, then suggest how some present historical trends might play themselves out during the coming years, and, finally, evaluate the extent to which Texas government measures up to the ideals of democracy now and is likely to measure up in the future.

The Texas Political System

POLITICAL CULTURE

Texas's history and the political culture that grew out of it are unique. Texas has a mystique unequalled by any of the other forty-nine states, born of the nature of the people who settled it, its size, and the fact that for over a decade it was an independent nation. It also has a unique political culture.

Historically, Texans have been characterized by optimism, self-reliance, self-confidence, pride, intolerance, candor, and personal generosity. The role models of the Texas imagination are the pioneers of the nineteenth century and the entrepreneurs of the twentieth. They were preoccupied with material progress and property—and particularly with taming the land. Growth and development were viewed as natural and normal. Having conquered a harsh and sometimes dangerous land, Texans have often been unsympathetic toward those who failed to achieve similar material success.

The basic conservatism of the Anglo settlers was reinforced, in the state's early days, by the social arrangements that they brought with them—the patrón system of Spanish Mexico and the plantation system of the American South. The two shared a hierarchical social scheme, with political power and authority in the hands of a tiny minority of the population. At the top were the owners of large landed estates; at the bottom were mestizos, Native Americans, and African Americans; and in the middle, still relatively powerless, were landless Anglos.

This traditional political culture, however, has always been in conflict with the culture of democracy, which values equality before the law, participation, majority rule, and minority rights. While the culture of inequality has dominated Texas through most of its history, it has gradually retreated before the advance of democratic values and practices. Although Texas is by no means an ideal democracy today, it has unsteadily but clearly improved over the course of the twentieth century. Whether it will continue to improve is an open question.

Texans dislike and distrust government. In general, their main request of government has usually been that it keep taxes low. As a consequence, the state's human services and economic regulatory programs pale beside those of the other large, populous states. Texas entrepreneurs have long worked successfully to minimize effective governmental regulation by influencing legislators and co-opting agencies. They also have succeeded in establishing a system of state taxation that is both low in rate and highly regressive. But they have never been above using government to protect and enhance their interests—for example, land grants of millions of acres to railroads, or regulation of petroleum production to stabilize markets and protect state producers from competition. The result is a pseudo laissez-faire economic culture. Dominant economic interests ask for government action when it is useful to them, while resisting government action when it might be inconvenient for them, regardless of how helpful that action might be to poor and powerless Texans or the natural environment.

Akin to pseudo laissez-faire is social Darwinism, the argument that those "at the top" deserve to be there, and those "at the bottom" deserve their place as well. Because the lower classes turn out to vote at such low rates, Texas politicians usually see their chief constituency as those at the top.

A consequence is that Texas, one of the richest states, has many governmental programs that are among the least generous in the nation—for example, Texas's welfare program currently ranks forty-eighth among those of the fifty states in benefits. Another result is that when the state government does act, it is often to aid business—those at the top rather than the bottom of the social scale. Even Democrat Ann Richards (1991–1995), the most liberal governor the state has had since the 1930s, spent much of her time trying, often successfully, to persuade business firms to locate in Texas. As a consequence, as was discussed in Chapter 1, Texas has a good "business climate" but a poor educational system, stingy health and welfare programs for needy citizens, and generally ineffective environmental protection programs.

THE INPUTS TO THE POLITICAL SYSTEM

For a century, from the 1870s to the 1970s, Texas was a one-party Democratic state. Texans voted Republican in presidential elections as early as the 1920s, but they remained solidly Democratic in state and local elections for decades after taking that small step toward a two-party system. Immigration from other states and from foreign countries, plus the national Democratic Party's liberal policies beginning in the 1960s, gradually broke down the Democratic dominance. Today, it is fair to say that Texas has a competitive two-party system, although it might be more accurately described as having a "three-faction system" because the Democrats are divided into liberal and conservative factions. The party system is one area in which prediction of the short-term future seems to be relatively unrisky, for the state is clearly moving in the direction of having ideologically homogeneous parties, with a conservative Republican Party taking most elections from a liberal Democratic Party.

Texas provides a nearly ideal setting for the exercise of interest-group influence, and the state's political system, despite its increasing size and diversity, remains heavily influenced by the dominant economic interests. Interest-group power is facilitated by the state's traditionally low voter turnout, especially among Mexican Americans and African Americans. Interest-group influence is also enhanced by a system of privately funded campaigns and by the short legislative sessions coupled with small staffs who need help in drafting bills. As was explained in Chapters 4, 5, and 6, wealthy individuals and groups are able to use the state's interest-group and electoral systems to rent the loyalty of politicians, so that private power often dominates public authority.

THE CONSTITUTION

As discussed in the first two chapters, the Texans who wrote the Constitution of 1876 had been emotionally scarred by the Union occupation that followed the defeat of the Southern states in the Civil War. They were determined to create a government that could never oppress them again. As a result, they created a document that was so long, restrictive, complicated, and detailed that it permitted only a very inefficient and weak state government. The Texas Constitution not only disperses power and impedes development of effective government, but makes it nearly impossible to determine who is responsible for developments when they occur. When Texas voters go to the polls on election day, they can never be certain whom to reward, whom to punish, or why. This lack of clear responsibility for public policy adds to the advantages that wealthy individuals and interest groups have in exercising influence behind the scenes.

Despite the inadequacies of the Texas document, however, constitutional reform is not a top priority. The many special-interest groups that benefit from the protections and opportunities afforded them by the current state constitution are in no hurry to see a new, streamlined document created. Moreover, ordinary citizens are skeptical about reform and fear that they might get something worse than what they have now. Thus, those who defend the status quo invariably have an advantage over those who try to bring about change.

THE INSTITUTIONS OF GOVERNMENT

Texas government reflects the provisions of the state's constitution and the purpose of its authors. The legislature, meeting in regular session for only 140 days every two years, is marked by extremely low salaries, insufficient research and committee staff support, and intermittent high turnover. Under these conditions, legislators are almost compelled to follow the lead of the powerful presiding officers and their usual allies, the dominant economic interest groups. The public policies enacted by the legislature reflect these conditions, but the frantic pace of activity and the chorus of loud, conflicting voices that characterizes a session tend to obscure the nature of the power relationships that produce the policies.

The inadequacies of the executive branch also can be traced to the state constitution. In terms of institutional powers, Texas's governor is widely regarded as one of the weakest in the nation. His or her effectiveness depends substantially on the ability to negotiate with the House speaker and the lieutenant governor, heads of state agencies, interest groups, and other political forces in the state. The governor is frequently stymied, since other state office-holders have their own goals and ambitions, and these often conflict with those of the governor.

The bureaucracy consists of more than two hundred agencies that have no common bond. Neither the governor nor the legislature is in command, and each agency seems to be responsive primarily to its own goals and clientele groups. In the early 1990s, Comptroller John Sharp supervised a comprehensive audit of all state functions and developed the Texas Performance Review to bring about better organization and cut government spending. The state administrative system is undoubtedly leaner and more efficient because of the comptroller's efforts. Nevertheless, power relationships have not changed. Special interests still work with administrative agencies to continue business as usual, and demands for efficiency and budgetary responsibility must be vigorous and perpetual.

Until the defeat of many Democratic judges in the elections of 1994 and 1996, the judiciary had maintained a certain distance from the other institutions of government. That independence had allowed Texas judges to force policy improvements on the legislature, most notably in the area of school finance. It will be worth watching to see if the judiciary persists in its progressive path, given the new electoral reality. Whatever its party balance, responsiveness to the people's wishes, or courageous independence, however, the judicial system will not be able to rid itself of major problems. The poor will still be at a comparative disadvantage when they attempt to get justice, the system will still be choked by more criminals than it can process, and its organization will still be complex and confusing.

Local government in Texas is also consistent with the constitution and other state institutions. County government, reflecting the values of 1876, is ill conceived and poorly organized for a twentieth-century urban state. Municipal government, characterized by nonpartisan politics and increasingly by appointed professional staffs, sometimes leaves citizens in a quandary as to how to solve political conflicts. Moreover, the thousands of special districts are confusing to even the most experienced observer.

In sum, the Constitution of 1876 does not provide Texans with all they might hope for in the way of state and local government.

The Coming Challenges

Despite its many imperfections, modern Texas government has functioned tolerably well in many areas. Texans have been able to build roads and bridges, educate a significant proportion of their children, lower the state's crime rate, and provide various kinds of services for themselves. In the areas in which the state has traditionally failed to serve its citizens—in environmental protection, for example—recent years have seen some improvement.[1] If Texans seem reluctant to change their structure of government and habits of behavior, it may be because they believe that government always falls short of the ideal and that reform may only make things worse.

They may be right. However, a political system that has worked adequately for the past and present may not be sufficient for the future. As the twenty-first century approaches, Texans face a set of challenges that will sorely test their capacity to respond. They have to ask themselves if the political culture and institutions that are good enough now will be good enough then.

THE ECONOMY

Economically, Texas has historically been a lucky state. Both its citizens and its government have been able to live off the petroleum that nature stored under the surface of the land. The citizens profited directly and indirectly from oil and gas, as entrepreneurs, executives, drillers, roustabouts, engineers, geologists, landmen, surveyors, accountants, attorneys, refinery workers, and gas station attendants earned salaries and then spent them on their spouses, children, churches, clubs, restaurants, auto dealers, movie theaters, retail stores, and every other business in the state. Texas government benefited through severance taxes, sales taxes, and land leases.

The oil and gas are not gone, and they will play an important role in the state's economy for decades to come. But they no longer dominate the Texas economy and government as they once did, and their importance will diminish each year. Once contributing at least a third of the state's total tax revenue, by 1997 petroleum's share was at 5 percent and falling.[2] Other industries will have to take its place if the state is to maintain its prosperity.

By the late 1990s, it seemed clear that Texas had survived the worst of the pain of the transition to a postpetroleum economy. High-tech manufacturing and trade with foreign countries were two of the industries that were replacing oil and gas as foundations of the economy. Sales taxes were up and unemployment benefits were down, and the state comptroller was reporting a budget surplus each year.

Partisans of the North American Free Trade Agreement (NAFTA), passed by Congress in 1994, argued that open commerce with Mexico would be a

---

1. Bill Dawson, "Texas Leads in Pollution Reduction," *Houston Chronicle*, March 28, 1995, A13.
2. Carolyn Barta, "As Bush Embraced Texas, GOP Gained a Toehold," *Dallas Morning News*, November 2, 1997, A32.

boon for both Texas and the country to the south. Indeed, even before the passage of NAFTA, Texas shipped almost 40 percent of its exports to Mexico, an activity that returned over $20 billion to the state. Trade with Mexico directly supported 247,000 Texas jobs and indirectly created another 217,000. The state comptroller's office estimated that such trade accounted for more than 15 percent of the new jobs created statewide from 1987 to 1993.[3]

Texas goods were also heading to other destinations. By 1996, Texas had become the second largest exporter among the fifty states. In that year, it sold $48.2 billion worth of goods abroad, an increase of 167 percent over the total in 1987.[4]

Thoughtful leaders in Texas know that the state must continue to diversify its economic base if it is to continue to prosper in the global marketplace that will be the world of the twenty-first century. One of the best ways to maintain competitiveness would be to create a first-rate educational system. If there is one fact that economists do not argue about, it is that an educated citizenry makes for a more vibrant economy.

As of the late 1990s, the evidence as to the adequacy of Texas's schools was mixed. On the one hand, the Scholastic Aptitude Test (SAT) scores of the state's high school students were rising, the school dropout rate had declined 40 percent in five years, and Texas was among four states judged to be making "significant progress" in educational goals by a national education panel. On the other hand, SAT scores remained below those of many other states, and over a quarter of Texas's citizens were functionally illiterate.[5] As discussed in several chapters of this book, Texas has been making efforts to both equalize and upgrade its schools. Whether these efforts will be continued and whether they will be enough are vital questions for the state's future.

Despite the fact that the state's economy was improving in the late 1990s, it still had a long way to go to pull many Texans out of dire straits. Although the state's poverty rate fell to 17.4 percent of the population in 1995, it was above the national average. Texas led the nation in the percentage of children lacking health insurance—46 percent—and ranked thirty-ninth among the fifty states and the District of Columbia in its response to child-care issues, according to a report by the Annie E. Casey Foundation.[6]

Although the future of any economy is one of the most difficult things to predict, Texans need to attempt to anticipate and plan for the employment situation that their children will face. In 1992 Robert Reich, a Harvard economist and later President Clinton's secretary of labor, published *The Work of Nations,* a useful look into the future of the workforce that has become highly influen-

3. Bruce Hight, "Texas Exports Rise 4.6%," *Austin American-Statesman,* May 4, 1994, E1; "Peso Fiasco," *Fiscal Notes,* (Austin: Texas Comptroller of Public Accounts, March 1995), 3.
4. Bruce Toal, "Fast Track to Economic Growth," *Austin American-Statesman,* November 6, 1997, A15.
5. Bob Dart, "Texas among Most Improved in Education Panel's Study," *Austin American-Statesman,* November 6, 1997, A2; Terence Stutz, "Texas Students Raise SAT Scores," *Dallas Morning News,* August 10, 1993, A34; "Texas Dropout Rate Declines 40% in 5 Years," *Dallas Morning News,* September 9, 1993, A22; Terence Stutz, "Texas Ranks Low in Survey on Literacy," *Dallas Morning News,* September 9, 1993, A1.
6. Bob Dart, "Texans' Income Up, Poverty Rate Down," *Austin American-Statesman,* September 27, 1997, A7; Chip Brown, "Texas Leads U.S. in Percentage of Uninsured Kids," *Austin American-Statesman,* March 29, 1997, B4; Clara G. Herrera, "Child Wellness Report Ranks Texas among 10 Worst States for Poverty," *Austin American-Statesman,* April 5, 1997, A1.

tial.[7] Reich argued that the increasing globalization of every nation's economy is tending to stratify national workforces into three classes of workers.

The members of Class One do the repetitive, simple tasks—assembling toasters, for example—that are needed to manufacture products that are increasingly sold on the international market. Because almost anyone can do these tasks, and because it is now easy to ship products long distances cheaply, the workers in one country are nearly interchangeable with those in another. If a corporation is dissatisfied with workers in the United States—if they join a union, for example—it can ship their jobs to Mexico; if Mexicans are not satisfactory, it can ship the jobs to Singapore, and so on. The ability of employers to manufacture anywhere tends to depress the wages of workers everywhere to the lowest possible level. In other words, Class One workers in the United States can in the future expect to earn no more than similar workers in Third World countries.

Class Two jobs consist of the provision of services that are also relatively simple and easy, but that require the provider to be physically in the presence of the consumer. Examples would be counter servers in fast-food restaurants, temporary workers, taxi drivers, child-care providers, secretaries, retail clerks, and security guards. Although these jobs cannot be sent overseas, there are very many people who want them and are able to do them. Class Two workers therefore have relatively little market power, and thus receive low wages and few benefits. According to Reich, an increasingly large number of Americans are employed in Class Two jobs.

Recent figures bear him out. From 1994 to 1995, for example, the number of *temporary* jobs in Texas increased by 20 percent. According to one projection, by early in the twenty-first century half of all workers will be temporaries, part-timers, or contract employees who are hired just to complete specific projects.[8] This scenario is disturbing because Class Two workers will mostly be without health insurance or retirement benefits.

Reich argues that the Class Three workers will be the winners in the economy of the future. These are highly educated "symbolic analysts" who have technical skills that the emerging "enterprise net" corporations will need. Examples of those workers who will be in demand are scientists, engineers, bankers, accountants, computer programmers, advertising executives, writers, and various kinds of consultants. These workers will have high incomes, adequate benefits, and a fulfilling, comfortable lifestyle.

Reich predicts that the higher the percentage of the American workforce that is employed in Class Three jobs, the better off the country will be. And once again, the number of Americans—and Texans—prepared to take their place in the new economy will depend upon their educational level. If Reich is even approximately correct about the trend in the national economy, then the key to creating a prosperous Texas in the twenty-first century is building a first-rate state educational system at the end of the twentieth. At present, it seems clear that some Texans are getting the right training to prevail in the next century, but there is a good deal of doubt that the state is doing all it can

7. Robert Reich, *The Work of Nations: Preparing Ourselves for 21st Century Capitalism* (New York: Random House, 1992).
8. L. M. Sixel, "Temporary Workers Here to Stay," *Houston Chronicle*, March 20, 1995, B1.

to maximize the number of its citizens who will be Class Three workers in the future.

Even if Texas manages to improve its educational system enough to prepare a significant number of workers for the next century, there will still be a large number left behind. Reich argues on humanitarian grounds that national and state governments will have to provide social services—health insurance, for example—to Class One and Two workers to prevent their falling into wretchedness and despair.

As of 1998, Texas was not doing all it could to meet the social challenges of the new century. The structure of state government, the low voter turnout of poor citizens, and the dominance of conservative political values all conspired to prevent Texas from doing much to improve the lives of its less wealthy residents. The future does not look bright for those who lack the skills and savvy to advance in a pseudo laissez-faire economy and a conservative political culture.

One possibility for Texas society over the next several decades, then, is a growing disparity between the income levels of those at the top and bottom of the social scale. A significant number of Texans will have access to all the comforts and toys of future living—personal computers, home entertainment centers, big houses, surplus income for travel—but an equally significant, and perhaps growing, portion of the population will sink farther into poverty and hopelessness.

If the present distribution of wealth and education remains unchanged, a further result would be that most of those on the top of the pyramid would be Anglo, and most of those on the bottom would be Mexican American and African American. It is by no means certain that such ethnic stratification will intensify, since there has been a surge of minority citizens into the middle classes in recent years. Whether or not the present *ethnic* divisions increase, however, there is a clear trend toward *economic* divisions becoming worse.

The impact these developments would have on public health, the crime rate, and other indices of civilized society would be grim. Consequently, one of the major tasks of the Texas political system in the immediate future will be to try to prevent such a social outcome by equalizing educational opportunity.

POPULATION

In late 1994 Texas passed New York and became the second most populous state, with over 19.5 million residents. The news that Texas was growing rapidly would not have surprised its citizens, who had become used to new subdivisions and shopping malls springing up around every city and former suburbs seeming to mutate into metropolises. One prediction that even von Mises would have to endorse is that the Texas population will continue to increase.

One scholarly estimate projects that Texas may have a population of almost 31 million by the year 2020.[9] Perhaps developers and construction workers view this prospect with delight, but the rest of the state's residents

---

9. Leon F. Bouvier and Dudley L. Poston, Jr., *Thirty Million Texans?* (Washington, D.C.: Center for Immigration Studies, 1993).

may feel more like the passengers on the hurtling bus in the motion picture *Speed,* unable to stop as the vehicle rushes toward destruction. The state is already wrestling with many problems caused by an expanding population. As more people move to Texas and are born here, the problems will get worse.

Pollution is one problem that becomes worse with increasing population. As each Texas family buys an automobile, and then perhaps a second car, and as ever more families want transportation, the noxious stuff that comes out of tailpipes builds to intolerable levels. The authors of *Thirty Million Texans?* calculate that, under moderate assumptions of population growth, by 2020 each Lone Star motorist will have to reduce his or her driving by 37.5 percent to avoid worsening the already unclean air of the state's cities.[10]

Given Texas's traditional love affair with driving—often, of course, in a pickup truck rather than a car—and given the state government's lackadaisical attitude toward pollution, it is unlikely that much will be done to keep Texas's air breathable. Houston already has the second worst air in the country, trailing only Los Angeles—which, ironically, has made progress in recent years in cleaning up its atmosphere.[11] Meanwhile, the federal Environmental Protection Agency is threatening Austin, San Antonio, and Longview-Tyler-Marshall with mandatory controls if they do not reduce the levels of ozone in their air.[12]

In the absence of a brake on population growth, which is unlikely, the only escape from some of the consequences of this growth would lie in a "technological fix." In 1995, some automakers announced that they had developed a car that not only emitted no pollutants, but actually made the air cleaner by removing its ozone. If this experimental vehicle proves to be both technically and economically feasible, it will dramatically ease the pressure on the environment as population increases. It will allow Texas policy makers to escape the responsibility for making many hard choices about population and pollution.

It will not allow them to escape every hard choice, however. Even cleaner vehicles won't solve the transportation problem that Texas has, especially in its major cities. There are now so many automobiles and pickup trucks on the roads of Houston and Dallas that at "rush hour" they often simply come to a halt. Some kind of mass transit is necessary if these and other cities are not to be paralyzed by gridlock much of every workday.

In the past, the transportation system—extensive roadways, modern airports, passenger rail lines—has fueled economic growth. The state will begin the new millennium, however, with the federal Department of Transportation unable to fund more than a small fraction of worthwhile highway projects, with passenger rail service threatening to disappear, with freight railroads in economic distress, and with airports that experience more congestion every year. Urban mass transit systems would be a way of easing some of the

---

10. Ibid., 87.
11. Robert Fisher, "Houston Air—It's More than You Expected," *Houston Chronicle,* November 16, 1997, C1; William Booth, "Los Angeles Finally Sees Through Smog," *Austin American-Statesman,* December 21, 1997, A21.
12. Nichole Monroe, "Tougher Air-Quality Standards Will Hit Austin," *Austin American-Statesman,* June 25, 1997, B1.

problems of bad air and traffic jams, but they are developing only very slowly in Texas cities.[13]

Whatever happens in the air and on the ground, the population explosion will continue to create problems for the water supply. A major difficulty arises from the fact that, although much of Texas is relatively wet, most people choose to settle where it is relatively dry. The huge Toledo Bend reservoir on the Texas-Louisiana border is untouched as a source of municipal water, while every drop of the Rio Grande, hundreds of miles to the west, is utilized. Although there is enough water in East Texas to satisfy West Texas's thirst for many years, transporting it out of its natural watershed ("interbasin transfer") would be very expensive and would certainly be opposed by the people who live in the moist areas.

Texans who reside in the relatively dry areas have traditionally utilized the aquifers, or "underground rivers," that underlie about three-quarters of the state's land area. For decades, many Texas cities have relied upon these aquifers for municipal use, but because of falling water tables they are becoming increasingly dependent upon surface reservoirs made by damming rivers. At the same time, however, citizens are ever more resistant to paying the taxes that building a reservoir requires. In the 1990s, for example, San Antonio has twice voted down the construction of the proposed Applewhite Reservoir. As cities grow, aquifers shrink, and citizens oppose the building of new dams, pressure grows to bring in water through interbasin transfers.

The attempt of some other group of citizens to "take our water" is certain to set off political fireworks. When, during the drought of 1996, Corpus Christi and San Antonio began exploring ways of transporting water from the seven Colorado River lakes in Central Texas to their municipal customers, the Lower Colorado River Authority and cities served by the river, including Austin, went ballistic. Journalists began to use such phrases as "the war for the Colorado" in reporting the passions provoked by the specter of interbasin transfers.[14] The end of the drought in the fall of 1996 and the advent of an unusually wet year in 1997 staved off a major political confrontation. Since future droughts are a virtual certainty, however, the issue will recur, and not just in the central and southern portions of the state.

In seeking to manage conflicts over water, the state constitution and the legislature have created more than thirty kinds of special water authorities, which together total more than a thousand separate governmental units. These include municipal utility districts, levee and flood control districts, drainage districts, underground water districts, irrigation districts, river authorities, and water improvement districts. Until 1997, however, there was no overall statewide agency coordinating all these mini-governments and planning for the future. In that year, the legislature passed a comprehensive state water statute aimed at allowing the three-member governing body of the Texas Natural Resource Conservation Commission to make contingency plans for future droughts, including the approval of interbasin transfers. Whether the TNRCC will be able to handle the many intense conflicting interests during the next drought, and the next, is a question certain to entertain students of Texas politics in the coming years.

---

13. Buses and Beyond," *Fiscal Notes* (1997), 1.
14. Helen Thorpe, "The War for the Colorado," *Texas Monthly*, May 1997, 98.

Whether or not the state's political institutions can handle the conflict over water, the population that drinks it is certain to increase. Moreover, not only is Texas's population expanding, it is changing in composition. In 1990 a quarter of the state's population consisted of Hispanics, who were overwhelmingly Mexican American in background. The Latino share of the Texas citizenry, however, is not stable, but growing rapidly. By the year 2020, Hispanics may make up over 42 percent of the total and outnumber Anglos.[15] Even in 1990, Mexican Americans were a majority in Corpus Christi, El Paso, and San Antonio, and constituted sizable minorities in other Texas cities.[16] The future of Texas is one in which the challenge of integrating this very large and growing Mexican American population into the Anglo-dominated political culture will become an inescapable focus of attention.

Mexican Americans are different from the traditional Southern Anglo citizen of Texas in several ways. Whereas most Anglo Texans are Protestant, Mexican Americans are overwhelmingly Catholic. Whereas most Anglos speak only English, most Mexican Americans are bilingual; a significant minority speak only Spanish. Whereas the great majority of Anglos identify only as citizens of the United States, an important proportion of Mexican Americans—especially, of course, immigrants—retain at least some loyalty to Mexico.

These differences have produced a great deal of cultural friction in the past, and will probably continue to do so in the future. There are, however, also economic differences between the two communities that promise even stronger disagreements. According to the 1990 census, the mean household income for Anglos was about twice that for Mexican Americans. Foreign-born Mexicans, in particular, were four times as likely to live below the poverty line as Anglos.[17] Thus, although there are wealthy Mexican Americans and poor Anglos, the centers of gravity of the two communities lie on opposite sides of an economic class divide.

Given the Anglo population's customary conservatism, the relative poverty of the Mexican American population, and that population's growing size and more liberal political leanings (see Table 6–3 in Chapter 6), the future will most likely hold many clashes between Anglo and Mexican American political values. Indeed, Latino voters will probably present Texas's customary political conservatism with its strongest challenge in history.

One particular political issue that is likely to divide the two communities is opposition to illegal immigration. Although there are illegal immigrants from many countries in Texas, the largest and most visible contingent comes from Mexico. It is estimated that of the roughly 3.5 million illegals in the country, 357,000 are in Texas.[18]

In 1994, Californians, themselves host to 1.4 million illegal immigrants, passed Proposition 187, which sought to prevent illegals from obtaining welfare payments and other state services. In a survey taken in 1997, 82 percent

15. Bouvier and Poston, *Thirty Million Texans?*, 36.
16. *Latinos in Texas: A Socio-Demographic Profile* (Austin: The Tomas Rivera Center, 1995), 66, 84, 111.
17. Ibid., 37
18. Josh Johnson, "Illegal Immigration Debate Is Hot despite Suspension," *Houston Chronicle*, April 2, 1995, A15.

of Texans reported that they considered illegal immigration a serious problem, 81 percent said that they would favor increasing the number of Border Patrol agents, and 52 percent endorsed using the U.S. military to patrol the border with Mexico.[19]

There is, of course, a great deal of difference between legal and illegal immigrants, and an even greater difference between illegal immigrants and native-born citizens. Still, many Mexican-American leaders are worried that Anglo hostility toward illegals will be generalized to all Latinos and result in legislation, or other political activity, contrary to their interests.

The Democrats, who count Mexican American voters among their core constituency (see Chapter 5), were trying hard to keep the immigration issue out of state political discussion in the 1990s. Republicans holding national office, however, were attempting to ride the Proposition 187 bandwagon to political advantage. U.S. Senator Phil Gramm, running for his party's 1996 presidential nomination, endorsed Proposition 187, but stopped short of recommending a national version of the plan. U.S. Senator Kay Bailey Hutchison was more forceful. "Illegal immigration is exacting a cost on this country we can no longer pay," she testified to a Senate immigration subcommittee in 1995.[20] She has sponsored a bill in the Senate that would

1. Provide funding for more federal agents and technology to guard the border with Mexico.

2. Establish a national database combining Immigration and Naturalization Service and Social Security Administration records to verify work eligibility.

3. Provide more severe punishments for employers who hire illegals.

4. Speed the deportation process.

The idea of a national registry full of Spanish surnames has created consternation in the Latino community. Activists imagine U.S. citizens of Hispanic heritage being checked for citizenship everywhere they go and having to produce documents to prove that they are not illegal. "What happens is that employers only check the documents of people they suspect of being illegal immigrants, and you can guess what those people look like," says Cecilia Munoz, immigration analyst for the National Council of La Raza. "The fact is that only certain people will be singled out because of their ethnicity."[21]

The national registry bill had not passed as of the beginning of 1998, but the mere fact that it could be proposed was disturbing to a large fraction of the Texas population. Similar legislation at the federal level is almost certain to be advocated in the future, and is just as certain to spark political controversy.

Within Texas, the anti-illegal immigrant wave in the rest of the country has yet to create a political issue. Unlike their party compatriots in other states and on the national stage, Texas Republicans have been reluctant to use the immigration issue to their advantage. Governor George Bush barely mentioned it in his 1994 campaign. Bush's hesitation may have been caused by

---

19. Christi Harlan, "Poll: Illegal Immigration Alarms Texans," *Austin American-Statesman*, November 17, 1997, B1.
20. Quoted in Johnson, "Illegal Immigration Debate."
21. Quoted in Ibid.

the fact that many of the state industries that would be the target of crack-downs on employers of illegals are important Republican campaign contributors. Or it may be that Republicans recognize that although Mexican Americans typically give about three-quarters of their voting support to Democratic candidates, the remaining quarter represents a significant number of voters and should not be antagonized.

Nevertheless, Texas Republicans may be unable to resist using an issue that has proved so potent in California. Given the attitudes of their core Anglo constituency, it is easy to foresee them attempting to wring whatever short-term advantage they can out of the illegal immigration issue. Growing political conflict between Anglos and Mexican Americans would seem to be likely in Texas's future.

African Americans are unlikely to be bystanders in this political struggle. Texas liberals have long dreamed of a "rainbow coalition" in which Anglo liberals, Mexican Americans, and African Americans would unite to seize power from the conservative Anglo establishment. Although this coalition has occasionally come together successfully—behind Ann Richards in 1990, for example—more often it has been defeated.

As discussed in Chapter 5, the liberal Democratic rainbow coalition has historically been an unstable one, partly because there are political divisions within and between Mexican American and African American groups. These cleavages were on display in 1997, for example, in the Dallas city council, where Mexican American and African American politicians often clashed bitterly. Moreover, the rainbow has often failed because of the usually low voter turnout of minority citizens. But as the minority population expands, the prospects for rainbow victory will improve. The prospects for this grouping's dominating Texas politics are uncertain, but they improve every year into the future.

In the near term, however, the dominant ethnic group in Texas politics will be Anglos, both because they constitute the majority of the population and because they turn out to vote at comparatively high rates. Although Anglos are clearly conservative in overall outlook, and although they are voting Republican with increasing frequency, they are not monolithic. Individual issues can divide the Anglo population and make the state's political discussion much more open than it sometimes seems.

Protection of the environment is a good example of an issue that divides the Anglo community. A public opinion poll taken in 1994 disclosed that 62 percent of Texans believed that the state government should do more to prevent or clean up water pollution; 59 percent said that more action is needed to deal with air pollution; and 80 percent agreed that they had "a moral obligation to protect the diversity of wildlife from pollution and extinction."[22] The proportions of the various ethnic groups who agreed with the statements was not reported, but such large majorities could not have been registered without very substantial agreement among Anglos. On this one issue, at least, the Anglo community's conservative attitudes are a thing of the past.

Texas politics is thus potentially far more open and complicated than it has often been in the past. The right political leader, arguing the right set of

---

22. "Poll: Texans Want Nature Protected," *Dallas Morning News,* October 11, 1994, A19.

issues, could change the complexion of the state's public policy debates and scramble its customary voter coalitions. And the emergence of strong, imaginative leaders is an occurrence no political scientist has been able to predict.

URBAN TEXAS

In Chapter 3 it was noted that Texas has gone from being one of the most rural states to being one of the most urban. While many rural attitudes still prevail, Texans live in cities, and more and more will face the realities of urban existence.

The rapid growth of the state means mainly the rapid growth of the cities. In the 1990s, Austin, Laredo, and McAllen were all among the ten fastest-growing metropolitan areas in the country. Predictions are that shortly after the turn of the new century, some 10 million Texans will inhabit a continuous urban strip along Interstate 35 from a point north of Dallas–Fort Worth southward through Waco, Temple, Austin, San Marcos, and New Braunfels to a point well south of San Antonio. A few years later, this megalopolis will extend farther south to Laredo and into Mexico. Another urban strip may extend from the Beaumont–Port Arthur–Orange area west through Houston to a point well beyond the western edge of San Antonio. Whether urban growth happens in precisely this way is unimportant. It will happen.

What will life be like in urban Texas thirty or forty years from now?

There are hints available from the older cities of the nation, particularly those of the Northeast. Many have experienced decay of the central city and a declining tax base, a movement of those who can afford it to the suburbs, problems of congestion and pollution, crime, unemployment, inadequate health care and abuse of drugs, and gang warfare, to mention only the most obvious. Surely this is a long way from the American—and Texas—dream of people owning their own land and living a semirural life, free, clean, and healthy. Yet many millions of Americans now live in this urban nightmare.

The traditional Texas attitude is that if government is kept small enough and taxes are low enough, then things will follow their beneficial natural course and all will be well. The cities of the Northeast, however, suggest that more thought and planning are needed to preserve urban livability. Will Texans learn from the mistakes of others and prepare for the problems of urbanization?

The answer to that question cannot be found in this book. But this survey of Texas society and politics should suggest that Texans must think hard about the future of their cities, and what can be done now to change the course of their development.

The Future of Texas Democracy

There have been many comparisons in this book of the ideal of the democratic polity to the reality of Texas politics. In summary, in a perfect democracy, all adult citizens participate in regularly scheduled elections contested by programmatic parties offering the voters clashing ideological visions. During the campaigns preceding these elections, the candidates discuss the problems facing the state and debate possible policies for dealing with them, the media fairly report the debate, and the citizens listen to it, using it as the basis for their own choices in the polling booth. This debate is not distorted by extremely unequal financing for the various points of view, and is enhanced by complete freedom of speech and of the press.

Once in office, the winners of the election carry out their pledges as a team, without being deflected from their purposes by wealthy special interests or an impossibly convoluted system of political institutions. Citizens pay attention to the performance of politicians in office and the effects of the policies they enacted, evaluate the incumbents, and take those evaluations into account during the next electoral cycle. As a consequence, the policies that emerge from the governmental system, while they are not necessarily either liberal or conservative, are at least a reflection of the well-considered preferences of the majority of the citizens. That is the ideal.

The Texas reality, as we have seen, is somewhat different. Barely two-fifths of Texas's eligible citizens can be counted on to vote even in major national elections, with sometimes less than 10 percent fulfilling their civic duty in municipal elections. This low turnout rate is strongly skewed toward the wealthier Anglo population. Much of Texas's minority population is conspicuous by its absence from the polling booth. The campaigns are noteworthy for the conservative bias of the media that report them and the distorting effect of campaign contributions on candidate behavior.

Once in office, the winners have difficulty functioning as a policy-making team because of the fragmented nature of the constitutional system and the distracting effect of special-interest lobbies that surround them. The output of this actual system is often a caricature of the preferences of the majority of Texans. It is biased—not always, but frequently—toward the conservative values of upper-class Anglos and the interests of corporations.

Texas democracy, as it stands, is therefore greatly flawed. As observers have pointed out throughout history, however, all human institutions are imperfect. To conclude that Texas institutions fall short of the ideal is not very helpful. A better question would be, Is Texas democracy moving closer to or farther from the ideal?

Looking back over the last century, there is reason to feel optimistic, for the Texas political system is far more defensible now than it was in, say, 1898. Then, African Americans, Mexican Americans, and poor Anglos were discouraged from political participation by a web of laws and informal practices that kept the ballot box a wealthy Anglo preserve. The reigning Democratic Party suppressed rivals and limited freedom of expression by potential dissenters. State government was so small that it had little ability to meet the challenges of the coming century. Corporations, particularly the railroads, dominated state policy making. The state scarcely deserved to be called a democracy. Compared with the Texas of 1898, the Texas of 1998 is practically a utopia.

Much of the improvement that has occurred in Texas over the past century is not the result of the efforts of Texans themselves, but was imposed on the state by the federal government. Still, whatever the reason, Texas is a better democracy than it was.

It is unlikely that the changes will be undone. The Texas of 1998 thus has the potential to improve as much in the twenty-first century as it did in the twentieth. Although voting turnout is low, that is the result of lethargy among the citizens, not suppression by the powers that be. Turnout could rise at any time, and in fact it has been increasing slowly and fitfully in recent years. An increase in the turnout rate could be a first step in an improvement in the quality of state government.

The increased party competition of recent years may lead to better government, also. Once political competition is established, it has a tendency to involve everyone. As Republicans and Democrats struggle over each election, both parties will see the need to appeal to more and more citizens. As a larger percentage of the people become involved, they may demand a state government that is more responsive to them and less to special interests. They may even decide to change the state constitution so that coordinated government action is possible. Once all varieties of citizens begin to vote, it could happen.

Summary

As in most politics, democracy in Texas falls short of the ideal. The conservative political culture that continues to dominate the state tends to favor government policies that make for a good business climate but a poor educational system, a stingy health and welfare program, and weak environmental protection. Although Texas is now a two-party state, its very strong interest-group system ensures that private power often overbalances public policy making. Its constitution disperses power, thus impeding the development of effective and responsible government. Voter turnout, especially among Mexican Americans and African Americans, is low, although it has been rising somewhat in recent decades. When measured against the standards of democratic theory, Texas government seems to be unsatisfactory, although not intolerable.

This imperfect political system will face a series of challenges in the future. The economy will need to continue diversifying. In order to help it do that, the state's educational system, which shows some signs of improvement but is still generally inadequate, will have to be improved. The population, which may reach 31 million by the year 2020, will generate many problems of pollution, water supply, and cultural conflict. The burgeoning cities will have to be managed so that they do not turn into cesspools of social pathology.

Judging Texas only in relation to ideal standards of democracy creates pessimism that the state can deal with its future. On the other hand, there is also evidence that Texas will be able to handle the opportunities and challenges that will come its way. Some trends in public opinion, voter turnout, and party competition hint that the state's political potential is more open and complicated than it often appears. Moreover, an evaluation of Texas in historical time makes it clear that the state has improved enormously in the twentieth century. This suggests that the potential for improvement in the twenty-first century is equally great.

Study Questions

1. Looked at from the perspective of democratic theory, what are the most discouraging aspects of Texas politics? What are the most encouraging aspects?

2. Over the last two decades, what aspects of Texas politics have changed the most? Has the change been for the better?

3. Over the last two decades, what aspects of Texas politics have changed the least? Is this stability good or bad?

4. What are some of the challenges the state is certain to face in the future? Which of these is Texas government best prepared to face? Which is it least prepared to face?

5. On a scale of 1 to 10, with 10 being perfect, rate Texas government in relation to democratic theory. On the same scale, rate the Texas of 1898. Are the two ratings similar or far apart? What explains the differences?

6. What trends make you most pessimistic about the future of Texas politics? What trends make you most optimistic? On balance, do you come down on the side of optimism or pessimism?

Internet Assignment

Internet site: http://www.austinlinks.com/Business/websites.html

Robert Reich's three classes of workers utilize: (1) Repetitive skills; (2) Service Skills; and (3) Symbolic skills. Go to the "Austinlinks" site where you can explore hundreds of different Texas businesses. Look for businesses of each class. It is probably no accident that few Class (1) businesses can be found, with many Class (2), and many more Class (3). For which of these firms would you prefer to work?

Appendix

A Research Guide to Texas Politics

The original research guide was written in 1983 by Arnold Fleischmann, then of the University of Texas at Austin. It was updated and rewritten in 1992 by Geneva Johnson of the University of Texas at Austin and by the text authors. Additional material has been added by the authors in 1995 and 1997.[1]

Texas Politics: A Great Place to Do Research

People frequently study Texas politics as part of a course, to further their interest in the subject, or because of personal involvement in an issue or campaign. No matter which applies to you, this essay can serve as a road map to help you do your research thoroughly and efficiently. The first part includes some common-sense reminders about doing research papers. The second section helps you to develop a bibliography that includes not only books but periodicals, newspaper articles, government documents, and other publications that can help you narrow your research topic and develop some background in it. The third section includes reference books and periodicals that can provide you with up-to-date statistics and other information about Texas politics. The fourth part of the essay will help you do original research by directing you to the great wealth of information that is generally not available in books. Finally, following this essay is a list of locations where you are most likely to obtain important references and competent assistance for your project.

Getting Started

You have an almost unlimited range of topics from which to choose. The most important thing to do at the outset of your project is to narrow the topic or question you want to investigate. You need not worry in the beginning about what information is available—you can do good research without burying yourself in the state archives. The important first step is to consult with your instructor and a reference librarian. They can provide you with sugges-

---

1. Copyright 1983, Arnold Fleischmann. My special thanks to Malinda Allison and Bonnie Grober for their encouragement, careful review, and suggestions.

tions or manuals on how to write a good research paper. They can also discuss the limitations of your library and other problems that you might encounter. Once you have defined your topic somewhat, you can begin to develop your bibliography, read to broaden your knowledge of the subject, and then narrow the questions to be examined in your paper. To some extent, the headings and citations in this book can serve as a starting point for developing a topic and a bibliography.

Developing a Bibliography

WHERE TO START

To cover a wide range of references and to avoid wasting time, you need a good library. A general source of information about the libraries in your area is the *American Library Directory,* which is arranged alphabetically by state and city. It includes the addresses of public, university, and some private libraries, along with information about their holdings and rules. If you will be looking for historical information, you can consult the *Directory of Historical Societies and Agencies in the United States and Canada.*

Much of the information you will need tends to be located in a library's reference area, periodicals section, documents department, or a special collection labeled "local history," "Texana," or some similar title. Your reference or research librarian can give you valuable advice about your library's card catalog or on-line catalog, reference works, special collections, documents, and the like. Getting professional advice early can save you time and improve the quality of your project, especially since your library may not have all the references that pertain to your research.

The best general guide to research about Texas is *Texas Reference Sources: A Selective Guide* (1978), which surveys general reference works, the humanities, the social sciences, history, and the physical sciences. Ask your librarian to order this volume if it is not available. It can be purchased for $8.50 from the Texas Library Association, 8989 Westheimer #108, Houston 77063. The 1984 Supplement can be purchased for $6.00 from the same source. The 1986 Supplement is available for $3.00 from the Texas Library Association, 3355 Bee Caves Road #603, Austin 78746. Suggestions and/or questions can be sent to the general editor, Lois Bebout, 3304 Bridle Path, Austin 78703. You can also locate valuable books and articles by using a variety of published bibliographies, indexes, and special library services, in addition to the card or on-line catalog in the library.

BIBLIOGRAPHIES

There is only one recent bibliography:

★ Arnold Fleischmann, Manley Elliot Banks, Richard H. Kraemer, and Allen Kupetz, *A Bibliography of Texas Government and Politics* (Policy Research Institute, The University of Texas at Austin, March 1985).

Other sources that can help you identify useful books and articles include those listed below.

★ Institute of Public Affairs, University of Texas, *Bibliography on Texas Government*, rev. ed. (1964). This book emphasizes history, government structure and organization, and the concerns of public officials. It represents the last effort at a comprehensive bibliography on the subject, but it was published prior to the social changes, population and economic shifts, and behavioral research of the past generation.

★ Robert B. Harmon, *Government and Politics in Texas: An Information Source Survey* (1980). This book provides a good overview of reference works and general books on Texas politics, but omits many articles. It is available for $8.75 (plus $2.00 for book-rate postage) from Vance Bibliographies, P.O. Box 299, Monticello, IL 61856 [phone (217) 762-3831]. A photocopy of the 1980 edition can be made; write a letter requesting P401 and enclose a check or money order for $7.60 plus $2.00 postage (no credit cards).

★ *Texas: A Dissertation Bibliography* (1978). This bibliography covers Texas-related doctoral dissertations and master's theses completed since the 1920s. The bibliography is divided into 142 categories, with authors listed alphabetically with their dissertation title, degree date, and institution. It frequently omits dissertations and theses, however, where the title does not indicate a Texas focus. The bibliography is available free from University Microfilms International, 300 North Zeeb Road, Ann Arbor, MI 48106, which also sells copies of the dissertations. The dissertation hot line [(800) 521-3042] operates 8:30 A.M. to 5:00 P.M., Eastern standard time; the fax number is (313) 973-1540. A Datrix search by subject is available at $20.00 for 500 titles; call extension 3732 to order by credit card. There is no update to the 1978 edition.

★ *Texas State Documents*. This valuable resource is published monthly and lists the publications of Texas state agencies, including annual reports, technical reports, and special studies. Documents are listed both by agency and in a subject/title index. The catalog also gives you information on how to borrow copies of the reports listed. Some have been photographically reduced and copied on microfiche cards, which can be purchased at a nominal charge (an order form is included). The monthly catalog also lists the forty-eight depository libraries around the state to which documents are shipped. (They are also listed following this essay.) If your library does not receive *Texas State Documents,* inform your librarian that it is sent free to libraries on request. You can also consult *Texas State Documents Periodicals Supplement,* which is published yearly and lists all periodicals received by the state library's Publications Clearinghouse.

★ *Catalogue of the Texas Collection in the Barker Texas History Center, the University of Texas at Austin* (1979). This fourteen-volume set is a reproduction of the Barker Center's subject and author/title card catalogs. Call ahead to make sure a library has this source, since many will not have spent the $1,375 to buy it. You may call the Barker Center directly at (512) 459-4515. Check to see if the material you want is available, whether it can be made available to your library on interlibrary loan, and if not, whether it can be duplicated. The sales agent for the catalogue, the

G. K. Hall Publishing Company in Boston, Massachusetts, can be reached at (800) 343-2806.

INDEXES

You are bound to do poor research if you limit your use of indexes to the *Reader's Guide to Periodical Literature*. While the *Reader's Guide* includes numerous references to popular magazines, it does not provide the necessary coverage of newspapers, documents, or the more detailed studies usually published in journals. You can locate such articles in the following sources.

★ *Social Sciences Index.* As the title suggests, this index covers books, articles, and reviews in history, political science, sociology, and related fields.

★ *P.A.I.S. Bulletin.* This index specializes in political science, public policy, selected law reviews, and some documents.

★ *Index to Legal Periodicals.* This index surveys law reviews and can be a great asset if you are interested in a legal issue or controversy.

★ *Current Law Index.* This index was begun in 1980 and provides good information on legislation and legal articles.

★ *Business Periodicals Index.* This index focuses on business and industry, but also includes topics related to government management and bureaucracy.

★ *Newspapers.* The *Houston Post,* which ceased publication in 1995, was the only Texas newspaper with a widely available index, which Bell and Howell published from 1976 to the year of the paper's demise. The *Post* gave extensive coverage to matters of statewide interest, but did not provide in-depth reporting on local politics outside the Houston area. However, do not despair if you are interested in some other city or region. Many newspapers are indexed, usually in a special card catalog at the main public library in the city in which they are published. For a list of newspaper indexes, their locations, and the years covered, see Anita Cheek Milner, *Newspaper Indexes: A Location and Subject Guide for Researchers* (1977), Volume II (1979), Volume III (1982), and subsequent volumes. Submit questions or suggestions to Anita Cheek Milner, 1511 Rivcon Villa Drive, Escondido, CA 92027. Also, almost all daily newspapers maintain libraries, which include files of articles according to subject matter. The larger dailies have librarians who maintain these files and who can answer questions. If you want to use newspapers that are not well indexed, you can often use the *Post* index to locate the date of an event and then scan other newspapers for the same period. You may also find it helpful to consult *Newspapers in Microfilm,* which the Library of Congress published for 1948–1972 and 1973–1977. The 1948–1983 volume combines the 1948–1972 publication, the 1973–1977 publication, the quinquennial issues for 1978–1982, and the report of 1983. There are annual issues for 1978 through 1982.

★ *Texas Observer Index.* Indexes have been published for 1954–1970 and 1971–1981. The *Observer* is a biweekly political magazine with a liberal perspective. Its stories cover national, state, and local political issues. It does a good job of covering the legislature and some of the larger state agencies.

★ *Access.* This index has been published since 1975 and concentrates on periodicals not covered by the *Reader's Guide,* including *The Texas Observer, Texas Monthly,* and local magazines.

★ *Texas Index* (Vol. III, No. 3, Spring 1990), Sharon Giles, ed. First published in 1987 with four issues per volume—fall, winter, spring, summer. It is a periodical index or reader's guide to more than 120 magazines and newsletters about Texas, Texans, Texana, and topics specifically of interest to Texans. The subject index is arranged into fifty-six broad categories with subheadings and extensive cross-referencing.

★ *Index to Texas Magazines and Documents* (1986, 1987, 1988, 1989, 1990, and current). A noncommercial venture of librarians on the Victoria College/University of Houston—Victoria library staff as a way to answer questions from students, the business community, and the general public about topics specific to Texas, with emphasis on business, education, and government. Magazines of general interest are included.

SPECIAL LIBRARY SERVICES

There are a number of ways in which your library can help you identify and obtain references. One is the bibliographic search. Usually for a fee, libraries will have a computer scan a national "card catalog" for books or articles that meet criteria that you specify. A second important service is the interlibrary loan mentioned above. Under such an arrangement, your library borrows or gets a photocopy of an item you want from another library. If your library does not have a reference that you want, ask the librarian to borrow it for you through interlibrary loan. Be sure to find out beforehand if there is a charge for this service. In addition, many libraries are becoming more and more electronic. Not only does that allow you to access the library catalog from a terminal, but it also allows you access to many materials located at other sites.

RESEARCH USING COMPUTERS

COMPUTER DATABASES

★ *Texas Innovation Network System (TINS).* This commercial service provides a number of services through Internet linkages. They include Texas Research Centers, a search through research installations across the state, and Texas Guide to Business Resources, a service for small businesses. In addition, if your university or college library is not equipped with a readily available computer search system, you might be interested in the Online Library Card Catalogue, which provides direct access to many university library catalogues. Other such services will continue to develop.

INFORMATION ON THE WORLD WIDE WEB

Extensive information is available to those with computer access to the World Wide Web. Since this area of cutting-edge technology changes rapidly, we can supply only the most basic Web addresses.

TEXAS GOVERNMENT WEB SITES

Any state government agency can be accessed at this address:
http://www.texas.gov/agency/agencies.html.

Once you get to this site, you will see a menu that will enable you to move anywhere in cyberstate. Here are the Web addresses of a few of the most important governmental institutions:

House	http://www.house.state.tx.us/
Senate	http://www.senate.state.tx.us/
Office of the Governor	http://www.state.tx.us/agency/301.html
Attorney General	http://www.state.tx.us/agency/302.html
Supreme Court	http://www.state.tx.us/agency/201.html
Court of Criminal Appeals	http://www.state.tx.us/agency/211.html
Ethics Commission	http://www.state.tx.us/agency/356.html

UNIVERSITIES

By logging on to university Web sites, you will be able to access their library files, plus much more. Here are addresses for some of the state's major universities:

Southwest Texas State	http://www.state.tx.us/agency/754.html
Texas Tech	http://www.state.tx.us/agency/733.html
Texas A & M	http://www.state.tx.us/agency/711.html
University of Houston	http://www.state.tx.us/agency/730.html
University of North Texas	http://www.state.tx.us/agency/752.html
University of Texas at Austin	http://www.state.tx.us/agency/721.html

Keeping Up with Texas Politics

STATISTICS AND BACKGROUND INFORMATION

★ Robert I. Vexler and William F. Swindler, eds., *Chronology and Documentary Handbook of the State of Texas* (1979). This is part of a series by Oceana Publications. This volume lists significant events from 1519 to 1977, as well as the names, birth and death dates, and years of service of Texans elected to the governorship and to Congress.

★ U.S. Department of Commerce, Bureau of the Census, *Statistical Abstract of the United States*. This volume is published annually and includes brief information about population, government, and the economy. It also lists its sources, so you can consult them for more detailed information. Information on Texas is available in the *1990 Census of Population*, vol. 1, *Characteristics of the Population*, Chapter A, *Number of Inhabitants*, and Chapter B, *General Population Characteristics* (Texas is part 45). These two volumes provide data about education, race, poverty, income, and similar economic or social characteristics for the state, counties, metropolitan areas, and municipalities. The bureau also publishes agricultural and economic (manufacturing, retail trade, etc.) censuses for years ending in 2 and 7. *The Census of Governments, County and City Data Book*, and *State and Metropolitan Area Data Book* provide detailed information on cities and counties, including population, economic activity, government finances and employment, and elections. Normally, you also can get such data by contacting the local chamber of commerce, city planning department, or regional council of government. The Census Bureau also publishes the *Congressional District Data Book,* which includes district maps, population and housing characteristics, and vote totals for recent elections. Your library may have much of the census information available on CD-ROM.

★ A. H. Belo Corporation, *The Texas Almanac and State Industrial Guide.* This "everything you ever wanted to know about Texas" book is published biannually and lists records and other statistical information about a wide range of subjects, including Texas elections.

★ Mike Kingston, Sam Attlesley, Mary Crawford, eds. *The Texas Almanac's Political History of Texas,* 1992 has election results since 1845, as well as sections on African American politics, women's political issues, and scandals. Veteran journalists have compiled noteworthy factual material.

★ Texas State Directory, Inc., *Texas State Directory.* This volume is published annually and is a great resource when you need to know something about a public official or agency. It has sections on each branch of state government; county, city, and federal officeholders; political party officials; and the state capital press corps. Useful information includes maps; officials' names, titles, addresses, telephone numbers, and brief biographies; and Texas House and Senate membership, seniority, committee membership, and county delegations. It features a compendium of state agencies, boards, and commissions, including administrative heads, board members, addresses, and phone numbers. Capitol employees consider it their "bible." The company also publishes, at the beginning of each regular session, a pocket-sized guide to the Texas legislature. In addition, it publishes *Capitol Update,* a political newspaper published twenty-five times a year, and the *Texas Legislative Manual,* a guide to the functions and inner workings of the legislative process.

★ Texas Advisory Commission on Intergovernmental Relations, *Handbook of Governments in Texas.* This was published until 1987, when the agency was dissolved. It contains information about the state, county, municipal, special, regional, and federal governments. The information includes agency descriptions, general responsibilities, membership qualifications, top officials, spending and employment levels, and laws governing operations. The Lyndon Baines Johnson School of Public Affairs *Guide to Texas State Agencies, 1990,* serves the same purpose.

★ Legislative Reference Library (LRL): *Chief Elected and Administrative Officials.* This list is updated regularly and includes the names of state and federal officeholders, the office locations and telephone numbers of Texas senators and representatives, and the membership of each House and Senate committee.

★ Roy R. Barkley, ed., *The New Handbook of Texas* (Austin: The Texas State Historical Association, 1996). Six volumes. Like the original *Hand-*

book discussed shortly, this work contains biographical data, but it also has information on the state's places, historical events, and institutions.

IMPORTANT PERIODICALS

There are several periodicals that you should review on a regular basis. Some publish cumulative or annual indexes that make your task easier.

★ *Texas Business Review* (six issues per year). Published by the Bureau of Business Research at the University of Texas at Austin, this journal consists of short, crisp articles on economic conditions, population changes, and public policy. Articles have examined the 1981 Houston mayoral election, the effects of federal cutbacks on Texas cities, and changes in the state's African American population. It includes an annual index.

★ *Southwestern Historical Quarterly.* This journal is published by the Texas State Historical Association and covers a wide range of subjects and historical periods. Its best feature is "Southwest Collection," a subject list of articles on Texas that have appeared in other recent publications. The *Quarterly* has a four-volume cumulative index covering its first eighty volumes. Students can join the association and receive the *Quarterly* for $10.00, half the regular rate. The association also sponsors the Walter Prescott Webb Society on college campuses to encourage the study of state and local history.

★ *Social Science Quarterly.* This journal covers all the social sciences, but concentrates on sociology and political science. Although it does not specialize in Texas-related research, it is the most likely of the regional political science journals to include topics on the state and the Southwest.

★ *Texas Journal of Political Studies.* This journal is published semiannually by Sam Houston State University and focuses on Texas state and local politics.

★ Law reviews. Each of the state's eight law schools publishes one or more journals with annual and occasional cumulative indexes. Law reviews specialize to some extent. If you want to focus on some key issues in Texas politics, it might be helpful to skim the "Annual Review of Texas Law" in the *Southwestern Law Journal,* published by the SMU Law School [phone (214) 692-2594].

★ Specialized periodicals. Periodicals that regularly include information about Texas government as well as the governments of other states include *Governing,* published monthly by Congressional Quarterly, Inc.; *State Legislatures,* published monthly by the National Conference on State Legislatures; *City & State,* published every two weeks by Crain Communications; *The Book of the States,* published in even-numbered years by the Council of State Governments; and *Significant Features of Fiscal Federalism,* published yearly by the U.S. Advisory Commission on Intergovernmental Relations.

★ *The Texas Poll Report.* This is the most important source of information about public opinion in Texas. The poll is a cooperative undertaking of the

Office of Survey Research in the College of Communications at the University of Texas at Austin and the Scripps-Howard Publishing Company. The directors make research data available to scholars. Call the Office of Survey Research at (512) 471-4980. Reports of Texas public opinion in the 1960s and 1970s can be found in some libraries in *The Belden Poll*.

★ Professional meetings. Another way to keep abreast of Texas politics is to attend conventions that discuss the subject. The Texas State Historical Association meets each spring. To find out the location and dates of its annual convention, ask a member of your history faculty, check the *Southwestern Historical Quarterly*, or contact the association. Another interesting conference is the annual convention of the Southwestern Social Science Association. The group meets each March, usually in Dallas, Fort Worth, Houston, or San Antonio, and includes political scientists, economists, sociologists, and other social scientists as well as historians. To find out about this meeting, ask a member of your government department, check *Social Science Quarterly*, or contact the Southwestern Social Science Association.

The above suggestions should help you to develop and get copies of a good set of secondary sources—other people's research. If, however, you would like to contribute something new to our knowledge of Texas politics, the following section should be useful.

Doing Original Research on Texas Politics

Doing original research is often more interesting than summarizing existing studies, as well as possibly giving you a chance to present your findings to a meeting or publish them in a newsletter, newspaper, or journal. This section contains suggestions for studying the electoral and policy processes at the state and local levels, the judicial and legal systems, or some aspect of a political figure's career.

STATE POLITICS: THE ELECTORAL PROCESS

There are a number of sources to help you do original research on state campaigns and elections.

★ Election data. The *Texas Almanac* includes state, district, and county vote totals for state and federal offices. Data for individual precincts are more difficult to obtain, however. Registration figures, precinct maps, and vote totals for primary and general elections for president, U.S. senator, governor, and lieutenant governor between 1966 and 1976 were published in two series of volumes, *Texas Precinct Votes* (1966, 1968, and 1970) and *TexaStats* (1972, combined volume for 1974 and 1976). These studies were discontinued, so you will have to get other election totals from the state archives, the secretary of state, or county clerks. In addition, you usually can obtain unofficial returns from your local newspaper the day following an election. The state archives has election tally sheets dating back to the days of the Texas Republic, while the secretary of state's Elections Division maintains more recent returns, some of which are computerized and are for sale. The elections division operates a nationwide toll-free number [(1-800) 252-8683], 8:00 A.M. to 5:00 P.M., Monday through Friday. You may leave a message for a callback. During primary, general, and constitutional amendment election times, Election Central [(512) 463-5701] is in operation, and callers can get raw data or percentages, plus polling places activity. The best source for precinct maps is your county tax assessor-collector, city clerk or elections administrator (Texas has nineteen combined city clerk and tax assessor-collector offices), planning department, or public works department. The Texas Legislative Council, located in the John H. Reagan building of the capitol complex, also has maps. Call (512) 463-1151 for information.

★ Campaign finances. Candidates and contributors are generally required by law to report their financial transactions. Newspapers are your best source of current information on who contributes large amounts to candidates and how candidates spend their money. News accounts are seldom very detailed, however. The election division of the secretary of state's office maintains the official, complete reports of candidates, lobbyists, and political action committees (PACs).

★ Candidates. You usually can get extensive information about candidates from newspapers. The Texas State Library also has two services that can help you if you want a reasonable amount of information. The state archives maintains an index to biography and can refer you to works about particular individuals. The Public Services Division maintains clipping files and can copy limited amounts of material at fifteen cents per page. This division can also send some materials through interlibrary loan.

★ Issues. Newspapers are undoubtedly the best source of information on the issues in a campaign. You should review them cautiously, however, since most newspapers are not completely unbiased in their reporting and normally endorse candidates. In addition, candidates and local political party officials may have copies of campaign literature that can help you identify election issues.

STATE POLITICS: THE POLICY PROCESS

There is a wealth of sources on the policy process in Texas. Where you turn for information, though, depends in part on whether you are interested in the development of alternative policies, the legislative or bureaucratic process of choosing a policy from a number of options, or the problems of implementing or enforcing a policy once it is enacted.

★ Newspapers and periodicals. Newspapers, of course, can help you understand the background of an issue. In addition to news stories, you should pay attention to editorials and columns by a newspaper's regular political writers, who often discuss the inner workings of the policy process. You can also obtain important information about policy alternatives and the legislative process from the publications of interest groups. Dozens of organizations such as the Texas Medical Association, the Texas State Teachers Association, and the Sierra Club publish magazines or newsletters for their members. Most of these are listed in *Legislative Library*

Resources, published by the legislative reference library, or *Texas Publishers and Publications Directory,* published by the S & S Press of Austin. Also try Georgia Kemp Caraway, ed., *Writers and Publishers Guide to Texas Markets, 1991,* for city and category indexes of book and magazine publishers; daily, weekly, and minority newspapers; publisher organizations; writers' groups; and radio and TV programs (some with public affairs content).

★ Legislative Reference Library, *Legislative Clipping Service.* The service includes copies of articles on government and politics clipped from newspapers throughout Texas. Each Friday the service also includes a section titled "Recent Articles of Interest," which lists articles in any newspaper or periodical that pertain to public policy in Texas. This service is an excellent source of information, but few libraries subscribe to it. If it is not available at your library, ask your librarian to inquire about obtaining it. The clipping service is distributed on a daily basis to each legislator's capitol office, one copy to each House member and three to each senator. Library copies cannot be checked out but can be read there. The LRL loans out items to state officials, members of the legislature, and their staffs. The LRL from time to time puts out a compilation of recent articles by issue and subject categories. This is also distributed to House and Senate capitol offices.

★ Legislative Reference Library (LRL), *Texas Legislative History: A Manual of Sources* (1980). This manual provides excellent tips for doing research on the legislative process and is a good place to turn before examining the history of specific legislation.

★ Texas House and Senate journals. These journals trace the history of all bills and resolutions considered by the legislature. They are limited, however, to actions that occur on the floor of each house or are reported there. Contact your state representative or senator if you want to get on his or her limited journal mailing list. The floor debate in both houses is recorded, and these tapes may be listened to in the LRL.

★ Legislative Information System of Texas (LIST). LIST is a database with basic information about bills and resolutions introduced in the legislature since 1973, including author, sponsor, short description, and the like. It also has a subject index, author and sponsor index, and committee index. Texts of proposed legislation can be printed out on a member's printer, or on the printer in the LRL, during the sessions. Material from the Seventy-first and Seventy-second legislatures, regular and special sessions, is in the LRL. Material prior to the Seventy-first Legislature is in hard copy in the LRL. During a legislative session, you can find out about the status of current legislation by calling a toll-free number, (800) 252-9693 (475-3026 in Austin), between 8 A.M. and 5 P.M. weekdays, or whenever either house is in session.

★ Original bill files. The state archives and legislative reference library also maintain complete files on all bills and resolutions introduced in the legislature. Each file contains not only the original bill, but often other documents such as notes on its fiscal effects, detailed explanations, and committee reports. Files on bills prior to 1973 are kept at the state archives; those since 1973 are at the legislative reference library.

★ House Research Organization reports. The House Research Organization (HRO), formerly known as the House Study Group, issues general reports on issues, as well as detailed analyses of individual bills that summarize the legislation, describe the arguments for and against it, and list its major supporters and opponents. Many reports are provided only to House members who belong to the study group. Its special legislative reports on general issues are distributed to depository libraries, and analyses of bills are usually included in the original bill files mentioned above.

★ Legislative hearings. The proceedings of committees in the legislature are tape-recorded, not written. The dates of hearings can be obtained from LIST. Hearings can be very instructive in understanding policy alternatives and decisions because of the testimony and debate that occur there. They can also provide information about the implementation of policies when legislators question officials of state agencies. Minutes of committee meetings are kept, however. Senate minutes are maintained by the legislative reference library and House minutes by the House committee coordinator. Because of the general inaccessibility of committee proceedings, you may be forced to rely on secondhand accounts of committee actions by the press, the House Research organization, or other sources. If you live in Austin, however, you can listen to tapes of the committee hearings, either at the LRL or in the House committee coordinator's office, once requests have been made and if the minutes and tapes are available. There is sometimes a rule-allotted time lag for the committee clerks to prepare documents for processing. While the minutes reflect only the action or nonaction taken, the tapes reveal interesting dialogue.

★ Interest groups. Lobbyists and political action committees are required to register and file reports with the elections division of the secretary of state. Their activities are often discussed in newspapers and periodicals such as *The Texas Observer* or *Texas Monthly*. The positions of groups are usually discussed in bill analyses and House study-group reports included in the original bill files. In addition, interest groups often publish their positions on issues in magazines or newsletters distributed to their members.

★ Legislative votes. Votes on the floor of the House and Senate are included in the journal of each house. In addition, the *Texas Government Newsletter* has published a *Voter's Guide* to recent legislative sessions. This volume does not cover all floor votes, but provides background on major votes along with the actual head count.

★ The Texas Legislative Council is a vital component of the entire legislative process. Drafts of legislation emanate from the staff of attorneys who put the members' concepts into proper form for introduction. The council publishes a cumulative number, subject, and author index throughout the session, with a final one at the end of the session (or special session), and after the session is over, it distributes a "Summary of the Legislative Session." It also publishes a *Legislative Manual*, showing how to correctly draft legislation. In 1988, it published the two-volume *District Profiles: Congressional, State Senate, and State Board of Education Districts* and the companion *District Profiles: State House of Representatives*. These show the configurations and composition of four types of districts drawn by the Texas legislature following each federal decennial census. For each type of district, there is a short history of the evolution of the statewide plan and a population/size analysis of the plan. For each individual district, there is a locator and detailed boundary maps and tables of selected 1980 census data. This first edition is a prototype for a district publication that the council plans to update for the 1990 census. The publication has not yet been printed because redistricting plans are in litigation.

★ Agency reports and hearings. The annual and periodic reports of state agencies are indexed in *Texas State Documents*. Hearings are listed by agency name in the *Texas Register,* which reports the activities and publishes the rules of bureaucratic agencies. These reports and hearings are a good way to gather information about the enforcement of policies.

★ Texas State Comptroller. The comptroller's office issues both regular and special reports. Among these is *Fiscal Notes,* which is a bimonthly publication on the economy and fiscal picture of the state.

★ Institute of Public Affairs, University of Texas. The institute published more than eighty-five books and monographs between 1950 and 1971, when it was disbanded. Included were summaries of several legislative sessions and an overview of the lieutenant governorship. Its activities have been continued by the Lyndon B. Johnson School of Public Affairs, which issues a variety of reports on issues facing the state. The school's publication office issues free cumulative and yearly catalogs of its publications.

★ Other bureaus, centers, and institutions. Many college and university campuses have research and public service bureaus, centers, and institutes that can provide you with valuable information. These are too numerous to list, but you should check your campus telephone directory to see what appropriate offices exist on your campus or on a nearby campus. Look for organizations with the word *Texas* in the title, as well as for such designations as "public management," "Texas culture," "economic development," and "urban affairs."

★ Contacting your legislators. The legislative reference library and legislative committees exist to serve the legislature and do not have time to do your research. If you need limited advice or information in Austin, however, you often can get some help by calling or writing your senator or representative, each of whom has staff members who can assist you. Use *Chief Elected and Administrative Officials* to find the correct spelling of your legislators' names if you do not find them listed on the editorial/opinion page of your local newspaper.

★ Contacting state agencies. State agencies frequently issue reports and conduct special studies that may be of interest to you. The Office of the Comptroller of Public Accounts is perhaps the most prolific. These offices are not equipped to do your research for you, but if you hear or read about a report issued by one of them, you may be able to obtain a copy. The comptroller's office can be phoned by dialing (800) 531-5441, extension 3-4900, or 463-4900 in Austin.

LOCAL POLITICS: THE ELECTORAL PROCESS

★ Election data. Voting returns are available from the city secretary (called city clerk in some municipalities). Precinct maps and voter registration totals can be obtained from the city secretary or county tax assessor-collector. This overlap occurs because counties draw precinct boundaries and oversee voter registration. The city secretary or planning department may have detailed census data about precincts, although this information has become generally available only recently as many cities have begun electing their council members from districts.

★ Candidates. One of the best ways to find out about candidates and issues is from the local League of Women Voters (LWV), which usually prints a "Voter's Guide" before each election. Although the league does not endorse candidates, it promotes voter education and occasionally takes positions on issues. Since the league is a volunteer organization, it does not always maintain a permanent office or old records. If you cannot reach the local chapter by phone or mail, ask if the city clerk knows the names, addresses, and phone numbers of its officers. Contacting the LWV is well worth the effort, since the "Voter's Guide" includes detailed biographical information about candidates and analyzes both sides of referendum, charter, and bond elections. You can also get information about the occupation and address of candidates from the alphabetical listing in the city directory.

★ Issues. Many libraries, newspapers, and interest groups maintain files of articles, press releases, letters, and similar material. These clipping files can hold a wealth of information and save you a lot of time, especially if the local papers are not well indexed. The first place to check for these clipping files is the main branch of the local public library. As with state and federal elections, candidates often keep material that can prove helpful to you.

LOCAL POLITICS: THE POLICY PROCESS

Local politics is often the easiest realm in which to do research, since you hear about it daily and the resources for a good project are readily available.

★ Newspapers. As mentioned earlier, indexes and clipping files are extremely important sources for understanding policy making. They can help you identify the nature of a controversy or issue, the people or groups involved in it, and their goals and political maneuvers.

★ Official records. City council minutes are valuable, since they indicate who made or seconded motions and how council members voted on specific questions. If verbatim minutes are kept, you can also analyze council debates to expand your understanding of an issue. Most city secretaries also maintain files on each ordinance and council meeting, which usually include substantial background information on issues. Most also have a subject index of council meetings and ordinances, copies of agendas, lists of citizens who sign up to address the council, and copies of petitions. All these records can help you identify significant participants in a policy decision and their positions and strategies. In larger cities, tapes or radio broadcasts may be available. Check with the city clerk's office.

★ Organizations. There are several things, in addition to lists of speakers at council meetings, that can help you analyze the role of organizations in the policy process. Neighborhood groups and other organizations often register with the city secretary, planning commission, or city manager. You can also find the names, addresses, and phone numbers of political and social organizations in a very handy source, the yellow pages of the telephone directory.

★ Reports and studies. Budgets, department reports, and board or commission studies often provide insights into the formulation and implementation of policies. Contacting the relevant department is usually the best way to gather such information about an individual city. Comparing cities is a somewhat more difficult task. *Texas Town and City,* the official publication of the Texas Municipal League, often reports data for the state's cities. In addition, the *Index to Current Urban Documents* covers reports and studies done by the nation's largest cities, many of which are available in the *Urban Documents Microfiche Collection.* A regional council of government (COG) may also have some of the information you need and be willing to assist you in your research.

★ Local magazines. Most large Texas cities have at least one local magazine. These are typically published by the chamber of commerce and promote economic activity in the area. They sometimes carry interesting accounts of local politics, however. Several of these magazines, including *D* and *Houston City,* are indexed in *Access.*

★ Interviews. Do not hesitate to ask questions of people who participate in local politics. You should do so, however, only after doing careful background research on an issue and consulting with one of your instructors who is experienced in interviewing.

LAW AND THE JUDICIAL SYSTEM

If your college library does not include a law collection, the county law library will include the basic volumes for doing research on the Texas legal system.

★ Marian Boner, *A Reference Guide to Texas Law and Legal History: Sources and Documentation* (1976). This is a good starting point if you intend to do research on some aspect of the law. It includes a detailed bibliography and helpful tips.

★ *Vernon's Texas Constitution.* These three volumes include the text of the Texas Constitution, commentary, citations of important court cases and articles, and a thorough subject index.

★ The most recent and most scholarly guide to the constitution is Janice C. May, *The Texas State Constitution: A Reference Guide* (Westport, Conn.: Greenwood Press, 1996).

★ *Vernon's Texas Codes Annotated, Vernon's Annotated Revised Civil Statutes, Vernon's Annotated Code of Criminal Procedure.* These volumes include the text of laws plus commentary, citations, and an index. Be sure to check the pamphlet supplement at the back for important developments since the volume was published.

★ *Southwestern Reporter.* Federal and state cases involving Texas are reported in this series. Citations are in the form: *City of San Antonio* v. *State ex. rel. Criner* 270 S.W.2d 460. To find the decision in the case involving these two parties, you would go to volume 270 of the *Southwestern Reporter* second series, and locate the beginning of the court's opinion on page 460. This is not a book for browsing—you need a case citation before referring to it.

★ *Shepard's Citations.* These citations to cases give the complete judicial history of every reported case as affected by decisions of both state and federal courts. If you are wondering if the decision in a particular case is still valid or has been superseded, *Shepard's Citations* answers your question. Check with your reference librarian about how to use *Shepard's.*

★ Texas Department of Criminal Justice, *Annual Report.*

★ The Office of Court Administration of the Texas Judicial Council, *The Texas Judicial System: Annual Report.*

BIOGRAPHIES

You may also want to study individual political careers. To a large extent, you can start by reviewing existing accounts of an individual and then supplementing them. A quick way to begin is to look up the individual in such biographical references as the following:

★ Walter Prescott Webb, ed., *The Handbook of Texas,* 2 volumes (1952), and Eldon S. Brandon, ed., *The Handbook of Texas: A Supplement* (1976). The *Handbook* contains important biographical information on deceased Texans in an alphabetical format.

★ Roy R. Barkley, ed., *The New Handbook of Texas* (Austin: The Texas State Historical Association, 1996). Six volumes. As noted previously, this series of books contains information on people, places, and institutions.

★ *Who's Who in the South and Southwest.* This volume includes brief biographical information about prominent persons.

★ *Dictionary of American Biography.* This series is published under the auspices of the American Council of Learned Societies, and has been updated frequently. Each entry includes a short life history and brief list of references. To locate someone, go to the most recent volume, which will refer you to the proper volume.

★ R. R. Bowker Company, *Biographical Books, 1950–1980* (1980). This collection includes subject/name, author, and title indexes.

You can supplement these sources with the materials mentioned above for studying local politics, particularly newspapers and clipping files. Another invaluable tool is personal papers, which many individuals donate to libraries.

In addition to the *American Library Directory,* there are several other ways to locate biographical information.

★ Texas State Archives, Biographical Index. You can contact the archives to find out what materials have been published on an individual and what sources are available.

★ Chester V. Kielman, ed., *The University of Texas Archives.* This includes the alphabetical list and index of the many manuscript collections at the University of Texas at Austin.

★ Library of Congress, *The National Union Catalogue of Manuscript Collection.* This annual series is organized by state and city, and will help you locate both personal papers and oral histories. Among the latter is the Oral History Collection at the University of North Texas, which includes interviews with Texas governors and legislators.

★ Philip M. Hamer, ed., *A Guide to Archives and Manuscripts in the United States* (1961). Although somewhat dated, this volume covers some major collections. It is organized by state and city, and includes a description of each institution's holdings.

Conclusion

Although none of the above suggestions guarantees a good research project—which requires some work on your part—this research guide should make your work easier. It should also allow you to analyze carefully some important political questions facing Texas citizens and their elected representatives.

Helpful Locations for Getting Information

TEXAS DEPOSITORY LIBRARIES

Abilene
Public Library, Documents Department
202 Cedar Street
Abilene 79601
(915) 677-2474

Alpine
Sul Ross State University
Bryan Wildenthal Memorial Library, Documents
   Department
Alpine 79832
(915) 837-8125

Amarillo
Public Library, Documents Department
P.O. Box 2171
Amarillo 79189-2171
(806) 378-3050

Arlington
University of Texas at Arlington Library,
   Government Publications/Maps Department
P.O. Box 19497
Arlington 76019
(817) 463-1252

Austin
Legislative Reference Library
1110 San Jacinto, Room 260
Box 12488
Austin 78711
(512) 463-1252

Texas State Library and Archives,
   Reference/Documents
Box 12927
Austin 78711
(512) 463-5455

University of Texas at Austin
Center for American History
2.109 Sid Richardson Hall
Austin 78713-7330
(512) 471-5961

Public Library, Reference Department
P.O. Box 3827
Beaumont 77704
(409) 838-6606

Lamar University
Gray Library, Documents Department
Box 10021, Lamar University Station
Beaumont 77710
(409) 880-8261

University of Texas at Brownsville Documents
    Department/LRC
1614 Ridgley Road
Brownsville 78520-4991
(956) 983-0295

West Texas State University Library, Documents
    Department
P.O. Box 748, WT Station
Canyon 79016
(806) 656-2204

Texas A&M University
Sterling C. Evans Library
Reference Division (Texas State)
College Station 77843-5000
(409) 845-5310

East Texas State University Library, Serials
    Department
Commerce 75249
(903) 886-5734

Public Library, Documents Department
805 Comanche Street
Corpus Christi 78401
(512) 880-7005

Corpus Christi State University Library,
    Documents Department
6300 Ocean Drive
Corpus Christi 78412
(512) 994-2341

Public Library, Government Publications Division
1515 Young Street
Dallas 75201
(214) 670-1460

Southern Methodist University
Fondren Library, Documents Department
Dallas 75275
(214) 692-2331

Public Library
300 West Gandy Street
Denison 75020
(903) 465-1797

University of North Texas Library, Documents
    Department
P.O. Box 5188, NT Station
Denton 76203-5188
(940) 565-3869

Texas Woman's University Library, Documents
    Department
P.O. Box 23715, TWU Station
Denton 76204
(940) 898-3708

University of Texas—Pan American Library,
    Documents Department
1201 W. University Drive
Edinburg 78539-2999
(512) 381-3304

Public Library, Documents Department
501 North Oregon Street
El Paso 79901
(915) 543-5475

University of Texas at El Paso Library, Documents and Maps Section
El Paso 79968-0582
(915) 747-5685

Fort Worth
Public Library, Government Publications
300 Taylor Street
Fort Worth 76102
(817) 871-7724

Texas Christian University
Burnett Library, Documents Department
P.O. Box 32904
Fort Worth 76129
(817) 921-7669

Houston
Public Library, Texas Room
500 McKinney Avenue
Houston 77002
(713) 247-1664

Rice University
Fondren Library, Documents Department
P.O. Box 1892
Houston 77251
(713) 523-2417

Texas Southern University Library, Documents Department
3100 Cleburne Street
Houston 77004
(713) 527-7147

University of Houston Library, Documents Department
4800 Calhoun Street
Houston 77204-2091
(713) 749-1163

University of Houston—Clear Lake Neumann Library, Documents Library
2700 Bay Area Boulevard
Houston 77058-1083
(713) 283-3910

Huntsville
Sam Houston State University
N. Gresham Library, Department of Government Documents
Huntsville 77341
(409) 294-1629

Kingsville
Texas A&I University Library, Documents Department
Kingsville 78363
(512) 595-2918

Laredo
Laredo State University Library, Documents Section
1 West End Washington Street
Laredo 78040-9960
(956) 722-8001, ext. 402

Lubbock
Texas Tech University Library, Documents Department
M. S. 2041
Lubbock 79409-0002
(806) 742-2268

Nacogdoches
Stephen F. Austin State University Library, Documents Department
P.O. Box 13055, SFA Station
Nacogdoches 75962-3055
(409) 568-1574

Odessa
Ector County Library, Documents Department
321 West 5th Street
Odessa 79761
(915) 332-0634

University of Texas of the Permian Basin Library
4901 E. University Boulevard
Odessa 79762
(915) 357-2313

Prairie View
Prairie View A&M University
John B. Coleman Library, Documents Department
Prairie View 77446
(409) 857-2612

Richardson
University of Texas at Dallas Library, Documents Department
P.O. Box 830643
Richardson 75083-0643
(214) 690-2627

San Angelo
Angelo State University
Porter Henderson Library
2601 West Avenue N
San Angelo 76909
(915) 942-2222

San Antonio
St. Mary's University Academic Library,
    Documents Department
One Camino Santa Maria
San Antonio 78228-8608
(512) 436-3441

Public Library (Main Branch)
Business and Science Department
203 South St. Mary's Street
San Antonio 78205
(512) 299-7802

Trinity University Library, Documents Unit
715 Stadium Drive
San Antonio 78212
(512) 736-7430

University of Texas at San Antonio
    Library/Documents
San Antonio 78249
(512) 691-4583

San Marcos
Southwest Texas State University Library,
    Documents Department
San Marcos 78666-4604
(512) 245-3686

Stephenville
Tarleton State University
Dick Smith Library/Education Library
Stephenville 76402
(254) 968-9869

Tyler
University of Texas at Tyler
Muntz Library, Documents Department
3900 University Boulevard
Tyler 75701
(903) 566-7344

Victoria
Victoria College/University of Houston at Victoria
    Library, Documents Department
2602 North Ben Jordan
Victoria 77901
(512) 576-3151, ext. 283

Waco
Baylor University (Texas Collection)
B.U. Box 97142
Waco 76798-7142
(817) 755-1268

Wichita Falls
Midwestern State University
Moffett Library, Documents Department
3400 Taft Street
Wichita Falls 76308-2099
(940) 692-6611, ext. 4165

Other Depository Libraries:
Library of Congress, State Documents Section
Exchange and Gift Division
Washington, DC 20540
(202) 707-9470

TEXAS STATE LIBRARY

P.O. Box 12927, Austin 78711
Reference: (512) 463-5455
Archives: (512) 463-5480
Public Services: (512) 463-5455

**THE LEGISLATURE AND LEGISLATIVE
AGENCIES**

The Honorable _____
Texas Senate
P.O. Box 12068,
Capitol Station
Austin 78711

The Honorable _____
Texas House of Representatives
P.O. Box 2910
Austin 78769-2910

Legislative Reference Library
P.O. Box 12488, Capitol Station
Austin 78711-2488
(512) 463-1252
Bill Status: (800) 253-9693
(463-1251 in Austin)

House Research Organization
Texas House of Representatives
P.O. Box 2910
Austin 78769-2910

SECRETARY OF STATE

Elections Division
P.O. Box 12060
Austin 78711-2060
(512) 463-5650

Texas Ethics Commission
P.O. Box 12070
Austin 78711-2070
(512) 463-5800

Support Services Division, Texas Register Section
P.O. Box 13824
Austin 78711-3824
(512) 463-5561

PROFESSIONAL AND EDUCATIONAL ORGANIZATIONS

Texas State Historical Association
2.306 Sid Richardson Hall
University of Texas
Austin 78712-1104
(512) 471-1525

Southwestern Social Science Association
P.O. Box 7998, University of Texas
Austin 78713-7998
(512) 471-4384

Office of Publications
Lyndon B. Johnson School of Public Affairs
Drawer Y, University Station
Austin 78713-7450
(512) 471-4962

TEXAS UNIVERSITY PRESSES

Seven universities in the state maintain presses that publish books on virtually all aspects of Texas: The University of Texas, Texas A&M University, The University of North Texas, Texas Christian University, Southern Methodist University, Rice University, and Texas Western. Each university press provides catalogs of its publications, and each can provide information on the publications of the other presses. Addresses and telephone numbers are available at your local library.

Glossary

Administrative discretion The freedom that administrators (bureaucrats) have in implementing and interpreting laws (Chapter 10).

Appellate jurisdiction The authority of a court to hear cases sent to it on appeal from a lower court. Appellate courts review only the legal issues involved and not the factual record of the case (Chapter 11).

Appointment and removal powers The governor's constitutional and statutory authority to hire and fire people employed by the state (Chapter 9).

At-large elections Elections in which each candidate for any given public office must run jurisdictionwide—in the entire city, county, or state—when several similar positions are being filled (Chapters 3 and 11).

Attorney general's advisory opinion A legal opinion as to the constitutionality of legislative proposals (bills), rules, procedures, and statutes (laws) (Chapter 11).

Bicameral For a legislative body, divided into two chambers or houses (Chapter 7).

Biennial Two years. Thus, a biennial legislative session occurs every other year and a biennial budget is one that directs spending for two years (Chapter 7).

Bill A proposed law written on a piece of paper and submitted to a legislature (Chapter 8).

Bills of rights Sections of constitutions, most famously the U.S. Constitution, that list the civil rights and liberties of the citizens and place restrictions on the powers of government (Chapter 2).

Block grants Federal funds that can be used for a broad range of programs; the state or local government recipient can determine specific uses within broad guidelines (Chapter 13).

Blue-collar crimes Crimes in which a criminal act is more or less directly perpetrated upon a victim, often violently.

Murder, rape, burglary, theft, and assault are common blue-collar crimes. Also called street crimes (Chapter 12).

Bureaucracy A type of organization that is characterized by hierarchy, specialization, fixed and official rules, and relative freedom from outside control (Chapter 10).

Campaign The period of time before an election during which the candidates and parties attempt to persuade citizens to vote for them (Chapter 6).

Casework A legislator's doing favors for constituents, such as troubleshooting or solving a problem (Chapter 7).

Categorical grants-in-aid Federal funds that can be used only for specific purposes (Chapter 13).

Checks and balances See **separation of powers.**

Civil jurisdiction The authority of courts that handle noncriminal cases, such as those dealing with divorce, personal injury, taxes, and debts (Chapter 11).

Civil liberties Individual freedoms such as speech, press, religion, and assembly. The protection of these liberties is essential to a vital democratic society. Generally, the protection of civil liberties requires forbidding government to take certain actions (Chapter 12).

Civil rights The constitutional claims all citizens have to fair and equal treatment under the law. Among the most important civil rights are the ability to vote in honest elections, to run for and serve in public office, and to be afforded a fair trial presided over by an impartial judge if accused of a crime. Civil rights refer to actions that government must take in order to ensure equal citizenship for everyone (Chapter 12).

Civil service system A personnel system in a government administrative agency in which employees are hired, fired, and promoted by the agency, rather than by elected politicians outside the agency. Individuals generally are hired and promoted through some sort of written examination. There are often restrictive rules that make firing an individual employee difficult. Often called the "merit system" (Chapter 10).

Clientele group The interest group or groups that benefit from or are regulated by an administrative agency (Chapter 10).

Closed primary A primary in which only voters who are registered members of that party may participate (Chapter 6).

Coalition A group of interests and individuals supporting a party or a candidate for office (Chapter 5).

Commissioners court The administrative and legislative body of a county; it has four elected members and is presided over by an elected county judge (Chapter 3).

Concurrent jurisdiction The authority of two or more different types of courts to hear the same type of case (Chapter 11).

Conference committee A temporary joint committee of both houses of a legislature in which representatives attempt to reconcile the differences in two versions of a bill (Chapter 8).

Conservatism A political ideology that, in general, opposes government regulation of economic life and supports government regulation of personal life (Chapters 1 and 5).

Constituent function The power of a legislative body to propose constitutional amendments and, in the case of a state legislature, to ratify amendments to the national constitution (Chapter 7).

Constitution The basic law of a state or nation that takes precedence over all other laws and actions of the government (Chapter 2).

Constitutional amendment A change in a constitution that is approved by both the legislative body, and, in Texas, the voters. National constitutional amendments are not approved directly by voters (Chapter 2).

Constitutional reform/revision Making major changes in a constitution, often including the writing of an entirely new document (Chapter 2).

Co-optation The process by which industries and their interest groups come to dominate administrative agencies that were originally established to regulate the industry's activities (Chapter 4).

Court of Criminal Appeals The highest state appeals court with criminal jurisdiction (Chapter 11).

Criminal jurisdiction The authority of courts that handle offenses punishable by fines, imprisonment, public service, or death. These offenses include murder, rape, assault, theft, embezzlement, fraud, drunken driving, speeding, and other acts that have been defined as criminal by the state legislature or municipal authorities (Chapter 11).

Democracy The form of government based upon the theory that the legitimacy of any government must come from the free participation of its citizens (Chapter 1).

District elections Elections in which a polity is divided into geographical areas; candidates for public office must run in one small area rather than in the whole polity; each district usually sends one representative. Also called single-member district elections (Chapters 3 and 11).

District system A system in which a candidate is required to live in the particular geographic area in which he or she runs for office (Chapter 3).

Dual-budgeting system A system in which both the executive branch and the legislative branch prepare separate budget documents (Chapter 13).

Elasticity The flexibility and breadth of the tax system so that state revenues are not seriously disrupted even if one segment of the economy is troubled (Chapter 13).

Equal protection clause The clause in the Fourteenth Amendment to the U.S. Constitution that declares that no state may "deny to any person within its jurisdiction the equal protection of the laws." This clause has been frequently used by the federal courts to protect the civil rights of American citizens, especially African Americans (Chapter 6).

Exclusive jurisdiction The sole authority of one court over a given type of case (Chapter 11).

Federal system A system of government that provides for a division and sharing of powers between a national government and state or regional governments (Chapter 1).

Filibuster An effort to kill a bill in a legislature by unlimited debate; it is possible in the Texas and United States senates, but not in the houses of representatives (Chapter 8).

Fiscal year The budget year for a government or a corporation; it may not coincide with a calendar year. In Texas, the state fiscal year runs September 1 through August 31. Municipal fiscal years run October 1 through September 31, the same as the federal fiscal year (Chapters 8 and 13).

Formal qualifications Qualifications for holding public office that are specified by law (Chapter 7).

General election An election in which voters choose government officeholders (Chapter 6).

General laws Statutes that pertain to all municipalities that do not have home-rule status (Chapter 3).

General revenue sharing A federal program that allowed state and local governments great flexibility in the use of federal funds. It expired in 1986 (Chapter 13).

Grand jury A legal body of twelve or more individuals convened at the county seat. The grand jury considers evidence submitted by prosecutors and determines whether there is sufficient evidence to indict those accused of crimes (Chapter 11).

Hierarchy Levels of authority in an organization, with the maximum authority on top (Chapter 10).

Home rule The ability of cities of 5,000 or more population to organize themselves as they wish within the constitution and laws of Texas (Chapters 2 and 3).

Hopwood v. State The case decided in federal court in 1996 that eliminated affirmative action in admissions to the University of Texas Law School and, through subsequent interpretation, in statewide public college admissions and scholarships (Chapter 14).

Ideology A system of beliefs and values about the nature of the good life and the good society, and the part to be played by government in achieving them (Chapter 5).

Impeachment The process of formally accusing an official of improper behavior in office. It is followed by a trial, and if the official is convicted, he or she is removed from office (Chapter 9).

Impresario In general, a promoter or organizer of an event; in the context of Texas history, a person who brought groups of settlers to Texas when it was Spanish or Mexican territory (Chapter 1).

Inflation A rise in the general price level, which is the same thing as a fall in the value of the dollar (Chapter 13).

Infrastructure The costly government investments in physical, nonhuman resources such as highways, bridges, water lines, and sewer systems; these make possible economic growth and a reasonable quality of life (Chapter 14).

Interest Something of value or some personal characteristic that people share and that is affected by government activity; interests are important both because they form the basis of interest groups and because parties attempt to form many interests into an electoral coalition (Chapter 5).

Item veto The governor's constitutional power to strike out individual items in an appropriations bill (Chapter 8).

Judiciary A collective term referring to the system of courts and its judges and other personnel (Chapter 11).

Juvenile courts Special state courts that handle accused offenders under the age of seventeen (Chapter 11).

Laissez-faire A French phrase loosely meaning "leave it alone." It refers to the philosophy that values free markets and opposes government regulation of the economy (Chapter 1).

Legislative oversight The legislature's supervision of the activities of state administrative agencies. Increasingly, the emphasis of oversight is on increasing efficiency and cutting back management—doing more with less (Chapters 7 and 10).

Legislative veto A provision in a law that allows a legislature, or one of its committees, to review and revoke the actions of a chief executive or other executive officer (Chapter 8).

Legitimacy The belief that people have that their government is morally just, and that therefore they are obligated to obey it (Chapter 1).

Liberalism A political ideology that, in general, supports government regulation of economic life and opposes government regulation of personal life (Chapters 1 and 5).

Lobby To try to influence government policy through face-to-face contact (Chapter 4).

Lobbyist A person who attempts to influence government policy through face-to-face contact (Chapter 4).

Mandate Action that the national government requires state and local governments to take or that the state requires cities, counties, and special districts to take (Chapter 14).

Message power The governor's means of formally establishing his or her priorities for legislative action by communicating with the legislature (Chapter 9).

Nonpartisan election One in which candidates bear no party label such as Republican or Democrat (Chapter 3).

Ombudsman A Scandinavian term that means "grievance man." Government ombudsman is an official who receives citizen complaints about government and tries to resolve the problems (Chapter 9).

One-party state A state that is dominated by a single political party. It is characterized by an absence of party competition, inadequate debate of public policy, low voter turnout, and usually conservative public policy (Chapter 5).

Open primary A primary in which all registered voters may participate, whether or not they are registered members of the party holding the primary (Chapter 6).

Original jurisdiction The authority to hear a case first, usually in a trial (Chapter 11).

Original trial courts Courts having the authority to consider and decide both criminal and civil cases in the first instance, as distinguished from appellate courts (Chapter 11).

Permanent party organization The small, fixed organization that handles the routine business of a political party (Chapter 5).

Place system A form of at-large election in which all candidates are elected citywide, but the seats on the council are designated Place One, etc., and each candidate runs only against others who have filed for the same place (Chapter 3).

Plea bargain The process in which an accused person agrees to plead guilty to a lesser crime and receives a lighter sentence. He or she avoids having to stand trial on a more serious charge, and the state saves the time and expense of a trial (Chapter 11).

Political action committee (PAC) A group formed by a corporation, trade association, labor union, or other organization or individual for the purpose of collecting money and then contributing that money to one or more political candidates or causes (Chapter 4).

Political culture A shared framework of values, beliefs, and habits of behavior with regard to government and politics within which a particular political system functions (Chapter 1).

Political interest group A private organization that attempts to influence politicians—and through them public policy—to the advantage of the organization (Chapter 4).

Political party An organization devoted to winning public office in elections, and thus exercising control over public policy (Chapter 5).

Political socialization The process by which we learn information, values, attitudes, and habits of behavior about politics and government (Chapter 5).

Pollutants Substances that are dumped into water supplies, landfills, or the atmosphere that are harmful to human, plant, and/or animal life (Chapter 14).

Populist Someone who believes in the rights, wisdom, and issues of the common people, and that those people should be protected from exploitation by corporations, rich people, and government (Chapter 9).

Poverty threshold The level of income below which a family is officially considered to be poor. It is established annually as the basis for determining eligibility for a variety of social programs. Also called the federal poverty line (Chapter 14).

Primary election An election held within a party to nominate candidates for the general election or choose delegates to a presidential nominating convention (Chapter 6).

Privately funded campaign A system in which candidates and parties must rely on private citizens to voluntarily donate money to their campaign chests; except partially at the presidential level, this is the system used in the United States (Chapter 6).

Privatizing Turning over public programs to the private sector to implement. For example, municipalities often contract with private waste management companies to dispose of solid waste. The state has contracted with a private firm to operate some Texas prisons (Chapter 7).

Progressive tax A tax that increases in rate with the wealth of the one paying the tax; the richer the person or institution, the higher the tax rate (Chapter 13).

Pseudo laissez-faire The tendency of entrepreneurs to oppose government involvement in the economy at the general philosophical level, but to seek government assistance for their particular business (Chapter 1).

Public policy The overall purpose behind individual governmental decisions and programs. It is the result of public officials' setting of priorities by creating the budget, making official decisions, and passing laws (Chapter 14).

Publicly funded campaign A system in which the government pays for the candidates' campaign expenses, either directly or through parties. This system is not used in the United States except partially at the presidential level (Chapter 6).

Reapportion To reallocate legislative seats, adding seats to areas with heavy population growth and taking away seats from areas without growth (Chapter 7).

Redistributive public policy Laws and government decisions that have the effect of taking wealth, power, and other resources from some citizens and giving those resources to others. Examples would be the graduated income tax and affirmative actions programs (Chapter 14).

Redistricting The designation of geographic areas that are nearly equal in population for the purpose of electing legislators—national, state, and local (Chapter 7).

Regressive tax A flat-rate tax that is not based on ability to pay; as a consequence, the poorer the payer of the tax, the larger the percentage of income that goes to the tax (Chapter 13).

Revenue shortfall A situation in which state revenues are not expected to be adequate to fund programs and services at current levels (Chapter 13).

Revolving door A name given by political scientists to the process in which government regulatory agencies hire their personnel from within the industry being regulated; after they leave the agency, employees are typically hired once more by the regulated industry (Chapter 4).

Select Committee on Higher Education A committee created by the legislature in 1985 to examine all aspects of higher education and make recommendations for action in 1987 (Chapter 14).

Seniority In a legislative body, the amount of time spent in continuous service in one house or committee (Chapter 7).

Separation of powers A phrase often used to describe the U.S. political system; it refers to the assigning of specific powers to individual branches of government. In the United States, separation of powers is accompanied by **checks and balances** that allow each branch to limit the other branches. As a result, the powers of the branches overlap. Consequently, "separate institutions sharing powers" would be a more accurate description of the U. S. system (Chapter 2).

Session power The governor's constitutional authority to call the legislature into special session and to set the agenda of topics to be considered in that session (Chapter 9).

Single-member district A designated geographic area from which only one representative is elected (Chapter 7).

Social Darwinism A philosophy, drawn from the biological theory of evolution, that holds that the rich are superior people and deserve their wealth, while the poor are inferior and deserve their poverty (Chapter 1).

Suffrage The legal right to vote in public elections (Chapter 6).

Sunset review The process by which the legislature reviews the performance of administrative agencies, then renews, reorganizes, or eliminates them (Chapter 10).

Sunshine law A law that provides for public access to the records of administrative agencies (Chapter 10).

Super Tuesday The second Tuesday in March, when Texas primary elections, both regular and presidential, and the primaries of many other states are now held (Chapter 6).

Supreme Court The highest state appellate court with civil jurisdiction (Chapter 11).

Tag A means by which an individual senator can delay a committee hearing on a bill for at least forty-eight hours (Chapter 8).

Tax equity The inherent fairness of a tax. As the term is used in this book, ability to pay is a factor in fairness (Chapter 13).

Temporary party organization The organization formed to mobilize the party's potential electorate and win an election (Chapter 5).

Third party A minor political party that fails to achieve permanence but frequently influences the major parties and, through them, public policy (Chapter 5).

Tort A private or civil wrong or injury resulting from a breach of a legal duty that exists by reason of society's expectations about appropriate behavior, rather than a contract. The injured party sues the alleged offender in order to receive compensation for his or her losses (Chapter 12).

Trial jury Six to twelve persons who determine the legal guilt or innocence of defendants in a criminal trial or the liability of defendants in a civil trial (Chapter 11).

Trickle-down theory A theory of economic development that maintains that government should create a very favorable climate to attract business and industry, and that the prosperity thus created will trickle down to the rank-and-file citizens (Chapter 1).

Turnover The proportion of the legislature that consists of first-term members because previous members retired, died, or were defeated at the polls (Chapter 7).

User fee A fee for a specific governmental service charged to the person who benefits from the service; a greens fee at a municipal golf course and college tuition are both user fees (Chapter 13).

Veto power The governor's constitutional authority to prevent the implementation of laws enacted by the legislature. The **item veto** allows the governor to delete individual items from an appropriations bill (Chapter 9).

Visual images The emotionally appealing symbols broadcast on television; they are dangerous in political advertising because they bypass the rational faculties and are therefore beyond argument (Chapter 6).

Voter registration The process used in every democracy to list the residents who are eligible to vote; it is necessary to prevent fraud but also discourages turnout by erecting a barrier between the citizen and the simple act of voting (Chapter 6).

Voter turnout The proportion of the eligible citizens who actually cast their ballots in an election (Chapter 6).

White-collar crimes Crimes in which a criminal act is perpetrated upon victims indirectly, often through an institution. Embezzlement, tax fraud, insurance fraud, and bribery are common white-collar crimes (Chapter 12).

Workers' compensation A program that provides income assurance for a worker injured on the job (Chapter 14).

Index